… ENGLISH LANG…
TITLE …

Rhythmic Phrasing …

ENGLISH LANGUAGE SERIES

General Editor: Randolph Quirk

Title no:

INVESTIGATING ENGLISH STYLE   1
David Crystal and Derek Davy

THE MOVEMENT OF ENGLISH PROSE   2
Ian A. Gordon

A LINGUISTIC GUIDE TO ENGLISH POETRY   4
Geoffrey N. Leech

AN INTRODUCTION TO   7
MODERN ENGLISH WORD-FORMATION
Valerie Adams

COHESION IN ENGLISH   9
M. A. K. Halliday and Ruqaiya Hasan

AN INTRODUCTION TO ENGLISH   10
TRANSFORMATIONAL SYNTAX
Rodney Huddleston

MEANING AND FORM   11
Dwight Bolinger

DESIGNS IN PROSE   12
Walter Nash

STYLE IN FICTION   13
Geoffrey N. Leech and Michael H. Short

THE RHYTHMS OF ENGLISH POETRY   14
Derek Attridge

MESSAGE AND EMPHASIS   15
Josef Taglicht

THE LANGUAGE OF HUMOUR   16
Walter Nash

GOOD ENGLISH AND THE GRAMMARIAN   17
Sidney Greenbaum

RHYTHMIC PHRASING IN ENGLISH VERSE   18
Richard D. Cureton

Rhythmic Phrasing in English Verse

RICHARD D. CURETON

LONGMAN
London and New York

Longman Group UK Limited
Longman House, Burnt Mill, Harlow,
Essex CM20 2JE, England
and Associated Companies throughout the world.

*Published in the United States of America
by Longman Inc., New York*

© Longman Group UK Limited 1992

All rights reserved; no part of this publication may be
reproduced, stored in a retrieval system, or transmitted in
any form or by any means, electronic, mechanical,
photocopying, recording, or otherwise without either the
prior written permission of the Publishers or a licence
permitting restricted copying in the United Kingdom issued
by the Copyright Licensing Agency Ltd, 90 Tottenham Court Road,
London, W1P 9HE.

First published 1992

British Library Cataloguing-in-Publication Data
A catalogue record for this book is available from the British
Library.

Library of Congress Cataloging in Publication Data
Cureton, Richard D., 1951–
　Rhythmic phrasing in English verse / Richard D. Cureton.
　　p.　cm. — (English language series ; 18)
　Includes bibliographical references and index.
　ISBN 0-582-55267-2
　1. English language—Rhythm.　2. English
language—Versification.
I. Title.　II. Series.
PE 1505.C87 1991
821'.009—dc20　　　　　　　　　　　　　　　　　　　　91–12981
　　　　　　　　　　　　　　　　　　　　　　　　　　　　CIP

Set in 10 on 12pt Times

Produced by Longman Singapore Publishers (Pte) Ltd.
Printed in Singapore

To Cath

Contents

Foreword ix

Preface x

Acknowledgements xiv

CHAPTER 1 CURRENT APPROACHES 1
1.1 Rhythm and multidimensional form 1
1.2 Prosodic theory 6
1.3 Current theories 7

CHAPTER 2 THE MYTHS OF TRADITIONAL PROSODY 77
2.1 Introduction 77
2.2 Myth 1: Verse rhythm is one-dimensional 79
2.3 Myth 2: Verse rhythm is physical/linguistic 98
2.4 Myth 3: Verse rhythm is regular 106
2.5 Myth 4: Verse rhythm is conventional 110
2.6 Myth 5: Verse rhythm is linear/flat 118

CHAPTER 3 CONTEXT 119
3.1 Rhythmic competence 119
3.2 Rhythm, prosody, versification, poetry and poetic experience 120
3.3 A definition of rhythm 121
3.4 Meter 126
3.5 Grouping 136
3.6 Prolongation 146
3.7 Interdisciplinary parallels: poetic rhythm and music theory 154

CHAPTER 4 THEORY: GROUPING 179
4.1 Preliminaries 179
4.2 Grouping well-formedness rules (GWFRs) 182
4.3 Grouping preference rules (GPRs) 191

CHAPTER 5 ANALYSIS		277
5.1	Free verse	277
5.2	'Sprung rhythm'	323
5.3	Pentameter	378
CHAPTER 6 IMPLICATIONS		423
6.1	Analysis	423
6.2	Rhythmic cognition	423
6.3	Rhythm and language	424
6.4	Rhythm and poetry	425
6.5	Shape and time	426
6.6	Meter	427
6.7	Metrical 'figures'	428
6.8	Prosodic history	429
6.9	Rhythmic phrasing	430
6.10	Prose rhythm and the rhythm of free verse	432
6.11	Poetic pedagogy	433
6.12	Poetry and music	434
6.13	Poetic rhythm and literary criticism	437
References		443
Index		461

Foreword

The study of rhythm involves complexity and breadth of a notoriously high order. It requires the ability to bring to bear on the subject an expert knowledge of several widely dispersed areas of scholarship. Thus one expects, of course, a wide reading in poetry and other literary genres; but this needs to be subjected to analysis with the tools of critical theory, of music, of linguistics – descriptive, generative, cognitive; nor can we afford to ignore aspects of physiology and acoustic physics.

This is a very tall order, since each of the disciplines concerned is itself dauntingly broad yet highly specialised, and practitioners in any one tend to have the time and skill to be little versed in any of the others. The result has been that studies in rhythm – however erudite and astute – have usually been firmly and rather exclusively located within one particular frame of scholarly reference, couched in a particular linguistic and theoretical mode that not merely ignores other relevant disciplines but is also, unsurprisingly, beyond the ready understanding of those whose disciplinary foundations are set in these other fields.

As those acquainted with Richard Cureton's previously published work will know, his strengths are many and obvious. But an outstanding one is his remarkable tenacity in achieving a mastery of the major disciplines that need to be co-ordinated for a successful fresh approach to understanding rhythm. In consequence, he has produced a book that provides insights from several different perspectives and presents us with a new and deeply challenging theoretical model.

University College London *Randolph Quirk*
March 1992

Preface

This book presents a theory of rhythmic phrasing for English verse. By *rhythmic phrasing* I mean those aspects of rhythmic response that are *not* metrical. Historically, most rhythmic criticism has focused on meter. The aim of this book is to move beyond this limited focus to a more inclusive account of verse rhythm, one that considers phrasing as well as meter.

As I draw it, the distinction between *phrasing* and *meter* is technical and can be specified in full only by the theory itself. The rhythmic intuitions that motivate this distinction are available to all readers, however, and have been commented upon for centuries, both in work on language and in work on rhythm in other media (e.g. music).

Broadly speaking, meters are regular, low-level configurations of largely physically controlled pulsations. Phrasal structures are more irregular, global organizations of rhythmic constituents. Meter presents the basic 'beat' of the verse. Phrasing represents how the text is segmented into parts and how those parts move, both in themselves and in relation to other parts. Historically, the referent of the word *meter* in rhythmic criticism has remained remarkably fixed. Phrasal rhythm has been called various other things: prose rhythm, word rhythm, sense rhythm, rhetorical sectioning, grouping, linkage, cadence or, most often, just rhythm.

The clearest motivation for the distinction between meter and phrasing comes from texts that are palpably rhythmic but not consistently metrical (e.g. much 'free' verse, prose poetry and, by definition, rhythmic prose). The most universally acknowledged examples are the mid- and high-level ('oratorical') rhythms of the King James translation of the Hebrew Bible and the free verse that it influenced (e.g. much of the poetry of Walt Whitman, Carl Sandburg and D.H. Lawrence).

24 The Earth is the Lord's, and the fullness thereof;
       the world, and they that dwell therein.
2   For he hath founded it upon the seas,
       and established it upon the floods.
3   Who shall ascend into the hill of the Lord?
       or who shall stand in his holy place?
4   He that hath clean hands, and a pure heart;
       who hath not lifted up his soul unto vanity, nor sworn
       deceitfully.
5   He shall receive the blessing from the Lord,
       and righteousness from the God of his salvation.

(Psalm 24)

Given the metrical focus of most rhythmic theories, the fairly regular high-level paralleling in these texts has usually been considered 'strange' and 'perplexing' because it does not count beats and syllables and therefore does not seem to be 'a matter of number', like meter (Hollander 1981: 26). But as Roman Jakobson taught us so thoroughly, mid- and high-level parallelism of this sort can be found in all verse, and in many cases these parallels are indeed numerically controlled. For instance, recently several prosodists have demonstrated that an important part of the rhythmic expressiveness of the great blank verse in the language derives from its orchestration of elaborate patterns of syntactic and rhetorical parallels arrayed in largely duple and triple patterns in cross-rhythm to metrical lines (Whaler 1952; Wright 1983, 1988; Cureton 1986a). These intonational, syntactic and rhetorical parallels are not submerged, esoteric designs. Their existence and effect are available to all readers and must be accounted for by any adequate rhythmic theory. The aim of this book is to make this possible.

This book is intended to be a *theory* of rhythmic phrasing, not merely a collection of observations or a tabulation of textual frequencies. In this respect it is unusual, if not unprecedented. As the generative metrists were quick to point out in the late 1960s, very little rhythmic criticism has aspired to theoretical claims. In fact, given the historical confusion in rhythmic study it is very much in question what a rhythmic theory should explain, much less what it should choose for its basic elements and relations.

Exactly what constitutes a theory is a complex philosophical issue, but it is one that needs to be discussed in cases such as this. As I use the term, a theory is an organized body of assumptions, principles and methods that explain the nature and behaviour of some specified set of phenomena. The major feature of a theory is its vulnerability, either to falsification or to supersession by a more valued theory. A theory is falsified if it fails to explain what it is designed to explain. A theory loses value as it fails to achieve desired levels of simplicity, naturalness, consistency, explanatory power, coherence and so forth. Descriptions and tabulations are weak theories because they only turn up false through carelessness and are no more consistent, coherent, natural, etc. than the phenomena they explain. Given this definition of *theory* one might claim that we have several theories of verse meter (although none of these has proven to be very strong). We have never had a theory of verse phrasing, however, and if rhythm includes both meter and phrasing we have also never had a theory of verse rhythm. Chapters 1 and 2 explore why this has been so. Chapters 3 to 5 fill this void.

Following parallel work in music theory (e.g. Lerdahl and Jackendoff 1983), I take the goal of a rhythmic theory to be a formal description of the rhythmic intuitions of the experienced reader. My goal is to produce a workable model of what we hear/see/feel/understand ('cognize') rhythmically when we read verse – and why. While these matters are seldom discussed explicitly, I think these experiential goals underlie the greater part of the rhythmic criticism and pedagogy in the English tradition.

These experiential goals distinguish this study sharply from several scholarly traditions in rhythmic study, however, and the reader should beware. Most scholarly approaches to verse rhythm in this century have been heavily influenced by linguistic methods. In fact, much of the most influential rhythmic theorizing in the last fifty years has been done by linguists for linguists in pursuit of largely linguistic (not critical/experiential) goals (Chapter 1). These linguistic studies have been largely text-oriented rather than reader-oriented. Their goal has been to predict/tabulate/investigate the occurrence or non-occurrence of certain linguistic forms given some known rhythmic response, not to build a theory of how (and why) we respond rhythmically given some configuration of language. This text orientation is no new departure in rhythmic study, either. It is continuous with the long philological tradition in English prosody, a tradition that has given us our standard typologies of poetic forms, stanzaic shapes, rhyme schemes, syllabic line counts, stress distributions and so forth (e.g. Schipper 1910; Hamer 1930). As both the title and contents of Brogan's massive bibliography attest

(Brogan 1981), a great deal of work on English prosody has focused on *versification* (the text), not verse *rhythm* (the reader).

Rhythm is one of our basic cognitive abilities; therefore, we might expect a prosodic theory to take the same basic form as theories of other cognitive abilities – for example vision (Marr 1982). As Marr explains, the most basic task of cognition is to process information; therefore, theories of cognition are basically theories of information processing. We use our cognitive abilities to construct useful representations of the external world. A rhythmic structure is one of these useful representations.

The dominant design feature of rhythmic response is its schematic, synthetic form. From formally diverse structures in a rhythmic medium we construct a usefully organized model of that medium's basic physical, structural and teleological energies: patterns of physical pulsations (beats vs off-beats), structural culminations (peaks vs valleys) and implied goals (arrivals vs departures). As with other cognitive theories, a theory of this information transformation will have three essential parts: (1) an explanation of *why* this transformation is useful; (2) a description of *what* is transformed into *what*; and (3) an account of *how* this transformation is performed. Part (1) confronts the problem of rhythmic *function*; (2), rhythmic *representation*; and (3), rhythmic *process*.

The organization of the book is straightforward, moving from an explanation of the theoretical problem and a review of comment to date (Chapters 1 and 2) to a solution to the problem (Chapters 3 and 4) and an application of this solution to critical practice (Chapter 5). Chapter 6 explores implications.

Acknowledgements

I would not have been able to complete this book without the help of many institutions and individuals. For all of this help, I am thankful. My working conditions were aided by teaching reductions at the University of Wisconsin at Milwaukee (1981–5) and by a junior leave from teaching at the University of Michigan (Fall, 1986). A deep personal thanks to Eleanor Berry, who gave my ideas about poetic rhythm hundreds of hours of her time and energy over the last decade. Special thanks to Donald Wesling, Marina Tarlinskaja, David Gil, Derek Attridge, Gilbert Youmans and Fred Lerdahl for their substantial responses to my ideas over the last five years. And thanks to those who commented on earlier drafts of this book: Randolph Quirk, David Crystal, Terry Brogan, Donald Freeman, Timothy Austin, James Winn, Reuven Tsur, George Wright, Dennis Taylor and Richard Bailey.

My greatest debts of gratitude are to those who made my academic life possible; to my parents for their example and inspiration; to Sidney Greenbaum for his personal generosity and professional support; and to my wife and children for their love and understanding. For these gifts, words fail.

We are grateful to the following for permission to reproduce poems;

Elizabeth Barnett, Literary Executor, for 'Spring' by Edna St Vincent Millay in *Collected Poems* (published by Harper & Row), copyright 1921, 1948 by Edna St Vincent Millay; Grafton Books, an imprint of HarperCollins Publishers, and Liveright Publishing Corporation for 'In Just–', 'be unto love as rain is unto colour; create' and 'so many selves (so many fiends and gods' in *Complete Poems, 1913–1962* by e e Cummings. Copyright © 1923, 1925, 1931, 1935, 1938, 1939, 1940, 1944, 1945, 1946, 1947, 1948, 1949, 1950,

1951, 1952, 1953, 1954, 1955, 1956, 1957, 1958, 1959, 1960, 1961, 1962 by the Trustees for the e e Cummings Trust, copyright © 1961, 1963, 1968 by Marion Morehouse Cummings; Penguin Books Ltd and New Directions Publishing Corporation for 'Without Invention' in Paterson by William Carlos Williams (published by Penguin Books, 1983/New Directions, 1963), copyright © William Carlos Williams, 1946, 1948, 1949, 1951, 1958, copyright © Florence Williams, 1963, US copyright © 1962 by William Carlos Williams; Random Century Group, on behalf of the Estate of Robert Frost & Henry Holt & Company, Inc. for 'Pertinax' and 'Nothing Gold Can Stay' by Robert Frost in *The Poetry of Robert Frost* edited by Edward Connery Lathem (published by Jonathan Cape Ltd/Henry Holt & Co, Inc.). Copyright 1923, © 1969 by Holt, Rinehart & Winston, copyright 1936, 1951 by Robert Frost, copyright © 1964 by Lesley Frost Ballantine and for permission to reproduce: George T. Jones for chart of overtones and circle of fifths (our pages 157 & 161) from *Music Theory* (1974) pp. 5 & 35; Charles Scribner's Sons, an imprint of Macmillan Publishing Company for 'to be or not to be' scansion from Lanier's *The Science of English Verse;* Music on our page 172, Leonard Meyer: *Explaining Music: Essays and Explorations*, one illustration from page 39, copyright © 1973 The Regents of the University of California; figures on our pages 176 and 177 © 1983 by The Massachusetts Institute of Technology from Fred Lerdahl and Ray Jackendoff's *A Generative Theory of Tonal Music*; Garland Publisher fox six pieces of material (on our pages 46, 47 & 48) from *The Intonational System in English* (1975) by Mark Liberman, pp. 35 & 37; Music (our page 166) from *Free Composition, Supplement: Musical Examples* by Henrich Schenker, translated and edited by Ernest Oster. Copyright © 1979. Reprinted with permission of Schrimer Books, a division of Macmillan Inc.; Illustrations (on our pages 158, 159 & 164) from *Music: A Listener's Introduction* by Kenneth Levy. Copyright © 1983 by Kenneth Levy. Reprinted by permission of HarperCollins Publishers.

Let chaos storm!
Let cloud shapes swarm!
I wait for form.

(Robert Frost
'Pertinax')

Semper idem sed non eodem modo

(Heinrich Schenker
Der freie Satz)

Work is repetition, without
differentiation, without salience,
putting down apples, making hay.
And music, the work
song? Gives shape,
lends emphasis. Groups
the repeated motions, turns
tick tick tick tick tick
into tick *tock*, tick *tock*, tick
tock – the halves of the gashed apple
fall asunder, releasing
the apple smell, white hearts
of apple flesh beaded
with juice, brown seeds bursting
from their split nest.

                              The halves
are halved again, etc. The brush
is dipped and lifted, full,
to the wall, and emptied
stroke by stroke, back and forth,
across each broad siding board.
Another bale and another is pitched
to the top of the stack in the rack wagon.
Hands and arms move to music,
to a music heard in the mind's ear
that groups the motions into steps,
the steps into parts, the parts into larger parts
of the task, that shapes the flow of energy
into minor and major tensions and resolutions.

(Eleanor Berry
'A Definition of Rhythm')

Chapter 1

Current approaches

> It is better to have weak answers to the right questions than to persist in asking the wrong questions.
>
> (Donald Wesling)[1]
>
> To make a good poem, meter is not enough.
>
> (Benjamin Hrushovski)[2]

1.1 RHYTHM AND MULTIDIMENSIONAL FORM

Rhythmic experience is essentially *multidimensional*. While the basic elements of a rhythmic pattern are often simple, each simple pattern can be combined in a variety of ways into comparable (or larger) patterns, with these further patterns arrayed variously within the rhythmic experience as a whole. When the rhythmic medium is complex, the formal *sources* of these patterns can also be various. Rhythmic responses can be elicited by many different phenomena, with the rhythmic effects of these phenomena converging or conflicting as they will.

Our rhythmic response to verse is one of these more complex cases. Language is a complex rhythmic medium, with many patterned forms of diverse shapes, sizes and textures: letters, punctuation, graphic layout (spacing, lineation, paragraphing), sounds, stresses, accents, pitch contours, words, phrases, sentences, meanings, arguments, etc.; and poets draw on all of these formal resources in realizing their rhythmic intentions. In fact, most poems are so intricately patterned in their rhythmic organization that they defy exhaustive analysis. Consider Blake's 'The Sick Rose'.

> O Rose, thou art sick.
> The invisible worm
> That flies in the night,
> In the howling storm:
>
> Has found out thy bed
> Of crimson joy:
> And his dark secret love
> Does thy life destroy.

Compared with other verse that we know, 'The Sick Rose' has a relatively simple rhythmic structure. It has a regular meter (two strong beats per line, alternating one or two non-prominent syllables between prominent syllables), a fairly normal syntax (unelaborated, uninverted, uninterrupted), a controlled graphic layout (lines and quatrains that follow the metrical structure, fairly normal punctuation, standard orthography), end rhyme (of various sorts) in a regular pattern (abxb), etc. The fact that the poem is short also contributes to this simplicity. All things being equal, more rhythmic complexity can be generated in a large space than in a short one. 'The Sick Rose' has only two sentences and thirty-four words.

In an absolute sense, the rhythmic structure of 'The Sick Rose' is anything but simple, however. The 'regular' features of the text that we have just noted *do* constrain its rhythmic volatility. The text's visual appearance gives it an orderly, symmetrical form. The meter gives it an engaging pulse and a large-scale repetitive frame. And the rhymes punctuate this frame with a pattern of sonic expectation and return. None the less, the real rhythmic action in the poem is something that develops more against and within this controlled structure than because of its presence. To equate the rhythm of 'The Sick Rose' with these few controlling regularities is to equate its movement with any syntactically regular eight-line poem with two beats per line, an abxb rhyme scheme, and a regular visual layout – for example 'Rock-a-bye, Baby'.

> Rock-a-bye, baby,
> Thy cradle is green,
> Father's a nobleman,
> Mother's a queen;
>
> And Betty's a lady,
> And wears a gold ring;
> And Johnny's a drummer,
> And drums for the king.

This equation is valid to a point, but in any serious rhythmic comparison this point is quickly passed.

As I experience it, the most dominant movement in 'The Sick Rose' derives from its 'sentencing'. The poem has two sentences. The first has five words and spans one line; the second has twenty-nine words and spans the remaining seven lines. This divides the text into two asymmetrical parts, parts whose skewed quantities generate a startling psychological acceleration in the second part. On some rhythmic level, the five words in the first line cover the same rhythmic span as the twenty-nine words in the next seven lines.

Part I: O Rose, thou art sick.

Part II: The invisible worm
That flies in the night,
In the howling storm:

Has found out thy bed
Of crimson joy:
And his dark secret love
Does thy life destroy.

This 'sentencing' also affects the directional movement of the text. The two sentences are not just formal parallels; they are parallels of sense and significance as well. In a flourish, the first sentence addresses the Rose and laments its state. Then the second sentence details cause, spreading out a scenario that sweeps precipitously from actor, to setting, to action, to effect. This narrative movement overwhelms the informational and emotive impact of the first line, giving the text a climactic movement, a movement that is supported further by the sheer physical weight and formal complexity of the second sentence.

At lower levels of structure, we find further instances of energizing asymmetry. Within the two sentences at the highest level, the first sentence has one main clause while the second has two. This asymmetry contributes further to the felt concentration of the first line and the felt expansion and activity of the next seven.

```
                    ┌─────────────────────┐
                    O Rose, thou art sick.
┌──────────────────────────────────────────────────────────────┐
    ┌──────────────────────────┐    ┌──────────────────────────┐
         The invisible worm              And his dark secret love
         That flies in the night,        Does thy life destroy.
         In the howling storm:
         Has found out thy bed
         Of crimson joy:
```

This binary second sentence is also unbalanced. It has an expanded first part and contracted second part, an apportioning that further heightens the rhythmic acceleration in lines 2–6 while delaying and concentrating the textual climax. The opposing distribution of informational strength and physical length is also important. The concentration of activity and physical weight in the informationally weak first conjoin tends to balance the rhythmic strength in the two parts of the sentence, partially muting the final climax.

The rhythmic energy in lines 2–6 is heightened further by lower levels of articulation. The most striking effect is the varying relations between syntactic expectation and visual/metrical parsing. Compared with the short, bare syntax of the first sentence, the subject of the first conjoin in the second sentence (*The invisible worm/That flies in the night,/In the howling storm:*) is dramatically extended, suspending the structural arrival of the sentence for three lines. In fact, for the structure to be completed, the syntax must ride over the stanza break, finding its predicate (*has found out thy bed . . .*) in line 5, with even this structure being surprisingly extended through line 6 (*. . . Of crimson joy*). These 'grammetric' relations produce a highly strained curve of rhythmic energy.

The interaction between intonational phrasing and metrical/visual structures contributes further to this prosodic contour. Throughout the poem, meter and intonational phrasing are kept closely in phase. Most of the lines end firmly with a strong pitch accent and tonal break. Five of the eight lines are blocked off with punctuation; the break between lines 7 and 8 occurs between subject and predicate and is reinforced with a syntactic inversion (*does thy life destroy*); and the break between lines 2 and 3 is between a phrasal head and a post-modifying clause, a syntactic juncture that often invites a tonal break as well. This tonal–metrical convergence drives the lines forward with a hypnotic regularity, further accentuating the rhythmic acceleration and crescendo generated by the syntax.

This rhythmic shape is also reinforced by *variations* in the intonational phrasing. Prosodic phrasing merges most completely with metrical articulation in lines 2–4. Line 1 begins with a stressed syllable in a metrically weak position (*O*) and is broken into two tone units; lines 5 and 7 have stressed syllables in metrically weak positions (*found*, *se*[-cret]); and line 6 is contracted to four syllables. These variations slow the perceived movement of the verse. On the other hand, lines 2–4 drive across the page in unimpeded duple units, units that are somewhat expanded at lower levels.

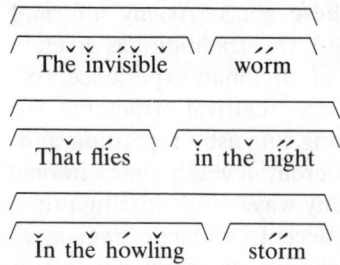

This pattern is not broken until line 5, where the intonational contour expands to three phrases at the lower level (*has found/ out /thy bed*), crests before the line break (at *out*), and then rides over into line 6. Like the syntax, structures at this level accelerate and energize lines 2–4, while slowing surrounding sections.

We could go on with this analysis, but even these few comments make the point. The rhythmic shape of 'The Sick Rose' does not result from a few conventional regularities imposed on a diffuse, unpatterned medium. This shape results from the simultaneous presentation of a diverse range of coherent patterning within a unified, multidimensional form. At the highest level, the asymmetric narrative structure gives the text an impulsive, rising movement. At middle levels, the suspended, asymmetric syntax both heightens and particularizes this movement, producing a maximum of tension and acceleration in lines 2–4, a dramatic structural arrival and extension in lines 5 and 6, and a muted, concentrated climax in lines 7 and 8. And lower intonational–metrical relations underscore this global contour with a hypnotic regularity. The rythm of 'The Sick Rose' is a product of all of this patterning – and more. The rhythm of most verse is similarly complex.

1.2 PROSODIC THEORY

The major task of a prosodic theory should be to model and motivate this coherent diversity, to detail in some efficient way the structure, sources and effects of these multidimensional experiences. The theory should be able to tell us what language structures characteristically produce a rhythmic response, how individual responses are combined into more complex organizations, and how these more complex structures in turn affect the perceiving subject (perceptually, emotively and conceptually).

To this point, the voluminous writing on verse prosody has made considerable progress towards these goals. As my informal comments on 'The Sick Rose' illustrate, this tradition has given us ways to talk about many dimensions of rhythmic experience. We have some illuminating ways to describe metrical structure. We have diverse terminologies for classifying linguistic repetition and parallelism as it occurs at many different levels (sonic, intonational, syntactic, semantic). We have many ways of identifying prominence in language (theories of stress, accent, syntactic emphasis, etc.). And we even have ways of analysing structural anticipation and arrival (theories of syntactic periodicity, narrative tension, textual closure, etc.).

The major difficulty has been to find some way to unify these diverse analytical tools and the phenomena they describe. While we have many ways of analysing certain parts of rhythmic response, we have been much less successful at making sense of our rhythmic response to language as a whole, as that response coheres as a larger, multidimensional experience. Rather, confronted with the diversity of individual rhythmic patterns, prosodists have tended to solve problems of rhythmic description as they arise, in a disjointed, piecemeal fashion, overgeneralizing solutions to problems in restricted domains into diverse systems of only loosely related principles and analytical procedures. Most prosodists have developed ways of describing phenomena unique to poetry (poetic forms, rhyme, etc.). Prose rhythmists have focused on rhythmic phenomena more characteristic of prose (syntactic parallelism, periodicity, narrative organization, etc.). Free verse prosodists have described non-metrical patterning in verse (visual layout; visual–syntactic 'scissoring'; syntactic fragmentation, elaboration and dislocation; lexical repetition, etc.). Linguists have analysed rhythmic aspects of grammatical organization (word stress, phonological phrasing, intonation, etc.). But historically, each of these analytical systems has been developed in relative isolation from the others and therefore with little attention to their relation. The result has been a huge body of writing, often useful in its particulars but lacking coherence and consensus on just those issues that should constitute its most fundamental concerns. We have many analyses of particular rhythmic phenomena in language, but no workable rhythmic theory.[3]

1.3 CURRENT THEORIES

At present there are many 'approaches' to English verse rhythm, each with relatively distinct assumptions, methods, textual foci and critical results. Some of our newer theories remain the proposals of isolated individuals or groups of individuals. But most of these theories have a long history and many followers. *Fifteen* of these theoretical 'approaches' are responsible for most of the achievements (and limitations) in our understanding of the rhythm of English texts. Before we proceed to develop a more workable alternative, it might be useful to review these 'approaches' here.

1.3.1 Foot-substitution prosodists[4]

The oldest and still most dominant approach to English verse rhythm derives from classical scansion and has come to be known as *foot-substitution prosody*. A foot-substitution scansion represents our rhythmic response to language by marking a line of verse into a series of sections ('feet'), each of which represents a normative spacing of beats with respect to off-beats at the most salient metrical level. For instance, given that most of the lines of 'The Sick Rose' begin with an unstressed syllable, end with a stressed syllable, and have two stressed syllables per line, a foot-substitution scansion divides each line into two feet, with the expected beat on the last syllable of each foot (I leave the beats unmarked; I mark feet with '/' within the line; I mark stresses with ' ´ ' above the line).

O Róse, / thou art sick.

The invi / sible worm

That flies / in the night,

In the how / ling storm:

Has found oút / thy béd
Of crím / son jóy:
And his dárk / sécret lóve
Does thy lífe / destróy.

In this tradition, rhythmic phrasing is most often represented by lexical stress. These lexical stresses constitute an 'actual' 'prose rhythm', which stands in opposition to a 'silent' 'metrical rhythm' (Fussell 1979: 32; Malof 1970: 1). The continuous opposition between these two rhythms creates a 'counterpoint, modulation, tension, syncopation, interplay, variation' (Fussell 1979: 32).

˘ ʹ ˘ ʹ ˘ ʹ ˘ ˘ ˘ ʹ   prose rhythm
˘ ʹ ˘ ʹ ˘ ʹ ˘ ʹ ˘ ʹ   metrical rhythm
And leaves /the world /to dark/ness and /to me

In addition to stress, foot-substitution prosodists also mark places where breaks in phrasing interfere with metrical continuity or where continuities in phrasing override metrical breaks. In this tradition, a *caesura* is a line-internal pause caused by a break in syntax/sense; *enjambment* is the *lack* of such a break at line end. The elusiveness of the textual correlate of 'pause' makes the scansion of these constructs unstable, however. In order to avoid these difficulties, most detailed studies of caesural positioning in this tradition (e.g. Oras 1960) have equated 'pause' with some overt graphic marker, deriving a hierarchy of caesural 'strength' from a hierarchy of punctuation, while most theoretical studies of the emotive *effects* of enjambment (e.g. Hollander 1985; Fowler 1966b; Cushman 1985) have derived a hierarchy of phrase–line 'counterpoint' directly from a syntactic hierarchy.

Syntactic constituent broken	*Effect*
morpheme	higher 'counterpoint'
word	
phrase	
clause	
sentence	lower 'counterpoint'
group of sentences	

For instance, using Robert Frost's 'Mending Wall', a partial punctuation/syntactic hierarchy might look like the following.

Between sentences/Across a period

(15–16)
We keep the wall between us as we go.
To each the boulders that have fallen to each.

Between clauses/Across a comma

(1–2)
Something there is that doesn't love a wall,
That sends the frozen-ground-swell under it,

Between phrases/No punctuation

(39–40)
Bringing a stone grasped firmly by the top
In each hand, like an old-stone savage armed.

The claim is that these enjambments are in increasing 'counterpoint' to the metrical 'frame'.

Central to all traditional work on caesurae and enjambment has been the claim that line-final breaks in phrasing are more 'normal' than line-medial breaks, and that line-medial breaks are in turn more 'normal' than breaks early and late in the line. For instance, the syntax of the following breaks in Donne's 'Love's Deity' are approximately parallel (both occur between a linking verb and a complement), but the break with the shorter segment after the line end (i.e. 13–14) is in 'stronger' counterpoint to the line.

Longer segment

(19–20)
Oh were wee wak'ned by this Tyrannie
To'ungod this child again, *it could not be*
That I should love, who loves not mee.

Shorter segment

Correspondencies
(12–14)
Only his subject was; *It cannot bee*
Love, till I love her, that loves mee.

In order to describe this phenomenon, many English prosodists (e.g. Golomb 1979; Linville 1984; Stein 1942) speak of a 'segment length' factor in enjambment, and following Grammont (1930), distinguish between *types* of phrase–meter imbalance. If the lesser part of a unit overflows on to the next line, this overflow is called a *rejet*; if the greater part of a unit overflows on to the next line, this overflow is called a *contre-rejet*. Milton is fond of strong rejets.

> Thus with the Year
> Seasons return, *but not to me returns*
> *Day*, or the sweet approach of Ev'n or Morn,
>
> (*PL* 3.41–3)

Shakespeare often uses strong contre-rejets:

> You have begot me, bred me, lov'd me. *I*
> *Return those duties back as are right fit*,
>
> (*King Lear* I,i,96–7)

In addition to enjambment and caesurae (points of phrase–meter interaction), many foot-substitution prosodists also mention phrasal structures in their own right. The most frequently analysed structures occur at the 'lowest' level and are given various names: 'simple phrasing' (Stewart 1930: 11–16), 'phrasal rhythm' (Shapiro and Beum 1965: 61; Baum 1922: 37–40), 'linkage' (Beardsley 1972: 241–5), 'word rhythm' (Malof 1970: 18–19), 'rhetorical sections' (Saintsbury 1910: 268–9), and others. These phrases are formed by grouping syntactically related unstressed syllables around one sonic prominence, and thus the breaks between these phrases differ from caesurae in being independent of pause. For instance, even though the line can be said without perceptible pauses, this phrasing leads one to perceive the first line of Gray's 'Elegy' in the following phrases.

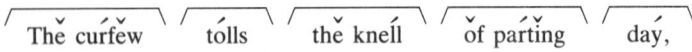

Or, as Stewart (1930: 13) hums it:

>   Ta-tumpty   tumm   ta-tumm   ta-tumpty   tumm

This line, then, has no caesurae and is not enjambed, but it is composed of five 'simple' phrases that crosscut metrical foot boundaries.

'simple phrasing'

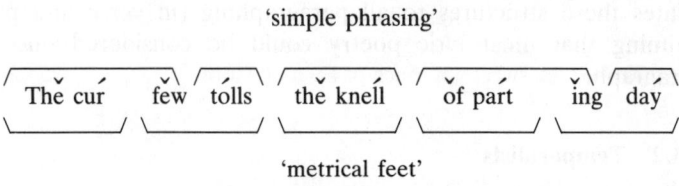

'metrical feet'

Within the foot-substitution approach, several prosodists have noticed that simple phrasing has a strong effect on rhythmic direction: perceptions of 'rising' movement vs 'falling' movement (Malof 1970: 19; Wimsatt and Beardsley 1959: 112–13; Creek 1920; Stewart 1925, 1930: 37–41). Many prosodists in this tradition also claim that the *boundaries* of these simple phrases can interact with metrical structures. For instance, in the following phrasal and metrical segmentation

'phrasing'

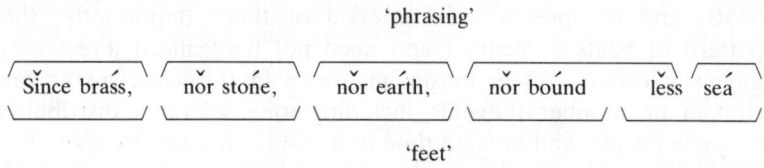

'feet'

Shapiro and Beum (1965: 61) claim that the word *boundless* 'tries to preserve its integrity' and 'refuses to be torn in two by the meter'. This creates 'a pleasing conflict (or counterpoint or tension)'. The result is an intralineal process that reproduces the interlineal process of enjambment: a unit of syntax/sense/prose rhythm overruns a metrical boundary.

Beyond simple phrasing, most foot-substitution metrists also recognize higher levels of phrasal organization. All recognize the *verse paragraph*, and most mention the *verse period*, although it would be difficult to formulate any consensus definitions of these structures. For instance, Saintsbury (1910: 33) defines verse paragraphs in terms of pause, E. Smith (1923: 213–27) defines them in terms of an organic cohesion of thought (a more common practice), and Hanford (1944: 293–325) adds syntactic and metrical considerations (sustained syntactic periodicity and line–syntax counterpoint). An unsigned entry in the *Princeton Encyclopedia of Poetry and Poetics* defines the verse paragraph as 'one or more sentences unified by a dominant mood or thought' (1974: 890) and relates these structures to all paragraphing (in verse and prose), claiming that most lyric poetry could be considered one verse paragraph.

1.3.2 Temporalists

Over the centuries, the most consistent rival of foot-substitution prosody has been *temporal prosody*.[5] Prosodists in this tradition reject the foot as a basis for scansion. The foot is neither a grouping of sound, nor a grouping of sense, nor a grouping of equal times, nor a grouping of equivalent shapes. Therefore, it has little relation to verse movement (e.g. Thomson 1923: 158–80).

As an alternative, this tradition divides verse into *measures*, like a musical score, and marks the relative duration (or *quantity*) of the linguistic events within these spans. As in music, each measure begins with a major beat, contains a regular pattern of subordinate beats, and occupies a fixed interval of time. Importantly, this pattern of beats is abstract and need not be realized directly by linguistic events. As in music, measures in the same meter can contain any number of events, including none, with time distributed between events, and unfilled time in measures marked by rests. For instance, if we use simple numbers to represent time intervals, Croll (1929: 392) scans the first line of *Paradise Lost* as follows:

```
2    4    2 2   2 2  3 12      2    2       2   4    2
Of/man's fi/rst diso/bedience/(rest) and the/fruit (rest)
```

In this scansion the line has a one-beat anacrusis (*of*) and five three-beat measures. In the first measure, *man's* takes the major beat and one following subordinate beat, with part of *first* getting the second subordinate beat. In the second measure, the second half of *first* gets the major beat, *dis-* gets one subordinate beat, and *o-* gets one subordinate beat. In the third measure, *bed-* gets the major beat and begins a subordinate beat, *-i-* completes this second beat, and *-ence* gets the third beat. In the fourth measure, the major beat falls on a rest, *and* gets the second beat, and *the* gets the third beat. And in the last measure, *fruit* gets the major beat and the following subordinate beat, with the final subordinate beat realized by a rest. Temporal metrists call this structure of beats, measures and quantities by various names (*rhythm* (Thomson), *meter* (Leech), *secondary rhythm* (Lanier)), but a scansion similar to this is common to most of the prosodists in this tradition.

Being freed from the foot and being conscious of musical parallels, prosodists in this tradition have also made fairly extensive comment on rhythmic phrasing. Lanier (1880) recognizes three types of what he calls *tertiary rhythm*: the phrase, the alliterative group, and the logical group (or 'emphatic word group'). *Phrases* are directly parallel to musical phrases and are indicated by pause. The *alliterative group* unites bars through repeated 'tone color' (83). Thomson (1923) makes parallel, but somewhat different, observations, isolating what he calls *sound groups* and *sense groups*. Thomson even offers two 'laws' of sound-group formation (143–4): (1) Syllables with weaker accents are attracted to syllables with stronger accents, and (2) proximate syllables are more attracted than distant syllables.

1.3.3 Phrasalists

A third tradition sees English verse as principally a phrasal patterning, with varying relations to meter. Some prosodists in this tradition deny the existence of meter entirely (e.g. Guest 1882; Skeat 1894, 1898; Nist 1964). Most prosodists in this tradition argue for phrasing without denying the existence of meter, however. Some stress the centrality of phrasing, even in metrical verse (e.g. Liddell 1902 and Scott 1925). Some argue for a more balanced treatment of meter and phrasing (e.g. La Drière 1943, 1974, and his various students: Berg 1962, Lindberg-Seyersted 1968, Barry 1969, and Dougherty 1973; and Cummings and Herum 1967). And some argue for a phrasal scansion in accentual verse and free verse, where meter is absent or less evident (e.g. Bridges 1921 on accentual verse; and Weeks 1921, Mitchell 1969, Jannacone 1973 and Berry 1981a on free verse).

The inventories of rhythmic units in these phrasal prosodies often overlap, but often differ as well. The most common unit is the 'simple rhythm phrase' of the foot-substitution and temporalist traditions, a phrase with one lexical stress and related proclitics and enclitics. With minor variations, some phrasalists (e.g. La Drière, Cummings and Herum) include only this unit, and therefore their phrasal systems differ in only minor ways from comments on phrasing in the central metrical traditions.

A more important contribution by the phrasalists is their treatment of phrasal sequences. For instance, Barry (1969) shows how T.S. Eliot often repeats combinations of phrasal shapes (what Barry calls *phrasal cadences*) and how these combinations organize lines into various phrasal symmetries (what she calls *lineal cadences*). For example, in 'La Figlia che Piange' she finds that amphibrachic groups often precede anapaestic groups.

Line
3 Weáve, / weáve / thĕ súnlĭght / ĭn yóur haír
6 Wĭth ă fŭgĩtĭve / rĕséntmĕnt / ĭn yóur eýes

Given geometrical patterns such as these, many phrasalists claim that the pleasures that we derive from verse rhythm are more spatial than temporal. Rhythm is a product of 'figured harmonies' of thought, as those thoughts are embodied in the fluctuating intensities, contractions and expansions of sound.

A few phrasalists also consider rhythmic units above the level of the 'pause-unit', units that leave the domain of sound entirely for more abstract levels of structure. For instance, Liddell (1902) finds the centre of verse rhythm not in sonic accents and emphases but in our ordered attention to units of meaning (what he calls 'thought-moments'). Several prosodists have made similar claims for free verse that displays rhythmic regularity at higher levels. Both Allen (1935) and Jannacone (1973) claim these structures for Whitman. Allen (253) scans the first two lines of 'Great are the Myths':

/ /	/

Great are the myths –   I too delight in them;
Great are Adam and Eve – I too look back and accept them.

Jannacone (78) scans lines 1140–3 of 'Song of Myself':

/ | | / Births have brought us richness and variety
     | And other births will bring us richness and variety.
     | / I do not call one greater and one smaller.
     | That which fills its period and place is equal to any.

Some phrasalists even work with more than one level of structure at a time. For example, in his analysis of Whitman, Mitchell (1969) develops a system that works with four phrasal levels. Stresses cluster into pause-groups, pause-groups cluster into lines, and lines cluster into verse paragraphs. Mitchell argues that the prosodic interest in Whitman is created by interactions among these grouping levels.

1.3.4 Prose rhythmists

There is also a long, if less rich, tradition in the study of English prose rhythm (e.g. Saintsbury 1912; Baum 1952; Scott 1926; Tempest 1930; Croll 1919; and other references in Brogan 1981: 125–9). The most influential work on English prose rhythm has been Saintsbury (1912). Parallel to his approach to verse, Saintsbury analyses prose rhythm into 'feet'. As with the 'groups' or 'simple phrases' of verse phrasalists such as La Drière, Saintsbury's prose feet are longer than verse feet, extending to five syllables (a dochmiac); however, unlike La Drière's groups, Saintsbury's feet can also contain several stresses (or 'long' syllables). This admission of multiple stresses and large spans demands a fairly substantial catalogue of foot types.

Saintsbury finds that the most felicitously rhythmical prose fashions its foot sequences into an *ordered variety*. Juxtaposed feet of the same shape are avoided; variety among foot shapes is maximized; and the various shapes that appear are ordered into coherent patterns: (1) *grades*, that move from long to short and short to long; (2) variations on some common shape; and (3) shaping that is appropriate in some way to its larger context (e.g. the use of 'rising' feet in inspirational contexts or 'falling' feet for endings). Saintsbury's recurring theme is the *opposition* between verse rhythm and prose rhythm. Verse presents recurring feet (with some variation); prose presents varied feet (with some recurrence).

In addition to 'feet' and their ordered variety, the classical tradition in the analysis of prose rhythm also recognizes a hierarchy of higher-level units. Four units are identified: the period, the phrase, the colon and the comma (Croll 1919: 324–8). Following Aristotle and Hobbes, Croll defines a period as 'a part as is perfect in itself, and has such length as may easily be comprehended by the understanding' (1919: 324). Croll stresses that the period is often a sentence but that it is essentially a rhythmical and psychological unit and therefore it can sometimes override syntactic boundaries. In his study, Croll analyses the translations of the Latin prayers in the English *Book of Common Prayer*, all of which are composed of one period.

Feet of two syllables	Of three	Of four	Of five
Iamb, ⌣ –	Amphibrach, ⌣ – ⌣	Antispast, ⌣ – – ⌣	Dochmiac
Pyrrhic, ⌣ ⌣	Anapaest, ⌣ ⌣ –	Choriamb, – ⌣ ⌣ –	A foot of five syllables, in which the possible permutations of long and short give a very large number of varieties. In English prose those containing *two* long and *three* short are perhaps the commonest, arranged in their different combinations. *One* long and *four* short, similarly varied, is not uncommon; and *three* longs with *two* shorts intervening may be found; but more than three longs, I think, never. For possible prolongations into *six* syllables see text.
Spondee, – –	Anti-Bacchic, – – ⌣	Di-iamb, ⌣ – ⌣ –	
Trochee, – ⌣	Bacchic, ⌣ – –	Dispondee, – – – –	
	Cretic, – ⌣ –	Ditrochee, – ⌣ – ⌣	
	Dactyl, – ⌣ ⌣		
	Molossus, – – –	Epitrite (four forms) { – – – ⌣ / – – ⌣ – / – ⌣ – – / ⌣ – – – }	
	Tribrach, ⌣ ⌣ ⌣		
		Ionic *a majore*, – – ⌣ ⌣	
		Ionic *a minore*, ⌣ ⌣ – –	
		Paeon (four forms) { – ⌣ ⌣ ⌣ / ⌣ – ⌣ ⌣ / ⌣ ⌣ – ⌣ / ⌣ ⌣ ⌣ – }	
		Proceleusmatic, ⌣ ⌣ ⌣ ⌣	

(Saintsbury 1912: xvi)

> Almighty and everlasting God who dost govern all things in heaven and earth; mercifully hear the supplications of thy people, and grant us thy peace all the days of our life.
> (2 Sun. after Ep.)

Of the next highest levels, the colon seems to be more basic and widespread. A period can be composed of only one colon, but most periods are divided into a number of cola, up to a maximum of eight. A colon is determined by 'the physiological laws of breathing' (1919: 325); therefore, some consider the colon to be the basic unit of oratorical style. Cola have an average of about ten syllables, usually no more than twenty-five, have one to four 'emphatic accents', and are usually arranged in physically and syntactically parallel patterns (isocola) against which the orator can deviate for expressive effect. For instance, in the following collect (4 Sun. after Ep.), Croll finds *five* cola. The first two are closely comparable in length (twenty and eighteen syllables); the last three all have nine syllables.

> O God, who knowest us to be set in the midst of so
>   many and great dangers
> that by reason of the frailty of our nature we cannot stand
>   upright;
> grant us such strength and protection
> as may support us in all dangers
> and carry us through all temptations.

Phrases group cola. If divided, most periods are divided into *two* phrases, often related by some important syntactic connection. For instance, in the collects Croll studies, the first phrase is an invocation composed of a vocative with a post-modifying relative clause and the second phrase is a supplication composed of an imperative main clause or a coordinated series of imperative main clauses.

> Almighty and everlasting God who dost govern all things in heaven
>   and earth;
> mercifully hear the supplications of thy people, and grant us thy
>   peace all the days of our life.

Cola are divided into *commata*. Croll stresses that commata are often purely 'melodic and rhythmic' (1919: 327), cutting across natural divisionings in syntax and sense. For instance, he claims that the second colon in the first phrase of the 4 Sun. after Ep. is divided into two commata, the first presenting an initial adverbial ('by reason . . .') and the second, the other clausal elements ('we cannot . . .').

> that by reason of the frailty of our nature
> we cannot stand upright

The other cola in the period remain undivided.

Prose rhythmists have also commented upon the *cursus*, a system of rhythmical formulae used at the end of commata and cola in Medieval Latin in order to give these rhetorical units a more perceptible rhythmic flow. As Croll (1919) describes them, the English *cursus* forms cover some portion of the last five to twelve syllables of an oratorical unit (period, phrase, colon or comma). The cursus begins with a strong accent, covers a relatively long span of unstressed syllables, encounters a second accent, one that is weaker than the first, and then covers a relatively short series of (optional) unstressed syllables. If the series of unstressed syllables after the first accent exceeds three, a secondary accent appears between the two major accents.

strong accent	optional secondary accent	weak accent	
//	. . . (\) . . .	/	. . .
	relatively long segment		relatively short segment (optional)

Croll names these patterns by numbering the position of the accents, counting from the end of figure (e.g. 6–2, 8–4–2, etc.).

In Latin, the *cursus* forms were conventionalized into explicitly named and regulated patterns of certain lengths and accentual positionings. *Planus* forms had no subordinate accent and ended with one unstressed syllable. Using Croll's numerical system, the English correlates to the Latin *planus* forms would be 5–2 or 6–2 figures.

Planus – 1   (5–2)   hélp and defénd us
                     5   4   3 2 1

Planus – 2   (6–2)   wrítten for our léarning
                     6 5   4   3 2   1

Tardus forms had no subordinate accent but ended with two unstressed syllables. In Croll's notation, the English correlates to tardus forms would be 6–3 and 7–3 figures.

Tardus – 1   (6–3)   góverned and sánctified
                     6 5   4   3 21

Tardus – 2   (7–3)   dángers and advérsities
                     7 6 5   4   3 21

Velox forms had a subordinate accent. Croll argues that there could be many English correlates of these forms: 7–4–2, 8–4–2, 8–5–3, 9–5–3, etc., and even forms with juxtaposed stresses (7–4–3, 7–4–2, 9–4–3, etc.) or final stresses (7–4–1, 7–3–1, etc.), forms that did not occur in Latin.

Velox   (7–4–2)   púnished for oùr offénces
                  7 6   5   4 3 2 1

Velox   (8–4–2)   wéakness of our mòrtal náture
                  8   7 6 5   4   3 2 1

Velox   (8–5–3)   defénd us from àll advérsity
                  8   7 6   5   4   3 2 1

Croll shows that both the collects and much rhythmical prose make considerable use of these *cursus* forms.

The other sort of 'periodicity' that has concerned prose rhythmists has been the rhythmic effects of anticipational and extensional articulation within the structure of the English sentence, independent of its scoring into oratorical units (e.g. Leech and Short 1981: 225–30; Christensen and Christensen 1978: 23–44; Corbett 1971: 443–58; J.M. Williams 1981: 79–162; Nash 1980: 111–19). The primary focus of this work has been on the linear ordering of substantial yet optional constituents (what Quirk *et al.* call *adverbials*) within the extended, elaborated sentence. Sentences that place adverbial elaboration *before* the mandatory elements of the main clause (i.e. subject, verb, objects and complements) are called *periodic* (or 'left-branching'); sentences that place adverbial elaboration *after* these mandatory constituents are called *loose* (or 'right-branching'). Sentences that contain both initial and final elaboration in approximately equal proportion are called *balanced*. Medial elaboration (between mandatory elements of the main clause) is less frequent and therefore is not generally named, but we might call these sentences *suspended* (or 'mid-branching'). The primary effects of these different sorts of elaboration are relatively obvious. Left-branching ('periodic') elaboration postpones the presentation of essential matter. Right-branching ('loose') elaboration broadens and deepens the articulation of an essentially completed structure, 'extending' both its structure and meaning. And mid-branching creates both of these effects simultaneously. In most artfully created sentences, these different sorts of elaborations are often symmetrically arrayed, comparable to isocola or verse lines (for example see Nash 1980: 116–17).

Finally, recent prose theorists have also suggested that the larger organization of a prose work can have a 'shape' that we might call rhythmic (Forster 1927; Brown 1950; Barthes [1970] 1974; Townsend 1983). For instance, Forster isolates two types of these larger rhythms – what he calls 'easy' and 'difficult'. 'Easy' rhythm is comparable to the recurrence of a musical theme, for example the 'di-di-di-dum' of Beethoven's fifth symphony. An action, an event, a scene recurs frequently, and with each recurrence gains new associations and significances, giving the fictional work as a whole an internal 'stitching' (1927: 165) independent of its larger compositional partitioning. This sort of 'easy' rhythm in fiction is explored in some detail by Brown (1950) and has been formalized in the semic, symbolic and referential 'codes' of Roland Barthes' *S/Z*. 'Difficult' rhythm is analogous to the structural organization of a musical composition as a whole, the overall relations between its movements. This is a movement 'which some people can hear but no one can tap to' (1927: 164), and Forster claims that most prose fiction resists this rhythm, striving for an opposing and often 'untidy' *expansion*, 'gutted of the common stuff that fills characters . . . and ourselves' (1927: 161). As McCreless (1988) points out, these 'difficult' rhythms in prose fiction are formalized by Barthes in his 'proaeretic' and 'hermeneutic' codes, the codes that represent (1) the normal sequencing of fictional events and behavior, and (2) the posing and solving of fictional enigmas, respectively.

1.3.5 Free verse prosodists

There is also a considerable body of comment on free verse that intersects, extends and complements this comment on conventional verse forms and prose.[6]

Within the major literary traditions, 'free verse' is defined negatively, in opposition to more 'regular' verse forms (i.e. 'meters'). One of the most exhaustive cataloguings of these oppositional relations appears in Ramsey (1968), who isolates ten: free verse is (1) unmetered, (2) metered but unscannable, (3) multiply metered, (4) partially metered, (5) loosely metered, (6) oppositionally metered, (7) accentual, (8) isochronous, (9) non-conventionally metered, or (10) multiply and non-conventionally metered. As Ramsey notes, (2) does not address verse form at all but the descriptive inadequacies of the prosodist, while (1) and (8) fail to distinguish free verse rhythmically from a lineated prose and therefore posit the visual *line* as definitional (more on this in a moment). On the other hand, (3), (4), (5), (6), (7), (9) and (10) define free verse as a novel or complex metrical verse, not as an entirely distinct rhythmic genre, and therefore imply that free verse can be described with traditional analytical tools. As might be expected, temporalists often approach free verse through definition (8) (e.g. Gall 1979 on Pound), while phrasalists often approach free verse through definitions (1) and/or (7) (e.g. Weeks 1921, Allen 1935 and Jannacone 1973 on Whitman; Mitchell 1970 and Cureton 1985a on various poets).

Definitions (3), (4), (5), (6), (7), (9) and (10) are important claims about the rhythms of free verse and have been pursued by various prosodists. These studies have been relatively few and disappointing, however – and for good reason. As 'generative' approaches to prosody have emphasized (e.g. 1.3.6–1.3.13 below) and as we will explore further at the end of this chapter, a foot-substitution scansion is more an analytical convenience, a way of getting around in a verse line (like a musical score), than a metrical *theory*, either of metrical response or of constraints on the linguistic input to a metrical response. In all analyses, a foot-substitution scansion must allow frequent 'variations' from a metrical norm, and unless 'permissible' variations can be distinguished rigorously from 'impermissible' variations, a linguistically volatile metrical text can be given any number of foot-based analyses of both the metrical variation and the metrical norm. Therefore, foot-substitution scansion is intrinsically ill-suited to describing the linguistic volatility that the meters of free verse texts often present (e.g. the relatively unilluminating analysis in Winters 1943; Hartman 1980: 106–29; Malof 1970: 160–3; Gross 1964: 130–214, etc.). In fact, one of the major results of applications of foot-substitution scansion to free verse has been a heightened awareness of the *general* difficulties of foot-based scansions – with versificationally 'regular' texts *and* 'free'.[7]

Free verse prosodists have achieved their most striking successes by following Ramsey's definition (2): free verse is unmetrical; linguistic structures in the free verse line present no normative organization. As I intimated above, this definition isolates the visual line as the definitional feature of free verse (*vis-à-vis* prose).[8]

While visuality has been a relatively peripheral concern in the history of poetry and prosodic criticism, over the past decade free verse prosodists have demonstrated the astonishing complexity of free verse visuality, a complexity that argues for visual form as the dominant 'versification' of our time. In her essay for the new edition of the *Princeton Encyclopedia of Poetry and Poetics*, Eleanor Berry gives 'visual prosody' 'at least' the following functions (Berry, forthcoming b: 2–3):

(1) to indicate juxtapositions of images and ideas;
(2) to signal shifts in tone, perspective, etc.;
(3) to present the reader with an image of form or chaos, crystallization or disintegration, expansion or contraction, or other abstract shape of energy;
(4) to render iconically the subject of the poem, an object referred to in it, the tenor or vehicle of its governing metaphor, etc.;
(5) to lend prominence to phonological, rhetorical or other kinds of patterns in the text;
(6) to signal a general or particular relation to poetic tradition;
(7) to allude to various kinds of printed texts, including ones (such as those of technical writing) that are not normally voiced;
(8) to engage and sustain reader attention by creating visual interest, visual texture;
(9) to engage the reader in the experience of different textual systems cutting across and/or lining up with each other;
(10) to heighten the reader's awareness of the reading process;
(11) to make the text an aesthetic object;
(12) to make manifest various aspects of language, writing and textuality.

As Berry explains as well, many aspects of traditional prosody are also significantly visual: syllabic verse, the stanza, punctuation, indentation, capitalization, word shapes, rhetorical 'schemes' (alliteration, assonance, etc.; repetition, chiasmus, parallelism, etc.), enjambment, the caesura, poetic forms, etc.

As many others have noticed (e.g. B.H. Smith 1968: 234–71; Frank and Sayre (eds) 1988), visuality is also an especially effective means to the ethical, ideological and aesthetic intentions of modern texts: variability, openness, irony, anti-climax, dissonance, volatility, surprise, tension, fragmentation, discontinuity, adirectionality, spatiality, self-referentiality, ambiguity, aconventionality, transparency, 'objectivity', etc. Unlike the effects of traditional versification systems, visual forms are not intrinsically continuous, directional, hierarchical and culminating; and visual forms often array themselves naturally in *opposition* to the conventional structure of the language and its dominant cognitive effects (e.g. meter and rhythmic phrasing), effects that free verse texts often aim to modify, distance or avoid.

These two results of the work of free verse prosodists – (1) their failure to describe the complex non-visual rhythms of free verse, and (2) their success in describing the effects of visual form – put this work in a complex relation to my intention in this book (i.e. the development of a general theory of verse rhythm). The first result intensifies the need for a more adequate rhythmic theory, one that can account for meters that result from both traditional versification and 'free'. It seems evident that free verse poets such as Whitman and Eliot, while taking increased advantage of visuality, draw on largely the same physical and linguistic material in the text, appeal to largely the same cognitive abilities of the reader, and elicit rhythms of largely the same basic shapes as poets who work in more recognizable and describable verse forms. It is also evident that many free verse texts that are intensely visual are *also* traditionally rhythmic and therefore cannot be accounted for with a theory of visual form alone.

On the other hand, the second result suggests that it is best to distinguish the effects of visual form in free verse from rhythmic response *per se*. Where visual forms blur or support rhythmic prominence and divisioning, these forms can be considered an input to rhythmic response. But where visual forms pervasively crosscut traditional rhythmic patterning – calling attention to language, modulating tone, linking sounds and meanings, and performing their many other functions – it seems unprofitable to call them rhythmic. In most cases these visual effects lack the distinguishing features of rhythmic organization: alternating pulsation, steep hierarchical ordering, culminating prominence, etc. Charles Hartman's bald claim that 'what . . . meter can do, lineation alone can also do' (1980: 60) is incomplete and dangerously misleading, if not overtly false. Rhythm and visual form can perform many of the same aesthetic functions, but many of their effects are different, if not oppositional, and many of the details of their formal organization – exactly the details for which a coherent theory of verse experience must account – are sharply distinct. A full theory of verse experience must provide accounts of both visual form and rhythm, but the most efficient path to this end leads through distinct theoretical intermediaries.[9]

1.3.6 Slavic metrists

In this century the most extensive tradition in verse analysis, both metrical and phrasal, has been sustained by Slavic metrists (for English readers useful overviews can be found in Wellek and Warren 158–73, Erlich 212–29, Zirmunskij, Tynianov, Jakobson 1979a, and Scherr). In recent decades, various scholars in this tradition have applied their analytical methods to English texts as well, establishing a major tradition in the study of English prosody (e.g. Jakobson 1960, 1964, 1970b; Jakobson and Jones 1970; Jakobson and Rudy 1977; Bailey; Tarlinskaja 1976, 1984, 1987a and b, 1989; Gasparov 1987).

In the Slavic tradition, meter/rhythm is essentially conventional, normative and linguistic rather than natural, categorical and psychological. Meter/rhythm exists when linguistic forms within a corpus of texts achieve some normative distribution, a distribution that suggests some general *verse design*. With this view of meter/rhythm, each distribution of linguistic forms represents a different meter/rhythm; therefore, no verse design/instance can be properly described without specifying the exact distribution of these forms. The task of the prosodist is to count these forms and tabulate the statistical occurrence of their configurations.

In their work on English verse, Slavic metrists have constructed statistical profiles of various structures in various verse corpora. The most frequently studied forms have been the distributions of stress in the poetic line and the relationship between this stressing and other structures in the text (e.g. words and syntactic structures). Profiles that tabulate frequency of stressing by syllabic position are termed *vertical*; profiles of sequential combinations are called *horizontal*.

Stress profiling allows prosodists in this tradition to specify statistical differences between the linguistic structure of various textual corpora (textual, authorial, historical, national or generic) within and across various verse designs. For instance, studying the non-dramatic iambic pentameter of some thirty authors (from Chaucer to Swinburne), Tarlinskaja (1976) finds that ictic stressing ranges from 74.9 per cent to 87.4 per cent, that non-ictic stressing ranges from 7.5 to 20.8 per cent, that non-ictic stressing in position 1 occurs three times as often as non-ictic stressing elsewhere, that non-ictic stressing progressively declines across the line, that unstressed icti are usually created by unstressed monosyllables, that lines avoid more than one non-ictic stress caused by a polysyllabic word, and so forth. Tarlinskaja constructs similar 'profiles' for the dramatic pentameter, for iambic tetrameter, and for other transitional forms (e.g. what Slavic metrists call the *dol'nik*, a four-beat form that maintains a loose control of intervals between ictic stresses). With this collection of generic 'profiles', Tarlinskaja can then report in some detail how different verse designs have differentially constrained the language of the texts in which they have historically appeared.

A major achievement of the Slavic approach has been its ability to show patterns of stressing *across* the line. While many approaches to meter claim that ictic positions are equally 'strong', the Slavic prosodists have demonstrated that verse designs tend to give lines distinctive contours, with some icti being stressed more often and some less.

Slavic metrists have also recognized the role of other aspects of language patterning in verse structure: words, intonation, sound orchestration, syntax, meaning and visual form. To distinguish these patterns from their central concern, they call these structures 'secondary rhythmic features' (Scherr 255–85). As in other approaches, the secondary feature most frequently studied by the Slavicists has been the 'phonological word', a prosodic unit composed of one lexical stress and associated proclitics and enclitics (e.g. Gasporov 1987; Tarlinskaja 1984).

Slavicists also recognize the larger structure of prosodic organization, the continuous segmentation of speech into a hierarchical array of informational equivalents – what Jakobson liked to call *syntactic prosody*. For instance, in their analysis of the Mordvinian folksong, Jakobson and Lotz (1941) propose a syntactic prosody that includes a five-level 'glottic' hierarchy: the *syllable*, the *word*, the *phrase-member*, the *phrase* and the *totality* (although we are not given clear definitions of these units or their relations). The 'phrase-member' is defined as 'the distance between two syntactic pauses'; the totality is an 'utterance' (161). In their analysis, Jakobson and Lotz interpolate various 'metric' units (e.g. *segment* and *verse*) within this 'glottic' hierarchy and then elaborate the constraints on the Mordvinian verse in terms of this expanded hierarchy. In his general survey of metrics, Zirmunskij (1925/1966: 91–3) suggests a similar hierarchy of 'phraseological groups', but also leaves these matters with a brief example and a disclaimer ('This question . . . has not yet been sufficiently studied in Russian metrics' (161)).

Like many recent prosodists (see the *grammetrists* below), the Slavicists have devoted most of their comment on higher levels to syntax. Although other Slavicists have also concerned themselves with these issues (e.g. Tarlinskaja 1984; Zirmunskij 1925/1966), the cornerstone of this work has been Jakobson's analyses of grammatical *parallelism* and its relation to other aspects of poetic form (e.g. Jakobson 1960, 1961, 1964, 1966b, 1970a, 1970c, 1981a; Jakobson and Lévi-Strauss; Jakobson and Jones; Jakobson and Rudy).

In essence, Jakobson's later treatment of parallelism is an attempt to wed his earlier work on metrics to a larger theory of semiotic organization in poetry (and literary discourse in general). The 'dominant' feature of literary discourse, Jakobson argues, is the linear ordering of various sorts of linguistic equivalents and contrasts: sounds, syllables, word shapes, morphological categories, prosodic phrases, syntactic constructions, narrative motifs, etc. In non-literary discourse, relations of similarity and difference are usually paradigmatic; they stand in a choice relationship to some position in the linear (syntagmatic) chain. In poetry, forms that are usually related as equivalent choices appear in a structured manner in the linguistic chain. Instead of using sequences to build equations (as we do in definitions, for instance), equations are used to build sequences. In Jakobson's famous formulation, the poetic function of language 'projects the principle of equivalence from the axis of selection into the axis of combination' (1960: 71). As Jakobson illustrates extensively in his later analyses, the rigorous application of this principle to poetic analysis yields a unique genre of critical discourse. With this theory of the 'poetic function', our most valued poetic texts become those that pattern complex webs of linguistic parallels into articulate structures. The task of the critic is to reveal this patterning.

1.3.7 Intonationalists

Many prosodists have also approached verse rhythm through intonation.[10] The most important of these have been influenced by the American structural linguists, especially (1) a short survey of English phonology and morphology by George L. Trager and Henry Lee Smith, Jr (Trager and Smith 1951), and (2) its precursor, a more extensive description of American intonation by Kenneth Pike (Pike 1947).

Trager and Smith argue that the 'suprasegmental' phonology of English is composed of symmetrical fourfold distinctions in stress, pitch and juncture.

Stress	Pitch	Juncture
´ = primary	4 = very high	+ = open
ˆ = secondary	3 = high	/ = sustained
` = tertiary	2 = mid	// = rising
ˇ = weak	1 = low	# = falling

They argue that three levels of stress are necessary to distinguish the loudness of syllables in words like *elevator*, *operator* and *operation*:

élevàtŏr   óperătŏr   ŏperátiŏn

and that a fourth distinction is needed to distinguish between the additional level of loudness perceptible when these words are compounded:

élevàtŏr–ôperătŏr

'Open' juncture ('+') accounts for differences in syllabification (e.g. nitrate vs night + rate). 'Double-bar' ('//') and 'hatch' ('#') juncture account for the basic directional contrast in contour-final pitch movement (between rising movement, as in most yes–no questions, and falling movement, as in most statements). And 'single-bar' ('/')

juncture accounts for the 'sustained' internal terminal in examples such as *Are you reading, / Macauley? //*.

Pitch levels in this system are not marked continuously but at points of significant movement ('contour points'), with the normal movement of a contour going from a beginning at pitch '2' to a height at pitch '3' and a termination at pitch '1':

   2   3   1
How do they study?

The fourth (and highest) pitch represents the pitch level attained by more emphatic and exclamatory utterances.

   4   1
Help!

This three-dimensional notation of stress, pitch and juncture combines easily into one formalism:

  2   3   1
How do they study? #

As with other advances in linguistic description, 'intonational' prosodists use this system in various ways. Some argue that the Trager–Smith notation provides an elegant way to represent the 'variation within regularity' that all agree is characteristic of metrical verse. Following Otto Jesperson's earlier arguments (Jesperson 1900), they claim that syllables in a 'regular' iambic line need only *alternate* in strength; these stress differences need not be maximal (i.e. '/' vs 'v').[11] Others use the Trager–Smith notation to represent regularities *within* this metrical variation (e.g. Stein 1956, 1968; Cummings 1965), others to describe metrical norms (e.g. Epstein and Hawkes 1959), others to detail phrasal morphology and phrase–meter interaction (e.g. Fowler 1966b; Stein 1968).

The most sophisticated and original work on verse rhythm using the Trager–Smith system has been done by Elizabeth Hewitt on the poetry of T.S. Eliot (Hewitt 1965). Hewitt's central achievement is to retain the hierarchical potential of the Trager–Smith description while adjusting units and levels to the particular needs of a rhythmic (rather than just a suprasegmental) analysis. Like Stein and Cummings, she finds rhythmic phrases (what she termed *cadences*) in close 'counterpoint' to metrical groupings. But by retaining a full detailing of juncture and pitch, she is able to define additional levels of rhythmic phrasing as well: a 'higher' level of cadence, which groups lower-level cadences and compares their prosodic strength, and a completely different kind of phrasing (what she terms *measure*), which groups syllables continuously *across* juncture boundaries. This yields a four-tiered system: metrical foot, measure, lower cadence, higher cadence. For instance, she scans line 38 of 'Ash Wednesday':[12]

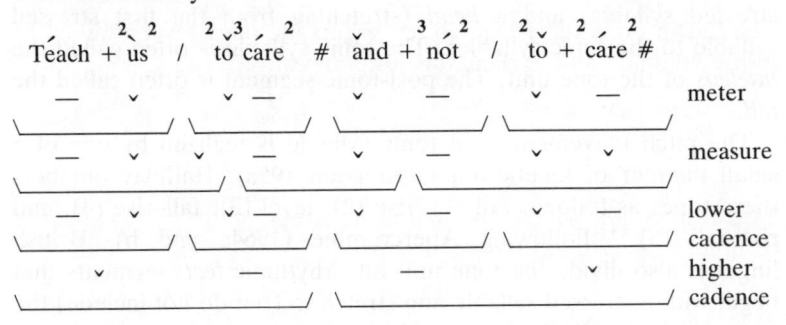

```
       2  2       2  3   2          3   2     2    2    2
Teach + us  /   to care   #   and + not  /   to + care #
    —    v      v   —       v    —        v     —            meter
  _____/ _____/   _____/    _____/
    —    v      v   —       v    —        v     v            measure
  _____/ _____/   _____/        _____/
    —    v      v   —       v    —        v     —            lower
  _____/ _____/   _____/    _____/               cadence
    v        —             —              v                  higher
  _____/  _____/               cadence
```

The American structuralist account of English intonation was both late and transient, however. While it has continued to influence work on versification, it was preceded by other accounts of English intonation, and once proposed it was quickly criticized and in the late 1970s universally rejected (e.g. Aronoff 1977). The historically primary and most enduring account of English intonation has been developed by British linguists and language teachers (see references in Note 10). While the American approach to intonation has been largely bottom up, moving from segment to phrase and from sound to meaning, the British approach has been top down, moving from meaning to sound and from phrase to segment (or phrasal constituent). In this tradition (e.g. Halliday 1985), intonation is the formal reflex of the *informational* organization of the language, with this informational organization combining with *theme* and *cohesion* to constitute the *textual* function within a multi-functional model of grammar (the grammar having *ideational*, *logical* and *interpersonal* functions as well).

The basic element in the British approach to intonation is the tone group (Palmer 1922; Schubiger 1935) or tone unit (e.g. Halliday), a unit somewhat larger than 'primary contour' or even a 'total contour' in the American approach to intonation.[13] Tone units divide a text into a continuous series of informational segments. Each tone unit culminates in a *tonic syllable* containing a prominent pitch movement marking the *information focus* of the tone unit (usually a point where the textually *new* information represented by the tone unit ends). The part of the tone unit that precedes the tonic syllable is the *pre-tonic* and usually marks information that is *given* (i.e. recoverable from context). The part of the tone unit that follows the nucleus is the *post-tonic* and is seldom extended. The pre-tonic is often divided into a *pre-head* (preceding the first stressed syllable) and a *head* (stretching from the first stressed syllable to the tonic syllable). The tonic syllable is often called the *nucleus* of the tone unit. The post-tonic segment is often called the *tail*.

The pitch movement on a tonic syllable is realized by one of a small number of kinetic *tones* (Kingdon 1958). Halliday numbers these tones as follows: fall (1), rise (2), level (3), fall–rise (4), and rise–fall (5).[14] Following Abercrombie (1964a and b), British linguists also divide the tone unit into rhythmic *feet*, segments that begin with a stressed syllable and stretch to (but do not include) the next stressed syllable, comparable to *measures* in the temporal approach to prosody reviewed above. Also following Abercrombie, 'stresses' in rhythmic feet can be 'silent', implied by the rhythmic structure but not sounded.

As in the American approach, this terminology and formalism combine easily into a graphic display. The tone unit is delimited with intralineal double slashes ('//'); rhythmic feet by intralineal single slashes ('/'); silent stresses with sub-lineal '^'; tones with iconic superscripts on the tonic syllable (e.g. '\' = falling; '/' = rising); and tonic syllables with **bold print**. Tone units are preceded by the number of their tone (e.g. 3 = level). Informational structure is notated below the intonational scansion. The following is an example (Halliday 1985: 283, 346).

pre-tonic (pre-head)	tonic (nucleus)	post-tonic (tail)	pre-tonic (head)	tonic (nucleus)	post-tonic (tail)
// 4 ˰ in /	**this**	job / Anne we're //	1 working with /	**sìl**	ver //i
	Focus New	Given	Given	Focus New	

The major use of the British approach to intonation has been the claim that the tone unit and its melodic contour can be used as an alternative to stress and 'syllable arithmetic' in defining the basic prosodic equivalences established by the poetic line in many versification systems.[15] For example, Taglicht (1971) suggests that most poetic lines end with a tonic syllable and a tone-unit boundary, although he recognizes that both of these also occur in line-internal positions. The best-known theoretical statement about intonation and the poetic line is in Crystal (1975b). Surveying historical approaches to meter/rhythm, Crystal laments the neglect of intonation and suggests that meter might be defined as 'the hierarchic system of continuous recurrent non-segmental phonological equivalences which constitute the organizing principle of the poetic text' (107) – with the relevant 'equivalences' pertaining mainly to the poetic line. He suggests that this definition might ease the 'unilluminating dichotomy' (11) in prosody theory between 'standard' types of versification and more 'esoteric' kinds by establishing certain phonological properties common to both. In a couple of short experiments, Crystal finds that readers do indeed expect poetic lines to be intonationally delimited, unified and parallel.

As Crystal suggests, we might suppose that the most promising poetic application of work on intonation might be exactly to more 'esoteric' systems of versification, but these applications have also been rare. The most significant might be Eleanor Berry's recent claim that William Carlos Williams' 'triadic-line' verse is essentially intonational in definition, with each visual lobe consisting (normatively) of a single tone unit (Berry forthcoming a). Berry claims that this continuous prosodic–visual merger gives this 'triadic-line' verse much of its characteristic *smoothness* and *stateliness*, effects that are sharply opposed to the 'jagged' effect created by most of Williams' other non-intonational visual–syntactic forms.

>   We have stood
>   from year to year
>   before the spectacle of our lives
>   with joined hands.
>   The storm unfolds.
>   Lightning
>   plays about the edges of the clouds.

> The sky to the north
>   is placid,
>   blue in the afterglow
> as the storm piles up.
>   It is a flower
>   that will soon reach
> the apex of its bloom.
>
> ('Asphodel, That Greeny Flower', Book I)

Within prosodic theory, most intonational analysis has been localistic and literal. Prosodists have simply adopted intonational analysis as metrical analysis (as Crystal suggests) or added intonational analysis to traditional metrical analysis (as Epstein and Hawkes suggest) without connecting this intonational analysis in any principled way to other aspects of prosodic form.

The exception is Kenneth Pike, who has expanded a consideration of intonation into a much broader theory of rhythmic organization in language. For Pike, rhythmic structures appear throughout all linguistic hierarchies and, taken together, constitute one of the three major 'standpoints' from which linguistic organization can be viewed: as a collection of *particles*, as a relational *field*, or as a series of *waves* (Pike 1959, 1982a: 19–38).

For Pike, linguistic rhythm is language as *wave*. From this 'standpoint', any linguistic 'particle' can be viewed as having a *nucleus*, which represents some focus of attention, surrounded by optional *margins*, which represent material of lesser interest. For example, in a 'grammar wave' a syntactic head might serve as nucleus, with pre- and post-modifiers serving as margins. In a 'referential wave' the climax of a story might serve as nucleus; the setting, developing action and dénouement might serve as margins. Each wave-like 'particle' in language appears as a member of a *class* of waves in hierarchical relationships with both superordinate and subordinate waves. And each of these waves is associated with both a non-linguistic *role* (i.e. a meaning) and contextualizing *field* of structural and functional expectancies. In his various writings Pike leaves much of this theory undeveloped, but he elaborates a detailed model of *phonological* waves (e.g. Pike 1962), and he applies this model several times to the analysis of one poem, Langston Hughes' 'Who but the Lord?' (Martin and Pike 1974; Pike 1982b; Pike and Pike 1983: 74–103). Pike identifies an expandable series of levels in his hierarchy of phonological waves. These levels stretch from the phone to discourse, with intermediate levels (other than the syllable) named according to their approximate match with units of syntax and meaning.

> discourse
> phonological paragraph-complex
> phonological paragraph
> phonological sub-paragraph
> phononological sentence
> phonological clause
> phonological phrase
> phonological word
> syllable
> phone

1.3.8 Barbara Herrnstein Smith: *poetic closure*

Prosodists have given little consideration to poetic rhythms at syntactic and intonational levels and even less attention to rhythmic movement 'above' these levels: movement *among* sentences and verse paragraphs, across the text as a whole. The only significant exception is Barbara Herrnstein Smith's study of poetic *closure* (B.H. Smith 1968).

One of the major pleasures we derive from poems (and from many art objects), Smith argues, is how they 'tease our tensions' (4), how they arouse our appetites and expectations, repeatedly defer and evade satisfaction of those appetites and tensions, and only then, at some distance, *close*. Given the fortuitousness of most ordinary experience, these 'enclosures' (2), Smith claims, can render a deep psychological (and even physiological) gratification (2–3).

Closure, Smith points out, depends crucially on a perception of structure. A poem closes when it arrives at a definite termination implied by the principles that generate its internal organization and linear progression. To close is not just to stop or cease but to conclude, to arrive at a point where a developing structure becomes 'integral: coherent, complete, and stable' (2).

Smith posits two major types of structural principles in poetry: *formal* and *thematic*. *Formal* structures arise from the 'physical nature of words' (6) and involve such things as sound schemata (e.g. rhyme and alliteration), meter, and the conventional arrangement of these structures into standard poetic 'frames' (the rhymed couplet, the sonnet, blank verse, free verse, etc.). *Thematic* structures arise from 'the symbolic properties of language' and involve such things as syntax, speech genres (e.g. meditation, description, narrative, etc.), references to events and states of affairs (both hypothetical and real), logical (or mock-logical) argumentation, sense imagery, and rhetorical figuration (metaphor, irony, hyperbole, etc.). Whether formal or thematic, a patterning of poetic elements must be 'systematic' (6) to be considered structural. Non-systematic patterning Smith terms *non-structural*.

While Smith demonstrates various ways that formal and thematic structures can *interact* to secure closure, one of her major claims is that 'there is no *formal* principle which in itself can prevent a poem from continuing indefinitely' (50). Given that formal patterning depends on repetition, no matter how large the pattern, the completion of one instance of a formal pattern can always be followed by another instance, and so on indefinitely. In fact, the major effect of all repetition, and therefore all formal structure, Smith notices, is not to close off but exactly the opposite: to increase the expectation for further repetition, for another instance of the pattern. Therefore, while formal structures can establish certain 'low-level' trajectories and teleologies, they cannot close themselves. They must be supplemented by other thematic or non-structural principles to reach a satisfying conclusion.

Ironically, formal patterns are most powerfully closural, Smith argues, not when they are satisfied but when they are broken (i.e. varied, etc.). As a formal pattern is repeated, Smith claims, our response to the repeating pattern becomes 'saturated' and we feel an increasing desire for change. If this change is then forthcoming, this desire for variation is satisfied and the pattern is (temporarily) closed off, renewed.

However, even in these cases, Smith argues, the closural effect of a break in formal patterning is usually more thematic than formal. While poems *do* often end with some significant 'terminal modification' of their formal patterning, these terminal forms, Smith demonstrates, are not random. Rather, they tend to be just those formal patterns that contribute rhetorically to the felt 'validity' (152) of the thematic 'revelation' at the poem's close: dense formal repetition (phonetic, lexical, syntactic), monosyllabic diction, metrical regularity, and so forth. Smith argues that these formal modifications pattern consistently with a range of non-structural thematic modifications that also tend to strengthen the authoritative tone of the poem's thematic conclusion: hyperbolic exaggeration, antitheses, puns, syntactic and semantic parallelism, aphoristic brevity, syntactic resolution, unqualified assertions, superlatives and so forth. Formal patterning can generate significant aspects of poetic structure, but poetic closure, Smith claims, is essentially thematic.

Smith's major contributions are: (1) to suggest a broad typology of discourse-level thematic structures in poetry; and (2) to investigate some of the typical ways poets bring these discourse patterns to a satisfying close.

The most basic thematic structures, Smith suggests, are *paratactic* (98–109). In a paratactic structure, equivalent thematic elements are arrayed in an unordered and (theoretically) expandable/contractable series: 'lists' and 'variations on a theme'. These paratactic structures are found in many song lyrics and other sorts of 'primitive and naive styles' (98). For example, Smith cites the repeated questions in the twenty-three verses of 'Billy Boy': Can she fry a dish of meat? Can she make a loaf of bread? Can she feed a sucking pig? and so forth (99).

Given that paratactically related elements are unordered and expandable, these structures also cannot close themselves. Rather, like formal patterning, they can be concluded only by some *other* principle external to their paratactic 'listing'. The most arbitrary ploy is just to announce closure, to frame the text with meta-references to the structural beginning and ending of the discourse, as in the following by John Skelton (101).

> I'll tell you a story
> About Jack a Nory,
> And now my story's begun;
> I'll tell you another
> About Jack and his brother,
> And now my story is done.

A more artful technique is to end the text with references to natural stopping places in our experience: sleep, winter, death, heaven, hell, etc. In most cases, however, it is just these paratactical structures that demand heavy 'terminal modification' to secure closure.

A second type of thematic development Smith calls *sequential*. These structures are produced by some principle of 'serial generation' so that their lines and verses follow one another in some ordered way. The most common and interesting sequential structures, Smith claims, are *logical* and *temporal*.

Temporal structures, Smith reminds us, are commonly found in narrative and drama, and Smith grants that some lyric poetry can incorporate what would be recognized as a conventional plot: references to events ordered into a series that defines a set of characters, a setting, complicating actions, a climax, and a resolution. None the less, Smith warns us against drawing any exact parallels between the use of temporal structures in poetry and the other literary genres. Dramas and novels, Smith claims, tend to represent or chronicle actions, while poems are more essentially representations of *utterances*. Poems often *use* narrative and dramatic ordering to some extent, but their global structure is usually not a chronicle of events but some sort of *comment* on such a chronicle. In poetry theme dominates plot, and therefore, even in narrative poems, poetic structure is still essentially thematic.

As a result, Smith claims that closure in narrative or dramatic poems is usually transitional in type. It is achieved by non-structural terminal modification (as in paratactic structures) or by some framing interpretation of the events narrated, as in logical and associative structures (which we will consider in a moment). In a narrative or dramatic lyric, Smith tells us, 'time is stopped *before* the conclusion and, as in a nonliterary anecdote, the speaker concludes by explaining its significance, adding some general or reflective comment, or otherwise "framing" the anecdote with some indication of why he told it in the first place' (124).

The other major sequential structure in poetry, Smith claims, is ordered by chains of reasoning closed by an appropriate conclusion. Smith terms these structures *logical*, and given her argument that narrative poems are also largely commentaries on events (rather than their presentation or representation), these logical structures must be considered the dominant sequential type.

Finally, if a thematic structure is neither sequential nor paratactic, it can be *associative/dialectal*. These structures represent interior monologue, 'the weavings and waverings of a mind pondering a specific matter of concern' (140). The major difficulty with these structures, Smith notes, is their duplicity. As with other artistic structures, they are controlled at every point by their 'expressive design' (141), by their effect upon the potential reader; but being interior monologue, they pretend to have no audience to affect. Smith reminds us that, freed from the constraints of communication, most sequences of thought are not 'trains', and few 'trains of thought' arrive at interesting destinations (141). Therefore, if at all realistic, most associative/dialectal structures should resist closure altogether. Smith does not attempt to resolve these difficulties, but she analyses closural processes in a number of dialectal/associative texts. Like most logical texts, some end by resolving their contradictions. Like many paratactic texts, others end by framing their inconclusiveness with meta-comment. And others end by just reaffirming their inconclusiveness (while heightening the closural force of this reaffirmation with 'terminal modification').

1.3.9 Generative metrists

In the mid 1960s, the rapid development of transformational–generative grammar, especially its extension to phonology (e.g. in Chomsky and Halle 1968), gave rise to a corresponding approach to the study of meter/rhythm, what has been called *generative metrics*.[16]

Parallel to work in generative grammar, the major concern of the generative metrists has been to define constraints on well-formedness. Comparable to well-formed sentences, certain linguistic structures are judged to be well-formed verse. Comparable to ungrammatical sentences, other linguistic structures are judged to be ill-formed verse. As in transformational–generative grammar, the major goal of the generative metrists has been to develop a set of principles that can provide structural descriptions for well-formed verse while at the same time excluding the ill-formed verse, a task that other approaches to prosody (foot-substitution, temporal, phrasal, etc.) often neglect.

Like the Slavic metrists, most generativists assume that verse meter/rhythm is essentially linguistic or algebraic rather than psychological. Meter/rhythm is not a series of experienced 'beats' but a series of 'positions' of varying degrees of abstractnesss, a verse design that 'corresponds' to the linguistic structure of the text in certain specified ways.[17] Again like the Slavicists, generativists tend to use the words *meter* and *rhythm* interchangeably, or if not interchangeably, in reference to different levels of abstractness in their analyses, again with *meter* referring to a more abstract level of organization and *rhythm*, to concrete realizations of this organization in particular verse instances. The great accomplishment of the generativists has been to make prosodic study a *theoretical* enterprise (in the modern sense of *theory*).[18] Using the terminology developed elsewhere in generative grammar (e.g. Chomsky 1965), the generativists have hoped to bring prosodic theory to at least *observational* and *descriptive* adequacy, perhaps even reaching *explanatory* adequacy on some matters.[19]

Like the generative grammarians, generative metrists couch their theoretical claims in systems of rules, rules that are often strictly ordered in their application. For instance, in their final proposal Halle and Keyser (1972) claim that iambic pentameter lines in English can be specified by a set of ordered *correspondence rules* that relate linguistic structures to the *metrical pattern* (W)SWSWSWSWS (X) (X), where each X position may be occupied only by an unstressed syllable and where the parentheses indicate optional elements. They suggest two sorts of correspondence rules, each with (ordered) subparts.

(1) A position (S, W or X) corresponds to a single syllable or to a sonorant sequence incorporating at most two vowels.
(2) Fully stressed syllables occur in S positions only and in all S positions, or
Fully stressed syllables occur in S positions only but not in all S positions, or
Stress maxima occur in S positions only but not in all S positions,

with a stress maximum being a fully stressed syllable occurring between two unstressed syllables in the same syntactic constituent. The theory forbids (constructed) lines such as *Ode to the West Wind by Percy Bysshe Shelley* and specifies both a 'simple' norm and a hierarchy of more 'complex' departures from that norm. Halle and Keyser even suggest that points in this 'complexity' cline can be quantified. They give headlessness, double occupancy and unexpected weakness a complexity value of 1. They give unexpected strength a complexity value of 2. And they give a misplaced stress maximum a complexity value of 3. (They claim that a different realization of the optional final positions has no effect on complexity.)[20]

One of the important proposals of the generativists is that 'metricality' is conditioned by word boundaries (Magnuson and Ryder 1970; Kiparsky 1975). Monosyllabic words can occur with relative freedom in English verse, but polysyllabic content words must usually place their lexical stress in a 'strong' position (except after a phrasal break), a constraint that the generativists call the 'monosyllabic word constraint' (MWC). The MWC accounts for the absence of many intuitively unmetrical lines that Halle and Keyser's 'stress maximum principle' (SMP) allow (e.g. *A little conceit? What a dangerous thing?* or *Introduced grandfather to amuse friends*), while accounting for the presence of some of the lines that the SMP forbid (e.g. *If I quench thee, thou flaming minister*). The MWC is especially important in predicting the placement of compounds.[21]

In formulating their constraints on weak positions, the generativists have also focused attention on more general aspects of verse phrasing, especially the nature of phrasal stress contours and phrasal breaks. In the late 1960s and early 1970s, generative metrists generally followed the theory of phrasal stress proposed in Chomsky and Halle (1968), a theory that assigns relative stress to words according to their syntactic context and linear positioning. In Chomsky and Halle's theory, phrasal stress is determined cyclically by giving highest stress to the rightmost lexical stress in a phrase and then repeatedly demoting other stresses, first within the most syntactically embedded constituent, and then within constituents at successively higher levels – a process that Chomsky and Halle call the 'Nuclear Stress Rule' (NSR). In their original formulation, Halle and Keyser define a stress maximum in terms of phrasal (rather than lexical) stress; therefore, the nature of phrasal stress played an important part in the early moments of the generative project (e.g. Beaver 1970, 1971).

The relative freedom of stress patterning after phrasal breaks in verse has long been observed, but with their desire for explicitly predictive rules the generativists have had to grapple with the fact that these phrasal breaks often do not correlate with any overt textual marking (as in the break between *proclaims* and *olives* in *And peace proclaims olives of endless age*). Because phrasal breaks loosen up the general constraints on weak positions found elsewhere in the line (i.e. the MWC and the SMP), these breaks have had to be explicitly defined if the more general conditions on weak positions were to be maintained.

Parallel to other approaches to prosody, Chomsky and Halle (1968) define a 'phonological word' consisting of a lexical stress on a major-category word plus syntactically associated unstressed syllables. The phrasal unit that seems to control metrical freedom in verse is a somewhat larger entity, however, what Chomsky and Halle call a 'phonological phrase' (1968: 371–2). Kiparsky (1975: 581–2) equates the phonological phrase with an 'optional intonational unit' and defines phonological phrase breaks as breaks between phonological words in different syntactic phrases. For instance, in a sentence such as *John sat with the old man*, which would be broken into *four* 'phonological words' (John / sat / with the old / man), there would be *three* phonological phrases (John // sat // with the old man). The break between *with* and *the* is syntactic but not phonological; the break between *old* and *man* is phonological but not syntactic. Kiparsky notes that most poets tend to put stressed syllables in weak positions only after breaks that are just this strong or greater, but not after breaks that are less severe (e.g. between phonological words within the same phonological phrase), although he notes that some poets (e.g. Pope) require stronger breaks.

The generativists have also argued that their work on phrasing can provide a more rigorous theory of the nature and effects of caesural and lineal breaks (e.g. Kiparsky 1975). In fact, using Kiparsky's distinctions, Dillon (1977) suggests a sevenfold hierarchy of phrasal breaks that can be used to quantify degrees of tension at points of phrase–meter asymmetry.

1.3.10 Reuven Tsur

One of the most sustained attempts to 'explain' and contextualize the findings of the generative metrists has been pursued over the past fifteen years by Reuven Tsur at Tel Aviv University (e.g. Tsur 1972, 1977, 1985). Tsur's work on poetic rhythm is part of his larger attempt to explore 'how poetic language, or critical decisions, are constrained and shaped by human information processing' (1983a: 3), a project that he and his colleagues at Tel Aviv call *cognitive poetics*.[22] The central thesis of Tsur's 'cognitive poetics' is that many aesthetic effects in literature are a result of 'some drastic interference with, or at least delay of, the regular course of cognitive processes' (1983a: 8). This thesis implies a three-part 'explanation' for poetic effects (such as rhythm): (1) a description of 'normal' cognitive processing; (2) a description of how 'normal' processing is disturbed (or delayed) by a poetic structure; and (3) a description of how the effects of this disturbance (or delay) are 'reorganized' for aesthetic use.

With respect to cognition, Tsur's central claims are: (1) that cognitive processing proceeds by successive 'recodings' of information at several levels of representation; (2) that these 'recodings' are motivated by informational economy and simplicity, and that 'simplicity' is defined, (3) differently on different levels of coding, and (4) (predominantly) from 'higher' levels to 'lower' levels within cognitive processing as a whole. As in Arnheim's theory of visual art or Meyer's theory of music, the controlling notion in these claims is 'simplicity', what the gestalt psychologists called *prägnanz*, or 'strong shape'. A structure is 'strong' if it presents 'clear-cut contrasts, distinct outlines', with these contrasts and outlines deriving from innate principles of perceptual/cognitive 'symmetry, similarity, regularity, and balance' (Tsur 1987: 18). All things being equal, it seems well established that we 'prefer' to perceive shapes that are 'strong' in this sense.

'Strong shape', Tsur claims, is paradoxically related to 'weak shape', both across levels of processing and through time: weak parts lead to strong wholes and strong parts to weak wholes. If the parts of a 'stimulus pattern' only *approximate* strong shape, they 'press toward' a more stable resolution, and when this resolution is achieved (either at higher levels of processing or at a subsequent point in the text), the shape of the whole is strengthened. On the other hand, parts that are 'strong' in themselves stand out as independent 'figures' and therefore weaken the integrity of the whole. In this view, a great deal of the 'affect' in poetic experience is generated by this paradoxical relationship between (what Tsur likes to term) the 'articulateness' of parts and the 'requiredness' of wholes (Tsur 1972).

Tsur isolates two major styles: *convergent/conclusive* and *divergent/suspensive*. Convergent/conclusive styles are marked by 'clear-cut shapes, both in contents and structure' (1977: 175). These styles 'incline towards definite directions' and convey 'a psychological atmosphere of certainty, a quality of intellectual control' (1977: 175). Divergent/suspensive styles are marked by 'blurred shapes, both in contents and structure' and convey 'an atmosphere of uncertainty, an emotional quality' (1977: 175). 'Convergence appeals to an actively organizing mind,' Tsur tells us, 'divergence – to a more receptive attitude' (1977: 175). Tsur illustrates these stylistic contrasts at some length (e.g. 1977: 175–238).

Tsur goes on to show that these general cognitive considerations bear crucially on detailed facts about rhythmic patterning in English verse. Following his immediate predecessors in the tradition (the generative metrists), Tsur's dominant concern is with rhythmic patterning in the pentameter line, in particular the statistical occurrence and distribution of stress maxima in weak positions. Tsur grants that the severe metrical tensions created by misplaced stress maxima are rarely tolerated, but he notes (1) that such tensions are tolerated with some frequency in poets with divergent styles, and (2) that these tensions are largely limited to position 7 in the pentameter line, as in the following from *Paradise Lost*.[23]

(6.866) Burnt after them to the bŏttŏmless pit
      w s w   s   w s w s   w   s
      1   2 3   4   5 6 7 8   9   10

Extending his 'top-down' theory of rhythm from style to metrical response, Tsur claims that these misplaced stress maxima can be 'explained' by considering the various 'dimensions' of cognitive processing that they elicit. In particular, Tsur claims that the processing of stresses and positions is integrated at higher levels into various performance 'groupings' determined by an amalgamation of the conventional and linguistic segmentations of the line (i.e. word boundaries and syntactic breaks on the one hand, and caesural expectation on the other). On the basis of frequency of occurrence, Tsur quantifies these 'grouping potentials', claiming that even positions have more 'grouping potential' than odd positions and that, among even positions, grouping potentials can be ranked as follows (with high numbers representing higher 'grouping potential'):

Grouping potential: 1 3 2 1   4
         Position: 2 4 6 8 10

Tsur also uses a range of detailed analysis to show how various sorts of linguistic patterning can influence 'performance grouping' in the pentameter line above and beyond the 'grouping potentials' of metrical positions.

1.3.11 Derek Attridge

In *The Rhythms of English Poetry* (*REP*) and supporting work, Derek Attridge has forged what is currently one of the most popular and widely respected approaches to English verse rhythm (e.g. Attridge 1982, 1987a, 1987b, 1988, 1989).[24] Attridge's major achievement is to combine a concern for rhythmic experience (the major focus of most literary prosodists) with a concern for well-formedness and universals (a focus more characteristic of linguistic prosodists). Parallel to the generative metrists, Attridge's goal is to write rules that specify the possible relations between language and rhythm, but he considers the rhythmic side of these relations to be a matter of reader *experience*, not the textual occurrence/frequency/distribution of linguistic forms.[25]

In terms of the general morphology of his theory, one of Attridge's major innovations over the generative metrists is to claim an additional construct on the rhythmic side of the rhythm–language dichotomy, a construct that he calls *underlying rhythm*. In Attridge's theory, *underlying rhythms* generate a small number of highly abstract patterns, patterns that are then particularized by the conventional *metrical patterns* of specific verse traditions. As in other generative theories, these metrical patterns are then related to the language of the text by a system of *realization rules* (and other *conditions*).

In Attridge's theory, 'underlying rhythms' reflect various aspects of rhythmic 'naturalness' and give this naturalness a separate representation. For Attridge, rhythm is a perceived temporal pattern reinforced by *repetition* (understood as perceived, rather than objective, equivalence) and *periodicity* (understood as perceived, rather than objective, isochrony) (1982: 77–8). The most powerful 'rhythm-inducing' events are perceived 'pulses of energy', pulses that are both cognitive and muscular in foundation. In the normal case, the mind 'prefers' to organize strong pulses (*beats*) and weaker pulses (*offbeats*) into alternating patterns. These alternating rhythmic patterns tend to be strongly self-perpetuating. Being 'regular', they 'project' (1982: 78) themselves into the future, and these more global expectations (*sets*) are only heightened by deviations from local patterning. Attridge represents a beat with a capital 'B', an off-beat with a small 'o'. In this formalism, the most 'natural' rhythmic pattern is represented: . . . BoBoBoBoBoB . . .

Within art forms at least, underlying rhythms also involve *grouping*. Rhythms outside of art, Attridge claims, tend to 'extend into infinity' (1982: 80), but art-rhythms require *shape*: 'middles should feel like middles and ends like ends' (1982: 80). As a result, art-rhythms are 'organized' (1982: 80). They tend to 'fall into groups, each of which the mind perceives as a whole' (1982: 80). In English verse the most popular groupings are in fours and fives, with a four-beat group (a duple of duples) being the more 'natural' of the two. Most English verse, then, has one of two 'underlying rhythms':

[...BoBoBoB...]   four-beat (4B)
[...BoBoBoBoB...]   five-beat (5B)

Attridge argues that four-beat verse differs systematically from five-beat verse, in both form and function. Four-beat verse is the dominant popular verse form and has a song-like structure. It is usually rhymed, dipodic, strophic, intonationally square ('end-stopped') and more syllabically unconstrained (i.e. 'accentual' rather than 'accentual–syllabic'). Five-beat verse is the dominant art-verse form, and it has complementary formal properties. It can be unrhymed and non-strophic (i.e. blank verse); it is syllabically constrained; it can tolerate heavy concentrations of enjambment; and it tends towards a less hierarchical, more speech-like patterning.

In addition to these 'underlying rhythms' Attridge also claims that experienced readers of a verse tradition internalize a group of *metrical patterns*. These metrical patterns define a number of rhythmic genres within verse of a certain underlying rhythm by specifying the nature of line peripheries, certain aspects of stanzaic form, and the number of beats per line (and the general relation of these beats to the language of the verse). Initial and final offbeats can be obligatory or optional (which he symbolizes with parentheses – '(o)'). Beats can be realized by language material or specified as unrealized (which he symbolizes with brackets – '[B]'). And the canonical structure of lines can have fewer or more than the four or five beats specified by the underlying rhythm.

Within Attridge's theory, the function of metrical patterns parallels the function of underlying rhythms. While underlying rhythms provide separate representations for 'natural' rhythmic responses of certain abstract 'shapes', metrical patterns provide separate representations of abstract perceptual schemata common to a number of superficially different verse forms. For instance, within Attridge's theory what foot-substitution prosodists identify as iambic tetrameter, anapaestic tetrameter and iambic–anapaestic tetrameter are assigned the same metrical pattern (i.e. oBoBoBoB(o)), and verse patterns that are traditionally identified as rising vs falling meters (i.e. iambic and anapaestic vs trochaic and dactylic) are distinguished only by different line peripheries (i.e. an obligatory initial or final offbeat).

Attridge captures further aspects of metrical 'naturalness' by distinguishing between various types of realization rules. Two *base rules* indicate the most natural relation between language and rhythmic response, a relation that he claims obtains in all 'regular' meters: that stressed syllables may realize a beat and that one or two unstressed syllables may realize an offbeat. A set of *deviation rules* then specifies where unstressed syllables may realize a beat (promotion), where stressed syllables may realize an offbeat (demotion), or where an offbeat can remain unrealized (*implied offbeats*). All 'regular meters' use some or all of these deviation rules. A set of *conditions* then specifies further relations between these deviations and options in the base rules, especially the position of unrealized offbeats (*implied offbeats*) with respect to offbeats that are realized by two syllables (*double offbeats*). Only the strictest duple verse invokes these conventions. In his scansions, Attridge indicates deviations and less natural base-rule choices with diacritics on the basic symbols for beats and offbeats:

double offbeat = ŏ   triple offbeat: ŏ̬

demotion = ȯ   promotion = B̄   ô = implied offbeat

The following scansion of line 438 of Milton's 'Comus' (1982: 179) illustrates the function of many of these symbols.

Antiquity from the old schools of Greece
o   B oB̄   ŏ   B ô B   o   B

Attridge admits that his metrical 'rules' are inadequate to provide a full account of metricality because they ignore many of the finer details of linguistic structure, but he claims that a full formalization of the rhythmic structure of verse language would be much too complex (214). Therefore, he chooses to represent the prosodic structure of language more loosely (215). He simplifies stress contours to a binary distinction: stressed (which he symbolizes '+s') and unstressed (which he symbolizes '−s'). Syllables that can be stressed or not he gives 'indefinite' stress and symbolizes 's'. Stress on syntactically unusual items he calls 'rhetorical stress' and symbolizes '*s*'. Deviantly placed but phrasally subordinate lexical stresses he terms 'metrical subordination' and symbolizes '[s]'. Possibilities of phonetic elision and coalescence he symbolizes '(s)'. And he marks various grouping linkages with a bracket above the relevant material. In his scansions, these formal representations of the prosodic structure of the language are placed above the line of verse, with the representation of rhythmic response below, as in the following scansion of line 4 of Shakespeare's Sonnet number 33 (1982: 362).

```
   +s–s   [s]    +s      –s +s (s)–s +s–s  –s
   Gilding pale streams with heavenly alchemy
     B     o     B      o    B    o B  o B̄
```

1.3.12 Metrical phonologists

In the last fifteen years, prosodic study has experienced an unprecedented number of theoretical and descriptive advances, advances that have unified the historical study of suprasegmental phenomena in language under a number of (relatively) agreed upon assumptions, methodologies, descriptive formalisms and empirical results.[26]

The turning point in this history came when linguists of various persuasions began to reverse the direction of influence between rhythmic/metrical and linguistic analysis, taking rhythmic/metrical analysis as the basis of linguistic prosody rather than linguistic prosody as the basis of rhythmic/metrical analysis. In this new disciplinary configuration, linguistic prosody has become a type of applied rhythmics/metrics rather than rhythmic/metrical analysis, a type of applied linguistics. Reflecting this reversal in disciplinary relations, this approach to prosody has been called *metrical phonology*.[27]

The initial impetus for this approach to prosody came from Mark Liberman's consideration of text–tune relations in simple calls, chants and children's games (Liberman 1975). Liberman noticed that stressed and unstressed syllables in these 'sung' forms line up in mandatory ways with strong and weak beats in the musical meter. For instance, in the standard musical form of the universal children's chant (Liberman 1975: 35, 38), the tonic syllable in the intonational unit must appear as the downbeat of the second measure, with the onset of the head of the intonational unit appearing as the downbeat of the first measure, and with other stressed syllables appearing as major subordinate beats (rather than as weak beats). Other text–tune alignments are ill-formed (Liberman 1975: 35, 37).

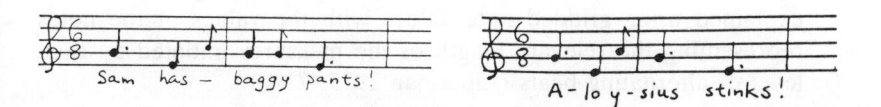

Liberman goes on to suggest that the musical pitch levels in chants such as this are related to the possible pitch levels in spoken language, that the patterns of 'congruence' between linguistic prominence and the placement of tones found in these sung forms also appear in the placement of intonational tones in spoken discourse, and that the patterns of linguistic prominence in spoken discourse are also heavily conditioned by their 'congruence' with ideal 'metrical' norms.

Liberman's more general observation was that constraints on prosodic structure can be stated very simply and naturally once the rhythmic bases of prosodic forms are recognized. For instance, in constraints on text–tune matching (and in rhythmic organization in general), *exact* levels of prominence are seldom an issue, but only *relative* prominence (within some specified domain). This radically simplifies the technical apparatus needed to describe prosodic structures and brings these structures back into the realm of the formal binary oppositions that control so much of the rest of linguistic organization. The realization that linguistic prosody is essentially rhythmic also separates the 'natural' motivations for prosodic structures from the less 'natural' historical conventions that actually appear. In text–tune matching, few texts provide a perfect realization of the musical meter. Rather, 'acceptable' texts simply *approximate* the ideal while avoiding certain sorts of unacceptable divergences.

Liberman's most influential suggestion has been his claim that this rhythmic approach to prosody can provide an elegant account of stress patterning in language. Following comparable representations in music theory, he suggests that stress contours in language be represented by two formalisms: (what he calls) *metrical patterns* and *metrical grids*.

Metrical grids are familiar from representations of meter in music theory. A metrical grid, Liberman tells us, represents subdivisions in *time itself*. It represents 'hierarchically-related periodicities' (282), as these periodicities are organized around patterns of regularly alternating prominences. In music theory, metrical grids are often explained using gridded note values with the values of the notes representing the relevant length of the measures initiated by each level of alternating beats (Liberman 1975: 73).

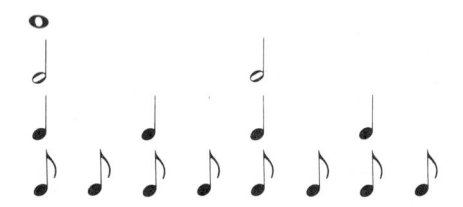

In this diagram, the taller the grid column, the stronger the beat (and the longer the measure initiated by the beat). Liberman observes that these grids are highly constrained formal structures. All high-level beats are also beats at all lower levels, and beats at the same level must be separated by one or two beats at the immediately subordinate level.

Metrical patterns, he tells us, are somewhat like the perceptual groupings in Leonard Meyer and Grosvenor Cooper's theory of musical rhythm (Cooper and Meyer 1960) and somewhat like musical meters (i.e. metrical grids), although he claims that they are distinct from both (47). Metrical patterns are composed of hierarchies of binary, 'weak–strong' oppositions operating over constituents defined partly by syntactic boundaries, partly by independently supplied well-formedness conditions for specific constituents, and partly by general conditions on representations. For instance, in the following children's chant (Liberman 1975: 48)

CURRENT THEORIES 49

Liberman claims that the syllables in the first measure are organized into two SW constituents coextensive with words, with the measure as a whole forming a larger SW constituent. He represents these constituents with a labelled 'tree', familiar from representations of syntactic structure in generative grammar.

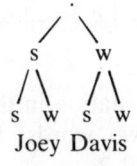

```
       /  \
      S    W
     /\   /\
    S  W S  W
      Joey Davis
```

Liberman claims that these metrical structures represent 'intuited structures of events in time' (266), with the hierarchical levelling representing how 'a more or less complex pattern, on one level, serves as a single aspect of a simple opposition on a higher level' (262). Liberman's initial suggestions have been enormously influential and, with various modifications, have been developed into major accounts of, first, English word stress (e.g. Liberman and Prince 1977; Selkirk 1980b) and then word stress in language in general (e.g. Hayes 1980/1985; Halle and Vernaud 1987).

Liberman also suggests that a metrical grid can account for the long-observed phenomenon of 'stress-shift' or the 'rhythm rule' in English (e.g. van Draat 1912; Bolinger 1965: 139–80), places where speakers move the normal position of lexical stress in the interest of a more 'eurythmic' phrasal stress contour, as in the following (taken from Bolinger 1965: 143).

> The word is misspélt   a mísspelt word
> Ábsolute power corrupts absolútely.

For instance, if we construct a grid that represents the linear flow of the strength contrasts in the metrical pattern of *anaphoric reference* (Liberman 1975: 296),

```
          •
     ┌────┴────┐
     W         S
    / \       / \
   W   S     S   W
  /\  /\    /\   |
 S W S W   S W   W
 anaphoric reference
```

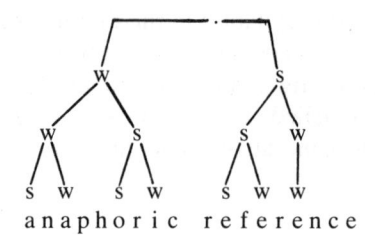

we find that the regular alternation in the grid is disturbed between the main stresses of the two words. Stresses at level 3 are not separated by a stress at level 2.

```
              4
       3      3
  2    2      2
  1 1  1 1    1 1 1
  anaphoric reference
```

But this violation of metrical alternation can be remedied by switching the second-level strength assignments in the two metrical constituents in the metrical pattern for *anaphoric*.

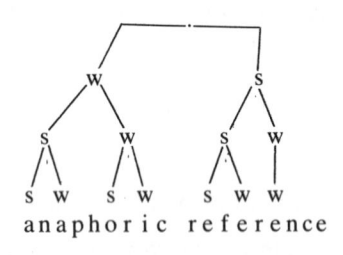

```
          •
     ┌────┴────┐
     W         S
    / \       / \
   S   W     S   W
  /\  /\    /\   |
 S W S W   S W   W
 anaphoric reference
```

```
              4
  3           3
  2    2      2
  1 1  1 1    1 1 1
  anaphoric reference
```

Hayes (1984a) suggests three additional principles of 'eurythmia': (1) a *quadrisyllabic rule* that claims a preference for a distance of *four* syllables between stresses/beats at some highly salient level in the grid; (2) a *disyllabic rule* that claims a preference for symmetrical division at the level below this salient level; and (3) a *phrasal rule* that prefers a polarization of stresses/beats at the highest level.

In more recent work, metrical phonologists have linked this early work on the stress hierarchies with a general theory of hierarchical phrasing in phonology. The initial impetus for this work on phrasing is attributed to Elizabeth Selkirk (1972, 1980a and b, 1981), but her original suggestions have been developed extensively by Marina Nespor and Irene Vogel (1982, 1983, 1986) among others.[28]

The basic argument in this work is that both economy and descriptive adequacy demand that phonological rules make reference to the edges and spans of a *strictly layered* hierarchy of phonological *domains* dependent on but distinct from syntactic phrasing. Hayes (1989) proposes five levels in this hierarchy:

U = utterance
I = intonational phrase
P = phonological phrase
C = clitic group
W = word

He illustrates:

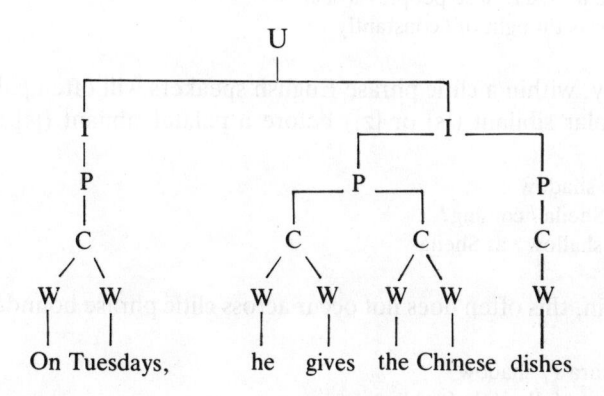

```
                              U
         ┌────────────────────┼────────────────────┐
         I                                 ─── I ───
         │                         ┌───── P ─────┐   │
         P                         │             │   P
         │                         C             C   │
         C                        / \           / \  C
        / \                      /   \         /   \ │
       W   W                    W     W       W     W W
       │   │                    │     │       │     │ │
    On Tuesdays,                he  gives   the  Chinese dishes
```

Studies such as Kahn (1976) present comparable evidence for the *syllable*.

The great contribution of the metrical phonologists has been to supply linguistic, rather than just perceptual, evidence for each of these levels. For instance, Nespor and Vogel (1982) show that the 'rhythm rule' is bounded by the phonological phrase. Phonological phrases centre on the head of a grammatical phrase and include determiners and pre-modifiers preceding the head plus one (optional) complement, if this complement does not branch. Constraining the rhythm rule to phonological phrases correctly predicts that the shift is possible in phrases such as *anaphoric reference* and *half-alive people*, but not in phrases such as **Tennesee will license them*. In the latter, a major syntactic phrase break occurs between *Tennesee* and *license*.

Hayes claims that there are a number of phonological processes in English that are bounded by the clitic phrase. For instance, within the clitic phrase English speakers often elide a [v] before a consonant (I indicate clitic phrase breaks with '/').

> Please / leave them / alone.
> Will you save me / a seat?
> a piece / of pie /

But this elision does not normally occur *across* a clitic phrase boundary.

> Give / Maureen / some.
> We'll save / those people / a seat.
> It was thought of / constantly.

Similarly, within a clitic phrase English speakers will often palatalize an alveolar sibilant ([s] or [z]) before a palatal sibilant ([š] or [ž]).

> his shadow
> Is Sheila / coming?
> as shallow / as Sheila

But again, this often does not occur across clitic phrase boundaries.[29]

> Laura's / shadow
> Those fellas / shafted him.
> Mrs / Shaftow

Other units in the hierarchy also bound phonological processes, although it seems unnecessary to cite all of this evidence here. Rules of syllabification (and therefore aspiration) in English make reference to word boundaries. 'Intrusive [r]' in British English is bounded by the utterance unit. And the grammatical and phonological significance of the intonational unit needs no (further) justification. This significance has been studied extensively, independent of its relation to other levels in the hierarchy (see 1.3.7 above).

To this point, the major use of metrical phonology has been to continue the scholarly project of the generativists (i.e. to define well-formedness conditions on verse language). For instance, Kiparsky (1977) uses Liberman's metrical patterns to claim an enriched hierarchical representation of the rhythmic structures of both verse instance and verse norm in metrical verse, from the level of the foot to the level of the line. He claims that the pentameter norm has a structure

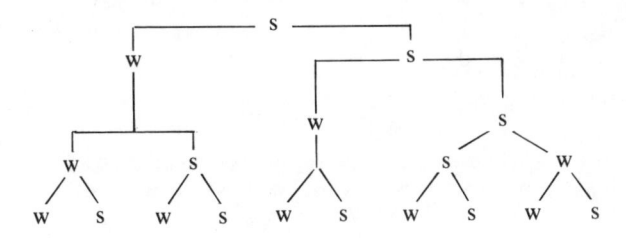

and that the 'normal' triple foot in triple meter has a binary structure with an SW subconstituent.

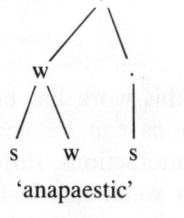

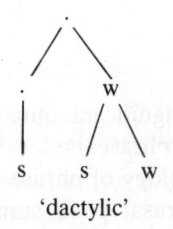

'anapaestic'   'dactylic'

In Kiparsky's 'metrical' theory, well-formedness, tension and ill-formedness become matters of arboreal 'matching' between the architectural structure of the verse instance and the architectural structure of the verse design, and Kiparsky finds that many of the constraints on 'metrical styles' can be stated elegantly in these arboreal terms.[30]

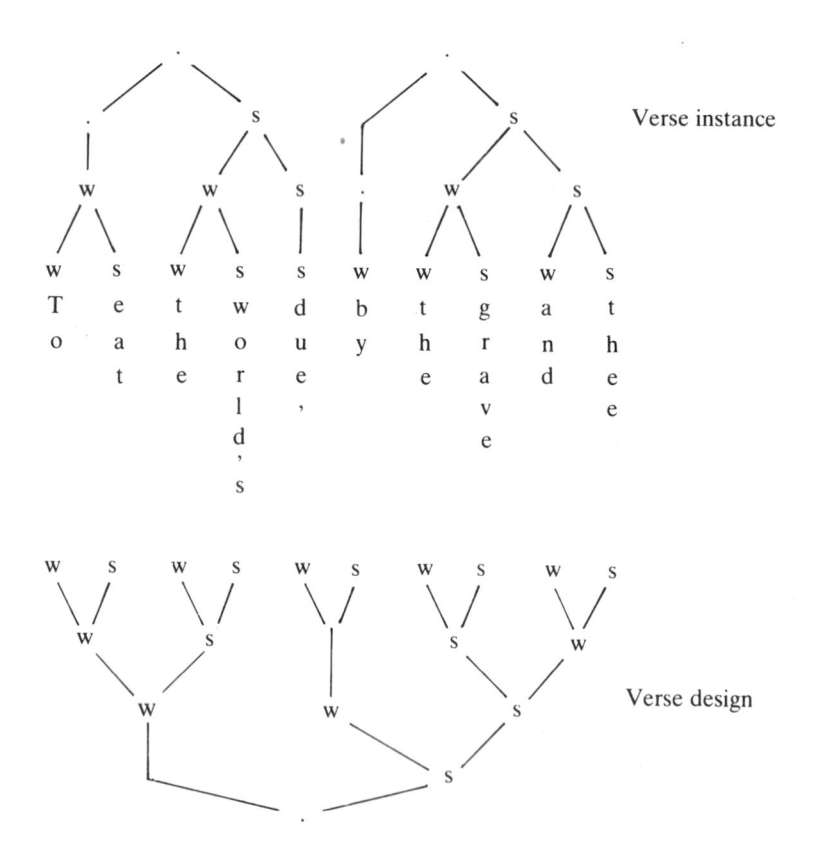

```
        /\                          /\
       /  \  s                     /  \  s          Verse instance
      |   /\                      |   /\
      w  /  \                     w  /  \
     /\  w   s                   /\  w    s
    /  \ /\  |                  /  \ /\  /\
   w  s w s  s    w     w  s   w  s
   T  e t w  d    b     t  g   a  t
   o  a h o  u    y     h  r   n  h
      t e r  e          e  a   d  e
          l  ,             v       e
          d                e
          ,
          s
```

```
  w   s   w   s   w   s   w   s   w   s
   \ /     \ /     \ /     \ /     \ /
    w       s       |       s       w         Verse design
     \     /        |        \     /
      \   /         |         \   /
       \ /          |          \ /
        w           w           s
        |            \         /
        |             \       /
        |              \     /
        |               \   /
        |                \ /
        └─────────────────s
```

The most significant outcome of this work has been Hayes' claim that these phrase–meter interactions can be generalized into an overall typology of phrase–meter interactions. Ill-formedness occurs when a phrasal peak stands in a weak metrical position. Hayes proposes three types of rules: (1) bounding rules; (2) right-edge rules; and (3) left-edge rules. Bounding rules restrict themselves to phrasal peaks within a given prosodic category. For example, Kiparsky's MWC is a bounding rule. It forbids the peak of a word to appear in weak position, as in line 44 from Frost's 'Design'.

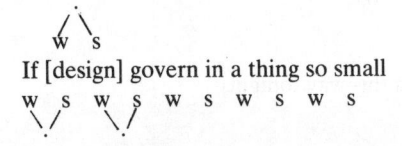

```
    /\
   w  s
If [design] govern in a thing so small
w  s  w  s  w  s  w  s  w  s
 \./   \./
```

Right-edge and left-edge rules work as inverses. Right-edge rules forbid peaks at the ends of phrases from appearing in weak metrical positions. Left-edge rules overrule right-edge rules and allow peaks in weak positions at the beginnings of phrases. These constraints are gradient and relative to the vertical position of the phrase in the prosodic hierarchy. Phrase-final peaks (if preceded by an unstressed syllable) are progressively more unacceptable in weak positions as one proceeds up the prosodic hierarchy.

> By [their rank] thoughts my deeds must not be shown
>   w   s
>
> (Son. 121)
>
> Give [my love] fame faster than time wastes life
>   w   s
>
> (Son. 100)
>
> [Like a child], half in tenderness and mirth
>   w   s
>
> (Shelley, 'The Revolt of Islam' 5.32.1)

Phrase-initial peaks are progressively more acceptable in weak positions as one moves up the hierarchy.

> Universal reproach, far worse to bear
>   s w
>
> (*PL* 6.34)
>
> Burnt after them to the [bottomless] pit
>   s w
>
> (*PL* 6.866)

And see the brave [day] sunk in hideous night
       s   w

(Son. 12.2)

Can vengeance be pursued [further than death]?
            s   w

(*Romeo and Juliet* 5.3.55)

What cursed foot [wanders this way tonight]
           s   w

(*Romeo and Juliet* 5.3.19)

Good night, good night! [Parting is such sweet sorrow]
                          s   w

(*Romeo and Juliet* 2.2185)

The major generalization about phrasal constraints on English meter, then, is this: the ends of phrases are metrically strict, the beginnings of phrases lax. As Hayes (1989) notes, this phrasal relationship is reproduced within meter itself. As Slavic metrists such as Tarlinskaja have demonstrated, the ends of lines and stanzas are also metrically strict and the beginnings of lines and stanzas lax.

1.3.13 David Gil *et al.*

Some of the most innovative work to emerge from the 'generative' paradigm has been done by David Gil and his associates, David Stein and Ronit Shoshani, at Tel Aviv University (Stein and Gil 1980; Gil 1980, 1985, 1986, 1987, forthcoming; Gil and Shoshani 1984a and b, forthcoming; Shoshani 1986).

Gil *et al.* argue that the verse forms studied in the generative tradition have been ill chosen. If we are interested in man's general 'competence' with verse, Gil *et al.* claim, the place to look is not in art verse but in 'non-canonical' forms. They also argue that the linguistic focus of the generativists has been ill chosen, claiming that the linguistic features that define non-canonical verse types, what they call *prosodic markers*, are not limited to suprasegmental structures but range across *all* levels in the linguistic hierarchy (phonological, lexical, syntactic, semantic, pragmatic, etc.) and even extend to non-linguistic units and relations (e.g. visual form).

In Gil *et al.*'s theory, the rhythmic organization of a text is represented by a *prosodic structure*. In some ways these prosodic structures resemble Liberman's metrical patterns, and in other ways Liberman's metrical grids. Like Liberman's metrical patterns, Gil *et al.*'s prosodic structures are *constituent hierarchies*, with constituents composed of one 'strong' unit and one or two 'weak' units. But like Liberman's metrical grids (and unlike Liberman's metrical patterns), they are also *strictly levelled, horizontally uniform* hierarchies. Units on the same level stand in a principled relation to each other and the hierarchy as a whole, and all constituents on the same level are composed of identical configurations of weak and strong subconstituents (i.e. WS or *iambic* (I), SW or *trochaic* (T), WWS or *anapaestic* (A), WSW or *amphibrachic* (H), or SWW or *dactylic* (D)), a formal limitation that Gil *et al.* call the *Horizontal Uniformity Constraint*.

Gil *et al.* label levels according to traditional metrical terminology. The central level is the *line* and is numbered '0'. Higher levels receive lower numbers. Lower levels receive higher numbers.

Level	Constituent name	Span (in duple patterning)
−4	bi-super-stanza	16 lines
−3	super-stanza	8 lines
−2	stanza	4 lines
−1	sub-stanza	2 lines
0	line	1 line
1	hemistich	½ line
2	foot	¼ line
3	position	⅛ line
4	sub-position	¹⁄₁₆ line

Within levels, constituents are numbered sequentially from the beginning of the text to the end.

Within the hierarchy as a whole, constituents are identified by a 'P', superscripted for level and subscripted for linear position within the level. For instance, in a text with duple patterning, P^{-1}_{6} would represent the second distich in the third quatrain, while P^{3}_{13} would represent the first position in the third foot of the second line.

Because these structures are horizontally uniform, their shape as a whole can be uniquely specified by listing the shape of the constituents at each level that is rhythmically organized. For example, $I^{-2}T^{-1}T^{0}T^{1}I^{2}$ would represent a rhythmic structure with five levels of prosodic organization, stretching from the stanza to the foot, with stanzas and feet being WS (or iambic) and distichs, lines and hemistichs being SW (or trochaic). This verse type would contrast with, say, verse types that control the same levels but with different directional movement on some or all levels (e.g. $T^{-2}I^{-1}I^0I^1T^2$), or with verse types that control a different number of levels (e.g. $T^{-2}I^{-1}I^0$), or with verse types that control different levels (e.g. $T^{-3}I^{-2}I^{-1}I^0T^1$), or in the usual case, with verse types that combine these differences in some way. Gil *et al.* claim that all verse types organize a *continuous* series of levels, a formal limitation that they call the *Continuity Constraint*. If the whole text is prosodically organized, its rhythmic organization is *upwards-exhaustive*. If the text organizes syllables into immediate prosodic constituents, its rhythmic structure is *downwards-exhaustive*. They find that much non-canonical verse is both upwards-exhaustive and downwards-exhaustive, with a strong preference for binary patterning. (For example, Gil *et al.* find no texts that have ternary patterning on contiguous levels.) They find that non-canonical verse can organize up to *eight* levels (from the position to the bi-super-stanza).

Gil *et al.* also observe that prosodic structures are binary in their *vertical* organization. Even levels (e.g. the stanza, line and foot) are more salient than the odd levels (e.g. the distich and the hemistich). Among the more salient levels, the line is also more salient than the stanza and foot. If we call the more salient levels 'dominant' and the less salient levels 'recessive', these intuitions establish a multilevelled binarism operating vertically in prosodic structure:

```
−3 super-stanza
−2 stanza          − dominant  \
−1 sub-stanza      − recessive /  − recessive
 0 line            − dominant  \
 1 hemistich       − recessive /  − dominant
 2 foot            − dominant  \
 3 position        − recessive /  − recessive
 4 sub-position
```

In non-canonical verse, Gil *et al.* find one important manifestation of this vertical organization. Levels are only horizontally uniform and therefore, in most cases, prosodic constituents can vary in shape from level to level. However, Gil *et al.* find that the prosodic dominance of the line tends to spread to contiguous (recessive)

CURRENT THEORIES 59

levels, upwards to the sub-stanza and downwards to the hemistich. In most non-canonical texts, these three levels (which Gil *et al.* call the 'uniformity levels') tend to have the same prosodic shape. Gil *et al.* call this formal limitation the *Vertical Uniformity Constraint*.

Gil *et al.*'s evidence for prosodic structure does not come from perception but from linguistic organization. They find that certain linguistic features will 'mark' this organization by appearing so that they are consistently associated with either weak constituents or strong constituents, but not both. In rare cases, these features are *obligatory* and *regular* in a verse type. They will occur in all texts of that verse type and will consistently mark one type of prosodic strength (strong or weak, but not both). But in most cases these markers are only *optional*, and in many cases they are *idiosyncratic*. They appear in some texts of a certain verse type but not others, and they mark different strength assignments from text to text. None the less, within a given text Gil *et al.* find that these markers will be rigorously arranged. All 'markers' of one type will occur in strong constituents and all 'markers' of another type will occur in weak constituents. And in most cases, if a marker is 'regular' in a certain verse type, it will tend to have a fairly 'natural' relationship to prosodic strength/weakness. For example, 'markers' of strength in English non-canonical verse tend to represent some sort of linguistic quantity, complexity or ornamentation: more syllables, more stresses, more obstruency, more sound play, more syntactic complexity, more semantic 'import', and so forth. Markers of weakness tend to represent the opposite (i.e. diminished quantity, complexity or ornamentation: repetition, parallelism, sonorancy, semantic and syntactic 'normality', etc.).

For instance, consider Gil and Shoshani's scansion of the first two lines of the following:

> One, two, three, four, five,
> Once I caught a fish alive,
> Six, seven, eight, nine, ten,
> Then I let it go again.

60 CURRENT APPROACHES

	Sub-stanza (couplet)								$\acute{P}_1^{-1}$							
	Lines				$\breve{P}_1^0$							$\acute{P}_2^0$				
	Hemistichs		$\breve{P}_1^1$			$\acute{P}_2^1$				$\breve{P}_3^1$				$\acute{P}_4^1$		
	Feet	$\breve{P}_1^2$		$\acute{P}_2^2$		$\breve{P}_3^2$		$\acute{P}_4^2$		$\breve{P}_5^2$		$\acute{P}_6^2$		$\breve{P}_7^2$		$\acute{P}_8^2$
	Positions	$\breve{P}_1^3$	$\acute{P}_2^3$	$\breve{P}_3^3$	$\acute{P}_4^3$	$\breve{P}_5^3$	$\acute{P}_6^3$	$\breve{P}_7^3$	$\acute{P}_8^3$	$\breve{P}_9^3$	$\acute{P}_{10}^3$	$\breve{P}_{11}^3$	$\acute{P}_{12}^3$	$\breve{P}_{13}^3$	$\acute{P}_{14}^3$	$\breve{P}_{15}^3$	$\acute{P}_{16}^3$
			One		two		three	four	five		Once	I	caught	a	fish	a-	live
	STRESS		3		2		3	˘	1		3	˘	2	˘	3	˘	1
	WORD STRESS		/		/		/	/	/		/	˘	/	˘	/	˘	/

```
                  0 1     0 1     0 1  1 1    0 1   1 1    1 1   1 1
NUMBER OF        ├─1─┤   ├─1─┤   ├─1─┤├─2─┤  ├─1─┤ ├─2─┤  ├─2─┤ ├─2─┤
SYLLABLES        ├── 2 ──┤       ├─── 3 ────┤├──── 3 ───┤ ├──── 4 ───┤
                 ├──────────── 6 ──────────┤├────────── 7 ────────────┤
```

SYNTACTIC COMPLEXITY ├──────── less ────────┤ ├──────── more ────────┤

SEMANTIC IMPORT ├──────── less ────────┤ ├──────── more ────────┤

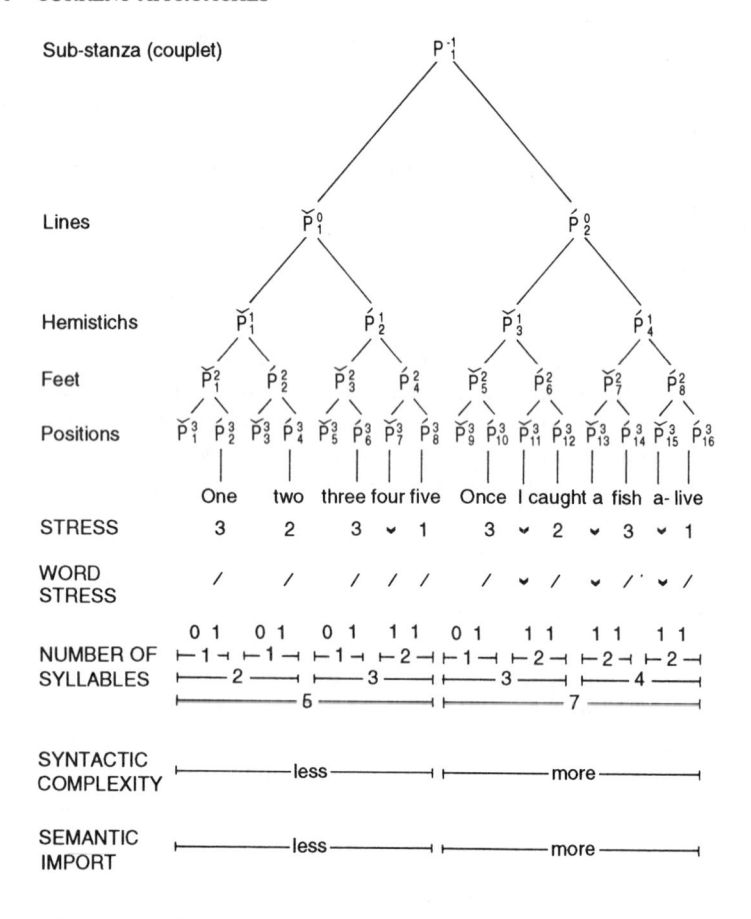

As indicated in the graphs below the scansion, Gil *et al.* claim that stress,[31] word stress, number of syllables, syntactic complexity and semantic import 'mark' this couplet as iambic at all four prosodic levels: couplet, line, hemistich and foot. Stress marks iambic structure at the three lower levels. All weak positions are filled with unstressed syllables (or no syllables at all), and all stressed syllables occur in strong positions. Only strong feet contain level-2 stresses and only strong hemistichs contain level-1 stresses. Word stress reflects iambic structure at the foot level. All strong positions contain word stresses, but word stresses occur in only one weak position. Number of syllables marks iambic structure at all four levels. The second line has seven syllables; the first line, five. The even hemistichs have three and four syllables; the odd hemistichs,

CURRENT THEORIES   61

two and three. Strong feet in the second and third hemistichs have two syllables; the weak feet in these hemistichs have only one. And strong positions are all filled with syllables; four weak positions are empty. Syntactic complexity and semantic import mark iambic structure at the couplet level. The first line contains a syntactically structureless list of numbers unrelated to the content of the verse. The second line contains a clause and refers to a specific event.

The startling confirmation of this analysis is the realization that this patterning is not just fortuitous but is demanded by our intuitions of well-formedness for verse of this sort. For instance, it sounds odd to place the 'unstressed' numeral in the first line in the first, third or fifth positions, rather than in the seventh.

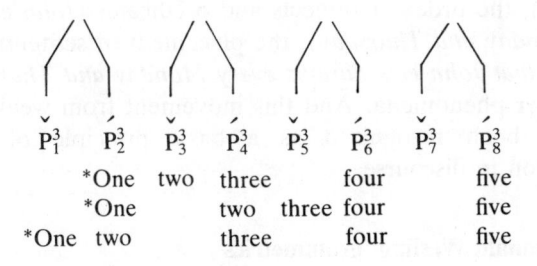

$$P_1^3 \quad P_2^3 \quad P_3^3 \quad P_4^3 \quad P_5^3 \quad P_6^3 \quad P_7^3 \quad P_8^3$$

	*One	two	three		four		five
		*One		two	three	four		five
	*One	two		three|	four|	five

Using this sort of analysis, Gil et al. are able to show that many common types of English non-canonical verse fall into distinct genres, and that these genres also appear in the non-canonical verse forms in many other languages.

Gil et al. claim that the structures that they describe are not linguistic but derive from an independent capacity of mind, what they call *prosodic competence*. Unlike most work on verse rhythm, however, Gil et al.'s arguments for a 'universal prosody' are not based on formal qualities such as isochrony, regularity, binary alternation, and other formal features which are normally associated with *meter*, but on such things as the 'small-precedes-large principle' and the 'principle of end-focus', principles that have long been observed in phonological, intonational and narrative organization in language (and in many other non-linguistic phenomena) but which are seldom associated with metrical organization. Given Gil et al.'s theory of prosodic markers and prosodic structures, the 'small-precedes-large' principle and the 'principle of end-focus' become instances of a larger principle of 'iambicity', a movement from weak to strong that pervades English syntax, many other languages (e.g. see Gil 1986), some other temporal art forms (such as music), and many other phenomena (e.g. algebraic equations). In fact, Gil argues that the influence of the 'iambicity' principle in English is so extensive that its relegation to prosody severely restricts what has usually been thought to constitute 'universal grammar'. For instance, in English syntax this movement from weak to strong appears in the structure of binominal freezes (e.g. *pins and needles*), the placement of adverbials (e.g. *John seldom eats durians on Mondays and Thursdays*), the basic ordering of topics and comments (e.g. *As for durians, John eats them every Monday and Thursday*), the order of subjects and predicates (*John eats durians every Monday and Thursday*), the placement of sentential subjects (*It seems that John eats durians every Monday and Thursday*), and many other phenomena. And this movement from weak to strong has long been recognized as a basic principle of rhetorical organization in discourse.

1.3.14 Donald Wesling: grammetrics

Among literary prosodists in the English tradition, the most embracing and explicit alternative to a predominantly metrical prosody has been developed over the past twenty years by Donald Wesling and his students at the University of California at San Diego (Wesling 1971, 1975, 1980a and b, 1981, 1982, 1985, forthcoming; Bollobas 1986).

Like Meschonnic (see 1.3.15), Wesling's major concern is with the 'historical fate' (forthcoming: 2) of prosodic theory, the intellectual and political positioning of prosodic analysis within literary criticism and the humanities in general. Like many of the 'schools' of prosody we have reviewed, Wesling finds the central tradition in prosodic comment excessively narrow and shallow. Preoccupied with sound, the tradition has neglected meaning. Preoccupied with structure, the tradition has neglected perceptual process. Preoccupied with form, the tradition has neglected the relations between form and artistic intention. And preoccupied with the individual text and historical continuity, the tradition has neglected the dynamics of prosodic evolution/revolution and the relations between these historical dynamics and literary value. The result, Wesling maintains, has been disciplinary alienation and peripheralization. As scholarship and humanistic endeavour, prosodic comment has been 'severed from poetry and thrust to the margins of poetics' (forthcoming: 2), divorced from the central concerns of the poet, critic and general reader alike.

Methodologically, the central difficulty with the tradition, Wesling argues, has been an inability to connect exegesis and formalization. Linguistic prosodists have elaborated 'scientific' prosodies that are 'brilliant in [their] own terms' (forthcoming: 35) but that lack 'hermeneutical first principles' (69). They only 'relate sign to sign – not sign to signifier' (50) and therefore they 'fail to ask questions which . . . lead beyond tautology into formulations productive for thought and analysis' (97). Literary scholars have developed 'interpretive' prosodies, but these prosodies have neglected language. They make a 'fetish' (63) of a metrical regularity that 'massacres reality and reconstitutes it in a drastically simplified model' (132). With their mutual concern for strong explanations, both literary and linguistic prosodists have been deeply suspicious of 'expressionist theory' (32), the 'broad end' of prosodic theory where form 'vaporizes out into cognition' (32). Therefore, neither has been able to build a prosodic theory that can 'bridge several levels of discourse' (97) to provide the 'trans-coding from meter to meaning' (35) that any adequate account of prosodic technique must describe.

The solution to these difficulties, Wesling suggests, is to abandon the goal of strong explanations to weak questions and be satisfied with weak explanations to stronger questions, to develop a prosody that aims at the broadest possible scope and the deepest possible explanatory results but that is content to arrive at only partial answers and tentative conclusions. This prosodic theory would not be a 'science of versification', as many prosodists advertise, but 'a non-prescriptive poetics of technique' (6) that could provide direct aid to those concerned with the making and reading of poems.

In terms of prosodic analysis, Wesling suggests a shift in focus from rhetoric (e.g. meter and rhyme) to language (e.g. sound, syntax, intonation, meaning). To achieve a workable poetics, the modern prosodist must recognize that one of the major aims of modern writers is to efface stable forms, in effect to dissolve genre and technique back into 'ordinary language'. In the modern poem, the traditional rhetoric of poetry is overthrown and *all* of the linguistic structures in the poem, 'down to the most minute pauses and punctuation marks, [become] indexes of personality . . . and correlations between the work and the universe' (1985: 72). Wesling's favourite designation for this linguistic 'index of personality' is *voice*.

Given these definitions of *prosody* and *voice*, Wesling's technical questions become: How is voice realized (1) in the reader's experience of the poem, (2) in the language of the text, and (3) in the relation between these two?

For an answer to (1), Wesling suggests that the function of prosodic form in poetry is to control the reader's processional cognition of the text, its cognitive 'eventfulness', unexpectedness, intensity and 'strangeness'. Wesling claims that poetic form 'contravene[s] the gestalt postulate that the most satisfactory forms are those which result from simple, stable commands' (1985: 109). It 'defamiliarizes', 'defacilitates' and retards the reader's normal frames of formal, semantic and referential expectation (1980a: 24–5).

In developing his theory of artistic 'tension', Wesling makes extensive use of the theoretical work by Jan Meijer (1973). Meijer claims that all works of verbal art contain two different sorts of organization: a cognitive structure ('verbal') and an aesthetic structure ('beauty'). He claims that there are three possible ways to view a work of art with respect to these two structures: as

(a) . . . an aesthetic structure which is somehow filled with words.
(b) . . . a cognitive structure on which an aesthetic structure is somehow projected; so that the basic cognitive structure does not really need the aesthetic structure to serve its end.
(c) . . . an aesthetic and a cognitive structure . . . so that there is no one-way dependence of one upon the other.

(Meijer 1973: 315–16)

Meijer claims that (a) and (b) 'have been discarded long ago'; therefore, we are 'forced' to accept (c).

In Meijer's theory of the art work, both cognitive and aesthetic structures use certain 'structural principles' to organize the bare 'matter' of the text (i.e. undeveloped thoughts, disordered forms). Cognitive structures create unequal relations of dependence and tend towards closure. Aesthetic structures create relations of equivalence and tend towards self-perpetuation. In the dynamics of the art work, cognitive and aesthetic structures mutually 'interfere'.

CURRENT THEORIES 65

The result is artistic 'tension'. This tension, together with its aesthetic and structural sources, is coextensive with a text's 'style', and this style is the major manifestation of the poet's 'voice'.

For an answer to (2), Wesling looks primarily to syntax, especially as this syntax interacts with other aspects of the language of the text (e.g. sound orchestration, visual form, etc.), with special concern for the relations between syntax and those linguistic structures associated with conventional poetic 'devices' (meter, lineation, stanzaic structure, rhyme schemes, etc.). Prosodic reading in Wesling's approach centres on the reader's sequential experience of the 'figures of grammar' in the text – subordination, apposition, modification, tense, mood, sentence types (e.g. questions, statements, etc.), anaphora, etc. – and all of the various figures caused by the linear positioning and processing of syntactic units – deletions, transpositions, inversions, parentheses and so forth – as these 'figures' play within and across the other prosodic 'structures' in the reader's acts of attention. Following Wexler (1964, 1966),

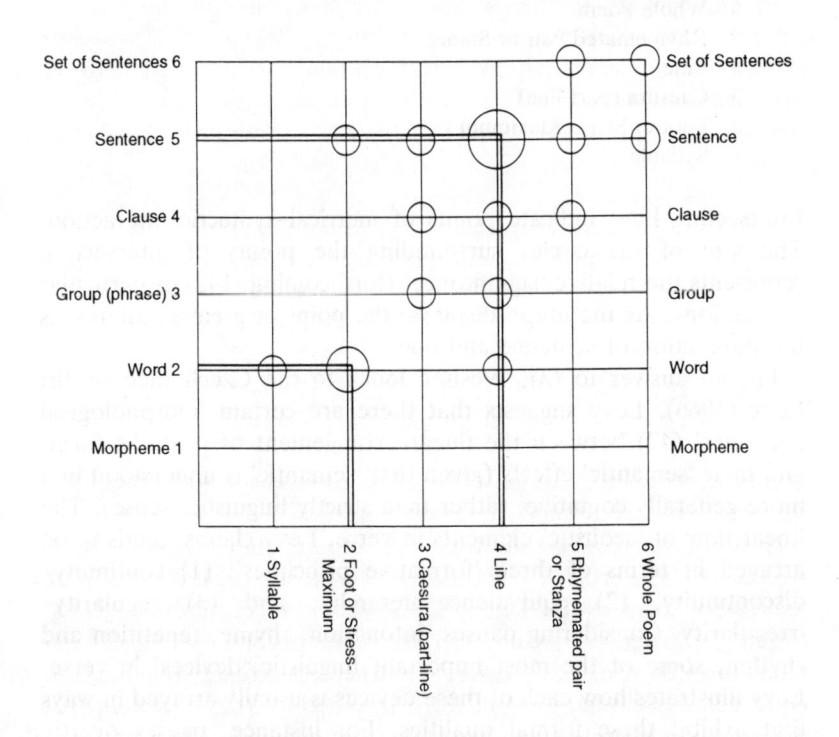

Wesling calls this analysis of syntactic–metrical 'scissoring' *grammetrics*.

To particularize his version of 'grammetrics', Wesling suggests a number of analytical procedures. The centre of these procedures is a grid of interactions between metrical and grammatical hierarchies, what he calls the 'grammetrical coordinates' (forthcoming: 141).

On one axis is a hierarchy of grammatical levels:

6 Set of Sentences
5 Sentence
4 Clause
3 Group (phrase)
2 Word
1 Morpheme

On the other axis is a corresponding hierarchy of metrical levels:

6 Whole Poem
5 Rhymemated Pair or Stanza
4 Line
3 Caesura (part-line)
2 Foot or Stress Maximum
1 Syllable

Intersecting lines indicate points of metrical–syntactic interaction. The size of the circles surrounding the points of intersection represents the relative 'significance' (forthcoming: 142) of particular interactions. As the graph displays, the point of greatest interest is the interaction of sentence and line.

For an answer to (3), Wesling looks to the Czech theorist Jiri Levy (1966). Levy suggests that there are certain 'morphological analogies' (47) between the linear arrangement of prosodic forms and their 'semantic' effects (given that 'semantic' is understood in a more generally cognitive, rather than strictly linguistic, sense). The linear flow of 'acoustic' elements in verse, Levy claims, tends to be arrayed in terms of three 'formative principles': (1) continuity–discontinuity, (2) equivalence–hierarchy, and (3) regularity–irregularity. Considering pauses, intonation, rhyme, repetition and rhythm, some of the most important linguistic 'devices' in verse, Levy illustrates how each of these devices is usually arrayed in ways that exhibit these formal qualities. For instance, pauses overtly break up the linear stream of speech, contributing to discontinuity; these discontinuities isolate speech segments, making the isolated segments more prominent than surrounding material; and these discontinuities, given that continuity is considered 'regular', contribute to formal irregularity. Levy claims that these 'formative principles' stand in an 'ideal' (53) 'homomorphism' (47) to certain 'forms of meaning'.

Acoustic principle of arrangement	Forms of meaning
continuity–discontinuity	coherence–incoherence
equivalence–hierarchy	lack of intensity–intensity
regularity–irregularity	predictability–unexpectedness

For instance, the fragmentation of the speech stream by pauses has a 'formal analogue' (46) in a 'dissolute organization of context' (46); prominent speech fragments tend to be intensified or emphasized; and irregular, fragmented entities tend to be less predictable, more unexpected.

In his grammetrical analyses, Wesling uses Levy's theory to guide his selection of comment and, in some measure, to validate his form–effect correlations. Wesling recommends 'studying' Levy's three 'semantic functions' (and their formal analogues) at every rank level in his 'grammetrical coordinates'. This 'grammetrical inspection' can then be used to form hypotheses about higher-level, interpretive responses (e.g. point of view and tone of voice). The result of this process, Wesling claims, is to 'load stylistic concepts with semantic possibilities' (forthcoming: 152).

1.3.15 Henri Meschonnic

Finally, no survey of writings about rhythm, especially non-metrical aspects of rhythm, can neglect Henri Meschonnic's massive *Critique du rythme* (1982), by far the most extensive discussion of these matters to date.

Meschonnic's *Critique* is part of his larger attempt to renovate the philosophical foundations of the human sciences (linguistic, literary, anthropological, historical). He argues that traditional writing about rhythm reveals with particular clarity the 'stakes' of theory in the humanities. To Meschonnic, a critique of rhythm entails a critique of language, society and the individual; therefore, a new theory of rhythm demands a new historical anthropology of language.

Meschonnic's large claims for prosodic theory derive most directly from his broad (re-)definition of *rhythm*. Meschonnic finds that most definitions of rhythm have been vague, narrow or just wrong, and he spends most of the *Critique* rejecting these historical alternatives. Rhythm in language is not just sound; it involves *all* of discourse. It is not just binary, periodic and repetitive; it can be asymmetrical, aperiodic and varied. It is not just a product of *langue*; it 'overflows' linguistic description. It is not just a realization of meter; it is a positive organization – a form, a matrix, a pattern. It is not just a feature of versification; it pervades all literary genres. It is not just quantitative; it is a qualitative shape, a textual 'body'.

Given his larger philosophical project, Meschonnic is especially eager to debunk traditional views of the *function* of rhythm in discourse. Rhythm is not valued because it is mnemonic; it is mnemonic because it is valued. It is not socially or biologically determined; it is an *activity*, a dialectical interchange between the embodied subject and socio-historical givens. It is not an aesthetic category, a hedonistic ornamentation that simply repeats what the text signifies; it is a central component of discourse 'meaning'. It is not a transcendental mimeticism, a 'celestial pantomime' of Pythagorean numerology; it is essentially historical, varying across writers, literary traditions and languages. And it is not some ineffable emotion; it is *in* language, and therefore, theoretically at least, it is accessible and describable, if not empirically demonstrable.

To avoid these pitfalls in previous definitions of rhythm, Meschonnic turns to etymology, in particular the exploration of the Greek etymon *ruthmos*, as presented by Benveniste (1971). Benveniste rejects the usual derivation of *ruthmos* from *rein*, 'to flow' (with this 'flowing' associated with the movement of ocean waves). He shows that (in its earliest occurrences) *ruthmos* was never used for the movement of waves but had a much broader meaning – not 'measured movement' but 'form' in general ('proportioned figure', 'arrangement', 'disposition', 'the characteristic arrangement of parts in a whole'). In particular, he finds that the modal suffix *-(th)mos* gave *ruthmos* an original meaning opposed to our normal conception of rhythm as 'periodic return', 'measure'. *Ruthmos* was not used to refer to such fixed forms but to 'form in the instant that it is assumed by what is moving, mobile, and fluid, the form of that which does not have organic consistency . . . the pattern of a fluid element, of a letter arbitrarily shaped, of a robe which one arranges at one's will, of a particular state of character or mood . . . form as improvised, momentary, changeable' (Benveniste 285–6).

This historical meaning of *rhythm* is more suited to Meschonnic's project. For Meschonnic, *rhythm* in language is nothing less than the full 'figured sense' of a discourse (94), a synthetic collection of all of the non-significational (i.e. non-lexical) aspects of discourse meaning – what he calls *signifiance*. This *signifiance*, he argues, is involuntary and anterior to signification, in fact anterior to anthropology. It is the most archaic part of both language and human subjectivity. Rhythm is not just a linguistic form (although it is this as well); it is a *'forme-sujet'*, an ontological merger of speaker and spoken, historical subject and linguistic object. It is the organization of the speaking subject as discourse, in and by discourse.

Formally, this rhythmic *'signifiance'* is open-ended; therefore Meschonnic doesn't attempt an exhaustive list of its linguistic realizations. In fact, he claims that this open-endedness is exactly the strength of its definition. Like the speaking subject, rhythm is not a homogeneous totalization; it is fragmentary, diverse.

In the course of his discussion, Meschonnic does mention various particulars, however, and these suggest his intent. On a large scale, he isolates three sorts of rhythms: (1) *linguistic* rhythms (e.g. rhythms of words, phrases and sentences); (2) *rhetorical* rhythms (e.g. rhythms of cultural traditions); and (3) *poetic* rhythms (e.g. the rhythmic organization of modes of writing). Within the *Critique* he elaborates only on (1). Linguistic rhythms seem to involve all aspects of discourse organization that presently escape rigorous linguistic description: paralinguistic gesture, visual form, sound orchestration, intonational forms and meanings, and various aspects of the syntactic and semantic organization in discourse – metaphor, lexical fields, register (e.g. formal vs conversational styles), parallelism, periodicity, syntactic and lexical neologism, ambiguity, real-time reanalysis (garden-path effects), and various statistical patternings of syntactic choices (e.g. nominal vs verbal styles). Included under linguistic rhythm are also the descriptions he provides of more conventional rhythmic articulation: the position of phrasal accents, the length and placement of pauses, the unexpected juxtapositioning of accents, various 'closed' rhythmic figures (e.g. choriambic patterns), vocalic hiatus, the accentual 'onset' of syntactic constituents, and other matters.

Given the diversity of these forms, Meschonnic does not attempt any full formalization of his rhythmic observations, and he actually presents very little analysis (some detailed comment on a couple of isolated lines – e.g. pp. 252–3 – and a handful of analyses that present very selective comment on complete texts or larger textual corpora – e.g. pp. 359–89, 507–18). Most of his analytical comment is also fairly standard, with few descriptive advances. His major descriptive innovation is to provide linguistic forms with 'ties' that represent their formal linkages, and 'marks' that represent their relative accumulation of rhythmic articulation (of various sorts). Meschonnic spends very little time motivating or illustrating this new descriptive system, however, and admits that it is only suggestive of the inadequacy of more traditional scansion.

NOTES

1. Wesling forthcoming: 284
2. Hrushovski 1960: 179
3. Brogan (xix) claims that 'versification among all the other various humanistic disciplines is a field exceptionally confused and incoherent about basic principles and procedures', one that 'has been prey to more eccentricity and confusion, more nonthink and doubletalk, than probably any other discipline in the realm of letters' (xvii).
4. Most of Brogan's 300 or so entries under 'traditional stress metrics' (233–89) present some version of foot-substitution metrics. The most important scholarly study using this system is George Saintsbury's three-volume history (1906–10). For handbooks, see Fussell, Shapiro and Beum, and Malof. For popular pedagogies, see Brooks and Warren, Ciardi and Williams, Kennedy, Perrine and Proffitt. To my knowledge there is no verse pedagogy that does not use some version of this system. I review the work in this tradition in Cureton 1986a.
5. For a selection of studies in this tradition, see Steele 1779, Patmore 1856, Lanier 1880, Thomson 1923, Prall 1936, Croll 1929, Abercrombie 1964a and b, Leech 1969 and Stevenson 1970. For a review of methods in this tradition, see Sumera 1970.
6. Considering the position of free verse as the dominant verse form for English poetry in this century, this comment is surprisingly small, however. For references to 1980, see Brogan 1981: 402–16; for subsequent studies see Brogan's updates through to 1985 in *Eidos* 1:2 (1984) and the bibliographical supplement to *Eidos* 2 (March 1986).

   Until recently, most of the comment on free verse has been little more than posturing and polemicizing, usually by free verse poets

themselves, especially the great moderns (Pound, Williams, Eliot, Lawrence, etc.; see Allen and Tallman (eds) 1973) and their lesser lights (e.g. Charles Olson 1950). These polemics have yielded little insight into the structure of free verse and have now been explicitly deflated by various hands (e.g. Perloff 1973, 1981; Lieberman and Lieberman 1972; Cushman 1985; Steele 1990). The only full-length study of English free verse is Hartman 1980, and this is largely non-technical. Most of the original detailed work on free verse has focused on individual poets, of whom William Carlos Williams has been an overwhelming favourite (e.g. Berry 1981a and b, 1985, forthcoming a; Sayre 1983; Cushman 1985; Perloff 1985: 88–118). Significantly, none of the linguistic approaches to prosody (see 1.3.9–1.3.13 below) has taken a general interest in free verse (the major exceptions being Crystal 1975b and Luecke 1983, who attempt some intonational analysis). The only literary tradition to concern itself centrally with free verse is Wesling's grammetrics (see 1.3.14 below), and his major volume of technical theory and analysis still remains unpublished (Wesling forthcoming). Prosodic handbooks consistently slight free verse (e.g. Shapiro and Beum 148–52; Fussell 1979: 76–89), usually speak in disparaging terms, and when technical are only chaotically so (e.g. Malof 146–63). Free verse is omitted entirely from Wimsatt's collection of survey essays *Versification: Major Language Types* (1972). As Wesling and others have argued, this weakness and paucity of comment on the major verse form of our time is disturbing and stands as a striking indication of the inadequacy of traditional approaches to verse rhythm.
7. As Attridge (1982: 11) and many others have noted, one of the major weaknesses of a foot-based prosody is its treatment of seven-syllable tetrameter lines, which can often be analysed arbitrarily as either iambic (but acephalic) or trochaic (but catalectic).

> Hére / the án/ them doth / comménce (iambic)
> Hére the / ánthem / doth com / ménce (trochaic)

> ('The Phoenix and Turtle', line 20)

Difficulties such as these arise constantly in the scansion of syllabically variable free verse meters. (For further discussion of these difficulties, see 2.2 below.)
8. The experiential effects of the visual free verse line have now been extensively studied, most brilliantly and exhaustively by Eleanor Berry in her writing on William Carlos Williams, but significantly by a number of other commentators as well. In addition to the references in Note 1 above, see M. Williams 1978, Frank and Sayre (eds) 1988, Perloff 1981, Berry forthcoming b, Hollander 1985: 245–87, Cureton 1986b, Ranta

1976, 1978, and the special section on 'the theory and practice of the line in contemporary poetry' in *Epoch* 29 (1980: 161–224).

9. Taken together, the ongoing polemics for free verse and the recent defence of traditional versification by Steele (1990) inscribe the fate of a prosodic theory that stays at a high level of generality, mixing incompatibles and avoiding particulars. Neither side of the debate displays a sound and detailed understanding of either their own practice or the practice of the opposing side. The free verse polemicists reject traditional verse for its rhythmic regularity when much traditional verse is highly volatile rhythmically, claim that free verse overthrows traditional meter when much of free verse is significantly metrical, and claim that free verse creates a new measure, when what free verse creates is not a new measure at all but expressive visual form. Steele justifies metrical verse largely in terms of its metrical regularity when all metrical verse derives much of its aesthetic interest from its phrasing, accuses the moderns of writing 'unmeasured' verse when much free verse is significantly metrical, and disregards entirely the major find of the free verse poets in this century: visual form.

10. For a compact survey of early comments on intonation by English grammarians and American elocutionists, see Pike 1947: 2–3. For the British tradition, see Jones 1909, Palmer 1922, Armstrong and Ward 1926, Schubiger 1935, 1958, Kingdon 1958, O'Connor and Arnold 1961, Halliday 1963, 1966, 1967, 1970, 1985, Crystal 1969, 1975b, Crystal and Davy 1969, 1975, Crystal and Quirk 1964, Quirk 1968: 121–35, 36–47, Brazil 1975, 1985, and Taglicht 1984. For the American tradition, see Pike 1947, 1959, 1962, 1967, Trager and Smith 1951, Hill 1958: 13–29, Hockett 1958: 33–61, Gleason 1961: 167–70, Bolinger 1965, 1986, Liberman 1975, Bing 1979, Ladd 1980, Selkirk 1984 and Pierrehumbert 1987. For overviews of these traditions, see Cruttenden 1986 and Couper-Kuhlen 1986.

11. For these arguments, see Whitehall 1951, Sutherland 1958, Pace 1961 and Fowler 1966c. Most American structuralists also claim that syllables with the same phonemic stress are *allophonically* iambic (e.g. H.L. Smith 1959).

12. In the interest of clarity, I reduce some of the complexity of Hewitt's scansion. She also develops a complex system of symbols that mark *types* of strength in cadence groups. These symbols represent various combinations of pitch and stress.

13. These intertheoretical comparisons are hard to make, but the British 'tone unit' seems comparable to Pike's 'rhythm unit' (Pike 1947: 34), a unit unbroken by pause, containing one or more 'primary contours'. Pike's 'simple rhythm unit', a 'rhythm unit' with one 'primary contour', seems comparable to what metrical phonologists have come to call a phonological phrase (see 'Metrical Phonologists' below). In the British

approach to intonation, there is nothing comparable to the phonological phrase.
14. Halliday also identifies two 'compound tones'. These tones combine a fall (1) or rise–fall (5) early in the tone unit with a final level tone (3) on the tonic syllable. In Halliday's system the first is numbered 13, the second 53.
15. This claim has also been made in other prosodic traditions (e.g. Mukarovsky 1933; Kopczynska and Pszczolowska 1960). To my knowledge, there have been no extensive applications of the British approach to English intonation to rhythmic analysis. Most suggestions have remained theoretical. Halliday's 'functional grammar' has been applied extensively in poetic analysis (e.g. Birch and O'Toole (eds) 1988; Hasan 1985), but this application has been directed almost exclusively towards interpretation and the articulation of meaning rather than towards aesthetic evaluation and rhythmic figuration. The British approach to intonation has also been applied extensively to the practical analysis of non-poetic texts (e.g. Crystal and Davy 1969), but within these more extensive stylistic applications, poetic texts do not appear. Most theoretical and pedagogical presentations of the 'London School' grammar also provide some brief mention of the relevance of intonation to rhythm and meter (e.g. Cummings and Simmons 1983: 43–59; Halliday 1985: 5–18), but these comments are invariably cursory and suggestive rather than theoretical. Faure 1970 draws on work in the British tradition but settles for a partial representation of intonation, one that marks pitch levels and movements (fives static tones and seven dynamic tones) but not juncture (i.e. pauses, tone-unit boundaries, etc.) or dependency relations (e.g. tonic syllables vs non-tonic syllables). Therefore, his intonational scansion neither segments the text nor marks points of informational culmination, an approach that is difficult to relate to rhythmic articulation.
16. The original study in this approach (Halle and Keyser 1966) generated an enormous response which led to immediate revisions and 'defences' by the original authors (Halle 1970; Keyser 1969; Halle and Keyser 1971a and b, 1972) as well as competing proposals by other prosodists (e.g. Beaver 1968a and b, 1969, 1970, 1971, 1973; Freeman 1968, 1969; Magnuson and Ryder 1970, 1971; Hascall 1971, 1974; Youmans 1974; Bernhart 1974; Devine and Stephens 1975; Kiparsky 1975; Chisholm 1977; Heller 1977, 1978). For a review of the accomplishments of generative metrics as seen from several historical perspectives, see Freeman 1972, Beaver 1974, Hayes 1988 and Youmans 1989. For some critical reviews, see Wimsatt 1971, Cable 1972, 1976, Klein 1974, Standop 1975, Ihwe 1975, Attridge 1982: 34–5, 1989 and Abrams 1983.
17. Representations of metrical patterns in generative theories have not been consistent. For example, in Halle and Keyser's original theory

(Halle and Keyser 1966), the verse design (or metrical pattern) is completely abstract, a series of counted 'positions' ('odd' vs 'even') with no linguistic or psychological content. In their final revision (Halle and Keyser 1972), however, these positions are defined psychologically ('strong' vs 'weak'). In Kiparsky 1975 they are defined linguistically (1 stress vs 4 stress). Some of the criticism of the generative approach has focused on this vacillation (e.g. Devine and Stephens 1975; Chisholm 1977).

18. The major precursors of the generativists' theoretical aspirations are Jesperson 1900 and Bridges 1921.
19. In Chomsky's formulation, a theory reaches observational adequacy if it accounts for the available data. A theory reaches descriptive adequacy if its assigns the data structural descriptions on the basis of explicit formal principles. A theory reaches explanatory adequacy if it can arbitrate between theories with equal descriptive adequacy.
20. Some of the discussion following the appearance of Halle and Keyser's proposals focused on counter-examples that violate their rules but none the less occur (e.g. Barnes and Esau 1979; Tsur 1977; Koelb 1979). The more significant fact, however, is how few of these lines have been found. For some interesting studies of how the predictive power of the generativists' rules can be verified indirectly (by examining syntactic inversions), see Youmans 1982 and 1983.
21. Some of the response to this suggestion has also focused on counter-examples (e.g. Barnes and Esau 1979). But again the more significant fact is the relative strength of this generalization, not its occasional vulnerability.
22. For a general discussion of Tsur's theoretical project, see Tsur 1983a. For various studies within this project, see Tsur 1983b, 1987a, b and c and 1989.
23. In an appendix to his major work on rhythm (1977: 243–4), Tsur lists some fifty instances of stress maxima in weak positions taken from the verse of Shakespeare, Donne, Milton, Shelley and Hopkins.
24. Bjorklund 1985 makes much of the derivative nature of the *parts* of *REP*, missing entirely the important methodological and theoretical innovations of the theory as a whole.
25. For an interesting discussion of this point, see Hayes 1984b.
26. To my knowledge, the first overview of historical work on English prosody has just appeared: Couper-Kuhlen 1986.
27. For an overview of the results of this approach to linguistic prosody, as argued from various perspectives, see Hayes 1980/1985, Selkirk 1984, Giegerich 1985, Halle and Vernaud 1987 and Hogg and McCully 1987. For several studies that apply this model to verse rhythm, see Kiparsky and Youmans (eds) 1989.
28. Ironically, Selkirk has recently changed her mind about how many of

her earlier observations should be explained, but space does not permit me to pursue these further considerations here. In my discussion I follow those who have furthered Selkirk's earlier work rather than followed her new approach. For a compact review of this work, see Hayes 1989.

29. Hayes also cites a range of phonological evidence for clitic phases from other languages. Some versification systems seem to make specific reference to clitic phrase constituency (e.g. Devine and Stephens 1978, 1981, 1983 on metrical 'bridges' in ancient Greek).

30. The most important issue under debate is whether these constraints should be represented with grids or trees. Hayes (1984a, 1989) favours grids; Kiparsky (1977) favours trees. This debate reproduces the uncertainty about these matters within the theory of metrical phonology itself. For a review of this issue, see Prince 1983.

31. What Gil *et al.* call 'stress' is problematic and is never clearly defined. As they use the term, 'stress' seems to correlate with the relative prominence of the syllables in some performance of the line. Needless to say, this definition opens various cans of worms (most of which Gil *et al.* do not consider).

Chapter 2

The myths of traditional prosody

2.1 INTRODUCTION

The body of writing we have just reviewed has contributed in many ways to our understanding of English verse rhythm, and my intention is not to overlook or discount these contributions here. The foot-substitution tradition has isolated and catalogued most of the significant prosodic phenomena that require attention by any prosodic theory and thus have given the field of study most of its basic concepts and analytical vocabulary. The temporalists have provided some of the most illuminating treatments of meter and have explored most extensively the relation between rhythm in poetry and rhythm in music. The phrasalists have paid most attention to the relation between verse rhythm and meaning. The Slavic metrists have broadened our knowledge of the normative placement and semantic functions of the 'metrical figures' long described by foot-substitution prosodists, and in their syntactic studies have set a new standard for descriptive rigour and intensity. The intonationalists have provided the descriptive means and theoretical context for representing intonational segmentation and its informational functions. The generative metrists have demonstrated the complexity of metrical well-formedness and have provided ways of specifying constraints on metrical styles. The metrical phonologists have explored the formal relationships between rhythmic structure and linguistic structure and have demonstrated the role of phrasing in metrical well-formedness. The grammetrists have looked more closely at enjambment and its experiential effects. Prosodists such as Gil have noted the pervasiveness of hierarchical patterning in meter and have investigated its diverse textual sources. The free verse prosodists have explored the role of visual form in rhythmic response. And critics such as Wesling, Tsur, Smith and Meschonnic have broadened the literary scope of prosodic comment and provided detailed ways of talking about the structure and effects of prosodic organization at high levels.

None the less, it is also evident that no single 'school' of prosodic theory, traditional or recent, presents a strong, unified theory of verse rhythm. In fact, it is evident that even all of these 'schools' taken together do not present such a theory.

The outstanding support for this claim is the lack of critical productivity of this theoretical tradition. Despite this huge body of theoretical writing and the real advances it has achieved, detailed critical studies of individual texts and authors have been lacking and therefore this theoretical writing has had little influence on critical practice or prosodic pedagogy in the schools. For instance, to my knowledge, no study uses the temporal approach to meter in an analysis of an extensive body of text. No study provides complete scansions of a substantial corpus of English prose using the classical phrasal hierarchy of feet, commata, cola, phrases and periods, together with a close consideration of syntactic periodicity and discourse hermeneutics. I know of only one extensive attempt to describe the function of intonation in the rhythm of an extended body of text (Faure 1970), and this study is twenty years old. As far as I am aware, the results of the generative metrists and metrical phonologists have never been extensively applied in textual analysis. As Jakobson himself lamented, Slavic metrists have generally avoided extensive analyses of individual texts and authors. To my knowledge, Smith's detailed theory of poetic closure has never been extended beyond her suggestions or extensively applied. Besides Wesling's own work, I know of only one extensive application of grammetric methods (Berry 1981a), a study that is still unpublished. Attridge's analysis is only brief, suggestive and partial. Tsur and Meschonnic's proposals are almost entirely theoretical; they present no complete analyses. And no verse pedagogy that I know of presents anything other than foot-substitution metrics. Despite the many theoretical advances by this tradition, scholarship and pedagogy in prosodic analysis are still pursued with traditional theoretical and descriptive tools (e.g. Wright 1988).

While we might see this limited productivity as accidental, as simply a lack of time and energy devoted to these more practical affairs, this judgement would be generous. Rather, it is my claim here that this lack of productivity can be traced to a number of deep philosophical and methodological difficulties, difficulties that recur in various forms throughout this tradition of writing and that, in this recurrence, have prevented *in principle* the development of a strong theory of English verse rhythm. I like to call these difficulties 'the myths of traditional prosody'. Before we proceed to develop a more workable set of basic assumptions and methodologies, it might be useful to review these traditional philosophical and methodological difficulties here.

2.2 MYTH 1: VERSE RHYTHM IS ONE-DIMENSIONAL

In terms of our opening discussion, the most obvious difficulty with many traditional approaches to verse rhythm has been their avoidance of the major dilemma of all rhythmic description: an account of multidimensional form. In their detailed proposals, the majority of the 'approaches' in the tradition (e.g. foot-substitution metrics, temporal metrics, Slavic metrics, generative metrics, Tsur, Attridge, the metrical phonologists, Gil) are not theories of verse rhythm at all, but theories of *meter*. These approaches isolate this one aspect of rhythm for description and implicly claim that other rhythmic patterning is disordered 'variation' against this one coherent form. Phonological patterns are reduced to stress and lead to metrical substitution and tension. Intonational patterns are reduced to caesurae and occasion metrical inversion and delay. Syntactic patterns are reduced to enjambment and establish 'counterpoint' between line and phrase. And many other linguistic patterns (e.g. above the level of the sentence) are not mentioned at all. No attempt is made to provide complete rhythmic descriptions of these other patterns, and any descriptions that are attempted are couched in metrical terms. Faced with multidimensional patterning, these traditions describe only one dimension. This does not solve the basic problem of rhythmic description; it avoids it.

When present, a metrical response is a prominent component of any rhythmic experience. No theory of rhythm can neglect its effect. Besides its own shape and movement, a metrical response will usually pervade our experience of a text and with its pervasive influence will constrain other rhythmic patterns to attend to its more rigid form. Phonological phrasing will take shape around the basic metrical beat, intonational phrasing around the line, the clause around the distich, the sentence around the stanza, the argument around the poetic form, and so forth throughout the text. The visual form of a text will usually follow metrical divisions as well, a fact that has proved increasingly important in recent times.

There is no justification for *equating* rhythm and meter, however, and no prosodic theory can be adequate that is based on such an equation. While all meters constrain somewhat the other rhythmic patterning in a text, a meter will not determine these other patterns. The same rhythmic pattern can co-occur with many different metrical forms, and many different rhythmic patterns can co-occur with the same metrical form. In fact, language is such a complex rhythmic medium that no two lines of poetry will have either entirely distinct or entirely identical rhythmic forms.

Consider lines 4 and 8 of 'The Sick Rose': *In the howling storm:* (4); *Does thy life destroy.* (8). As even casual analysis reveals, these lines share many rhythmic features. Both lines are visual units, of about the same length, beginning with a capital, ending with punctuation, preceded by a block of type, and followed by white space. Both lines have five syllables and two major metrical beats, on the third and fifth syllables, realized by stress, with the stress on the second beat stronger than the stress on the first, and with all offbeats realized by unstressed syllables. Both lines end with an intonational break, a significant syntactic arrival, a rhyme, and a quatrain break. Both lines are composed of two simple phrases (*In the howling / storm*; *Does thy life / destroy*). Both lines have exactly one disyllabic word (*howling, destroy*). Both lines have a phonetic link between the first and fourth syllable (*In-ing*; *Does/de-*). Both lines begin their second syllable with [ð] and their fifth syllable with [st]. And so forth.

In many other ways, however, these lines are rhythmically distinct. Line 4 is syntactically suspensive; it is the last extension of an already extended subject. Line 8 is a syntactic arrival; it is the completing predicate in the last clause of the last sentence in the text. Line 4 is divided into heavily asymmetric phrases at the lowest level (*In the howling / storm*). Line 8 is more symmetrical (*Does thy life / destroy*). Line 4 is more coherent phonologically and syntactically; syntactically it is a prepositional phrase that divides phonologically between a pre-modifier and the head noun of the noun phrase object. Line 8 is less coherent phonologically and syntactically; syntactically it is a predicate that divides phonologically between a preposed object and the main verb (a main verb that is syntactically isolated from its associated auxiliary). Line 4 has only a partial rhyme (*storm–worm*). Line 8 has a full rhyme (*joy–destroy*). Line 4 is part of a relatively expanded clause, a clause that overruns metrical boundaries (including a quatrain boundary). Line 8 is part of a relatively contracted clause, a clause that is coextensive with a distich (a common grammetric norm for a poem with short lines). The disyllabic word in line 4 (*howling*) is stressed on the first syllable and occurs in the first phrase in the line. The disyllabic word in line 8 (*destroy*) is stressed on the second syllable and occurs in the second phrase in the line. Line 4 follows a metrically regular line, a line with the same number of syllables and phrases but a more symmetrical arrangement. Line 8 follows a metrically strained line, a line with an expanded number of both phrases and syllables in a similarly contracting arrangement. The stressed syllables in line 4 have tense vowels and diphthongs that end with back glides ([aw], [ow]). The stressed syllables in line 8 have diphthongs that end with front glides ([ay], [oy]). And so forth.

The point is: only a couple of these rhythmic similarities and differences are determined by the meter – the basic two-beat line, the regular realization of the beat by stress, and the differing metrical contexts (the more deviant realization of the meter in line 7 vs the more regular realization of the meter in line 3). All of the other rhythmic similarities and differences are non-metrical: the similar yet different phrasings, the similar yet different phonetic articulation, the differing syntactic articulation, the similar yet different word shapes, and so forth. A rhythmic theory that overlooks this other rhythmic patterning overlooks the better part of verse rhythm. If we are to understand how meters organize texts, we must understand what they organize. And if we are to have an adequate theory of rhythm, we must be able to confront rhythm in its non-metrical forms. A great deal of language is engagingly rhythmic without being metrical, and all metered language contains exactly those structures that are used for rhythmic effect in non-metrical forms. The phenomena demand a unified account; most traditional theories of verse rhythm ignore this demand.

The assumption that verse rhythm is one-dimensionally metrical severely restricts the critical usefulness of a rhythmic scansion. If a prosodic system defines rhythm as meter, a critic using this system must find the shapely movement of the verse in its meter, rather than in a rhythmic response to the language of the verse as a whole. The usual result is an exaggeration of the contribution of meter to that movement, as in the following analysis of 'The Sick Rose' offered by Paul Fussell (1979: 103–4), one of our most respected foot-substitution prosodists.

William Blake's 'The Sick Rose' is perhaps an even more impressive metrical achievement, for the whole poem depends upon one crucial substitution. Here the base against which the substitution has power to operate is iambic–anapestic:

O Rose, thou art sick!
The invisible worm
That flies in the night,
In the howling storm

Has found out thy bed
Of crimson joy,
And his dark secret love
Does thy life destroy.

All goes swimmingly until line 7. Until we arrive there the meter has kept us in the world of some possibility, a world in which escape is thinkable and in which even salvation may be engineered. If we have been shown an invisible worm flying in the night, if we have experienced a howling storm, we have also been conducted to a bed of compensating crimson joy. But after line 7, hope is no longer possible, and the cause that extinguishes hope is a spondaic substitution, the only one in the poem:

And hĭs / dárk sĕc / rĕt lóve[1]

It is this line that consummates the love, and it is this central spondaic foot that is the metrical consummation of the whole structure. The meter conducts the argument. The meter is the poem.

'The meter is the poem.' This is the central difficulty with many approaches to verse rhythm. The meter is *never* the poem. Fussell's comments here are typical of the reductive analyses found throughout the history of comment on English verse.

Ironically, phrasal approaches to rhythm, which in principle escape the reduction of verse rhythm to meter, often embrace Myth 1 as well, but with a complementary gesture. They reduce verse rhythm to phrasing, omitting an independent representation of meter. For instance, this reduction of meter to phrasing has pervaded the phrasalists' treatment of Whitman's verse, most of which is palpably metrical. In all but the most obvious metrical contexts, prosodists such as Mitchell, Allen and Jannacone scan for phrases, omitting any representation of meter.

This complementary realization of Myth 1 also pervades the temporalist tradition. As many have argued, the *physical* movement of most English verse is more dominantly controlled by the placement of lexical stresses than the placement of metrical beats. This asymmetry between meter and physical time is particularly severe when metrical beats are not realized by stress. In these situations, the structure of the meter plays against, rather than with, the natural stress-timing in the language, a conflict that is difficult to represent in temporal terms. The temporal prosodist must either structure measures with the beat, misrepresenting the physical movement of the line, or align measures with the stresses, misrepresenting both the metrical structure and its regulating temporal influence. Lanier often takes the former option, as in his scansion of *Hamlet* (172–3), a scansion that Gross (1964: 7) rightly claims 'scatters sand in the eyes and pours wax in the ears'.

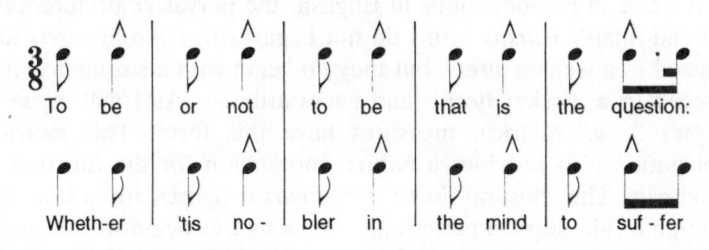

| To be | or not | to be | that is | the question: |
| Wheth-er | 'tis no-| bler in | the mind | to suf-fer |

Most temporal prosodists take the latter course, however, presenting scansions of the pentameter that abandon the five-beat norm for an analysis with more or fewer measures. For example, Cobb (1913, 1917) claims that many pentameters have four measures; Prall (1936), three. Cobb (1913: 144) scans

> A / thing of / beauty is a /joy for / ever

and announces the existence of the 'heroic tetrameter'. Finding the physical movement of non-metrical rhythms in conflict with the meter, many temporal prosodists abandon the meter and let measures vary freely with phrasing.

This reduction of meter to phrasing also pervades the work of the prose rhythmists. As with Whitman's verse, most rhythmical prose (and ordinary conversation) is at least sporadically metrical, but one of the primary arguments of the prose rhythmists has been to deny this metricality. In fact, Myth 1 is a controlling assumption in this tradition even when the prose analysed is most obviously metrical. For example, it seems evident that the *cursus* is best explained in metrical, rather than phrasal, terms. *Cursus* forms represent the metrification of the ends of rhetorical units. Contrary to Croll's claims, in most *cursus* forms the initial stress in the cadential figure is *not* stronger than the final stress. The most natural rendition of a phrase such as *His treatment of the vanquished Saxons*, an 8–4–2 velox, is not

His tréatment of the vànquished Sáxons

as Croll claims, but

His tréatment of the vànquished Sáxons.

At the end of prosodic units in English, the pervasive preference is for 'end-focus'. *Cursus* forms do not begin with a strong *stress* and proceed to a weaker *stress*, but they *do* begin with a strong *beat* and proceed to a weaker *beat* – and necessarily so. As I will argue in chapter 3, *all* metrical measures have this form. This metrical explanation also provides a natural motivation for the function of the *cursus*. The 'closural' force of the *cursus* figures arises from the function of all metrical patterning. These figures begin with a strong beat, project a measure, and then play out their structural inertia to a predictable close.

This complementary reduction of meter to phrasing is also the natural result of the philosophical critiques of metrical approaches to rhythm by the intonationalists, Wesling, and Meschonnic. Wesling openly acknowledges the limitations of his grammetric analysis; one of these major limitations is exactly the lack of a strong theory of meter. Given that French verse is predominantly non-metrical, it is understandable that Meschonnic criticizes metrical approaches to French verse. But given the multicultural focus of his *Critique*, Meschonnic indulges in Myth 1 when he extends his critique of meter to other verse traditions. Any adequate theory of verse rhythm must contain a theory of meter. Crystal's suggestion that we provide an intonational definition for metrical lines is another case in point. It is indeed normative to have lines delimited by intonational breaks. But there are perfectly acceptable metrical texts where this is not the case (e.g. *Paradise Lost*). It also seems evident that metrical lines in most art-verse have no consistent intonational composition. Rather, being metrical they are defined metrically and therefore their linguistic composition is best specified exactly by the sort of 'syllable arithmetic' that Crystal deplores. In English at least, truly intonational versification systems are rare (e.g. Williams' 'triadic-line' verse) and readers respond to these systems immediately as 'esoteric' rather than 'normal'.

Some of the most complex realizations of Myth 1 appear in the more recent linguistic approaches to rhythm: the metrical phonologists and Gil. In these approaches, meter is not reduced to phrasing or phrasing to meter; rather, some new structure is proposed that is a mélange of the two.

The source of difficulty in metrical phonology seems to derive from a misinterpretation of various constructs in music theory: (1) Cooper and Meyer's theory of musical grouping/phrasing; and (2) metrical grids. In his initial formulations Liberman limits his metrical grids to duple and triple patterning, a commonly recognized limitation on metrical structure. As metrical phonology has developed, however, Liberman's original intentions and definitions have been altered. Given their hierarchical form, grids have been used as an alternative to trees in the modelling of stress patterns, or in a more reduced ('flattened') form they have been used as a way of representing simple strong–weak alternations (as in the verse norms of the Slavicists or metrical patterns of the generativists). For instance, translating his grid formalism into Liberman's, Hayes would scan:

```
                            4
                3           3
        2   2   2       2       2           Verse instance
    1   1 1 1   1   1   1 1 1   1
    And life is too much like a pathless wood
        2   2           2   2       2       Verse norm
    1   1 1 1   1   1   1 1 1   1
```

In this representation, the verse norm is assumed to be a flat grid (that falls within Liberman's constraints on grid well-formedness). The verse instance is assumed to be a more vertical grid (that falls outside of Liberman's constraints on well-formedness). It is questionable whether either of these grids represents a system of 'hierarchically-related periodicities', however; therefore, it is questionable whether either of them represents Liberman's original use of grids. As Hayes (1984a) points out, the grid formalism, because it provides a more direct representation of locality, seems to be a more convenient way to represent constraints on the language of verse lines. But experientially, Hayes' grids are very close to being just formal reflexes of arboreal representations.

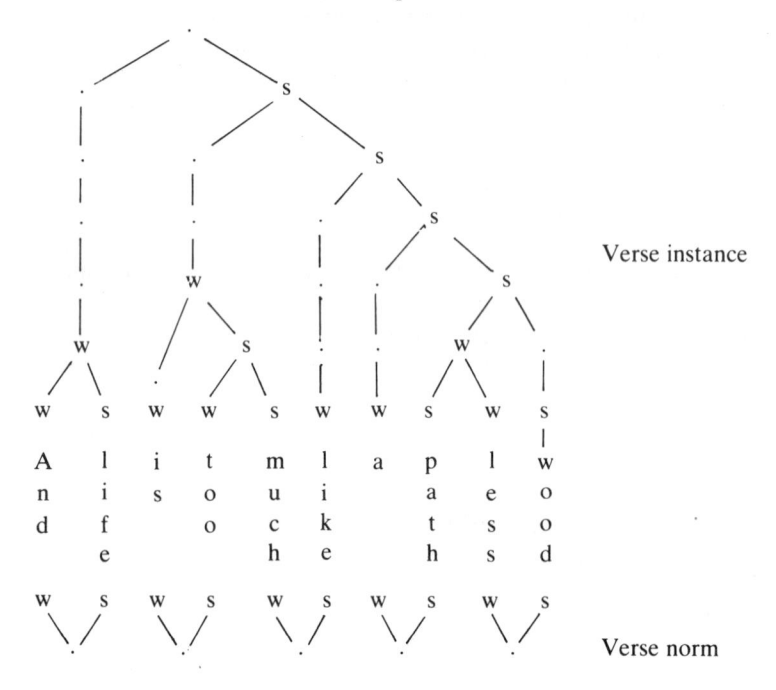

```
                    .
               /  \
              /    s
             /   /  \
            .   .    s
            |   |   / \
            .   .  .   s
            |   |  |  / \
            |   w  |  .  s
            |  / \ |  |  / \
            w /   s|  |  w  .
           /\ .  /\|  | / \ |
          w  s w  s w w  s w  s
          A  l i  t m l  a p  l w
          n  i s  o u i  a e  o
          d  f    o c k  t s  o
             e    o h e  h s  d
          w  s w  s w s  w s  w  s
          \ / \ / \ /  \ /  \  /
           .   .   .    .    .
```
Verse instance

Verse norm

Used in this fashion, it is hard to see the relation between these grids and the grids that are used to represent musical meter.

On the other hand, Liberman himself seems to misunderstand Cooper and Meyer's theory of musical grouping/phrasing. Cooper and Meyer's groups/phrases are highly abstract, 'natural', psychologically real, vertically unlimited and horizontally irregular shapes segmented out of the perceptual stream in response to the summative effects of various local and global features of the rhythmic medium (structural parallelism, proximity, symmetry, continuity, etc.). That is, Cooper and Meyer's theory is a theory of rhythmic phrasing. But Liberman (and his collaborators and followers) have used these phrasal representations to describe relatively concrete, conventional, horizontally uniform and vertically constrained patterns *in* language – i.e. stress – while naming these representations *metrical* patterns. This is a clear mistake. As later metrical phonologists have gone on to claim (with the prosodic hierarchy), the patterns of constituency represented by Liberman's arboreal 'metrical patterns', being coextensive with syntactic structure, have little relation to rhythmic phrasing at these phonological levels. In the line from Frost diagrammed above, the following are considered binary, rising phrases:

```
         w                    s
    ⎧ and life    ⎫  ⎧ is too much like a pathless wood  ⎫
      is              too much
      like            a pathless wood
      a               pathless wood
```

These phrasings make some syntactic sense, but they represent little about the line's *rhythmic* phrasing. On the other hand, as many have argued (for both language and music), an arboreal representation of meter overspecifies metrical constituency. In fact, as I understand them, most metrical phonologists recognize that foot boundaries are only analytical conveniences marking the placement of metrical beats, not perceptual forms.

Gil also posits one structure to represent both phrasing and meter. Although Gil is aware of the metrical phonologists, he makes no mention of the prosodic hierarchy (clitic phrases, phonological phrases, tone units, etc.). Therefore, his representations have little relation to rhythmic phrasing, at least as this phrasing has been described in other theoretical traditions. At the same time, Gil dismisses as relatively fixed (and therefore unimportant) the 'accentual structures' that have been usually equated with meter. Therefore, his prosodic structures are not meant as representations of meter, either. If Gil *et al.*'s structures are neither metrical nor phrasal, they become novel, if not questionable. With their perceptual opaqueness, uniform segmentation and often 'empty' realization, they resemble 'measures' in the temporalist tradition. With their directionality, they resemble 'feet' in the foot-substitution tradition. And with their ranked strength (independent of metrical patterning), they resemble phrases in the phrasalist and intonationalist traditions. In sum, they are *ranked, directional measures*. The question is: Do such hybrid theoretical entities have sufficient support to be put at the foundations of a prosodic theory?

Within the tradition, the most pervasive construct that conflates meter and phrasing is the *metrical foot*, a construct that is unique to analyses of meter in language and therefore a construct that should be immediately doubted on interdisciplinary grounds. While it is evident that meter does indeed 'stave' a text in certain ways, it is questionable whether the foot is a significant part of this 'staving' (as is, for instance, the hemistich or the line). More significantly, it is questionable whether this metrical 'staving' should be equated theoretically with other aspects of rhythmic phrasing (e.g. divisioning into the prosodic hierarchy, syntactic units and discourse organization).

In general, comment on the metrical foot within the tradition has reflected these doubts and uncertainties. Those theorists who posit the foot as more than an analytical convenience often speak only ambiguously and tentatively of its existence (e.g. Chatman 1965: 114–19), and as we have reviewed, many traditions (the temporalists, the phrasalists, the Slavic metrists, the generative metrists, Attridge) reject the foot as a perceptual construct (or even as an analytical convenience). None the less, even our most sophisticated recent prosodists (e.g. the intonationalists, metrical phonologists, Gil, and Wesling) continue to find arguments for the foot, and being the central concept in 'foot-substitution' metrics, the foot continues to play a central role in rhythmic analysis in almost all verse pedagogy and practical verse analysis in the English profession. Arguments for the foot derive from many of the 'myths' in the tradition; therefore we will return to the foot repeatedly in our discussion of these difficulties (below). Some of the strongest motivations for the foot rely on Myth 1, however, and we can take up those arguments here.

The strongest arguments for the foot, over and above its representation of a metrical beating, claim that it accounts in a consistent way for significant aspects of our experience of metrical verse, in particular for (1) rhythmic direction, (2) rhythmic tension, and (3) rhythmic pace (e.g. Fussell 1979). However, as the temporalists, phrasalists and others have argued, these claims have little basis and should be rejected.

One of the major arguments from rhythmic direction claims that texts with beat-final feet have a 'rising' rhythm while texts with beat-initial feet have a 'falling' rhythm (e.g. Brooks and Warren 1976: 505; Proffitt 1981: 173; Malof 1970: 29). For instance, this argument claims that the consistently 'rising' rhythm of a line such as the following derives from its consistently iambic feet.

MYTH 1: VERSE RHYTHM IS ONE-DIMENSIONAL 89

At ŏnce / wĭth jóy / ănd feár / hĭs heárt / rĕboúnds.

(*PL* I, 788)

As many have noted, however, the perception of rhythmic inclination ('rising' vs 'falling') derives from a variety of sources, many of which extend beyond the spacing and placement of beats (e.g. Creek 1920; Cummings and Herum 1967; Stewart 1925; Attridge 1982: 108–14; Stevenson 1970). In a line such as *PL* I, 788, foot shape and perceived shape coincide. But in most cases, perceived shape varies relatively freely within a metrical norm. In fact, within any metrical pattern, rhythmic direction is so free that it constitutes its own pattern, one that demands an independent description. For example, while they are all in the same meter (at low levels), *PL* I, 540 largely 'falls'.

Sonorous mettal blowing Martial sounds.

PL VI, 795 moves symmetrically from 'falling' to 'balanced' to 'rising'.

Kingdom and power and Glorie appertain.

PL II, 405 moves progressively from 'rising' to 'balanced' to 'falling', and then to 'rising' again.

The dark unbottom'd infinite Abyss

PL IV, 293 first 'falls' then 'rises'.

Truth, Wisdom, Sanctitude severe and pure,

Another argument from rhythmic direction claims that the rhythmic direction of the verse is 'inverted' if the position of the stresses in the foot is inverted, as in the first foot of 'Lycidas', line 5.

Shátter / your leaves / before /the mel / lowing year.

However, while we do feel a change in rhythmic inclination in line 5, we feel no change in inclination in many other lines in 'Lycidas' that have the same 'inverted feet' in initial position in the line.

24 Féd thĕ /same flock by fountain, shade, and rill
63 Dówn thĕ /swift Hebrus to the Lesbian shoar.
70 Fáme ĭs /the spur that the clear spirit doth raise
75 Cómes thĕ /blind Fury with th'abhorred shears
78 Fáme ĭs /no plant that grows on mortal soil

Again, the perception of rhythmic inclination is not dependent only on foot shape, but on other matters as well (word shape, phonological phrasing, etc.).

The argument from metrical tension claims that the relative tension in a line of metrical verse can be predicted from the quality and distribution of its 'foot-substitutions'. As many have pointed out, this argument also runs into difficulties, however. For instance, Attridge (1982: 13–15) rightly observes that a foot-substitution scansion implicitly claims that line 1 in the first quatrain of Shakespeare's Sonnet 29 is less regular (and therefore 'tenser') than line 3, even though perceptually line 3 is clearly a greater point of rhythmic tension and strain.

1 Whén in / disgráce / with Fór / tune and / mén's eyés,
2 I all alone beweep my outcast state,
3 And troú / ble deáf / heáv'n with / my bóot / less criés,
4 And look upon myself and curse my fate

In foot-substitution terms, line 1 has three substitutions (feet 1, 4 and 5); line 3 has only one (foot 3).

In part, this incorrect prediction is produced by the asymmetric treatment of juxtaposed stresses (vv//, //vv) in a foot-based system. The juxtaposed stresses in line 1 (*men's eyes*) lead to two foot-substitutions. The juxtaposed stresses in line 3 (*deaf heav'n*) lead to only one. The other difficulty involves the minimal representation of phonological constituency in the foot-substitution formalism. In line 3 a major phrase ends on *heav'n* (where a beat is not expected), but in line 1 the major phrase ends on *eyes*, where a beat is expected. As we have just reviewed, metrical phonologists such as Kiparsky and Hayes have been demonstrating that our impressions of metrical tension (and well-formedness) appear to arise from various sorts of mismatches between meter and this type of phonological phrasing. As in the other cases, this phrasing has its own organization independent of meter and demands a separate description.

The argument from rhythmic pace claims that spondaic feet move slowly, pyrrhic feet more quickly. In fact, this argument claims that quick and slow movement in verse finds its major cause in the relative number and distribution of these different foot types. For instance, Fussell (1979: 40) cites line 87 of Gray's 'Elegy' to illustrate how spondaic substitution 'is enlisted to lengthen the lingering backward look which the dying cast on the 'warm precincts' of their lives.

> For who, to dumb Forgetfulness a prey,
> This pleasing anxious Being e'er resign'd.
> Left the warm Precincts of the cheerful Day,
> Nor cast / one long / ing ling'ring Look behind?

However, Fussell fails to note that this metrical effect is created in part by juxtaposed stresses (a phrasal phenomenon) and that the larger phrasal context also contributes significantly to the delay. In this line, the syntax interpolates a noun phrase composed of four minimal prosodic phrases between the two parts of the phrasal verb *cast behind*.

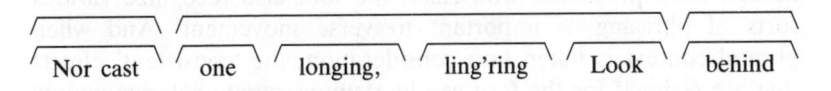

| Nor cast | one | longing, | ling'ring | Look | behind |

Even in a non-metrical context, this structure is heavily delaying.

> Nor cast loving, longing, ling'ring Looks behind

Notice that if *one* in the original line is weakened to an indefinite article, thus eliminating the spondaic substitution, much of the 'delaying' effect remains.

> Nor cast a longing, ling'ring Look behind

On the other hand, if the spondaic substitution is preserved but the phrasal delay is reduced, the felt 'delay' is greatly reduced as well.

> For who to dumb Forgetfulness a prey,
>   This pleasing anxious Being e'er forsook,
> Left the warm Precincts of the cheerful Day,
>   Nor, ling'ring cast behind one longing Look.

The argument for the relative speed of a pyrrhic runs into similar difficulties. As with a spondee, the accelerating effect of a pyhrric derives from its phrasal context. Of necessity, a pyrrhic represents a lower-level expansion in phrasing (an effect that occurs in both prose and verse). Within this phrasal context, the effect of meter is usually to *oppose* this accelerating effect, however, as in the retarded movement of the expanded clitic phrase *Immortality* in the closing line of Emily Dickinson's 'Conscious am I in my chamber', which, in any foot analysis, must be given two pyrrhic feet.

> Neither if He visit other
> Do He dwell – or Nay – know I –
> But Instinct esteem Him
> Immortality –

Other examples could be cited, but there is little need. Throughout the tradition, the consistent experiential effects of the foot have been defined without controlling for the effects of phrasing, even though most prosodists who claim the foot also recognize various sorts of phrasing as important to verse movement. And when phrasal context is taken into consideration, the 'consistent' effects that are claimed for the foot can be demonstrated to derive mainly from consistent patterns of phrasing, with meter often *opposing* these phrasal effects. That is, the theoretical 'need' for the foot is not a need for a 'foot-based' formalization of meter, but a need for a fully explicit theory of phrasing, one that escapes Myth 1 by disinguishing phrasing and meter in a principled way, demonstrating their independent (though interacting) contributions to verse movement. A representation of meter in terms of feet does not and cannot explain the effects that the foot has been posited to explain. The experiential motivations for the foot are overtly misleading – simply wrong.

The conflation of meter and phrasing in the metrical foot has led to enormous analytical confusion in traditions that use this formalization. For example, in attempting to account for rhythmic direction with metrical feet, foot-substitution prosodists will often propose metrical scansions in which feet vary freely with lower-level phrasing, as in the following from a well-known pedagogy (Proffitt 1981: 107).

> One more bit of terminology can be useful: iambic and anapestic meters, which are related, are often called *rising*, because the beat of each comes at the end of the foot; conversely, trochaic and dactylic meters, also related, are called *falling*. These terms can be particularly useful in characterizing metrical effect. For example, the last line of Wallace Stevens's 'Sunday Morning' begins with a falling feeling and ends on a rising note:
>
> Dównward tŏ dărkness ŏn extĕndĕd wíngs.
>
> We could analyze this mixed line as containing two dactyls followed by two iambs, or a dactyl and a trochee followed by an anapest and an iamb. In either case, falling yields to rising, and the shift is very much in keeping with what is being expressed: that we all go down to death (falling), but that we can do so with grace and purpose (rising).

While Proffitt's rhythmic intuitions are right here (the verse *does* appropriately fall and then appropriately rise), the readings he proposes are not metrical.

| Downward to | darkness on | extend | ed wings |
| Downward to | darkness | on extend | ed wings |

Both of these scansions have only four feet, and thus they assert that one of the most admired endings of one of the most acclaimed pentameter poems in the language ends, clunk, with a missing beat. In trying to make the meter account for too much, these scansions miss both phrasing and meter.

In the worst case, this confusion of meter and phrasing can lead to analytical pandemonium, as in the following from Ciardi and Williams (1975: 326–7), one of our most respected verse pedagogies. After scanning the last line of Yeats' 'After Long Silence',

We loved / each other // and were ig / norant

94 THE MYTHS OF TRADITIONAL PROSODY

they note:

> The second line of the Yeats excerpt is metrically very complicated. One may also scan the line as follows:
>
> We loved / each o / ther // and / were ig / norant
>
> with the third foot rendered as a pyrrhic containing a caesura within it. If the line must be brought to five feet at all costs it seems far more reasonable to take the caesura as a foot all by itself (a full-measure rest) than to render a 'split pyrrhic,' whatever that might be. The fact is that Yeats' line (it is the last line of the poem) is constructed for a deliberately falling rhythm. And might almost be rendered:
>
> We loved / each other // and were ignorant
>
> Certainly the stress on the last syllable of 'ignorant' is hardly more than formal as compared to the stress on the first syllable. Note, however, that despite all variation, the syllable count is full and the mechanical scansion presents no difficulties:
>
> We loved / each o / ther and / were ig / norant

While alternative scansions are often possible, if not necessary, the four scansions that Ciardi and Williams suggest have little to do with variant readings of the meter. Rather, they reflect different ways that the metrical foot can be manipulated to account for both meter and phrasing simultaneously. The last scansion represents the major level of metrical expectation. It has five units and two levels of prominence. The third scansion represents segmentation and prominence at one level of lower phrasing, and just segmentation at a higher (intonational) level. It has three lower-level units, two higher-level units and two levels of prominence. The second scansion represents the major level of metrical expectation, segmentation at a higher (intonational) level, and prominence at an even higher (syntactic) level. It has five lower-level units, two higher-level units and three levels of prominence. And the first scansion is an even more incoherent blend of meter and phrasing. The last foot boundary splits a word (and therefore marks a metrical rather than a phrasal boundary), but the line as a whole is given only four lower-level phrases, not the full five demanded by the metrical norm. Intonational segmentation and syntactic prominence are indicated as in the second scansion. This first scansion has four lower-level phrases, two higher-level phrases, and three levels of prominence. Like many foot-substitution prosodists, Ciardi and

Williams present these scansions as *metrical alternatives* rather than as *phrasal simultaneities*. Like Proffitt in the previous example, they try to make meter do too much, and in the process miss both meter and phrasing.

While recognizing (1) the difficulties with 'foot-based' representation of meter, and (2) the need for an independent theory of phrasing are important preliminaries to a more adequate account of verse rhythm, it is also important to understand the consequences of this recognition for prosodic theory as a whole. Traditionally, those who have argued against the foot have asssumed that it is just an analytical construct that can be discarded without significant consequences. This is also a mistake. As I have demonstrated above, the loss of the foot results in a severe *contraction* of what a metrical prosody can accomplish. In particular, a footless metrics makes a clean distinction between the component of rhythm that articulates beats and their linear ordering (i.e. meter) and the component that articulates direction, shape, speed and so forth (i.e. phrasing). If a footless prosody does not add a theory of phrasing, it becomes more responsible but less useful. In fact, it cannot account for most of the traditional experiential motivations for rhythmic analysis cited throughout the 400 years of comment on English verse. That is, again, the major difficulty in developing a critically useful theory of verse rhythm is not to clarify the nature of meter (although we must do that as well) but to construct a more embracing rhythmic theory that can account in a principled way for our full experience of the movement of verse.

This is the central difficulty with theoretical projects such as Attridge's, our most respected analysis of verse rhythm to date. Attridge's major accomplishment is exactly to escape from Myth 1 and the theoretical conflations entailed by the metrical foot without falling into *other* difficulties encountered by the temporalist and generativist treatments of meter (see below). He defines rhythm as a physical pulsation, and thus clearly separates meter from other sorts of rhythmic response. He eliminates the metrical foot, and thus relegates considerations of rhythmic direction (i.e. rising and falling meter, 'metrical inversions', etc.) to phrasing. He omits any treatment of the caesura, and thus avoids the frequent confusions between meter and line-internal phrasing. He puts off discussions of intonation and syntax, and thus avoids the confusions between language structure and rhythmic response in the intonational and grammetric 'schools' of verse analysis. He omits discussion of stanzaic structure and poetic forms, and thus avoids traditional confusions between metrical response and other aspects of versification. He limits his discussion to metrical verse, and thus avoids the temptation to 'scan' free verse and prose in some quasi-metrical formalism. And so forth. Taking meter as his subject, Attridge – as he should – describes only meter.

This limitation of the scope of his theory, however, is unprecedented and especially ironic, given Attridge's primary aims, the development of a strong theory of rhythmic experience. Attridge achieves the degree of theoretical clarity and simplicity that he does by eliminating from consideration most of our rhythmic response to verse. If we regard Attridge's theory as a full representation of verse rhythm, it is one of the most exclusive and restrictive representations of rhythmic response to verse in the history of comment on English prosody.[2] Contrary to most discussions of these matters in the tradition, meter/rhythm for Attridge is just a temporally regular beating, with patterns limited to the span of a line, with beats usually occurring on the same level of structure, and with only one sort of grouping of beats (at the line level). With this theory, many of the local effects of meter can indeed be described, but most of our experiential motivations for describing rhythmic organization in verse are lost.

As might be expected, Attridge gets round this difficulty by including other considerations in his demonstrations and discussions of rhythmic function none the less, even though these considerations are explicitly legislated out of his theory. For example, in his analysis of Geoffrey Hill's 'The Kingdom of Offa' he notices the predominantly falling rhythm realized at several levels: in compound words, simple phrases and sentences. In his analysis of a section from 'Epistle to a Lady' he focuses on Pope's manipulation of phrasal balance and congruence in his pentameter lines. In his analysis of Sonnet 73, he notices the controlled, duple rising phrases in the opening and how the phrasal modulation in the first quatrain is echoed in the second. And so forth. Attridge also blends these comments on phrasing with various observations about syntactic structure, sound patterning, narrative development and other matters – all of which contribute to rhythmic articulation and must be considered by any full theory of the rhythmic organization of verse.

In his discussion of general rhythmic functions, he also moves well 'beyond meter', especially in his consideration of internal pattern

MYTH 1: VERSE RHYTHM IS ONE-DIMENSIONAL 97

and cohesion. These comments give Attridge's discussion a fullness and adequacy that his theory itself cannot deliver.

> Rhythm contributes to the sense of momentum not just on its own, but also in the interplay between the rhythmic sequence and the other sequential features of the poem; the continuous confirming or contradicting of metrical expectations overlaps with other patterns of expectation and satisfaction to impel the verse forward and to delay a sense of closure. Metrical relaxation may occur at a point at which the syntactic pressure for continuation is high (the obvious example is enjambment), or vice versa (the syntactic pause within the line); rhythmic parallelism may be accompanied by syntactic variation, or syntactic repetition by metrical changes; a stanza may end with a structural resolution but leave strong semantic expectations; iambic openings and masculine endings may encourage a rising rhythm while the contours of words and phrases encourage a falling one. All such effects may contribute to the meaning of the poem, whether through imitation, affective embodiment, emphasis, or connection; but they also have an important non-semantic function, creating a form that is experienced not as a static object but as a sequential progression, alternately disturbing and satisfying, challenging and calming, and usually ending with a sense, however momentary, of conflict resolved. Music offers a close analogy: a composer can draw on a common stock of melodic, harmonic, and rhythmic material to create a series of expectations at several levels, whose simultaneous fulfilment is postponed until the end of the work. The satisfaction experienced at the close of a heroic couplet, for instance, is not merely the sum of the separate satisfactions provided by the completion of patterns in meaning, syntax, metre, and rhyme, but the experience, on reaching the final word of the couplet, of *simultaneous* completion of all these levels. And a poem as a whole may achieve completeness by setting up a series of expectations, whether emotional, narrative, syntactic, logical, rhetorical, or formal, which are only completely and simultaneously fulfilled at the end.
>
> (Attridge 1982: 309)

In this excellent summary of the global effects of rhythmic form in verse, Attridge mentions enjambment, caesurae, the shapes of words and phrases, syntactic repetition, semantic expectation, stanzaic structure, rhyme, and other matters. But none of these considerations forms a principled part of his theory of verse rhythm. The question is: How should we view the theoretical status of

Attridge's basic assumptions and definitions when the system he develops describes so little of our experience of verse?

2.3 MYTH 2: VERSE RHYTHM IS PHYSICAL/LINGUISTIC

A second assumption in much of the tradition is that verse rhythm is essentially physical, or if not physical, then at least linguistic.

There is some support for this view. As we know from music theory and elsewhere, there is indeed a connection between metrical response and physical stimulation – both physical prominence and physical time. Our metrical response generally increases as recurrent prominences in a medium approach isochrony, and isochronous recurrence is usually physical (e.g. recurrent stresses, pitches and durations in music and languages) rather than abstract (e.g. the recurrence of points of tonal stability in music or points of syntactic and semantic 'centrality' in language). It is also evident that verse rhythm, both meter and phrasing, is strongly controlled by the structure of the text's language, even if this language has no consistent *physical* manifestation. All recognize that meter is strongly conditioned by lexical stress (and to a lesser extent by sublexical and phrasal stress). The metrical phonologists have also demonstrated the clear relationship between phonological phrasing and metrical well-formedness. And many traditions have noticed the strong correlation between phonological phrasing and rhythmic phrasing, as well as the rhythmic effect of large-scale syntactic and narrative divisioning.

To equate rhythm and physical/linguistic patterning is a clear mistake, however, and, like the conflation of meter and phrasing in Myth 1, leads to enormous theoretical and practical confusion. As music theorists have argued for the better part of this century (see Chapter 3), the dominant feature of our rhythmic capacities is their ability to unify complex and diverse phenomenal input into relatively simple and comparable forms. In meter, these comparable forms are various sorts of pulses, what most prosodists call *beats*. With phrasing, these comparable forms involve points of structural salience and expectational arrival, what many prosodists call 'peaks' and 'goals'. To equate rhythmic forms and phenomenal/linguistic forms, however, is exactly to deny this centre of 'rhythmic cognition', to eliminate the synthesizing cognitive powers of the perceiving subject and therefore to dissolve prosodic theory back into physical and linguistic analysis, defeating the whole enterprise.

MYTH 2: VERSE RHYTHM IS PHYSICAL/LINGUISTIC

Despite these consequences, Myth 2 has none the less been a controlling assumption in most of the traditional approaches to English verse rhythm. Temporalists overtly claim that meter is physically controlled; measures are composed of equal *times*. Most linguistic approaches to meter (the Slavicists, the intonationalists, the generative metrists and the metrical phonologists) also conceive of verse rhythm as some sort of reproduction or schematized model of the linguistic structure of the text. And even the most influential phrasalists, La Drière and his students, conceive of rhythmic phrasing as points of *sonic* concentration (after Scripture's acoustical 'centroids') and therefore limit phrasing to *physical* form.

There is nothing necessary about Myth 2, however, and there is much evidence against it. For meter, the most convincing evidence against Myth 1 comes from (what the tradition has called) 'dipodic' meters, meters with many levels of salient beating. As many have observed (e.g. Attridge 1982: 114–21), these meters are predominantly, if not exclusively, 'falling' in their structure, even if the pattern of linguistic stressing is 'rising'. Within metrical lines, the first major beat is strongest with subsequent beats declining in strength, usually against the text's physical and linguistic form. (I indicate the strength of beats with dot columns; the higher the dot column, the stronger the beat).

No more pencils, no more books,

No more teacher's ugly looks,

No more things that bring us sorrow,

'Cos we won't be here tomorrow.

    .

   .   .

  .   .   .   .

 . . . .

However, if meter is (exclusively) a schematic organization of the physical and linguistic substance of the text, these rhythmic reactions are inexplicable. In *none* of the lines in this quatrain is the first lexical stress, the point of the strongest beat in the line, the strongest stress in the line as well. One might argue that there is also no physical or linguistic motivation for our responding to the strongest beat in the first and third lines as metrically stronger than the strongest beat in the second and fourth lines, or for our responding to the strongest beat in the first line as metrically stronger than the strongest beat in the third line. If, indeed, we respond this way to verse of this sort, this response refutes Myth 2. In the tradition it is generally recognized that 'actual' stressing can deviate from the metrical norm, but to my knowledge, all traditions assume that the metrical norm derives from some schematic simplification of the physical or linguistic patterning in the text. Examples such as these show that this assumption is unfounded. In these cases, the metrical pattern runs pervasively *against* the linguistic and physical saliences in the text – at many levels of structure. Therefore, this metrical response must derive from some independent source.

For phrasing, the major evidence against Myth 2 comes from the many prosodists who have perceived comparable rhythmic 'shapes' at many levels of linguistic structure. Included here would be many of the phrasalists (Hewitt, Liddell, Allen, Jannacone, etc.), the prose rhythmists, Pike, Gil, and to some extent Wesling. If all rhythmic phrasing is linguistic/physical, sharply different linguistic forms should necessarily elicit sharply different rhythmic responses, and the rhythmic perceptions of these prosodists should not be possible. Additional evidence against Myth 2 derives from other disciplines. The synthetic rhythmic perceptions that these prosodists are confessing are directly represented for music in Cooper and Meyer's theory of musical grouping/phrasing (and in several other aspects of contemporary music theory; see Chapter 3).

Myth 2 has had a devastating effect on both prosodic theory and practical prosodic analysis. If we assume that rhythm is physical/

MYTH 2: VERSE RHYTHM IS PHYSICAL/LINGUISTIC

linguistic, we must assume that prosodic description advances to the extent that we can develop finer and finer systems for describing the surface of language – a goal that might describe exactly the intention of many foot-substitution metrists, temporalists, Slavic metrists, intonationalists and grammetrists. However, as many have expressed in relation to the work in these prosodic traditions, the finer our descriptions of the surface of language, the more distant the relation between these descriptions and our synthetic rhythmic perceptions.

For instance, marking 'The Sick Rose' for stress, we might get something like this (/ = strongest stress; ^ = strong stress; \ = weaker stress; ˇ = weakest stress).

> Ô Róse, thòu àrt sick./
> The ĭnvîsiblĕ wórm
> That flíes ĭn thĕ níght,
> In thĕ hôwlĭng stórm:
>
> Hàs fôund óut thy̆ bèd
> Ǒf crîmsŏn jóy:
> And his dàrk sêcrĕt lóve
> Dòes thy̆ lífe destróy.

Marking the text for levels of pause, we might get this (/ =short pause, // = longer pause, /// = longest pause).

> O Rose, / thou art sick. ///
> The invisible worm /
> That flies in the night, /
> In the howling storm: /
>
> Has found out thy bed
> Of crimson joy: //
> And his dark secret love /
> Does thy life destroy. ///

Concerned with syntax, we might label the grammatical constituency of the lines.

O Rose, thou art sick.	(sentence)
The invisible worm	(part of noun phrase subject)
That flies in the night,	(relative clause)
In the howling storm:	(prepositional phrase post-modifier)

Has found out thy bed	(predicate [unfinished])
Of crimson joy:	(prepositional phrase post-modifier)
And his dark secret love	(noun phrase subject)
Does thy life destroy.	(predicate)

Marking the text for 'phonetic words' (or clitic phrases), we might get this.

O / Rose, / thou art sick. /
The invisible / worm /
That flies / in the night, /
In the howling / storm: /

Has found / out / thy bed /
Of crimson / joy: /
And his dark / secret / love /
Does thy life / destroy. /

Concerned with phonetic quality, we might note the pattern of stressed vowels in the text.

[o] [o] [I]
[I] [3]
[ay] [ay]
[aw] [o]
[aw] [aw] [E]
[I] [oy]
[a] [i] [ʌ]
[ay] [oy]

And so forth. But being disparate and therefore incommensurate, these descriptions can never give us the shape of the text as a piece of rhythmic language. As linguistic descriptions, these formal patterns imply no theory of rhythmic organization. In essence, most of our respected work on English verse rhythm has resembled 'analytical heaps' of this sort (e.g. Tarlinskaja's metrical profiles, Jakobson's syntactic studies, the intonational descriptions of the structural metrists, the 'constraints' on metrical form of the generative metrists and metrical phonologists, Wesling's grammetric analyses, etc.).

These issues raised by Myth 2 bear heavily on the standard methodological assumptions of much prosodic analysis, especially the methodological assumptions of recent linguistic approaches.

Many of the more recent approaches to prosody (e.g. the Slavicists, intonationalists, metrical phonologists and Gil) have valorized the 'objectivity' of their methods, criticizing other approaches to prosody for their impressionistic analysis while striving to achieve more detailed and 'scientifically' valid descriptions of the physical and linguistic texture of the verse. When questions of subjective response arise, these issues are avoided, and the only questions that are asked are those questions that yield themselves to 'objective' description.

If the argument I have presented here has any validity, however, this valorization of 'objectivity' is simply a more complete indulgence in Myth 2, an indulgence that only obscures the central questions of prosodic organization. While no one can lament precise, informed description, description is valuable only to the extent that it bears on the object of investigation. If rhythm is abstract, a collection of cognitive schemata inferred from language, then the object of investigation is inherently 'subjective' and an approach to rhythm that eliminates from consideration the constructive activities of the perceiving subject can only lead away from a productive representation of this subjectivity.

This critique of Myth 2 also casts doubt on those projects that recognize the subjectivity of rhythmic response but still cling to textual study as a possible 'window' into rhythmic organization – a case that might apply to 'softer' advocates of Slavic metrics and metrical phonology. For instance, one of the most attractive qualities of the metrical phonologists is their willingness to ask larger questions about their scholarly project, to move beyond observation and description to explanation. While he has few answers to these larger questions, Kiparsky (1977) ends his study:

> A question that I have been able to say nothing about here, though I hope that this work will eventually contribute toward answering it, is: What is the function of rhythm in poetry? What esthetic ends are served by the formal patterns that I have tried to uncover here? And second, we have to ask *why* the metrical rules work as they do . . . . No doubt the formal organization of meter is determined in a complex way by the interacting demands of esthetic function and linguistic form. But how?

Hayes (1989: 258) also ends his study with larger considerations. He notes the striking similarities between the prosodic hierarchy in language and metrical hierarchies in verse and asks: 'Why is bracketing, both in the linguistic representation and in the metrical pattern, a necessary ingredient of metrical form?'

From an external perspective, however, this further questioning only raises further questions, questions that the metrical phonologists themselves are beginning to ask. For instance, in a recent survey of the generative project, Hayes (1988) reasserts that his goal is to achieve explanatory adequacy, but he suggests that explanatory principles in metrical theory might be very different from explanatory principles in linguistics. In fact, he suggests that there may be no such field as 'universal metrics' at all (245). Rather, he suggests that most explanatory principles in metrics are most likely to come from a more general consideration of our 'rhythmic competence', and therefore he warns metrists against developing principles that are too 'specific to metrics' (rather than more generally applicable to rhythmic activity in other domains).

Given their methods and formalisms, it is difficult to see how the project of the metrical phonologists can ever achieve these more general results, however. Metrical phonology is essentially a study of texts rather than a study of rhythmic responses to texts. It considers only textual phenomena. Its formalisms are designed to 'generate' only textual patterns. Its more 'general principles' are generalizations about only textual patterns. If metrical phonologists do not study rhythm but can reach explanatory adequacy only by doing so, how can the terms in this contradiction be reconciled? How can the metrical phonologists ever explain what they describe?

Lurking behind this question is a more difficult one which applies to all linguistic approaches to rhythm. If the explanatory principles governing verse systems lie in 'rhythmic competence' rather than in 'linguistic competence', how can linguistic approaches to rhythm even describe what they observe? How can they know when they have discovered a 'significant' generalizaton about rhythmic organization rather than just a fortuitous linguistic pattern? And if they discover several 'significant' generalizations about the rhythmic organization of linguistic units, how can they link these generalizations into a larger theory?

For instance, as he states them at least, Hayes' principles of 'eurythmia' have very little generality, and, in the end, seem to be steps *backwards* from Liberman's original observations. Hayes tells us that he formulates his quadrisyllabic rule as he does so that it accounts for the gradient nature of 'rhythm rule' judgements: grids become eurythmic if beats at some salient level are *close to* four syllables apart (1984a: 46). On this basis, he claims that five-syllable intervals are no improvement on three-syllable intervals, while four-syllable intervals are best. But as Liberman defined grids (and as we know from other work on meter), five-unit metrical intervals are in a different universe from three- and four-unit intervals. As twice two, four is a natural grid interval if a grid is uniformly structured in twos. A three-syllable interval is also natural and can be multiplied to six, nine and so forth. But if grids are limited to duple and triple alternation, five-syllable intervals demand horizontal irregularity (2–3 or 3–2). This is a very unnatural metrical structure (and one that Hayes already weighs against with his 'disyllabic rule'). Consequently, it is not only the explanation of the phenomena that eludes Hayes, but the description of the phenomenon as well.

A similar problem arises in Hayes' formulation of the 'phrasal rule'. As Hayes states it, the phrasal rule claims that a grid is more eurythmic if it is *asymmetrical* (i.e. polarized at the highest level). Given what we know about the regularity of metrical organization, shouldn't this be disturbing? As it turns out, the major structures that Hayes 'explains' with the phrasal rule are structures in triple time, where shifts place major beats *six* beats apart, a structure whose stability is predicted by grid well-formedness, independent of any additional principles.

```
                         4
                 3   *   3
         2       2       2
     1 1 1 1   1 1 1   1   1
     the Saginaw, Michigan Journal   »
                         4
             3           3
         2       2       2
     1 1 1 1   1 1 1   1   1
     the Saginaw, Michigan Journal
```

Other structures also seem to have polarized stresses, but should these observations justify discarding the basic constraints on grid organization? If Hayes' descriptive system were based in principles derived from 'rhythmic competence', wouldn't his first impulse be to look for an alternative explanation for the recalcitrant data? Again, issues of explanation cannot be kept separate from issues of description.

At the close of his survey of metrics and phonological theory, Hayes (1988: 246) claims that, even if the principles of 'universal metrics' are *entirely* derivative from principles in other domains, the study of language patterning in verse can still serve an important function. It can 'serve as very direct evidence for what those [rhythmic] principles are'. This is optimistic. It comes close to assuming that theoretical principles are there to be 'discovered' in our observations. In most cases, we find only what we are looking for. If we don't know how to look for something that something becomes very hard to find.

2.4 MYTH 3: VERSE RHYTHM IS REGULAR

Another assumption in the tradition is that rhythm is a *regular* recurrence, while other phenomena are more 'irregular' in some way. The favourite illustration of a rhythm within the tradition is a ticking clock (e.g. Perrine 1982: 166; Brooks and Warren 1976: 493) or some other simple, highly regular repetition (for example, X.J. Kennedy mentions an alarm clock and a telephone engaged tone (140)). In fact, the ticking clock is so often the first illustration of rhythmic form among prosodists that John Dewey (1934: 163) calls this approach the 'tick-tock' theory of rhythm.

As we just encountered in our discussion of Myth 2, there is indeed a connection between meter and various sorts of regular recurrence. None the less, it is again questionable whether regularity should occupy a central position in the study of rhythm. The difficulty is specifying what is meant exactly by *regularity*. In most simple examples (e.g. a heartbeat, an engaged tone), *regularity* usually means 'isochronous repetition'. The stimuli approach identity, and the period between their recurrence approaches some constant duration. As we all know, however, rhythms of this sort are fairly rare. In most cases the recurrent stimuli that give rise to a rhythmic response are very different and the period between their recurrence is variable. Even the recurrent linguistic forms that give rise to linguistic meters are demonstrably variable in quality and temporal spacing, and extending this definition to non-metrical rhythms is even more problematical. Patterns of recurring intonational, syntactic and semantic forms generate powerful rhythmic responses even though they depart wildly from physical isochrony and exact repetition, and most non-linguistic rhythms that we experience are more like these non-metrical forms than their metrical counterparts. We have rhythmic responses to an enormous amount of our everyday experience: our internal physiology (breathing, hunger, anger, sex, fatigue, tension, etc.), our physical environment (heat, light, noise, etc.), our activities (work, play, social interaction, etc.), and so forth. These rhythmic responses are not just spurious, metaphorical extensions of some more technical meaning of *rhythm*. The problem is not with the unity of rhythm as a cognitive phenomenon; the problem is with our standard description of that unity.

If we maintain a physical definition of *regularity*, the complementary difficulties arise as well. Many exact physical recurrences are not felt to be rhythmic, even though they approach isochrony. For instance, I have little rhythmic response to a machine-gun blast, or a steam drill, or a woodpecker, or the recurrent triggering of my watch alarm each day at noon. The more we scrutinize our rhythmic perceptions, the more inadequate *regularity* seems as a central explanatory principle.

If we give up a physical definition of *regularity*, however, we encounter even more serious difficulties. For instance, considering Myth 2 we might propose that the requisite regularity need not be physical, but more abstract. To recur 'regularly', phenomena need not be identical and isochronous, they need only be *equivalent* (in some definition of *equivalence*) and *patterned* (in some definition of *pattern*). The problem is: with this approach, the notion 'regular' no longer depends on the stimuli at all. Any series of events can be seen as equivalent and patterned. A judgement of equivalence does not depend on the things compared but on the standard of comparison (tadpoles and elephants are both animals). Similarly, what constitutes a 'regular' pattern of events does not depend on the events but on the structure of the activity in which the events occur. The pattern of events that occur in a regular baseball game are very different from the pattern of events that occur in a regular wrestling match. In sum, if we give up a physical definition of *regularity*, *regularity* becomes just a pseudonym for rhythmic structure, and therefore it no longer makes an independent contribution to a definition of that structure. Recurrent events are rhythmically regular when they are rhythmically equivalent and pattern rhythmically. Rhythmic equivalence and patterning are determined by rhythmic structure. The question is: What is rhythmic structure?

As with Myths 1 and 2, Myth 3 has severely hindered attempts to justify the critical significance of prosodic analysis. The assumption that rhythm is a regular recurrence focuses critical attention on significant but relatively peripheral aspects of rhythmic expressiveness: disciplined constraint, hypnotic regularity, framing artificiality, mnemonic ordering, normative measuring and so forth. As regular recurrence, rhythm is relegated to an invariant background against which significant textual events occur, and prosodic criticism becomes a type of form recognition, accompanied by local and sporadic error analysis, as we found in Fussell's comments on Blake: 'The Sick Rose' is iambic–anapaestic; the central deviation occurs in the seventh line.

If we give up the theoretical centrality of regularity (together with Myths 1 and 2), however, these difficulties do not arise. If rhythms are complex forms of various sorts (rather than repeating forms with local variation), critical focus can shift to the shape of the forms themselves. With this shift, the major prosodic question changes from 'Is this text regular enough to be judged rhythmic?' to 'What rhythmic shape does this text achieve?' Once described, these rhythmic shapes can then be connected with a larger critical response to the text as a whole. With this approach, regular recurrence is not a definitional feature of rhythm but just the achievement of a certain sort of rhythmic shape (to be described along with the achievement of other rhythmic shapes). This alternative approach lays a much firmer foundation for critical comment. Given the multidimensionality of rhythm, most poems achieve many different rhythmic shapes simultaneously. In most cases, some of these shapes are 'regular', some are not.

The need for this switch in focus from 'regularity' to 'shape' further underlines (1) the weakness in current approaches to prosody, and (2) the necessity of a medium-independent characterization of rhythmic organization. As we have just discussed, most current approaches to prosody have tried to specify, with greater and greater delicacy, the linguistic/physical structure of 'rhythmic' texts. In these linguistic/physical characterizations, however, the *rhythmic* shape of the text is often neglected, or if mentioned, is represented in some simple, schematic form (e.g. a simple series of weak and strong positions, a procession of 'regular' feet, etc.). Following Myth 3, prosodists have generally assumed that rhythmic 'regularity' is a given, leaving only the task of specifying how the 'actual' organization of the text 'realizes' or 'deviates from' this 'regularity'. If we give up Myths 2 and 3, the difficulties in this approach become evident. If rhythm is something other than the 'actual' linguistic/physical organization of the text and, at the same time, something other and more complex than the simple rhythmic 'norms' assumed in these textual studies, this physical/textual approach to rhythm misses the object of study entirely.

This argument applies (in differing ways and to differing degrees) to many of our most respected approaches to verse rhythm. For instance, we must assume that some characterization of 'regularity' is the major goal of the 'generative' traditions in verse analysis (the Slavic metrists, the generative metrists, Attridge, the intonationalists, the metrical phonologists, Tsur and, to some extent, Gil). In attempting to specify how the language of certain rhythmic texts is 'constrained', these approaches contribute to our understanding of their linguistic 'regularity', and therefore, by Myth 3, their 'rhythmicality'.

If we define rhythm in terms of 'shape' rather than 'regularity', however, the peripheral nature of this demonstration becomes evident. As many have pointed out with respect to the generative metrists, detailing the constraints on linguistic well-formedness is only an indirect and negative characterization of rhythmic shape.[3] Specifying constraints on textual well-formedness provides ways of excluding unacceptable linguistic realizations of some (unspecified) rhythm, but it offers no way of building up rhythmic structure. As Wimsatt (1971: 200) laments, the generativist representation of rhythm bears the same relation to the reader's experience of rhythm that 'a negative for a photogragh does to a positive print'. In this sense, the generative approach to rhythm comes dangerously close to misunderstanding the basic motivation of a 'generative' grammar, which, as generative grammarians themselves repeatedly stress, does not investigate boundary conditions on well-formedness as a theoretical end but as a means for inferring and verifying structure.

In terms of a parallel with generative grammar and structural linguistics in general, the missing element in the generative enterprise is any mechanism for judging the 'sameness' or 'difference' of the phenomena they are investigating, a central aspect of any phonological or syntactic analysis in linguistic theory. In both phonological and syntactic analysis, the basic motivation for units and relations is their functional equivalence, their ability to distinguish/represent similar meanings/logical forms. Functional grammars try to present a positive representation of these 'underlying' functional relations, but even exclusively formal grammars must use these judgements of functional sameness or difference to motivate formal representations. In the generative metric/rhythmic paradigm, however, judgements of rhythmic sameness or difference play little or no part in the construction of representations. This motivation of structural relations exclusively on the basis of well-formedness judgements confuses discovery procedure with theory construction, an accusation that generative grammarians have often levelled at their theoretical predecessors.

If prosodic theory is to develop theoretically significant 'constraints on representations', it must not develop constraints on *linguistic* form but constraints on *rhythmic* form. That is, it must develop a principled theory of the nature of rhythm and its characteristic organization. It is only in this theoretical universe that a notion of prosodic 'regularity' can play a significant role.

2.5 MYTH 4: VERSE RHYTHM IS CONVENTIONAL

Another guiding assumption of the tradition is that verse rhythms are *conventional*. In this view, verse rhythms are largely historical phenomena, systems of linguistic constraints that develop to a certain conventional shape and then perpetuate themselves through time. As conventions, these constraints remain somewhat arbitrary, and therefore fluid, in their composition. While they may originate naturally, in any given historical period poets may omit certain parts of these constraints or include others. In fact, in this view, all poets fashion their own sort of constrained language, language that may differ significantly from that of both their contemporaries and the rhythmic tradition as a whole. In this view, the major goal of prosodic study is to describe these linguistic constraints as they appear in verse corpora of various sizes: a single text, a small group of texts, the texts of one author, the texts of an historical period, or the texts of a rhythmic tradition as a whole. Once constructed, these linguistic descriptions can then be used in practical criticism by detailing the global and local relations between these linguistic norms and their textual realization. This is the major focus of the philological tradition in foot-substitution metrics and the linguistic tradition of the Slavicists, intonationalists and generativists.

The basic motivations behind Myth 4 are unobjectionable, if not laudable. Convention plays a significant role in all cognitive response, and rhythmic response is no exception. Everything that we experience is affected in significant ways by what we are used to experiencing, and to describe conventional phenomena is to describe our most persistent habits of mind. Convention also plays an especially important role in artistic experience. One of the major functions of art, it has been argued, is to invoke, expose and unsettle our habitual modes of perceiving, thinking, feeling and acting; and artistic conventions are a natural means to that artistic end. Stylistic conventions in verse can infuse even the most insignificant linguistic choice with conservative, anarchic or revisionary value. Given the inherent connection between rhythm and formal expectation, we might assume that rhythmic conventions would be especially sensitive to these considerations.

None the less, it is again questionable whether convention should be given the central position in prosodic theory that Myth 4 implies. While our rhythmic response to verse is always influenced by convention, rhythmic response in general is very natural. It is not limited to poetry, to literature or to art. Therefore it has little about it that is arbitrary or 'art-ificial'. Rather, it is one our most deep-seated and far-reaching cognitive abilities. Our rhythmic responses to the language of poems all have relatively clear analogues in our responses to other artistic and non-artistic media. Therefore any discussion of rhythm in verse must necessarily transcend its local context. It must be responsible to what we know about rhythmic response wherever it occurs. To claim that verse rhythm is essentially conventional obscures the naturalness of the phenomenon and divorces prosodic description from its larger theoretical context.

This argument is not just philosophical; it has a direct bearing at every stage of prosodic description and explanation, from our basic assumptions about the nature of verse rhythm to the particular constructs we choose to include in our scansional formalisms. For instance, if there is a disagreement over whether or not we should represent verse rhythm in feet, the question should immediately arise: What is the analogue of the verse foot in our rhythmic response to other media? If no analogue is forthcoming, this is strong evidence against the verse foot. If there are many analogues elsewhere, this is strong support for that representation. Many of the other issues in prosodic theory could benefit from a similar scrutiny: What is the analogue of our response to poetic syntax in our rhythmic response to dance? What is the musical counterpart of the poetic line? And so forth.

The difficulties created by Myth 4 converge at an early point with the difficulties created by Myth 2. If the major task of prosodic theory is to detail the conventional constraints poets have placed on the language of their verse, it becomes unclear which constraints should be described and how. With these goals, the prosodist reaches for finer and finer descriptions of the linguistic structure of texts while the descriptions achieved become increasingly diffuse and disorganized. In this theoretical universe, description begins to dominate explanation to the point that even major prosodic concepts begin to blur and lose their meaning. In the most extreme cases, the *rhythm* of a text is even taken to embrace *all* of the linguistic features that co-occur with a rhythmical response (e.g. Slavic metrics). In this situation, prosodic analysis dissolves back completely into linguistic analysis. The rhythm of a text becomes its constrained language.

All poets tend to construct rhythms with certain characteristic shapes. To construct these shapes, they must constrain the composition and distribution of forms in their language. The purpose of a prosodic analysis is not to describe that constrained language, however, but to describe those characteristic shapes (and how they arise from those forms). If a prosodic analysis just describes the constrained language, it misses its subject: rhythmic response.

Within the normal terminology used in prosodic study this contrast between conventional textual pattern and natural response is a contrast between *versification* and *rhythm* – and almost all substantial studies of English verse have been studies of the former. The major instance, certainly, is the foot-substitution tradition. Virtually all of the basic concepts and terminology we have inherited from this tradition are versificational, not rhythmic. For instance, the normal array of terms used to classify meters in this tradition (syllabic, accentual, accentual–syllabic and 'free') are not rhythmic characterizations. They refer to conventional textual patterns, and even so, they often misrepresent what they are intended to describe. If we take 'meter' to refer to an experience of a certain sort of pulsation, much syllabic verse is not metrical at all and much 'free' verse is demonstrably metrical. If we take 'accentual' to refer to 'lexical stress', almost no verse is 'accentually' 'regular'. And, as all descriptions in this tradition go on to detail, almost all accentual–syllabic verse is syllabically variable. The basic terminology we have inherited from this tradition to refer to patterns of rhythmic grouping/phrasing and to metrical 'staving' (the foot, the line, the stanza, the poetic form, etc.) is also versificational, not rhythmic. As we have discussed, metrical feet are often not perceived and therefore, by definition, are not rhythmic. As Attridge and others have argued, most trimeters contain four metrical beats, not three. If we take meter to refer to a patterned pulsation, many verse 'lines' are not metrical units at all, nor are stanzas or poetic forms. In fact, in the exceptional case stanzas are not even phrasal units, as they can be framed *against* the dominant rhythmic phrasing in the text. The dominant definition of the 'hemistich' in this tradition (i.e. a part of a line delimited by a syntactic intonational break) is not a rhythmic description either – metrical or phrasal. The symmetrical distribution of metrical beats in a line is often not intonationally or syntactically defined and the parts of a verse line that are divided by a major intonational or syntactic break are often not rhythmic phrases.

Of course, the study of versification has its own justification. Therefore, this distinction between rhythm and versification is not a criticism of the study of versification as such. It is a significant fact about poetry that all verse traditions develop conventional linguistic patterns within which poets frame their rhythmic creations. The basic problem is that, as with the metrical foot, these versificational descriptions are often not taken as such but as descriptions of rhythmic experience, and that, minus this versificational vocabulary, the tradition has developed few concepts to describe rhythm *per se*. As with Myth 3, a principled theory of prosody must go beyond these descriptions of linguistic conventions to a description of rhythmic experience itself. It is only in this theoretical universe that the role of convention in verse experience can be fully and productively explored.

2.6 MYTH 5: VERSE RHYTHM IS LINEAR/FLAT

Finally, most traditional approaches to prosody assume that verse rhythm is structurally flat, or if not flat, composed of a small collection of loosely related 'levels', often of disparate definition and composition. The ultimate example, certainly, is the generative metrist conception of the pentameter line as an alternating series of weak and strong positions. The Slavic metrists seem to embrace this view as well. For pentameter, at least, Attridge's view of meter is also flat (i.e. oBoBoBoBoB), as is Tsur's. This flat, linear view of rhythmic organization is perhaps the major obstacle that has prevented the development of a workable theory of rhythm in the tradition.

As Liberman gleaned from music theory, hierarchical structure is the most central definitional feature of rhythmic organization. It is hierarchical structure that gives rhythmic events their very existence and perceptual quality. It is hierarchical structure that provides the formal architecture that allows rhythmic structures to organize diverse phenomenal input into comparable representations. It is hierarchical structure that gives rhythmic structures their culminative scope and therefore propulsive and anticipational powers. It is hierarchical structure that gives rhythm structures their culminative and completive functions. And so forth. A linear conception of rhythm conceives of rhythmic organization as a simple speeding up and slowing down, as a linear array of 'varying' shapes, or in the worst case as a metronomic ticking – conceptions of rhythm that enormously impoverish the scope and significance of rhythmic cognition in human experience. Given these acknowledged facts, the pervasiveness of a linear (or only weakly hierarchical) conception of rhythm in the English prosodic tradition is a telling measure of the theoretical limitations of these historical approaches to prosody.

As I will argue in Chapter 3, a strong theory of verse rhythm depends crucially on clarifying the nature of rhythmic hierarchies, both their internal structure and their external relations. Rhythmic structures (1) present a certain sort of hierarchical design, and (2) elaborate this hierarchical design in several distinct ways, each of which is (3) extended to different vertical depths, (4) correlated with different sorts of phenomenal input, and (5) aligned in different ways with other rhythmic hierarchies. Those prosodic traditions that have couched their rhythmic representations in hierarchical form have gone awry on one or more of these five points. They have claimed the wrong hierarchical design, the wrong number of distinct hierarchies, the wrong vertical depths, the wrong phenomenal correlations, and/or the wrong alignment with other rhythmic hierarchies.

The rhythmic hierarchies posited by the foot-substitution tradition are versificational, not rhythmic. Hemistichs, lines and stanzas in this tradition are represented with no point of salient rhythmic

MYTH 5: VERSE RHYTHM IS LINEAR/FLAT   115

action (a major beat, peak or goal); therefore these units are not rhythmic. Hierarchies proposed in this tradition are also highly attenuated. In the normal case, this tradition recognizes only two or three levels of meter and two or three (loosely organized) levels of phrasing.

Following Myth 2, temporalists limit their rhythmic perceptions to concrete differences in sound; therefore, their phrasal and metrical hierarchies can extend to only three or four levels. Thomson and Lanier also give only sketchy characterizations of their phrasal units ('sound groups', sense groups, etc.).

Most phrasalists neglect metrical hierarchies altogether. Levels in Mitchell's phrasal hierarchy (i.e. syllables, tone units, lines and verse paragraphs) stand in no principled relation and are presented only as versificational staves. La Drière's structures are totally flat.

Both the classical prose hierarchy and the *cursus* are versificational. Units in the former (commata, cola, etc.) contain no point of rhythmic action. The latter details syllables and stresses, not beats and peaks. Discussions of syntactic periodicity and narrative hermeneutics have also been conceptualized in linear, rather than hierarchical, terms.

Trager–Smith intonationalists view their representations in linear terms. British intonationalists conflate meter and phrasing (i.e. the foot and the tone unit) within the same hierarchy. Pike's phrasal hierarchies proliferate unnecessarily. His phonological hierarchy is impeccable, but he proposes many other hierarchies as well, most of which seem not to bear on rhythmic organization. As with many of the intonationalists, Pike also reduces meter to phrasing; therefore, his hierarchies are also too few.

Liberman's metrical structures conflate both meter with phrasing and phrasing with syntax. Hayes' metrical grids are 'true' but too flat. The prosodic hierarchy is versificational, not rhythmic. Its units contain no significant point of rhythmic action. Gil's prosodic structures conflate phrasing and meter. Wesling's hierarchy is versificational (i.e. syntactic).

The remaining traditions (the Slavic metrists, the generative metrists, Tsur, and Attridge) conceive of verse rhythm as essentially flat. The exception might be the hierarchies claimed or implied by Jakobson in his syntactic studies and studies of 'syntactic prosody'. These hierarchies are versificational.

All of the myths of the tradition have conspired to support Myth 5. Recognizing that meter is relatively flat and equating the centre of verse rhythm with meter (Myth 1), prosodists have naturally conceived of other rhythmic forms in verse as structurally flat. Conceiving of rhythm as largely physical (Myth 2), prosodists have generally represented non-metrical rhythms in terms of physical interference with metrical patterning (patterns of pause, pitch and duration) rather than in terms of abstract (hierarchical) structuring inferred from these physical forms. Conceiving of rhythm as a 'regular' recurrence (Myth 3), prosodists have tended to search for one central level of linguistic organization that could be identified as the poem's rhythm (Whitman's verse has 'syntactic rhythms' and the like) rather than seeing rhythmic organization as a more general hierarchical organization of differences into sames. And intent on detailing the conventional linguistic differences between verse corpora (Myth 4), prosodists have been led away from considering the natural form of rhythmic perception that underlies and organizes all these differences: hierarchical form.

A rigorously hierarchical view of verse rhythm, such as I will develop in Chapter 3, is a radical revision of the normal conception of rhythm in the prosodic tradition. Instead of viewing rhythm as the regulation of one abstract pattern of formal repetition superimposed with diverse concrete 'variation', this approach demonstrates how diverse formal patterning in the medium contributes positively to comparable rhythmic shapes at differing levels of textual subordination, with shapes at one level clarifying and contributing to shape at neighbouring levels and with the whole hierarchy standing in a complex balance. Unlike the normal conception of verse rhythm, prosodic form in this view is not a concrete patterning of linguistic/physical forms (Myth 2) but a cognitive response. This response is not linear/flat (Myth 5) but hierarchical and therefore architectonically deep. This response is not 'regular' (Myth 3) but 'shaped'. These shapes are not simple and static (Myth 1) but multidimensional and interactive. And these interactions are not arbitrary/conventional (Myth 4) but arise as a natural product of our innate rhythmic competence.

NOTES

1. While poems can be read many ways, I find it odd that Fussell gives line 7 three major beats, when all of the other lines clearly have two. I would give beats to *dark* and *love* while placing the first syllable of *secret* on a subordinate beat.

2. For further elaboration of this point, see Easthope 1983 and Cureton 1985b.
3. For discussions of this difficulty, see Wimsatt 1971, Bernhart 1974, Ihwe 1975, Klein 1974 and Abrams 1983.

Chapter 3
Context

> The phenomenon of form in the foreground can be described in an almost physical–mechanical sense as an energy transformation – a transformation of the forces which flow from the background to the foreground through the structural levels.
> Heinrich Schenker[1]

> There are countless ways of achieving variety. What is crucial is the way in which the particular form of variety shapes musical experience.
> Leonard Meyer and Grosvenor Cooper[2]

> Many writers have treated the subject of rhythm inadequately because they have tried to reduce its many aspects to a few simple notions. We have proposed instead that rhythm is multidimensional and interactive.
> Fred Lerdahl and Ray Jackendoff[3]

3.1 RHYTHMIC COMPETENCE

Following Gil, I assume that the structure of rhythmic experience is the product of a relatively autonomous capacity of mind, a capacity that I will call *rhythmic competence*. As a working hypothesis, I assume that this rhythmic competence is universal and medium-independent, that *all* rhythmic experience is a product of its forms of representation and preferences for correspondence with rhythmic media (of all sorts).

Theoretically, the major consequence of this claim is that I assume no theory-independent relations between poetic rhythm and the structure of the linguistic or physical events presented by the poem. In this theory, the basic principles of rhythmic organization in poetry need not be controlled exclusively by linguistic or physical form. Salient aspects of rhythmic articulation (beats, peaks, arrivals, etc.) need not reflect (mimic, 'stylize', etc.) salient aspects of linguistic or physical articulation. Rhythmic experience can be structured, in part, by its own internal imperatives.

3.2 RHYTHM, PROSODY, VERSIFICATION, POETRY AND POETIC EXPERIENCE

To formalize this claim, in my more technical discussions, I will make principled distinctions among the references of the terms *rhythm, prosody, versification, poetry* and *poetic experience*. In the theory presented here, *poetry* is a literary genre, a certain set of linguistic objects that occasion a characteristic complex of aesthetic responses. *Poetic experiences* are our aesthetic responses to the generic qualities of poems. *Versification* refers to pervasive, conventionalized textual patterns that enable a certain aspect of poetic experience. *Rhythm* is the response of our rhythmic competence to internal and external events. *Prosody* is a certain type of linguistic organization, one that includes syllabification, stress, tonicity, tonality and related phenomena.

With these distinctions, a text can be poetry without being especially rhythmic (e.g. much imagistic poetry), rhythmic without being poetry (e.g. all novels by Joyce or Beckett; most oratory; much oral narrative, and some conversation), poetic without being versified (most prose poetry), versified without being poetry (e.g. most chants, cheers, slogans, jingles and doggerel), prosodic without being poetic or especially rhythmic (e.g. most expository prose), and versified without being prosodic (e.g. some concrete poetry).

The implications of these distinctions for a theory of poetic rhythm are many. First, contrary to much of the tradition, a theory of poetic rhythm in this definition will always entail a general theory of rhythm, including a theory of prose rhythm, free verse rhythm, rhythm in the prose poem, and rhythm in other artistic media, such as music. Second, contrary to all linguistic approaches to poetic rhythm, a theory of versification in this approach will not be a theory of verse rhythm, much less a theory of poetic rhythm. Third, contrary to the intonationalists and temporalists, a theory of prosody in this approach will not be a theory of versification, a theory of verse rhythm or a theory of poetic rhythm. And fourth, contrary to Wesling and Meschonnic, this theory of poetic rhythm will not (and should not) be a full theory of poetic experience.

3.3 A DEFINITION OF RHYTHM

3.3.1 Prominence and hierarchy

In this theory I assume that rhythmic structures are cognitive representations of the flow of energy in the stream of our experience. The essential feature represented in these structures is *relative prominence*, and the major vehicle for this structuring is the well-formed *hierarchy*.

The essential fact about hierarchical form is that it is *vertically continuous*. In a hierarchical representation, phenomena are ordered into continuous levels defined by relations of subordination/superordination. The paradigm instance might be the military chain of command.

```
'higher'    etc.
            General
       ^    Lieutenant General
       ^    Major General
       ^    Brigadier General
            Colonel
            Lieutenant Colonel
       ˅    Major
       ˅    Captain
       ˅    1st Lieutenant
            2nd Lieutenant
'lower'     etc.
```

Notice that a hierarchical structure of this sort demands both the ranking and the continuous levelling. If a general outranked a major but not a colonel, and a colonel outranked a captain but not a major, we probably would not consider the chain of command to be a well-formed hierarchy (or a 'chain' for that matter), even though discontinuous relationships of this sort might be arranged so that it would still make sense to assign officers a system of ranks. In rhythmic structure, relative prominences are ranked into continuous levels.

In language (and many other phenomena), some of the most important hierarchies are based on *constituency*, where ranking within the hierarchy is defined in terms of internal composition. Units at superordinate ranks are 'composed of' units at immediately subordinate ranks. For example, most theories of syntax claim that syntactic structures are organized into a constituent hierarchy (at some level of abstraction), as in the following (adapted from Halliday 1985: 24).

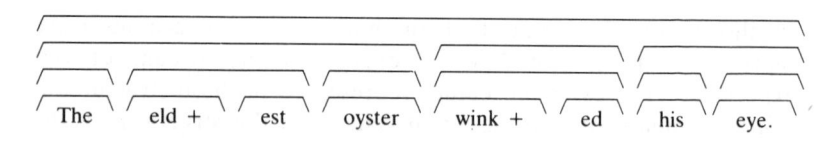

```
┌─────────────────────────────────────────────────────────────┐
├──────────────────────────┬──────────────────────────────────┤
├──────┬───────────┬───────┼───────┬──────────┬──────┬────────┤
│ The  │  eld +    │  est  │ oyster│  wink +  │  ed  │  his   │  eye.
```

In this 'minimal bracketing', morphemes (e.g. *-ed*) are constituents of words (e.g. *eldest*), words are constituents of groups/phrases (e.g. *his eye*), and groups/phrases are constituents of the one clause that forms this simple sentence. Rhythmic structures are constituent hierarchies of this sort.

Following Lerdahl and Jackendoff (1983), I assume that rhythmic hierarchies are also strictly levelled, horizontally continuous and recursively defined. Prominences represented in a rhythmic structure stand as structural *equivalents* by virtue of their occurrence at the same level in a rhythmic hierarchy (strict levelling). Units at all levels are subject to the same structural constraints (recursive definition). And units at the same level are juxtaposed (horizontal continuity).

One of the significant results of this definition of rhythm is that syntax is not a rhythmic form. For instance, it seems evident that syntax is not recursively defined. In syntax, constituents at different ranks usually have different well-formedness conditions (e.g. clauses have a different structure to phrases). As Chomsky has taught us, syntax is also horizontally discontinuous (e.g. the constituents of phrases in the clause *Which one did Paul go to?*). And syntax is not strictly levelled, either. In a syntactic hierarchy, all superordinate units are 'composed of' immediately subordinate units, but the hierarchical layering throughout the text need not occur in any particular order or consistent depth of elaboration. In syntax, constituents can undergo 'rank shift', so that clauses appear as parts of phrases or phrases as parts of other phrases (e.g. the prepositional phrases in *I vacationed at my home in the country*); and in syntax one part of a structure can have many levels of subordinate articulation without affecting the syntactic quality of less articulated parts of the structure. (When we say that a syntactic structure has many levels of articulation, we don't mean that *all* superordinate constituents in the structure have many levels of articulation, only that *some* do.)

While these constraints on rhythmic form seem few and simple, their implications are significant. First, these constraints mean that rhythmic structures present a continuous shaping, a shaping that is echoed in similar forms both horizontally and vertically in the rhythmic representation. Second, these constraints mean that rhythmic structures are pervasively relational. Articulation at one point in a rhythmic structure can disturb the whole structure. All units are related to all other units through their participation in the levelled hierarchical form.

3.3.2 Rhythmic components

Following contemporary music theorists, I also assume that rhythmic structure is *componential*. Rhythmic perception is not monolithically hierarchical; it is composed of a small number of different hierarchies. Given this organization, the complexity of a rhythmic response can come from three different sources: (1) interactions among rhythmic forms (both horizontally and vertically) within the same rhythmic hierarchy; (2) interactions among rhythmic forms (both horizontally and vertically) across different rhythmic hierarchies; and (3) interactions among rhythmic forms and the presentation of phenomena by the perceptual medium.

In this theory, I claim *three* rhythmic components, what I will call *meter*, *grouping* and *prolongation*. An experience is rhythmic if it contains any *one* of these components. Most rhythmic perception involves more than one rhythmic component, however, and poetic rhythm (and rhythm in other art forms, such as music) often contains all three. In rhythmic experiences that contain all three components, grouping seems to be the most basic and central; prolongation the most embracing and cognitively advanced; and meter the most primitive and physically controlled. For reasons that will become evident later, I call grouping and prolongation the *phrasal* components.

Meter represents our rhythmic response to (relatively) regular pulsations in a perceptual medium, to moment-to-moment alternations of inactivity and activity, stasis and change – a response that seems to be deeply embedded in all biological organization (Fraisse 1963: 17–48). Technically, meter divides the text into a hierarchy of *measures* articulated by a hierarchy of metrical *beats*.

Grouping represents our rhythmic response to points of structural culmination within delimited structural spans – a response that is also widespread in the animal world but seems more characteristic of higher organisms than those lower on the evolutionary scale (Fraisse 1963: 67–98). Technically, *grouping* divides the text into a hierarchy of *groups*, each of which contains a grouping *peak*.

Prolongation represents our rhythmic response to the teleology of the medium, to anticipated points of structural resolution/completion – a response that seems to be more uniquely human (Fraisse 1963: 151–98). Technically, prolongation divides the text into a hierarchy of prolongational *regions* defined by a point of structural *arrival/departure*.

As Fraisse argues, these three components are elegantly complementary ways of structuring time. All three components segment a medium into a hierarchy of spans with respect to certain foci of perceptual prominence. But they represent responses to somewhat different structural actions; they present different orientations; and they achieve different scopes of representation.

Meter represents a relatively objective time, projective in action, retrospective in orientation and local in scope. Metrical response is strongly influenced by physical salience, is affected in significant ways by preceding patterns of regularity, is strictly limited to duple and triple patterns, and is usually restricted to lower levels of structure.

Grouping represents a more structural time, centripetal/centroidal in orientation and considerably broader in scope. Grouping extracts more irregular shapes from structures (more) inherent in the medium, looks both backwards and forwards from some point of structural culmination, and orders these shapes into hierarchical structures in a continuous layering from the most local levels to the level of the rhythmic structure as a whole.

Prolongation represents a more subjective time, prospective in orientation and global in scope. It represents a response to goals that are strongly dependent on the perceiver's imaginative positing of future events and therefore more dependent on the perceiver than the medium itself, and more dependent on global context than on local articulation.

Rhythmic components

Dimension	Meter	Grouping	Prolongation
action	projection	culmination	completion
scope	local	both	global
orientation	retrospective	centroidal	prospective
time	objective	structural	subjective

The theoretical centrality of grouping in rhythmic structure comes from its strong influence on both rhythmic segmentation and rhythmic direction in the other components and, therefore, its strong influence on the general 'shape' of a rhythmic structure as a whole. As a hierarchy of alternating beats, meter has no inherent segmentation and thus no inherent direction. To borrow Lerdahl and Jackendoff's metaphor (1983: 28), meter is like wallpaper: it can begin and end anywhere. Similarly, prolongation is strongly directional but, like meter, it is only weakly segmented. At any point in a text, we are continually moving towards or away from a hierarchy of structural goals, but both the existence of these goals and their phrasal relations are often heavily influenced by the positioning of points of rhythmic culmination, matters that are determined primarily by grouping. It is only in grouping that parts of the text are inherently delimited from other parts of the text by their centroidal gathering around a common point of rhythmic action; therefore it is only grouping that is both strongly segmented and strongly directional.

The validity and productivity of the componential theory of poetic rhythm stands or falls on several considerations: (1) the perceptual reality of the separate experiences claimed by the separate components; (2) the ability of the theory to specify in a principled way the structural differences between these components and their various relations both to each other and to phenomenal input from the text; and (3) the ability of this experiential anatomy to account for our more synthetic experience of rhythmic structure as a whole – 'impulsion', 'tension', 'climax', 'closure', 'acceleration', 'rise and fall', 'reversal', etc. To explore these matters we must look more closely at the internal organization of each of the components.

3.4 METER

The basic metrical unit is a *beat*; the basic metrical span, a *measure*. Like all of the rhythmic components, meter organizes its basic units into well-formed hierarchies. Perceptually 'stronger' beats result from additional levels of beating. Following the music theorists, metrical hierarchies are most efficiently represented by a *dot grid*.

```
    .
    .     .
    .  .  .  .
 .  .  .  .  .  .  .
```

Each row of dots in the grid represents a series of metrically 'equivalent' beats. Taller dot columns represent 'stronger' beats; shorter dot columns, 'weaker' beats. Spans from (and including) a beat at some level to (and excluding) the next beat at that level form a *measure*.

```
    .
    .     .
    .  .  .  .  .
 .  .  .  .  .  .  .
 |–|              one-dot measure
 |———]            two-dot measure
 |————————]       three-dot measure
```

In addition to the general constraints on rhythmic hierarchies (i.e. vertical and horizontal continuity, strict levelling, etc.), the major constraints on metrical form are: (1) a limitation to duple and triple patterning (with a preference for duple over triple); and (2) a strong preference for horizontal uniformity. In a metrical structure, adjacent beats at a given level must be separated by either one or two beats at the next lower level (with a strong preference for just one and only one, or if need be, two and only two). These constraints, we might assume, are the structural analogues of the less explicit notions 'periodicity' and 'regularity'.

These conditions severely limit the shape that metrical response can achieve. For example, the constraint on duple and triple patterning permits (a) and (b) but forbids (c) and (d).

(a) . . . .

(b) . . . .

*(c) . . . .

*(d) . . . .

The strong preference for horizontal uniformity also weighs strongly against (b), as well as a structure such as (e).

(e) . . . .

Beats within metrical structure are not inherently grouped and therefore meter has no inherent direction ('rising', 'falling', etc.). When placed in a phrasal context, however, meter has a strong preference for 'falling' movement across phrases. Within rhythmic structure as a whole, this preference for falling movement across groups combines with the preference for horizontally uniform and alternating movement to make many meters strongly 'projective' in their articulation of certain metrical spans.

Starting at some salient level of beating, just one level of articulation presents a salient pulse.

. . . . pulse

A second level of beating presents alternating prominences (strong–weak–strong–weak).

```
    .    .    .    .    .        alternation
.  .  .  .  .  .  .  .  .  .     pulse
```

But a third level of beating presents a point of metrical obtrusion and therefore a more salient point of metrical segmentation/demarcation   (weak–strong–weak–STRONGER–weak–strong–weak–STRONGER).

```
         .         .             obtrusion
    .    .    .    .    .        alternation
.  .  .  .  .  .  .  .  .  .     pulse
```

At some levels in some meters, these 'obtrusive' beats become salient points of metrical action, and if they are aligned with the *beginnings* of phrases (in a strictly alternating meter), this metrical patterning will 'project' a grouping span of *four* pulses before the next major point of metrical action (and, given the suggested alignment with grouping, the beginning of the next phrase).

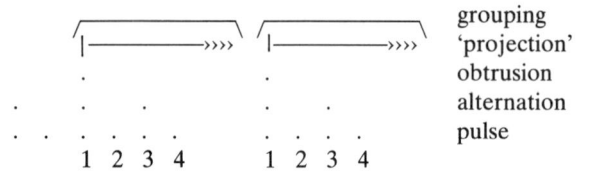

```
    ┌─────────⟍  ┌─────────⟍
    |───────→»»» |───────→»»»    grouping
                                  'projection'
         .              .        obtrusion
    .    .    .    .    .        alternation
.  .  .  .  .    .  .  .  .      pulse
    1  2  3  4    1  2  3  4
```

This patterning explains the salience and pervasiveness of 'four-beat' measures throughout metrical patterning. In these 'projective' actions, the obtrusive beat and the salient pulse (two levels below) are perceptually highlighted while the alternating level of articulation in between is perceptually dampened. This patterning also explains Gil's observation that, vertically in a metrical hierarchy, we often find that measures alternate in salience as well.

Ironically, meter combines the most abstract and the most concrete aspects of rhythmic response. As many have noted, metrical response is strongly influenced by physical considerations. Metrically, we respond most strongly to overtly phenomenal prominences (stresses, etc.), and in many cases metrical response itself affects us bodily (we snap our fingers, tap our toes). Many have also noted that we respond most strongly to beats that come every three-quarters of a second or so (about the rate of the normal heartbeat), a fact that also seems best motivated in physical terms. This inherent physicality of meter seems to explain its fairly limited vertical scope. In most music and poetry, for instance, there are seldom more than seven or eight levels of salient metrical beating, while phrasal articulation is theoretically unlimited in its vertical elaboration.

On the other hand, because of the structural uniformity of meter, most metrical response must stand in an oblique relation to the actual structure of phenomenal prominences in a rhythmic medium, and therefore, in this sense, meter is relatively 'abstract' (in the sense 'self-generating' and 'self-perpetuating'). Few phenomena in our experience are strictly duple or triple in structure; therefore, our metrical response to most phenomena must be maintained more by suggestion from the rhythmic medium than by direct causation. When we respond metrically, phenomena in a rhythmic medium only *approximate* an acceptably duple or triple pulsation at some salient level, and in following this pattern we elaborate a hierarchically duple or triple response (a *metrical set*) that we maintain through occasionally conflicting input at that salient ('tactical') level and through *considerable* conflicting input at other (super- and sub-tactical) levels. As we will see, it is just this 'abstract' aspect of meter that makes it so useful as a poetic/musical 'measure'.

As Attridge argues, the inherent physicality of meter also gives meter a somewhat ironic position in poetic rhythm as a whole, a position that distinguishes the role of meter in poetic rhythm fairly sharply from the role of meter in musical rhythm. With its physicality, a strong meter can be one of the most salient components of a poetic rhythm and therefore it can make a significant contribution to rhythmic expressiveness. Unlike music, however, many languages conventionally mark structural prominences (i.e. points of informational salience) with overt phenomenal prominences (i.e. stresses, pitch slides, etc.), and these structural prominences are the major determinants of rhythmic shaping in the phrasal components. Therefore, a strong linguistic meter will constrain the quality and linear ordering of the rhythmic phrasing at low levels, in addition to disturbing (with its strong physical pulsation) the shapes of the variously articulated phrasing that *does* appear – a result that most art verse poets would like to avoid.

No more pencils, no more books
   .
   .
   .
   .   .
   .   .   .   .
  . . . .

No more teacher's ugly looks,
   .
        .
  .   .   .
 . . . .

No more things that bring us sorrow,
   .
   .
   .   .
  .   .   .   .
. . .   .

'Cos we won't be here tomorrow.
   .
   .   .
  .   .   .   .
 . . . .

If an art verse poet does use a highly vertical meter, then, it is usually in a rhythmic setting that maintains an irregular placement of linguistic material along the metrical grid, for example as in 'rap' and what the Slavicists call *dol'nik* verse (a triple meter that uses an irregular distribution of one and two syllables between tactical beats).

Have you dug the spill
    .
    .
    .
    .
    .   . ..   .
  . . ..

METER 131

Of Sugar Hill?

Cast your gims

On this sepia thrill:

Brown sugar lassie,

Caramel treat,

Honey-gold baby

Sweet enough to eat.

(Langston Hughes, 'Harlem Sweeties', 1–8)

A pity beyond all telling

Is hid in the heart of love:

The folk who are buying and selling,

The clouds on their journey above,

The cold wet winds ever blowing,

And the shadowy hazel grove

Where mouse-grey waters are flowing,

>   Threaten the head that I love.
>
>   (W.B. Yeats, 'The Pity of Love')

Another result is that many art verse traditions (e.g. syllabic versification systems, free verse traditions, the prose poem) avoid meter altogether, while many other traditions use only a very *weak* (non-vertical) meter. The alliterative tradition in English verse is a case in point. Anglo-Saxon alliterative verse (and its modern analogues) use only three levels of beating, the minimal number of levels needed to 'project' a lineal measure.

>   Hrothgar mathelode helm Scyldinga:
>
>   (*Beowulf*, 1321)
>
>   Bosque taketh blossom, cometh beauty of berries,
>
>   (Ezra Pound, 'The Seafarer', 48)

As I will argue in Chapter 5, at least some of Hopkins' 'sprung rhythm' texts use this (lineally) four-beat, three-level meter as well.

>   . . . how he rung upon the rein of a wimpling wing
>
>   (Gerard Manley Hopkins, 'The Windhover', 4)

As Attridge argues, the so-called 'iambic pentameter' tradition in Western European poetry is a another case in point. In fact, iambic pentameter might be the most extreme effacement that a poetic meter with a regular grid alignment can endure without being totally eliminated. 'Iambic pentameter' creates non-uniform measures at the hemistich level and seldom extends beyond four levels of beating, with the higher level asymmetry severely weakening the metrical 'projection' at the two highest levels. This relatively 'effaced' meter greatly reduces the influence of the metrical set on the ordering of lower-level informational prominences, freeing the poet to use a wide range of phrasal shaping. It is a significant statement about the role of meter in art verse that the most popular art verse meter, by an overwhelming margin, is one of the weakest meters imaginable.

> No more be grieved at that which thou hast done:
>
> Roses have thorns, and silver fountains mud,
>
> Clouds and eclipses stain both moon and sun,
>
> And loathsome canker lives in sweetest bud.

(William Shakespeare, Sonnet 35, 1–4)

This view of meter differs radically from the 400 years of discussion of meter in the English tradition, and in this revised view, many of the traditional problems in the description of meter in English poetry dissolve.

First, the whole notion of 'metrical variation' and 'metrical style' is discarded. In this view, meter, by definition, is a highly stable form, consisting of a rigid grid of duple or triple prominences. While a poem can indeed 'vary' its meter, this seldom happens; in fact, it is extremely rare. A true instance of 'metrical variation' must vary the meter itself, not just the prosodic structure of the language – as in Emily Dickinson's 341 ('After great pain, a formal feeling comes'), which mixes (lineally) four-beat and (lineally) five-beat measures:

> This is the Hour of Lead –
>
> Remembered, if outlived,
>
> As Freezing persons, recollect the Snow –
>
> First – Chill – then Stupor – then the letting go –
>
> (Emily Dickinson, 341, 10–14)

In terms of this theory, the long study of what has been called 'metrical variation' or 'metrical style' in English tradition has been a study of patterns of metrical–phrasal *alignment* in poetry, without a principled theory of either meter or phrasing.

The most significant revisionary claim in this theory of meter is that higher levels of metrical articulation in poetry normatively 'fall' across rhythmic groups. In the tradition, it has generally been assumed that metrical prominence at high levels follows ('models', 'stylizes', etc.) grouping prominence (e.g. the hierarchical scansions by Gil, the stress profiling of the Slavicists, the 'verse designs' of the metrical phonologists, etc.). In particular, it has been assumed that, as phrasal rhythms reach towards culmination, metrical structures culminate as well, leading to a release in tension (and therefore the impression of rhythmic closure).

The theory of meter I am advocating here rejects this view. In fact, following the music theorists, I claim that the very possibility of 'metrical projection' in verse (and music) depends on meter's *oppositional* relation to grouping at high levels. In the theory here, strong metrical beats canonically signal the *beginnings* of groups, and in doing so, 'project' the measures through which rhythmic groupings move to culmination. Then, as grouping culminates, meter dissipates, exhausting its 'measured' projection.

3.5 GROUPING

Grouping represents our rhythmic response to points of structural culmination within delimited structural spans. In essence, grouping 'chunks' a rhythmic medium into parts (and those parts into further parts), ordering the parts into a well-formed hierarchy according to their relative prominence. The basic element in a grouping hierarchy is a *group*, each of which contains a grouping *peak*.

The name *grouping* comes from the 'centroidal' operation of grouping segmentation. In responding rhythmically to a medium, we organize the medium into parts by recursively grouping a small number of juxtaposed and structurally equivalent parts around one superordinant part of greater prominence. At the lowest level, some minimal unit of segmentation and prominence serves as a baseline and is gathered into parts (and those parts into further parts) from the 'bottom up', while the text as a whole is divided into parts (and those parts into further parts) from the 'top down'.

Following the music theorists, the grouping hierarchy that results is best seen as a schematic representation of structural *elaboration* in the rhythmic medium. At all levels in the grouping hierarchy, grouping peaks at that level represent a 'rhythmic sketch' of structurally 'central' aspects of our experience of the medium at that level of abstraction, a kind of rhythmic 'outline'.

    I.
        A.
            1.
            2.
                a.
                b.
                c.
                . . .

B.
   1.
     2.
       a.
       b.
       c.
       . . .
II.
   . . .
.
.
.

Comparable to using an outline, in analysing a grouping structure we can isolate the contribution of individual levels of grouping to the grouping structure as a whole by repetitively 'factoring out' subordinate elaboration. Music theorists call this analytical process *reduction*. In Chapter 5 I will make extensive use of grouping reduction as an analytical tool.

As in meter, the shape of our grouping response to an experience comes from: (1) general constraints on the organization of rhythmic hierarchies (strict levelling, horizontal continuity, etc.); (2) constraints on the number and distribution of prominent and non-prominent elements in the individual group; and (3) preferences for certain grouping shapes and certain correspondences between these canonical shapes and input from the rhythmic medium.

With respect to grouping, the general constraints on rhythmic hierarchies demand that grouping hierarchies be cleanly and continuously tiered structures composed of cleanly and completely segmented material at each level of representation.

These structures can be formalized in various ways. The most revealing formalizations are familiar from syntactic analysis in linguistics: (1) a bracketing, or (2) a tree. The constraint that rhythmic hierarchies be recursively defined requires that groups at all levels have the same morphological specifications; therefore, constituent groups in these bracketings/trees need not be 'labelled' for structural type. On the other hand, the constraint that rhythmic hierarchies be strictly levelled permits a labelling of the *levels* formed by the grouping arrays.

In this book I will label grouping levels according to their numerical position in the grouping hierarchy, counting from the bottom up. For some levels I will replace these numbers with names that are mnemonic of the correspondence of groups at this level with the rhythmic medium (e.g. 'syllables' or 'tone units'). These more informative names will always be equivalent to a number, however, and can always be replaced by the numerical labelling. The only other notation necessary to represent a grouping hierarchy is an indication of the relative prominence of constituents within groups. Following the generative metrists, I will use 's' (strong) for 'more prominent' and 'w' ('weak') for 'less prominent'. With these symbols, grouping hierarchies in the two formalisms will look something like the following:

Grouping hierarchy: bracketing formalization

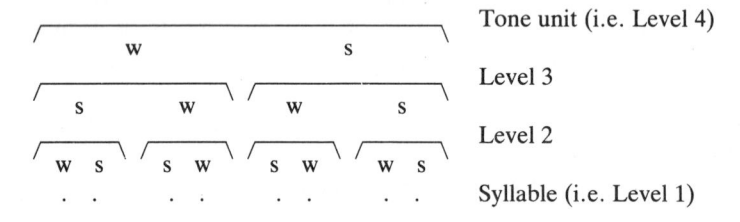

```
⌐─────────────────────────────────⌐   Tone unit (i.e. Level 4)
          w              s
⌐──────────────⌐⌐──────────────⌐   Level 3
    s      w        w      s
⌐─────⌐⌐─────⌐⌐─────⌐⌐─────⌐   Level 2
  w  s    s  w    s  w    w  s
  .  .    .  .    .  .    .  .   Syllable (i.e. Level 1)
```

Grouping hierarchy: tree formalization

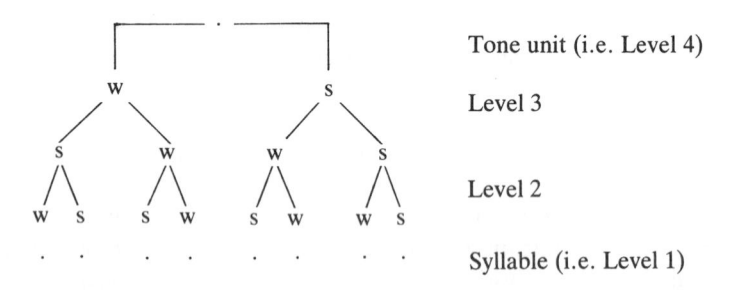

```
         ⌐──────·──────⌐           Tone unit (i.e. Level 4)
         w             s
        / \           / \
       s   w         w   s         Level 3
      /\  /\        /\  /\
     w s s w       s w w s         Level 2
     . .  . .      . .  . .        Syllable (i.e. Level 1)
```

These formalisms have complementary virtues. The bracketing notation is more useful in representing proportional relations in horizontal spans. The tree notation is more useful in indicating vertical relations.

In grouping, numerical constraints are somewhat looser than in meter, and distributions of prominence are constrained in terms of centroidal positioning rather than hierarchical spacing. The maximum number of units in a group seems to be seven; each group has one and only one peak; and no more than three weak elements can appear in succession. If we use parentheses to indicate an optional unit, the basic structure of a group can be represented as follows:

⌐_____¬
    (w)   (w)   (w)   s   (w)   (w)   (w)

The strong unit in a group is the *peak*; the weak units before the peak form the *rise*; and the weak units after the peak form the *fall*.

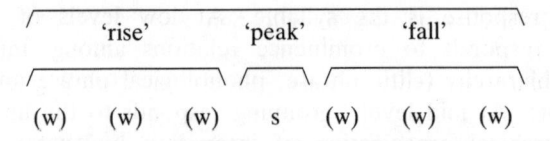

⌐_____¬
      'rise'   'peak'   'fall'
  ⌐_____¬ ⌐__¬ ⌐_____¬
    (w)   (w)   (w)   s   (w)   (w)   (w)

A group with more units in its rise than its fall is a *rising* group. A group with more units in its fall than in its rise is a *falling* group. A group with a medial peak is *waved*. In their morphology, groups resemble traditional poetic 'feet' and therefore grouping shapes can be most conveniently named with traditional foot-substitution terminology (ws = iambic; sw = trochaic; wsw = amphibrachic; wws = anapaestic, etc.).

Grouping structures allow for a much more variable array of shapes than metrical structures. Like meter, groups show some preference for binary and ternary form, but this preference is weaker. The segmented and centroidal organization of grouping also separates its numerical preferences from linear imperatives. Unlike meter, a grouping structure can be rigorously binary, but, given that the relative positioning of prominent and non-prominent elements is still unconstrained, the structure can still present a highly various shaping (as in the binary tree structure and bracketing above).

Compared with meter, grouping segmentation also allows for a much more variable shaping even when equivalent grouping prominences are equally spaced. For instance, in the series of thirteen events below, every third event is strong, but the grouping of the events creates no repeating shapes.

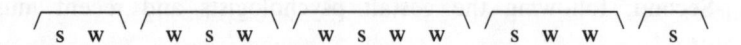

⌐___¬ ⌐_____¬ ⌐_____¬ ⌐_____¬ ⌐__¬
  s w   w s w   w s w w   s w w   s

This inherent segmentation allows grouping to craft successive shapes into engagingly dynamic processes: expansion, contraction, inversion, chiasmus, alternation and so forth (what I will call *grouping schemes*; see 4.3.3.2). In a grouping hierarchy as a whole, these schemes can be presented on many levels simultaneously.

In our response to language and therefore our response to poetry, the major input to grouping is the informational organization of the text. While meter responds primarily to the shape and distribution of phenomenal prominences in the medium, grouping responds to the shape of a text's meaning.

As in meter, the smallest linguistic unit that gives rise to a grouping response is the syllable. At low levels of structure, grouping responds to prominence relations among units in the prosodic hierarchy (clitic phrase, phonological phrase and intonational unit). At mid levels, grouping responds to the linearization and hierarchical organization of intonation by syntax. At high levels, grouping responds to prominence relations among sentences within discourse units (e.g. verse paragraphs). And at the highest level, grouping responds to prominence relations among discourse units themselves. The peak of a poem as a whole is usually its closural image or argument.

The hierarchical scope and morphological flexibility of grouping and its basis in informational (rather than phenomenal) relations make it a much more complex and 'interpretive' component of our rhythmic response than meter. In some cases grouping relations are clear, but in most cases they are somewhat blurred or ambiguous, even where readers are giving the text the same general 'reading'. While we must grant this variability, we must nevertheless recognize that grouping responses can be remarkably stable across readers as well. To the extent that this stability occurs, it has several sources.

First, considerable stability in the interpretation of grouping derives from constraints on grouping well-formedness. In many cases the sheer possibility of realizing a group of a certain shape can resolve a potential uncertainty. For instance, given a string of four equally non-prominent groups, grouping morphology strongly pressures us to perceive one of the groups as more prominent. Similarly, when confronted with random, local elaboration, our grouping competence will try to adjust the whole grouping hierarchy in order to represent the local irregularities.

Second, following the gestalt psychologists and recent music theorists, I claim that a great deal of this stability comes from a set of universal grouping preferences, both for grouping morphology itself and for grouping-language correspondences. For instance, more so than for meter, grouping segmentation is strongly influenced by formal parallelism (semantic and non-), by concentrated unities or discontinuities of formal texture (semantic and non-), and by uniformities in grouping morphology itself (e.g. the continuation or completion of a grouping scheme). On the other hand, the relative prominence of two groups can be strongly influenced by their (non-semantic) 'weight', their position in the immediately superordinate group, their formal density, and their relation to more global formal patterning (e.g. an earlier occurrence of exactly the same form or a previous departure from a regular pattern of forms). In ambiguous contexts, grouping realization is also strongly influenced by its relation to the other rhythmic components.

Finally, grouping response is stabilized in some degree by the language of the text itself – at low levels by the canonical relations between syntax and units in the prosodic hierarchy; at mid levels by the placement of major syntactic breaks (clauses, sentences) and the canonical relations between types of syntactic structuration (modification, subordination, apposition, etc.) and informational prominence; and at high levels by conventionalized procedures of literary interpretation (e.g. Smith's theory of poetic discourse and its relation to closure), conventions that are ultimately motivated by our deeply shared sensibilities as similar beings who bring to the act of reading a poem both a (relatively) similar biological endowment and a (relatively) common cultural tradition.

As in the other components, the expressive power of a grouping hierarchy comes from (1) its own shape, (2) interactions between that shape and the other rhythmic components, and (3) interactions between that shape and the rhythmic medium.

As to (1), the most striking contribution of grouping to rhythmic perception as a whole is its ability to present coherent asymmetry. Meter, when it presents perceptible segments at all, is almost always symmetrical. Therefore, it can articulate only a type of constant time. Grouping, however, is able to present units that are both equivalent (i.e. 'at the same level') and volatile; therefore, grouping can be a powerful force for articulating textual time and energy (through structural expansions, contractions, etc.).

For instance, to take one of Barbara Herrnstein Smith's examples, one of the striking effects of Frost's 'Nothing Gold Can Stay' is its startling sequence of, first, easy, evenly paced movement in lines 1 to 4, then crushing descriptive contraction in line 5, then jolting physical acceleration *together with* logical condensation in lines 6 and 7, and then pure fermata (logical *and* physical hold) in the last line – none of which has much to do with meter.

Rather, this jolting manipulation of textual time and energy is created by the heavily asymmetrical grouping structures at high levels, which (moving from top to bottom) first divide the text into two heavily asymmetrical halves (after line 7), then articulate the first half into a top-heavy triplet, then articulate the first unit of that triplet into a highly asymmetrical doublet, then articulate the first unit of that doublet into a perfectly balanced doublet of doublets (congruent with the meter).

Nothing Gold Can Stay

1 Nature's first green is gold,
2 Her hardest hue to hold.
3 Her early leaf's a flower;
4 But only so an hour.
5 Then leaf subsides to leaf.
6 So Eden sank to grief.
7 So dawn goes down to day.
8 Nothing gold can stay.

Higher Level Grouping Structure

1 Nature's first green is gold,   w
                                       s
2 Her hardest hue to hold.   s
                                           w
3 Her early leaf's a flower;   w
                                       w   w   w
4 But only so an hour.   s

5 Then leaf subsides to leaf.   s

6 So Eden sank to grief.   w

7 So dawn goes down to day.   s

8 Nothing gold can stay.   s

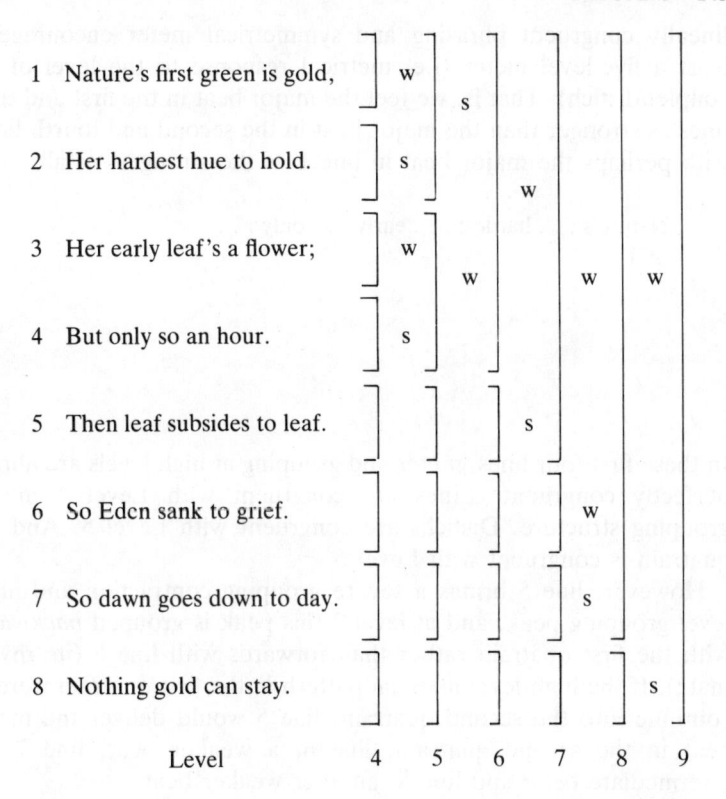

                  Level   4   5   6   7   8   9

As to (2), it is the shape of our grouping response that creates the quality of the tensions and resolutions that are characteristic of expressive interactions between grouping and meter in metrical verse. As I have argued in Chapter 1 (and will demonstrate at length in Chapter 5), much of the tradition's inability to develop a defensible description of the expressive qualities of (so-called) 'metrical variation', caesural placement and enjambment has stemmed from its lack of a workable theory of grouping.

For instance, to return to 'Nothing Gold Can Stay', relations between grouping and meter make a significant contribution to the feeling of contraction and rhythmic disturbance in line 5. In lines 1 to 4, the couplet rhyme scheme, syntactically unified distichs,

144 CONTEXT

lineally congruent phrasing and symmetrical meter encourage at least a five-level meter (i.e. metrical response to the level of the couplet/distich). That is, we feel the major beat in the first and third lines as stronger than the major beat in the second and fourth lines, with perhaps the major beat in line 1 as the strongest of all.

    Nature's . . . hardest . . . early . . . only . . .
    (.)
    .
    .   .   .   .
    .   .   .   .
    .   .   .   .

In these first four lines, meter and grouping at high levels are almost perfectly congruent. Lines are congruent with Level 4 in the grouping structure. Distichs are congruent with Level 5. And the quatrain is congruent with Level 6.

However, line 5 brings a severe grouping contraction and high-level grouping peak, and at level 7 this peak is grouped *backwards* with the first quatrain rather than forwards with line 6 (its rhyme mate). If the high-level metrical pattern in the first quatrain were to continue into the second quatrain, line 5 would deliver the major beat in the second quatrain; line 6, a weaker beat; line 7, an intermediate beat; and line 8, another weaker beat.

The grouping non-congruences and asymmetries in the second quatrain upset this pattern, however. With the delivery of the major grouping peak in line 5, the metrical projection of the second quatrain is disturbed, and when we try to begin it again in line 6, the metrical projection now goes against the rhyme scheme, as well as against continuing 'single', non-branching movement in the grouping structure. Trying again in line 7, we are further frustrated, as line 7 again delivers a major grouping peak, this time the peak of the first half of the text and therefore a peak that again looks *backwards* for its complement. Then, in line 8, the poem abruptly ends.

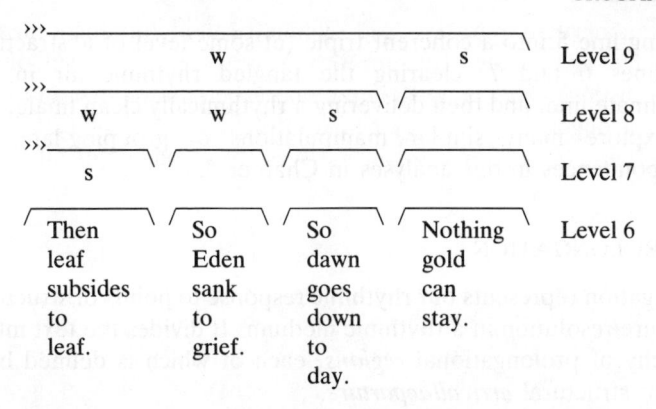

```
>>>_____
                    w                     s    \  Level 9
>>>_____
      w         w         s    \ /              \  Level 8
>>>_____
      s    \ / \ / \ / \               Level 7
   /Then  \/So   \/So    \/Nothing\   Level 6
    leaf    Eden   dawn    gold
    subsides sank  goes    can
    to      to     down    stay.
    leaf.   grief. to
                   day.
```

A large part of the jolting, disturbing movement in the second quatrain of 'Nothing Gold Can Stay' is due to the asymmetrical structure of its grouping alone (and the interaction between this asymmetry and the rhyme scheme). But a significant amount of additional rhythmic disorder is added by the high-level metrical-grouping relations.

Finally, poets throughout the English tradition often achieve expressive effects by frustrating preferences for grouping-language correspondence. Of all of the components, grouping responses are the easiest for poets to blur or violate altogether.

For instance, to return again to 'Nothing Gold Can Stay', the disturbing effect of line 5 is increased further by its ambiguous relation to preceding and following material. Logically, line 5 'concludes' the description of the first instance of decline. But while it repeats (twice) the concrete noun *leaf* from line 3, it delivers an abstract verb ('subsides') that provides a strong link to the series of verbs to follow ('sank', 'goes down', etc.), and given that the next two lines form parallel grouping peaks at Level 6, it is strongly associated with the second quatrain in the grouping 'reduction' (at this level of abstraction) as well. When the physical position and rhyme connections of line 5 are added to these semantic considerations, the grouping relations between line 5 and preceding and following material become almost perfectly balanced. The poem lands crushingly on line 5, destroys its higher-level meter, drastically changes its grouping movement, wrenches its logical development against the rhyme scheme, but *none the less* succeeds in maintaining cognitive and formal coherence by pivoting smoothly on line 5, grouping line 5 into a coherent triple (at some level of abstraction) with lines 6 and 7, clearing the tangled rhythmic air in the penultimate line, and then delivering a rhythmically clean finale. We will explore many similar manipulations of grouping-language correspondences in our analyses in Chapter 5.

3.6 PROLONGATION

Prolongation represents our rhythmic response to points of structural departure/resolution in a rhythmic medium. It divides the text into a hierarchy of prolongational *regions*, each of which is defined by a point of structural *arrival/departure*.

Prolongation is the most global, and therefore embracing, component of rhythmic response, but for various reasons it is the rhythmic component that has been given the least attention in the prosodic tradition. Prolongation has long been identified as rhythmic in music theory, however, and its function in poetry is precisely analogous, and therefore it will be given an appropriate position here. In both music and poetry, prolongational regions are closely coordinated with groups and measures, and within rhythmic perception as a whole, prolongational energies usually provide an important continuity and modulation to what are often oppositional energies articulated by grouping and meter.

A description of prolongation depends most crucially on the notion *structural goal*. Structural goals control our global impressions of structural anticipation and resolution in our experience of a rhythmic medium. In grouping and meter, certain sorts of goals are indeed established and achieved, but these goals are more experiential by-products than the central concerns of these components. For example, in driving from one beat to the next, meter indeed generates its projected measure. But this generation is not achieved by hermeneutical suggestiveness but by patterned regularity. Similarly, in proceeding through a grouping experience we entertain many structural hypotheses, some of which indeed build and then relieve tension, but these hypotheses are more a product of our general expectations for canonical grouping form than our positing of definite structural goals.

The distinguishing feature of prolongation is that it is *essentially* hermeneutical. In prolongation, present experience leads to the establishment of a structural problem and a projection of a future resolution, and we experience the rest of the text as an exploration of that problem and a movement towards that projected resolution.

As music theorists have demonstrated, hermeneutic forces in art are not rigorously hierarchical; therefore, hermeneutical energies, in their full complexity, are not thoroughly rhythmic, or at least not obviously or demonstrably so. But much hermeneutical organization can indeed be represented in hierarchical terms, especially our hermeneutical response to poetry, and to the extent that this occurs, this hierarchical organization makes a significant contribution to rhythmic experience.

Terminologically, I will refer to structural goals in prolongation as *arrivals* and, comparable to 's' in grouping, I will label them 'r'. Parts of the text that move towards these structural goals I will call *anticipations* and label them 'a'; parts of the text that move *away* from a structural goal, elaborating and complicating its implications, I will call *extensions* and label them 'e'. Following Lerdahl and Jackendoff (1983), the complex of relations established by a prolongational arrival and its associated anticipations and extensions I will call a prolongational *region*. As in grouping, prolongational arrivals need not have anticipations or extensions. Again, using parentheses to indicate optionality, the structure of a prolongational region can be represented as follows:

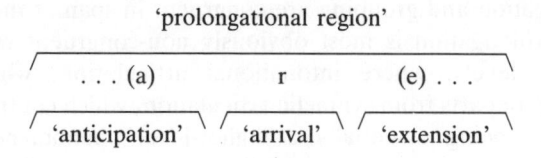

```
              'prolongational region'
        ┌─────────────────────────────────┐
            ... (a)        r        (e) ...
        ┌──────────────┐┌─────────┐┌──────────────┐
         'anticipation'   'arrival'    'extension'
```

Following Smith, the music theorists, and new work in functional linguistics, I will also distinguish between three types of prolongational anticipation and extension: (1) equative, (2) additive, and (3) progressional.

Equative prolongation is anticipational and extensional movement that does not significantly move. In poetry, this 'pausal' movement is usually articulated by overt repetition or apposition. In moving towards or away from a goal, the text pauses on the path to name and rename some part of the path rather than getting on to the journey's end. I will indicate equative prolongation with '='. For example, '=e' will indicate an equative extension.

Additive prolongation is anticipational or extensional movement that progresses by presenting some structurally analogous experience.

In poetry, additive prolongation is usually articulated by parataxis or conjunction. I will indicate additive prolongation with '+'. For example, '+r' will indicate an additive arrival.

Progresssional prolongation is anticipational or extensional movement that progresses by presenting some strikingly new experience. Progressional movement in poetry is usually articulated by subordination, both syntactic and conceptual. Following the mathematical symbolism used for the other types of prolongation, I will indicate progressional prolongation with 'x'. For example, 'xr' will indicate a progressional arrival.

It is important to note that these subclassifications are essentially qualities of the *second* of two constituents in a prolongational relation; therefore, some prolongational constituents will receive no subclassifications. For example, an anticipation, being necessarily the first unit in a prolongational relation, will never be subclassified.

As I have encountered them, most hierarchically organized prolongational regions in poetry tend to be congruent in span with groups. For instance, at mid levels prolongation is determined primarily by syntax, and grouping at these levels usually follows syntax as well. Unlike prolongation in music, large-scale prolongational regions in poetry for the most part follow the contours of discourse divisions in the text, divisions that also control grouping; therefore prolongation and grouping are congruent in span at these levels as well. Prolongation is most obviously non-congruent with grouping at low levels, where intonational articulation, which controls grouping, departs from syntactic articulation, which controls prolongation. But being essentially a higher-level phenomenon, prolongational articulation at these levels is not as significant; therefore, for now at least, we might overlook these non-congruences.

This convergence between grouping spans and prolongational regions is convenient and simplifies our difficulties in representing prolongational response. It means that prolongational energies are largely felt in waves across groups, with each group eliciting a prolongational contour that terminates as the group terminates and is initiated again as the next group is initiated. This also means that the basic architecture of prolongational rhythm follows the basic architecture of grouping. As we gather together local grouping contours and combine them into more global contours, we also gather together the local prolongational contours that are associated with these groups, gathering them into more global prolongational regions.

This (relative) congruence between grouping and prolongational spans in poetry also permits us to combine graphic displays of grouping and prolongation. Prolongational movement can just be added to the 'weak' and 'strong' labellings of grouping brackets and trees. I will adopt this convention. For instance, a bracket labelled 's–xr' will indicate a grouping peak that coincides with a progressional arrival.

Our prolongational responses to poetry are controlled by various linguistic structures and conventions of reading.

At the highest level, prolongational goals are usually not generated by the text at all but derive from our generic expectation for a certain sort of canonical global movement. We don't infer these expectations from the rhythmic medium; we bring them with us and assume that they will be satisfied.

In Western tonal music and English poetry, the most common prolongational expectation at the highest level is for an 'arc' of movement from some *structural beginning* early on in a text/piece to some *structural ending* near its termination.

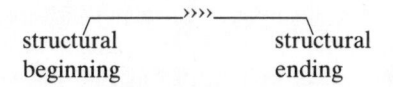

structural beginning >>>> structural ending

In poetry, this 'arc' of movement is usually hermeneutical. The structural beginning of the text raises some identifiable issue about human experience (what we might traditionally identify as a *theme*). The body of the text explores this issue with description, narrative or argument, complicating and elaborating the hermeneutical problem. Then the structural ending resolves these complications and elaborations in some satisfying way. In essence, Barbara Herrnstein Smith's theory of poetic closure is largely a theory of high levels of prolongation in poetry.

This movement from setting, to extensional complication, to resolutional ending seems to pervade prolongational articulation in both English poetry and Western tonal music, and, together with a penultimate anticipation of closure, constitutes what Lerdahl and Jackendoff (1983) identify as *Canonical Prolongational Form*.

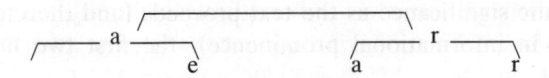

a e   a r   r

This canonically chiastic organization provides a perfect formal complement to the canonically falling structure of meter and the canonically rising structure of grouping. In many textual units, meter begins with a strong beat, projects a measure, and then winds down. Grouping builds steadily and peaks at the end of the measure. And prolongation suggests a structural goal, then tensely departs from that suggestion, then anticipates a goal, and then achieves it. The first metrical line of Hopkins' 'The Windhover' (analysed in Chapter 5) is a case in point.

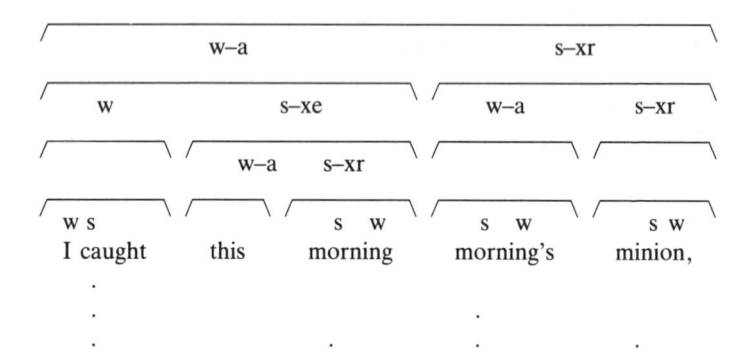

```
⌐                    w–a                    ⌐               s–xr              ⌐
⌐       w               s–xe        ⌐    w–a          s–xr       ⌐
⌐     ⌐     w–a     s–xr    ⌐           ⌐          ⌐
⌐  w s  ⌐         ⌐  s  w   ⌐  s   w    ⌐  s   w
   I caught    this     morning    morning's      minion,
     .          .          .          .            .
```

I take this result as one of the strongest possible arguments for a componential theory of rhythm. This elegantly complementary relation between the three components does not seem accidental.

As in classical Western music (e.g. sonata form), it is largely at high levels in poetry that the complementary, medially tensing function of prolongation in rhythmic experience as a whole is most salient. For instance, to return to Frost's 'Nothing Gold Can Stay', we might guess very early on that the poem is about the transient beauty of 'first fruits', even though this thematic conclusion is not stated explicitly until the last line. In fact, we might infer this theme after the first two lines, experiencing the next five lines as extensions of this implication, played out in further meanings and wordings. In this reading, the contours of high-level discourse expectation in the poem, while capped in the last line, are largely backward-looking (e.g. elaborational) in orientation, even though the grouping structure continues to rise. While the repeated examples of decline deepen in thematic significance as the text proceeds (and therefore continue to rise in informational prominence), the first two lines establish the basic frame of expectation for this further discourse development.

Higher levels of prolongation

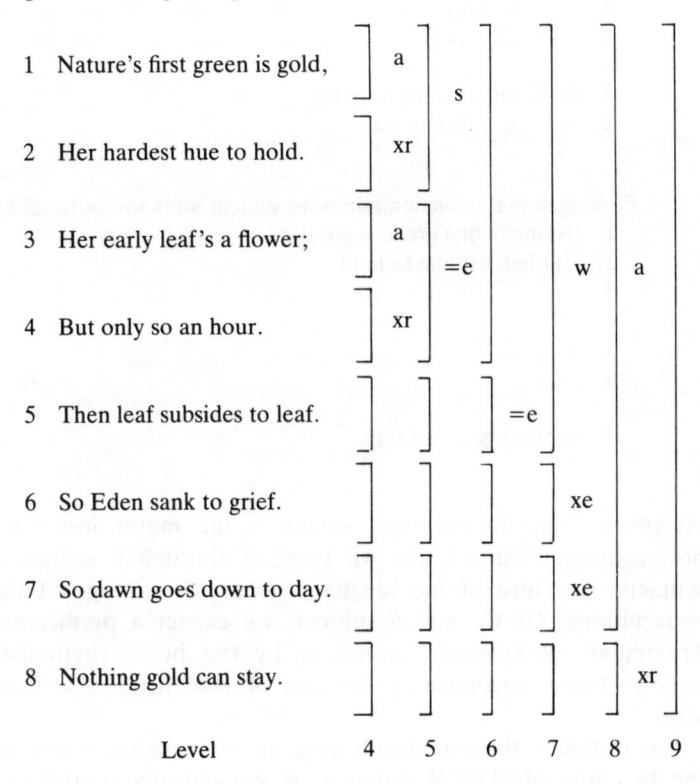

```
1  Nature's first green is gold,    a
                                        s
2  Her hardest hue to hold.         xr

3  Her early leaf's a flower;       a
                                        =e           w    a
4  But only so an hour.             xr

5  Then leaf subsides to leaf.                  =e

6  So Eden sank to grief.                            xe

7  So dawn goes down to day.                         xe

8  Nothing gold can stay.                                      xr

         Level                  4    5    6    7    8    9
```

This means that contrary to grouping, the prolongational structure arcs between lines 1–2 and the last line, progressively tensing the rhythmic energies in the discourse with equational and progressional extension before the text resolves abruptly in line 8.

It is crossing lines of force such as these that can be illuminated with special clarity by reductional analysis. In its most global movement, grouping proceeds from the peak of the first half of the text (in line 7) to the peak of the text as a whole (in line 8), but in its most global movement prolongation arcs across the poem from the structural beginning of the text (in line 2) to the structural ending of the text (in line 8).

Grouping reduction minus dependent units within Level 8
1
2
3
4
5
6
7 So dawn does down to day.
8 Nothing gold can stay.

Prolongational reduction minus dependent units within Level 8
1 [Nature's first green is gold]
2 Her hardest hue to hold.
3
4
5
6
7
8 Nothing gold can stay.

At other levels in the text, syntax is the major instrument of prolongational control. As we proceed through a sentence, the syntactic structure of the language generates a range of definite expectations. (If we find a subject, we expect a predicate, etc.) Treatments of syntactic branching by the prose rhythmists are largely (loose, incomplete) theories of prolongation at syntactic levels.

For instance, the canonically chiastic prolongational structure in the first line of 'The Windhover' is syntactically controlled. The transitive main verb *caught* anticipates its direct object *morning's minion*; the adverbial *this morning* intrudes an optional, tensing extension between subject and object; and the genitive determiner *morning's* in the noun phrase object provides a penultimate anticipation for the arrival of the head noun in the object noun phrase, *minion*, which completes the syntactic requirements of the clause.

The advances of this theory of prolongation over previous treatments of syntactic periodicity are its placement of these phenomena within the context of the other rhythmic components, its definition of individual prolongational regions and architecture in terms of grouping spans and architecture, and its demonstration of the complementary (chiastic) function of syntactic energies within our rhythmic experience of the poem as a whole.

One of the important and natural consequences of this theory of prolongation is an efficient and synthetic enrichment of traditional treatments of enjambment. As many prosodists have noted (e.g. Hollander, Golomb, Wesling and Berry), syntactic expectation makes an important contribution to the transitional energies generated by the scissoring of grouping by meter at the ends of metrical lines. But the tradition has had difficulty integrating these considerations with the traditional definition of enjambment as the lack of an end-line pause (i.e. an intonational, and therefore grouping boundary). The componential theory of rhythm developed here solves this difficulty by defining these line-terminal syntactic expectations as mid-level prolongational energies that exist in analogous forms at other levels as well (e.g. between discourse units).

The theory of prolongation presented here also provides a six-part subclassification of *types* of prolongational movement (i.e. a › =r ; a › +r ; a › xr ; (r) › =e ; (r) › +e ; (r) › xe). Therefore, it provides a delicate system for describing these prolongational expectations involved in enjambment, a system that can be added to the considerable delicacy entailed by this theory's more thoroughly hierarchical and directional treatment of grouping, the other phrasal component involved in metrical–phrasal 'scissoring' at line end.

Despite these mid-level achievements, the major contribution of this theory of prolongation, however, is its integration of a theory of closure and discourse prolongation with a theory of rhythmic articulation at low levels. In its central concerns, the prosodic tradition has been preoccupied with non-informational, low-level, linguistically based phenomena. This preoccupation has divorced more richly synthetic comment on the rhythmic energies generated by sense rhythms at high levels from detailed analyses of the rhythmic energies generated by lower levels (i.e. sound, intonation, etc.). As in other matters, the theory of rhythm developed here integrates these concerns and gives them a principled motivation.

3.7 INTERDISCIPLINARY PARALLELS: POETIC RHYTHM AND MUSIC THEORY

My primary subject is poetic rhythm, but my approach to rhythm in language has been strongly influenced by recent work in music theory, and I regard this interdisciplinary parallel both as a significant argument for the productivity of my approach and as an important heuristic for understanding my basic assumptions and claims. To this point, I have not investigated these music–poetry parallels in sufficient depth to give them a self-standing presentation (e.g. as a separate chapter), but given the extent that these parallels have informed my thinking, they deserve some detailed consideration here as a significant part of the theoretical context of my approach.

Historically, there has been little productive interaction between music theory and prosodic theory. As we reviewed in Chapter 1, the most time-honoured use of musical parallels in prosodic theory has been the temporalists' claim that poetic meter is isochronous, a claim that has been repeatedly refuted by both psychological experiment and sensitive listening. This claim has been a major component of Myth 2 (Poetic rhythm is physical/linguistic) and Myth 3 (Poetic rhythm is regular) and has appeared in various guises in other approaches to prosody as well (e.g. Derek Attridge). Recent uses of music theory by linguistic prosodists have been more extensive and technical, but even here serious misunderstandings have persisted. In their musical analogies, linguistic prosodists (such as Liberman, Hayes and Gil) have consistently misinterpreted both the experiential referents of musical formalisms (such as Cooper and Meyer's theory of phrasing) and the theoretical and methodological claims these musical formalisms entail. As Meschonnic laments, the more general (and always non-technical) claim that prosodists are exploring/revealing 'the music of poetry' has also been little more than a front to hide, with a type of mystical aestheticism, the deep conceptual difficulties and practical ineffectualities of the prosodic tradition. In my experience, the most illuminating discussions of poetic–musical parallels in literary study have been historical rather than theoretical (e.g. Pattison 1948; Winn 1981; Jorgens 1982), but for reasons of audience or otherwise, these discussions have all assumed a traditional (and therefore problematical) theory of poetic rhythm and a relatively atheoretical approach to musical rhythm. Most of the technical analysis in these historical studies also concerns itself with text–tune relations, a phenomenon in its own right and therefore one that confronts the problem of rhythmic parallels in the two arts from a highly specialized perspective.

Within literary criticism, careful technical treatments of rhythmic parallels in music and poetry have been rare to the point of non-existence (see Stevenson 1970 and Beardsley 1972 for welcome exceptions), and those studies that have been attempted have generally been brief and isolated. Speaking as late as 1984, Lawrence Kramer, in his study of musical–poetic relations since the nineteenth century, laments the divorce between modern literary theory and modern music theory, and assessing the interdisciplinary models that have been developed to study the relations between music and poetry, concludes: 'None exists' (4). Despite his engaging theory of 'gestural temporality' (to which I will return later) and his illuminating analyses of various sorts of musical–poetic parallels, Kramer also succeeds in avoiding any technical discussion of rhythmic parallels in the two arts.

Given the technical sophistication of modern music theory, it is surprising that music theorists haven't made progress with these interdisciplinary issues. As we will discuss in more detail below, music theorists have long adopted terms and notational symbols from prosodic theory. For instance, Eugene Narmour (1977: 137–8) traces the use of poetic 'feet' by music theorists to Saint Augustine, and in the analysis of tonal music, to a continuous tradition stretching back to the middle of the eighteenth century. However, in their interdisciplinary endeavours in rhythmic analysis, music theorists have been severely hampered by the lack of a workable theory of rhythm in language. To extend a theory of musical rhythm to poetry, music theorists do not just need to connect theories in two areas of study; they first have to found a workable theory of poetic rhythm – a formidable task for those whose principal training is in music rather than literature or linguistics.

Given the late development of tonal music in the West and the less conventional (and therefore less codified) structure of music compared with language, music theorists have naturally looked to language study for general musical terminology (musical 'syntax', 'semantics', 'intonation', etc.). In recent times, music theorists have also been strongly influenced by the successes of modern linguistic theory (especially Chomskyan linguistics) and have therefore adopted linguistic methods and formalisms. As recent theorists (e.g. Narmour 1977: 109–21; Jackendoff 1977) have been arguing, however, these linguistic analogies are often based heavily on a version of what I am calling Myth 2 (Poetic rhythm is physical/ linguistic). They assume that the structural organization of our response to music, much of which is based on very general principles of perception and rhythmic cognition, is comparable to the structural organization of language, most of which is only partly and peripherally influenced by perceptual and rhythmic considerations. As Narmour argues (167–208), many quasi-linguistic music theories also indulge in a version of what I am calling Myth 4 (Poetic rhythm is conventional). They conflate style and criticism, and therefore, like the Slavic metrists, severely underestimate the uniqueness of the individual work of art, the 'secrets of the singular' (171). They forget the history of linguistic stylistics, which has had to face the fact, argued repeatedly by literary critics who have opposed such superficial interdisciplinary endeavours, that statistical tabulations of phonological and syntactic structures in poetic corpora, however exact, can tell us very little about our experience of an individual poem. As Narmour (169) puts it, 'Artworks only exhibit style. They are not assimilated by it.' Ironically, in their interdisciplinary endeavours, the music theorists that have most influenced my thinking, Fred Lerdahl and Ray Jackendoff, also limit themselves to musical–linguistic (rather than musical–poetic) relations and therefore stand firmly within this (problematical) interdisciplinary tradition (e.g. Jackendoff and Lerdahl 1980, 1982; Jackendoff 1989).

In sum, the history of comment on musical–poetic relations demonstrates the difficulty of establishing any extensive and technically explicit connections between poetic and musical rhythm. Therefore, if the theory of poetic rhythm I am presenting here claims to establish such connections – as it does – this claim deserves some detailed explanation.

Three seminal ideas in the theory of Western tonal music have influenced the theory of poetic rhythm I have presented here: (1) Heinrich Schenker's theory of prolongational elaboration/reduction; (2) Leonard Meyer and Grosvenor Cooper's gestalt theory of phrasal rhythm; and (3) Fred Lerdahl and Ray Jackendoff's componential theory of metrical–phrasal–prolongational interaction in musical cognition. My knowledge of these musical theories is limited; therefore my discussion will be only brief and suggestive. None the less, both literary and musical readers should find these parallels engaging and worthy of further study.

3.7.1 The 'language' of Western tonal music (WTM)

The formal organization of the musical idiom we are most familiar with, the idiom that produced the great works of classical Western music (Bach, Mozart, Beethoven, etc.) as well as the folk music of the last 300 years (including the folk music of our time), is a relatively 'natural' form with a strong base in our biologically determined perceptual reactions to the relative unity or clash among the waveforms produced by vibrating objects. When an object (e.g. a string) vibrates, it sets up not one but a *series* of sound waves. The most salient sound, called the *fundamental*, is created by the vibration of the whole string. The other sounds, called *partials* or *overtones*, are created by parts of the string: halves, thirds, quarters, etc. Together, these sounds form what is called an *overtone series*. For instance, given a string the correct length to produce the pitch that we call 'C', this overtone series is the following.

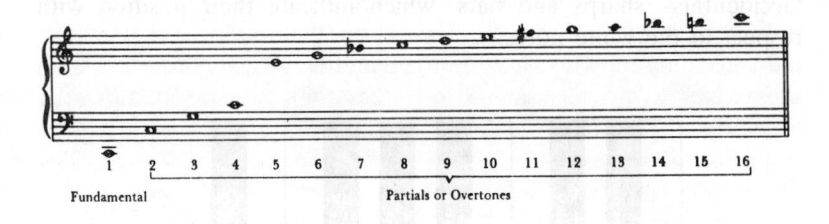

(Jones 1974: 5)

For those of us who 'speak' the musical idiom of Western tonal music (WTM), much of our response to the relative unity or clash of two tones sounded simultaneously comes (first) from their position in the overtone series, in particular their inclusion or exclusion from the first five tones in this series (the other tones being present but less salient). The dominant overtone duplicates the quality of the fundamental and is called the *octave*. The second overtone (here, G) is called the *dominant*. The third overtone produces the octave once again. And the fourth overtone (here, E) is called the *mediant*. The fundamental tone is called the *tonic*. Arranged within the same octave with the fundamental as the lowest note, these 'pitch classes' (here, C–E–G) form what music theorists call a 'root-position triad'. Our response to simultaneously sounded pitches in WTM, our judgements of their contextual *consonance* or *dissonance*, come (first) from the relation of the sounded notes to this triad of tones. Various aspects of our response to tonal music are conventional, but this triadic relation seems to be 'natural'.

158 CONTEXT

In a piece of WTM (or a section of a piece), a composer will use various 'collections' of pitches. From the earliest times, theorists have extracted these tones, arranged them into linear *scales*, and named both the *intervals* between points in the scale, and depending on the notes in the scale and their distribution, the scale itself. In WTM, the most important scales, the *chromatic* and *diatonic* scales, involve thirteen- and seven-pitch classes respectively (with the eighth and fourteenth pitches representing the octave). The chromatic scale with a tonic of C is represented by all the piano keys (black and white) between two Cs separated by an octave. The diatonic scale is represented by just the white notes in the same interval. The white notes are given simple letter names in the series CDEFGAB and the black notes are given names by adding 'accidentals', sharps and flats, which indicate their position with respect to the white notes.

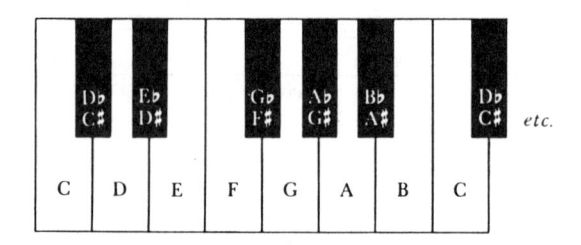

	Db/C#	Eb/D#		Gb/F#	Ab/G#	Bb/A#		Db/C# *etc.*
C	D	E	F	G	A	B	C

(Levy 1983: 414)

In WTM, composers use all of the pitches of the chromatic scale, but use them with respect to diatonic collections (seven out of the full thirteen). Diatonic pitch collections come in two major varieties, *major* and *minor*, defined by the ordering of pitch intervals in the scale. Adjacent keys on the piano define *half-step* intervals, with two half-steps making a *whole step*. In their more advanced talk, music theorists refer to points on the diatonic scale by number (superscripted with a 'caret'), with the tonic being $\hat{1}$ and the octave $\hat{8}$. Major diatonic scales have half steps between the third and fourth and between the seventh and eighth points on the scale. Minor diatonic scales have half-steps between the second and third and between the fifth and sixth points on the scale. For instance, the C major and C minor scales would be organized as follows:

INTERDISCIPLINARY PARALLELS 159

MAJOR SCALE
Interval: 1   1   ½   1   1   1   ½
Pitch: 1̂   2̂   3̂   4̂   5̂   6̂   7̂   8̂
Example: C   D   E   F   G   A   B   C
(C major)

MINOR SCALE
Interval: 1   ½   1   1   ½   1   1
Pitch: 1̂   2̂   3̂   4̂   5̂   6̂   7̂   8̂
Example: C   D   E♭ F   G   A♭ B♭ C
(C minor)

C MAJOR SCALE: C·····C   D·····D   E⌐F   G·····G   A   B⌐C

C MINOR SCALE: C·····C   D⌐E♭   F   G⌐A♭   B♭   C

1 = Whole-step interval
½ = Half-step interval

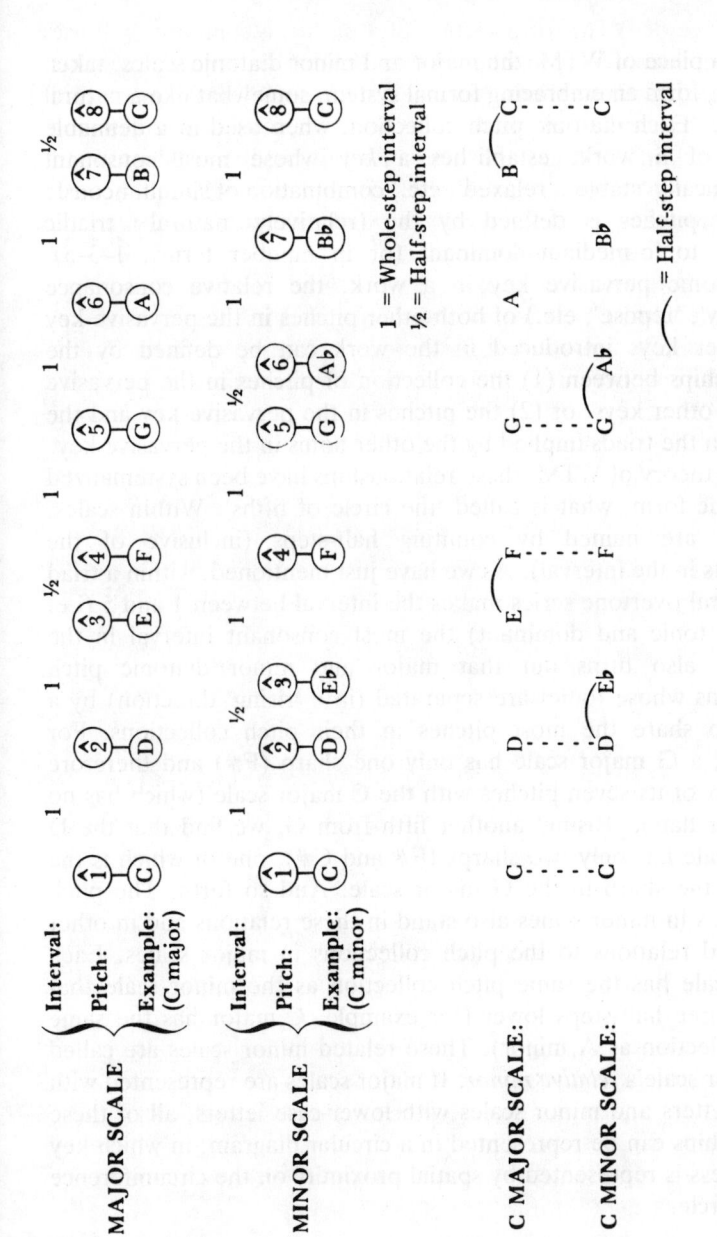

(Levy 1983: 441)

Within a piece of WTM, the major and minor diatonic scales, taken together, form an embracing formal system, somewhat like a natural language. Each diatonic pitch collection, when used in a definable section of a work, establishes a *key* whose most consonant (harmonically 'stable', 'relaxed', etc.) combination of simultaneously sounded pitches is defined by the (relatively 'natural') triadic relation: tonic–mediant–dominant (or in number terms, $\hat{1}$–$\hat{3}$–$\hat{5}$). Given some pervasive key in a work, the relative consonance ('stability', 'repose', etc.) of both other pitches in the pervasive key and other keys introduced in the work can be defined by the relationships between (1) the collection of pitches in the pervasive key and other keys, or (2) the pitches in the pervasive key and the pitches in the triads implied by the other notes in the pervasive key.

In the theory of WTM, these relationships have been systematized in graphic form, what is called 'the circle of fifths'. Within scales, intervals are named by counting half-steps (inclusive of the endpoints in the interval). As we have just mentioned, within a triad the natural overtone series makes the interval between $\hat{1}$ and $\hat{5}$ (i.e. between tonic and dominant) the most consonant interval in the triad. It also turns out that major and minor diatonic pitch collections whose tonics are separated (in a 'rising' direction) by a fifth also share the most pitches in their pitch collections. For instance, a G major scale has only one sharp (F#) and therefore shares six of its seven pitches with the C major scale (which has no sharps or flats). 'Rising' another fifth from G, we find that the D major scale has only two sharps (F# and C#), one of which is the same as the sharp in the G major scale. And so forth. The pitch collections in minor scales also stand in these relations and in other principled relations to the pitch collections in major scales. Each major scale has the same pitch collection as the minor scale that begins three half-steps lower (for example, C major has the same pitch collection as A minor). These related minor scales are called the major scale's *relative minor*. If major scales are represented with capital letters and minor scales with lower-case letters, all of these relationships can be represented in a circular diagram, in which key relatedness is represented by spatial proximity on the circumference of the circle.

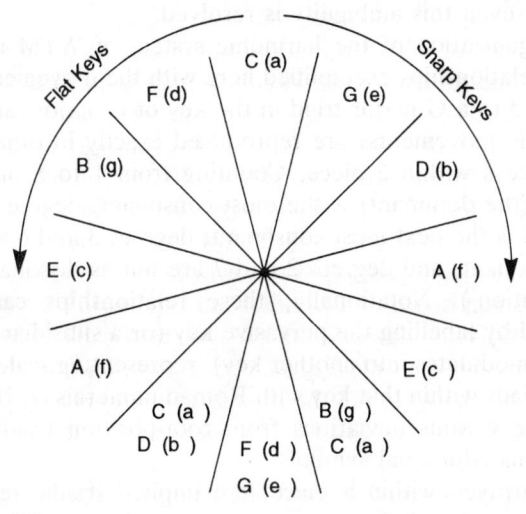

```
              C (a)
       F (d)         G (e)
  Flat Keys              Sharp Keys
     B (g)               D (b)
   E (c)                   A (f )
      A (f)              E (c )
         C (a )     B (g )
        D (b )     C (a )
          F (d )
           G (e )
```

(Jones 1974: 35)

Given these relationships (and many others), this system provides a relatively precise account of our impression of the consonance/dissonance (i.e. 'relative stability', 'repose', etc.) conveyed by both (1) simultaneously sounded pitch events, and (2) linearly ordered pitches or pitch combinations within a given pervasive key in the 'language' of WTM. Within a triad, consonance/stability is defined in terms of the relation to the lowest note in the triad. For instance, a 'root-position' C major triad (which would read C–E–G from lowest to highest pitch) would be more consonant than a C major triad with the E or the G as the lowest note (these other orderings are called 'inversions'). Other pitch combinations can be ranked for relative stability according to (1) the triadic relations they imply and the position of these relations on the circle of fifths, and (2) some measure of the relative distortion of triadic relations (a complex issue that I can't go into here). For instance, in the key of C major, a 'root-position' major triad beginning on G (G–B–D, reading from lowest pitch to highest pitch) would be a fairly stable event (although not as stable as any of the C major triads (root-position and non-). G major is one of two juxtaposed major keys to C major on the circle of fifths (the other being F). Within WTM it has also been a historical development that keys in a 'rising' direction of the circle of fifths have been conventionalized as more 'stable' than keys the same distance away on the circle in a 'descending' direction;

therefore, even this ambiguity is resolved.

The organization of the harmonic system of WTM makes it so that the relationships exemplified here with the movement from a C major triad to a G major triad in the key of C major (and all other comparable movements) are reproduced exactly in other keys and between keys within a piece. Counting from $\hat{1}$ to $\hat{8}$ on the scale, degree $\hat{5}$ (the dominant) is the most consonant, degree $\hat{4}$ (the subdominant) is the next most consonant, degrees $\hat{3}$ and $\hat{6}$ are the next most consonant, and degrees $\hat{2}$ and $\hat{7}$ are felt as dissonant (in need of 'resolution'). Notationally, these relationships can then be formalized by labelling the pervasive key (or a subsidiary key when the piece modulates into another key), representing scale degrees of implied triads within that key with Roman numerals (I, II, III, etc.), and noting various deviations from root-position triadic relations with various additional symbols.

When arrayed within a piece, the implied triadic relations can form phrases by defining certain standard moves between the harmonic relations (what are called *harmonic progressions*), with the limits of phrases defined by a conventional movement from V to I (called a cadence). These cadenced phrases usually have subparts (called *motifs*) defined by various sorts of repeated/varied melodic motion. Phrases can then be combined into phrase-groups or *periods*, periods can be combined into sections, sections can be combined into movements, and movements can be moulded into certain standard musical forms (e.g. the sonata), defined by various considerations (usually thematic/melodic in focus). Almost all tonal music ends with a cadential formula.

In addition to these harmonic relations, it is also characteristic of WTM to articulate certain types of *thematic content* defined by melodic movement. Most of WTM continues to reflect its historical roots in song and therefore most of the pieces in this idiom highlight an upper voice that defines a horizontal figure of pitches, usually dominated by step-wise motion. Through repetition and variation, this thematic content plays an important role in both phrasing and sectioning, and, as we just mentioned, is a dominant consideration in defining musical forms. Melodic variation in WTM is usually described in terms of certain structural and rhythmic *transformations* of the basic melodic motif (inversion, ornamentation, augmentation, diminution, fragmentation, repetition, etc.).

Of course, these harmonic and melodic structures in WTM are also arrayed rhythmically in the linear flow of the work. Traditionally, the rhythmic structure of music has usually been described much the same way as the temporalist tradition describes the rhythmic structure of poetry. The basic beat of the music, if there is one, is called *meter* and is defined in terms of the predictable and regular sectioning of the music into short, identical patterns of beating (i.e. *measures*) created by the imposition of a hierarchy of regularly spaced, higher-level prominences on some baseline throbbing (i.e. a *pulse*). Five 'commonly used' metric figures are recognized, all based on duple and triple patterns. *Duple* and *triple* meters simply group beats into one-level, beat-initial measures containing two and three beats. Duple meter is claimed to be the meter of pieces such as 'Frère Jacques' and 'Three Blind Mice'. Triple meter is claimed to be the meter of pieces such as 'Silent Night' and 'America'.

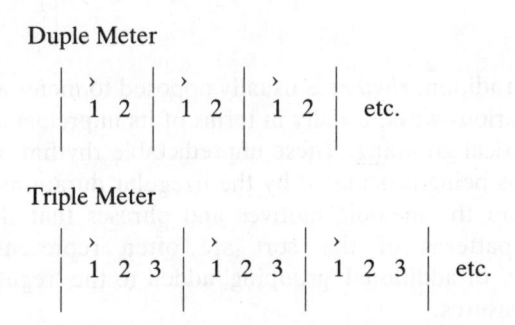

Duple Meter

```
|  >    |  >    |  >    |
|  1 2  |  1 2  |  1 2  |  etc.
|       |       |       |
```

Triple Meter

```
|  >      |  >      |  >      |
|  1 2 3  |  1 2 3  |  1 2 3  |  etc.
|         |         |         |
```

Common meter groups pulses in *fours*, doubling the pattern of duple meter and therefore adding another level of organization. Common meter is claimed to be the meter of pieces such as 'America the Beautiful' and 'Way Down upon the Swanee River'.

```
|           |           |           |
|  >        |  >        |  >        |
|  >    >   |  >    >   |  >    >   |
|  1 2 3 4  |  1 2 3 4  |  1 2 3 4  |
|           |           |           |
```

Compound duple meter groups pulse in *sixes*, dividing measures at two levels, first into twos and then into threes. Compound duple meter is claimed to be the meter of pieces such as 'Row, Row, Row your Boat'.

164   CONTEXT

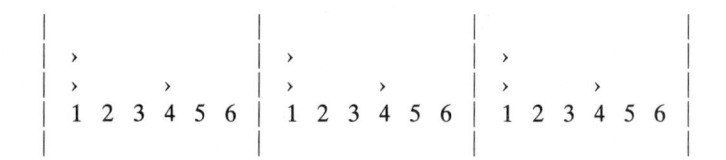

```
|           |           |           |
|  >        |  >        |  >        |
|  >    >   |  >    >   |  >    >   |
| 1 2 3 4 5 6 | 1 2 3 4 5 6 | 1 2 3 4 5 6 |
|           |           |           |
```

And *compound triple meter* groups pulses into *nines*, dividing measures into three groups of three. Compound triple meter is claimed to be the meter of pieces such as 'My Darling Clemintine' and 'Down in the Valley'.

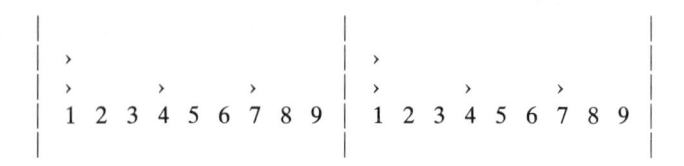

```
|                    |                    |
|  >                 |  >                 |
|  >    >    >       |  >    >    >       |
| 1 2 3 4 5 6 7 8 9  | 1 2 3 4 5 6 7 8 9  |
|                    |                    |
```

As in the prosodic tradition, *rhythm* is usually opposed to meter and is talked about in various ways, usually in terms of its unpredictable variations from metrical grouping. These unpredictable rhythms are usually thought of as being articulated by the irregular durations of individual notes (and the melodic motives and phrases that they form). Rhythmic patterns of this sort are often represented graphically as a 'tier' of additional 'grouping' added to the 'regular' flow of metrical measures.

```
Tier 3: Rhythm  ━━━ ━ ━━    ━━━  ━  ━━
                Si  -  lent  night     Ho  -  ly   night
                >            >         >          >
                1   2   3    1   2   3  1   2   3  1   2   3   1
Tier 2: Meter:  ▮   |   |    ▮   |   |  ▮   |   |  ▮   |   |   ▮

Tier 1: Pulse   |   |   |    |   |   |  |   |   |  |   |   |   |
```

(Levy 1983: 450)

Conflict between metrical beats and phenomenal stresses is called *syncopation*.

3.7.2 Heinrich Schenker and prolongational reduction[4]

If I understand the history of these matters correctly, this sketch of musical structure (and the theory of musical rhythm that this structure implies) was the standard view of the formal organization of WTM before the work of the great German theorist Heinrich Schenker in the first three decades of the twentieth century (and, as my references indicate, this view is still presented in non-professional, low-level theory classes in the music curriculum).

What is so interesting about this sketch is that this theory of musical rhythm is exactly comparable to the contemporary view of the rhythm of English poetry, a view that was also codified in the nineteenth century in the great historical surveys by prosodists such as Saintsbury and Schipper. As in the prevailing theory of poetic rhythm, the global structure of music in this pre-Schenkerian theory is largely a matter of thematic variation, as that variation is contained within and moulded by pre-existent stylistic frames, and the part that rhythmic organization plays in this structure is largely local and limited (i.e. relatively 'concrete' variation and syncopation of some 'regular' metrical norm).

However inadequate the details of Schenker's theory have turned out to be as a complete theory of WTM, it is generally recognized that he convincingly refuted this relatively flat, concrete and localistic view of musical structure, developing as an alternative a hierarchical, abstract and global view of the organization of WTM that is directly comparable to the view of poetic rhythm I am suggesting in this book.

Schenker's great accomplishment was to develop a relatively explicit theory of the abstract, hierarchically structured teleology of tonal 'syntax' in classical WTM, a theory that closely resembles the prolongational component of the theory of poetic rhythm I have just suggested above. Schenker's fundamental insight was his demonstration that the goal-oriented movement in classical WTM is essentially a rhythmic process (Schenker 1935: 15, 32), articulated by the recursive elaboration, with a relatively small number of formal trajectories at various levels of cognitive abstraction, of an embracing frame of melodic–harmonic expectation. In this dimension of rhythmic articulation at least, this demonstration argued, with unprecedented articulateness and detail, for the 'organic coherence' (1979: xxi) of WTM, for its explicit 'composing out' of tonal structures so that their hierarchically organized, goal-ordered movements (in both their architectural elaboration and their linear projections and delays) produce a formal simulacrum of the subjective energies embodied in the artistic vision of the work.

Historically, the most significant aspect of Schenker's theory is his demonstration that WTM is largely *vertical* in its organization, that the 'masterworks' of the musical idiom embody the workings of an over-archingly synthetic formal imagination that transcends the linear flow of a work and its surface variation in a way that is almost inconceivable in its complexity and that, to comprehend and represent adequately, takes an intensity of analytical attention that can be achieved only with a significant amount of training in structural 'hearing'. As in my critiques of the prosodic tradition, this view of musical rhythm argues that attention to local, surface variation simply misses the point by not addressing the embracing unity of the artwork and the flow of formal energies from this embracing unity through the structural levellings in the work to the physical detail of the 'textual' surface.

The parallels between Schenker's theory of goal-oriented movement in WTM and the theory of poetic prolongation I have suggested above are close. In fact, if taken at the proper level of abstraction and adjusted for the modifications suggested by contemporary music theorists, they can be considered tight formal analogues.

In rough outline, Schenker's detailed claim is that all WTM is a hierarchical elaboration of a *fundamental structure* in which melodic descent of a major third, perfect fifth or octave to the tonic is coordinated with a lower-voice rise from tonic to dominant and back to dominant. With the three-step melodic descent, this fundamental structure is the following.

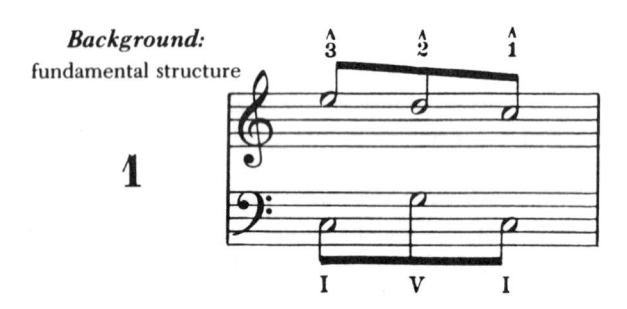

Background: fundamental structure

1

(Schenker 1935: Fig. 1)

This *fundamental structure*, Schenker claims, constitutes a *background level* in all work in this musical idiom and therefore provides an embracing frame of formal expectation in terms of which more detailed formal articulation in the work is necessarily heard. While I must refrain from analysing complex examples here, the most significant result of this claim is that the over-arching rhythmic structure of a piece of WTM, at least in this prolongational aspect, is usually wildly asymmetrical and relatively free of large-scale thematic divisioning, phrasal segmentation (throughout the rhythmic hierarchy) and metrical organization on the musical surface. Like our closural expectations in poetry, this fundamental structure pre-exists the work, is invoked early on in the work's linear flow, and therefore provides an embracing formal continuity, impulsion and expectation to the more symmetrical and parallelistic formal patterns at lower hierarchical levels in prolongation and in the other rhythmic components.

At mid levels and lower, Schenker demonstrated that this fundamental structure is systematically elaborated by relatively 'free' and equally asymmetrical melodic trajectories whose cognitive positioning is determined by principles of strict counterpoint, principles that amount to assessing at each point in the individual melodic trajectory the relative consonance/stability of the harmonic support for the projected voice involved. As in his positing of the background structure, Schenker claimed that these mid- and low-level elaborations occur in only a small set of patterns that are found repeatedly throughout the corpus of WTM. For our purposes here, the most striking aspects of these mid-level structures are their abstractness, controlled hierarchical organization, and asymmetry. As in poetry, these mid-level and low-level elaborations swell the body of the fundamental prolongational expectation of the work, shaping the piece with a unique structure of inner tensions and resolutions. In essence, each tonal elaboration, at the level where it occurs, indicates a unique shape of 'prolonged' anticipation/extension of the next element in the immediately superordinate melodic trajectory (thus the term 'prolongation'), and that superordinate trajectory, to the extent that it is elaborated, adds another level of shaped anticipation/extension to its immediately superordinate trajectory – and so on, to the fundamental trajectory that embraces the whole.

It is this hierarchical organization of our prolongational intuitions that permits the 'reductional' analysis of prolongation that I have claimed for poetic prolongation in this chapter. In exploring these structures, the analyst can adjust a 'sketch' of these prolongational trajectories to any desired level of elaboration, leaving out subordinate levels if these levels obscure the heuristic purposes of the analysis. One of Schenker's most influential contributions has been his claim that 'sketches' of these prolongational intuitions and their various realizations can be productively graphed, and he develops a complex system of visual conventions to illustrate this. In these graphic displays, Schenker makes various distinctions between prolongational processes, distinctions that amount to a detailed theoretical anatomy of prolongational movement.

The major criticisms of Schenker's graphic system (and his analytical work in general) have been directed at its combination of complexity and incompleteness, and its frequent lack of principled motivation. While Schenker's theory is clearly hierarchical in organization, in his explicit graphic analysis he chooses to isolate just a couple of levels for representation, leaving it unclear how these levels are connected. In general, the particular prolongational structures that he posits for individual works also outrun his analytical principles, leaving unclear the basis of his analytical decisions (including the possibilities of alternative readings). It has been the significant contribution of Lerdahl and Jackendoff (1983) to demonstrate that the representation of these prolongational intuitions can be simplified and clarified if they are represented (1) in a continuously hierarchical manner, and (2) in a way that relates them to an explicit system of prolongational preferences governing ambiguous and/or alternative readings. This is the approach I have recommended for poetry. In this book I do not attempt an explicit theory of prolongational preference for poetry, but I recognize that such a theory is possible, and in anticipation of its future development I provide a more loosely motivated representation of prolongational energies in my analyses in Chapter 5.

Lerdahl and Jackendoff's elegant suggestion is that prolongational hierarchies in music (and therefore in poetry as well) can be represented by unlabelled 'angle' graphs, in which tensing motions (i.e. prolongational extensions) are represented by right branches, and relaxing motions (prolongational anticipations) by left branches. Following the general tradition in Schenkerian analysis, Lerdahl and Jackendoff distinguish between three types of prolongational movement. *Strong prolongation* is produced by formal repetition (and is represented with an open circle on their angle graphs). *Weak prolongation* is produced by intra-harmonic movement (and is represented by filled circles on their angle graphs). *Progressions* are produced by inter-harmonic movement (and are represented by simple line mergers on their angle graphs). As explained earlier in this chapter, I adopt this three-way classification and this graphic method for my analyses in Chapter 5, relating equational movement in poetry to weak prolongation and additive movement to strong prolongation, while adopting the musical term *progression* for more hypotactic, subordinating movement.

To give a short example of these graphic conventions as Lerdahl and Jackendoff use them for music, consider my attempt below to graph our prolongational response to the first four measures of Mozart's A-major sonata below.[5]

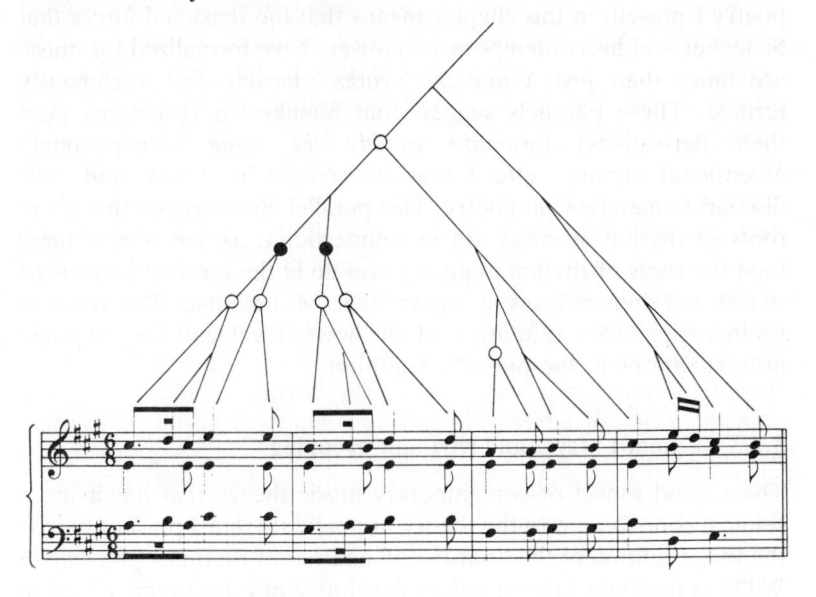

At the highest level, this graph represents the progression of the initial tonic harmony and melodic C# to the final dominant harmony and melodic B. The second level represents the 'strong' recapitulation of the initial C#. The third level represents the lower-neighbour to upper-neighbour elaboration of the opening C#, articulated first with a progressional extension to the dominant and melodic B on the downbeat of measure 2 and then with an anticipational progressional movement that skips from the melodic D and tonic harmony to the final melodic B and dominant harmony in the fourth measure. The fourth level represents the parallel triplet of rising motions (with largely echoic lower levels): the harmonically 'weak' extensional skips from C# to E in the first measure and from B to D in the second measure, followed by the two-level progressional and anticipational rise (also with lower-level echos) from melodic A through melodic B to the recapitulated melodic C# on the downbeat of the fourth measure. The parallel between prolongational representations of this sort for WTM and the representation of our prolongational response to poetry in the theory presented in this chapter is evident.

This parallel has significant implications for our conception of the rhythmic relations between the two arts. The claim that Shenkerian analyses are comparable to the prolongational representations for poetry I present in this chapter means that the tensional forces that Schenker and his contemporary followers have formalized for music are more than just a musical 'syntax', loosely and analogously termed. These parallels suggest that Shenkerian reductions (and their derivatives) formalize *exactly the same* anticipational–extensional rhythmic effects that are created by syntax (and their discourse analogues) in poetry. This parallel also suggests that if the roots of rhythm in music are in counterpoint, as Schenker claims, then the roots of rhythm in poetry also lie in the tensional effects of syntax and their reflexes at higher levels of discourse. This result is again a significant refutation of the lower-level and largely sonic preoccupations in the prosodic tradition.

3.7.3 Leonard Meyer and rhythmic grouping

The second aspect of contemporary music theory that has made a seminal contribution to the theory of poetic rhythm I present here is the long tradition of the 'foot-based' analysis of rhythmic phrasing in WTM, a tradition whose modern development is best represented in the work of Leonard Meyer (Meyer 1956, 1967, 1973; Cooper and Meyer 1960).

Meyer's work has also been a seminal input to the general rationale and discourse organization of the rhythmic analysis I present in Chapter 5. Given the critical weakness of the prosodic tradition, one of the great voids in literary study is any critical *format* for rhythmic comment, any conventional discourse model to motivate the linear ordering, level of detail, and rhetorical texture of an extended critical elucidation of complex rhythmic patterning in a poem. The format of Meyer's critical analysis of WTM, I think, can fill this void.

A major contribution of Meyer's approach is his careful explanation of the *interpretive*, rather than just *descriptive*, nature of rhythmic analysis. In Meyer's intellectual project, the major goal of rhythmic criticism is not to formulate rigid rules of analysis, but to demonstrate in specific cases how and why general rules of rhythmic structuring are actualized the way they are (1973: 14). The aim is to elucidate the psychological–stylistic *choices* available to the composer and to evaluate the consequences of the choices realized against the background of the unchosen alternatives. This aim leads to a discourse in which probings of the textual and psychological sources of a rhythmic scansion are as prominent as an elucidation of the effects of the scansion proposed. Unlike much prosodic analysis in the tradition, rhythmic analysis with these aims becomes not a matter of a cursory checking for well-formedness, a mechanical tabulation of frequently occurring structures, or a disjointed marking of rhythmico-stylistic 'deviances', but a process of rhythmic *reading* in the fully pregnant, literary sense. Meyer invests his critical discourse with the necessary indecidability, ambiguity and evaluative relativity that are a part of any complex interpretive activity. The result is a style of rhythmic analysis that has no analogues in the history of comment on poetic rhythm.

The heavily intepretive discourse that Meyer advocates is not just a critical preference, however; it is also motivated theoretically. As Meyer describes them, the structures that he is most concerned with in his analysis, what he calls *rhythm*, emerge necessarily from a preferential weighing of a wide range of perceptual input presented by many different aspects of the musical surface: duration, melody, meter, instrumentation, dynamics, harmony, phrasing/slurs and others (e.g. Cooper and Meyer: 12–57). The rhythmic structures that result from these preferential weighings are far from clear, presenting various overlappings, fusions, blurrings and ambiguities (e.g. Cooper and Meyer: 60–86). A particularly difficult problem in isolating these structures involves repetition and parallelism, what Meyer likes to call *conformant relationships* (Meyer 1973: 45–79). Perceptions of conformant relationships, Meyer demonstrates, are necessarily complex, multidimensional and somewhat indeterminate. The following disclaimer (Cooper and Meyer: 9) is a useful summary of these considerations:

> Rhythmic grouping is a mental fact, not a physical one. There are no hard and fast rules for calculating what in any particular instance the grouping is. Sensitive, well-trained musicians may differ. Indeed, it is this that makes performance an art – that makes different phrasings

and different interpretations of a piece of music purposefully ambiguous and must be thus understood rather than forced into a clear decisive pattern. In brief, the interpretation of music – and this is what analysis should be – is an art requiring experience, understanding, and sensitivity.

The rhythmic structures that Meyer defines for music ('the way in which one or more unaccented beats are grouped to an accented one' (Cooper and Meyer: 6)) are virtually identical to those I have proposed for the grouping component of our rhythmic response to poetry and therefore need no further discussion here. Meyer distinguishes these structures from both *pulse* ('one of a series of regularly recurring, precisely equivalent stimuli' (Cooper and Meyer: 3)) and *meter* ('the number of pulses between more or less regularly recurring accents' (Cooper and Meyer: 4)), and, as I have done for poetry, he stresses grouping's (1) hierarchical organization, (2) recursive elaboration, and (3) indirect relationship to the musical surface (Cooper and Meyer: 6–7). Meyer also adopts a bracketing formalism to represent these hierarchical groupings, although he uses the conventional prosodic markings '/' and 'v' to mark grouping peaks and valleys, rather than the 's' (strong) and 'w' (weak) markings I have adopted from the metrical phonologists (I reserve the traditional prosodic markings to indicate linguistic stress). For instance, he indicates the 'rhythmic' structure of the first eight measures of the theme of Mozart's A-major sonata as follows.

(Meyer 1973: 39)

This diagram claims a regular series of trochaic groupings at the lowest level, following the afterbeating meter in half-measures. A second level groups these trochees into a series of four trochees and two anapaests, with the anapaests coming every third unit (and with the second anapaest resolved into a two-level triple). At a third level, these six units are grouped into two anapaests. And at the highest level, these two anapaests are grouped into an iamb.

The major difference between the formal organization of Meyer's rhythmic structures and the grouping structures I propose for poetry is that Meyer recognizes only duple and triple structures and therefore only five grouping shapes (i.e. iamb, trochee, anapaest, dactyl, amphibrach). I permit groups to expand to seven units. The practical differences between these claims might be minimal, however. Expanded groupings in poetry usually occur only at low levels, and Meyer *begins* his analysis at a fairly high level (somewhat above the occurrence of individual notes). This difference may have some theoretical importance, however. A theory of grouping that limits groups to duples and triples erases one of the major structural differences between the two components. In general, Meyer also gives some representation to retrospective patterning and real-time reanalysis, while I refrain from representing these matters (though I recognize their existence). For instance, in Meyer's Mozart analysis, the double markings on the first unit of (1) the anapaests at lower levels, and (2) the iamb at the highest level indicate that we first hear these units as strong and then revise this reading to weak as we proceed. Again, the tight parallel between Meyer's theory of musical grouping and the theory of grouping I present in this chapter is clear.

With respect to rhythmic theory (prosodic and musical), one of Meyer's major accomplishments is to isolate general preferences (1) for grouping shape, and (2) for correspondences between grouping shapes and phenomena presented by the musical surface. He notes that we prefer groups to be binary (especially at high levels (Cooper and Meyer: 22)), end-focused (61), ornamented at lower levels (21–2), and arrayed in a regular pattern (33). He notes that we usually group together phenomena on the musical surface that are physically and melodically proximate (14) and cohesive in their internal texture (16). He notices that abrupt changes in the musical texture tend to produce grouping breaks (Meyer 1973: 52). He notes the pervasive effects of formal parallelism on grouping segmentation (Meyer 1973: 44–79). (Formal parallels tend to be preserved by grouping segmentation, but immediate repetition tends to lead to grouping breaks.) He notes that the vertical organization of a grouping hierarchy is largely a matter of the relative stability of groups – their relative closural force and their relative position as structural vs ornamental material (Meyer 1973: 80–105). And he notes a pervasive tendency to coordinate grouping structures with both metrical beating and goal-oriented movement (the *other* components of rhythmic response).

While all of these grouping preferences are fairly general and can occur in seemingly infinite combinations and realizations, they provide a strong basis for a rich practice of phrasal reading. In Chapter 3 I extend Meyer's musical grouping preferences to language.

As with Schenker's theory of prolongation, it has been one of the significant accomplishments of Lerdahl and Jackendoff (1983) to formalize these grouping preferences into a system of named and numbered 'preference rules' for (1) grouping segmentation (what they call 'grouping'), and (2) hierarchical ordering (what they call 'time-span reduction'). In Chapter 3 I will make use of Lerdahl and Jackendoff's method, although I realize that the substance of their claims has its source in Meyer's less formalized practice.

3.7.4 Fred Lerdahl and Ray Jackendoff and rhythmic cognition

Despite the significant advances by Schenker and Meyer (and their predecessors and followers), these theories of rhythmic organization in music remain sketchy and indeterminate. They provide a basis for detailed critical analysis, but that analysis must still be based heavily on discretionary moves by the analyser, moves that receive no explicit theoretical motivation.

As in prosodic theory, the major difficulty is the exact relation between the components of musical rhythm described by Schenker and Meyer. Schenker makes a number of interesting comments about meter and phrasing, but these comments are brief and undeveloped; and while Meyer refers frequently to meter and prolongation, it is generally unclear how these other considerations relate to his theory of grouping. In particular, given the relatively loose form of both Schenker and Meyer's analysis, it is unclear what is *shared* by these components of rhythmic organization – and what is not.

The first contribution of Lerdahl and Jackendoff (1983) is to give all of the components a rigorously hierarchical representation and thus provide a rich formal criterion for defining the nature of rhythmic forms. In LJ's theory, constraints on hierarchical organization become the major well-formedness conditions on rhythmic form in all of the components. Consequently, it is largely this hierarchical organization that defines what rhythms are, with the relations between these hierarchical forms and the surface having a more peripheral theoretical status. The discussion of hierarchy I present in this chapter derives directly and with little alteration from LJ's suggestions.

LJ's second contribution is their development of a principled theory of meter. While meter seems to be one of the better understood components of musical rhythm, before LJ many aspects of metrical organization still remained unclear (e.g. the nature of meter above the level of the measure and the effect of meter on grouping and prolongational organization). For example, Cooper and Meyer see rhythmic grouping as a grouping of *beats* and provide only one term, *accent*, to refer to grouping and metrical prominences at higher levels of structure. In most cases Cooper and Meyer also discuss meter and grouping separately, so that it is sometimes unclear which of Cooper and Meyer's representations are meant to be metrical and which phrasal, and in all cases it remains unclear how complete metrical and grouping structures interact.

LJ overcome these difficulties by distinguishing carefully between a *structural accent*, 'an accent caused by melodic/harmonic points of gravity in a phrase or section', and a *metrical accent*, 'a beat that is relatively strong in its metrical context'; and they distinguish both of these from a *phenomenal accent*, 'an event at the musical surface that gives emphasis or stress to a moment in the musical flow' (1983: 17). They then go on to develop principled theories of each of the rhythmic components, theories that refer to these different accents in different ways. For instance, LJ represent meter as more sensitive to phenomenal accents; grouping and prolongation, less so. Structural accents are then freed to serve as (1) the defining frame for the global arc of prolongational expectation in cadenced phrases, and (2) points of structural stability within the hierarchically ornamented grouping segmentation.

A major contribution of LJ's theory of meter as well is their definition of the *oppositional* relation between directional motion in metrical and phrasal accentuation. It is largely this insight that defines the complementary roles of the components within rhythmic cognition as a whole, the fact that I take as the most convincing proof of the productivity of a componential approach to rhythmic description in poetry. As in their treatment of hierarchy, the theory of metrical organization in poetry I present in this chapter derives with little alteration from LJ's suggestions.

A third contribution of LJ's theory over Schenker's and Meyer's is their explicit extension of reductional analysis to grouping. In most cases with which I am familiar, reductional analysis in music theory is applied only to prolongation. Following Schenker, these reductional 'sketches' represent goal-oriented movement across medially tensing motion. In their theory, however, LJ provide explicit 'sketches' of hierarchies of *grouping* ornamentation as well. They split the segmenting action of grouping (which they call *grouping*) from its ordering of structural prominences (which they

INTERDISCIPLINARY PARALLELS 177

call *time-span reduction*). These time-span reductions isolate an explicit vertical ordering of grouping peaks that can be presented at various levels of abstraction, as in Schenkerian reduction. The result is a series of grouping 'sketches', graded for hierarchical level.

For instance, given a 'reduction' of the first four measures of the theme of Mozart's A-major sonata to the score represented in the stave labelled 'e', the staves 'd' to 'a' represent a progressive 'factoring out' of ornamentation at successive levels of grouping represented by the 'angle graph' above (Lerdahl and Jackendoff 1983: 227). LJ then represent grouping segmentation by a simple bracketing (without indications of relative prominence).

(Lerdahl and Jackendoff 1983: 120)

I resist LJ's splitting of grouping into two components. To my intuition, grouping is largely a centroidal process and groups are coherent shapes ('waves' of motion), not segmentations whose peaks are ranked for prominence. In poetry, much of grouping segmentation depends on the placement of structural prominences, so a theory that separates grouping segmentation from the ranking of those structural prominences would have difficulty. The existence of an unranked grouping segmentation is also an anomaly within rhythmic cognition as a whole and upsets the strictly complementary relationships among the components within a three-component theory of rhythm. All of the other components involve both spans and relative prominences.

The notion of a grouping reduction, however, is very powerful and can be a major heuristic for probing the organization of complex rhythms. Therefore, I adopt this feature of LJ's theory as well. In principle, there is nothing to prevent a reduction of a Meyer-like grouping hierarchy. Applied to a Meyer-like scansion, a grouping reduction just factors out subordinate *groups* rather than subordinate *peaks*. This is the strategy I adopt in Chapters 4 and 5.

LJ's theory of music has a beguiling elegance that has no peer in rhythmic study. With its pithy constraints on hierarchy, its small number of cleanly articulated components, its short lists of psychologically 'natural' preference rules, and its revealing graphic displays, this theory offers the rhythmist an analytical tool that combines an unprecedented degree of clarity, simplicity and descriptive power. My central argument in this book is that prosodists should accept these generous offerings.

NOTES

1. Schenker 1935/1979: 162.
2. Cooper and Meyer 1960: 38.
3. Lerdahl and Jackendoff 1983: 283.
4. Schenker's most mature and synthetic work is considered to be Schenker 1935/1979, together with the graphs presented in Schenker 1932/1969. Schenkerian theory is now a regular part of music pedagogy at higher levels in the music curriculum. The most respected pedagogical presentation is Forte and Gilbert 1982. An earlier presentation is Salzer 1952. For an overview of the place of Schenkerian analysis within music theory as a whole, I find Cook 1987 useful.
5. Lerdahl and Jackendoff discuss this example in various places (1983: 32–3, 63, 70–1, 88, 118–23, 134–5, 138, 140–1, 156–7, 162–5, 167–8, 171–4, 194, 227–32, 276; Jackendoff 1977: 890–2).

Chapter 4
Theory: grouping

> Rhythmicalized material in essence is a fiction. In verse we do not face material which needs to be rhythmicalized and deformed. It is not *rhythmicalized material*, but *material in rhythm*.
>
> (Yuri Tynianov)[1]
>
> The peculiar pleasure of English poetry consists, not in a rhythmical arrangement of accents and emphases, but in a rhythmical arrangement of attention-stresses which produce accent and emphasis . . . . The poet when he makes his verse does not take a given series of notions and clothe them one by one with rhythmic speech sounds in regular successions, but forces his ideas themselves to flow in rhythmic series, whose waves are the waves of thought rising and falling with the intensity of his ideation . . . . The poet's idea forges its own rhythm, and with it batters its way through the gates of speech to the inmost core of human experience.
>
> (Mark Liddell)[2]

4.1 PRELIMINARIES

4.1.1 Cognitive competence

To specify the input to a grouping response, I assume a reader with a rich complex of non-rhythmic cognitive abilities. When constructing a grouping response to a poem, we do not respond to a bare, physical experience but to the interpretive product of innumerable structure-producing capacities of mind and body, capacities that function in reciprocal exchange with our grouping competence. Important here is the ability to construct a perceptual representation of the poem on the page; to abstract patterns from this perceptual representation and from the products of our linguistic, rhythmic and literary competences; to remember these patterns for certain periods of time; to project hypotheses about future events on the basis of these perceptual, linguistic, literary and rhythmic experiences; to integrate these patterns into more abstract representations; to modify hypotheses on the basis of new information; to compare and contrast different patterns both within the same cognitive mode and across different modes; and so forth. These capacities form a 'lower' endpoint for the input to our grouping competence and imply (1) that many sorts of animals (and machines) which lack these complex mental abilities would be incapable of a grouping response, and (2) that research methods that omit consideration of these abilities would be incapable of developing an adequate theory of grouping.

4.1.2 Literary competence

I also assume an experienced reader with a significant literary competence (e.g. Culler 1975). Included here is a certain volume of life experience; a certain level of perceptual, emotional, linguistic and intellectual subtlety; a rich knowledge of literary history based on wide reading in English poetry and the poetry of other literatures; an understanding of the historical constraints on poetry as a literary genre; a substantial knowledge of conventions of literary reading, poetic reading in particular; and so forth. These literary competencies establish an 'upper' endpoint for the input to our grouping response and imply (1) that readers who have not developed these capacities might be incapable of some aspects of grouping response, and (2) that prosodic theories that exclude these capacities would be incapable of an adequate account of grouping.

For the moment, I assume an interpretive community in the great aesthetic tradition in the West (as discussed by, for instance, Krieger 1988). I assume that poems are aesthetic objects whose major intention is a relatively 'disinterested' exploration of human sensibility within the limited materials of the art. I assume that a major part of this intention is a certain sort of artistic achievement, one that is defined by certain universal aesthetic criteria of formal unity, economy, complexity and intensity, and certain culturally relative considerations of humanistic 'truth' (emotional validity, moral vision, social relevance, etc.) and historical positioning (e.g. level of imaginative and formal invention within a specific artistic tradition). I also assume certain standard generic expectations: a novel and unusually elaborated linguistic surface; an 'organic'

PRELIMINARIES 181

coherence of formal patterning across levels of linguistic structure and between language and the 'world' of people, objects and events semiotically presented or implied; an unusual economy of expression and indirection of statement; a complex semiotic intention, inviting interpretive exploration on many levels (mimetic, moral, metaphysical, artistic, etc.); and (1) a characteristic hermeneutic development that moves from a thematic problem to an exploration of that problem, to a closural 'solution', and (2) a characteristic projection by detailed stylistic means of a pervasive and consistent subjective presence, a poetic 'voice'. It is my belief that most of the historical discussions of rhythmic organization in English poetry have assumed this interpretive community.

4.1.3 Linguistic competence

I also assume for my reader a rich linguistic competence. This competence will include the abilities described by the most advanced work in twentieth-century linguistics, in addition to the long Western tradition of language study in the literary and philosophical traditions (e.g. logic, rhetoric, poetics, etc.). In particular, I assume a rich system of conventions for interpreting the visual shape of the poem (e.g. Berry forthcoming b; Cureton 1986b), a rich phonological and syntactic competence, and a rich system of linguistic prosody (as described by the sections on the linguistic 'schools' in Chapter 1). This prosodic competence will include a principled theory of syllabic segmentation and representation (e.g. Hogg and McCully 1987: 31–61); a quasi-metrical organization of stress (e.g. Halle and Vernaud 1987); a hierarchical organization of prosodic domains (e.g. Nespor and Vogel 1986; Hayes 1989); a rich system of formal and functional principles governing intonational segmentation, structure and use (e.g. Crystal 1969; Halliday 1985; Couper-Kuhlen 1986); and some familiarity with the normative relations between these prosodic structures and other aspects of the linguistic and literary form of poems (e.g. Crystal 1975b; Byers 1977, 1979, 1980, 1983). In my prosodic representations I will in.di.cate syl.la.ble seg.men.ta.tion with full stops. I will indicate tone unit nuclei with **bold print**. I will not present a rigorously hierarchical representation of stress but, following many, will represent stress with four 'levels'. I will use primary stress ('´') to mark the peaks of clitic phrases. I will use secondary stress ('ˆ') sparingly to indicate a strengthened tertiary stress. I will use tertiary stress ('ˋ')

to indicate syllables with full vowels within the rise and/or fall of a clitic phrase. I will use weak stress ('ˇ') to indicate syllables with reduced vowels.

4.1.4 Rhythmic competence

Finally, I assume for my reader the rhythmic competence outlined in Chapter 3. That is, I assume that the reader articulates a grouping response in close conjunction with the other components of rhythmic response (i.e. meter and prolongation). The major consideration here is the notion of *Canonical Form* (as described in Chapter 3). I assume (1) that all of the components serve a relatively distinct function within rhythmic cognition, (2) that these functions are largely oppositional/complementary, and (3) that stability/coherence of a rhythmic form as a whole takes precedence over stability/coherence of a *part* of that form. Following Lerdahl and Jackendoff (1983), I assume that rhythmic form is essentially multidimensional and interactional, with the individual components adjusting their shapes so that they contribute productively to the multidimensional whole.

4.2 GROUPING WELL-FORMEDNESS RULES (GWFRs)

Following Lerdahl and Jackendoff (1983), I will specify categorical constraints on grouping form with a battery of *grouping well-formedness rules* (GWFRs). GWFRs for verse must specify two aspects of grouping form: (1) the categorical constraints on the structure of the rhythmic group, and (2) the categorical constraints on the relations among rhythmic groups (i.e. the organization of grouping hierarchies).

4.2.1 Grouping well-formedness rules (GWFRs): the individual group

In the theory of rhythmic cognition developed in Chapter 3, rhythmic groups have the following form (where 's' = strong unit, 'w' = weak unit, and parentheses indicate an optional unit).

```
                        'group'
          ┌───────────────┼───────────────┐
        'rise'          'peak'          'fall'
      ┌────┬────┬────┐    │    ┌────┬────┬────┐
     (w)  (w)  (w)        s   (w)  (w)  (w)
```

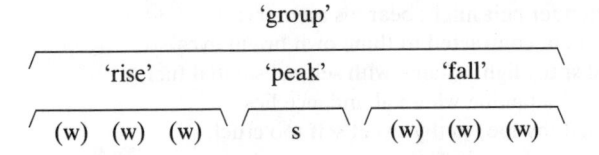

Groups contain one strong unit and up to six optional weak units, three optional weak units being possible before the strong unit, and three optional weak units being possible after the strong unit. The weak units preceding the strong unit form the *rise* of the group; the strong unit forms the *peak*; and the weak units following the strong unit form the *fall*.

This grouping schema can be accounted for with a small collection of GWFRs:[3]

> GWFR1 (Contiguity): Constituents of groups must be contiguous.
> GWFR2 (Peak): Groups with relatively weak constituents must contain one and only one relatively strong constituent.
> GWFR3 (Magic 7): Groups have a maximum of seven constituents.
> GWFR4 (Tri-weak): Groups have a maximum of three contiguous weak constituents.

GWFR1 (Contiguity) specifies that grouping is a 'chunking' process. Grouping relates only units that are juxtaposed in our experience of the text. This is an important constraint, because many perceptual and linguistic processes can associate items across experiential gaps and interruptions. GWFR1 (Contiguity) claims that rhythmic grouping crosscuts these more discontinuous processes.

This contiguity constraint on grouping might be regarded as an expressive liability, but it is often just the opposite. As rhetoricians have long noted, one of the most effective ways of scoring a syntactic structure into rhythmical phrases is to manipulate the position of mobile syntactic constituents. That is, rhythmic control is often secured by bending syntactic discontinuity to the service of grouping expressiveness.

For instance, in the fifth line of Sonnet 1, Shakespeare heightens the emphatic force of *thou* by separating it from its associated predicate with an adverbial clause:

> From fairest creatures we desire increase,
> That thereby beauty's rose might never die,
> But as the riper should by time decease

His tender heir might bear his memory:
5 But thou, contracted to thine own bright eyes,
Feed'st thy light's flame with self-substantial fuel,
Making a famine where abundance lies –
Thyself thy foe, to thy sweet self too cruel.

In constructing a grouping structure, we cannot relate *But thou* directly to *Feed'st thy light's flame with self-substantial fuel*. We must first relate it to the following adverbial *contracted to thine own bright eyes*. This interaction between syntactic discontinuity and grouping contiguity creates much of the distinctive rhythmic structure of the verse. *But thou* is established as a short (and therefore concentrated) phrase. *Thou* is forced into the position of an intonational nucleus. The following adverbial adds another level of rhythmic intensification. And only then is the subject of the clause grouped with its predicate.

GWFR2 (Peak) distinguishes this theory from rhythmic theories that allow phrases with more than one strong unit (spondees (ss), cretics (sws), choriambs (swws), di-iambs (swsw), dispondees (ssss), ditrochees (swsw), ionic a majores (ssww), ionic a minores (wwss), etc.). The intuitions that motivate these multi-peak phrasings are real, but I will claim that these phrases have more than one level of structure.

The stipulation 'with relatively weak units' in GWFR2 (Peak) is necessary to account for units with no internal structure (a perfectly acceptable possibility that occurs frequently). Groups with just one constituent unit ('singles') have no internal strength assignment. Elements of units with one constituent do not appear relative to any other elements and therefore cannot be labelled strong or weak on this level.

GWFR2 (Peak) has significant theoretical implications. It claims that strength within a group is strictly relative. GWFR2 (Peak) also clarifies the intuitive motivation for the rhythmic group. Rhythmic groups surround one relatively strong unit with one or more relatively weak units (Cooper and Meyer 1960: 6).

GWFR3 (Magic 7) distinguishes this theory from some versions of metrical phonology which claim that rhythmic phrases are strictly binary and therefore can have only one weak unit. This also has significant theoretical implications. It claims that readers experience rhythmic groups of significantly different spans, each of which makes a different contribution to rhythmic expressiveness. It also claims that the hierarchical organization of a grouping structure is relatively independent of the spans of its constituent groups. It claims that we determine group boundaries by other means (i.e. we do not count two and then break).

GWFR3 (Magic 7) follows from GWFRs 2 (Peak) and 4 (Tri-weak), but I give it independent status. If a group can have only one peak and three contiguous weak constituents, the maximum realization of the group is necessarily wwwswww, seven units. GWFR3 (Magic 7) claims that the deviance of a longer group is not just a matter of its longer rise or fall, however. The absolute length of the group also contributes to its rhythmic order/disorder. Given the importance of the number 7 in cognitive psychology, it might be possible to relate this constraint to limitations on short-term memory.

GWFR4 (Tri-weak) seems to be a constraint on the limits of our perception of coherent temporal 'shape' in a rhythmic 'wave'. A string of more than three weak units seems to exceed the limits of our perception of rhythmic stasis within change. Stasis that is prolonged to this extent becomes difficult to relate to a preceding or subsequent change in prominence.

4.2.2 Grouping well-formedness rules (GWFRs): grouping hierarchies

GWFRs 1–4 (Contiguity, Peak, Magic 7, Tri-weak) account for categorical constraints on the shape of the individual group. Additional GWFRs are needed to account for constraints on relationships *among* groups. Again following Lerdahl and Jackendoff (1983) and Cooper and Meyer (1960), I claim that rhythmic groups are perceived in the form of a strict, non-overlapping, recursive hierarchy.

The most radical part of this claim is that readers try to organize an entire text into a well-formed grouping hierarchy. With respect to a tree-structure formalism, this amounts to a claim that grouping structures are 'rooted' trees, that branches in a tree-structure representation of a grouping hierarchy are tied together by one superordinate node representing the grouping peak of the text as a whole. This radical claim is embodied in GWFR 5 (Root):

GWFR5 (Root): The text is a group.[4]

Other constraints on grouping relations are defined by GWFRs 6–9.

> GWFR6 (Levelling): All groups occur at a labelled level in the grouping hierarchy.[5]
> GWFR7 (Recursion): If a constituent of a group is partitioned, it must itself be a group.[6]
> GWFR8 (Non-overlapping): If a group contains part of another group, it must contain all of that group.[7]
> GWFR 9 (Horizontal Continuity): If a group is partitioned, it must be exhaustively partitioned.[8]

GWFR6 (Levelling) demands that the grouping hierarchy relate each peak to its vertical 'equivalents' within the hierarchy as a whole. It demands that grouping structures be *levelled* hierarchies.

GWFR7 (Recursion) demands that all complex units in the hierarchy be subject to the constraints on grouping form (GWFRs 1–4). In a well-formed grouping structure, there can be no units at superior levels in the hierarchy that have eight weak constituents, four strong constituents, discontinuous constituents, and the like.

GWFR8 (Non-overlapping) prevents grouping overlap within and between levels, situations represented by (a) and (b).

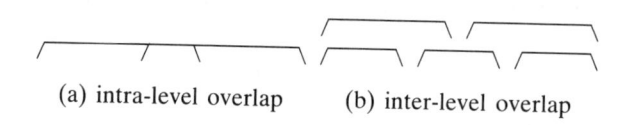

(a) intra-level overlap   (b) inter-level overlap

As both Cooper and Meyer (1960: 62–3) and Lerdahl and Jackendoff (1983: 38) point out, situations like (b) are excluded logically, but situations that resemble (a) occur quite often in our response to both music and verse. Nevertheless, these situations are not the norm, and there are other arguments that support excluding them from canonical grouping form. To perceive an overlap such as (a), we must recognize the overlapping groups as independent structures at some point in processing. An overlap presupposes two overlapping entities; the basic perception is of the independent groups. Following comparable situations in linguistic theory, Lerdahl and Jackendoff account for (a) with transformational rules. Groups with a 'pivot' (Cooper and Meyer: 62) of this sort, they claim, result from an operation *upon* canonical grouping form. I adopt this suggestion here.

In most cases in verse, situations such as (a) involve real-time reanalysis. A group is perceived as the last constituent in a phrase and then is reinterpreted as the initial constituent in the next phrase as well.

A particularly kinetic example of such a grouping overlap occurs at high levels in e.e. Cummings' 'In Just-'.

1	In Just-
2	spring when the world is mud-
3	luscious the little
4	lame balloonman
5	whistles far and wee
6	and eddieandbill come
7	running from marbles and
8	piracies and it's
9	spring
10	when the world is puddle-wonderful
11	the queer
12	old balloonman whistles
13	far and wee
14	and bettyandisbel come dancing
15	from hop-scotch and jump-rope and
16	it's
17	spring
18	and
19	the
20	goat-footed
21	balloonMan whistles
22	far
23	and
24	wee

At the highest level, 'In Just-' is built on a tight discourse triple whose immediate constituents are progressively pared away as the text approaches closure. In its fullest realization (lines 1–9), this discourse motif has five parts (ignoring for the moment intermediate phrasing). In its next realization (lines 10–17), one of these parts is lost. And in the final realization (lines 18–24), only one of these parts appears.

		Narrative triple	
Parts	*First*	*Second*	*Third*
(a)	In Just-spring	[and it's spring]	[and it's spring]
(b)	when the world is mud-luscious	when the world is puddle-wonderful	
(c)	the little lame balloonman whistles far and wee	the queer old balloonman whistles far and wee	and the goat-footed balloonMan whistles far and wee
(d)	and eddieandbill come running from marbles and piracies	and bettyandisbel come dancing from hop-scotch and jump-rope	
(e)	and it's spring	and it's spring	

This repeating, yet diminishing, form contributes variously to the poem's effect. The exact repetition enhances its child-like tone and song-like simplicity. The diminishing form gives it movement and development. And the much-diminished final repetition secures closure. The pervasive repetition also enables Cummings' symphonic graphics. Repeating forms appear in varying visual shapes and positions, to various effects.

As I have indicated with brackets in the table above, the exact formal shape of the narrative triple also leads to a salient grouping overlap. The formal resemblance between parts (a) and (e) of the narrative repetition (i.e. *In Just-spring* and *and it's spring*) encourages the reader to hear the end of the last part of the first and second narrative repetitions simultaneously as the first part of the second and third narrative repetitions.[9] This is particularly effective because, in the grouping hierarchy, part (a) of the narrative repetition is a strong unit three levels below the level at which part (e) is a strong unit; and part (a) is relatively equal in span with its rhythmic equivalents while part (e) is a severe contraction.

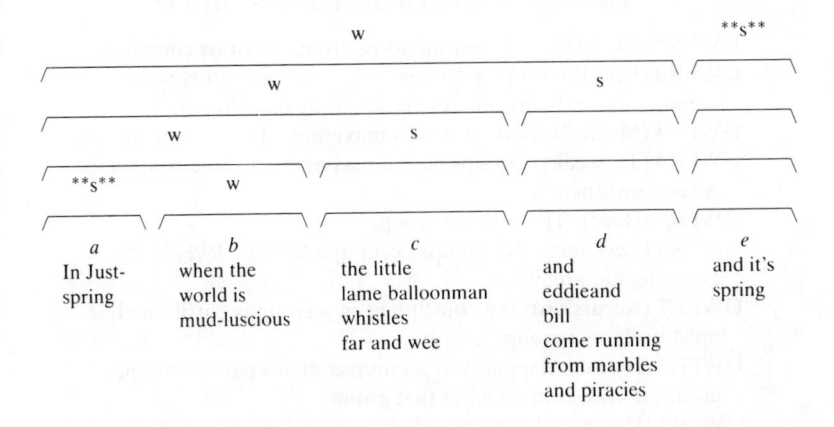

```
                                    w                          **s**
                    ┌───────────────────────────────┐     ┌──────────┐
                    w                         s
           ┌──────────────────────┐     ┌──────────┐     ┌──────────┐
           w              s
      ┌──────────┐    ┌──────────┐     ┌──────────┐     ┌──────────┐
     **s**      w
   ┌──────┐  ┌──────┐ ┌──────────┐    ┌──────────┐     ┌──────────┐

     a          b         c                d              e
  In Just-  when the   the little       and           and it's
  spring    world is   lame balloonman  eddieand      spring
            mud-luscious whistles        bill
                        far and wee     come running
                                        from marbles
                                        and piracies
```

This causes the highly charged, concentrated ends of the narrative units to overlap with their relatively weak, relaxed beginnings. The result is a type of rhythmic chord in which we experience simultaneously both the 'high-pitched' *and it's spring* and the 'low-pitched' *In Just-spring*. The joyful cry celebrating the onset of spring is subjectively prolonged and hangs in the air in a higher register like an echo, while the text gambols on.

GWFR9 (Horizontal Continuity) prevents the occurrence of stray, ungrouped constituents in the hierarchy, situations such as (a), (b) and (c) below.

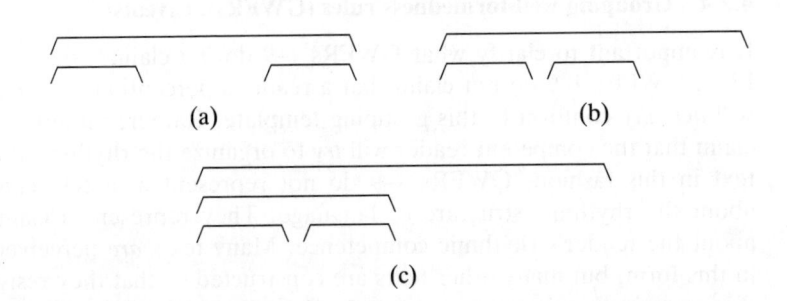

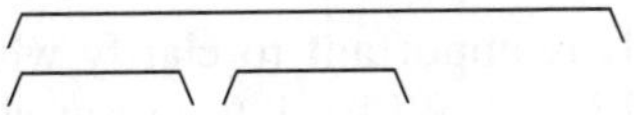

```
   ┌──────────────┐         ┌──────────┐ ┌──────┐
   ┌──────┐                 ┌──────┐
      (a)                         (b)

           ┌──────────────────────┐
           ┌──────────────┐
           ┌──────┐ ┌──────┐
                    (c)
```

4.2.3 Grouping well-formedness rules (GWFRs): summary

GWFRs 1–9 represent the categorical constraints on grouping form. For the reader's convenience, I recollect them here.

GROUPING WELL-FORMEDNESS RULES

GWFR1 (Contiguity): Constituents of groups must be contiguous.
GWFR2 (Peak): Groups with relatively weak constituents must contain one and only one relatively strong constituent.
GWFR3 (Magic 7): Groups have a maximum of seven constituents.
GWFR4 (Tri-weak): Groups have a maximum of three contiguous weak constituents.
GWFR5 (Root): The text is a group.
GWFR6 (Levelling): All groups occur at a labelled level in the grouping hierarchy.
GWFR7 (Recursion): If a constituent of a group is partitioned, it must itself be a group.
GWFR8 (Non-overlapping): If a group contains part of another group, it must contain all of that group.
GWFR9 (Horizontal Continuity): If a group is partitioned, it must be exhaustively partitioned.

GWFRs 1–9 represent a substantive claim about a reader's rhythmic competence. The rules claim that readers try to segment poems continuously and cleanly into a system of rhythmic phrases, each of which has one structurally prominent constituent and 0–6 less prominent constituents, such that these phrases form a recursive, levelled hierarchy from the smallest unit in the text to the text as a whole.

4.2.4 Grouping well-formedness rules (GWFRs): caveats

It is important to clarify what GWFRs 1–9 do *not* claim, however. First, GWFRs 1–9 do not claim that a reader's perception of a text will *actually* conform to this grouping template. Rather, these rules claim that the competent reader will *try* to organize the rhythms of a text in this fashion. GWFRs 1–9 do not represent a direct claim about the rhythmic structure of language. They represent a claim about the reader's rhythmic competence. Many texts *are* perceived in this form, but many other texts are constructed so that they resist this organization in various ways. In these cases as well, GWFRs 1–9 make a substantive claim about reader experience, however. They claim that texts which resist this canonical form will be perceived as partially arhythmic. Many texts maintain rhythmic coherence on a number of levels while letting other levels vary freely into arhythmic forms. Many texts establish coherent rhythms on some level and then let them lapse into arhythmia. Some texts resist this rhythmic template as much as possible (and this is often a significant expressive effect). The theory of grouping I am proposing here claims only that all texts invoke this template. All texts achieve their rhythmic form by means of an interaction with this aspect of the reader's rhythmic competence.

Second, these GWFRs do not claim that all readers *prefer* texts that conform to this formal shape. Most readers do, I think, but *de gustibus non disputandum est*. Some readers may consistently judge texts of this shape to be rhythmically derivative and therefore of little aesthetic worth. This theory still makes a significant claim about these readers as well, however. It claims that what these readers reject as a criterion of aesthetic value is exactly (a major dimension of) rhythmic form.

4.3 GROUPING PREFERENCE RULES (GPRs)

GWFRs 1–9 specify the general constraints on a well-formed hierarchy, but they still fall far short of an adequate theory of rhythmic grouping. In particular, GWFRs 1–9 (1) specify only *negative* conditions on grouping, and (2) provide no way of connecting the rhythmic schemata they define with the language of the text. These rules describe the limits of what readers will judge to be rhythmic. They do not specify what grouping structures readers will actually realize given these broad possibilities. And they specify exclusively formal, rather than substantive, constraints on a reader's grouping competence. In GWFRs 1–9, all of the major theoretical primitives (strong, weak, group boundary, level, etc.) remain undefined in linguistic terms.

The problem is: competent readers do not just look for a minimal rhythmic organization when they read a text; they try to *maximize* the rhythmic expressiveness of the text. A strong theory of rhythmic grouping, then, must also be a strong theory of grouping expressiveness. It must be explicitly *teleological*.

These two inadequacies are closely related and must be considered together. As we will investigate further as our discussion proceeds, levels in the grouping hierarchy are often not coextensive with recognized linguistic hierarchies (syntactic, prosodic, etc.), and grouping prominences and boundaries are not 'given' in any overt way by the structure of the text. Rather, in coming to a relatively stable conception of the grouping structure of a text, readers use what is given by the text to construct grouping schemes they prefer, as these schemes fall within the constraints of the grouping template defined by GWFRs 1–9. In terms of the normal orientation one finds in, say, linguistic theory, the innovation is that the objects of analysis are *preferences*, a small set of realized entities selected from a large number of equally possible, but unrealized, entities.[10]

If a theory of grouping is going to advance beyond the GWFRs, then, it must develop a battery of *grouping preference rules* (GPRs) that specify how readers make their rhythmic choices. Of course, if the basis for these choices were entirely individual and idiosyncratic, there would be no point in proceeding (other than the anecdotal point of comparing notes on differing strategies). But given what we know about shared rhythmic responses to poems, it makes sense to assume that at least *some* of these principles might be shared by most readers.

This case might be strengthened, too, by what we know of how subjects make forced choices among a range of alternatives in other perceptual and cognitive domains. If readers tend to choose grouping boundaries and prominences according to the same principles across domains, it might be reasonable to claim that these principles have some general cognitive motivation and that they would therefore play a part in grouping segmentation and prominence in verse as well.

The most frequently cited work on these issues was done by the gestalt psychologists, in particular Wertheimer (1923). Wertheimer studied 'figural stability', the emergence of visual wholes from their conflicting or incomplete parts. He found that there are a number of demonstrable principles controlling this visual grouping and that these principles seem to be of a very general nature that makes them applicable across perceptual domains.

The most important principles that he found are (what he calls) 'The Factor of Proximity' (74) and 'The Factor of Similarity' (75). Visual phenomena that are closer together (such as the pairs of dots below) or similar in form (such as the pairs of os and Os below) are viewed as groups.

. .   . .

o o O O o o O O o o O O o o O O o o O O o o O O o o O O o o

The significant result here is that I need not mark where these visual groups are in order to demonstrate how these principles operate.

We share these grouping preferences.

Wertheimer demonstrates several other important grouping principles.

> 'The Factor of Objective Set' – grouping sequences tend to prolong their order
> 'The Factor of Uniform Density' – a change affecting part of a group is expected to affect all of the group
> 'The Factor of Direction' – parts connected by a common direction tend to be grouped
> 'The Factor of Closure' – closed forms are preferred over open forms
> 'The Factor of Habit' – familiar forms are preferred over unfamiliar forms

Taken together, these principles provide strong evidence for the 'top-down', 'subjective' nature of perception (i.e. perceptual wholes are often greater than the sum of their parts). Therefore they relieve a grouping theory of the burden of trying to derive all actualized grouping perceptions in a direct way from categorical constraints on grouping form or unambiguous structuring in the phenomenal surface of the text. Where more than one grouping structure is formally possible, these principles claim that readers will prefer to group forms that are proximate and similar into forms that are established, familiar, closed, unidirectional and so forth.

Significantly, Wertheimer found that the effects of grouping 'factors' are graded and summative. For instance, he found that objects that are *very* proximate tend to be grouped more strongly than objects that are less proximate, and that objects that are both proximate and similar tend to be grouped more strongly than objects that are proximate but dissimilar. He also found that these 'factors' differ in relative strength. For instance, he found that in grouping dissimilar objects at varying distances the 'factor of proximity' usually dominates the 'factor of similarity', as in the figure below.

o O O o o O O o o O O o

However, he found that there is usually a point where these principles balance, yielding an indeterminate grouping, as in the next figure.

o O O o o O O o O o O o

Here the dissimilar letters are one space closer to one another than the similar letters. To my intuition, this balances proximity and similarity. If the dissimilar letters are two spaces closer, proximity begins to dominate.

o O   O o   o O   O o   o O   O o

In the original figure, the dissimilar letters were three spaces closer. In that case, proximity clearly dominates.

o O   O o   o O   O o   o O   O o

Lerdahl and Jackendoff (1983: 36–67) show how the musical analogues of Wertheimer's 'factors' (together with a small number of additional grouping preferences) can be used to develop a workable theory of musical grouping preferences. The musical correlate of Wertheimer's 'Factor of Proximity' (in a negative formulation) claims that two notes with more widely separated attack-points, separated by a greater rest or pulled apart by preceding and/or following slurs, will tend not to be grouped. The musical correlate of Wertheimer's 'Factor of Similarity' claims that any two notes separated by a relatively large change in pitch, dynamics, articulation and/or length will also tend not to be grouped.

Morphologically, grouping articulates rhythmic shapes in two dimensions, what we might metaphorically term *vertical* and *horizontal*. A grouping structure represents how we cognize relative *prominence* (a 'vertical' dimension) across structural *spans* (a 'horizontal' dimension). Both the peak of the individual group and the position of individual groups in the grouping hierarchy as a whole are determined by relative prominence. The horizontal influence of each centroidal peak is represented by its grouping span.

```
              ^
              ^
              |
              p
              r
              o
              m
              i
              n
              e
              n
              c
              e
      span    |    span
   <<<_____|_____>>>
```

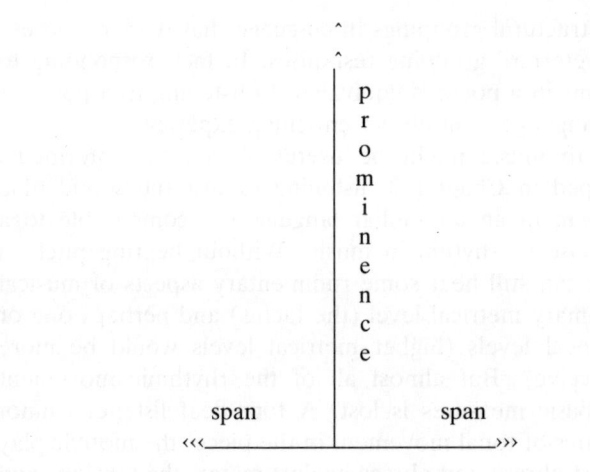

4.3.1 Grouping preference rules (GPRs): prominence

4.3.1.1 GPR1 (Information)

As we have seen in Chapter 1, many prosodists over the centuries have claimed that poetic rhythms are largely patterns of *sound*, a position that I like to call the 'tongs and bones' theory of verse rhythm.[11] However, as I have also argued in Chapter 1, a 'tongs and bones' theory of verse rhythm is radically exclusionary and, when articulated explicitly as a rhythmic theory, is both inadequate and inefficient. All verse rhythms do indeed group sounds and do indeed determine some rhythmic prominences in terms of sonic salience. But many of our central responses to verse rhythm have little to do with sound. Many rhythmic prominences in verse are not determined in any significant way by sound, and much of verse segmentation is not sonically determined either. In fact, sound is the source of only a small fraction of the hierarchical organization of verse. The first fact we need to recognize about our preference for grouping prominence in poetry, then, is its relative independence of sound.

This relative independence of grouping prominence from sound expands (1) the scope of phenomena that can be considered as input to a grouping response, and (2) the scope of the grouping response itself. Most of language organization (syntax, discourse, etc.) is not sonic. Therefore, a sonic theory of verse rhythm excludes from consideration many of the prominences, equivalences, hierarchical

196 THEORY: GROUPING

orderings and structural groupings in language that readers can use to construct 'preferred' grouping responses. In fact, responding to the sonic rhythms in a poem is equivalent to listening to a poem in an unfamiliar language – hardly an enriching experience.

An analogy to music might be useful. Given the intermedia parallel developed in Chapter 3, listening to just the sound of a poem (or a poem in an unfamiliar language) is comparable to a tone-deaf response to rhythm in music. Without hearing pitch, a musical listener can still hear some rudimentary aspects of musical rhythm: the primary metrical level (the tactus) and perhaps one or two other metrical levels (higher metrical levels would be more difficult to perceive). But almost all of the rhythmic movement through these basic measures is lost. A tone-deaf listener cannot feel the larger arcs of tonal movement in the piece, the motivic play of phrase against phrase and phrase against meter, the tensions and resolutions in the melodic and harmonic articulation, and the structure of tonal elaboration and ornamentation. Without pitch, a tone-deaf listener has no way to make judgements about structural prominence and constituency and therefore cannot hear most of the hierarchical organization of the music. Musical listening becomes a bare percussive response to the beating of 'tongs' on 'bones'.

These hypothetical situations and analogies are useful but unnecessary. The simple facts of our rhythmic reading of verse also strongly support this argument for non-sonic rhythms in poetry. For example, we don't feel that the third quatrain of Shakespeare's Sonnet 12 is more prominent rhythmically than the first two quatrains because we perform it at a higher pitch or drag it out for a longer duration or scream it at the top of our lungs.

> When I do count the clock that tells the time,
> And see the brave day sunk in hideous night,
> When I behold the violet past prime,
> And sable curls all silvered o'er in white,
> When lofty trees I see barren of leaves,
> Which erst from heat did canopy the herd,
> And summer's green all girded up in sheaves
> Borne on the bier with white and bristly beard,
> Then of thy beauty do I question make
> That thou among the wastes of time must go,
> Since sweets and beauties do themselves forsake,
> And die as fast as they see others grow,

And nothing 'gainst time's schythe can make defence
Save breed to brave him when he takes thee hence.

The third quatrain in this text creates a different sort of rhythmic prominence, established on different grounds. In performance we could modify our voices in an attempt to indicate this prominence sonically, but there would be little point. Sonnet 12 can be said in many ways, but the rhythmic prominence of the third quatrain remains none the less.

The rhythmic prominence of this third quatrain is not sonic but semantic, or better *informational*. It is perceived by weighing the contextual significance of the third quatrain with respect to what precedes. This informational prominence is 'coded' in many ways in the text. The most important 'coding' is not tied in any direct way to language structure. It derives from our developing sense of the literary and linguistic pragmatics at this point in the text: the relation between speaker and addressee, the argumentative line, the conceptual relationship between the speaker's observation of natural and cosmic decline in the first two quatrains and his use of these observations in his musings about his 'friend' in the third quatrain. These pragmatic considerations are also supported semantically. The first eight lines overtly indicate 'time-when' and therefore 'set the scene' for the information presented in the third quatrain. This semantic coding is also supported syntactically. The first two quatrains present parallel subordinate clauses that overtly indicate a structural subordination to the main clause that follows in the third quatrain.

As with sonic considerations, however, the additional support that semantics and syntax give to the rhythmic effect of the contextual pragmatics is not necessary to determine rhythmic relations. This linguistic articulation helps to clarify the prominence relationships among the quatrains, but it does not have the final say. Even these semantic and syntactic considerations are effective only as they contribute to the articulation of the larger informational structure of the text. Shakespeare could have placed a full stop after the second quatrain and still preserved a 'rising' movement and a rhythmic equivalence between the first two quatrains and the third (as he and innumerable other sonneteers have done). Notice that considerations of *physical* 'weight' can also be misleading. As one often finds at higher levels of rhythm in poetry, the 'strong' constituent in this rhythmic grouping is physically *contracted* and therefore is physically 'weaker' than its rhythmically 'weak' counterpart.

Given the history of comment on these matters, these hypothetical situations, intermedia analogies and rhythmic intuitions lead to a fairly radical claim: *all prominence relations in our rhythmic grouping of language are primarily informational relations.* In searching for a global criterion to establish grouping segmentation and prominence, readers have little option but to choose an aspect of textual organization that crosscuts linguistic form *per se*. This criterion is meaning, or better, contextual 'significance'. A sonic criterion would be ineffectual at higher levels. A syntactic criterion would be ineffectual at both high and low levels. The only productive choice is a criterion that follows the global teleology of language. Language structures exist so that we can communicate with ourselves and others in context. Consequently, all rhythmic prominence in grouping arises, first and foremost, from an assessment of the rhythmical organization of this global teleology. As Tynianov would have it, poetry is not 'rhythmicalized material'. It is 'material in rhythm'. In form, our grouping responses to verse are levelled hierarchies. In substance, they represent our response to the ordering of a text's *informational* prominences.

Perceptions of informational prominence are a central part of our rhythmic response to verse, and it has been largely the lack of a general theory of informational prominence in language that has prevented the development of a workable theory of verse grouping.

An adequate treatment of grouping prominence demands that we have more than a theory of syntax. It demands that we have a theory of discourse prominence. This theory would not describe the text's grammar; it would specify how we infer informational prominence (at all levels) from such a grammatical description.

Needless to say, this is no easy demand. In fact, to my knowledge, no such theory exists. None the less, as I hope to detail shortly, recent work in phonology, syntax, text linguistics and literary criticism has had enough to say about informational prominence at various levels of discourse to permit us to suggest the direction that such a theory might take.

The major preconditions of a theory of discourse prominence are that it be *top-down*, *pragmatic* and *linear*. All informational inference is strongly conditioned by the reader's developing awareness of the over-arching teleology of the text and the informational means that the poet is employing to articulate that teleology. The local evaluation of information, then, is always relative to an evaluation of its global articulation (it is a top-down process). The global articulation of information always extends beyond language (it is pragmatic). And the relative prominence of a structure at a given point is always relative to the prominence of structures that have preceded and will follow (these judgements are linear). The major implication of these preconditions is that all grouping response depends on a 'reading' of the text, in the rich, literary sense of 'reading' (i.e. the reader's assessment of the poet's global intentions with respect to theme, voice, audience, setting, poetic argument, imagery, allusion and so forth).

Given these preliminaries, the question we need to ask is: How do poems characteristically realize their informational teleologies in rhythmic form?

The answer that I would like to suggest is that most grouping peaks in a poem represent some sort of *informational containment* of (1) subordinate peaks in the grouping structure as a whole, and (2) weak units in their own group. Comparable to structural notes in music, grouping peaks in verse encompass/entail/imply/etc. the informational movement of their associated grouping valleys and therefore, also like structural notes in music, serve as points of informational stability. Conversely, grouping valleys and subordinate peaks, like grace notes and other structural ornamentation in music, represent informational elaborations of their associated grouping peaks, elaborations that 'play out' the informational substance of their associated and superordinate peaks with further meanings and wordings (i.e. qualifications, exemplifications, renamings, analogical extensions, etc.). Let's call this principle grouping preference rule (GPR) 1.

> GPR1 (Information): Prefer a grouping peak that informationally contains other groups.

Given that grouping is largely a top-down process, this amounts to the common claim that most poems have a semiotic core (a 'matrix', 'theme', etc.) whose structure is 'played out' ('modelled', 'projected', etc.) in an organized way into the hierarchical structure of the text at lower levels.[12] This globally 'centroidal' organization is what gives poetry much of its characteristic unity and formal 'monumentality'. While prose texts tend to articulate their arguments with a looser semiotic and formal structure, the semic content of a rhythmic text tends to be reproduced synonymically, hyponymically and antonymically throughout the poem. Forms and meanings chosen at one point in the poem tend to 'overdetermine' the possibilities of formal and semantic articulation at other points in the poem. Semiotic and formal choices that are usually presented paradigmatically as alternative expressive choices are 'projected' syntagmatically into the linear flow of the text. The result is a complex network of formal and semiotic 'equivalences' at various levels of structure. Arhythmic texts tend to begin, move forward, and end; rhythmic texts tend to say the same thing (or related things) over and over, and in the same (or related) forms, saturating the textual space with formal and semiotic relationships which explore both the formal limits for realizing 'equivalent' sayings and the semantic limits for re-presenting 'equivalent' forms.

This semiotically 'centroidal' organization of rhythmic discourse at high levels presents the clearest instance of a grouping peak in language, and we can use this instance to characterize the textual sources of grouping peaks at lower levels. In general, grouping peaks look towards the centre of the text, its semiotic core. At all levels of structure, grouping peaks represent semiotic 'centrality', while grouping valleys indicate less 'central' informational elaboration. Throughout a grouping structure, textual segments of relatively equivalent informational 'centrality' are grouped and compared at the same level. Groups that represent more 'central' information appear at high levels. Groups that represent more 'peripheral' information appear at lower levels.

4.3.1.1.1 Grouping reduction

It is largely GPR1 (Information) that makes possible grouping *reduction*; therefore, it might be appropriate to introduce reductional analysis here.

As mentioned briefly in Chapter 3, a *reduction* is an analytical technique used in music theory to reveal the layers of elaboration within a phrasal hierarchy (either grouping or prolongation). Applied to linguistic grouping, a reduction begins with the text as a whole and repeatedly rewrites the text so that each rewrite removes all of the 'weak' constituents at exactly one level of grouping elaboration, beginning with the lowest level and proceeding to the level of the text as whole. Given GPR1 (Information), each rewrite should 'read' as a 'reduced' version of the original. Each rewrite removes only rhythmically parallel units and leaves all parallel units;

therefore it preserves the levelled form of the original, a remainder that, by GPR1, should 'contain' both the semiotic gist and general rhythmic shape of the original. The result is a series of rhythmic 'sketches' that isolate the contributions of individual levels of phrasal elaboration to the rhythmic movement of the whole.

Rhythmic reduction can be a useful heuristic for 'validating' the claims of a complex phrasal analysis. By isolating individual levels of elaboration, reductional sketches free the analyser from the burden of keeping all of the levels in a phrasal analysis explicitly in mind when working with an individual level, and by translating the effects of individual levels into a 'natural' textual form, these sketches convert subtle judgements of rhythmic prominence into judgements of textual modelling (i.e. same text? or different text?).

There are some difficulties with translating this musical technique to language, but these can be overcome with minor adjustments.

The most pervasive difficulty is that reductional sketches are still *rhythmic* sketches, not linguistic summaries/outlines. Therefore, some levels of reduction might not produce well-formed texts. Music, one might argue, is essentially rhythmic. Therefore, most reductions of music should produce something musical. Language is not essentially rhythmic, however; therefore, a rhythmic sketch of a text might not read like a well-formed text. As I have argued throughout, the notion 'information' referred to in GPR1 (Information) is not a syntactic notion. At some levels, informational articulation in language crosscuts syntax. Therefore, a reduction that preserves informational relations can disturb syntactic relations, and with this disturbance, the coherence of a reductional rewrite.

A second problem is that GPR1 is not a constraint on well-formedness but just a preference, and just one of many preferences. Grouping response is also subject to the constraints on grouping well-formedness and a number of other grouping preference rules. Therefore all grouping peaks need not informationally 'contain' subordinate articulation in a grouping structure. For instance, at the lowest levels of structure, rhythmic grouping operates on the internal structure of syntactic phrases. Even at this level, grouping is heavily conditioned by informational considerations, but the notion of 'containment' is no longer relevant (or at least not obviously so).

A final problem is that, unlike music, syntactic structures in language are often (1) pervasively elliptical, and (2) explicitly connected. In syntax, 'old' information is conventionally represented in reduced form (e.g. with pronouns or not at all), while 'new' information is often explicitly linked to the 'old' information that has preceded with conjunctions, deictics, conjunctive adverbials and other formal 'connectors'. Therefore, if a rhythmic reduction disturbs these explicit markers of discourse connection, it might not 'read' like a well-formed text.

Considering our purposes here, these difficulties are not overwhelming, however. The first problem can be solved by beginning a rhythmic reduction at a level where minimal syntactic relations are still maintained. In most of the reductions in this book, I adopt the *intonational unit* (or slightly above) as the lowest level. The second problem can be solved by checking any odd-sounding reductions for complicating influences from other rhythmic considerations. The third problem can be solved by adding and subtracting connecting material in reductional sketches, as this connecting material is needed to maintain syntactic and discourse coherence. In reductional analyses in this book, I will indicate changes in connective material with brackets '[ ]'.

A reduction explores/validates a complete grouping analysis; therefore a thorough illustration of the method here is premature (until the other grouping preference rules have been enumerated). None the less, if the reader can tolerate an incomplete motivation of the structures claimed in the analysis, a short example will illustrate both the analytical power of the technique and the support it gives to GPR1 (Information).

Consider section 3 of Whitman's 'When Lilacs Last in the Dooryard Bloom'd' (lines 12–17).

> In the dooryard fronting an old farm-house near the white-wash'd palings,
> Stands the lilac-bush tall-growing with heart-shaped leaves of rich green,
> With many a pointed blossom rising delicate, with the perfume strong I love,
> With every leaf a miracle – and from this bush in the dooryard,
> With delicate-color'd blossoms and heart-shaped leaves of rich green,
> A sprig with its flower I break.

At the highest level, this section breaks into two groups, following the contours of the two conjuncts of its compound sentence.

> In the dooryard fronting an old farm-house near the white-wash'd palings,
> Stands the lilac-bush tall-growing with heart-shaped leaves of rich green,
> With many a pointed blossom rising delicate, with the perfume strong I love,
> With every leaf a miracle –
>
>   and from this bush in the dooryard,
> With delicate-color'd blossoms and heart-shaped leaves of rich green,
> A sprig with its flower I break.

Within this two-part structure, we might argue that the second group informationally 'contains' the first group, and therefore that grouping contours at this level 'rise' with a ws (iambic) shape. The first conjunct introduces the lilac-bush, its various 'fruits' (blossoms, leaves, etc.), and the speaker's evaluative reaction to these 'fruits'. The second conjunct repeats this introduction and reaction (in many of the same words and phrases: *bush, in the dooryard, delicate, blossoms, heart-shaped leaves of rich green*) and presents the major focus of the section: the ritual 'breaking' of the lilac 'sprig'. This ritual breaking is the thematic centre of the section. The breaking of the lilac sprig (a symbol of eternal spring, the masculine erotic, and the poet's love) is the first action by the speaker in the poem and harbingers the 'giving' of the sprig to Lincoln's coffin (and all coffins) in sections 6 and 7, which in turn harbingers the symbolic death carol of the hermit thrush to the fallen Western star that occupies most of the body of the poem.

> Here, coffin that slowly passes,
> I give you my sprig of lilac.
> (Nor for you, for one alone,
> Blossoms and branches green to coffins all I bring,
> For fresh as the morning, thus would I chant a song for
>   you sane and sacred death.
>
> (44–48)

At a third level, I read six units, three in each of the two 'halves' of the text we have just isolated at the level above.

> In the dooryard fronting an old farm-house near the white-wash'd palings,

> Stands the lilac-bush tall-growing with heart-shaped leaves of rich green,
>
> With many a pointed blossom rising delicate, with the perfume strong I love,
> With every leaf a miracle –
>
> and from this bush in the dooryard,
> With delicate-color'd blossoms and heart-shaped leaves of rich green,
>
> A sprig with its flower
>
> I break.

Within these triplets, I read the middle constituents as strong, yielding two wsw (amphibrachic) contours. In the first triple, the middle constituent presents the mandatory elements in the first clause (subject: *the lilac-bush*; verb: *stands*; subject complement: *tall-growing*), together with a closely related adverbial enumerating thematically important attributes of the lilac-bush (i.e. the *heart-shaped* leaves and their rich *green*). The preceding and following constituents place the bush in space (*In . . . near . . .*) and elaborate on the lilac's attributes (*With . . . with . . . with . . .*). Therefore, I read these constituents as subordinate. In the second triple, the central constituent presents the focus of the passage as a whole, the lilac sprig, while the preceding and following constituents present the sources of the sprig, the bush itself and the speaker's action. The prominence of *A sprig with its flower* with respect to *I break* is also heightened by its size and by the inverted syntax, which presents *A sprig with its flower* syntactically as a marked topic. The structure as a whole is also stabilized by the repeating amphibrachic pattern between the two triples and by the chiastic morphology of this repeating pattern. The first triple has a heavily weighted final weak segment; the second triple has a heavily weighted initial weak segment.

> With many a pointed blossom rising delicate, with the perfume strong I love,
> With every leaf a miracle –
>
> and from this bush in the dooryard,
> With delicate-color'd blossoms and heart-shaped leaves of rich green,

GROUPING PREFERENCE RULES   205

As we will see, the internal morphology of these weighted segments is also parallel in span and partially parallel (and partially chiastic) in prominence. This further stabilizes this reading.

At the next level I read eight units, with this level adding one local binary elaboration in each of the weighted weak constituents at the level above.

> In the dooryard fronting an old farm-house
> near the white-wash'd palings,/
>
> Stands the lilac-bush tall-growing
> with heart-shaped leaves of rich green,/
>
> With many a pointed blossom rising delicate, ⎤
> with the perfume strong I love, / ⎦ w ⎤
>
> With every leaf a miracle – ⎤ s ⎦
> ⎦
>
> and from this bush in the dooryard, ⎤ s ⎤
> ⎦ ⎦
>
> With delicate-color'd blossoms ⎤ w
> and heart-shaped leaves of rich green,/ ⎦
>
> A sprig with its flower
>
> I break.

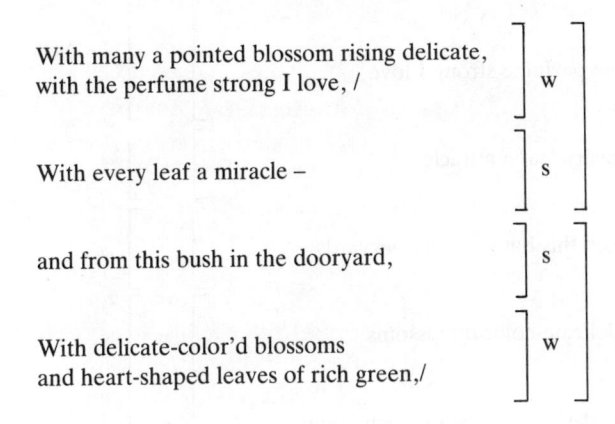

As I just intimated, these local elaborations are parallel duples, chiastic in inclination. The first duple rises in an evaluative crescendo from the 'lovely perfume' of the lilac's blossoms to its 'miraculous' leaves. The second duple falls from a mention of the bush to a reiteration of its qualities. The other units at this level remain unelaborated.

Finally, at the lowest level I will analyse here, I read twelve units, eight of which are organized into duple units at the next level and four of which remain singles.

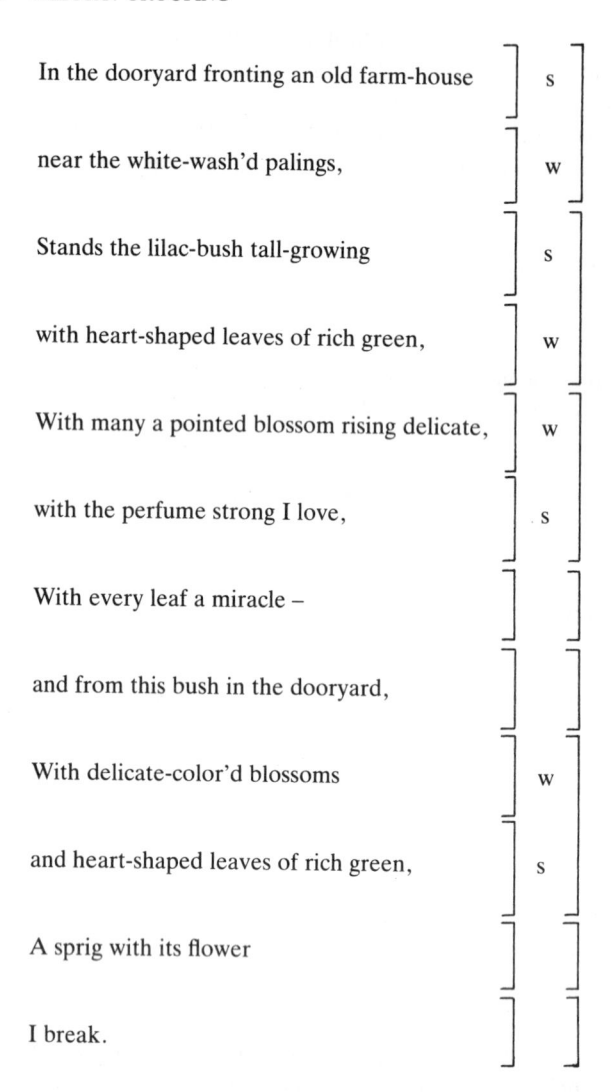

In the dooryard fronting an old farm-house] s]
near the white-wash'd palings,] w]
Stands the lilac-bush tall-growing] s]
with heart-shaped leaves of rich green,] w]
With many a pointed blossom rising delicate,] w]
with the perfume strong I love,] s]
With every leaf a miracle –
and from this bush in the dooryard,
With delicate-color'd blossoms] w]
and heart-shaped leaves of rich green,] s]
A sprig with its flower
I break.

The first two duples fall, the second two rise. In the first duple, the spatial placement of the lilacs (*In* . . .) is further elaborated (*near* . . .). In the second duple, the main elements of the first clause (*Stands* . . .) are elaborated with an adverbial (*with* . . .). And the last two duples both rise from the lilac's delicate blossoms to its more potent qualities: its strong, lovely perfume and its green, 'heart-shaped' leaves.

GROUPING PREFERENCE RULES 207

This level completes the grouping structure to a level sufficient to illustrate the workings and heuristic power of reductional analysis. The grouping structure we have read is the following:

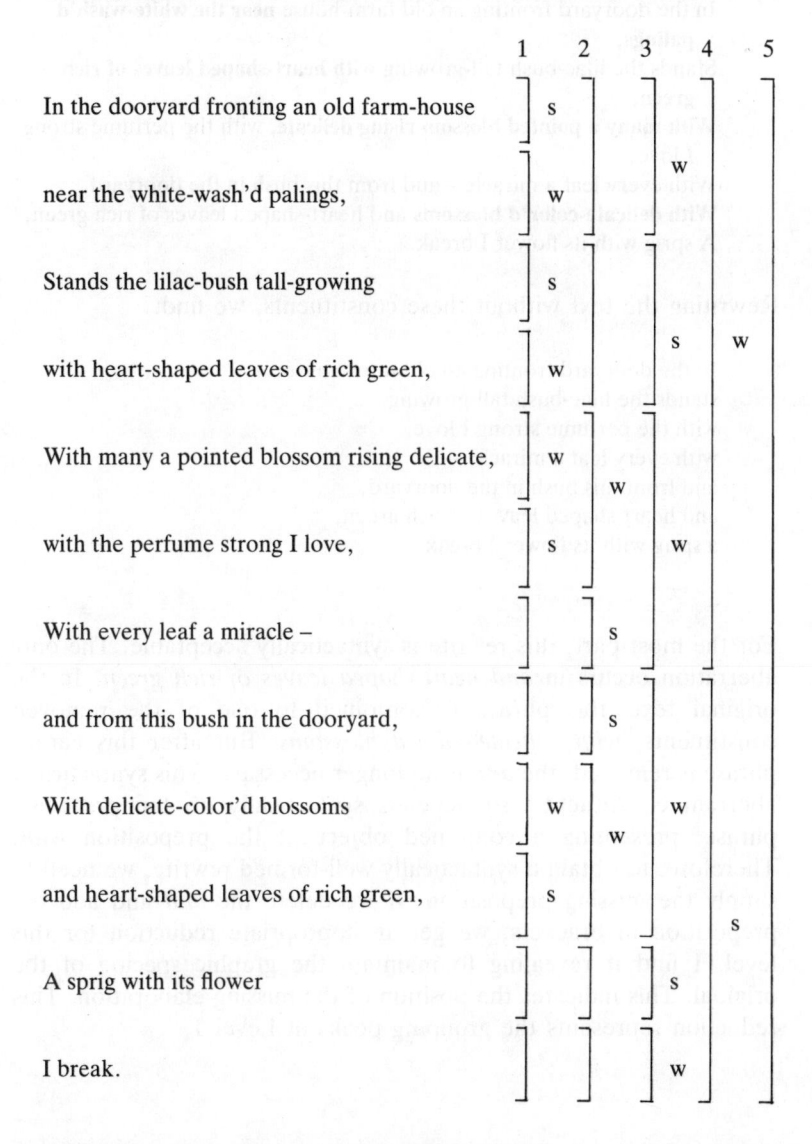

	1	2	3	4	5
In the dooryard fronting an old farm-house	s				
				w	
near the white-wash'd palings,	w				
Stands the lilac-bush tall-growing	s				
				s	w
with heart-shaped leaves of rich green,	w				
With many a pointed blossom rising delicate,	w				
		w			
with the perfume strong I love,	s		w		
With every leaf a miracle –		s			
and from this bush in the dooryard,		s			
With delicate-color'd blossoms		w		w	
			w		
and heart-shaped leaves of rich green,		s			
					s
A sprig with its flower			s		
I break.			w		

To construct a reduction for this grouping structure, we begin at the lowest level and rewrite the text, removing the weak constituents at that level. At the lowest level we have analysed, these constituents are marked below in **bold print**.

> In the dooryard fronting an old farm-house **near the white-wash'd palings**,
> Stands the lilac-bush tall-growing **with heart-shaped leaves of rich green**,
> **With many a pointed blossom rising delicate**, with the perfume strong I love,
> With every leaf a miracle – and from this bush in the dooryard,
> **With delicate-color'd blossoms** and heart-shaped leaves of rich green,
> A sprig with its flower I break.

Rewriting the text without these constituents, we find:

> In the dooryard fronting an old farm-house,
> stands the lilac-bush tall-growing,
> with the perfume strong I love,
> with every leaf a miracle –
> and from this bush in the dooryard,
> and heart-shaped leaves of rich green,
> a sprig with its flower I break.

For the most part, this rewrite is syntactically acceptable. The only aberration occurs in *and heart-shaped leaves of rich green*. In the original text, this phrase is conjoined to one of the removed constituents, *with delicate-color'd blossoms*. But after this earlier phrase is removed, the *and* is no longer necessary. This syntactically aberrant constituent also depends syntactically on the preceding phrase, presenting a conjoined object of the preposition *with*. Therefore, to obtain a syntactically well-formed rewrite, we need to supply the missing preposition. If we delete the *and* and add the preposition in brackets, we get an appropriate reduction for this level. I find it revealing to maintain the graphic spacing of the original. This indicates the position of the missing elaboration. This reduction represents the grouping peaks at Level 1.

Minus dependent units at Level 1

> In the dooryard fronting an old farm-house
> Stands the lilac-bush tall-growing
>   with the perfume
>   strong I love,
> With every leaf a miracle – and from this bush in the dooryard,
> [With]   heart-shaped leaves of rich
>   green,
> A sprig with its flower I break.

The second reduction operates upon the first, removing weak constituents at the next highest level. Within the first reduction there are two weak constituents at Level 2. I again mark these constituents in **bold print**.

> In the dooryard fronting an old farm-house
> Stands the lilac-bush tall-growing
>   **with the perfume**
>   **strong I love,**
> With every leaf a miracle – and from this bush in the dooryard,
> **[With]**   **heart-shaped leaves of rich**
>   **green,**
> A sprig with its flower I break.

Removing these constituents, we obtain a syntactically well-formed and therefore appropriate reduction for this level. This reduction represents the grouping peaks at Level 2.

Minus dependent units at Level 2

> In the dooryard fronting an old farm-house
> Stands the lilac-bush tall-growing
>
>
> With every leaf a miracle – and from this bush in the dooryard,
>
>
> A sprig with its flower I break.

The third reduction operates on the second, removing weak constituents at the next highest level (Level 3). At Level 3, there are *four* weak constituents. Again, I mark these in **bold print**.

> **In the dooryard fronting an old farm-house**
> Stands the lilac-bush tall-growing
>
> **With every leaf a miracle – and from this bush in the dooryard,**
>
> A sprig with its flower **I break**.

Removing these constituents, we obtain the following.

> Stands the lilac-bush tall-growing
> A sprig with its flower

Again, this rewrite is elliptical in its syntax. The difficulty is that *A sprig with its flower* is the direct object of the final clause in the passage, but the subject and verb in the clause (*I break*), being rhythmically subordinate at this level, have been deleted. Again, to obtain an appropriate reduction, we need to supply (some semblance of) these mandatory syntactic constituents. Doing this, we obtain an appropriate reduction. This reduction represents the grouping peaks at Level 3.

Minus dependent units at Level 3

> Stands the lilac-bush tall-growing
>
>
> A sprig with its flower [I break].

The final reduction operates upon this two-constituent unit, removing the weak unit at Level 4, *Stands the lilac-bush tall-growing*. This final reduction yields the grouping peak of the passage as a whole (i.e. Level 5).

Minus dependent units at Level 4

A sprig with its flower [I break.]

Reductional analysis reveals with particular clarity the shape of the multilevelled rhythmic organization of this passage. The first reduction lets us appreciate the rhythmic contribution of the parallel and chiastic articulation within the weighted middle of the passage. The second reduction lets us appreciate the rhythmic contribution of the once-repeated, lilting movement of the passage at Level 3. The third reduction isolates for our appreciation the climactic and symmetrical structure of the passage as a whole. And the fourth reduction isolates the grouping peak of the passage, *A sprig with its flower [I break]*, and its relatively late (climactic) positioning.

4.3.1.1.2   High discourse levels

Textual information is articulated with different means and in different canonical patterns at different levels of structure. Therefore, GPR1 (Information) has many textual sources. A short survey of some of these canonical patterns might be useful at this point.

While I can cite no statistical evidence, it is my experience that many of our canonical English texts present alternating layers of rising and falling grouping patterns. At high narrative levels, most poems present consistently rising grouping contours. At low narrative levels, grouping contours often fall. At high syntactic levels, contours usually rise. At low syntactic levels, contours again often fall. At high intonational levels, contours again usually rise. And at low intonational levels, contours again often fall (although rising movement is largely predominant throughout intonational levels).

At the highest level, information in the text almost always rises towards some point of thematic centrality and generality. In essence, Barbara Herrnstein Smith's theory of closure is a well-developed theory of the formal characteristics of textual peaks. As Smith claims, textual peaks usually present types of informational absolutes: references to elemental experiences (life, death, sleep, love, beauty, truth, time, etc.), universal quantifiers (*all, never, ever, everywhere, everything, always, none,* etc.), antitheses, paradoxes, superlatives (*most, best, worst,* etc.), timeless conditions (equations, definitions, etc.) and so forth. These closural forms usually appear towards the end of the text, coinciding with the arc of prolongational anticipation. For example, the universal quantifier and modal in the title and last line of Frost's 'Nothing Gold Can Stay' are classically closural.

To work through another example, consider 'Spring' by Edna St. Vincent Millay.

> To what purpose, April, do you return again?
> Beauty is not enough.
> You can no longer quiet me with the redness
> Of little leaves opening stickily.
> I know what I know.
> The sun is hot on my neck as I observe
> The spikes of the crocus.
> The smell of the earth is good.
> It is apparent that there is no death.
> But what does that signify?
> Not only under ground are the brains of men
> Eaten by maggots.
> Life in itself
> Is nothing,
> An empty cup, a flight of uncarpeted stairs.
> It is not enough that yearly, down this hill,
> April
> Comes like an idiot, babbling and strewing flowers.

In 'Spring' the direction of grouping contours at high narrative levels follows the informational movement of the text from assertion (weak) to reason (strong), observation (weak) to conclusion (strong).

On the highest level, 'Spring' is an expanding duple, rising from a jolting rejection of the beauty of Spring to a justification for that rejection.

GROUPING PREFERENCE RULES 213

> To what purpose, April, do you return again?
> Beauty is not enough.
> You can no longer quiet me with the redness   w
> Of little leaves opening stickily.
> I know what I know.

> The sun is hot on my neck as I observe
> The spikes of the crocus.
> The smell of the earth is good.
> It is apparent that there is no death.
> But what does that signify?
> Not only under ground are the brains of men   s
> Eaten by maggots.
> Life in itself
> Is nothing,
> An empty cup, a flight of uncarpeted stairs.
> It is not enough that yearly, down this hill,
> April
> Comes like an idiot, babbling and strewing flowers.

At a second level, the asymmetrically large strong constituent at the highest level also presents a rising duple structure, this time proceeding from a rejection of the significance of vernal sensuousness and physical rebirth to a justification for this rejection.

> The sun is hot on my neck as I observe
> The spikes of the crocus.   w
> The smell of the earth is good.
> But what does that signify?

> Not only under ground are the brains of men
> Eaten by maggots.
> Life in itself
> Is nothing,   s
> An empty cup, a flight of uncarpeted stairs.
> It is not enough that yearly, down this hill,
> April
> Comes like an idiot, babbling and strewing flowers.

However, as in many texts, low narrative levels in 'Spring' have more varied movements. The opening five lines move in two levels of falling duples. The speaker's overt rejection of April is presented first in a bluntly confrontational rhetorical question followed by a negative. Compared with this confrontational and rhetorically indirect opening, the more direct and declarative statements that follow, as Christensen and Christensen would have it, 'pirouette' within the opening statement, particularizing and explaining.

To what purpose, April, do you return again?
Beauty is not enough. ⎫ s

You can no longer quiet me with the redness
Of little leaves opening stickily.
I know what I know. ⎫ w

But the constituents in this duple are also clearly duples, and with similarly falling contours. As in the poem as a whole, the speaker's overt rejections of spring's motives and powers are followed by 'explanations', but here these 'explanations' are brief, general and cryptic. Therefore they remain informationally weak. The contracted lengths of these 'explanations' also contribute to their relative weakness.

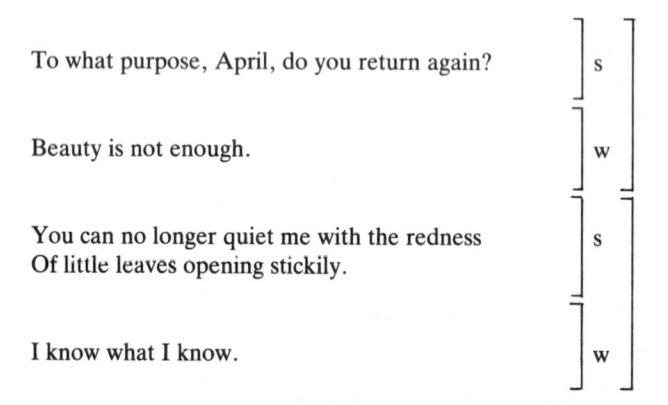

To what purpose, April, do you return again? ⎫ s

Beauty is not enough. ⎫ w

You can no longer quiet me with the redness
Of little leaves opening stickily. ⎫ s

I know what I know. ⎫ w

The weak constituent at the second level of structure in the poem forms a *rising* duple, however. The speaker concedes the sensuous presence of spring and its cyclical triumph over death, but again bluntly rejects the significance of the concession with another rhetorical question.

The sun is hot on my neck as I observe	
The spikes of the crocus.	
The smell of the earth is good.	w
It is apparent that there is no death.	
But what does that signify?	s

Given the relative balance in the rhythmic quatrain in the first five lines, this duple division is skewed both structurally and physically, concentrating rhythmic force on the question ('But what . . .'). At the next lower level, the weak constituent in this duple is a triple, while the strong constituent is a single. The triple in the weak constituent also rises. Two parallel observations of spring's sensuous presence lead to a conclusion (the rejection of hibernal death).

The sun is hot on my neck as I observe	w	
The spikes of the crocus.		
		w
The smell of the earth is good.	w	
It is apparent that there is no death.	s	

The strong constituent at the second level (the concluding lines of the poem) also continues this triple movement, but at the third (rather than fourth) level of structure.

216 THEORY: GROUPING

Not only under ground are the brains of men   ⎫
Eaten by maggots.   ⎬ w

Life in itself   ⎫
Is nothing,   ⎬ s
An empty cup, a flight of uncarpeted stairs.

It is not enough that yearly, down this hill,   ⎫
April   ⎬ w
Comes like an idiot, babbling and strewing flowers.

There is considerable informational balance in these three final constituents at Level 3. All three statements are informationally climactic, revelatory. Each has its own shocking truth and imagistic strength. And each provides the same 'ultimate' motivation for the rejection of spring's sensuous rebirth: the spiritual primacy of human existence. In terms of closure, the second constituent is classically absolute, universal, timeless, unqualified, aphoristic. The flanking constituents are also significant as well, however: the stark portrait of spiritual death/decay in the first constituent and the macabrely ineffectual portrait of vernal 'idiocy' in the final unit. The progressively expanding lower levels and a general preference for end-focus also tend to favour the final constituent. But the statement in this final constituent, at least in part, is a restatement of what has preceded (i.e. 'The sun is hot . . . . But what does that signify?'). If I am forced to make a choice from slim differences, I might choose to read this final triple with medial strength. This reading balances human spiritual torment against the ineffectuality of spring to alleviate that torment, with these two flanking the physical non-presence of life, vividly rendered in the image of the uncarpeted stairs. The 'reading' above is represented in the following grouping structure.

GROUPING PREFERENCE RULES   217

	Level 5	Level 4	Level 3	Level 2	Level 1

To what purpose, April, do you return again?   — s

Beauty is not enough.   — w | s

You can no longer quiet me with the redness
Of little leaves opening stickily.   — s · w | | | w

I know what I know.   — w

The sun is hot on my neck as I observe
The spikes of the crocus.   — w · w

The smell of the earth is good.   — w | | w

It is apparent that there is no death.   — s

But what does that signify?   — s | s

Not only under ground are the brains of men
Eaten by maggots.   — w | | | s

Life in itself
Is nothing,
An empty cup, a flight of uncarpeted stairs.   — s | s

It is not enough that yearly,
    down this hill,
April
Comes like an idiot,
    babbling and strewing flowers.   — w

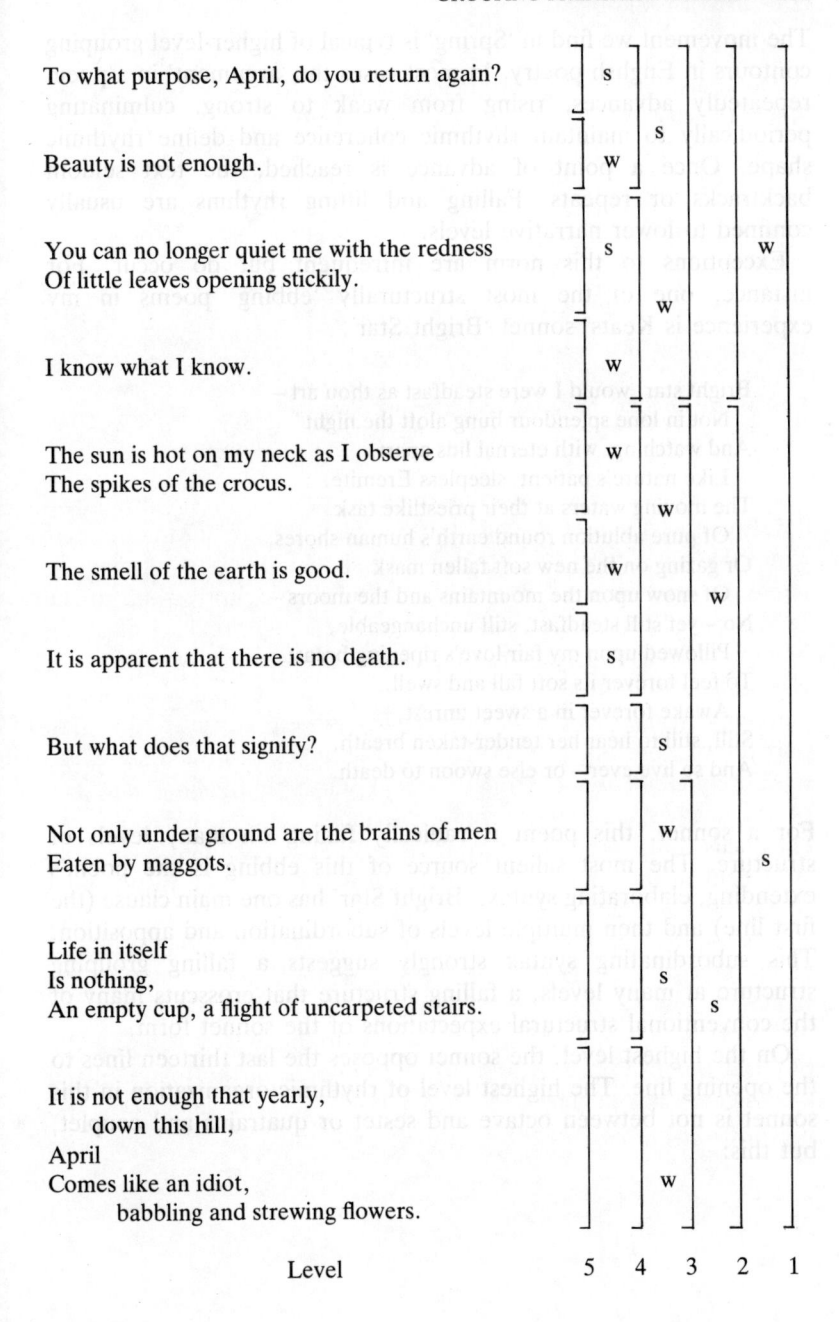

Level   5   4   3   2   1

The movement we find in 'Spring' is typical of higher-level grouping contours in English poetry. In most cases the 'argument' in a poem repeatedly advances, rising from weak to strong, culminating periodically to maintain rhythmic coherence and define rhythmic shape. Once a point of advance is reached, the text seldom backtracks or repeats. Falling and lilting rhythms are usually confined to lower narrative levels.

Exceptions to this norm are infrequent but do occur. For instance, one of the most structurally 'ebbing' poems in my experience is Keats' sonnet 'Bright Star'.

> Bright star, would I were steadfast as thou art –
>   Not in lone splendour hung aloft the night
> And watching, with eternal lids apart,
>   Like nature's patient, sleepless Eremite,
> The moving waters at their priestlike task
>   Of pure ablution round earth's human shores,
> Or gazing on the new soft fallen mask
>   Of snow upon the mountains and the moors –
> No – yet still steadfast, still unchangeable,
>   Pillowed upon my fair love's ripening breast,
> To feel forever its soft fall and swell,
>   Awake forever in a sweet unrest,
> Still, still to hear her tender-taken breath,
> And so live ever – or else swoon to death.

For a sonnet, this poem is radically falling on many levels of structure. The most salient source of this ebbing is the poem's extending, elaborating syntax. 'Bright Star' has one main clause (the first line) and then multiple levels of subordination and apposition. This subordinating syntax strongly suggests a falling grouping structure at many levels, a falling structure that crosscuts many of the conventional structural expectations of the sonnet form.

On the highest level, the sonnet opposes the last thirteen lines to the opening line. The highest level of rhythmic organization in this sonnet is not between octave and sestet or quatrains and couplet, but this:

Bright star, would I were steadfast as thou art –] s

    Not in lone splendour hung aloft the night
And watching, with eternal lids apart,
    Like nature's patient, sleepless Eremite,
The moving waters at their priestlike task
    Of pure ablution round earth's human shores,
Or gazing on the new soft fallen mask   w
    Of snow upon the mountains and the moors –
No – yet still steadfast, still unchangeable,
    Pillowed upon my fair love's ripening breast,
To feel forever its soft fall and swell,
    Awake forever in a sweet unrest,
Still, still to hear her tender-taken breath,
And so live ever – or else swoon to death.

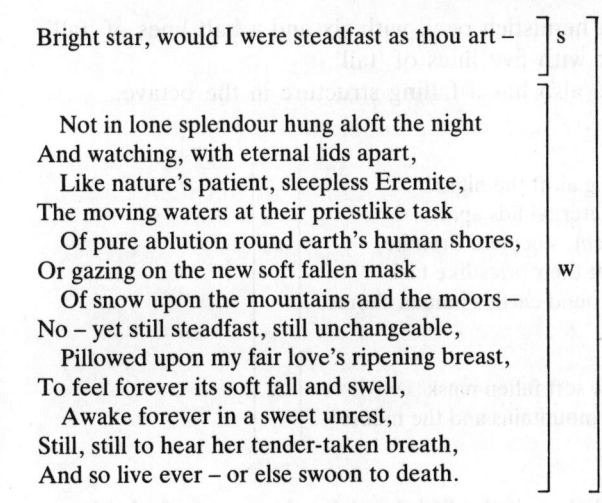

This divisioning is wildly skewed, especially considering its ebbing, strong-to-weak movement.

At a third level of organization (I omit Level 2 for the moment), there is also a highly asymmetrical, consistently falling structure, this time running parallel in octave and sestet.

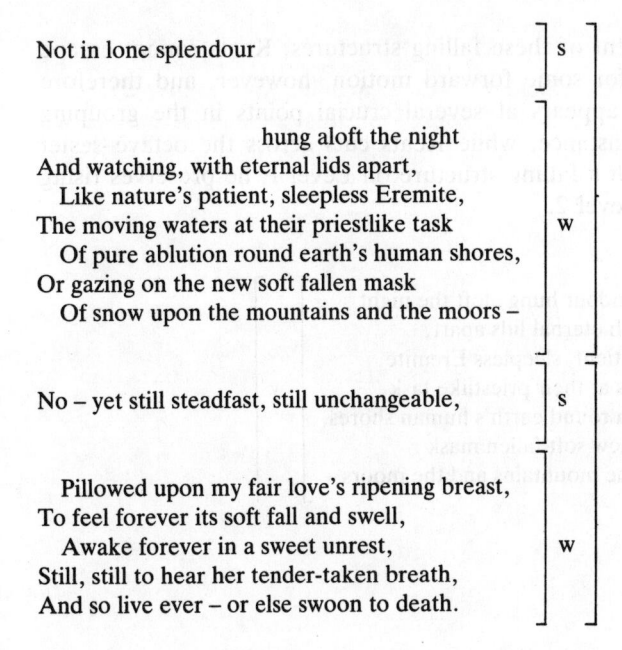

Not in lone splendour   s

               hung aloft the night
And watching, with eternal lids apart,
    Like nature's patient, sleepless Eremite,
The moving waters at their priestlike task   w
    Of pure ablution round earth's human shores,
Or gazing on the new soft fallen mask
    Of snow upon the mountains and the moors –

No – yet still steadfast, still unchangeable,   s

    Pillowed upon my fair love's ripening breast,
To feel forever its soft fall and swell,
    Awake forever in a sweet unrest,   w
Still, still to hear her tender-taken breath,
And so live ever – or else swoon to death.

These units pair a hemistich peak with six and a half lines of 'fall', then a lineal peak with five lines of 'fall'.

The fourth level also has a falling structure in the octave.

>   hung aloft the night
> And watching, with eternal lids apart,
>   Like nature's patient, sleepless Eremite,
> The moving waters at their priestlike task
>   Of pure ablution round earth's human shores,   s
>
> Or gazing on the new soft fallen mask
>   Of snow upon the mountains and the moors –   w

And the sixth level (I omit the fifth level for the moment) also has a falling structure, this time a balanced echo of line against line.

> To feel forever its soft fall and swell,   s
>
> Awake forever in a sweet unrest,   w

Despite the extent of these falling structures, Keats cannot escape the imperative for some forward motion, however, and therefore rising grouping appears at several crucial points in the grouping hierarchy. For instance, while Keats cuts across the octave–sestet organization with a falling structure on Level 1, he preserves rising movement on Level 2.

>   Not in lone splendour hung aloft the night
> And watching, with eternal lids apart,
>   Like nature's patient, sleepless Eremite,
> The moving waters at their priestlike task   w
>   Of pure ablution round earth's human shores,
> Or gazing on the new soft fallen mask
>   Of snow upon the mountains and the moors –

> No – yet still steadfast, still unchangeable,
>   Pillowed upon my fair love's ripening breast,
> To feel forever its soft fall and swell,
>   Awake forever in a sweet unrest,
> Still, still to hear her tender-taken breath,
> And so live ever – or else swoon to death. } s

And while the poem has falling structures at Level 3, Keats reverses the last unit on Level 4 to a rising movement to achieve closure. The grouping rises here from position ('pillowed upon') to result/purpose ('to feel . . .', 'to hear . . .').

> Pillowed upon my fair love's ripening breast, } w
>
> To feel forever its soft fall and swell,
>   Awake forever in a sweet unrest,
> Still, still to hear her tender-taken breath,
> And so live ever – or else swoon to death. } s

This reversal is supported further at Levels 5 and 6. The semantic intensification 'Still, still' in the couplet suggests that it be read as stronger than its parallel in lines 11–12.

> To feel forever its soft fall and swell,
>   Awake forever in a sweet unrest, } w
>
> Still, still to hear her tender-taken breath,
> And so live ever – or else swoon to death. } s

And the last line, with its universal quantifiers ('ever'), thematic absolutes ('live', 'death') and resultative semantics ('and so'), suggests that it be read as stronger than the first line in the couplet.

222 THEORY: GROUPING

Still, still to hear her tender-taken breath,   ] w

And so live ever – or else swoon to death.   ] s

This reading yields the following grouping structure at these high levels.

Bright star, would I . . . as thou art –

Not in lone splendour

                hung aloft the night
and watching, with eternal lids apart,
Like nature's patient, sleepless Eremite,
The moving waters at their priestlike task
Of pure ablution round earth's human shores,

Or gazing on the new soft fallen mask
Of snow upon the mountains and the moors –

No – yet still steadfast, still unchangeable,

Pillowed upon my fair love's ripening breast,

To feel forever its soft fall and swell,

Awake forever in a sweet unrest,

Still, still to hear her tender-taken breath,

And so live ever – or else swoon to death.

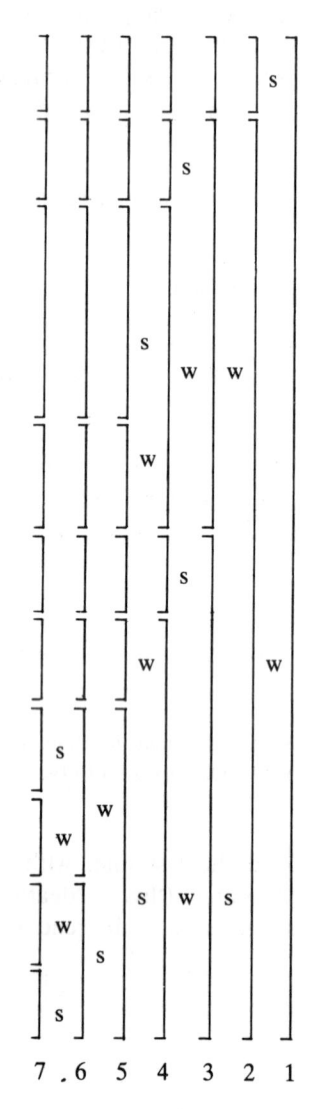

                                        7 .6   5   4   3   2   1

GROUPING PREFERENCE RULES 223

Lilting contours also displace the textual peak from final position. Therefore, they are also rare at high levels. A possible candidate might be the following from e.e. Cummings.

> be unto love as rain is unto colour;create
> me gradually(or as these emerging now
> hills invent the air)
>   breathe simply my each how
> my trembling where my still unvisible when.   Wait.
>
> if i am not heart,because at least i beat
> – always think i am gone like a sun which must go
> sometimes, to make an earth gladly seem firm for you:
> remember(as those pearls more than surround this throat)
>
> i wear your dearest fears beyond their ceaselessness
>
> (nor has a syllable of the heart's eager dim
> enormous language loss or gain from blame or praise)
> but many a thought shall die which was not born of dream
> while wings welcome the year and trees dance(and i guess
>
> though wish and world go down,one poem yet shall swim

In my reading, this poem peaks at the centrally placed, visually isolated *i wear your dearest fears beyond their ceaselessness*. The rest of the poem generalizes the speaker's initial entreaty and confession, but more as a parenthetical or afterthought. At the highest level we might see the poem as duple, breaking after line 9. But this duple is falling, and at a second level the text's three-part structure has a lilting, strong–medial contour.

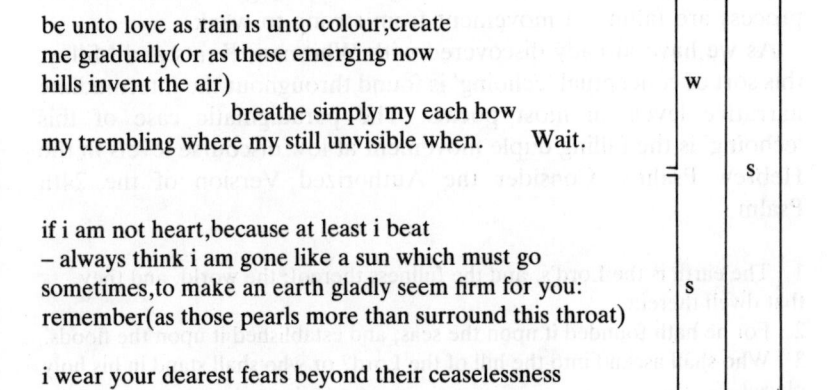

> be unto love as rain is unto colour;create
> me gradually(or as these emerging now
> hills invent the air)
>   breathe simply my each how
> my trembling where my still unvisible when.   Wait.   ⎤ w
>
> if i am not heart,because at least i beat
> – always think i am gone like a sun which must go
> sometimes,to make an earth gladly seem firm for you:
> remember(as those pearls more than surround this throat)   ⎤ s
>
> i wear your dearest fears beyond their ceaselessness

(nor has a syllable of the heart's eager dim
enormous language loss or gain from blame or praise)
but many a thought shall die which was not born of dream   w
while wings welcome the year and trees dance(and i guess

though wish and world go down,one poem yet shall swim

4.3.1.1.3 Low discourse levels

As we move away from the highest levels in a text, canonically rising movement is complicated by the linear flow of the information. In the body of a poem's argument, information is often developed in parallel. An idea or image is introduced, and then the implications of this idea are explored in a range of forms, contexts, conceptual domains, emotive colourings, vocal inflections and so forth – with this development presented at roughly the same level of informational prominence. The linear flow of information strongly influences our perceptions of relative strength among constituents in these higher-level parallels. Given two prominences of equal informational strength, we usually prefer the final prominence as a peak. However, if information presented later on in the text *duplicates* information presented earlier on, the information that is presented first 'shadows' the information that occurs later. In terms of the global informational teleology, the later information merely translates the informational infrastructure of the earlier information into new contexts, new words, new images, new sounds. This later information, then, is a type of discourse apposition, a renaming and renaming, and the contours of rhythmic energy enacted by this process are falling, a movement from strong to weak.

As we have already discovered with Whitman, Keats and Millay, this sort of conceptual 'echoing' is found throughout the intermediate narrative levels in most poems. The paradigmatic case of this 'echoing' is the falling duple movement at low discourse levels in the Hebrew Psalms. Consider the Authorized Version of the 24th Psalm.

1 The earth is the Lord's, and the fullness thereof; the world, and they that dwell therein.
2 For he hath founded it upon the seas, and established it upon the floods.
3 Who shall ascend into the hill of the Lord? or who shall stand in his holy place?

4 He that hath clean hands, and a pure heart; who hath not lifted up his soul unto vanity, nor sworn deceitfully.
5 He shall receive the blessing from the Lord, and righteousness from the God of his salvation.
6 This is the generation of them that seek him, that seek thy face, O Jacob. Se-lah.
7 Lift up your heads, O ye gates, and be ye lift up, ye everlasting doors; and the King of glory shall come in.
8 Who is this King of glory? The Lord strong and mighty, the Lord mighty in battle.
9 Lift up your heads, O ye gates; even lift them up, ye everlasting doors; and the King of glory shall come in.
10 Who is this King of glory? The Lord of hosts, he is the King of glory. Se-lah.

Like many texts, Psalm 24 is a symmetrically rising duple at the highest level. Verses 1–5 define the conditions for salvation, verses 6–10 the consequences of satisfying those conditions, the coming of salvation itself.

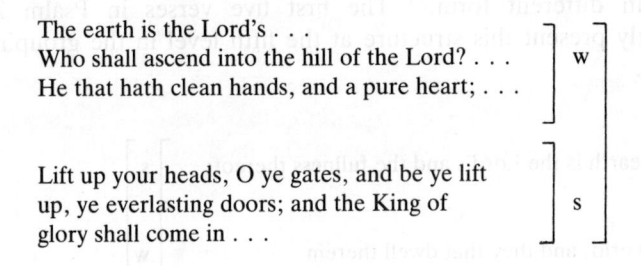

> The earth is the Lord's . . .
> Who shall ascend into the hill of the Lord? . . .   ⎤
> He that hath clean hands, and a pure heart; . . .   ⎦ w
>
> Lift up your heads, O ye gates, and be ye lift
> up, ye everlasting doors; and the King of   ⎤ s
> glory shall come in . . .   ⎦

As we move down the rhythmic hierarchy, however, we find a broadening of this basic argumentative line. At the second level, the text is a pair of duples, parallel in span and chiastic in inclination. The first two verses (1–2) establish the omnipotence of the Lord and rise to the next three verses (3–5), which define the Lord's conditions for salvation. But the second half of the text reverses this rising movement. Verses 6 and 7 present the rhythmic height of the poem (the consequences of spiritual purity), while the last three verses recapitulate the narrative line (i.e. the omnipotence of God, the consequences of obeying his commands, etc.).

226   THEORY: GROUPING

The earth is the Lord's . . .	w
Who shall ascend . . .?	s	w
This is the generation . . .	s
Who is this King . . .?	w	s

This narrative redundancy and recapitulation are typical of prayer, invocation, incantation.

The repetitively falling rhythms we are interested in, however, occur three levels lower down in the rhythmic hierarchy. As has been widely discussed, each of the verses in the Psalms tends to have a duple, falling structure. The first part of the verse presents a thought; the second part of the verse presents basically the same thought in different form.[13] The first five verses in Psalm 24 consistently present this structure at the fifth level in the grouping hierarchy.

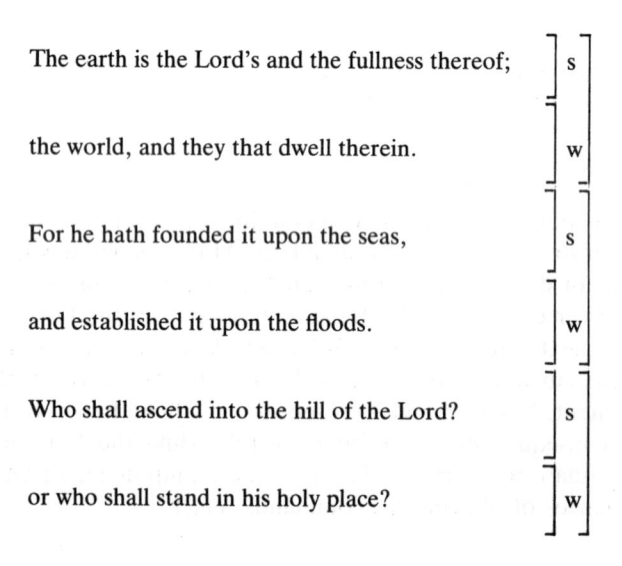

The earth is the Lord's and the fullness thereof;	s
the world, and they that dwell therein.	w
For he hath founded it upon the seas,	s
and established it upon the floods.	w
Who shall ascend into the hill of the Lord?	s
or who shall stand in his holy place?	w

| He that hath clean hands, and a pure heart; | s |
| who hath not lifted up his soul unto vanity, nor sworn deceitfully. | w |

| He shall receive the blessing from the Lord, | s |
| And righteousness from the God of his salvation. | w |

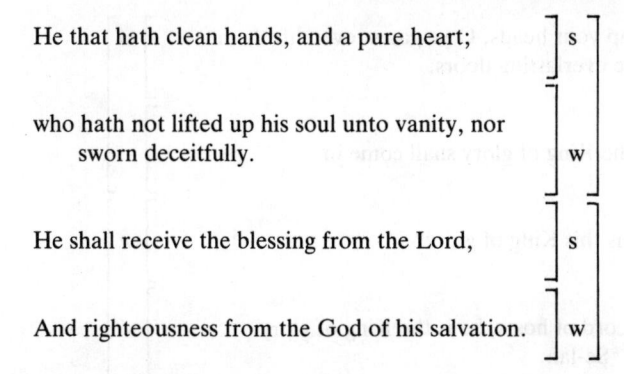

As is usually the case, however, these consistently falling rhythms are not perfectly regular. They are modulated to support and counterpoint the flow of rhythmic energies at higher levels. As the grouping structure rises to the second half of the text, these lower-level duples also reverse and rise. Verse 6 begins with a falling duple.

| This is the generation of them that seek him, | s |
| that seek thy face, O Jacob. Se-lah. | w |

But from then on, these rhythms rise (condition rises to consequence, question to answer).

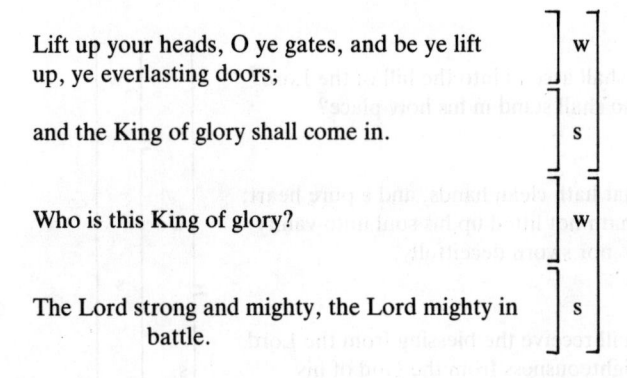

| Lift up your heads, O ye gates, and be ye lift up, ye everlasting doors; | w |
| and the King of glory shall come in. | s |

| Who is this King of glory? | w |
| The Lord strong and mighty, the Lord mighty in battle. | s |

Lift up your heads, O ye gates; even lift them } w
up, ye everlasting doors;

and the King of glory shall come in. } s

Who is this King of glory? } w

The Lord of hosts, he is the King of glory. } s
Se-lah.

This change in rhythmic direction at the fifth level is also supported and modulated by articulation at the third and fourth levels. In the rising duple at the second level (the first half of the text), the weak constituent is supported at a third level with falling articulation.

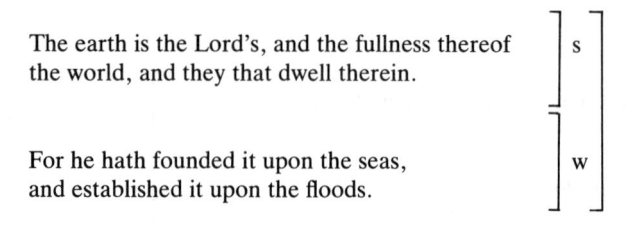

The earth is the Lord's, and the fullness thereof } s
the world, and they that dwell therein.

For he hath founded it upon the seas, } w
and established it upon the floods.

But as this second-level constituent rises, the third level turns and rises, and the poem presents a fourth level that also rises, deepening the crescendo.

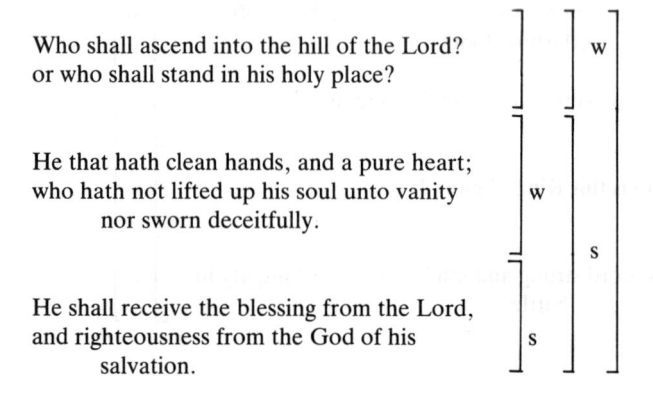

Who shall ascend into the hill of the Lord? } w
or who shall stand in his holy place?

He that hath clean hands, and a pure heart; } w
who hath not lifted up his soul unto vanity
    nor sworn deceitfully.

He shall receive the blessing from the Lord, } s
and righteousness from the God of his
    salvation.

GROUPING PREFERENCE RULES 229

The rhythmic turn from falling to rising at the fifth level (in verse 7, 'Lift up . . .') is also supported by rising articulation at the third level and strength at the first and second levels.

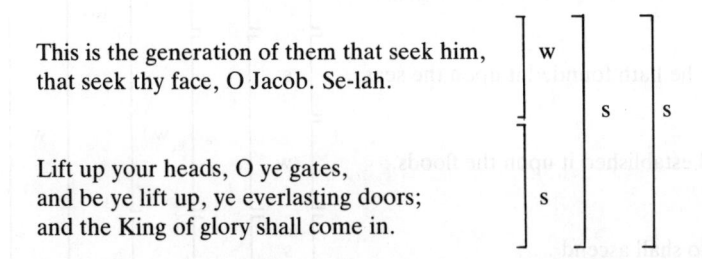

> This is the generation of them that seek him, w
> that seek thy face, O Jacob. Se-lah.
>   s   s
>
> Lift up your heads, O ye gates,
> and be ye lift up, ye everlasting doors;   s
> and the King of glory shall come in.

Then the intermediate-level rhythms at the second and third levels modulate back into a falling, echoic movement, and the text achieves closure with a medially strong triple at the third level (the only triple in the higher-level rhythms in the poem). The interactions among these motifs create a muted, yet strong and satisfying, close.

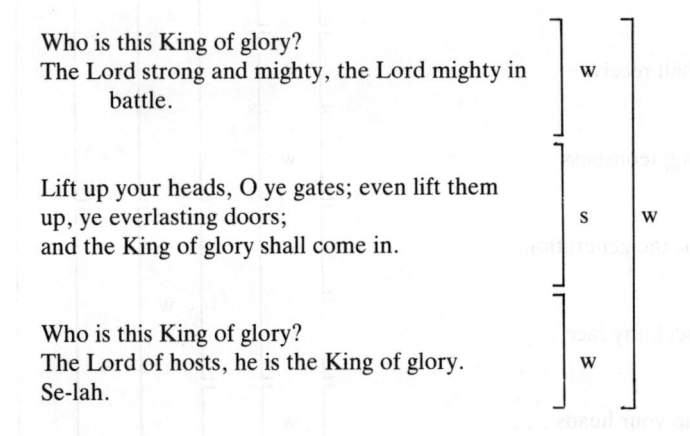

> Who is this King of glory?
> The Lord strong and mighty, the Lord mighty in   w
>   battle.
>
> Lift up your heads, O ye gates; even lift them
> up, ye everlasting doors;   s   w
> and the King of glory shall come in.
>
> Who is this King of glory?
> The Lord of hosts, he is the King of glory.   w
> Se-lah.

The grouping structure we have read is the following.

230   THEORY: GROUPING

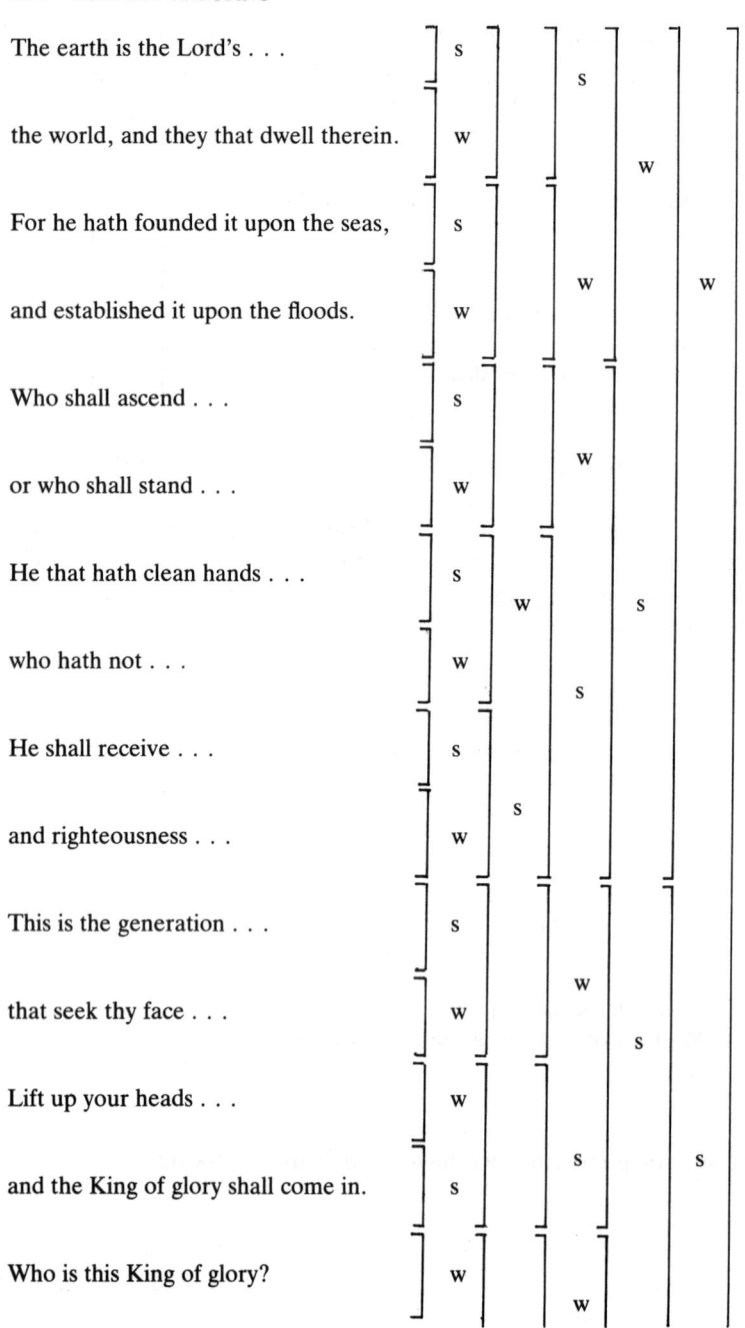

The earth is the Lord's ...	s			
the world, and they that dwell therein.	w	s		
For he hath founded it upon the seas,	s		w	
and established it upon the floods.	w	w		w
Who shall ascend ...	s			
or who shall stand ...	w	w		
He that hath clean hands ...	s		s	
who hath not ...	w	w		
He shall receive ...	s		s	
and righteousness ...	w	s		
This is the generation ...	s			
that seek thy face ...	w	w	s	
Lift up your heads ...	w			
and the King of glory shall come in.	s	s		s
Who is this King of glory?	w		w	

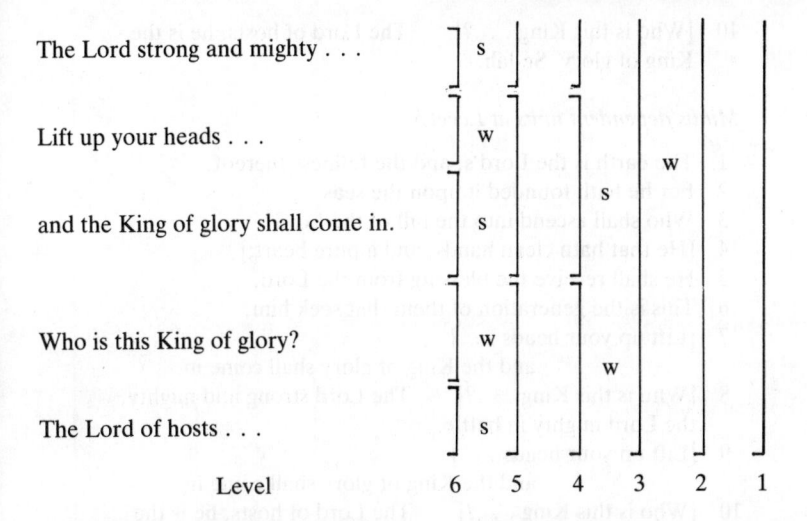

The Lord strong and mighty . . .	s					
Lift up your heads . . .	w			w		
		s				
and the King of glory shall come in.	s					
Who is this King of glory?	w		w			
The Lord of hosts . . .	s					
Level	6	5	4	3	2	1

A grouping reduction is useful in demonstrating the effects of this varied, levelled movement. The first reduction removes the pulsing trochaic movement in the first half of the text within Level 5 and its reversal to rising contours in verses 7–10. The second reduction squares up the text, removing the local rise that cadences the first half of the text within Level 4. The third reduction removes the contrasting choriambic and amphibrachic movements in the two halves of the text within Level 3, leaving just a chiastic ws sw figure. The fourth reduction reduces this chiastic figure to a single binary rise. And the fifth reduction yields the peak of the text within verse 7.

Minus dependent units at Level 6

1 The earth is the Lord's, and the fullness thereof;
2 For he hath founded it upon the seas
3 Who shall ascend into the hill of the Lord?
4 He that hath clean hands, and a pure heart;
5 He shall receive the blessing from the Lord,
6 This is the generation of them that seek him,
7 [Lift up your heads . . .]
         and the King of glory shall come in.
8 [Who is this King . . .?]   The Lord strong and mighty,
   the Lord mighty in battle.
9 [Lift up your heads . . .]
         and the King of glory shall come in.

10 [Who is this King . . .?]   The Lord of hosts, he is the King of glory. Se-lah.

Minus dependent units at Level 5

1 The earth is the Lord's, and the fullness thereof;
2 For he hath founded it upon the seas
3 Who shall ascend into the hill of the Lord?
4 [He that hath clean hands, and a pure heart;]
5 He shall receive the blessing from the Lord,
6 This is the generation of them that seek him,
7 [Lift up your heads . . .]
       and the King of glory shall come in.
8 [Who is this King . . .?]   The Lord strong and mighty, the Lord mighty in battle.
9 [Lift up your heads . . .]
       and the King of glory shall come in.
10 [Who is this King . . .?]   The Lord of hosts, he is the King of glory. Se-lah.

Minus dependent units at Level 4

1 The earth is the Lord's, and the fullness thereof;
4 [He that hath clean hands, and a pure heart;]
5 He shall receive the blessing from the Lord,
7 [Lift up your heads . . .]
       and the King of glory shall come in.
9 [Lift up your heads . . .]
       and the King of glory shall come in.

Minus dependent units at Level 3

4 [He that hath clean hands, and a pure heart;]
5 He shall receive the blessing from the Lord,
7 [Lift up your heads . . .]
       and the King of glory shall come in.

Minus dependent units at Level 2

7 [Lift up your heads . . .]
       and the King of glory shall come in.

4.3.1.1.4 Syntactic and prosodic levels

As we move even lower in the rhythmic hierarchy, the influence of informational redundancy on rhythmic articulation is even more important. While the focal potential of constituents at these levels is also determined informationally, the prominence of this information will depend crucially on how this information is integrated semantically and pragmatically into the discourse. Discourse at lower levels is pervasively redundant. The demands of textual cohesion and syntactic well-formedness often require that one constituent be linked redundantly to the next, that what is new (and therefore prominent) be presented within the structural scaffolding of what is old (and therefore less prominent). Informational 'containment' still determines grouping prominence, but this prominence is often not so much a matter of the thematic centrality of the information as its 'packaging' within the conventional informational structure of the syntax and prosody at the grammatical level being considered.

One of the major achievements of recent work in functional linguistics has been its success in teasing out the various ways that a sentence can 'package' information simultaneously in grammatical form.[14] These formal 'wrappings' adapt the message to the temporary state of the listener's beliefs and knowledge at that point in the discourse, while indicating those parts of the message that are of most interest. The modes of information 'packaging' I will be concerned with are represented in the following table.

Informational Packaging

Syntactic structure:	Subject	Verb	Complement
Semantic structure:	Agent	Action	Goal
Thematic structure:	Theme		Rheme
Topical structure:	Topic		Comment
Oppositional structure:	(Focus & Frame)		

The *syntactic* structure of a sentence represents its traditional grammatical form. Sentences have subjects and predicates, 'parts of speech' or lexical categories, phrases, clauses, etc. In some cases these formal constraints are fairly arbitrary informationally. But in most cases the syntactic form of an utterance is an important informational choice. For instance, syntactic categories are associated with centres of informational value. Nouns are used to convey 'thingliness'. Verbs are used for actions and states. Adjectives convey qualities. Clauses convey propositions.

234   THEORY: GROUPING

For our purposes here, one of the most important syntactic processes is *subordination*. As in rhythmic structures, information in sentences is 'packaged' in layers. For instance, while clauses are associated with propositions, most complex sentences are composed of clauses within clauses within clauses. We saw the rhythmic importance of this in a poem like 'Bright Star'. 'Bright Star' is composed of one sentence. But it has eleven 'predicates' (*to be steadfast, to hang aloft, to watch, to gaze, to be unchangeable, to be pillowed, to feel, to be awake, to hear, to live* and *to swoon*), each of which can form the centre of a clause at some level of syntactic structure. This syntactic layering of information strongly affects a reader's judgement of informational prominence. Rhythmic levels are not coextensive with syntactic levels. But all things being equal, superordinate syntactic constituents tend to be perceived as rhythmically superordinate. For instance, in 'Bright Star' the basic syntactic scaffolding of its one sentence is rhythmically superordinate, even though the shape and disposition of this scaffolding run against both the canonical preferences for grouping form (end-focus, symmetry, etc.) and the discourse interest of the reader (i.e. in the speaker's humanization of his stellar 'constancy' from a 'lone splendour' to the 'sweet unrest' of aesthetic and emotional response).

> **Bright star, would I were steadfast as thou art –**
>   **Not in lone splendour** hung aloft the night
> And watching, with eternal lids apart,
>   Like nature's patient, sleepless Eremite,
> The moving waters at their priestlike task
>   Of pure ablution round earth's human shores,
> Or gazing on the new soft fallen mask
>   Of snow upon the mountains and the moors –
> **No – yet still steadfast, still unchangeable,**
>   Pillowed upon my fair love's ripening breast,
> To feel forever its soft fall and swell,
>   Awake forever in a sweet unrest,
> Still, still to hear her tender-taken breath,
> And so live ever – or else swoon to death.

Sentences also have a *semantic* structure. For instance, in addition to controlling verb agreement, pronominalization and other matters, grammatical subjects can represent agents (intentional actors), affected entities (entities that are operated upon by the action expressed), beneficiaries (human recipients of an action), places, times, goals and other semantic notions. Most grammatical entities have a similar range of semantic 'roles'. These are not in a one-to-one correspondence with the syntax; therefore, they can represent another stratum of informational choice.

Sentences also have a *thematic* structure. In most sentences, this structure is binary. One part of the sentence will refer back to what has been said, and therefore will represent old information; another part will add some new information. The part that conveys the old information is the *theme*. The part that conveys the new information is the *rheme*. For instance, if asked 'Where is John?' a speaker might respond, 'Oh, John is in the bathroom.' In this response, *John* is the theme; *is in the bathroom* is the rheme. As we might expect, rhematic information, being 'new', is usually felt as rhythmically superordinate to thematic information.

Thematic structure correlates in many ways with the other modes of 'packaging'. For instance, old information tends to be syntactically *reduced*, the most important reductional process being pronominalization. For example, in the exchange above, speakers questioned about John's whereabouts would probably not bother to reiterate John's name. They would respond with a pronoun: 'Oh, he's in the bathroom.' Old information also correlates with the linear flow of the sentence (i.e. with its *topical* structure). Speakers usually put 'backward-looking' information first, new information later. Themes also tend to be subjects. As Chafe (1976) notices, speakers tend to make their propositional 'pegs' (i.e. their subjects) their discourse 'pegs' (i.e. their themes) as well.

Sentences also have a *topical structure*. Topical structure refers to the linear flow of a sentence in time – what comes first, what later. Many linguists have claimed a binary structure on this level as well. Material that comes first in a sentence is the *topic*; material that comes later, the *comment*. Linear ordering in English is complicated by the conventional semantic functions of linear positioning in the language (e.g. *Bob hit Bill* vs *Bill hit Bob*). But this topical structure is also an important and relatively independent mode of informational 'packaging'. As Bolinger (1952) and others have pointed out, sentences in English tend to proceed from general to specific. Constituents early on in a sentence tend to 'set the scene' for constituents later on, and as a sentence proceeds, these later constituents tend to 'modify' ('specify', 'particularize', 'fill in', etc.) earlier information. As Bolinger argues, the influence of topical 'packaging' is often clearly evident in adverb positioning. To use one of Bolinger's examples (1952: 283), a speaker who asks 'Why did you abruptly back away?' more likely questions the listener's 'backing away', while a speaker who asks 'Why did you back away abruptly' more likely questions the listener's 'abruptness'. As in most cases in the English sentence, 'the differentiator, the contrasting element comes last'.

The major exception to these correlations between linguistic and rhythmic structure involves what I will term *oppositional structure*: situations involving 'contrastive differentiation' with binary oppositions. There are many discussions in the literature on these issues that demand an independent consideration of limited contrast. For example, work in prosody has traditionally isolated 'contrastive stress' as an independent category, and various functional analyses of English syntax have reserved a separate place for 'contrastiveness', 'parallelism' and the like (e.g. Chafe 1976; Bardovi-Harlig 1986).

Limited contrast is the trump card in the determination of informational prominence. If a speaker can unambiguously communicate that the focus of a statement is not *this* but *this*, considerations of topicality, thematicity, semantics and syntax are overruled (e.g. *Only YOU can prevent forest fires*). There are also some unambiguous ways of indicating such contrast syntactically: clefting (*It was JOHN who broke the window*; *What John did was break the WINDOW*; *The one who broke the window was JOHN*); fronting (e.g. topicalization: *BEANS, I LIKE*); focusing adjuncts (e.g. *Only JOHN could have broken the window*; *Even JOHN knew about the broken window*); emphatic auxiliaries (*John DID know about the broken window*); correlative parallels (*It wasn't JOHN, but MARY, who broke the window*).

These 'packaging' considerations do not specify an algorithm for determining prominence from the form of the English sentence. But they *do* indicate that poets have considerable means for suggesting their rhythmic intentions through linguistic structure. Texts do not yield in a facile manner to the rhythmic preferences of the reader. They resist the reader and demand that that resistance be respected.

Consider again the first four lines of Frost's 'Nothing Gold Can Stay'.

Nature's first green is gold,
Her hardest hue to hold.
Her early leaf's a flower;
But only so an hour.

Starting with the first line, we have a clear discourse slate. No information is new, no information is old (we will put aside for the moment the effect of the title of the poem). From topical and syntactic structure, we expect the predicate in this clause (*is gold*) to be more prominent than the subject (*Nature's first green*). The predicate hangs some propositional clothes on 'Nature's first green' and comments further on some topical realm. *Within* the subject and predicate of this clause, oppositional structure makes prominent 'green' and 'gold' (two contrasting colours). *First* is more overtly contrastive, however. Given a 'first' green, we ponder 'second' and 'third' greens. *Nature's* seems to be less contrastive. As the poem proceeds, 'natural' green is compared with other sorts of 'greenness' ('innocence', etc.). But at this point, *Nature's* does not reach the same contrastive status as *first*. As a result, 'information packaging' in this first line suggests that we read *gold* as more prominent than *first*, and *first* as more prominent than *Nature's*.

The second line is in apposition to the first line. This syntactic subordination mutes its prominence. This second line advances the discourse informationally, however, and this is a major consideration. Our normal presuppositions about gold or the onset of spring do not automatically include transience. Therefore, I read line 2 as rhythmically superordinate to line 1. On the other hand, there are aspects of this second line that are informationally redundant. 'Hue' is 'contained' semantically in 'green' ('green' is a 'hue'). This weakens the prominence of 'hue' with respect to 'hardest', even though *hue* occurs after *hardest* and is the head noun of the noun phrase and thus is made prominent by both syntactic and topical structure. Again, however, the most influential consideration is oppositional structure. The superlative 'hardest' evokes a contrastive reading. This makes 'hardest' somewhat more prominent than 'hue'. Syntactic and semantic relations complicate the rhythmic status of *to hold*. *To hold* is a clausal modifier of *her hardest hue*, and *her hardest hue* is an affected entity and the syntactic object of *to hold*. In English, noun phrases tend to be more prominent than verb phrases and syntactic objects more prominent than syntactic subjects. And syntactically superordinate constituents tend to be more prominent than subordinate constituents. These considerations give *her hardest hue* more prominence than *to hold*. None the less, *to hold* is again just the bit of information that advances the discourse and makes line 2 informationally stronger than line 1. Therefore, its informational value is still high. Its final position also gives it topical prominence. Giving superordinate prominence to *to hold* also makes the rhythmic contours in line 2 closely parallel to those in line 1; therefore this reading is favoured by another grouping preference. These considerations suggest that we read *hold* as more prominent than *hardest* and *hardest* as more prominent than *hue*.

The third line invokes many of the same considerations. Line 3 is informationally parallel to line 1. Therefore it is narratively weak. *Early* again invokes contrast. And now we have a tight syntactic parallel with the first line that reinforces this contrast. *Leaf* is informationally redundant, however. 'Leafing' is a generic term for the 'greening' of nature. This reading also produces parallel 'falling' constituents in the first three lines (***first green***, ***hardest hue***, ***early leaf's***); therefore this reading is favoured by another grouping preference. On the other hand, as in the other lines, the final constituent in the line, *a flower*, remains superordinate. *A flower* is the main constituent in the predicate, and it gives some appropriate topical narrowing of the subject. The image of the flower as a 'first fruit' also teems with metaphorical richness, in addition to introducing the theme of death in birth ('in the beginning is the end'). Together, these considerations suggest that we read *flower* as more prominent than *early* and *early* as more prominent than *leaf's*. This reading also makes line 3 almost the exact rhythmic counterpart of line 2; therefore it is favoured by another grouping preference.

Line 4 continues the phrasal shaping we have found in the noun phrase subjects in lines 1–3. In this case, the constituent that competes with *only* for prominence is pronominalized (to *so*) and therefore is overtly presented as old information. Then *hour* gives us just the 'linear modification' that we expect of a rhythmically strong comment and rheme: the transience of nature is given an exact (and startlingly brief) specification. This reading also makes line 4 almost the exact rhythmic counterpart of lines 1–3, which in turn are almost the exact counterparts of one another; therefore this reading is also supported by another grouping preference.

4.3.1.2 GPR2 (Weight)

GPR1 (Information) is the dominant determinant of grouping prominence in poetry. Other considerations also affect our placement of grouping peaks, however, and when GPR1 (Information) is equivocal or irrelevant, these other considerations can be important.

The first we might mention is sheer physical/linguistic *weight*. In general, we not only prefer grouping peaks to be informationally 'richer' than grouping valleys; we prefer them to be *physically* 'richer' as well – louder and longer. In this respect, grouping peaks resemble metrical beats. Let's call this preference GPR2 (Weight).[15]

> GPR2 (Weight): Prefer a peak that is linguistically/physically 'heavy'.

GPR2 (Weight) is an influential preference throughout the grouping hierarchy. For instance, at low levels this preference is reflected in our placement of the peaks of clitic phrases on the main stress of polysyllabic content words. Stressed syllables are not informationally richer than their unstressed counterparts. They are just louder (higher pitched, longer, etc.).

At mid levels, GPR2 (Weight) is also evident in our preference for expanding constituents within climactically ordered groups of various sorts. These expanding 'grades' have long been observed by prose rhythmists and rhetoricians, and Gil *et al.*'s studies of chants and nursery rhymes reveal a strong preference for weighted peaks in non-canonical verse as well. Climactically ordered chants and cheers pervasively resist weighting weak groups (e.g. 'Ho Ho / Ho Chi Mihn' not 'Ho Ho Ho / Chi Mihn'; 'One two / three four five' not 'One two three / four five'), as do many nursery rhymes ('Rain, rain, go away, / Come again another day' not 'Windy weather, go away, / Come back some day'). Most manuals of prose style also make a special effort to recommend 'short-to-long' order both within sentences and within larger rhetorical crescendos (e.g. J.M. Williams 1981: 95–8).

In responding to a grouping structure, GPR2 (Weight) can be influential in both muting and clarifying grouping contours. For instance, the grouping contours of informationally balanced conjoins, appositives or paratactically related discourse units are often clarified if one of the constituents is significantly weighted. Weighting can be particularly important and effective early on in a text before thematic relations, the major considerations in determining informational prominence in context, have been clearly established. For instance, my reading of a falling movement within the first line of the Whitman passage we examined earlier is at least partially due to the disparity in physical/linguistic weight between the two units.

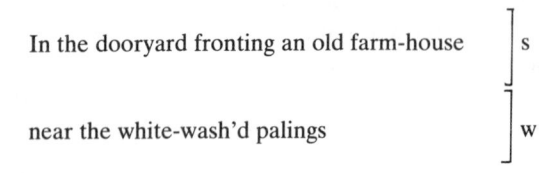

> In the dooryard fronting an old farm-house ⎤ s
>
> near the white-wash'd palings ⎦ w

Weight also influences my reading of falling (rather than rising) duples in the first five lines of Millay's 'Spring'.

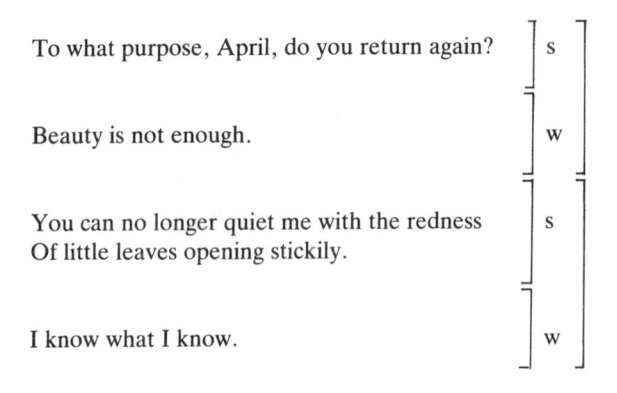

> To what purpose, April, do you return again? ⎤ s ⎤
>
> Beauty is not enough. ⎦ w ⎦
>
> You can no longer quiet me with the redness
> Of little leaves opening stickily. ⎤ s ⎤
>
> I know what I know. ⎦ w ⎦

Grouping structures in art verse often run *against* GPR2 (Weight). Grouping peaks are often physically *lighter* than the units in their associated rises and falls. As a result, any attempt to draw a categorical correlation between physical weight and grouping 'strength' for art verse, as Gil suggests for non-canonical verse, is frustrated at every turn. This fact does not refute either the reality or the importance of GPR2, however. It just underlines the summative, preferential nature of grouping response. In many cases, GPR2 is overruled by other preferences.

4.3.1.3 GPR3 (End-focus)

Another important grouping preference is for group-final peaks. The basic function of grouping within canonical rhythmic form is to move to a peak at the end of a measure projected by an after-beating meter. Our preference for 'rising' movement in verse grouping is general, however, and is evident in our response to non-metrical texts as well. Following the terminology used by functional linguists, let's call this preference *end-focus* and list it as GPR3.[16]

GPR3 (End-focus): Prefer a peak that is in final position in a group.

End-focus seems to be near mandatory at the highest level in art verse. Very few poems are anti-climactic. As Robert Frost (1949: 56) describes it, most poems 'ride on their own melting', like 'ice on a hot stove', like love.

> No one can really hold that the ecstasy should be static and stand still in one place. It begins in delight, it inclines to the impulse, it assumes direction with the first line laid down, it runs a course of lucky events, and ends in a clarification of life – not necessarily a great clarification, such as sects and cults are founded on, but in a momentary stay against confusion. It has denouement. It has an outcome that though unforeseen was predestined from the first image of the orginal mood – and indeed from the very mood.

In English poetry the most significant influence of GPR3 (End-focus) derives from the canonical organization of informational peaks within English grammar, in both syntax and prosody. Grammarians have long noted that English syntax has a pervasive preference for end-focus. In fact, in the last twenty years or so, many functional grammarians have argued that a large number of the 'transformational' options within English syntax (passive, extraposition, 'heavy noun phrase' shift, existentials, clefts, etc.) can be motivated in terms of their informational effect. These options allow the placement of informationally rich, communicatively 'dynamic' constituents in final position (for a summary see Quirk *et al.* 1985: 1353–1419). As Gil argues (1985, 1986, 1987), the Prague School notion of 'communicative dynamism' and the London School theory of theme–rheme and topic–comment relations in syntactic ordering formalize the various ways in which English (and other languages) have grammaticalized this rhythmic preference.[17]

It is also clear that prosodic structures in English have pervasively grammaticalized GPR3 (End-focus). David Crystal (1969: 224) reports that only 10 per cent of the intonational units in his corpus of some 30,000 words do not have a nucleus on the final stressed lexical item in the unit, 'a remarkably low proportion', he says, that makes the generalization that intonational units are usually strong-final 'a most reliable one'. Similarly, phonological phrases are so often end-focused that generations of generative–transformational grammarians have claimed that levels of phrasal stress can be predicted structurally (rather than informationally) by mechanically assigning strong stress to rightmost constituents within syntactic constituents (i.e. Chomsky and Halle's Nuclear Stress Rule), a claim that has given rise to years of controversy (see Chapter 1).

Given these prosodic and syntactic preferences within the English language itself, we have considerable motivation for assuming that a final constituent within a linguistic structure in a poem is intended to be read as a grouping peak. And given that there is a pervasive preference for groups to align themselves with linguistic structures (see below), this preference provides strong support for GPR3 (End-focus).

Together, GPR1 (Information) and GPR3 (End-focus) have the effect of emphasizing structural beginnings and endings at the expense of structural middles, an effect that is also furthered by the componential organization of rhythm itself (i.e., meter marks structural beginnings; grouping and prolongation mark structural endings). By GPR1 (Information), information presented by structural beginnings 'shadows' (i.e. makes 'old') equivalent information that occurs later on, encouraging a falling movement. But by GPR3 (End-focus) we assume that information presented in final position is intended as superordinate.

A major effect of these contradictory preferences is the retrospective reanalysis that often occurs within grouping triples. As we move through a triple, we often read the first constituent as superordinate to the second constituent (perceiving a falling movement). Then we read the third constituent as the peak of the triple, reanalysing the initial falling movement into a rising triple. Cooper and Meyer (1960) choose to represent this process explicitly with double markings on the first constituent of the triple, a subscripted accent mark to indicate the initial hypothesis (influenced by the musical correlates of GPR1 (Information)) and a superscripted breve to indicate the final result (influenced by the musical correlates of GPR3 (End-focus)).

$$\underset{1}{\underline{v}} \quad \underset{2}{v} \quad \underset{3}{\underline{}}$$

GPR3 (End-focus) cannot and should not be regarded as categorical. In general, groups within a poem are highly varied in inclination. Directional movement is one of the two major dimensions of grouping shape and thus grouping expressiveness (the other dimension being grouping *span*). In fact, prosodic structures tend to ride against GPR3 (End-focus) at several places in our grouping response to poetry. At low levels, the conventional placement of lexical stress is often non-final, and given the relatively fixed positioning of these stresses, the reader is often given no opportunity for alternative readings. Therefore, clitic phrases in English often fall, especially if they encompass just one polysyllabic word. As many have argued, constraints on linguistic processing, within both syntax and discourse, also seem to favour right-branching and deductive structures and therefore falling grouping contours. Consequently, poets who strive to maintain a 'natural' syntactic and discourse ordering must often resort to falling structures at mid and high levels. It also seems evident that emotively and rhetorically 'marked' structures in English conventionally favour falling grouping contours. Given the norm of end-focus, English syntax often secures unusual emphasis by various *preposing* processes (e.g. topicalization, left-dislocation, etc.). Overtly ungrammatical syntactic inversions in poetry are often 'read' as preposings and therefore are often interpreted as rhythmically falling. Consequently, poets who want to achieve an artificially 'heightened' rhetoric must also resort to falling structures.

GPRs 2 (Weight) and 3 (End-focus) combine to generate a pervasive preference for *end-weight*, a preference that has been widely observed by grammarians and rhetoricians.

4.3.1.4 GPR4 (Density)

As David Gil and Barbara Herrnstein Smith observe, another important grouping preference is for linguistically *dense* grouping peaks. Grouping peaks, especially if they are closural, tend to concentrate formal patterning: sonic and lexical repetition, syntactic and morphological parallelism, word play (e.g. puns), gnomic and aphoristic brevity, and so forth. It is significant that most conventional poetic forms in English encourage contracted and/or formally marked grouping peaks (e.g. the contracted final couplet of the Shakespearean sonnet and *ottava rima*, the abxb rhyme scheme of ballad stanza, the juxtaposed double refrain at the end of the villanelle, the shortened final line of the sapphic and *rime couée*, and so forth). Let's call this grouping preference *density* and list it as GPR4.

> GPR4 (Density): Prefer a peak that is linguistically dense.

Theoretically, GPR4 (Density) usually runs against GPR2 (Weight) and, to some extent, GPR1 (Information). Expanded and therefore informationally rich groups are often not very dense in their formal patterning. In practical terms, however, GPRs 4 (Density) and 2 (Weight) often apply in different circumstances and therefore operate independently. GPR2 (Weight) is often important in determining grouping peaks at low levels (where physical substance is an important consideration and formal patterning has less scope for significant concentration), while GPR4 (Density) is often more influential at high levels (where significant strands of formal patterning can be brought together and concentrated and where physical weight is less important in determining grouping 'strength').

4.3.1.5 GPR5 (Return)

A fifth preference is for a grouping peak to be a formal *return*. In general, major types of formal return in poetry (e.g. refrains, metrical-grouping congruences, the end of narrative or syntactic digressions, normative patternings of grouping shapes and spans, repetitions of opening words or phrases, etc.) are significant signals of grouping peaks, especially if these formal 'returns' are combined and compounded. Let's call this preference *return* and list it as GPR5.

GPR5 (Return): Prefer a peak that is a formal return.

GPR5 (Return) has been discussed and illustrated at some length by both literary and music theorists (e.g. Barbara Herrnstein Smith, and Cooper and Meyer) and therefore needs no further documentation here. In many aspects of its operation, GPR5 (Return) is motivated by the general emotive teleology of artistic organization. Most art works begin placidly, generate tension through formal departures and conflicts, and then resolve those conflicting tensions with some satisfying formal synthesis. Grouping peaks at lower levels of structure (e.g. at the ends of textual divisions or sentences) often just reproduce in miniature this larger emotive teleology.

The canonical organization of metrical-grouping relations within the poetic line is also an instance of this emotive teleology working at local levels. Metrical-grouping non-congruences (i.e. promotions, demotions, 'foot substitutions', etc.) are more frequent *early* in the line than at the canonical position for a grouping peak, line end.

The canonical structure of the eighteenth-century couplet also follows GPR5 (Return). The second hemistich in the first line in a Popean couplet is often syntactically inverted with an initial (often nominal) grouping peak and a weak (often verbal) ending; the second hemistich of the second line in the couplet (almost always the peak of the couplet as a whole) is often uninverted and peak-final, as in the following from Pope.

> Favors to none, to all she smiles extends;
> Oft she rejects, but never once offends.
>
> ('The Rape of the Lock', Canto II, 11–12)

The conventional organization of some of our most popular non-canonical forms fixes GPR5 (Return) as a categorical demand. For instance, the lengthened, visually divided, intonationally duple, and differently and internally rhymed third metrical line in the limerick form generates a startling formal 'departure'. After this 'departure' the textually normative last line, which is mandatorily the textual peak, is necessarily felt as a formal return.

> A flea and a fly in a flue
> Were imprisoned, so what could they do?
>   Said the fly: 'Let us flee'
>   Said the flea: 'Let us fly'
> So they flew through a flaw in the flue.
>
> (Anonymous)

GPR5 (Return) overlaps with both GPR4 (Density) and our general preference for componential congruence. Many returns recall previous patterning and therefore contribute to formal density. And a formal return re-establishes normative patterning, some of which is rhythmic.

4.3.1.6 GPR6 (Change)

The formal texture of most art verse is highly varied. Consequently, we prefer formal markings of grouping peaks to indicate some positive aspect of aesthetic, linguistic or physical prominence: weight, density, unity, etc. However, in some isolated instances or unusually homogeneous verse textures, a simple *change* in formal patterning can also mark a constituent for notice and therefore suggest its superordinate structural value. Let's call this preference *change* and list it as GPR6.

> GPR6 (Change): Prefer a peak that is a linguistic change.

Support for GPR6 can be marshalled from various aspects of our response to poetry. Gil notices that in non-canonical verse formal repetition often patterns with other markers of prosodic weakness. Barbara Herrnstein Smith's notion of 'terminal modification' in closural gestures is also an invocation of formal change as a marker of grouping peaks. Many poetic forms mandatorily require formal change in their closing gestures (e.g. the alexandrine at the end of a Spenserian sonnet).

If a change in formal texture is multidimensional and created against the texture of preceding parallels, it can add considerable prominence to a group. One of the clearest instances in the English canon might be the fourth stanza of George Herbert's 'Vertue', which Smith (1968: 67–70) also cites. After tight parallelistic patterning in the first three stanzas, Herbert changes the mood, the directional movement from life to death, the sonic quality of the rhymes, the rhythmic texture, the syntax, indeed almost every dimension of poetic form, to indicate the textual peak in the fourth stanza.

Vertue

Sweet day, so cool, so calm, so bright,
The bridall of the earth and skie:
The dew shall weep thy fall to night;
    For thou must die.

Sweet rose, whose hue angrie and brave
Bids the rash gazer wipe his eye:
Thy root is ever in its grave,
    And thou must die.

Sweet spring, full of sweet dayes and roses,
A box where sweets compacted lie;
My musick shows ye have your closes,
    And all must die.

Onely a sweet and vertuous soul,
Like season'd timber, never gives;
But though the whole world turn to coal,
    Then chiefly lives.

Herbert also uses formal change to mark the peaks of the individual stanzas (i.e. the shortened stanza-final lines), and as Smith notes, to mark the third stanza as rhythmically superordinate to the first two (e.g. the textually unique feminine endings in the odd lines).

4.3.1.7 GPR7 (Beats)

We also prefer for grouping peaks to coincide with metrical beats. Metrical response, especially the metrical *tactus*, is significantly influenced by the occurrence of phenomenal stress in the rhythmic medium. In poetry, this normative alignment of tactical beats and stress has been documented at length by the Slavic metrists, is the implicit claim of the 'metrical' patterns posited by almost all of the approaches to meter we surveyed in Chapter 1, and is one of the major bases for the various 'constraints' on metrical well-formedness posited by generative metrists and metrical phonologists. Let's call this preference *beats* and list it as GPR7.[18]

GPR7 (Beats): Prefer a peak whose strongest syllable is a strong beat.

Historically, prosodists have most often invoked GPR7 (Beats) when reading the contextually flexible stressing of prepositions, conjunctions, demonstratives, pro-forms, negatives and so forth. The most common assumption has been that contextually sensitive items such as these are intended as stressed if they appear in tactical positions and as unstressed if they don't.

The most radical invocation of GPR7 (Beats) has been the claim by some foot-substitution metrists (e.g. Wright 1988) that meter *always* rearranges low-level grouping peaks so that they conform to an alternating metrical pattern, an argument that seems an unsupportable valorization of meter over grouping within rhythmic response as a whole. As Attridge (1982: 222–30) argues, it makes sense to assume that lines in a metrical context are intended to be metrical. Therefore, if possible, we should give such lines a prosodic structure that maintains the meter. But given the wide disparity between meter and grouping in many contexts, there seems little motivation to demand that our preference for metrical-grouping congruence always dominate other grouping preferences. Within the theory I am proposing here, GPR7 (Beats) is a rhythmic preference, one preference among many, not a categorical constraint on rhythmic response.

The role of GPR7 (Beats) in rhythmic reading is complex and cannot be considered at length here. The most significant complication is that GPR7 (Beats) will vary with the strength of the meter. In general, our reading of grouping structures in verse with a highly vertical and symmetrical (and therefore perceptually salient) meter will be strongly influenced by GPR7 (Beats) while our readings of grouping structures with a less vertical or symmetrical (and therefore less salient) meter will be less strongly affected.

For instance, in a tetrameter context I have a strong tendency to read function words in tactical positions as stressed and therefore as peaks of clitic phrases.

> To-day, the road all runners come,
> Shoulder-high we bring you home,
> And set you *at* your threshold down,
> Townsman *of* a stiller town.
>
> (A.E. Housman, 'To an Athlete Dying Young', 5–8)

In most cases I consider this reading (as in scansion (a) of line 8 below) to be only one alternative, however. I usually entertain other readings as well. For instance, I still find it *possible* to give the underlined prepositions in the Housman stanza above both a tactical beat and weak stress (as in scansion (b) of line 8 below). I also find it possible to syncopate the lines, giving the prepositions weak stress and placing them *after* the second tactical beat (as in scansion (c) of line 8 below).

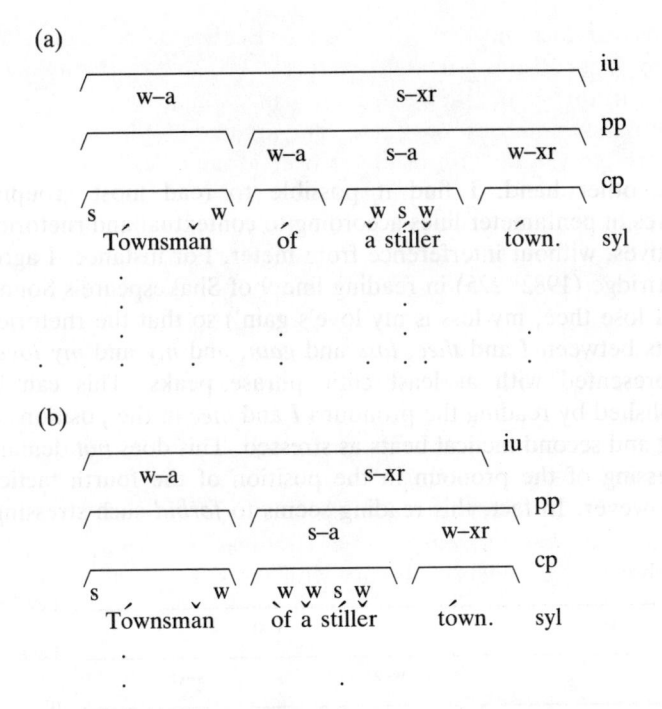

(a)

```
                                                              iu
   ┌─────────┐┌─────────────────────────┐
   │  w–a    ││         s–xr            │
                                                              pp
   ┌─────────┐┌──────┐┌──────┐┌─────────┐
             │ w–a   ││ s–a  ││  w–xr   │
                                                              cp
   ┌────┐┌───┐┌──────┐┌──────┐┌─────────┐
   │ s    w ││  ́   ││ w s w││   ́      │
   Townsman    of     a stiller  town.              syl
```

(b)

```
                                                              iu
   ┌─────────┐┌─────────────────────────┐
   │  w–a    ││         s–xr            │
                                                              pp
              ┌──────┐┌─────────┐
              │ s–a  ││  w–xr   │
                                                              cp
   ┌────┐┌───┐┌──────────┐┌─────────┐
   │ s    w ││ w w s w  ││   ́     │
   Townsman    of a stiller   town.               syl
```

.
.   .
.   .   .
.   .   .   .

250 THEORY: GROUPING

(c)

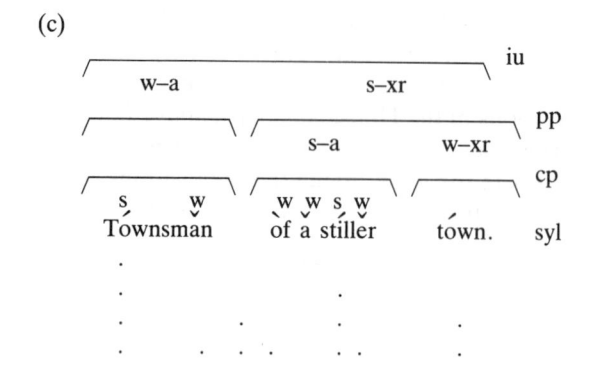

```
                                                                iu
    ┌─────────────────┬──────────────────────┐
    │      w–a        │        s–xr          │
    ┌────────┬────────┬──────────┬───────────┐  pp
             │        │   s–a    │   w–xr    │
    ┌────────┬────────┬──────────┬───────────┐  cp
    │  s   w │ w w s w│          │           │
     Townsman  of a stiller   town.           syl
```

On the other hand, I find it possible to read most grouping structures in pentameter lines according to contextual and rhetorical imperatives, without interference from meter. For instance, I agree with Attridge (1982: 225) in reading line 9 of Shakespeare's Sonnet 42 ('If I lose thee, my loss is my love's gain') so that the rhetorical contrasts between *I* and *thee*, *loss* and *gain*, and *my* and *my love's* are represented with at least clitic phrase peaks. This can be accomplished by reading the pronouns *I* and *thee* in the positions of the first and second tactical beats as stressed. This does *not* demand the stressing of the pronoun in the position of the fourth tactical beat, however. In fact, this reading seems to *forbid* such stressing.

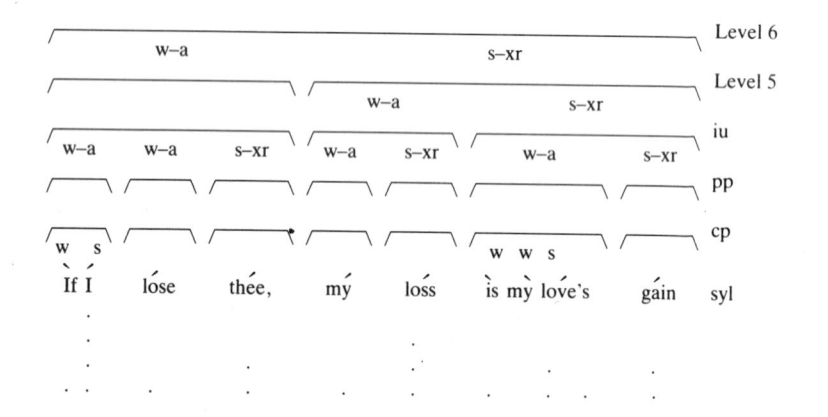

```
                                                                         Level 6
    ┌───────────────────────┬──────────────────────────────────┐
    │         w–a           │              s–xr                │
    ┌──────────┬────────────┬──────────────┬──────────────────┐  Level 5
                            │     w–a      │       s–xr       │
    ┌────┬─────┬────┬───┬───┬──────┬───────┬────────┬─────────┐  iu
    │w–a │ w–a │s–xr│w–a│s–xr│ w–a         │ s–xr             │
    ┌────┬─────┬────┬───┬───┬──────┬───────┬────────┬─────────┐  pp
    ┌────┬─────┬────┬───┬───┬──────┬───────┬────────┬─────────┐  cp
    │w  s│     │    │   │   │      │ w w s │        │         │
     If I  lose  thee,  my  loss   is my love's     gain       syl
```

The canonical structure of rhythmic form prevents GPR7 (Beats) from being a strong determinant of grouping preference at high levels. At high levels, grouping peaks usually occur on relatively weak metrical beats. For example, *gain* in line 9 of Sonnet 42 above is the strongest syllable in a sixth-level peak but appears on a two-dot beat, while *I* is a second-level peak but appears on a four-dot beat. At these levels, grouping peaks are determined predominantly by informational considerations, considerations that are not significantly affected by physical stressing and meter.

4.3.1.8 GPR8 (Arrivals)

At high levels, another preference is for an alignment of grouping peaks and prolongational arrivals. Grouping and prolongation in language traverse similar spans and, in many cases, run in concert. For example, while grouping and meter are opposed in many ways in line 9 of Sonnet 42, grouping and prolongation are aligned. In the reading I suggest, the grouping structure consistently rises; the prolongational structure is consistently anticipatory. Grouping and prolongation also articulate similar sorts of energy in similar ways. Therefore, a significant action in one of these components often affects our interpretation of action in the other. While prolongational arrivals do not mark informational prominences *per se*, a prolongational arrival has a strong feeling of structural 'culmination' that is closely comparable to the feeling of informational culmination marked by grouping peaks. Therefore, ambiguous or indeterminate grouping patterns can often be clarified by unambiguous prolongational articulation. Let's call this preference *arrivals* and list it as GPR8.

> GPR8 (Arrivals): Prefer a peak that is a prolongational arrival.

GPR8 (Arrivals) plays a significant role in various aspects of grouping response. For instance, the successful shaping of many poetic forms (e.g. the sonnet, the couplet, the limerick, etc.) depends crucially on maintaining climactic grouping contours, even though the images, arguments and/or events presented in the form may be closely parallel and therefore only slightly differentiated in informational value. As Smith (1968: 137) notes, one way to solve this difficulty is to direct anticipational energies towards the constituent that is intended as a grouping peak. For instance, many

Shakespearean sonnets are constructed so that the first two quatrains are parallel subordinate clauses directed at a main clause delivered in the third quatrain or so that the first three quatrains are parallel subordinate clauses directed at a main clause delivered in the couplet. This is an effective (albeit heavy-handed) way to strengthen our grouping response to the textual units presented in the main clauses, as in the third quatrain of Shakespeare's Sonnet 15.

> When I consider everything that grows
> Holds in perfection by a little moment,
> That this huge stage presenteth nought but shows
> Whereon the stars in secret influence comment;
> When I perceive that men as plants increase,
> Cheered and checked ev'n by the selfsame sky,
> Vaunt in their youthful sap, at height decrease,
> And wear their brave state out of memory;
> Then the conceit of this inconstant stay
> Sets you most rich in youth before my sight,
> Where wasteful time debateth with decay
> To change your day of youth to sullied night;
>   And all in war with time for love of you,
>   As he takes from you, I engraft you new.

In the following, e.e. Cummings mutes this heavy-handedness somewhat by using a *so* ... (*that*) correlative that is only ambiguously (and retrospectively) anticipatory. At first, we interpret the *so* as a syntactically complete (non-correlative) intensifier (i.e. 'A man is so many selves . . .'); only later do we see its possible function as a correlative comparative (so many . . . (that) how should . . .').

> so many selves(so many fiends and gods
> each greedier than every)is a man
> (so easily one in another hides;
> yet man can,being all,escape from none)
>
> so huge a tumult is the simplest wish:
> so pitiless a massacre the hope
> most innocent(so deep's the mind of flesh
> and so awake what waking calls asleep)

so never is most lonely man alone
(his briefest breathing lives some planet's year,
his longest life's a heatbeat of some sun;
his least unmotion roams the youngest star)

– how should a fool that calls him "I" presume
to comprehend not numerable whom?

4.3.2 Grouping preference rules (GPRs): segmentation

GPRs 1–8 influence our reading of grouping peaks. In general, we prefer peaks that are informationally rich (GPR1), physically heavy (GPR2) and linguistically dense (GPR4); that present a local change (GPR6) and a global return (GPR5); that coincide with a strong beat (GPR7) and a prolongational arrival (GPR8); and that occur in final position in a group (GPR3).

Several preferences also influence our reading of grouping *spans*.

4.3.2.1 GPR9 (Binary Form)

First, we have a strong preference for duple segmentation. Let's call this preference *binary form* and list it as GPR9.

> GPR9 (Binary Form): Prefer a group with two constituents.[19]

A preference for binary form pervades rhythmic organization, including the phrasal components, grouping and prolongation. The motivations for this preference are many and need only be suggested. A binary group represents the minimal configuration of a relative weighting (strong–weak). A binary group maximizes symmetry. A binary group presents a minimal unit of movement (weak-to-strong, strong-to-weak). A binary group must place its peak on the periphery of the group; therefore it maximizes group cohesion (peripheral weak units tend to be attracted away to surrounding groups). A binary group maximizes phasal congruence with binary meters, another important rhythmic preference. Binary contrast is a fundamental part of the biology of perception and cognition. Binary form pervades the structure of language at all levels (subject–predicate, topic–focus, modifier–modified). And so forth. All English poetry is overwhelmingly binary in its phrasing, even those texts that intensively concentrate grouping patterns of other spans. Almost all of our standard poetic forms favour duple organization at all levels: couplets, quatrains, octaves, sestets (which are usually quatrains plus a couplet), sonnets (octave plus sestet or three quatrains and a couplet), and so forth.

The most important effect of GPR9 (Binary Form) is that texts need to present very little actual segmentation in order to be perceived as rhythmically segmented. With the slightest encouragement, we will divide a text into duples (and those duples into further duples). In fact, a more significant feat is for a text to *resist* binary segmentation.

This preference for binary segmentation has important consequences for the relation between rhythmic structure and the informational organization of a text. In particular, our rhythmic response to a text is often more highly divided (and therefore vertically elaborated) than a bare outline of the conceptual content of the text would seem to warrant. With our grouping competence, we do not respond transparently to the semantic organization of the text. We make waves, structures that culminate between discernible endpoints, a process that differs significantly from conceptual construal.

In most cases, a text can resist binary segmentation only by (1) presenting strongly cohesive local patterning that weighs persuasively against segmentation, or (2) participating in global patterns that weigh against the vertical elaboration of a binary hierarchy at the point of segmentation involved. Both of these situations indeed arise and will be mentioned frequently in both our enumeration of the other grouping preferences and in our analyses in Chapter 5.

4.3.2.2 GPR10 (Tri-max) and GPR11 (Singles)

Among grouping spans other than duples, triples are the overwhelming preference. A few poetic forms have a triple organization (e.g. the tercet, the triple organization of the classical ode, etc.). Some have even claimed that the pentameter line is normatively triple in its phrasing (e.g. Prall 1936; Youmans 1989; Tarlinskaja 1984).

> Contrite designs / invite / divine delight
> And mighty hearts / are held / in slender chains
> The busy Sylphs / surround / their darling Care

It is questionable, however, whether we actually *prefer* phrasal triples, as we do duples. In meter, triples can be a more positive preference because of the temporal balancing of one 'long' against two 'shorts'. But in grouping, such temporal considerations are less influential. Rather, given a text that resists duple segmentation, we just *accept* triples more readily than other grouping spans. Triples enable many of the canonical functions of grouping form that are excluded by duple segmentation: rise *and* fall (i.e. directional balance rather than just directional movement), extended rise and extended fall (i.e. differential horizontal movement rather than just horizontal movement), internal parallels (rather than just external parallels), and so forth.

As many have noticed, our strong preference for duples makes triples relatively unstable, however. In particular, most triples are threatened by a two-level duple representation, as in the following.

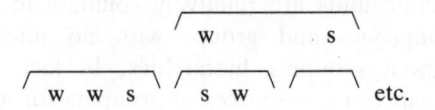

```
              w       s
    w   w   s    s   w          etc.
```

The two-level duple representation retains many of the rhythmic qualities of the triple (e.g. asymmetry, internal pairing, etc.). Therefore, given a linguistic structure that suggests a triple, grouping perceptions often shimmer between a triple reading and its two-level binary analogue. In the analyses in Chapter 5 I will sometimes refer to this two-level duple representation of a triple as a 'two-level triple'.

In our battery of preference rules, our preferential acceptance of triples is best represented by rules that specify an *avoidance* of other alternatives, in particular singles and spans of over three units. Let's call these (negative) preferences *singles* and *tri-max* and list them as GPRs 10 and 11.

> GPR10 (Singles): Avoid a group with only one constituent.

> GPR11 (Tri-max): Avoid a group with more than three constituents.

GPR11 (Tri-max) is supported by the *dearth* of poetic forms with more than three units (without internal, hierarchical organization). For instance, to my knowledge we have no octave forms that require an aaabcccb rhyme scheme (or the like). It has often been noticed that rhythmic prose frequently favours a third paeonic phrasing at the clitic phrase level, but we might see this more as an *avoidance* of triple and duple phrasing (which threaten to become metrical) than as an achievement of a rhythmic norm. As far as I am aware, no texts, poetic or prosaic, present a predominantly paeonic phrasing at any level.

The motivation for GPR10 (Singles) is more basic. A rhythmic unit with no constituency articulates no distinction in prominence and therefore establishes no rhythmic movement. A single can be effective as a *variation* for some grouping norm, but it can establish no rhythmic norm of its own. To my knowledge, we have no one-line poems. At the highest level of structure, the couplet seems to be the minimal phrasal frame.

Unlike the comparable constraints on meter, GPRs 10 (Singles) and 11 (Tri-max) cannot be taken as categorical. Contrary to the claims of Cooper and Meyer (1960) for music, at low levels phrasings of more than three units are relatively common in our rhythmic response to language, and groups with no internal consistency occur throughout grouping hierarchies. In fact, the single is one of the great expressive resources of grouping form. A single presents no articulation at some level of structure and therefore is the major vehicle of *contraction* in rhythmic phrasing. Because of the demand for alternating form, meter cannot present singles (i.e. juxtaposed beats, one-hemistich lines, etc.). Therefore the various effects of singles represent some of the most significant contributions of grouping to rhythmic expressiveness.

4.3.2.3 GPR12 (Proximity)

Texts influence our perception of grouping spans by presenting types of formal cohesion or divisioning that yield readily to certain types of grouping segmentation while resisting others. As the gestalt psychologists discovered, one of the major textual influences on grouping segmentation is the physical *proximity* of units in the medium.

In an abstract medium such as language, the notion 'proximity' is complex and ultimately ill defined. Language presents many continuities and discontinuities, and it is difficult to discern which of these are relevant to rhythmic response and why. Proceeding pragmatically, however, we might suggest that our rhythmic response to poetry is especially sensitive to *prosodic* units in the language. In fact, we might make the mild claim that some of the flexible constraints on prosodic realization in language are largely constraints on grouping segmentation. Given the preferential nature of grouping and the diverse functions of prosodic organization in language, this does not claim that the prosodic hierarchy *is* a rhythmic form. It just claims that the rhythmic *effects* of the prosodic hierarchy are part of what constrains its structural organization.

If we assume that prosodic segmentation is coextensive with grouping segmentation, we can claim that all grouping responses to texts contain four levels of segmentation at the lowest levels: *syllable* (syl), *clitic phrase* (cp), *phonological phrase* (pp) and *intonational unit* (iu).

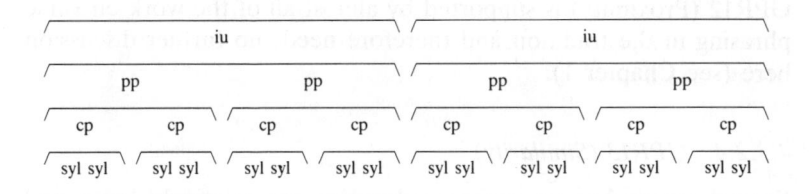

```
        iu                              iu
   pp         pp              pp              pp
 cp    cp   cp    cp       cp    cp       cp      cp
syl syl syl syl syl syl syl syl syl syl syl syl syl syl syl syl
```

While these matters are still poorly understood (see Selkirk 1984 for some speculations), we will assume that these linguistic units control our impression of the lower-level *proximity* of textual spans and therefore that boundaries between these units create rhythmic effects comparable to the rhythmic effects of perceptual gaps in music established by pauses, slurs, and differences in the temporal value of pitch events. In the case of phonological phrases and intonational units, this claim is very mild, because constraints on the linguistic composition of these prosodic units are very loose. In particular, I do not claim that the text 'presents' these units. Rather, I just claim that we prefer that our grouping response to a text include textual segments at low levels that fall within the bounds of the (loose) linguistic constraints on these units. I won't reproduce a discussion of these units here. I refer my reader back to Chapter 1.

In addition to prosodic proximity, we might also acknowledge here the effects of visual segmentation. Prosodic units in poems often override visual breaks, but we still *prefer* prosodic units to align themselves with visual units and therefore we might claim that visual discontinuity contributes to prosodic discontinuity.

We must also acknowledge that at higher levels continuities and discontinuities in syntactic form heavily influence grouping segmentation. Above the level of the intonational unit, groups often run parallel to the syntax, breaking at major points of syntactic discontinuity (e.g. the ends of sentences) and running continuously within syntactic continuities (e.g. extended phrases and clauses).

These acknowledgements lead to a multidimensional and multimedia formulation of the grouping preference we are considering. Let's call this preference *proximity* and list it as GPR12.[20]

> GPR12 (Proximity): At low levels, prefer a group that is a prosodic domain, especially a prosodic domain that is visually unbroken. At high levels, prefer a group that is a syntactic constituent.

GPR12 (Proximity) is supported by almost all of the work on verse phrasing in the tradition and therefore needs no further discussion here (see Chapter 1).

4.3.2.4 GPR13 (Similarity)

Formal constraints on prosodic domains are relatively loose and within textual organization as a whole, syntax has a fairly limited scope. Therefore, poets must control formal cohesiveness and divisiveness in other ways if they are significantly to influence a reader's phrasing of a text.

One of these ways is to craft the formal texture of the language so that continuities in texture are coextensive with groups, and discontinuities in texture coextensive with group boundaries. As the gestalt psychologists investigated at some length, we strongly prefer to group formal similarities and to separate formal differences. Let's call this preference *similarity* and list it as GPR13.[21]

> GPR13 (Similarity): Prefer a group that contains similar linguistic forms.

At high levels, such continuities and discontinuities are a natural product of discourse organization and occur in all texts. As recent work in text linguistics has demonstrated (e.g. Halliday and Hasan 1976), all high-level textual units will show a considerable number of cohesive linguistic 'ties' (continuities in reference, phoric connections, lexical repetitions, etc.). From a literary perspective, all thematic analysis of poetic discourse (in the sense developed by Barabara Herrnstein Smith) is based on continuities and discontinuities in imagery, argument and narrative line.

At mid and low levels, poets often use continuities and discontinuities in syntactic and phonetic texture to reinforce or blur our impressions of textual divisioning. These effects have been noticed throughout the tradition. For instance, many of Jakobson's arguments for structural organization in poetry are based on these considerations (e.g. left-branching syntax in the peripheral quatrains of Yeats' 'Sorrow of Love', right-branching in the central quatrain). The temporalists' notion of 'alliterative grouping' in 'tertiary rhythm' is another case in point.

These patternings of forms at mid and low level can be complex and subtle, but they are often an essential determinant of phrasal clarity in poetry. In fact, one might suggest that it is exactly the relative *lack* of such patterning in prose that leads to a blurring of prose rhythms at low levels.

For example, consider the first quatrain of Shakespeare's Sonnet 12.

> When I do count the clock that tells the time,
> And see the brave day sunk in hideous night;
> When I behold the violet past prime,
> And sable curls, all silvered o'er with white;
> When lofty trees I see barren of leaves,
> Which erst from heat did canopy the herd,
> And summer's green all girded up in sheaves,
> Borne on the bier with white and bristly beard,
> Then of thy beauty do I question make,
> That thou among the wastes of time must go,
> Since sweets and beauties do themselves forsake
> And die as fast as they see others grow;
>   And nothing 'gainst time's scythe can make defence
>   Save breed, to brave him when he takes thee hence.

At low levels, I perceive the first quatrain as a pleasing alternation of ternary and duple phrasings. The odd lines move more quickly, in asymmetric triples; the even lines resolve this ternary movement into more symmetrical duples.

260 THEORY: GROUPING

```
⌐ When I    ⌝ ⌐ do count the clock ⌝ ⌐ that tells the time ⌝
  When I        behold the violet       past prime,
⌐ And see the brave day ⌝ ⌐ sunk in hideous night       ⌝
  And sable curls,           all silvered o'er with white;
```

These perceptions are anything but stable and categorical, however, and I am sure my intuitions here differ from those of many of my readers. My intuitions derive from my personal balancing of various grouping preferences, one of which is GPR13 (Similarity).

The general difficulty is that the syntactic structures of these lines often pull against canonical grouping form. In lines 1 and 3, the subject–predicate break is off-centre (2:8).

> When I // do count the clock that tells the time,
> When I // behold the violet past prime,

And there is no stronger, compensating break near the formal centre of the line. *The clock* has firm syntactic connections with both the preceding main verb *count* and the following relative clause *that tells the time*. And the complex-transitive structure (Subject–Verb–Direct Object–Object Complement) in line 3 is particularly cohesive.

As is often the case, however, Shakespeare laces this quatrain with phonic patterning that helps articulate rhythmic grouping at this blurry, intermediate level. For instance, by GPR9 (Binary Form), a preferred reading of line 1 might split the predicate into two, and that duple into further duples at the next lower level.

> When I // do count/ the clock // that tells/ the time

And Shakespeare gives us phonetic patterning that supports this phrasing. The alliterations *count–clock* and *tells–time* are very prominent. The vowels in *count* and *clock* are back, while the vowels in *tells* and *time* have (at least partially) front articulations. And this parsing places the assonantal pair *I* and *time* in parallel (final) positions in groups (a patterning that is favoured by another preference that we will discuss shortly). The phrases *do count the clock* and *that tells the time* are also parallel syntactically. They both are (or have) transitive predicates, containing a finite verb and a direct object, which in turn has a definite determiner and no premodification. Both phrases begin with function words (*do, that*). And both are composed exclusively of monosyllabic words (as is the whole line).

The major competing reading divides the line after the sixth syllable.

When I/ do count/ the clock // that tells / the time

And this reading also has considerable motivation. It is a duple reading and therefore is supported at this level by GPR9 (Binary Form). It maintains the separation of the alliterations in [k] and [t] and therefore is supported by GPR13 (Similarity). And it distributes the two [ay] diphthongs evenly among prosodic constituents and thus is supported further by considerations of parallelism.

However, unlike the other phrasing, this divisioning roughs up the tight syntactic parallel between *do count the clock* and *that tells the time* and skews the positioning of sonic parallels. One way of avoiding these difficulties would be to add another level of phrasing, breaking the line into two intonational units and *four* phonological phrases.

When I // do count the clock /// that tells // the time ///

To my informational ear, this is somewhat unnatural, however. The line has an intonational unity that drives towards and culminates on *time*. Adding an additional intonational nucleus at *clock* breaks up this informational unity.

Grouping structures are multilevelled, while much formal patterning is structurally 'flat'. Therefore, most formal patterning suggests grouping divisions on many levels simultaneously, and in many cases these 'suggestions' can be contradictory. A famous case is Whitman's use of anaphoric structures in his rhetorical 'catalogues'. Both the catalogues and the anaphora are rhetorically heightening and broadening and therefore functional. In some cases, the anaphoric cataloguing is so intense and unvaried that it can blur rhythmic phrasing, however, creating an undifferentiated, arhythmic 'rush' (that many critics have found somewhat grotesque), as in the following section from 'Song of Myself' (674–83).

> In vain the speeding or shyness,
> In vain the plutonic rocks send their old heat against my approach,
> In vain the mastodon retreats beneath its own powder'd bones,
> In vain objects stand leagues off and assume manifold shapes,
> In vain the ocean settling in hollows and the great monsters, lying low,
> In vain the buzzard houses herself with the sky,
> In vain the snake slides through the creepers and logs,
> In vain the elk takes to the inner passes of the woods,
> In vain the razor-bill'd auk sails far north to Labrador,
> I follow quickly, I ascend to the nest in the fissure of the cliff.

Here, Whitman presents a nine-item catalogue, with little formal differentiation to suggest an internal phrasing. In this case, one might suggest that the arhythmic effect of this undifferentiated catalogue is contextually effective. It dramatizes the irresistible force of the poet's ego as it searches out contact with the infinite particularity of the environment. A rhythmic structure of this sort has a fairly limited expressive range, however. It loses its organized, directional movement.

Catalogues such as this must be distinguished carefully from most of Whitman's practice, however. In most cases, Whitman's anaphoric parallels contain other means for organizing the verse into coherent phrasal shapes. For instance, to my intuition, the following passage (663-9) is only superficially similar to 674-83.

> I believe a leaf of grass is no less than the journey-work of the stars,
> And the pismire is equally perfect, and a grain of sand, and the egg of the wren,
> And the tree-toad is a chef-d'oeuvre for the highest,
> And the running blackberry would adorn the parlors of heaven,
> And the narrowest hinge in my hand puts to scorn all machinery,
> And the cow crunching with depress'd head surpasses any statue,
> And a mouse is miracle enough to stagger sextillions of infidels.

Here, Whitman varies clausal structures so that they divide the passage into a pleasing triple, itself composed of a pair of triples anchored by a single.

a leaf of grass	is no less . . .
the pismire	is equally perfect . . .
the tree-toad	is a chef-d'oeuvre . . .

the running blackberry	would adorn . . .
the narrowest hinge	puts to scorn . . .
the cow	surpasses . . .

a mouse   is miracle enough   to stagger . . .

The first three structures are copular, the next three are transitive, and the final line is both copular *and* transitive (with the copular verb finite and the transitive verb non-finite). These structural differences subtly differentiate groups of lines syntactically and semantically and therefore by GPR13 (Similarity) suggest a tightly organized (and therefore more diversely expressive) phrasing.

4.3.2.5 GPR14 (Parallelism)

Closely associated with GPR13 (Similarity) is a general preference for grouping to respect formal *parallelism*. Given a series of formal parallels, we try to construct grouping parallels that are segmented and linearly ordered in accord with the formal parallels. Let's call this preference *parallelism* and list it as GPR14:[22]

> GPR14 (Parallelism): Prefer a grouping structure in which parallel forms appear as parallel parts of groups.

GPR14 (Parallelism) utilizes the same formal patterning as GPR13 (Similarity) but achieves an opposite result. Instead of interpreting formal repetition as an indication of grouping cohesion, GPR14 'reads' a repetition as an indexical marking relating two *different* groups. In general, GPR13 (Similarity) and GPR14 (Parallelism) respond to different sorts of formal repetition, however, so their results seldom conflict. GPR13 (Similarity) is sensitive to continuous repetition (the structure of repeated clauses, the continuous modulation of vocalic quality, etc.) while GPR14 responds to highly salient but discontinuous forms (e.g. lexical echoes, verbatim phrasal repetitions, etc.). For instance, in the Whitman passages from 'Song of Myself' we use GPR14 (Parallelism) to interpret the sporadic anaphoric repetitions ('In vain the . . .' in 674–83) and 'And the . . .' in 674–83) as indexical markers of the beginnings of different groups (i.e. the lines) while we use GPR13 (Similarity) to interpret the continuous modulation of the clausal structure in 674–83 (from copular, to transitive, to both) as an indication of grouping continuity and discontinuity among groups of these smaller lineal units.

Formal parallelism has a pervasive influence on all rhythmic response (meter and prolongation as well as grouping) and therefore is one of the strongest grouping preferences. As all would acknowledge, rhythm itself is a type of parallelism, one that represents parallels in our cognitive response to (1) alternating local saliences (meter), (2) global patterns of informational segmentation and culmination (grouping), and (3) global patterns of informational anticipation and extension. GPR14 (Parallelism) specifies the influence of formal parallels on our 'reading' of grouping spans. The influence of parallels on our 'reading' of grouping peaks is specified formally by GWFR6 (Levelling) and substantively by GPR1 (Information). Peaks of the same informational 'richness' (GPR1 Information) tend to gravitate to the same level in a grouping hierarchy (GWFR6 Levelling).

GPR14 (Parallelism) is multidimensional, drawing upon the entire system of 'associational' connections we construct in our response to the language of a text. Almost all of the formal 'schemes' isolated and named in classical rhetorical theory (e.g. Leech 1969: 73–102; Corbett 1971: 462–95) represent some type of formal parallelism.

From a historical perspective, however, the most important claim of GPR14 (Parallelism) is not its relative *strength* but its relative *weakness*. Following Myth 2 (Rhythm is linguistic/physical), many prosodists through the centuries have regarded GPR14 (Parallelism) as a categorical constraint on rhythmic response, representing rhythms directly as linguistic parallels. As I have argued at length in Chapter 1, the disparity between the formal coherence of rhythmic response and the relatively diffuse and overlapping patterning of formal parallels on the surface of a text weighs heavily against this approach. As in other matters, GPR14 (Parallelism) is just a preference that conditions grouping-language correspondences, not a definitional feature of grouping form.

Demonstrating the effect of formal parallelism on our grouping response to a text is a heavily contextual process that necessarily involves all of the grouping preferences. I reserve such demonstrations for Chapter 5.

4.3.2.6 *GPR15 (Measures)*

Analogous to GPRs 7 (Beats) and 8 (Arrivals), grouping segmentation is also influenced by canonical rhythmic form. Given that we have defined prolongational regions in terms of grouping spans, this influence is mainly metrical. We have a general preference for measures to coincide with grouping spans. Let's call this preference *measures* and list it as GPR15.

GPR15 (Measures): Prefer a group whose span coincides with a metrical projection.

GPR 15 (Measures) is supported by most of the approaches to meter in the tradition and is the (indirect) analogue of the metrical 'norms' proposed by the intonationalists (e.g. Epstein and Hawkes; Crystal, etc.), metrical phonologists (e.g. Kiparsky; Youmans, etc.), Slavicists (e.g. Tarlinskaja), and grammetrists (e.g. Wesling). All of the discussions in the tradition of the 'tensional' effects of enjambment and asymmetrically placed caesurae provide intuitional support for GPR15 (Measures) as well.

As with GPR14 (Parallelism), GPR15 (Measures) differs from these traditional discussions, however, in that it maintains a strict separation between (1) meter and grouping, and (2) rhythm and language. For example, GPR15 (Measures) does not claim that we prefer an intonational unit to be a metrical line (rather than some other metrical unit higher or lower in the metrical hierarchy). It just claims that we prefer grouping boundaries to coincide with *some kind of* metrical boundary. In this theory, the 'tensional' effects of more particular correspondences between language, grouping and meter are attributed to other sources (e.g. shaping within grouping itself, constraints on metrical realization, other grouping preferences, 'norms' within particular verse traditions, etc.).

GPR15 (Measures) also links metrical-grouping correspondence specifically to a metrical projection and therefore a certain level of metrical patterning, a specification that differs somewhat from traditional comment on these issues as well. In particular, GPR15 (Measures) does not claim that we prefer the textual spans between tactical beats to line up in any particular way with lower-level groups (or if we do, GPR15 (Measures) claims that this preference will have some other source). The spans between tactical beats are related by only one level of metrical articulation and are therefore not maintained by a metrical projection. This correctly predicts that lines are more rigorously constrained. It also correctly predicts the relatively free inclusion or exclusion of a lineal 'upbeat' and/or 'afterbeat' at a subtactical level. These subtactical beats are not a part of the lineal projection (which extends only from the four-dot to the two-dot level).

GPR15 (Measures) also predicts both (1) the 'segment-length' factor in enjambment, (2) the more severe effect of enjambment in a tetrameter than in a pentameter, and (3) the asymmetry between the relatively mild tensional effects of a contre-rejet vs the relatively severe effects of a rejet in the pentameter. A mid-line to mid-line enjambment runs against GPR15 (Measures) at the lineal level but maintains GPR15 (Measures) at the hemistich level. A rejet or contre-reject runs against GPR15 (Measures) at both levels. On the other hand, a contre-rejet in a pentameter with a four–six divisioning occurs outside of the 'natural' imperatives of the metrical projection *per se*, which is satisfied at the eighth syllable. According to GPR15 (Measures), this leaves the last two syllables free to serve as an optional 'upbeat' to the next line.

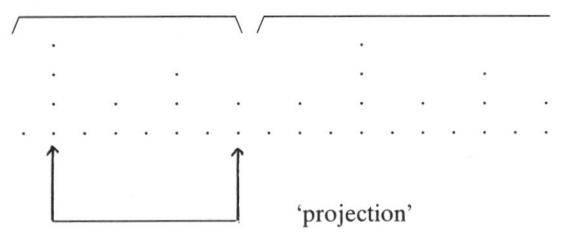

'projection'

Because of its symmetrical structure, a tetrameter cannot offer this option. A contre-rejet in a pentameter is jolting, however, because it usually denies the projection of both the second line in the figure and the first hemistich of this second line (in addition to denying the expected cadential completion of the projection of the first line in the figure).

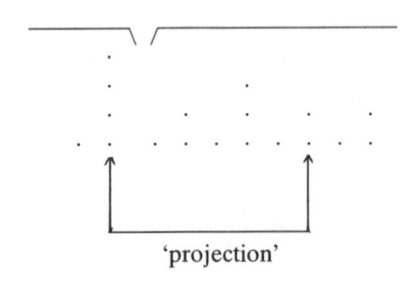

'projection'

4.3.3 Grouping preference rules (GPRs): textual pattern

GPRs 9–14 influence our reading of grouping spans. In general we prefer groups with duple spans (GPR9), while we avoid groups of just one (GPR11) or more than three (GPR10) constituents, and we prefer grouping spans that coincide with metrical projections (GPR15), that embrace formal similarities (GPR13), and that follow the morphology of formal parallels (GPR14).

There are also a couple of grouping preferences that influence our reading of *both* peaks and spans. These preferences refer to the distribution of grouping shapes within the grouping structure as a whole.

4.3.3.1 GPR16 (Unity)

First, we have a general preference for grouping unity, a preference for similar grouping shapes, both sequentially (on the same level of structure) and simultaneously (on different levels of structure). Let's call this preference *unity* and list it as GPR16.

> GPR16 (Unity) : Prefer a group that conforms to the predominant shape of other groups, both groups preceding and following as well as groups superordinate and subordinate.

GPR16 (Unity) is the grouping correlate of constraints on horizontal and vertical uniformity in meter and derives ultimately from more general preferences that operate in all perception and cognition (e.g. Wertheimer's 'Factor of Objective Set'). Within the structure of my literary assumptions, I also consider GPR16 (Unity) to be the foundation of one of the major functions of grouping (i.e. its contribution to organic form). Therefore, I would claim that readers that share my assumptions would seek out such grouping unities for other reasons as well and would generally prefer groups that contribute to such unities over other alternatives.

I have invoked GPR16 (Unity) in most of the (partial) analyses presented in this chapter, and we will see the influence of GPR16 (Unity) throughout the analyses in Chapter 5. For example, in our analysis of the first quatrain of Frost's 'Nothing Gold Can Stay' we saw how a preference for grouping unity contributes to our reading of informational prominences at low levels (the repeated falling contours early in the line – '**first** green', '**hardest** hue', '**early** leaf's', and '**only** so' – within the larger structure of rising prominence in the line as a whole – '**is gold**', '**to hold**', '**a flower**', '**an hour**'). In our analysis of lines 12–17 of Whitman's 'When Lilacs Last in the Dooryard Bloom'd' we saw how GPR15 influences our reading of the repeated amphibrachs at the third level, the structures that give the text its engaging lilt ('In . . . / **stands** . . . / with . . .'// 'and from . . . / **a sprig** . . . / I break'). We also saw how GPR15 (Unity) influences our reading of the falling contours of the paired duples at the opening of Millay's 'Spring' ('**To what purpose . . .**? / Beauty is not enough'. // '**You can no longer . . .** / I know what I know'). Most texts suggest an intricate system of multilevelled grouping unities. GPR16 (Unity) claims that we prefer to maximize this result.

4.3.3.2 GPR17 (Schemes)

Finally, it seems evident that our preference for grouping unities goes beyond a favouring of simple repetition. As the prose rhythmists, phrasalists and grammetrists have investigated at some length, we also prefer certain grouping *patterns*, what I will call grouping *schemes*. Grouping schemes include both static patterns, which present types of geometrical arrangement, and dynamic patterns, which present smooth modulations of grouping morphology. Let's call this preference *schemes* and list it as GPR17.

> GPR17 (Schemes): Prefer a group that completes a grouping scheme.

Grouping schemes are constructed out of the elements of grouping morphology: the two qualitative constrasts 'strong' and 'weak', the number of elements in the group (i.e. group's *span*), and the position of the strong element with respect to weak elements (i.e. the group's *inclination*). Together, span and inclination define *shape*.

Most static grouping schemes can be described with familiar terminology. Geometrical patterning is common in other aspects of poetic form (sound, syntax, etc.) and has been described for centuries. For instance, grouping shapes can repeat, alternate, invert or form chiastic or concentric patterns. One of the most significant aspects of these geometric schemes is that they can be constructed over isolated aspects of grouping morphology (e.g. span but not inclination, inclination but not span, etc.). For example, a grouping structure can be predominantly 'duple' or predominantly 'falling'. The first characterizes only span; the second only inclination.

Following the prose rhythmists and phrasalists, we might call dynamic grouping patterns *grades*. Graded spans can contract, expand, or both (either from small-to-large-to-small or from large-to-small-to-large). A convenient term for a scheme that both expands and contracts might be a *span pyramid*. Graded inclinations can *advance* the position of the peak from early in the group to late in the group, *retract* the position of the peak from late in the group to early in the group, or both (either from late-to-early-to-late or from early-to-late-to-early). We might call these inclinational schemes *advancing grades*, *retracting grades* and *inclinational pyramids*, respectively. The most effective grades modulate one aspect of grouping morphology (e.g. inclination) while keeping the other aspect constant (e.g. span), or modulate both span and inclination simultaneously. Advancing and retracting grades that maintain span we might call *perfect* (advancing and retracting grades). We might name expanding and contracting grades that maintain inclination by the part of the group that expands/contracts (e.g. *expanding rise*). We might name grades that modulate both span and inclination by combining descriptions for span with descriptions for inclination (*expanding advancing*, etc.).

Finally, we might regard meticulous variation also as a scheme. In most cases, *some* aspect of grouping morphology repeats occasionally. Therefore, for a poet to craft a passage that presents minimal repetition is a significant accomplishment. We might also note the effect of variation in a very homogeneous texture. In this context, a variation is felt as a *departure-and-return*. Departure-and-return figures, if they involve inclination, are often felt as *inversions*. Of course, departure-and-return figures could be heavily subclassified according to the nature of the grouping texture and 'departing' variation.

Collecting these comments, we might propose the following as a tentative 'typology' of grouping schemes. Of course, such typologies are always just suggestive; they can be expanded or contracted as required.

Grouping schemes

I. **Span**
   A. **Repetition**
      1. single (e.g. S, S, S)
      2. duple (e.g. WS, SW, WS, SW, SW)
      3. triple (e.g. WWS, SWW, WSW)
      4. large (all others) (e.g. WWSW, WWSWWW, WSWW)
   B. **Geometric patterns**
      1. parallel (e.g. . . .abc. . .abc. . .)
      2. alternating (e.g. abab. . .)
      3. chiastic (e.g. abba)
      4. concentric (e.g. abc. . .cba. . .)
   C. **Grades**
      1. expanding (e.g. 1–2–3)
      2. contracting (e.g. 3–2–1)
      3. span pyramid
         a. small-to-small (e.g. 1–2–3–2–1)
         b. large-to-large (e.g. 3–2–1–2–3)
   D. **Departure–Return**
      1. contraction (e.g. 3–3–1–3)
      2. expansion (e.g. 2–2–5–2)
   E. **Variation**

II. **Inclination**
   A. **Repetition**
      1. strong-final (e.g. WS, S, WWWS, WWS)
      2. strong-initial (e.g. SWW, S, SWW, SW)
      3. strong-medial (e.g. WSW, S, WWSWW)
   B. **Geometric patterns**
      1. parallel (same as for span)
      2. alternating
      3. chiastic
      4. concentric
   C. **Grades**
      1. advancing (e.g. WSWWW, WSW, WS)
      2. retracting (e.g. WWWSW, WSW, SW)
      3. inclination pyramid
         a. final-to-final (e.g. WWS, WSW, SW, WSW, WS)
         b. initial-to-initial (e.g. SW, S, WS, WSW, SW)
   D. **Departure–Return** (i.e. inversion)
      1. final-to-initial (e.g. WWS, WS, SWW, WWWS)
      2. initial-to-final (e.g. SW, SWW, WS, SWWW)
   E. **Variation**

III. **Shape**
  A. **Repetition**
   1. iambic (e.g. WS, WS, WS)
   2. trochaic (e.g. SW, SW, SW)
   3. dactylic (e.g. SWW, SWW, SWW)
   4. anapaestic (e.g. WWS, WWS, WWS)
   5. amphibrachic (e.g. WSW, WSW, WSW)
   6. single-rise (e.g. WS, WSWWW, WSW, WS, WSWW)
   7. single-fall (e.g. WSW, SW, WWSW, WWSW)
   8. double-rise (e.g. WWS, WWSW, WWSWW, WWSWWW, WWSW)
   9. double-fall (e.g. SWW, WWSWW, WSWW)
  B. **Geometric patterns**
   1. parallel (same as for span and inclination)
   2. alternating
   3. chiastic
   4. concentric
  C. **Grades**
   1. perfect advancing (e.g. SWW, WSW, WWS)
   2. perfect retracting (e.g. WWS, WSW, SWW)
   3. expanding advancing (e.g. SW, WSW, WWWS)
   4. expanding retracting (e.g. WS, WSW, SWWW)
   5. contracting advancing (e.g. SWWW, WSW, WS)
   6. contracting retracting (e.g. WWWS, WSW, SW)
   7. expanding rise (e.g. S, WS, WWS, WWWS)
   8. expanding fall (e.g. WSW, WSWW, WSWWW)
   9. contracting rise (e.g. WWWS, WWS, WS)
   10. contracting fall (e.g. SWWW, SWW, SW)
  D. **Departure–Return**
   1. perfect final-to-initial inversion
     a. double (e.g. WS, WS, SW, WS)
     b. triple (e.g. WWS, WWS, SWW, WWS)
   2. perfect initial-to-final inversion
     a. double (e.g. SW, SW, WS, SW)
     b. triple (e.g. SWW, SWW, WWS, SWW)
  E. **Variation**

4.3.4 Grouping preference rules (GPRs): summary

GPRs 16 (Unity) and 17 (Schemes) complete our discussion of grouping preference rules. For convenience, I reproduce these rules here, together with the grouping well-formedness rules discussed earlier.

Grouping well-formedness rules

GWFR1 (Contiguity): Constituents of groups must be contiguous.
GWFR2 (Peak): Groups with relatively weak constituents must contain one and only one relatively strong constituent.
GWFR3 (Magic 7): Groups have a maximum of seven constituents.
GWFR4 (Tri-weak): Groups have a maximum of three contiguous weak constituents.
GWFR5 (Root): The text is a group.
GWFR6 (Levelling): All groups occur at a labelled level in the grouping hierarchy.
GWFR7 (Recursion): If a constituent of a group is partitioned, it must itself be a group.
GWFR8 (Non-overlapping): If a group contains part of another group, it must contain all of that group.
GWFR9 (Horizontal Continuity): If a group is partitioned, it must be exhaustively partitioned.

Grouping preference rules

GPR1 (Information): Prefer a peak that informationally contains other groups.
GPR2 (Weight): Prefer a peak that is linguistically/physically 'heavy'.
GPR3 (End-focus): Prefer a peak that is in final position in a group.
GPR4 (Density): Prefer a peak that is linguistically dense.
GPR5 (Return): Prefer a peak that is a formal return.
GPR6 (Change): Prefer a peak that is a linguistic change.
GPR7 (Beats): Prefer a peak whose strongest syllable is a strong beat.
GPR8 (Arrivals): Prefer a peak that is a prolongational arrival.
GPR9 (Binary Form): Prefer a group with two constituents.
GPR10 (Singles): Avoid a group with only one constituent.
GPR11 (Tri-max): Avoid a group with more than three constituents.
GPR12 (Proximity): At low levels, prefer a group that is a prosodic domain, especially a prosodic domain that is visually unbroken. At high levels, prefer a group that is a syntactic constituent.
GPR13 (Similarity): Prefer a group that contains similar linguistic forms.
GPR14 (Parallelism): Prefer a grouping structure in which parallel forms appear as parallel parts of groups.
GPR15 (Measures): Prefer a group whose span coincides with a metrical projection.
GPR16 (Unity) : Prefer a group that conforms to the predominant shape of other groups, both groups preceding and following as well as groups superordinate and subordinate.
GPR17 (Schemes): Prefer a group that completes a grouping scheme.

Together, these well-formedness and preference rules represent a fairly detailed and explicit theory of grouping interpretation for English verse rhythm. The grouping well-formedness rules specify categorical constraints on our cognitive *representation* of grouping. The preference rules specify both representations that we prefer and the preferred *correspondences* between these representations and our non-rhythmic interpretation of texts.

By its very nature, a preference rule system makes relatively weak, and in practical terms relatively complex claims. None the less, following Lerdahl and Jackendoff (1983), I maintain that this system of rules makes substantial claims about our rhythmic reading of poetry, claims that are susceptible to refutation, by either intuitional evidence or more controlled, objective experiment. Therefore I maintain that these claims are technically theoretical, in the modern sense of the term. Given that I know of no competing theory, I offer these claims as a working hypothesis that can serve as a theoretical centre for the exploration of other components of rhythmic response (i.e. meter and prolongation).

The theory of grouping I have proposed here has significant implications for a range of general issues in prosodic theory and practice: philosophical, historical, critical, stylistic, pedagogical and so forth. However, a full consideration of these implications depends on a demonstration of the utility of the theory in practical analysis. This utility is the subject of Chapter 5. Therefore, I defer consideration of these implications until Chapter 6.

NOTES

1. Tynianov 1924/1981: 62.
2. Liddell 1902: 236–8.
3. GWFR1 (Contiguity) is the counterpart of Lerdahl and Jackendoff's GWFR 1. GWFR2 (Peak) is comparable to their TSWFR 1.
4. GWFR5 (Root) corresponds to Lerdahl and Jackendoff's GWFR 2.
5. GWFR6 (Levelling) has no counterpart in Lerdahl and Jackendoff's theory. Their grouping structures are not explicitly levelled, although their representations *imply* levelling. Cooper and Meyer's representations appear to be more explicitly levelled.
6. GWFR7 (Recursion) is the counterpart of Lerdahl and Jackendoff's GWFR 3.
7. GWFR8 (Non-overlapping) is the counterpart of Lerdahl and Jackendoff's GWFR 4.

8. GWFR9 (Horizontal Continuity) is the counterpart of Lerdahl and Jackendoff's GWFR 5.
9. The formal similarities between *in Just-spring* and *and it's spring* are many: *spring* is repeated; both phrases have three syllables; *in* and *it's* are assonantal; and *Just* and *it's* are consonantal, as are *in* and *and*.
10. Lerdahl and Jackendoff (1983: 307–14) argue that preferences may play a larger part in language structuring than is usually thought. They suggest that preferences are involved in conversational implicatures, quantifier scope, lexical semantics, markedness, parsing strategies and other matters.
11. I owe my label 'tongs and bones' to Lanier (1880: 246), who argues for the universality of rhythm on the basis of our strong response to percussive sound, citing the cry of the Ass in *A Midsummer Night's Dream* (IV, i, 28–9): 'I have a reasonable good ear in music. Let's / have the tongs and the bones.'
12. For comparable claims, one could cite Michael Riffaterre's theory of 'semantic overdetermination' in poetry (Riffaterre 1977, 1978) and Roman Jakobson's 'projection principle' for the poetic use of language (Jakobson 1960). Barabara Herrnstein Smith's theory of closure, as we will go on to discuss, also assumes that poetry has this 'centroidal' organization. GPR1 (Information) is the counterpart of Lerdahl and Jackendoff's TSPR 2 (Local Harmony).
13. For some discussions of Biblical prosody see Gray 1972, Yoder 1972 and Kugel 1981. The first full discussion is usually attributed to Lowth 1753: 200–16.
14. I borrow the term 'packaging' from Chafe 1976. There is now a considerable literature in text linguistics, too much to bring to bear on an interdisciplinary topic of this sort. Most useful to me has been the work by the Prague School (e.g. Jan Firbas), the English functionalists (e.g. M.A.K. Halliday), Dwight Bolinger, and the massive synthesis in Quirk *et al.* 1985. Taglicht 1984 and de Beaugrande and Dressler 1981 have also been useful. I have also been influenced by work in experimental psycholinguistics (e.g. the summary and references in Clark and Clark 1977).
15. GPR2 (Weight) might be seen as the counterpart of Lerdahl and Jackendoff's TSPR 3 (Registral Extremes), which prefers musical peaks with certain sorts of brute perceptual salience (rather than harmonic stability).
16. GPR3 (End-focus) is the counterpart of Lerdahl and Jackendoff's TSPRs 7 (Cadential Retention) and 9 (left unnamed), which prefer structural endings to structural beginnings. Cooper and Meyer (1960: 61) also notice this preference in Western tonal music.

Beginning groups, simply because they are beginnings, seem to be leading or moving toward a conclusion and therefore expectation is directed toward and emphasizes (accents) the completing groups or units. An antecedent appears to be directed toward the consequent which is its goal. And this goal is stable, focal, and accented in comparison with motion which precedes it. Second, this antecedent-consequent organization is so common in the literature with which we are dealing and the pattern is so well understood by the practiced listener that he tends if possible to organize groups in this way even though they have not been completed.

17. For the most extensive work on 'communicative dynamism' in language, see Firbas 1959, 1961, 1964, 1965, 1966, 1968, 1969, 1972, 1974, 1975a and b, 1976, 1979. I also recommend Bolinger 1952, 1957, 1958, 1972.
18. GPR7 (Beats) is the counterpart of Lerdahl and Jackendoff's TSPR 1 (Metrical Position).
19. GPR9 (Binary Form) is the counterpart of Lerdahl and Jackendoff's GPR 5 (Symmetry).
20. GPR12 (Proximity) is the counterpart of Lerdahl and Jackendoff's GPR 2 (Proximity).
21. GPR13 (Similarity) is the counterpart of Lerdahl and Jackendoff's GPR 3 (Change).
22. GPR14 (Parallelism) is the counterpart of Lerdahl and Jackendoff's GPR 6 (Parallelism).

Chapter 5

Analysis

> In the study of metrics, the philosphers' dictum, 'Not Meaning but Use,' formulates succinctly the most salubrious praxis. One must attend not to what a metrist *says* but to what he *does*, particularly in cases of discrepancy. Go to the scansion last, if not first – that is where the real principles appear.
>
> (T.V.F. Brogan)[1]

This chapter presents three rhythmic analyses applying the theoretical principles developed in Chapters 3 and 4. I present the three analyses in the same format.

(1) A summary graph with (a) a tree formalization of grouping and prolongation, and (b) a dot matrix formalization of meter.
(2) A bracketing formalization of higher levels of phrasing (to the level of the tone unit).
(3) A grouping reduction (to the level of the tone unit).
(4) A prolongational reduction (to the level of the tone unit).
(5) A 'top-down' commentary on higher levels of phrasing (to the level of the tone unit).
(6) A 'bottom-up', line-by-line commentary on lower levels of phrasing and their interaction with meter.

5.1 FREE VERSE

5.1.1 Text

 1 Without invention nothing is well spaced,
 2 unless the mind change, unless
 3 the stars are new measured, according
 4 to their relative positions, the
 5 line will not change, the necessity
 6 will not matriculate: unless there is
 7 a new mind there cannot be a new
 8 line, the old will go on
 9 repeating itself with recurring
10 deadliness: without invention
11 nothing lies under the witch-hazel
12 bush, the alder does not grow from among
13 the hummocks margining the all
14 but spent channel of the old swale,
15 the small foot-prints
16 of the mice under the overhanging
17 tufts of the bunch-grass will not
18 appear: without invention the line
19 will never again take on its ancient
20 divisions when the word, a supple word,
21 lived in it, crumbled now to chalk.

(William Carlos Williams)

FREE VERSE 279

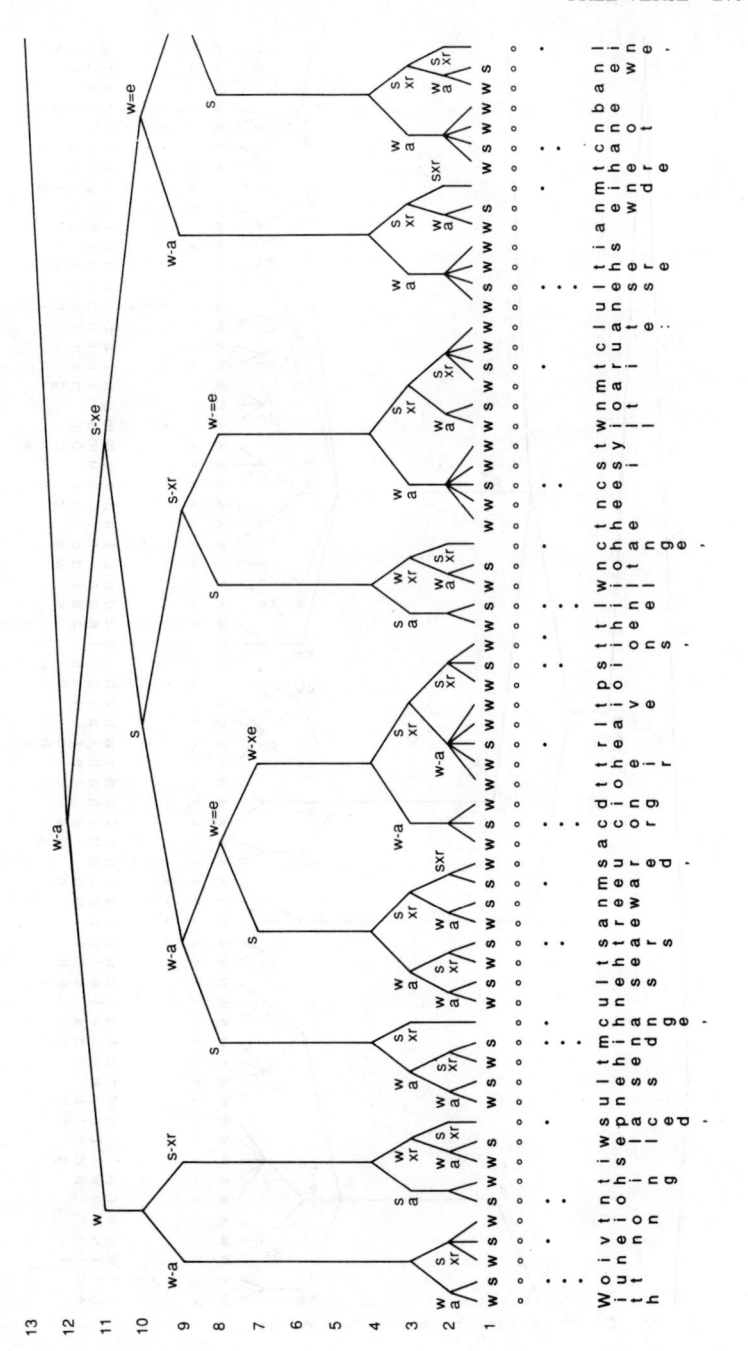

280 ANALYSIS

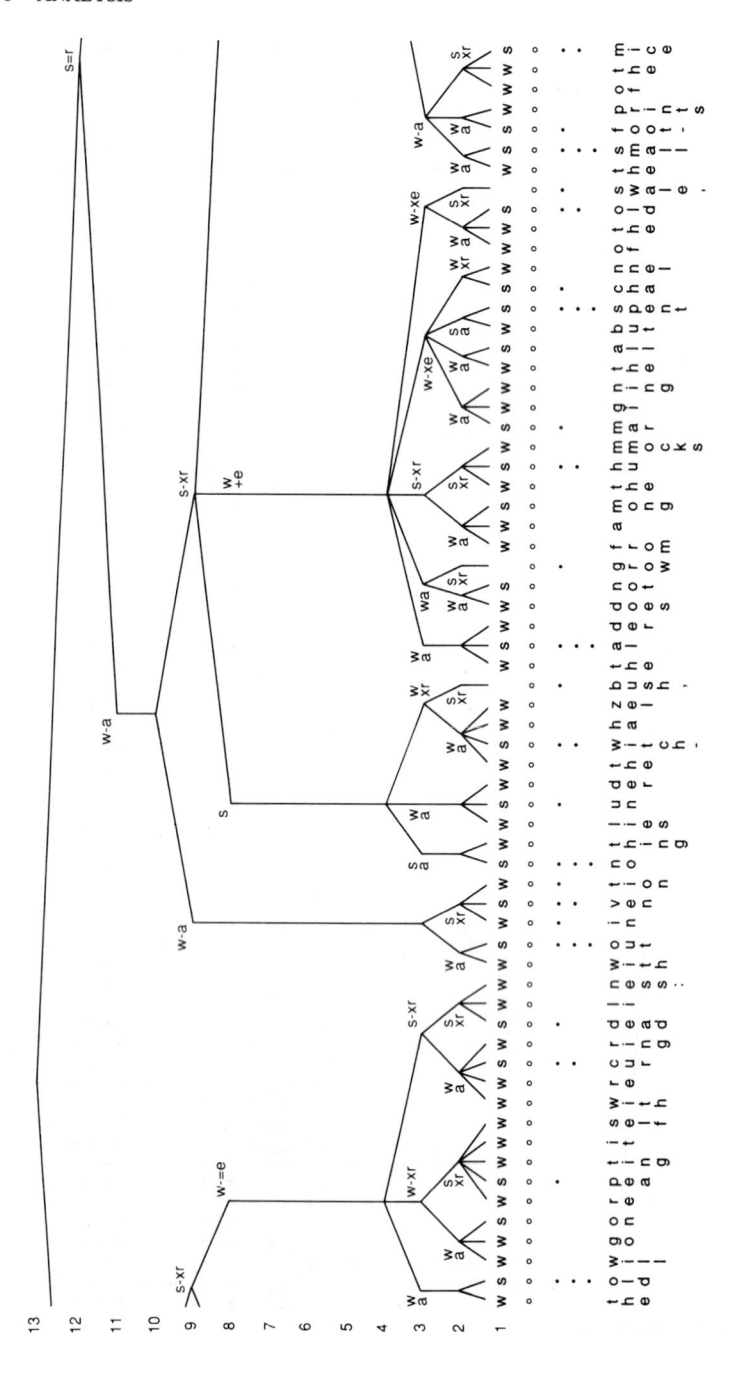

FREE VERSE   281

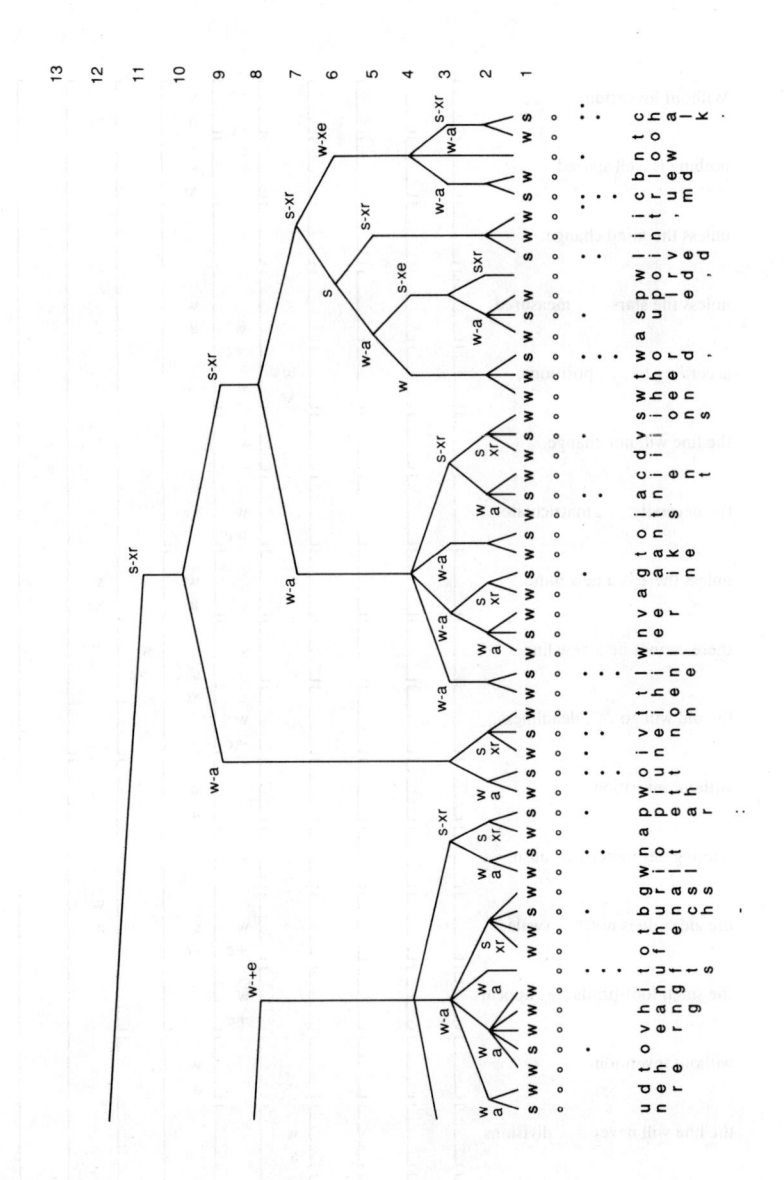

5.1.2. Higher levels of phrasing: bracketing formalization

282 ANALYSIS

5.1.2 Higher levels of phrasing: bracketing formalization

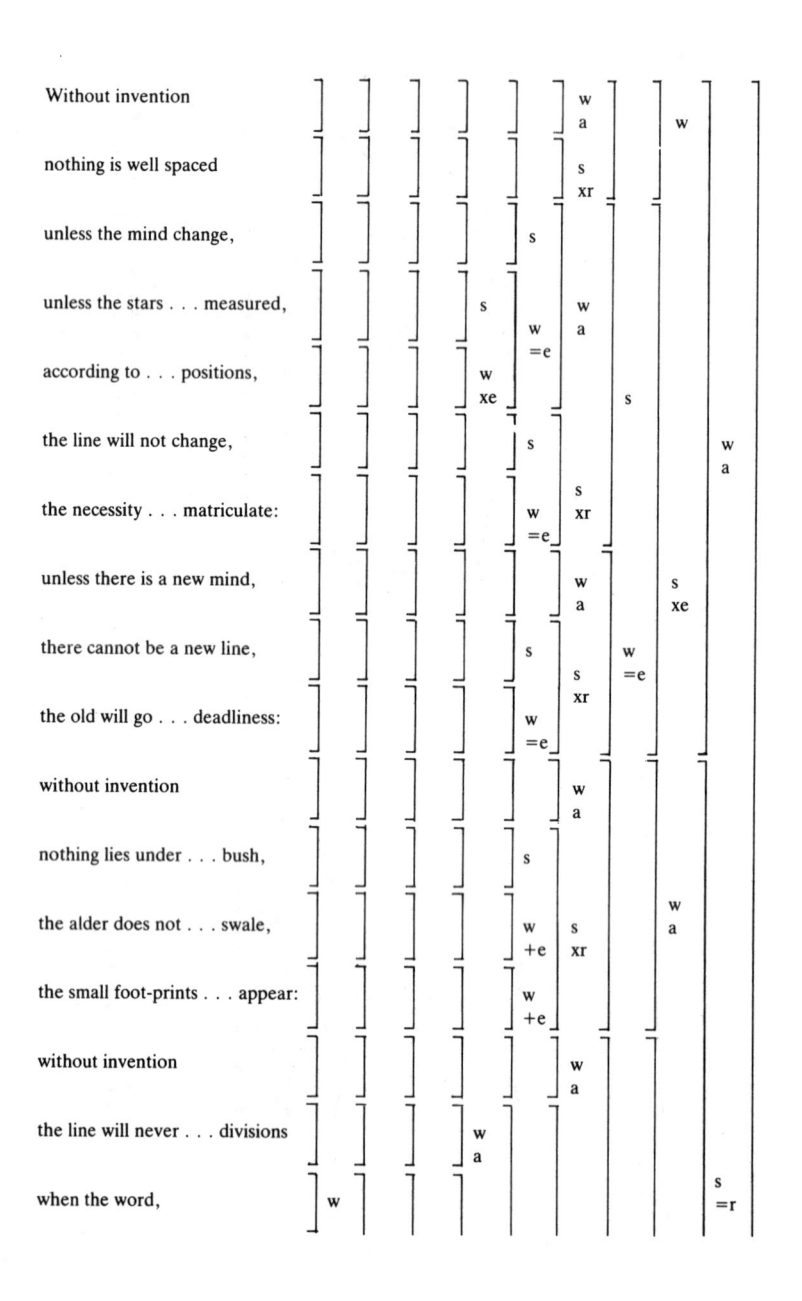

Without invention						w a		w
nothing is well spaced						s xr		
unless the mind change,					s			
unless the stars . . . measured,			s			w a		
according to . . . positions,				w xe	w =e		s	
the line will not change,					s	s		w a
the necessity . . . matriculate:						w =e	s xr	
unless there is a new mind,						w a		s xe
there cannot be a new line,					s	s xr	w =e	
the old will go . . . deadliness:						w =e		
without invention						w a		
nothing lies under . . . bush,					s			
the alder does not . . . swale,					w +e	s xr		w a
the small foot-prints . . . appear:					w +e			
without invention						w a		
the line will never . . . divisions			w a					
when the word,	w							s =r

FREE VERSE 283

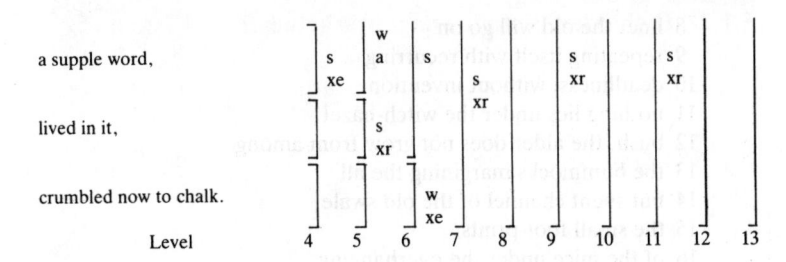

```
a supple word,          ⎤     w  ⎤      ⎤       ⎤ s  ⎤ s  ⎤
                        ⎥  s  a  ⎥ s    ⎥       ⎥ xr ⎥ xr ⎥
                        ⎥  xe    ⎥   s  ⎥       ⎥    ⎥    ⎥
                        ⎦        ⎦   xr ⎥       ⎥    ⎥    ⎥
lived in it,            ⎤        ⎤ s    ⎥       ⎥    ⎥    ⎥
                        ⎥        ⎥ xr   ⎥       ⎥    ⎥    ⎥
                        ⎦        ⎦      ⎥       ⎥    ⎥    ⎥
crumbled now to chalk.  ⎤        ⎤   w  ⎥       ⎥    ⎥    ⎥
                        ⎦        ⎦   xe ⎦       ⎦    ⎦    ⎦
       Level            4    5   6    7    8   9   10   11   12   13
```

5.1.3 Grouping reduction

Minus dependent units within Level 5

 1 Without invention nothing is well spaced,
 2 unless the mind change, unless
 3 the stars are new measured, according
 4 to their relative positions, the
 5 line will not change, the necessity
 6 will not matriculate: unless there is
 7 a new mind there cannot be a new
 8 line, the old will go on
 9 repeating itself with recurring
10 deadliness: without invention
11 nothing lies under the witch-hazel
12 bush, the alder does not grow from among
13 the hummocks margining the all
14 but spent channel of the old swale,
15 the small foot-prints
16 of the mice under the overhanging
17 tufts of the bunch-grass will not
18 appear: without invention the line
19 will never again take on its ancient
20 divisions [when]   a supple word,
21 lived in it, crumbled now to chalk.

Minus dependent units within Level 6

 1 Without invention nothing is well spaced,
 2 unless the mind change, unless
 3 the stars are new measured, according
 4 to their relative positions, the
 5 line will not change, the necessity
 6 will not matriculate: unless there is
 7 a new mind there cannot be a new

8 line, the old will go on
   9 repeating itself with recurring
  10 deadliness: without invention
  11 nothing lies under the witch-hazel
  12 bush, the alder does not grow from among
  13 the hummocks margining the all
  14 but spent channel of the old swale,
  15 the small foot-prints
  16 of the mice under the overhanging
  17 tufts of the bunch-grass will not
  18 appear: without invention the line
  19 will never again take on its ancient
  20 divisions [when]   [a supple word],
  21 lived in it, crumbled now to chalk.

Minus dependent units within Level 7

   1 Without invention nothing is well spaced,
   2 unless the mind change, unless
   3 the stars are new measured, according
   4 to their relative positions, the
   5 line will not change, the necessity
   6 will not matriculate: unless there is
   7 a new mind there cannot be a new
   8 line, the old will go on
   9 repeating itself with recurring
  10 deadliness: without invention
  11 nothing lies under the witch-hazel
  12 bush, the alder does not grow from among
  13 the hummocks margining the all
  14 but spent channel of the old swale,
  15 the small foot-prints
  16 of the mice under the overhanging
  17 tufts of the bunch-grass will not
  18 appear: without invention the line
  19 will never again take on its ancient
  20 divisions [when]   [a supple word],
  21 lived in it,

Minus dependent units within Level 8

   1 Without invention nothing is well spaced,
   2 unless the mind change, unless
   3 the stars are new measured,
   4   the

```
 5 line will not change, the necessity
 6 will not matriculate: unless there is
 7 a new mind there cannot be a new
 8 line, the old will go on
 9 repeating itself with recurring
10 deadliness: without invention
11 nothing lies under the witch-hazel
12 bush, the alder does not grow from among
13 the hummocks margining the all
14 but spent channel of the old swale,
15 the small foot-prints
16 of the mice under the overhanging
17 tufts of the bunch-grass will not
18 appear: without invention [the line
19 will never again take on its ancient
20 divisions] [when]     [a supple word],
21 lived in it,
```

Minus dependent units within Level 9

```
 1 Without invention nothing is well spaced,
 2 unless the mind change,
 3
 4                       the
 5 line will not change,
 6                            unless there is
 7 a new mind there cannot be a new
 8 line,
 9
10              without invention
11 nothing lies under the witch-hazel
12 bush,
13
14
15
16
17
18         without invention [the line
19 will never again take on its ancient
20 divisions] [when]     [a supple word],
21 lived in it,
```

Minus dependent units within Level 10

```
 1 [Without invention] nothing is well spaced,
```

2 [unless the mind change,]
 3
 4   the
 5 line will not change,
 6   [unless there is
 7 a new mind] there cannot be a new
 8 line,
 9
10   [without invention]
11 nothing lies under the witch-hazel
12 bush,
13
14
15
16
17
18   [without invention] [the line
19 will never again take on its ancient
20 divisions] [when]   [a supple word],
21 lived in it,

Minus dependent units within Level 11

 1 [Without invention] nothing is well spaced,
 2 [unless the mind change,]
 3
 4   the
 5 line will not change,
 6
 7
 8
 9
10   [without invention]
11 nothing lies under the witch-hazel
12 bush,
13
14
15
16
17
18   [without invention] [the line
19 will never again take on its ancient
20 divisions] [when]   [a supple word],
21 lived in it,

Minus dependent units within Level 12

```
 1
 2  [unless the mind change,]
 3
 4                          the
 5  line will not change,
 6
 7
 8
 9
10
11
12
13
14
15
16
17
18           [without invention] [the line
19  will never again take on its ancient
20  divisions] [when]      [a supple word],
21  lived in it,
```

Minus dependent units within Level 13

```
 1
 2
 3
 4
 5
 6
 7
 8
 9
10
11
12
13
14
15
16
17
18           [without invention] [the line
19  will never again take on its ancient
```

288 ANALYSIS

   20 divisions] [when]   [a supple word],
   21 lived in it,

5.1.4 Prolongational reduction

Minus dependent units within Level 5

1 Without invention nothing is well spaced,
2 unless the mind change, unless
3 the stars are new measured, according
4 to their relative positions, the
5 line will not change, the necessity
6 will not matriculate: unless there is
7 a new mind there cannot be a new
8 line, the old will go on
9 repeating itself with recurring
10 deadliness: without invention
11 nothing lies under the witch-hazel
12 bush, the alder does not grow from among
13 the hummocks margining the all
14 but spent channel of the old swale,
15 the small foot-prints
16 of the mice under the overhanging
17 tufts of the bunch-grass will not
18 appear: without invention the line
19 will never again take on its ancient
20 divisions when the word
21 lived in it, crumbled now to chalk.

Minus dependent units within Level 6

1 Without invention nothing is well spaced,
2 unless the mind change, unless
3 the stars are new measured, according
4 to their relative positions, the
5 line will not change, the necessity
6 will not matriculate: unless there is
7 a new mind there cannot be a new
8 line, the old will go on
9 repeating itself with recurring
10 deadliness: without invention
11 nothing lies under the witch-hazel
12 bush, the alder does not grow from among
13 the hummocks margining the all
14 but spent channel of the old swale,

15 the small foot-prints
16 of the mice under the overhanging
17 tufts of the bunch-grass will not
18 appear: without invention the line
19 will never again take on its ancient
20 divisions [when the word]
21 lived in it, crumbled now to chalk.

Minus dependent units within Level 7

1 Without invention nothing is well spaced,
2 unless the mind change, unless
3 the stars are new measured, according
4 to their relative positions, the
5 line will not change, the necessity
6 will not matriculate: unless there is
7 a new mind there cannot be a new
8 line, the old will go on
9 repeating itself with recurring
10 deadliness: without invention
11 nothing lies under the witch-hazel
12 bush, the alder does not grow from among
13 the hummocks margining the all
14 but spent channel of the old swale,
15 the small foot-prints
16 of the mice under the overhanging
17 tufts of the bunch-grass will not
18 appear: without invention the line
19 will never again take on its ancient
20 divisions [when the word]
21 lived in it

Minus dependent units within Level 8

1 Without invention nothing is well spaced,
2 unless the mind change, unless
3 the stars are new measured,
4   the
5 line will not change, the necessity
6 will not matriculate: unless there is
7 a new mind there cannot be a new
8 line, the old will go on
9 repeating itself with recurring
10 deadliness: without invention
11 nothing lies under the witch-hazel
12 bush, the alder does not grow from among

13 the hummocks margining the all
14 but spent channel of the old swale,
15 the small foot-prints
16 of the mice under the overhanging
17 tufts of the bunch-grass will not
18 appear: without invention [the line
19 will never again take on its ancient
20 divisions] [when the word]
21 lived in it

Minus dependent units within Level 9

1 Without invention nothing is well spaced,
2 unless the mind change,
3
4   the
5 line will not change,
6   unless there is
7 a new mind there cannot be a new
8 line,
9
10   without invention
11 nothing lies under the witch-hazel
12 bush,
13
14
15
16
17
18   without invention [the line
19 will never again take on its ancient
20 divisions] [when the word]
21 lived in it

Minus dependent units within Level 10

1 [Without invention] nothing is well spaced,
2 [unless the mind change,]
3
4   the
5 line will not change,
6   [unless there is
7 a new mind,] there cannot be a new
8 line,
9

```
10          [without invention]
11 nothing lies under the witch-hazel
12 bush,
13
14
15
16
17
18          [without invention] [the line
19 will never again take on its ancient
20 divisions] [when the word]
21 lived in it
```

Minus dependent units within Level 11

```
1 [Without invention] nothing is well spaced,
2 [unless the mind change,]
3
4                    the
5 line will not change,
6
7
8
9
10          [without invention]
11 nothing lies under the witch-hazel
12 bush,
13
14
15
16
17
18          [without invention] [the line
19 will never again take on its ancient
20 divisions] [when the word]
21 lived in it
```

Minus dependent units within Level 12

```
1 [Without invention] nothing is well spaced,
2
3
4
5
6
```

7
8
9
10
11
12
13
14
15
16
17
18   [without invention] [the line
19 will never again take on its ancient
20 divisions] [when the word]
21 lived in it

Minus dependent units within Level 13

1
2
3
4
5
6
7
8
9
10
11
12
13
14
15
16
17
18   [without invention] [the line
19 will never again take on its ancient
20 divisions] [when the word]
21 lived in it

5.1.5 General comments

Thematically, this passage from *Paterson* laments the loss of imaginative order in the modern world and the dependence of that loss on the lack of imaginative 'invention', in particular prosodic invention. As Cushman (1985) and others have argued, this is a recurrent theme in Williams' poetry and other writing and can be viewed as an artistic reflex of Williams' frequent prosodic theorizing (about the 'variable foot', the formal bases of poetic invention, the centrality of 'measure' to the poetic imagination, etc.).

These thematic relations between order and disorder, loss and redemption, metaphysics and metapoetics, provide the overall architecture for the passage at discourse levels, an architecture that appears at the five highest levels in the text's phrasing (i.e. Levels 9–13). Structurally, the most central realization of this theme appears at Level 9 in the grouping structure, a level that corresponds to the major syntactic figure in the passage: a clause complex with a negative conditional subordinate clause followed by a negative consequent main clause (i.e. 'Without/unless X, no/not Y'). With its fivefold appearance, often supported by verbatim wordings, this syntactic figure organizes the most salient and the regular movement in the text's phrasing. This movement is normatively duple and rising.

These five syntactic parallels provide the major rhythmic control from which Williams constructs the more 'irregular' and therefore energizing dimensions of the text's rhythm. At high levels of phrasing, Williams places the unpairable fifth unit at this central level in the first half of the text, producing a discourse prolongation that adds some high-level tension within the text's normative 2x2 structure at the highest levels. At low syntactic levels, Williams then expands these central syntactic parallels with weak, equative/additive extensions, extensional echoes that first crescendo in length and complexity, reaching a maximum in the wildly expanded double extension at the opening of the second half of the text, and then cadence with a severe syntactic contraction supported by a multilevelled anticipatory rise at lower (intonational) levels. The firmly closed crescendoing movement in the text gives the verse its didactic, oratorical tone. The falling extensional movement renders the text's elegiac sentiment.

The syntactic and intonational parallels within these central duples at Level 9 also provide the basic structural frame for the text's meter. Occasionally, one of these ninth-level parallels in itself suggests a metrical line.

> Without invention nothing is well spaced.
> unless there is a new line, there cannot be a new line,

Sometimes a *part* of one of these central parallels suggests a metrical line.

> nothing lies under the witch-hazel bush
> the line will never again take on its ancient divisions

Sometimes a part of one of these central parallels pairs with an elaboration to suggest a metrical line.

> unless the mind change, unless the stars are new measured,

And sometimes an elaboration alone suggests a metrical line.

> according to their relative positions
> the old will go on repeating itself with recurring deadliness
> when the word, a supple word, lived in it
> crumbled now to chalk

Given the visual and intonational variation in the text, this meter is not insistent, however, and to be effective must be both cognitively natural (i.e. a four-beat form) and somewhat forcibly maintained. Many readers may choose to relinquish it at times; others may choose not to maintain it at all. I find a metrical response to this text an important rhythmic possibility, however. Therefore, I include this possibility in my rhythmic analysis below.

Tactical beats in my metrical response to the text are stabilized most forcibly by the distribution of phonological phrase peaks within the intonationally and syntactically 'natural' lines I have suggested above.

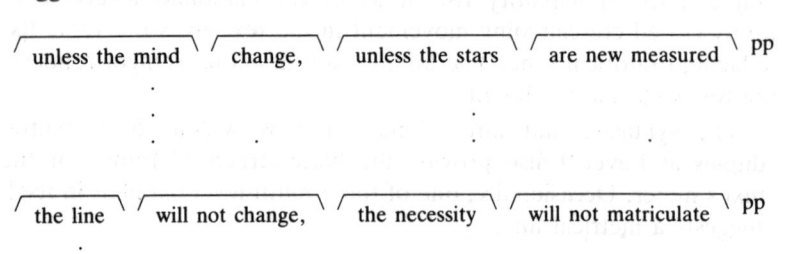

| unless the mind | change, | unless the stars | are new measured | pp |

| the line | will not change, | the necessity | will not matriculate | pp |

This meter does not align syllables but responds to a higher prosodic level. This high-level positioning gives the meter a prosaic air. If continuously maintained, this meter must articulate its own structural spaces at times, sometimes in a relatively forceful resistance to grouping. For instance, the last two metrical lines have only three realized beats, with a fourth beat implied.

> when the word, a supple word, lived in it
> .
> .   .
> .   .   .   [.]
> crumbled now to chalk
> .   .   .
> .   .   [.]

I also read the last two instances of *without invention* as metrical lines, even though this reading departs wildly from the normative correspondence in the text of tactical beating and the phonological phrase.

> without invention
> .
> .   .
> .   .   .   .

These cases of metrical strain are aesthetically functional, however; therefore, they are supported by a range of broader considerations that mitigate their local difficulty. For instance, the odd metrical readings of the last two instances of *without invention* further enhance the physical and cognitive retardation produced independently by high-level grouping contraction at these points. And the implied beats in the last two metrical lines add prosodic solidity and 'terminal modification' to the firm closure produced independently by rhythmical articulation of other sorts at other levels.

As in most of Williams' mature practice, this text is also significantly visual. Some of this visual form is aesthetically 'objective', calling attention to language itself and to the text's 'arbitrary' arrangedness. Line 2 both begins and ends with *unless*; and *new* is both the first and last content word in line 7.

2 unless the mind change, unless
7 a new mind there cannot be a new

Like line 2, many lines also place function words in either initial or final position, calling attention to their existence and meaning, a favourite practice of Williams.

3 the stars are new measured, according
4 to their relative positions, the
6 will not matriculate: unless there is

The general blocklike appearance of the text on the page could also be regarded as functionally 'arbitrary'.

Many other visual lines produce iconic/mimetic effects, reinforcing/enacting what they say. Line 8 begins a new line with a break between *new* and *line*.

6   unless there is
7 a new mind there cannot be a new
8 line,

Line 8 'goes on' intonationally into line 9.

8   the old will go on
9 repeating itself with recurring

The 'small footprints' in line 15 are given the shortest line in the text.

15 the small foot-prints

The *overhanging tufts* in lines 16–17 'hangs over' from line 16 into line 17.

16   the overhanging
17 tufts of the bunch-grass

Appear in line 18 'appears' after a line break and a negative.

17   will not
18 appear:

The noun phrase *its ancient divisions* is divided across a line break.

```
18                    the line
19  will never again take on its ancient
20  divisions,
```

In many cases, the text's visual lines also link and oppose lexical meanings across the syntax. The peripheries of line 5 link *line* and *necessity*; line 6, *will* and *is*; line 9, *repeating* and *recurring*; line 10, *deadliness* and *invention*; and the last line, *lived* and *chalk*.

This arbitrary and/or mimetic visuality is important to the aesthetics of the text. In my reading, most of these visual effects are not significantly rhythmic, however. The effects of the text's visual lines are not *completely* arhythmic. The first visual line is coextensive with the first metrical line, and five of the visual lines break between tone units (lines 1, 10, 14, 20 and 21). But in comparative terms this is a very low correspondence of visual and rhythmic form – in fact, low enough to be almost negligible. In this text, visual form runs pervasively *against* rhythmic form. For example, *no* visual lines are tone units.

This arhythmicity of the text's visual lines frees up visual form in the text so that it can present a continuously revisionary and 'inventive' comment on metrical and phrasal form. One significant dimension of this revisionary comment is the appearance of strong grouping peaks in line-initial position, a rare occurrence in texts in which visual and rhythmic form are coextensive (or reinforcing). Line-initial *lived* (in line 21) is the grouping peak of the text as a whole (at Level 12). Line-initial *line* is a grouping peak at Level 11 (in line 5) and at Level 10 (in line 8). Line-initial *deadliness* (in line 10) and *appear* (in line 18) are grouping peaks at Level 7. And line-initial *divisions* (in line 20) is a grouping peak at Level 6.

This independent and oppositional visuality, together with the possibility of a meter, gives this text a three-dimensional 'staving': visual, metrical and phrasal – a situation that we will encounter again in our analysis of Hopkins' 'The Windhover' in the next section. If we represent the phrasal staving of the text in tone units, my reading below suggests sixteen metrical lines and twenty phrasal lines, most of which cross both each other and the twenty-one visual lines.

Visual lines

1 Without invention nothing is well spaced,
2 unless the mind change, unless
3 the stars are new measured, according
4 to their relative positions, the
5 line will not change, the necessity
6 will not matriculate: unless there is
7 a new mind there cannot be a new
8 line, the old will go on
9 repeating itself with recurring
10 deadliness: without invention
11 nothing lies under the witch-hazel
12 bush, the alder does not grow from among
13 the hummocks margining the all
14 but spent channel of the old swale,
15 the small foot-prints
16 of the mice under the overhanging
17 tufts of the bunch-grass will not
18 appear: without invention the line
19 will never again take on its ancient
20 divisions when the word, a supple word,
21 lived in it, crumbled now to chalk.

Metrical lines

1 Without invention nothing is well spaced,
2 unless the mind change, unless / the stars are new measured,
3 according to their relative positions,
4 the line will not change, the necessity will not matriculate:
5 unless there is a new mind there cannot be a new line,
6 the old will go on repeating itself with recurring deadliness:
7 without invention
8 nothing lies under the witch-hazel bush,
9 the alder does not grow from among the hummocks margining
10 the all but spent channel of the old swale,
11 the small foot-prints of the mice under the overhanging
12 tufts of the bunch-grass will not appear:
13 without invention
14 the line will never again take on its ancient divisions
15 when the word, a supple word, lived in it,
16 crumbled now to chalk.

Phrasal lines

1 Without invention

2 nothing is well spaced,
3 unless the mind change,
4 unless the stars are new measured,
5 according to their relative positions,
6 the line will not change,
7 the necessity will not matriculate:
8 unless there is a new mind
9 there cannot be a new line,
10 the old will go on repeating itself with recurring deadliness:
11 without invention
12 nothing lies under the witch-hazel bush,
13 the alder does not grow from among the hummocks margining the all but spent channel of the old swale,
14 the small foot-prints of the mice under the overhanging tufts of the bunch-grass will not appear
15 without invention
16 the line will never again take on its ancient divisions
17 when the word,
18 a supple word,
19 lived in it,
20 crumbled now to chalk.

Most of the 'story' of this text's rhythmic effect will consist of a narrative rendering of (1) the cognitive events that occur as these these three different 'stavings' interact, and (2) the position of these events within the superstructure of the text's grouping and prolongational hierarchies.

I read almost all of the prolongational contours as congruent with grouping contours. This phasal coordination within the phrasal components accentuates the heavy-handed, didactic tone of the text. The only major departure from this phasal congruence occurs at Level 12, which I read as canonically extensional and then anticipatory in prolongation but canonically rising in grouping. Even this non-congruence is only faintly motivated, however, and could be read as congruent as well. My reading claims that we anticipate the primacy of metaprosody over metaphysics only in its second textual repetition. Many readers may make this inference earlier and therefore feel the conclusion of the first half of the text as a major prolongational arrival.

5.1.6 High levels of phrasing: commentary

5.1.6.1 Level 12

At the highest level (Level 13), the text is a canonically rising duple, with the grouping break near the text's prosodic and visual centre: in the middle of the tenth visual line. Prolongational contours at this level are anticipatory, although the arrival in the second half of the text is fairly equative (there is very little discourse movement).

The effect of this shaping is stasis and symmetry. Volatile expansion and contraction at lower levels is reined in here, giving the text a stiff formality. This static prolongation is the rhythmic reflex of the textual genre – meditation, not description, narrative or argument. The text speaks its message, and then speaks it again (in heightened tones).

The segmentation within the tenth visual line is motivated by several textual patterns. The most obvious is lexical repetition (GPR 14 Parallelism). The opening of the text *Without invention nothing* reappears verbatim in lines 10–11: *without invention /nothing*. The first two words of this phrase, *without invention*, appear again in line 18, but with a variation on the following negative ('never again'). In the first half of the text, the negative condition–negative consequent figure appears two other times, but with an introductory *unless* rather than an introductory *without* and with various paraphrases of *invention* and *nothing* rather than with these very words.

This medial break is also motivated by the rhythmic texture of lower levels (GPR 13 Similarity). Up to line 10, tone units remain controlled (e.g. five to eleven syllables), with only the last unit being expanded (for 'terminal modification'). After line 10, tone units (first) wildly expand (then) severely contract, presenting a much more volatile prosodic texture.

1 Without invention
2 nothing is well spaced,
3 unless the mind change,
4 unless the stars are new measured,
5 according to their relative positions,
6 the line will not change,
7 the necessity will not matriculate:
8 unless there is a new mind
9 there cannot be a new line,
10 the old will go on repeating itself with recurring deadliness:

11 without invention
12 nothing lies under the witch-hazel bush,
13 the alder does not grow from among the hummocks margining the
    all but spent channel of the old swale,
14 the small foot-prints of the mice under the overhanging tufts of
    the bunch-grass will not appear
15 without invention
16 the line will never again take on its ancient divisions
17 when the word,
18 a supple word,
19 lived in it,
20 crumbled now to chalk.

The significance of this modulation in tone units is heightened by their symmetrical distribution. There are exactly ten tone units in each half of the text. Line 10 and following also brings the only high-level triple in the text (i.e. the witch-hazel bush, the alder, the foot-prints), an event that also signals a grouping break (GPR 13 Similarity).

The rising inclination at this level is also well motivated. The second half of the text presents more descriptive intensity (GPR 1 Information), syntactic complexity (GPR 4 Density) and rhythmic volatility (GPR 6 Change). One might also argue that the metaphorical contrast presented in the last line between 'supple living' and 'crumbled chalk' is also the most explicit and intense realization of the text's theme: the loss of prosodic imagination/ invention (GPR 1 Information).

At this level, the multidimensional staving discussed earlier serves various functions. While the grouping division at this point produces phrasal symmetry, it divides the text after the sixth metrical line (leaving ten metrical lines to follow). This metrical asymmetry adds weight to the text's conclusion (GPR 2 Weight) while controlling its prosodic volatility. Visual form stitches together the two halves of the text (the grouping break at this level occurs at mid-line), maintaining the text's unitary, blocklike structure on the page.

5.1.6.2 Level 11

Level 11 is shaped by the repeated discourse movement in the text from metaphysical change to metapoetic change, the world to the line (GPR 13 Similarity, GPR 14 Parallelism). In each case, the reference to the line is stronger, yielding another level of duple, rising movement. The prolongational contours are chiastic, however, first extensional and then anticipatory. Together, these grouping and prolongational contours produce canonical phrasal form, a shaping that, like Level 12, restrains and frames the more volatile and various shaping at lower levels while highlighting for attention the basic proportional relations in this lower-level activity.

Quantitatively, the most striking feature of these proportional relations is the severe six- to eightfold expansion in the middle two units at this level, followed by a milder (2–1) contraction in the last unit. These chiastic quantities give physical support to the chiastic inclination of the prolongational contours at this level, highlighting with points of physical concentration the text's structural beginning and ending against its more expanded (and therefore dilute) centre of prolongational extension and anticipation.

With respect to immediately adjacent levels, the most salient function of Level 11 is to place a square frame around the repeated references to prosodic invention in visual lines 2–10, preventing an overtly asymmetrical triple–duple articulation at this level, an organization whose asymmetry would blunt and mute the text's dichotomous thematics and heightened oratorical tone.

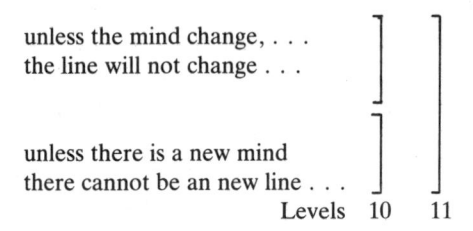

```
    unless the mind change, . . .   ⎤ ⎤
    the line will not change . . .  ⎦ |
                                      |
    unless there is a new mind      ⎤ |
    there cannot be an new line . . . ⎦ ⎦
                            Levels  10  11
```

Grouping segmentation at this level is relatively clear, both conceptually and formally. The fourth unit at this level is clearly marked by the third appearance of *without invention* (GPR 14 Parallelism) and by the sharp change in rhythmic quality and quantity after the expansive triple (i.e. the witch-hazel, alder and foot-prints) in visual lines 11–17 (GPR 13 Similarity). The first unit at this level is even more sharply bounded. It is the only visual line that forms a metrical line (GPR 15 Measures); it is one of the few visual lines that is bounded by a tone unit break (GPR 12 Proximity), and this visual–metrical–tonal unit, by itself, stands as a group at Level 11, a significant textual compression that sets itself

FREE VERSE 303

aside for notice (GPR 13 Similarity).

If there is any uncertainty in the segmentation of this level it is exactly with the second unit. Segmentation at Level 9 is so strong that one might want to dissolve Level 10 altogether, reading a triple in the second unit at Level 11. Several considerations weigh against this, however. In addition to roughing up the parallel with the second half of the text (GPR 16 Unity), this reading denies the many textual features that set aside visual lines 2–10 from surrounding material. It is only in this section of the text that *unless* appears in parallel with the negative condition *without* elsewhere. It is also only in this section of the first half of the text that Level 8 is elaborated. This level of elaboration is held in strict parallel with various syntactic and lexical echoes/oppositions and therefore is highly salient.

> unless the stars are new measured
> according to their relative positions
>
> the necessity will not matricuate
>
> the old will go on repeating itself with recurring deadliness:

Many other lexical and syntactic echoes also set aside this section of the text: for example, *new* (repeated three times), *change* (twice repeated), and the existential construction with *there* (twice repeated). Some of these echoes are also distributed in internal parallels, adding further to their perceived unity (GPR 13 Similarity).

> unless   the   mind change
> unless the stars   are   new   measured
> unless there   is   a   new mind
>   there cannot be   a   new   line

Prolongationally, Level 11 gives the text a major stratum of progressional movement that will be intensified at Level 9 but then delayed and prolonged with equational and additive movement at middle levels in the text. With the equational movement that appears at Level 10 (see 4.3.6.3 below), this shaping produces an alternate layering of progressional and non-progressional movement in the vertical structuring of the text, an organization that seems canonical for this rhythmic genre (i.e. 'oratorical' rhythm).

304   ANALYSIS

5.1.6.3   *Level 10*

Level 10 isolates the local, equative elaboration of the reference to prosodic invention in the first half of the text, the only unpaired local elaboration before the closural syntactic elaboration at end of the text. Together with the elaboration at Levels 7 and 8, this local elaboration expands the second unit at Level 11, further differentiating it from the structural beginning of the text while extending further the delaying, tensing prolongation of the first half of the text before the onset of its thematic recapitulation (in lines 10–21). This elaboration also adds another level of falling, equative movement between the rising movement at Levels 11 and 9, developing further the layered alternation of falling and rising movement in the vertical organization of the grouping.

The segmentation at this level is one of the clearest in the text. The five units articulated here present the repeated negative condition–negative consequent figure that is at the centre of the rhythmic organization of the text (GPR 13 Similarity, GPR 14 Parallelism).

This expansion and delay at Level 10 is matched in the second half of the text with different sorts of shaping at different levels of structure: a triple at Level 8 and wildly expanded articulation at the tone unit and below (Levels 2–4). This parallel in the second half of the text produces about the same syllabic volume with exactly half the number of tone units (8–4).

   1 unless the mind change,
   2 unless the stars are new measured,
   3 according to their relative positions,
   4 the line will not change,
   5 the necessity will not matriculate:
   6 unless there is a new mind
   7 there cannot be a new line,
   8 the old will go on repeating itself with recurring deadliness:

   1 without invention
   2 nothing lies under the witch-hazel bush,
   3 the alder does not grow from among the hummocks margining the
       all but spent channel of the old swale,
   4 the small foot-prints of the mice under the overhanging tufts of the
       bunch grass will not appear:

Such cross-level unity-in-variety seems more characteristic of verse than prose and perhaps differentiates the oratorical rhythms in this text from similar oratorical rhythms in unlineated forms with less explicit poetic intentions.

5.1.6.4 Level 9

Level 9 presents the most regular and salient level of rhythmic movement in the text. The ten units articulated at this level are all paired into duple, rising, progressional and anticipatory units at Level 10. This movement is unique at these mid levels in the grouping hierarchy; therefore it is foregrounded with special prominence. Both above and below in the hierarchy, movement is falling, extensional and non-progressional (i.e. additive and equative). This level is also the only global level of articulation at mid levels in the grouping hierarchy, a fact which further enhances its perceptibility and centrality.

Movement at this level gives the text its drivingly didactic and 'oratorical' tone. The pervasive anaphora and syntactic parallelism that marks the units articulated at this level might also be considered more typical of rhythmic prose than of verse. Therefore, in both form and effect, it might be this level that connects the rhythm of this text most directly with oratorical rhythms in other genres.

5.1.6.5 Level 8

Level 8 articulates the most extensive level of local elaboration in the text. The ten units at this level that are grouped at Level 9 all form falling, extensional and non-progressional contours – a remarkably regular level of movement for a local level of elaboration. This regularity enhances even further the 'oratorical' tone of the text and its relation to rhythmic prose.

The major function of this falling, equative movement is to give the text its ebbing, elegiac tone, a tone that achieves its most intense realization in the falling triple at the opening of the second half of the text, the only triple movement at high levels.

> nothing lies under the witch-hazel bush
> the alder does not grow from among the hummocks margining the all
> but spent channel of the old swale,
> the small foot-prints of the mice under the overhanging tufts of the
> bunch-grass will not appear:

This triple movement will be picked up again at low levels, especially the clitic phrase level, another instance of interlevel harmony that relates this text more closely to poetry than to prose.

While the falling movement at this level is indeed salient and somewhat heavy-handed (especially in the first half of the text), Williams does not make this level global by excluding it from the structural beginning and ending of the text. He also varies the paralleling by omitting this level in the negative condition within the local elaboration at Level 10.

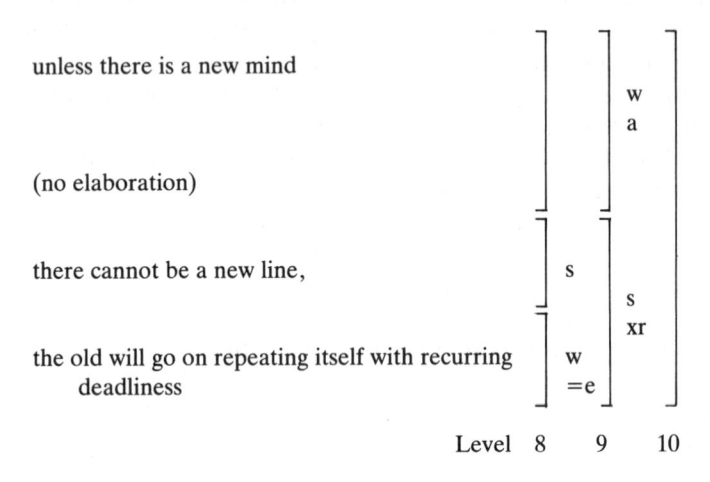

```
unless there is a new mind                        ⎤  ⎤  ⎤
                                                  ⎥  ⎥  w
                                                  ⎥  ⎥  a
                                                  ⎥  ⎥
(no elaboration)                                  ⎥  ⎥
                                                  ⎦  ⎦
                                                  ⎤  ⎤
there cannot be a new line,                       ⎥ s⎥
                                                  ⎦  ⎥  s
                                                     ⎥  xr
                                                  ⎤  ⎥
the old will go on repeating itself with recurring⎥ w⎥
       deadliness                                 ⎦=e⎦  ⎦

                              Level  8   9   10
```

This selective omission adds to the felicity of the relatively dense and regular elaboration that does appear.

Both the segmentation and the salience of this level are heightened by the homogeneous syntax of the five extensional elaborations at this level. All of these elaborations present exactly one finite clause, usually an independent clause.

> unless the stars are new measured,
>   according to their relative positions
> the necessity will not matriculate:
> the old will go on repeating itself with recurring deadliness
> the alder does not grow from among the hummocks margining the all
>   but spent channel of the old swale,
> the small foot-prints of the mice under the overhanging tufts of the
>   bunch-grass will not appear:

This homogeneous syntax affects the tone and generic relations of the text. Many poets (e.g. Wordsworth) elaborate their texts at high levels with falling, equative structures, but these poetic elaborations are more often phrasal than clausal. The high-level falling articulation in this text is not a repetitive renaming but a reiterated *asserting*. This again relates the text more directly to prosaic, oratorical genres than to poetry.

The contribution of Level 8 to both the emotion and the elegiac tone of the text is clearly evident in the grouping reduction for this level. Without the falling movement articulated at Level 8, the text is deprived of both its countermotion and its quantitative variation. It becomes flatly and coldly assertive.

Minus dependent units within Level 9

```
 1 Without invention nothing is well spaced,
 2 unless the mind change,
 3
 4                the
 5 line will not change,
 6                      unless there is
 7 a new mind there cannot be a new
 8 line,
 9
10            without invention
11 nothing lies under the witch-hazel
12 bush,
13
14
15
16
17
18            without invention [the line
19 will never again take on its ancient
20 divisions] [when]    [a supple word],
21 lived in it,
```

5.1.6.6 Level 7

Level 7 isolates two chiastically related elaborations, one in each half of the text. The first is falling and extensional; the second, rising and anticipatory. The major function of this local level is to oppose the two halves of the text, first enhancing the falling and extensional contours in the first half, as the text departs from its structural beginning, then enhancing the anticipational and rising contours in the second half, as the text comes to a close.

Because of their textual distance, these two elaborations are only faintly related. Both the structural imperatives of the grouping hierarchy (GWFRs 1–9) and the aesthetic organization of the text (GPR 17 Schemes) strongly suggest their rhythmic relation, however. Syntax also relates these elaborations across their physical separation (GPR 14 Parallelism). Both could be construed as in apposition to preceding pre-modifiers.

> unless the stars are *new* measured
> according to their relative positions,
>
>> the line will never again take on its *ancient* divisions
>> when the word, a supple word lived in it . . .

Of these two elaborations, the second is the more important, as it contains the cadential formula that brings the text to a close. Given the relatively slight discourse movement at the highest level, this cadential formula is essential to provide some forward impulsion and shape to the text as a whole. Without this closural gesture the text gapes open in rhythmic limbo, a shaping that could be effective in another context but which would be inappropriate here.

1 Without invention nothing is well spaced,
2 unless the mind change, unless
3 the stars are new measured, according
4 to their relative positions, the
5 line will not change, the necessity
6 will not matriculate: unless there is
7 a new mind there cannot be a new
8 line, the old will go on
9 repeating itself with recurring
10 deadliness: without invention
11 nothing lies under the witch-hazel
12 bush, the alder does not grow from among
13 the hummocks margining the all
14 but spent channel of the old swale,
15 the small foot-prints
16 of the mice under the overhanging
17 tufts of the bunch-grass will not
18 appear: without invention the line

19 will never again take on its ancient
20 divisions.

Being syntactically appositional, the final elaboration at this level is only weakly anticipatory and progressional. None the less, the imperatives of canonical rhythmic form become so pressing at this point that we expect this closural gesture even though this expectation is not suggested by either the text's argument or the syntax. Under the influence of this closural gesture, the first elaboration at this level becomes similarly progressional, although more weakly so.

5.1.6.7 Levels 4–6

Williams brings the text to a close with a two-level step-wise crescendo and a final coda, three levels of rhythmic 'deepening' that do not appear elsewhere in the text.

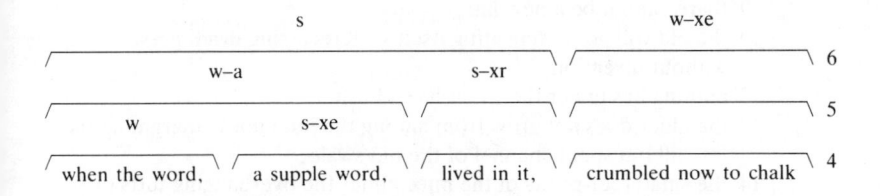

	s		w–xe	
w–a		s–xr		6
w	s–xe			5
when the word,	a supple word,	lived in it,	crumbled now to chalk	4

Within this local syntactic elaboration, intonational units are sharply contracted, with the syntactic and rhythmic relations achieved concentrating and recapitulating many of the dominant rhythmic motifs in text. The first 'step' (at Level 4) presents a rising appositional figure that recapitulates the movement that appears elsewhere at Level 12 (the text as a whole) and at Level 7 (the cadential figure as a whole). The second 'step' (at Level 5) presents a rising anticipational figure that echoes the strongest and most regular contour in the text, the rising duple movement at Level 9. And the coda (at Level 6) presents a falling, extensional figure that echoes the falling counter-movement that appears in a vertically alternating pattern at several higher levels. Any reduction in this final figure is less effective.

the line will never again take on its ancient divisions,
when the word lived in it,
crumbled now to chalk.

the line will never again take on its ancient divisions,
when the word lived in it.

the line will never again take on its ancient divisions,
crumbled now to chalk.

Level 4 presents the twenty tone units in the text.

1 Without invention
2 **no**thing is well spaced,
3 unless the mind **change**,
4 unless the stars are new **mea**sured,
5 according to their relative positions,
6 the **line** will not change,
7 the necessity will not ma**tri**culate:
8 unless there is a new **mind**
9 there cannot be a new **line**,
10 the old will go on repeating itself with recurring **dead**liness:
11 without invention
12 **no**thing lies under the witch-hazel bush,
13 the alder does not grow from among the **hum**mocks margining the all but spent channel of the old swale,
14 the small foot-prints of the mice under the overhanging tufts of the bunch-grass will not ap**pear:**
15 without invention
16 the line will never a**gain** take on its ancient divisions
17 when the **word**,
18 a **supple** word,
19 **lived** in it,
20 crumbled now to **chalk**.

Both in segmentation and in prominence, tone units in this text present many alternatives for rhythmic interpretation, most of which are not significantly constrained by textual patterns. Where the rhythmic structure of a text verges on prose, is only loosely metrical and is relatively free from visual contraint, as the text is here, this is to be expected. Under the influence of the first half of the text, I choose to render tone units in this passage with a relatively quick, 'sweeping' motion that segments only at overt marks of punctuation or other major points of syntactic discontinuity. Fifteen of the twenty units in my reading are bounded by punctuation. Four of the five remaining units segment between an initial adverbial (in one case a clausal adverbial) and the rest of a clause, a common point of intonational segmentation in the language. These breaks involve the three instances of *without invention* and the unpunctuated break after *unless there is a new mind* in visual line 7 (whose parallel, *unless the mind change* in visual line 2, *is* bounded by punctuation). The remaining break involves the final cadential figure *when the word . . .* (whose parallel in the first half of the text, *according to their relative positions*, is also punctuated).

The major effect of this intonational 'style' is to allow some tone units to run to considerable length, in particular the units in the middle of the text. The last tone unit in the first half of the text (the tenth) runs to seventeen syllables. The third and fourth tone units in the second half of the text (the thirteenth and fourteenth) run to twenty-five and nineteen syllables, respectively.

In addition to textual pressures (e.g. the close correlation of tone-unit breaks with punctuation), I make this choice on the basis of rhythmic genre and my aesthetic preferences. The prose-like movement of the verse encourages a more expansive movement, as does the text's dense repetition (and therefore informational redundancy). The long tone units are also expressive, both locally and globally. The expanded units in the second half of the text present the major flowering of descriptive detail in the passage. This detail does not directly participate in the major rhetorical oppositions elsewhere in the text (old vs new, mind vs line, invention vs deadliness, supple vs crumbled, etc.) but comes exactly as a rush of lament for the loss of the world; therefore, it is arbitrary to emphasize some parts of this description at the expense of others. Given a decision to avoid such selective emphasizing, the result is exactly to render intonational units with a descriptive rush, an effect that is pleasingly iconic in its larger context.

My choices of tonic syllables are relatively uncontroversial, though other choices are certainly possible. Because of the universal claims and rhetorical force of the negatives in the passage, I choose to render as tonic both instances of *nothing* (in tone units two and twelve) and the negative *never again* (in tone unit sixteen), even though these readings run against end-focus. My other decisions follow end-focus or clear discourse patterning. In tone unit six, I read *line* as tonic (instead of *change*) because of the earlier focus on *change* (in tone unit three). In tone unit eighteen, I read *supple* as tonic because of the earlier focus on *word* (in the immediately preceding unit).

I have discussed how the distribution of tone-unit segmentation affects the rhythmic shape of the text. Some patterns in inclination are also significant. The reversals in inclination caused by the negatives are important to the insistent tone of the text. These reversals create strong-initial contours with unusually forceful onsets. Tone-unit inclination is also carefully modulated in the cadential figure in the text, a patterning that is also echoed downwards in the prosodic hierarchy. In the grouping crescendo in the last four tone units, tonic syllables move from final, to second, to initial, and then again to final position. This 'capped' retracting grade further heightens both the emphatic, exclamatory tones of the rhythmic crescendo at higher levels and the inclinational reversal at the textual close.

when	the	**word**		
a	**su.**	pple	word	
lived	in	it		
crum.	bled	now	to	**chalk**.

5.1.6.8 *Levels 2 and 3*

As in most rhythmic prose, lower-level phrasing in this text is only loosely controlled, with only occasional global regularities or local schematic patterning. One noticeable pattern is a texture of triple movement at the clitic phrase level, often with medial prominence, especially in the latter parts of the text – a patterning that gives the text a lower-level lilt that supports its lyric intent. This pattern is not quantitatively dominant, but it is salient because it includes the triple repetition of *invention*, one of the key words in the passage.

in	ven.	tion
the	al.	der
from	a.	mong
the	hum.	mocks
mar.	gi.	ning
of	the	old
of	the	mice
in	ven.	tion
will	ne.	ver
its	an.	cient

```
di.     vi.    sions
when    the    world
a       su.    pple
lived   in     it
```

There are some occasional grades at the clitic phrase level. The text opens with a retracting grade, culminating on the negative *nothing*.

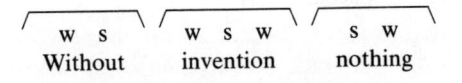

```
┌─────────┐ ┌───────────┐ ┌─────────┐
  w   s       w   s   w     s   w
  Without     invention     nothing
```

And the retracting intonational grade in the cadence is extended to the clitic phrase level.

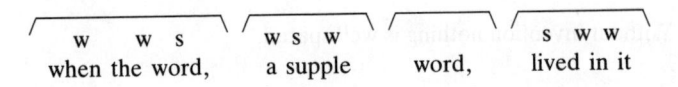

```
┌──────────────┐ ┌───────────┐ ┌──────┐ ┌─────────────┐
   w     w  s      w  s  w              s    w   w
  when the word,   a supple    word,    lived in it
```

This selective marking of structural beginnings and endings with low-level patterning is typical of most rhythmic crafting.

5.1.7 Meter

As mentioned earlier, I give the text a canonical four-beat, three-level meter, but with this pattern responding to a fairly high level of prosodic patterning.

5.1.7.1 Metrical Line 1

The first two tone units form a metrical line.

Metrical Line #1

Tone unit one

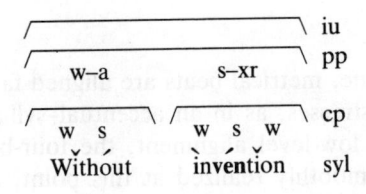

```
                               iu
  ┌──────────────────────────┐ pp
     w–a          s–xr
  ┌─────────┐ ┌───────────┐    cp
    w   s       w  s   w       syl
    Wĭthóut     invĕntĭon
    ·
    ·
    ·
```

Tone unit two

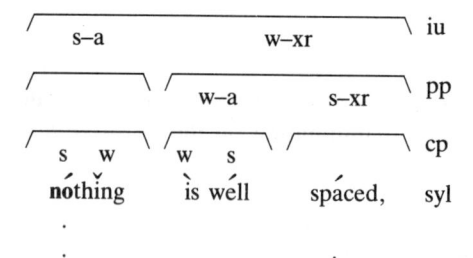

```
         ┌─────────────────────────┐ iu
         │  s-a          w-xr      │
         ┌──────────┐┌─────────────┐ pp
         │          ││ w-a   s-xr  │
         ┌────┐┌────┐┌─────────────┐ cp
         │ s  w││w  s │
          nŏthíng  ìs wéll  spáced,   syl
           .         .          .
           .
```

With its ten syllables and five clitic phrases, this line can be read as a pentameter, a possibility that most experienced readers undoubtedly hear.

    Without invention nothing is well spaced,

        .
        .   .   .   . .
   . . . .

Only two other prosodic units can be read as pentameters, however, and only one of these is also a line in the dominant meter in the text. Therefore, these pentameters only lurk in the background.

    according to their relative positions,

        .
      .   .
     . .   . . .
   . . . .

    the necessity will not matriculate

        .
           .   .
      . .   .   . .
    . . . .

None the less, in this opening line, metrical beats are aligned fairly closely to syllables and lexical stresses, as in an accentual–syllabic meter. In fact, because of this low-level alignment, the four-beat reading I give the text is not smoothly realized at this point, but stumbles somewhat on *well spaced*, uncertain where to place the fourth beat.

In this first metrical line, meter generally supports phrasing, however, even in the four-beat reading. Hemistichs are tone units and beats are generally placed on phonological phrase peaks. Given this alignment of beats and peaks, metrical tension is fairly low and the propulsive effect of the meter relatively mild.

5.1.7.2 Metrical lines 2–6

In the remainder of the first half of the text, the relation between metrical beats and syllables becomes looser. It is common to find four or even five syllables between tactical beats; therefore, the meter tends to accelerate the text's lower-level movement.

As in the first metrical line, the norm in this part of the text matches tone units with metrical hemistichs. Two tone units are matched with full lines: metrical line 3 and tone unit five, metrical line 6 and tone unit ten. These metrical–prosodic mergers divide the first half of the text into two tercets. With this loose relation between syllables and beats, it is just the more expansive tone units that become potential metrical lines (e.g. tone unit ten). This metrical support for long tone units might further justify my 'expansive' reading of the intonational structures in the text.

These metrical–phrasal relations have the effect of fusing and separating groups that are related, sometimes horizontally, sometimes vertically, in the grouping hierarchy. Metrical line 1 further unifies a grouping at Level 10, the most salient rhythmic level. Metrical line 2 pulls together groups at Levels 9 and 8. Metrical Line 3 unifies a group at Level 7. Metrical line 4 unifies a group at Level 9. Metrical line 5 again pulls together groups at Levels 8 and 9. And metrical line 6 unifies a group at Level 8.

ANALYSIS

Metrical line 2

Tone unit three

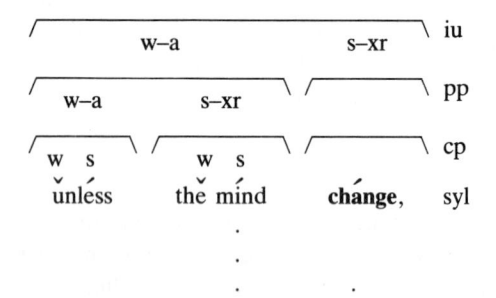

```
          ┌─────────────────────────┐ iu
          │   w–a       s–xr        │
       ┌──┴──────────┐┌─────────────┤ pp
       │ w–a   s–xr  ││             │
    ┌──┴──┐┌──┴──────┐┌─────────────┤ cp
    │ w s ││  w  s   ││             │
    │unless││the mind││  change,    │ syl
              .
              .
              .
```

Tone unit four

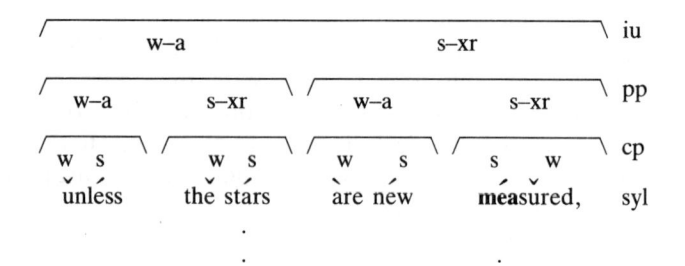

```
          ┌────────────────────────────────────────┐ iu
          │     w–a                 s–xr           │
       ┌──┴────────────┐┌──────────────────────────┤ pp
       │ w–a    s–xr   ││  w–a          s–xr       │
    ┌──┴──┐┌──┴────────┐┌──┴──┐┌────────────────────┤ cp
    │ w s ││  w  s     ││ w s ││  s   w             │
    │unless││ the stars││are new││ measured,        │ syl
                .                        .
```

Metrical line 3

Tone unit five

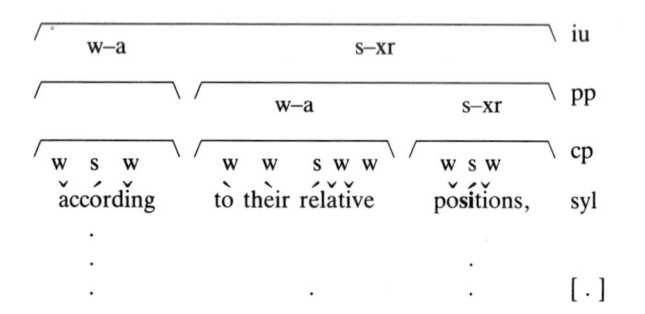

```
          ┌────────────────────────────────────────┐ iu
          │   w–a              s–xr                │
       ┌──┴───┐┌──────────────────────────────────┤ pp
       │      ││     w–a              s–xr         │
    ┌──┴──────┐┌──┴──────────────┐┌────────────────┤ cp
    │ w s w   ││ w  w   s w w    ││  w  s w        │
    │according││to their relative││ positions,     │ syl
       .                              .
       .                              .
       .            .                 .      [ . ]
```

Metrical line 4

Tone unit six

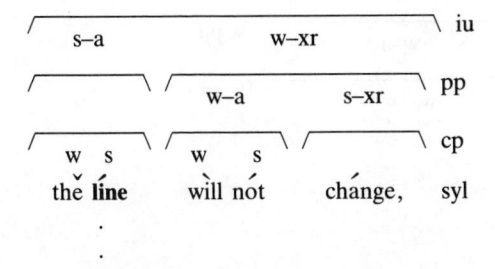

```
  ┌─────────────────────────────┐ iu
  │  s–a           w–xr         │
  ┌────────┐┌───────────────────┐ pp
             │  w–a      s–xr   │
  ┌────────┐┌──────────┐┌───────┐ cp
  │ w   s  ││ w    s   ││       │
  │the líne││will nòt  │change, │ syl
```

Tone unit seven

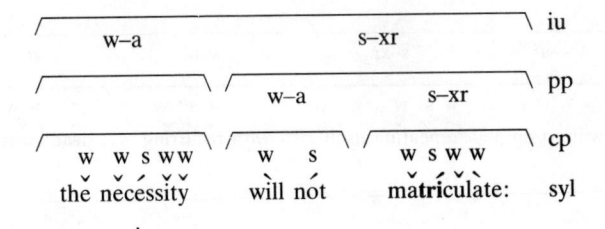

```
  ┌──────────────────────────────────┐ iu
  │   w–a            s–xr            │
  ┌──────────────┐┌──────────────────┐ pp
                   │  w–a      s–xr  │
  ┌──────────────┐┌────────┐┌────────┐ cp
  │ w  w s w w   ││ w   s  ││w s w w │
  │the necèssity ││will nòt││matrículate:│ syl
```

Metrical line 5

Tone unit eight

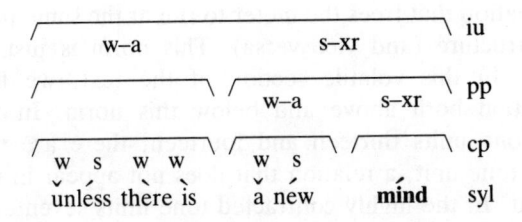

```
  ┌─────────────────────────────────┐ iu
  │   w–a            s–xr           │
  ┌─────────────┐┌──────────────────┐ pp
                  │  w–a      s–xr  │
  ┌─────────────┐┌────────┐┌────────┐ cp
  │ w s w w     ││ w   s  ││        │
  │unless there ìs││a néw ││ mínd   │ syl
```

318 ANALYSIS

Tone unit nine

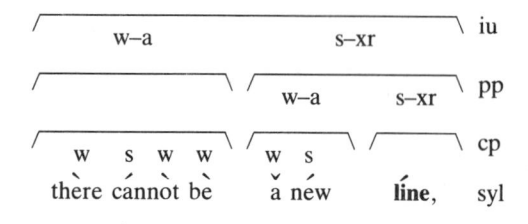

```
                                            iu
       w–a              s–xr                
                                            pp
              w–a           s–xr            
                                            cp
   w  s  w  w    w  s                       
  there cannot be  a new    line,     syl
```

Metrical line 6

Tone unit ten

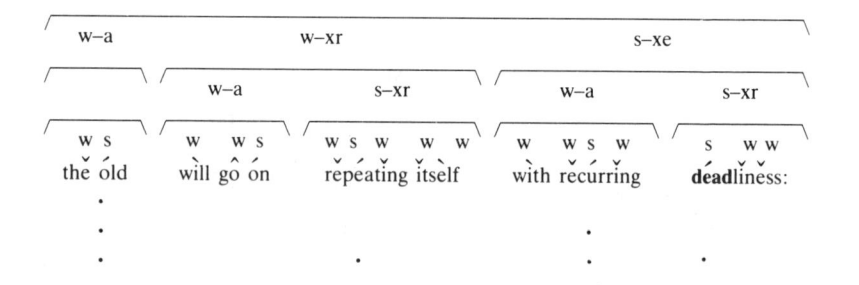

```
   w–a          w–xr                s–xe
         w–a          s–xr     w–a        s–xr
  w s   w   w s   w s w  w w  w  w s w   s  w w
  the old  will go on repeating itself with recurring deadliness:
```

5.1.7.3 Metrical lines 7–16

The norm in the second half of the text is to match tone units with metrical lines, a relation that frees the meter to run at the same pace as the grouping structure (and vice versa). This norm is just an average, however. In this volatile section of the text, we find considerable variation both above and below this norm. In the highly expanded tone units thirteen and fourteen, there are two metrical lines to a tone unit, a relation that does not appear in the first half of the text. In the highly contracted tone units seventeen, eighteen and nineteen, there are three tone units to a metrical line, a relation that also does not occur in the first half of the text. In both cases, the function of the meter is regulatory, making somewhat more acceptable to the ear the descriptive rush presented by tone units thirteen and fourteen (by parcelling this run into two metrical lines) and making somewhat more acceptable the cramped crescendo in the textual cadence (by encasing this cadence in one metrical line).

The oddest (and therefore most questionable) part of my reading is my metrical interpretation of the two instances of *without invention* in the second half of the text. As I mentioned before and graph explicitly below, I prefer to read these phrases by slowing down and readjusting the meter so that syllables correspond to tactical beats. The only other alternative is to read these phrases as metrical suspensions, outside of the metrical patterning elsewhere.

Metrical line 7

Tone unit eleven

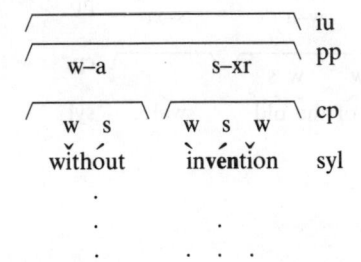

Metrical line 8

Tone unit twelve

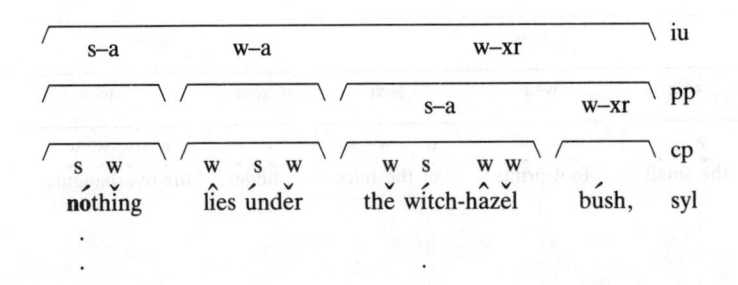

320 ANALYSIS

Metrical lines 9 and 10

Tone unit thirteen

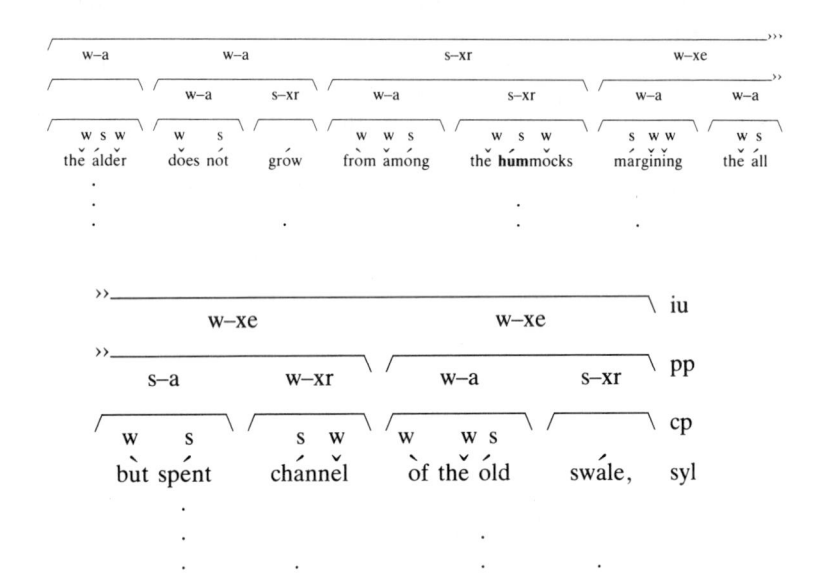

```
                                                                              ⟩⟩⟩
    ┌──────────────────────────────────────────────────────────────────────
    │  w–a            w–a                      s–xr                w–xe
    │  ┌──────────────────────────────────────────────────────────────────⟩⟩
    │  │              w–a       s–xr    w–a         s–xr    w–a        w–a
    │  │  ┌────────────────────────────────────────────────────────────────
    │  │  │ w s w     w   s      \  w  w s     w  s  w    s  w w     w  s
       the alder   does not    grow  from among   the hummocks  margining   the all
         ·           ·                              ·              ·
         ·           ·                              ·              ·
```

```
    ⟩⟩_____  iu
              w–xe                     w–xe
    ⟩⟩_____      pp
         s–a           w–xr      w–a        s–xr
                                                         cp
         w   s       s   w     w   w s
       but spent   channel    of the old   swale,        syl
         ·           ·          ·            ·
         ·           ·          ·            ·
```

Metrical lines 11 and 12

Tone unit fourteen

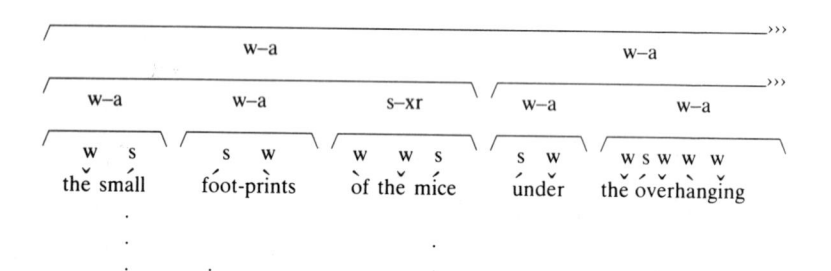

```
    ┌──────────────────────────────────────────────────────────────────⟩⟩⟩
    │            w–a                              w–a
    │  ┌────────────────────────────────────────────────────────────────⟩⟩⟩
    │  │ w–a         w–a         s–xr       w–a           w–a
    │  │  ┌─────────────────────────────────────────────────────────────
    │  │  │ w  s       s   w      w  w  s    s  w     w s w w  w
       the small   foot-prints   of the mice   under   the overhanging
         ·           ·             ·            ·         ·
         ·           ·             ·                      ·
```

FREE VERSE 321

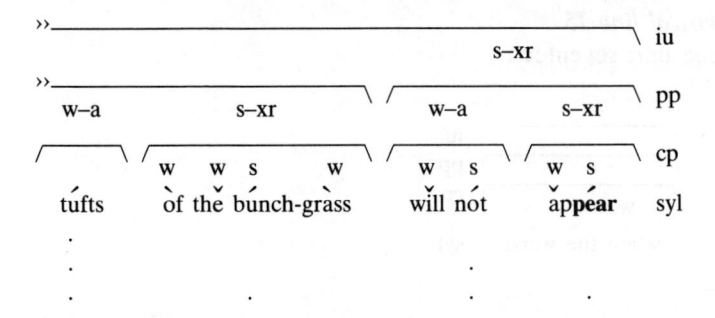

```
          »————————————————————⟍ iu
                          s–xr
          »——————————————⟍ ⟋————————⟍ pp
            w–a      s–xr    w–a    s–xr
         ⟋——⟍ ⟋—————————⟍ ⟋———⟍ ⟋———⟍ cp
           w   w  s   w   w  s   w  s
          tufts of the bunch-grass will not appear  syl
```

Metrical line 13
Tone unit fifteen

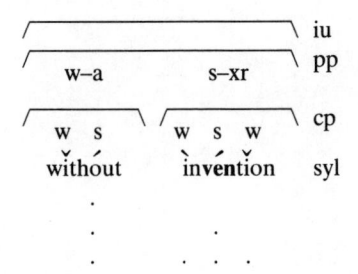

```
                  ⟋————————⟍ iu
                   w–a   s–xr   pp
                  ⟋——⟍ ⟋———⟍ cp
                   w  s  w  s  w
                  without invention  syl
```

Metrical line 14
Tone unit sixteen

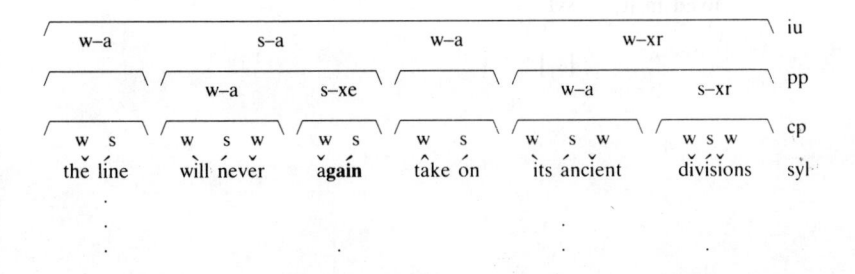

```
  ⟋————————⟍ ⟋————⟍ ⟋————⟍ ⟋——————————⟍ iu
   w–a      s–a    w–a      w–xr
  ⟋——⟍ ⟋————⟍ ⟋——⟍ ⟋———⟍ ⟋——————⟍ ⟋————⟍ pp
         w–a    s–xe           w–a    s–xr
  ⟋——⟍ ⟋——⟍ ⟋——⟍ ⟋——⟍ ⟋————⟍ ⟋——————⟍ cp
   w s   w s  w  w s  w  s  w  s  w   w  s  w
  the line will never again take on its ancient divisions  syl
```

322 ANALYSIS

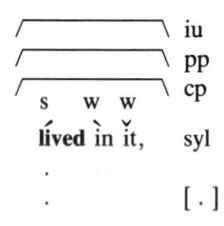

Metrical line 15
Tone unit seventeen

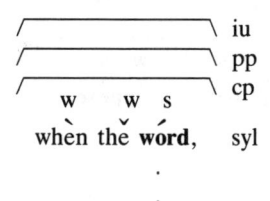

```
         ┌─────────────⟍ iu
       ┌──────────────⟍ pp
     ┌────────────⟍ cp
       w    w    s
     when the  word,    syl
              ·
              ·
              ·
```

Tone unit eighteen

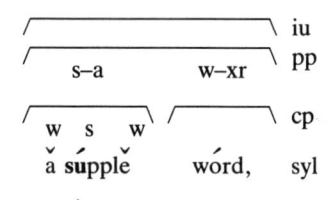

```
         ┌─────────────⟍ iu
       ─────────────⟍ pp
        s–a       w–xr
     ┌────────⟍ ┌──────⟍ cp
       w  s  w
     a supple    word,   syl
       ·
```

Tone unit nineteen

```
         ┌─────────────⟍ iu
       ┌────────────⟍ pp
     ┌──────────⟍ cp
       s   w   w
     lived in it,   syl
              ·
              ·        [ · ]
```

Metrical line 16

Tone unit twenty

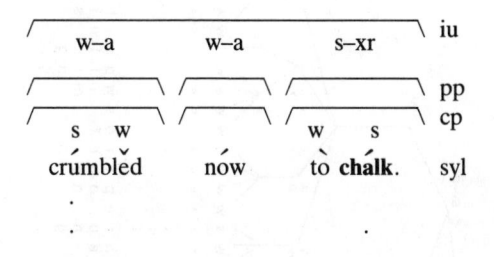

```
                                    iu
    ⌐─────────────────────⌐
    │ w–a      w–a    s–xr │
    ⌐──────⌐ ⌐─────⌐ ⌐─────⌐  pp
    ⌐──────⌐ ⌐─────⌐ ⌐─────⌐  cp
    │ s   w │ │     │ │ w  s│
     crúmblĕd   nòw    tò chálk.   syl
    ·         ·
    ·    ·   ·   ·
```

5.2 'SPRUNG RHYTHM'

5.2.1 Text

The Windhover
To Christ Our Lord

1 I caught this morning morning's minion, king-
2   dom of daylight's dauphin, dapple-dawn-drawn Falcon, in his riding
3   Of the rolling level underneath him steady air, and striding
4   High there, how he rung upon the rein of a wimpling wing
5   In his ecstasy! then off, off forth on swing,
6   As a skate's heel sweeps smooth on a bow-bend: the hurl and gliding
7   Rebuffed the big wind. My heart in hiding
8 Stirred for a bird, – the achieve of, the mastery of the thing!

9 Brute beauty and valour and act, oh, air, pride, plume, here
10   Buckle! AND the fire that breaks from thee then, a billion
11 Times told lovelier, more dangerous, O my chevalier!

12   No wonder of it: sheer plod makes plough down sillion
13 Shine, and blue-bleak embers, ah my dear,
14   Fall, gall themselves, and gash gold-vermillion.

(Gerard Manley Hopkins)

324 ANALYSIS

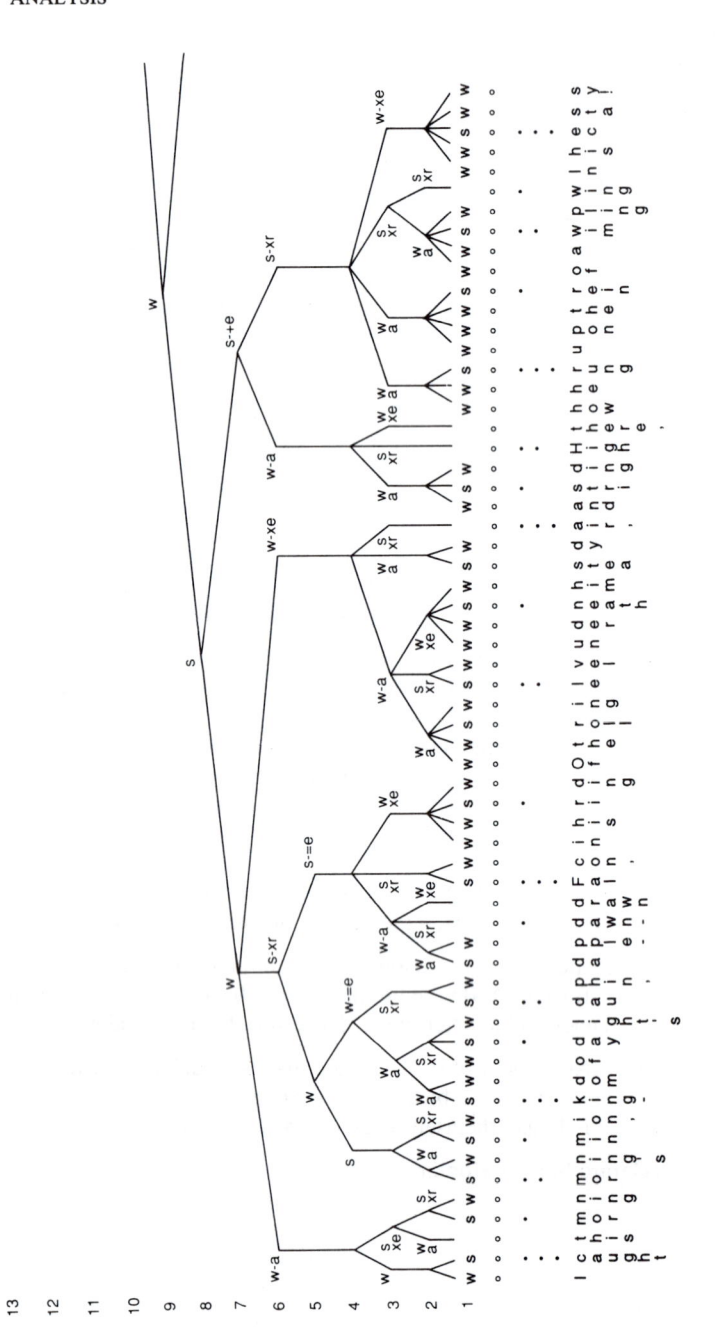

'SPRUNG RHYTHM' 325

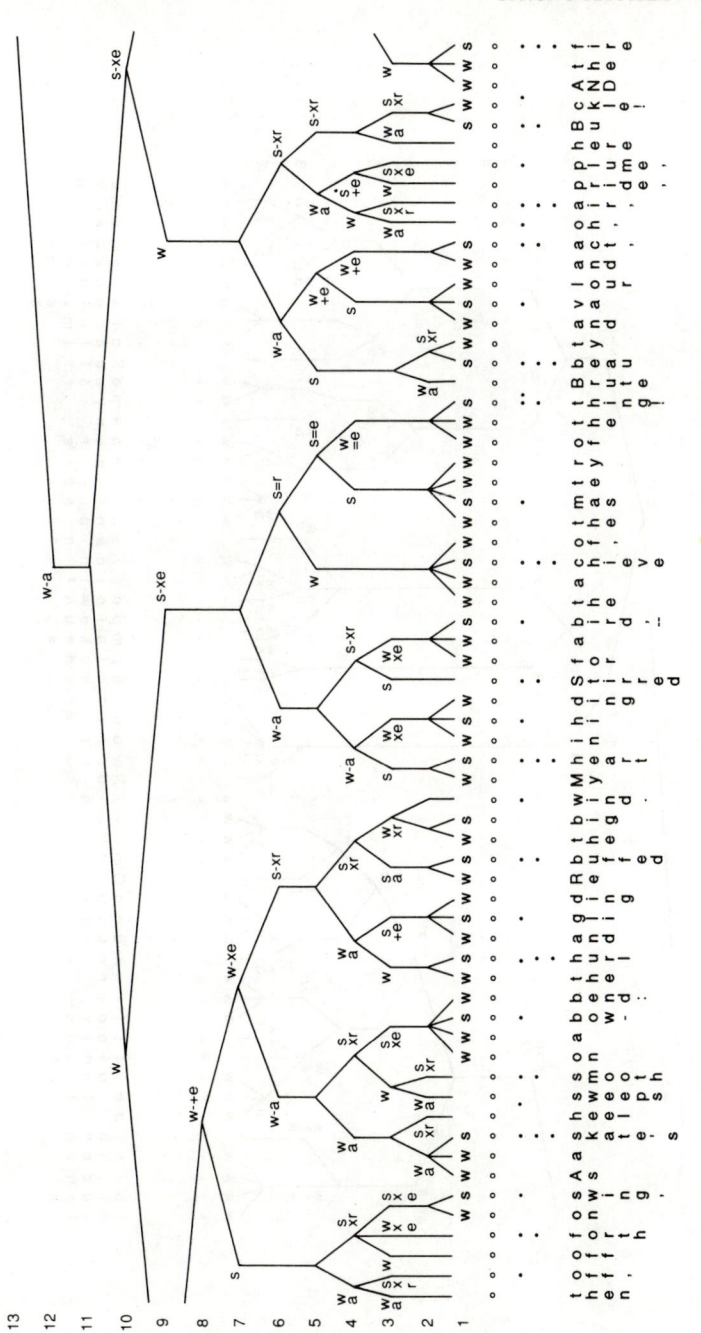

326 ANALYSIS

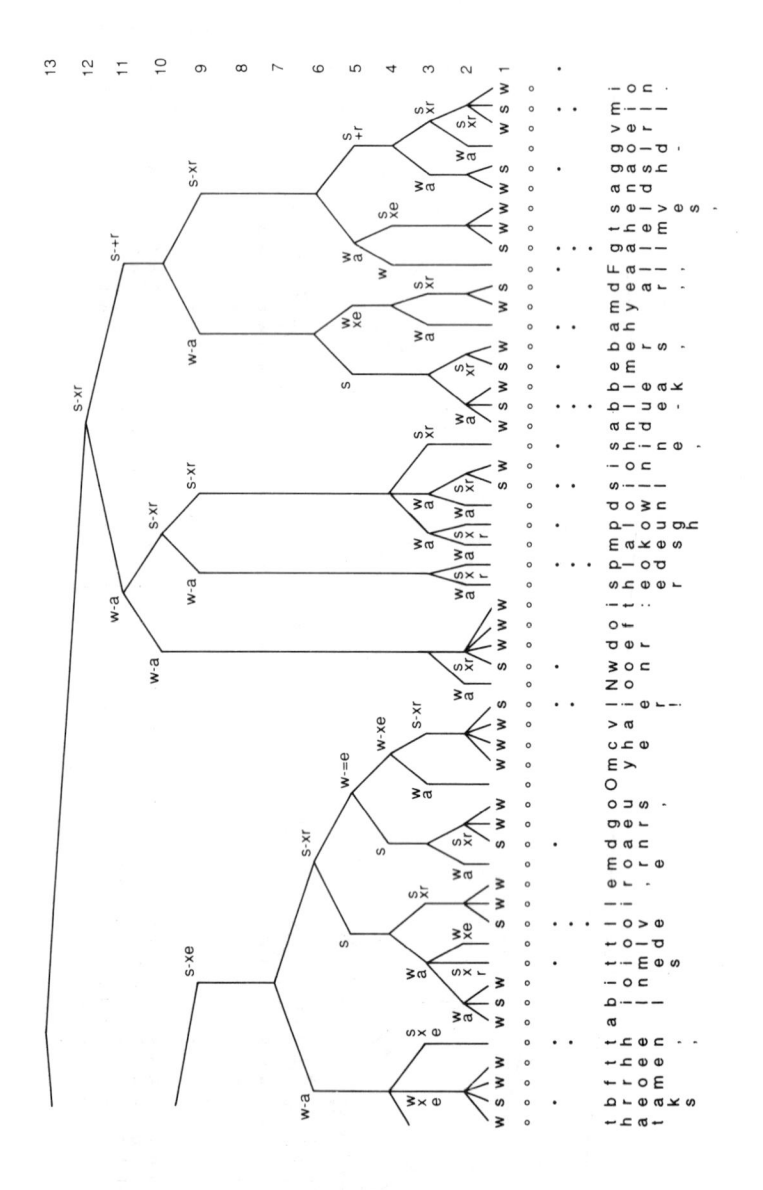

5.2.2 Higher levels of phrasing: bracketing formalization

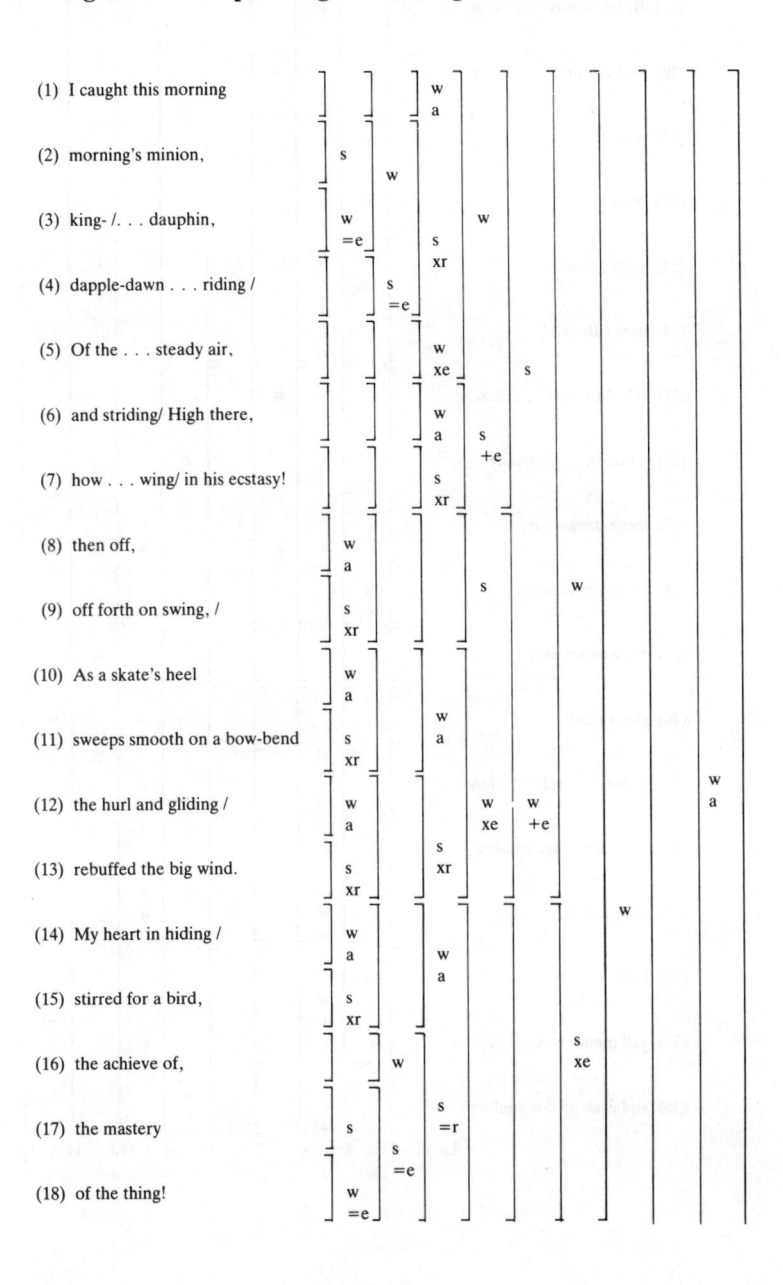

```
 (1) I caught this morning      ⎤    ⎤  w        ⎤          ⎤    ⎤    ⎤    ⎤
                                ⎥    ⎥  a        ⎥          ⎥    ⎥    ⎥    ⎥
 (2) morning's minion,        s ⎥    ⎥           ⎥          ⎥    ⎥    ⎥    ⎥
                                ⎦  w ⎥           ⎥          ⎥    ⎥    ⎥    ⎥
 (3) king- /. . . dauphin,    w ⎤    ⎥         w ⎥          ⎥    ⎥    ⎥    ⎥
                                =e ⎦ ⎥       s   ⎥          ⎥    ⎥    ⎥    ⎥
                                     ⎥       xr  ⎥          ⎥    ⎥    ⎥    ⎥
 (4) dapple-dawn . . . riding/  ⎤  s ⎥           ⎥          ⎥    ⎥    ⎥    ⎥
                                ⎥   =e ⎦         ⎥          ⎥    ⎥    ⎥    ⎥
 (5) Of the . . . steady air, ⎦      ⎤  w        ⎥          ⎥    ⎥    ⎥    ⎥
                                     ⎥  xe       ⎥  s       ⎥    ⎥    ⎥    ⎥
 (6) and striding/ High there,⎤      ⎥  w        ⎥          ⎥    ⎥    ⎥    ⎥
                              ⎥      ⎦  a        ⎥          ⎥    ⎥    ⎥    ⎥
                                       s         ⎥          ⎥    ⎥    ⎥    ⎥
                                       +e        ⎥          ⎥    ⎥    ⎥    ⎥
 (7) how . . . wing/ in his ecstasy! ⎤ s         ⎥          ⎥    ⎥    ⎥    ⎥
                                     ⎦ xr ⎦      ⎥          ⎥    ⎥    ⎥    ⎥
 (8) then off,                w ⎤                ⎥          ⎥    ⎥    ⎥    ⎥
                              a ⎥                ⎥          ⎥    ⎥    ⎥    ⎥
                                ⎥              s ⎥  w       ⎥    ⎥    ⎥    ⎥
 (9) off forth on swing, /    s ⎥                ⎥          ⎥    ⎥    ⎥    ⎥
                              xr⎦                ⎥          ⎥    ⎥    ⎥    ⎥
 (10) As a skate's heel       w ⎤                ⎥          ⎥    ⎥    ⎥    ⎥
                              a ⎥    ⎤ w         ⎥          ⎥    ⎥    ⎥    ⎥
 (11) sweeps smooth on a bow-bend s ⎥ a          ⎥          ⎥    ⎥    ⎥    ⎥
                              xr⎦    ⎥           ⎥          ⎥    ⎥  w ⎥    ⎥
 (12) the hurl and gliding /  w ⎤    ⎥       w|w ⎥          ⎥    ⎥  a ⎥    ⎥
                              a ⎥    ⎥      xe +e⎥          ⎥    ⎥    ⎥    ⎥
                                ⎥  s ⎥           ⎥          ⎥    ⎥    ⎥    ⎥
 (13) rebuffed the big wind.  s ⎥  xr⎦           ⎥          ⎥    ⎥    ⎥    ⎥
                              xr⎦                ⎥          ⎥  w ⎥    ⎥    ⎥
 (14) My heart in hiding /    w ⎤    ⎤ w         ⎥          ⎥    ⎥    ⎥    ⎥
                              a ⎥    ⎥ a         ⎥          ⎥    ⎥    ⎥    ⎥
 (15) stirred for a bird,     s ⎥    ⎥           ⎥          ⎥    ⎥    ⎥    ⎥
                              xr⎦    ⎦           ⎥          ⎥    ⎥    ⎥    ⎥
 (16) the achieve of,         ⎤    w             ⎥  s       ⎥    ⎥    ⎥    ⎥
                              ⎥                  ⎥  xe      ⎥    ⎥    ⎥    ⎥
                              ⎥              s   ⎥          ⎥    ⎥    ⎥    ⎥
 (17) the mastery           s ⎥              =r  ⎥          ⎥    ⎥    ⎥    ⎥
                              ⎥   s              ⎥          ⎥    ⎥    ⎥    ⎥
                              ⎥   =e             ⎥          ⎥    ⎥    ⎥    ⎥
 (18) of the thing!         w ⎦                  ⎦          ⎦    ⎦    ⎦    ⎦
                              =e
```

328 ANALYSIS

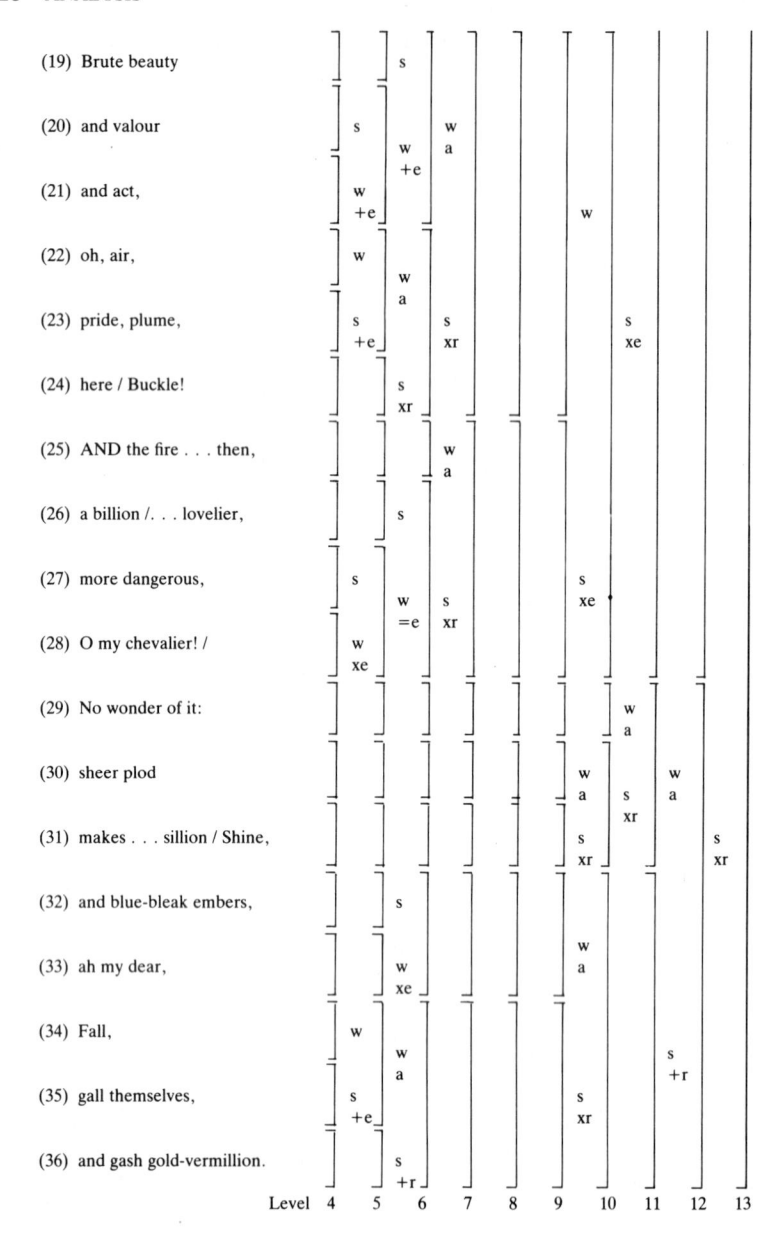

	Level 4	5	6	7	8	9	10	11	12	13
(19) Brute beauty		s								
(20) and valour	s	w +e	w a							
(21) and act,	w +e					w				
(22) oh, air,	w	w a								
(23) pride, plume,	s +e		s xr				s xe			
(24) here / Buckle!		s xr								
(25) AND the fire . . . then,			w a							
(26) a billion /. . . lovelier,		s								
(27) more dangerous,	s	w =e	s xr			s xe				
(28) O my chevalier! /	w xe									
(29) No wonder of it:							w a			
(30) sheer plod						w a	s xr	w a		
(31) makes . . . sillion / Shine,							s xr			s xr
(32) and blue-bleak embers,		s								
(33) ah my dear,		w xe				w a				
(34) Fall,	w	w a					s +r			
(35) gall themselves,	s +e					s xr				
(36) and gash gold-vermillion.		s +r								

5.2.3 Grouping reduction

Minus dependent units at Level 6

1 [I caught this morning]
2   dapple-dawn-drawn Falcon, in his
     riding
3   Of the rolling level underneath him steady air, and striding
4 High there, how he rung upon the rein of a wimpling wing
5 In his ecstasy! then off, off forth on swing,
6   As a skate's heel sweeps smooth on a bow-bend: the hurl and
     gliding
7   Rebuffed the big wind. My heart in hiding
8 Stirred for a bird, –   the mastery of the thing!

9 Brute beauty [and valour . . .]
     here
10   Buckle! AND the fire that breaks from thee then, a billion
11 Times told lovelier

12   No wonder of it: sheer plod makes plough down sillion
13 Shine, and blue-bleak embers,
14   gash gold-vermillion.

Minus dependent units at Level 7

1 [I caught this morning]
2   dapple-dawn-drawn Falcon, in his
     riding
3
4   how he rung upon the rein of a wimpling wing
5 In his ecstasy! then off, off forth on swing,
6   the hurl and
     gliding
7   Rebuffed the big wind.
8   the mastery of the thing!

9 [Brute beauty and valour. . .]
     here
10   Buckle! [And the fire that breaks from thee then,] a billion
11 Times told lovelier

12 No wonder of it: sheer plod makes plough down sillion
13 Shine, and blue-bleak embers,
14   gash gold-vermillion.

Minus dependent units at Level 8

1 [I caught this morning]
2   [dapple-dawn-drawn Falcon, in his riding]
3
4   how he rung upon the rein of a wimpling wing
5 In his ecstasy! then off, off forth on swing,
6
7
8   the mastery of the thing!
9 [Brute beauty and valour . . .]
    here
10 Buckle! [AND the fire that breaks from thee then,] a billion
11 Times told lovelier

12 No wonder of it: sheer plod makes plough down sillion
13 Shine, and blue-bleak embers,
14   gash gold-vermillion.

Minus dependent units at Level 9

1 [I caught this morning]
2   [dapple-dawn-drawn Falcon
3   in his riding]
4   how he rung upon the rein of a wimpling wing
5 In his ecstasy!
6
7
8   the mastery of the thing!
9 [Brute beauty and valour . . .]
    here
10 Buckle! [AND the fire that breaks from thee then], a billion
11 Times told lovelier

12 No wonder of it: sheer plod makes plough down sillion
13 Shine, and blue-bleak embers,
14   gash gold-vermillion.

Minus dependent units at Level 10

1 [I caught this morning]
2   [dapple-dawn-drawn Falcon
3   in his riding]
4

'SPRUNG RHYTHM' 331

5
6
7
8   the mastery of the thing!
9
10   [the fire that breaks from thee then], a billion
11 Times told lovelier,
12   No wonder of it: [sheer plod] makes plough down sillion
13 Shine, [and blue-bleak embers]
14   gash gold-vermillion.

Minus dependent units at Level 11

1
2

3
4
5
6

7
8

9
10   [the fire that breaks from thee then,] a billion
11 Times told lovelier

12   [sheer plod] makes plough down sillion
13 Shine, [and blue-bleak embers]
14   gash gold-vermillion.

Minus dependent units at Level 12

1
2

3
4
5
6

7
8
9

10   [the fire that breaks from thee then,] a billion
11 Times told lovelier

12
13   [and] blue-bleak embers]
14   gash gold-vermillion.

Minus dependent units at Level 13

1
2

3
4
5
6

7
8

9
10
11

12
13   [blue-bleak embers]
14   gash gold-vermillion.

5.2.4 Prolongational reduction

Minus dependent units at Level 6

1 I caught this morning morning's minion, king-
2   dom of daylight's dauphin,
          [in his riding]
3   Of the rolling level underneath him steady air, and striding
4 High there, how he rung upon the rein of a wimpling wing
5 In his ecstasy! then off, off forth on swing,
6   As a skate's heel sweeps smooth on a bow-bend: the hurl and
          gliding
7   Rebuffed the big wind. My heart in hiding
8 Stirred for a bird, – the achieve of, [the thing!]

9 Brute beauty [and valour . . .]
       here
10   Buckle! AND the fire that breaks from thee then, a billion
11 Times told lovelier

'SPRUNG RHYTHM' 333

12　No wonder of it: sheer plod makes plough down sillion
13　Shine, and blue-bleak embers,
14　　　　　　　　　　　　gash gold-vermillion.

Minus dependent units at Level 7

1　[I caught this morning] morning's minion, king-
2　　dom of daylight's dauphin,

3
4　　　　　how he rung upon the rein of a wimpling wing
5　In his ecstasy! then off, off forth on swing,
6　　　　　　　　　　　　　　the hurl and
　　gliding
7　Rebuffed the big wind.
8　　　　　　　　the achieve of [the thing!]

9　[Brute beauty and valour . . .]
　　　here
10　Buckle! [AND the fire that breaks from thee then], a billion
11　Times told lovelier

12　No wonder of it: sheer plod makes plough down sillion
13　Shine, and blue-bleak embers,
14　　　　　　　　　　　　gash gold-vermillion.

Minus dependent units at Level 8

1　[I caught this morning] morning's minion, king-
2　　dom of daylight's dauphin,

3
4
5　　　　　　　off, off forth on swing,
6

7
8　　　　　　　　the achieve of [the thing!]

9　[Brute beauty and valour . . .]
　　　here
10　Buckle! [AND the fire that breaks from thee then], a billion
11　Times told lovelier

12　No wonder of it: sheer plod makes plough down sillion
13　Shine, and blue-bleak embers,
14　　　　　　　　　　　　gash gold-vermillion.

Minus dependent units at Level 9

1 [I caught this morning] morning's minion, king-
2   dom of daylight's dauphin,

3
4
5
6

7
8   the achieve of [the thing!]
9 [Brute beauty and valour . . .]
       here
10 Buckle! [AND the fire that breaks from thee then], a billion
11 Times told lovelier

12 No wonder of it: sheer plod makes plough down sillion
13 Shine, and blue-bleak embers,
14   gash gold-vermillion.

Minus dependent units at Level 10

1 [I caught this morning] morning's minion, king-
2   dom of daylight's dauphin,

3
4
5
6

7
8

9 [Brute beauty and valour . . .]
       here
10   Buckle!
11

12 No wonder of it: [sheer plod] makes plough down sillion
13 Shine, and [blue-bleak embers],
14   gash gold-vermillion.

Minus dependent units at Level 11

1 [I caught this morning] morning's minion, king-
2   dom of daylight's dauphin,

3
4
5
6

7
8
9

10
11

12   [sheer plod] makes plough down sillion
13 Shine, and [blue-bleak embers],
14   gash gold-vermillion.

Minus dependent units at Level 12

1 [I caught this morning] morning's minion, king-
2   dom of daylight's dauphin,

3
4
5
6

7
8
9

10
11

12
13   [blue-bleak embers],
14   gash gold-vermillion.

Minus dependent units at Level 13

1
2

3
4
5
6

336 ANALYSIS

      7
      8

      9

     10
     11

     12
     13   [blue-bleak embers],
     14   gash gold-vermillion.

5.2.5 General comments

The nature of Hopkins' 'sprung rhythm' versification is a topic in its own right, one that I cannot consider at length here. As Kiparsky (1989) notes, Hopkins subjects the distribution of his prosodic forms to complex constraints on stress, quantity and phrasing (as well as other matters). Kiparsky's theory suggests the following 'scansion' for 'The Windhover'. I indicate icti with underlining and outrides (i.e. extrametrical syllables) with ' ~ '.

> I c<u>au</u>ght this m<u>o</u>rning m<u>o</u>rning's m<u>i</u>nion, k<u>i</u>ng-
> dom of d<u>ay</u>light's d<u>au</u>ph<u>i</u>n, dapple-d<u>aw</u>n drawn F<u>a</u>lc<u>o</u>n, in his
>   r<u>i</u>ding
> Of the r<u>o</u>ll<u>i</u>ng level <u>u</u>nderne<u>a</u>th h<u>i</u>m steady <u>a</u>ir, and str<u>i</u>ding
> H<u>i</u>gh th<u>e</u>re, how he r<u>u</u>ng upon the r<u>ei</u>n of a w<u>i</u>mpling w<u>i</u>ng
> In his <u>e</u>cstasy! then <u>o</u>ff, <u>o</u>ff f<u>o</u>rth on sw<u>i</u>ng,
> As a sk<u>a</u>te's h<u>ee</u>l sweeps sm<u>oo</u>th on a b<u>ow</u>-bend: the h<u>u</u>rl and
>   gl<u>i</u>ding
> Reb<u>u</u>ffed the b<u>i</u>g w<u>i</u>nd. My h<u>ea</u>rt in h<u>i</u>ding
> St<u>i</u>rred for a b<u>i</u>rd, – the ach<u>ie</u>ve <u>o</u>f, the m<u>a</u>stery of the th<u>i</u>ng!
> Brute b<u>eau</u>ty and v<u>a</u>lour and <u>a</u>ct, oh, air, pr<u>i</u>de, plume, h<u>e</u>re
> Buckle! <u>A</u>ND the f<u>i</u>re that br<u>ea</u>ks from thee th<u>e</u>n, a b<u>i</u>llion
> T<u>i</u>mes told l<u>o</u>vel<u>ie</u>r, more d<u>a</u>nger<u>ou</u>s, O m<u>y</u> cheval<u>ie</u>r!
> No w<u>o</u>nd<u>e</u>r <u>o</u>f <u>i</u>t: sh<u>ee</u>r pl<u>o</u>d makes pl<u>ou</u>gh down s<u>i</u>llion
> Sh<u>i</u>ne, and bl<u>ue</u>-bleak <u>e</u>mbers, <u>a</u>h my d<u>ea</u>r
> Fall, g<u>a</u>ll thems<u>e</u>lves, and g<u>a</u>sh g<u>o</u>ld-verm<u>i</u>llion.

As many critics have noted, this versification leads to severe perceptual difficulties. The following can be noted.

(1) Stressed monosyllables in non-ictic position are left metrically ambiguous (e.g. *off* in line 5 and *sheer* in line 12, which Hopkins' versification demands that we read as ictic).

    5 In his ecstasy! then off, off forth on swing,
   12 No wonder of it: sheer plod makes plough down sillion

(2) Long syllables in multiple offbeat positions are left metrically ambiguous. For example, in the last line Hopkins' constraints on quantity forbid the demotion of *-selves* and *gold*, even though this forbids many 'natural' readings of the line.

   14 Fall, gall themselves, and gash gold-vermillion.

Constraints on quantity also determine the highly 'unnatural' demotion of 'Bu-' and promotion of 'AND' in line 10.

   10 Buckle! AND the fire that breaks from thee then, a billion

Various special conditions Hopkins places on quantity also allow the unnatural demotion of *oh* in line 9.

   9 Brute beauty and valour and act, oh, air, pride, plume, here

(3) Hopkins' positional constraints on stress in 'offbeat' position are also unnatural. For example, these constraints prevent the demotion of *un-* in line 3 and *big* in line 7.

   3 Of the rolling level underneath him steady air, ...
   7 Rebuffed the big wind. My heart in hiding

(4) Hopkins' definition of extrametrical outrides produces metrical ambiguity. For instance, he counts *heel* as an extrametrical outride, even though it is both a phrasal stress and a long syllable.

   As a skate's heel sweeps smooth on a bow-bend: the hurl ...

(5) Hopkins pushes the natural limits of non-congruence between phrasing and meter, for example in the demotion of *Fall* in line 14 and *oh* and *air* in line 9.

> 14 Fall, gall themselves, and gash gold-vermillion.
> 9 Brute beauty and valour and act, oh, air, pride, plume, here

As all have noted, enjambment in 'The Windhover' is also extreme, as in the splitting of the word *king-/dom* between the first two lines. *No* lines in Hopkins' versification of 'The Windhover' are clauses or sentences.

(6) Hopkins' versification also crosscuts perceived metrical 'onsets' (i.e. projectional beats).

> . . . **KING-**/dom of daylight's . . .
> . . . how he **RUNG** upon the rein . . .
> . . . the **HURL** and gliding . . .
> . . . My **HEART** in hiding . . .
> . . . the a**CHIEVE** of, the mastery . . .
> . . . Brute **BEAU**ty . . .
> . . . oh **AIR**, pride, plume, . . .
> . . . And the **FIRE** that breaks from thee . . .
> . . . sheer **PLOD** makes plough . . .

(7) Hopkins' versification also runs against phonetic patterning. The alliteration of [m] in line 1 (*morning, morning's, minion*) ends at the comma blocking off the first syntactic unit.

> I caught this morning morning's minion,

The alliteration of [r] in line 2 begins at the *end* of the line and connects to the *beginning* of line 3.

> in his riding / Of the rolling level . . .

The internal rhyme *air–there* and the prominent assonance in [ay] *strid–high* cuts *across* lines 3 and 4.

> air and striding / High there

The mid-vowel assonance in *hurl–(re-)buffed* cuts *across* lines 6 and 7.

> the h*u*rl and gliding / Reb*u*ffed the big wind

The prominent assonance in *fire* and *times* cuts *across* lines 10 and 11.

> AND the f*i*re that breaks from thee then, a billion / T*i*mes told

The prominent alliteration *sheer–shine* cuts *across* lines 12 and 13.

> *s*heer plod makes plough down sillion / *S*hine . . .

And the final echoing [g]s begin *after* the opening stressed syllable *fall*.

> Fall, *g*all themselves, and *g*ash *g*old-vermillion.

For all of these reasons (and others that I will enumerate as the analysis proceeds), I scan 'The Windhover' into metrical lines that correspond with perceived onsets, syntactic constituencies and phonetic patterns – not into lines marked by rhyme and visual form. The meter I claim is a falling duple tetrameter, vertically organized to three levels.

> I caught this morning morning's minion,
> . . .
> . . .

In this revised scansion, almost all of the lines are closely related to the clausal syntax. The poem scans into *seventeen* of these lines. The sixty-eight beats within these seventeen tetrameter lines share fifty-four beats with the 'traditional' sixty-beat, fourteen-line, pentameter scansion. The two scansions periodically converge – at the end of lines 4, 5, 8 and, of course, 14 in the original scansion. The two scansions share one line, line 5 in the original scansion (line 6 in the 'revised' scansion). Using Kiparsky's format (just marking line boundaries and tactical icti), the 'revised' scansion is as follows.

I caught this morning morning's minion,
kingdom of daylight's dauphin, dapple-dawn-drawn
Falcon in his riding of the rolling level underneath him steady
air, and striding high there,   [–]
how he rung upon the rein of a wimpling wing
in his ecstasy! then off, off forth on swing,
as a skate's heel [–] sweeps smooth on a bow-bend:
the hurl and gliding rebuffed the big wind.
My heart in hiding stirred for a bird,
the achieve of, the mastery of the thing! [–]
Brute beauty and valour and act, oh
air, pride, plume, here Buckle! [–]
AND the fire that breaks from thee then, a billion times told
lovelier, more dangerous, O my chevalier! No wonder of it:
sheer plod makes plough down sillion shine,
and blue-bleak embers, ah my dear, fall
gall themselves, and gash gold-vermillion. [–]

5.2.6 Higher levels of phrasing: commentary

5.2.6.1 Level 12

At the highest level, the text breaks rhythmically in two (GPR9 Binary Form), with rising contours in the grouping structure (GPR3 End-focus) and anticipational, progressive contours in prolongation (Canonical Form). The opening description and interpretation of the sacrificial beauty of the Falcon leads to the concluding generalization of the inherent beauty of all sacrificial labour/performance/process, illustrated with first the plough and then the fire. The final lines tie up the mixture of natural, religious and human imagery in the poem and return explicitly to the ultimate example of sacrificial beauty: Christ. The 'gashing' fire unites the basic colours of the elements (earth, air, fire and water) with the colours of the bird's breast, chivalry and blood and brings together the actions of diving and bleeding, now richly interanimated by what has come before (GPR1 Information, GPR4 Density).

'SPRUNG RHYTHM' 341

With respect to the conventional sonnet frame, the most remarkable aspect of this level is its asymmetry. The usual 4–3 proportions of the Italian sonnet are skewed to (about) 7–2. The joyful ride of the Falcon is expanded to the extent of the octave, while the ironic implications of the ride (its culminating, sacrificial dive) are kept in reserve for the first three lines of the sestet. These proportions help render the general *extremity* of the text: the novelty of its prosodic form, the exclamatory accents of its rhetoric, the expansiveness of its descriptions, the magnitude of its theme.

The 'turn' in the text is heavily marked with a double exclamation: 'O my chevalier!', concluding the opening, and the 'No wonder of it', leading to closure (GPR14 Parallelism). These markings clearly signal the reversal in prolongational contours and lead to a multilevelled cadencing of rising, progressional contours, rendered in the physically compressed confines of the final three lines.

There is also a considerable 'turn' at the octave (a turn that is also marked with an exclamation: 'the mastery of the thing!'). But the opening of the sestet brings more description and action (not the expected interpretation of that description and action), and when the interpretation comes (in line 11), it is surprising and therefore rhythmically extensional rather than resolving. Only with the interpretive comment of the final three lines do the extensional contours of the poem turn round and anticipate closure. The joyful sacrifice of the bird is the typological revelation of the sacrificial beauty of all beings, whose individual inscapes are each instressed by the sacrificial beauty of Christ.

The reductions show that the text both peaks and arrives at the final sacrificial action: '[and blue-bleak embers] gash gold-vermillion' (Canonical Form).

5.2.6.2 *Level 11*

Level 11 presents the development of the three parallel examples of sacrificial beauty: the bird, the plough, and the fire (GPR1 Information). With respect to Level 12, this level adds a local articulation in the second 'half' of the text, adding further concentration and intensity to the culmination of the text in the last three lines (GPR2 Density).

The one complex articulation at this level is also rising and duple (GPR9 Binary Form, GPR3 End-focus), but now with additive prolongation ('and blue-bleak embers . . .'). By keeping his references to Christ implicit, Hopkins avoids a heavy 'logical' arrival, softening somewhat the text's (already abrupt) closure. The text closes 'naturally', tying together the thematic development of the poem with reference to a common terminal point in human experience, the dying fire (GPR1 Information).

The strong arrival in the last unit at this level is firmly end-weighted (GPR2 Weight, GPR3 End-focus) and exhibits most of the common marks of 'terminal modification' (GPR6 Change, GPR4 Density). The plough image is given just one tone unit; the fire image is given five. And the final line, one might claim, presents the most intense phonetic patterning in the poem (e.g. the internal rhyme (*fall–gall*), the prominent alliteration in [g] (*gall–gash–gold*), and the pervasive consonance in [l] (*fall–gall–themselves–gold–vermillion*).

The grouping reduction at this level shows how rhythmic phrasing highlights the parallel between the 'fiery' breast of the diving Falcon and the 'gold-vermillion' of the gashing fire. The first half of the text peaks at '[AND the fire that breaks from thee then,] a billion times told lovelier', and the second half peaks at '[and blue-bleak embers] gash gold-vermillion'.

On the other hand, the prolongational reduction shows the text arching from a structural beginning at 'morning's minion, king-dom of daylight's dauphin' to a structural ending at 'gash gold-vermillion', explicitly connecting the 'noble' flight of the bird (the opening sacrificial agent) to the gashing of the fire (the culminating sacrificial action).

5.2.6.3 Level 10

Level 10 isolates the rhythmic parallel between the description of the 'awe-ful' dive of the 'royal' Falcon in the opening eleven lines; the denial of wonder by the analogical connection of the 'fiery' bird to the 'shining' blade of the lowly plough; and a culminating synthesis in the elemental 'gash' of the Christ-fire (GPR1 Information). In physical substance this parallel is highly asymmetrical (and therefore perceptually submerged), but it appears clearly in the structural organization of the text as a whole.

With respect to Level 11, this level articulates two rising duple units (GPR3 End-focus, GPR9 Binary Form, GPR16 Unity) and one single. The first duple is highly expanded, extensional and front-weighted (about 3–1) and the second unit is heavily contracted, anticipational and end-weighted (in about the same proportions) – a multidimensional chiasmus.

This chiastic structure renders the chiastic shape of the text's double revelation: (1) the culmination of the magnificent ride of the Falcon in its sacrificial dive, and (2) the redeeming beauty of all sacrificial action, however lowly, as illuminated by the living Christ. The dive of the Falcon is a wonder, but really 'no wonder' when seen in this second 'light'.

The maintenance of this parallel is one of the beautiful rhythmic touches in the poem. The text 'turns' rhythmically at 'No wonder of it'. This phrase also occurs on a line-final, weak metrical beat, in a line with an especially large number of 'scudding' non-ictic syllables.

> lovelier, more dangerous, O my chevalier! No wonder of it:

And in the grouping parallel at this level, this phrase is put in opposition to the whole octave (which, in turn, has just moved to a dramatic extensional peak in the first three lines of the sestet).

This rhythmic articulation combines to make 'No wonder of it' especially salient. With its weak metrical position, contracted higher-level structure, expanded lower-level structure and explicit denial of the (seemingly undeniable) 'wonder' that the first eleven lines have just generated, it becomes an enormous anticipational anacrusis and upbeat to the concluding lines to follow.

The grouping reduction shows that the peaks of the strong units at this level highlight the three 'flaring' sacrifices: the fire of the Falcon is 'lovelier', the plough 'shines', and the fire 'gash[es] gold-vermillion' (GPR14 Parallelism). These peaks all occur within a span of four lines (GPR4 Density).

The prolongational reduction shows the three closely positioned 'arrivals' in the sestet (i.e. 'here/ Buckle!', 'shine' and 'gash gold-vermillion') after the long extensional articulation in the octave (Canonical Form).

5.2.6.4 Level 9

Level 9 isolates one of the most regular and important movements in the poem: the alternation of description and then evaluative comment (specific detail and then generalization, cause and then effect). This alternation is interrupted once – at the rhythmic fulcrum 'No wonder of it!' – and then it continues again.

Discounting this one interruption, Level 10 articulates four rising duples (GPR9 Binary Form, GPR3 End-focus, GPR16 Unity). Interpretive and evaluative comments serve as peaks for more neutral descriptions (GPR1 Information). Following the higher-level asymmetry, the second two duples are wildly contracted compared with the first two duples. The four duples as a whole shift regularly from beginning-weighted to end-weighted (about 2–1, 3–2, 1–1, and then 2–3, counting in tone units). This adds to the text's strong feeling of impulsion, smooth process and closure, which is articulated in other ways at other levels of structure as well (GPR2 Weight).

Prolongational contours shift from extensional progressions in the first two duples to progressional arrivals in the last two (Canonical Form). Hopkins makes these prolongational connections increasingly syntactic (and therefore explicit) as the text proceeds (GPR8 Arrivals). The first duple straddles a full sentence break. The second duple straddles a coordinating conjunction. The last two duples are broken between subject and predicate.

```
. . . the big wind.            My heart . . .
. . . here / Buckle!           AND the fire that breaks . . .
sheer plod                     makes plough . . .
and blue-bleak embers          Fall, gall themselves . . .
```

The interruption of this alternation at 'No wonder of it!' adds further to the prominence of this rhythmic turn (GPR6 Change).

At this level, the grouping reduction of the first half of the text highlights the parallel exclamatory rhetoric of the text (GPR14 Parallelism).

> How he rung upon the rein of a wimpling wing in his ecstasy!
> [Brute beauty and valour . . .] here buckle!
> [AND the fire that breaks from thee then] a billion times told lovelier
> . . .
> No wonder of it:
> etc.

The prolongational reduction at this level shows the temporary arrival at 'Buckle' before the final concentration of arrivals in the last tercet.

This prolongational reduction is especially effective in showing what would be lost if the text were deprived of the prolongational energy generated by its medial anticipations and extensions (Canonical Form).

> [I caught this morning] morning's minion, kingdom of daylight's dauphin. [Brute beauty and valour . . .] here buckle! No wonder of it: [sheer plod] makes plough down sillion shine, [and blue-bleak embers] gash gold-vermillion.

5.2.6.5 Level 8

Level 8 isolates a local, additive elaboration in the octave. This elaboration, together with the elaborations at Level 7, almost exactly doubles the weight of the octave relative to its parallel in the sestet, expanding the presentation of the actions of the 'riding' Falcon. The elaboration here is falling, a reversal in rhythmic direction that begins to articulate the more varied movement of the octave relative to the sestet.

5.2.6.6 Level 7

Level 7 isolates two local elaborations in the octave, both duple in span and chiastic in arrangement: ws and then sw (GPR9 Binary Form, GPR17 Schemes). The major effect of this articulation is mimetic. It kinaesthetically renders the varied movements in the soaring bird (and the varied effects of that movement on the thoughts and emotions of the observing speaker). This varied movement will be developed further at Levels 5 and 6. This pulsing rise and fall at mid levels in the octave disappears in the sestet, where detailed articulation occurs at high and low levels but is relatively sparse in the middle. This contrast renders the rhetorical development in the text as it shifts from the descriptive purposes of the octave to the more argumentative purposes of the sestet.

5.2.6.7 Level 6

Level 6 isolates a further tier of syntactic elaboration, one that is now extended into the sestet. Grouping movement at this level is varied in direction and (for the first time) in span, while prolongational movement is dominantly anticipational and progressional. The conjunction of these phrasal movements makes this one of the most highly charged levels of rhythmic articulation in the text. A major effect of this level is the lilting (amphibrachic) movement in the opening three lines, which rises to a peak at the triple appositive (minion–dauphin–Falcon) and then falls through the extending prepositional phrase (*of the rolling . . . air*). This level also begins to articulate the highly developed opening of the sestet, which showers the Falcon with superlative attributes: *beauty, valour, act, air, pride* and *plume*.

The grouping reduction for this level begins to show the tumultuous effect of the varied development of the octave.

> [I caught this morning] dapple-dawn-drawn Falcon in his riding. How he rung upon the rein of a wimpling wing in his ecstasy! then off, off forth on swing. The hurl and gliding rebuffed the big wind. The achieve of [the thing]!

5.2.6.8 *Level 5*

Level 5 isolates a final level of local syntactic elaboration. Level 6 groups these units into seven complex groups, all duple in span (GPR9 Binary Form). These groups are again arranged in various chiastic patterns (GPR17 Schemes, GPR16 Unity), for example in the attributes presented in line 9, and in the final cadence.

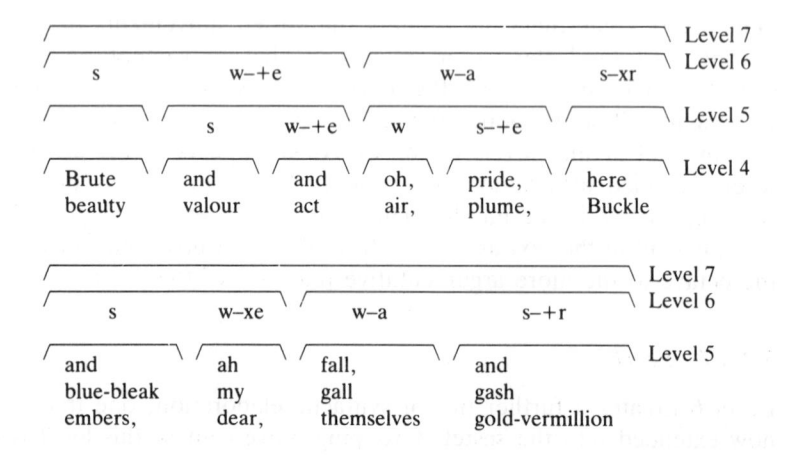

						Level 7
s	w–+e		w–a		s–xr	Level 6
	s	w–+e	w	s–+e		Level 5
Brute beauty	and valour	and act	oh, air,	pride, plume,	here Buckle	Level 4

				Level 7
s	w–xe	w–a	s–+r	Level 6
and blue-bleak embers,	ah my dear,	fall, gall themselves	and gash gold-vermillion	Level 5

'SPRUNG RHYTHM'   347

With minor exceptions, prolongational movement is extensional, with a predominance of equational (appositional) development.

$$=e$$

```
⌐──────────────────⌐ ⌐────────────────────────⌐
   morning's minion . . .    dapple-dawn drawn Falcon . . .
   the achieve of,           the mastery of the thing!
   . . . lovelier,           more dangerous . . .
```

Both of the chiastically ordered units at this level (in lines 9 and 13–14) are also chiastic prolongationally: first extensional and then anticipational (Canonical Form). The convergence of grouping and prolongation in the final cadence might be expected. The convergence in line 9 is more unusual. Therefore line 9 articulates a very strong perceptual figure. This figure helps to control the extreme hyperbole at this point, while presenting a strong shape that is (mimetically) 'broken' when the Falcon dives.

Where equational, the development at this level dots the text with rhythmic pauses, comparable to musical 'fermatas'. These appositional fermatas dwell briefly on (1) the bird itself, (2) its mastery, and (3) the 'loveliness' of its dive.

5.2.6.9 Level 4

Level 4 is articulated by the thirty-six tone units, ten pairs of which form duple units at Level 5 (GPR9 Binary Form); the rest remain singles.

Most of the paired tone units represent (the lower level in) two-level triples: (1) in the opening triple appositive, (2) in the multiple attributes at the opening of the sestet, and (3) in the double cadencing (a) at the end of the octave, (b) at the end of line 11, and (c) at the end of the text (GPR16 Unity).

> morning's minion,
> kingdom of daylight's dauphin
> dapple-dawn-drawn Falcon
>
> Brute beauty
> and valour
> and act
>
> oh, air,
> pride, plume,
> here Buckle!

> the achieve of,
> the mastery
> of the thing!
>
> a billion times told lovelier,
> more dangerous,
> O my chevalier!
>
> fall,
> gall themselves,
> and gash gold-vermillion.

The remaining pairs articulate the binary informational structure of the clauses in the second quatrain (GPR14 Parallelism, GPR16 Unity).

> As a skate's heel   sweeps smooth . . .
> the hurl . . .   rebuffed . . .
> My heart . . .   stirred . . .

The grouping reduction that just retains the peaks at Level 5 demonstrates what is lost when these two-level triples are omitted: the beginnings and ends of major phrases are blurred and blunted.

> I caught this morning dapple-dawn-drawn Falcon in his riding of the rolling level underneath him steady air, and striding high there, how he rung upon the rein of a wimpling wing in his ecstasy! then off, off forth on swing, as a skate's heel sweeps smooth on a bow-bend: the hurl and gliding rebuffed the big wind. My heart in hiding stirred for a bird, – the mastery of the thing! Brute beauty here buckles! and the fire that breaks from thee then, a billion times told lovelier. No wonder of it: sheer plod makes plough down sillion shine, and blue-bleak embers gash gold-vermillion.

There are exactly eighteen tone units in the octave and eighteen in the sestet. This symmetrical distribution recovers the architectural balance between the two traditional parts of the Italian sonnet.

In general these tone units are short, averaging less than five syllables. Discounting two or three very long units, this average is even less, about four syllables. The norm for speech is closer to six or seven syllables.

These spans are arranged in various productive patterns. Tone units at the beginning of the text progressively expand and (after a penultimate variation) reach a textual maximum (GPR17 Schemes).

'SPRUNG RHYTHM' 349

(1) I caught this **mor**ning
(2) morning's **min**ion,
(3) king- /dom of daylight's **dau**phin,
(4) dapple-dawn-drawn **Fal**con in his riding /
(5) Of the rolling level underneath him steady **air**,
(6) and striding/ **High** there,
(7) how he rung upon the rein of a wimpling **wing**/ in his ecstasy!

The tone units in the centre of the text are very short, a contraction that is not 'released' until the climactic 'buckling' of the diving Falcon (GPR17 Schemes).

(12) the hurl and **glid**ing /
(13) re**buffed** the big wind.
(14) My **heart** in hiding /
(15) **stirred** for a bird,
(16) the **achieve** of,
(17) the **mas**tery
(18) of the **thing**! /
(19) Brute **beau**ty
(20) and **val**our
(21) and **act**,
(22) oh, **air**,
(23) pride, **plume**,
(24) here / **Buckle**!
(25) AND the fire that burns from thee **then**,
(26) a billion / **Times** told lovelier,

An expanding series is then reinstated (in a more diminutive form) in the final three tone units.

(34) **Fall**,
(35) **gall** themselves,
(36) and gash gold-vermillion

Following normal preference, tonic syllables usually occur on the last clitic phrase in their tone units (GPR3 End-focus). The exceptions help render the insistent (peak-initial) 'tone' of the text as a whole (GPR16 Unity).

(4) dapple-dawn-drawn **Fal**con in his riding /
(6) and striding/ **High** there,
(7) how he rung upon the rein of a wimpling **wing**/ in his ecstasy!

(13) re**buffed** the big wind.
(14) my **heart** in hiding
(15) **stirred** for a bird,
(26) a billion / **Times** told lovelier,
(33) **ah** my dear,

5.2.7 Lower levels: scansion and commentary

5.2.7.1 Metrical line 1

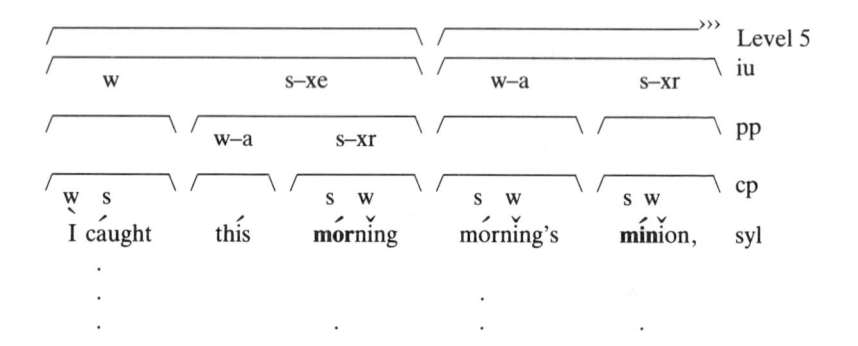

```
 ┌─────────────────────────────┐ ┌────────────────────>>>  Level 5
 ┌──────────────┐              │ ┌──────────┐              │   iu
 │   w          │    s–xe      │ │   w–a    │    s–xr      │
 ┌──────┐ ┌─────────┐          │ ┌──────────┐ ┌────────────┐   pp
 │      │ │  w–a    │   s–xr   │ │          │ │            │
 ┌───┐ ┌─────┐ ┌──────┐        │ ┌─────┐    │ ┌─────┐      │   cp
 │w  s│ │     │ │ s  w │       │ │ s w │    │ │ s w │      │
 │I caught│ │this│ │morning│   │ │morning's│ │minion,│  syl
```

The text begins with a relatively traditional tetrameter of nine syllables, phrasally complete (at the tone unit level), with a medial caesura, only one demoted lexical stress (*this*, a stress that is already subordinated in its phonological phrase *this morning*) and regular one-syllable offbeats. The line also begins with a conventional upbeat (*I*) and is heavily unified phonetically and lexically (e.g. the alliteration in [m] and consonance in *n* (*morning, morning's, minion*), the assonance in [I] (*this, minion*), and the repetition of *morning*).

Individual phrasal and metrical patterns are also largely canonical. At higher levels, grouping structures are duple and rising; prolongation is chiastic (extensional and then anticipational); and the meter is falling.

This line also exhibits some of the chiastic patterning that we have found so prevalent at higher levels (GPR16 Unity, GPR14 Parallelism). The line begins with an upbeat (*I*) and ends with an afterbeat (*-ion*); the opening clitic phrase is iambic (*I caught*) and the closing clitic phrase trochaic (*minion*); and the lexical repetition of *morning* ends the first intonational unit and begins the second.

This static and/or canonical patterning gives this line a feeling of emotional control.

5.2.7.2 Metrical line 2

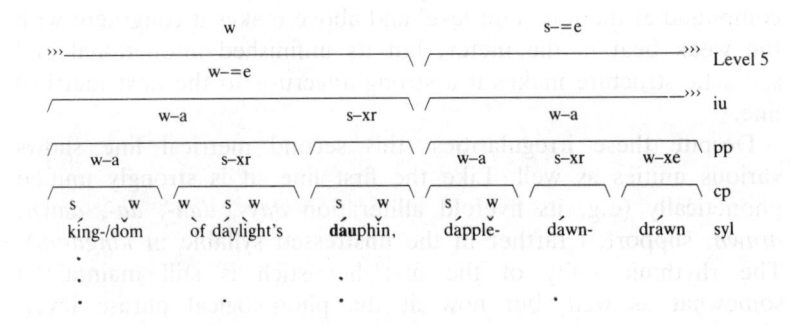

```
                    w                           s-=e
>>>─────────────────────┐    ┌──────────────────────────>>>  Level 5
             w-=e        \  /
┌────────────────────────┐\/┌──────────────────────>>>       iu
        w-a              s-xr       w-a
┌──────────────┐┌───────────┐┌──────────┐┌──────┐┌────┐      pp
   w-a           s-xr         w-a        s-xr    w-xe
┌─────┐┌──────┐┌─────┐┌─────┐┌─────┐┌──────┐┌────┐          cp
 s  w   w  s  w  s   w   s   w   s   w
king-/dom  of daylight's  dauphin,  dapple-  dawn-  drawn   syl
```

Metrical line 2 begins the more varied patterning that will render the tumultuous 'ride' of the Falcon in the rest of the octave.

In almost every respect that the first line is canonical, the second line is non-canonical (GPR13 Similarity). The line expands to eleven syllables and six clitic phrases. Grouping structures mix triple and single patterning with duple patterning. The caesura is placed off-centre, with the first intonational unit in the line culminating on the strong beat of the second hemistich (rather than the weak, concluding beat of the first hemistich). The ending of the line is strongly enjambed, breaking a phonological phrase and leaving the lineal measure with rising, anticipational contours. And metrical–phrasal relations at tactical levels become radically roughened: tactical offbeats are realized by 2, 1, 3 and then 1 syllable(s), with the three lexical stresses in *dapple-dawn-drawn* requiring two demotions. The visual form of the line also presents the famous breaking of the word *kingdom* across the first two visual lines, burying the first rhyme word *king-* both linguistically and metrically.

The peaking of the first intonational unit in the line on the strong beat of the second hemistich makes *dauphin* a considerable rhythmic convergence, a convergence that is also supported by the arrival in the prolongational contours at the tone-unit level (GPR7 Beats, GPR8 Arrivals). This rhythmic convergence is hardly complete, however, with grouping contours still being weak at

Levels 5, 6, 7, 9, 10 and 12 and prolongational contours being anticipational at Levels 6 and 12.

The Hopkinsian compound at the end of the line is typical of many of the rhythmic structures that will follow. The demotion of the stress on *dapple* takes the poem out of a duple meter (if this has been the reader's metrical response so far); the weakness of the compound at the tone-unit level and above makes it congruent with the weak beat in the meter; but its unfinished intonational and syntactic structure makes it a strong anacrusis to the next metrical line.

Despite these irregularities, this second metrical line shows various unities as well. Like the first line, it is strongly unified phonetically (e.g. its fivefold alliteration *day-, dau-, da-, dawn, drawn*, supported further in the unstressed syllable in *kingdom*). The rhythmic unity of the first hemistich is still maintained somewhat as well, but now at the phonological phrase level. *Kingdom of daylight's* peaks and arrives at the end of the hemistich (Canonical Form, GPR15 Measures, GPR8 Arrivals, GPR3 End-focus, GPR9 Binary Form).

Especially notable in this second metrical line are the amphibrachic contours. In this section of the text, these lilting contours will be presented simultaneously at *four* levels: within the clitic phrase, the phonological phrase, the intonational unit, and Level 7 (GPR16 Unity).

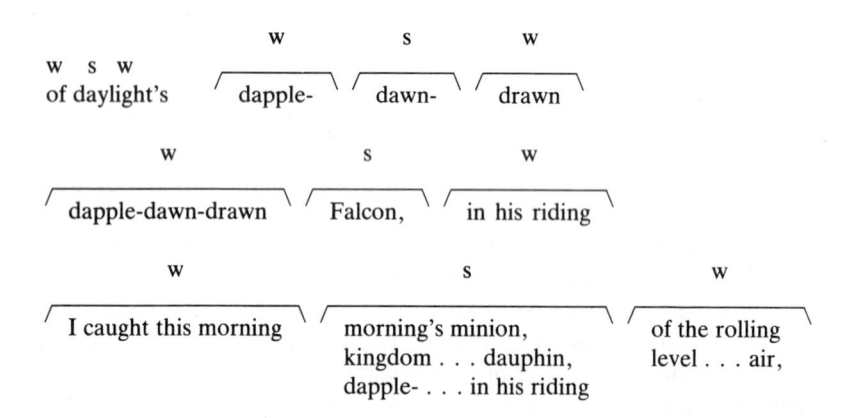

w s w	w	s	w
of daylight's	dapple-	dawn-	drawn

w	s	w
dapple-dawn-drawn	Falcon,	in his riding

w	s	w
I caught this morning	morning's minion, kingdom . . . dauphin, dapple- . . . in his riding	of the rolling level . . . air,

These amphibrachic contours are rare in the poem as a whole, but are very concentrated here, as they render both the lilting movement of the bird and the joyful celebration of that movement by the poetic speaker.

5.2.7.3 Metrical line 3

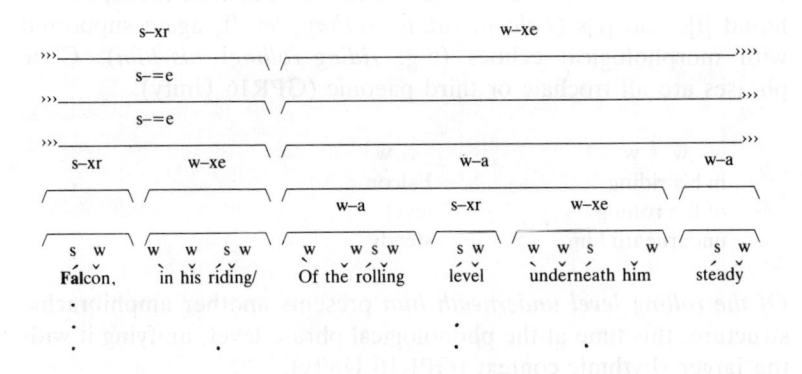

```
                    s–xr                              w–xe
>>>_____\ /_____>>>>
              s–=e
>>>_____\ /_____>>>
              s–=e
>>>_____\ /_____>>>
    s–xr       w–xe      \ /      w–a                   w–a
  /_____\ /_____\        /_____\ /_____\ /___\
                           w–a         s–xr      w–xe
                         /_____\ /_____\ /_____\ /___\
   s  w      w  w  s w    w   w s w    s w    w  w  s   w    s  w
   Falcon,  in his riding/ Of the rolling level underneath him steady
```

Rhythmically, metrical line 3 is one of the most disturbing lines in the poem, presenting many extremes, uncertainties and non-congruences – phrasal, metrical and visual.

At low levels in the grouping structure, the duple movement in the first line and triple movement in the second line now become third paeonic (GPR16 Unity), expanding the line to eighteen syllables, twice the syllables of the first metrical line.

```
   w   w  s    w
   in his rid. ing
   of the ro.    lling
   un.der.neath him
```

The long pre-modifying phrase *rolling level underneath him steady* is uncertain in its structure and could be read many ways, all of which yield relatively monstrous metrical and phrasal articulation (I group *rolling level underneath him* into one phonological phrase and put *steady* in a second). The line is intonationally incomplete at both extremities. And the runs of 'scudding' syllables at the tactical level become almost intolerable: 3, 5, 3 and 3. This takes the meter out of any possibility of triple movement at subtactical levels (if this was the reader's preference to this point), demanding a purely accentual reading (i.e. with subtactical levels uncontrolled). As we discussed earlier, the 'sprung rhythm' meter is also strained here, giving *un*(derneath) an ictus while denying ictus to the lexical stresses of both *le*(vel) (which precedes) and *stea*(dy) (which follows).

On the other hand, Hopkins still maintains various coherencies in the line. As before, he gives the line its own phonetic motif, now in liquid [l]s and [r]s (*Falcon, riding, rolling, level*), again supported with morphological echoes (e.g. *riding–rolling*; *his–him*). Clitic phrases are all trochaic or third paeonic (GPR16 Unity).

```
w   w  s  w                s   w
in his riding              Falcon
of the rolling             level
underneath him             steady
```

Of the rolling level underneath him presents another amphibrachic structure, this time at the phonological phrase level, unifying it with the larger rhythmic context (GPR16 Unity).

```
            w              s             w
        ┌─────────┐   ┌───────┐   ┌──────────────┐
         Of the rolling    level      underneath him
```

The prominent alliteration *riding–rolling* again links (chiastically) the ends and beginnings of hemistichs. And as in metrical line 2, *Falcon* resolves a higher-level group firmly on a higher-level beat, this time a sixth-level peak on a three-dot beat (GPR7 Beats).

One of the rhythmic niceties of this line is the perceptual fate of *in the riding*, given this rhythmic articulation. Considering the comma after *Falcon*, it seems clear that *in the riding* is connected syntactically with what follows, rather than what precedes. But given the large rhythmic convergence at *Falcon*, the metrical positioning of *in the riding* in the first hemistich (rather than the second), and the strong multilevelled pressure for amphibrachic structures, I find it impossible to read *in the riding* as a new intonational unit (GPR7 Beats, GPR15 Measures, GPR16 Unity). Rather, I read it as (what Hopkins might call) a phrasal outride attached to what precedes.

5.2.7.4 Metrical Line 4

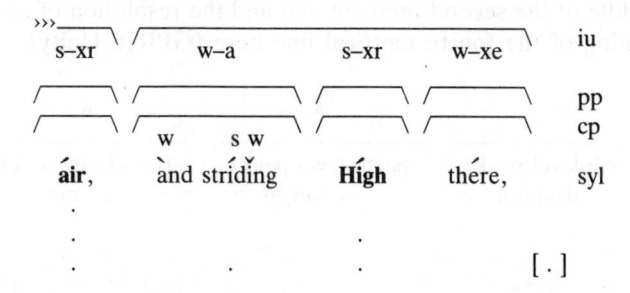

```
    >>>⌒
   ⌒―――⌒  ⌒―――――――――――⌒
   s–xr     w–a        s–xr    w–xe    iu
   ⌒―⌒ ⌒―――⌒ ⌒―――⌒ ⌒―――⌒           pp
   ⌒―⌒   w   s w    ⌒―――⌒ ⌒―――⌒    cp
   áir,  ànd strídĭng  Hígh   thére,   syl
    .
    .        .    .
                              [ . ]
```

Globally, line 4 is transitional, articulating the end of the first unit at Level 7 and presenting a major anacrusis to the second (the first peak within Level 8).

The one complete tone unit in this line is relatively contracted, presenting a penultimate variation that breaks the pattern of expanding tone units to this point and prepares the way for the longest tone unit in the text, presented in the next two metrical lines (GPR6 Change). This line also breaks the pattern of expanding metrical lines, contracting to only six syllables, two-thirds of the number in the first metrical line and one-third of the number in the previous metrical line. Given that the complete tone unit in this line is also a complete unit at Level 6, this rhythmic articulation conspires to make this line very slow physically and cognitively. The text hovers in expectation of the line to follow, an expectation that is intensified by the prolongational anticipation generated by the subordinate clause presented here as well.

This contraction and hovering expectation are intensified by the implied tactical beat at the end of the line. In my reading, the fourth lexical stress (on *there*) is weakened by its post-tonic position and therefore it is too weak to support a preceding implied offbeat that would be necessary to make it a tactical beat. As a result, *there* arrives *between* the third and fourth tactical beats, leaving a true *metrical* pause at line end.

The transitional nature of this line ־ is also smoothed by articulation at the beginning of the line. Following the pattern established in the last two lines, the line begins by resolving the peak of a major phrase on a major beat, this time a peak at the fifth level on a three-dot beat (GPR7 Beats, GPR14 Parallelism). These three 'resolutions' also present an amphibrachic figure, with the resolution of *Falcon* at the beginning of the third metrical line experienced as a rhythmic peak flanked by the resolution of *dauphin* in the middle of the second metrical line and the resolution of *air* at the beginning of the fourth metrical line here (GPR16 Unity).

```
         w                    s                    w
┌────────────────┐ ┌────────────────┐ ┌────────────────┐
 (fourth-level peak)  (sixth-level peak)  (fifth-level peak)
    . . . dauphin        . . . Falcon         . . . air
         .                    .                    .
         .                    .                    .
         .                    .                    .
```

In its larger contours, this last resolution is comparable to the patterning found in many songs with four-measure phrasing, which often (1) end the first phrase of the lyric on the major beat in the fourth measure, (2) fill out the fourth measure with a musical continuation (with no words), and (3) begin the lyric again in the fifth measure. Such wordless continuations are more difficult in poetry, but Hopkins provides the next best thing: an anacrustic subordinate clause followed by a metrical pause.

> I caught this morning morning's minion,
>   1   2   3   4
> kingdom of daylight's dauphin, dapple-dawn-drawn
> 1   2   3   4
> Falcon, in his riding of the rolling level underneath him steady
>   1   2   3   4
> Air, and striding high there,
> 1   [2] [3]   [4]
> how he rung . . .
>   1

This line also provides an appropriately culminating peak to the amphibrachic and chiastic articulation that has preceded. This fourth metrical line is rigorously chiastic in sound, with assonantal [ay] diphthongs at the centre of the line and rhymes at the peripheries. The one intonational unit here is also amphibrachic and is articulated at lower levels by an amphibrachic clitic phrase (GPR16 Unity).

```
            w            s          w
          ┌────┐      ┌─────┐    ┌─────┐
            w    s  w
          air,   and striding    High    there
           ↑        ↑              ↑
           └────────┤              │
                    └──────────────┘
```

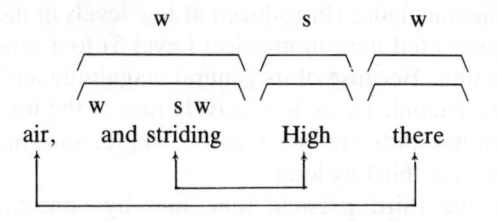

The visual form of the poem also breaks this fourth metrical line chiastically in half, with *striding*, the last word in the first half of the metrical line, completing both the third line and the first rhyme pair in the chiastically organized abba rhyme scheme of the first quatrain of the Italian sonnet form.

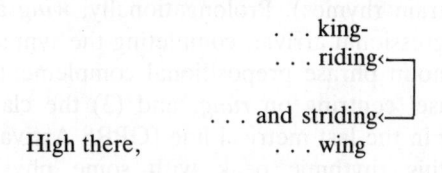

```
                              . . . king-
                              . . . riding‹─┐
                     . . . and striding‹─┘
          High there,         . . . wing
```

5.2.7.5 Metrical line 5

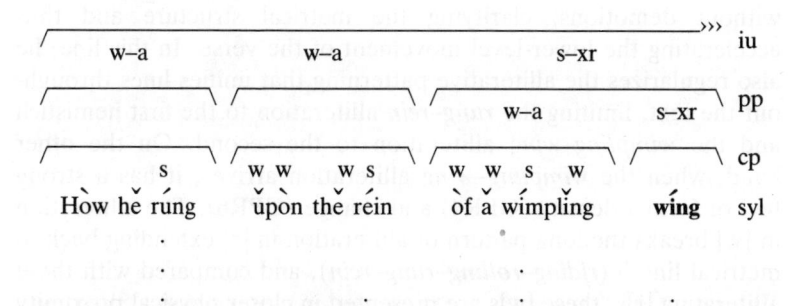

```
┌──────────────────────────────────────────────────»»  iu
  w–a           w–a                    s–xr
             ┌─────────────────────────────────────┐ pp
                              w–a          s–xr
             ┌──────┐ ┌──────────┐ ┌─────────────┐ cp
   s          w  w    w  s         w  w  s    w
  How he rung  upon the rein   of a wimpling  wing  syl
```

The grouping structures in metrical line 5 deliver the peak of the first unit at Level 8 and the end of (what might be seen as) the first verse period. Hopkins renders this peak by bringing to culmination the expansional processes in the first four metrical lines, presenting here (part of) the longest tone unit in the text (GPR2 Weight). In anticipation of the exclamation delivered in the next line, Hopkins also supports this expansion with largely rising contours at all levels: iambs, anapaests and third paeons (GPR2 End-focus).

Technically, Hopkins creates this expansional maximum by

moving the third paeonic figure (introduced at low levels in metrical lines 2 and 3 and presented here in metrical Level 5) to a relatively high level: the tone unit. Because of its general magnitude and post-tonic 'tail', this third paeonic figure is relatively rare at the tone-unit level. Most intonational units are end-focused, duple, and, measuring in syllables, about a third as long.

Hopkins creates the third paeonic tone unit by concentrating several sorts of formal patterning on *wing*, accentuating its status as a rhythmic peak, while delaying and weakening our experience of *in his ecstasy!* (which doesn't appear until the next metrical and visual line). *Wing* is the first place in the text where the two meters converge. *Wing* ends both the fifth line in the tetrameter meter and the first quatrain in the pentameter meter (including the envelope abba pattern of first quatrain rhymes). Prolongationally, *wing* also delivers a three-level progressional arrival, completing the syntactic requirements of (1) the noun phrase prepositional complement of *upon*, (2) the 'main clause' centring on *rung*, and (3) the clause complex begun at *striding* in the last metrical line (GPR8 Arrivals). Hopkins also delivers this rhythmic peak with some physical phonetic force. While he uses non-ictic runs of two and three syllables in metrical lines 2 and 3, here he presents these runs without demotions, clarifying the metrical structure and thus accelerating the lower-level movement of the verse. In this line, he also regularizes the alliterative patterning that unifies lines throughout the text, limiting the *rung–rein* alliteration to the first hemistich and the *wimpling–wing* alliteration to the second. On the other hand, when the *wimpling–wing* alliteration arrives, it has a strong feel of formal density (GPR4) and change (GPR6). The alliteration in [w] breaks the long pattern of alliteration in [r] extending back to metrical line 3 (*riding–rolling–rung–rein*), and compared with these alliterating [r]s, these [w]s are presented in closer physical proximity (on alternating syllables rather than every third or fourth syllable) and with further phonetic support (*wimpling* and *wing* do not just alliterate; they are full 'reverse rhymes' (in [wI]) and are partial rhymes as well, both having syllabic codas with a nasal consonant). He also reserves the only modification in the line for this climactic point, giving further weight (GPR2) to intermediate prosodic structures. *Wimpling* creates the only complex phonological phrase in the line, and this phonological phrase adds another level of anticipational rising movement that (also) arrives and peaks on *wing* (GPR8 Arrivals, GPR15 Measures).

5.2.7.6 Metrical line 6

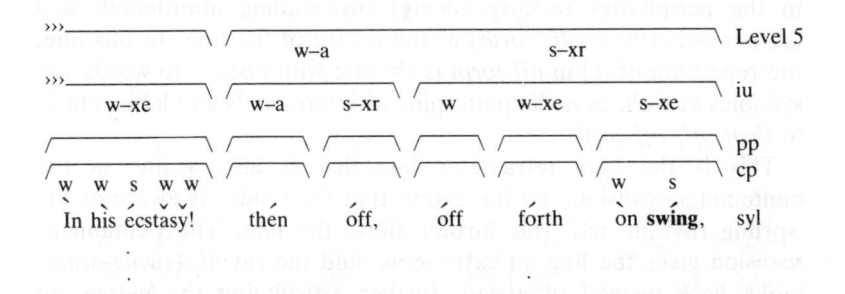

```
>>>————————\  /————————————————\  Level 5
            w–a              s–xr
>>>——\  /————\  /——\  /————\  /——\  iu
   w–xe   w–a   s–xr   w   w–xe   s–xe
/————————\ /——\ /——\ /——\ /————\ /——\  pp
 w  w  s w w                   w   s   cp
 In his ecstasy!  then  off,  off  forth  on swing,  syl
```

Given all of this patterning, when the end of this long tone unit arrives at the beginning of metrical line 6, it is felt as a maximum extension, appropriate to its content. Given normal grouping-metrical relations, the tone unit that *in his ecstasy* concludes 'extends over' the metrical and visual line break; it is a prolongational extension, adding an optional adverbial modifier to the clause centring on *rung*; it interrupts and disappoints metrical energies, preventing a strong metrical 'projection' in line 6, but now without bringing together grouping and metrical energies (as in the three previous 'resolutions' at *dauphin*, *Falcon* and *air*); and it delivers the only five-syllable clitic phrase in the poem.

After this enormous crescendo and then dissipation of energies, the additive extension in the next unit at Level 8 (beginning with *then off*, . . .) feels weak, and the verse resets itself, radically contracting and slowing. In this section, phrasing at low levels resists the meter, presenting five phonological phrases in six words, perhaps miming the change in the bird's movements as it starts 'off on swing'. In the context of the alternating meter, this staccato phrasing pulses with the metrical beating, giving the feel of the alternating beat of the bird's wings (or in the analogy here, a skater's stride). The medial repetition of *off* is particularly effective, presenting first the ictic tonic syllable in the initial weak tone unit, then the non-ictic non-tonic onset on the following strong tone unit. At the end of the line we finally get the tonic peak at Level 5, but now on a weak beat with congruent metrical segmentation, a rhythmic structure that also gives the feel of crossing contours of energy. This is the first lineal-grouping congruence since the first line.

Other formal patterning continues to be chiastic with relation to the line. In this line, fricatives are the phonetic motif, with sibilants in the peripheries (*ecstasy*, *swing*) surrounding interdentals and labiodentals (*then*, *off*, *forth*) at the centre of the line. In this line, the repetition of [f] in *off forth* is chiastic with respect to words and syllables as well, as is the patterning of interdentals and labiodentals in *then off, off forth*.

This is the only tetrameter line that is also a line in the pentameter scansion. To the extent that the reader is aware of the 'sprung rhythm' icti, this further slows the line. The pentameter scansion gives the line an extra ictus, and the rhyme (*swing–wing*) looks *back* instead of ahead, further articulating the merger in grouping and metrical segmentation at line end.

5.2.7.7 Metrical line 7

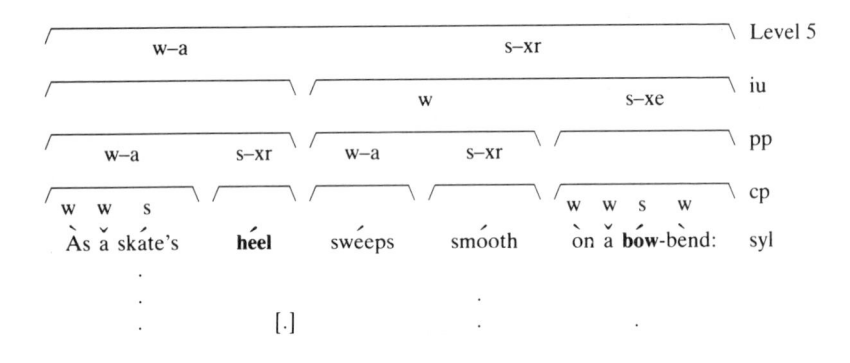

	w–a				s–xr			Level 5
			w			s–xe		iu
w–a		s–xr	w–a		s–xr			pp
w w s					w w s w			cp
As a skate's	**heel**	sweeps	smooth	on a **bow**-bend:	syl
	[.]							

Rhythmically, metrical line 7 is one of the most mimetic lines in the poem, enacting the energy contours of the 'sweeping' skate it describes.

At high levels, meter and grouping are congruent in their segmentation (GPR15 Measures). For the first time since metrical line 1, the line encompasses its tone units, without rejet or contre-rejet; and the two tone units in the ten-syllable line break 4–6 in syllable count, a canonical division. At these levels the line has largely rising and anticipational contours, also canonical patterning (GPR9 Binary Form, GPR3 End-focus). This canonical patterning gives the line relatively neutral emotive contours that are appropriate to its largely descriptive (rather than interpretive) content.

In this line, rhythmic interest is generated principally at low levels, where tactical beats and offbeats are syncopated against phrasal peaks and valleys. In my reading, *heel* is the tonic syllable in the first tone unit, but the prominence of *skates* (i.e. in both stress and phonetic 'weight') attracts the major beat in the line, leaving *heel* in a metrical gap before the arrival of the second tactical beat, a near maximal crossing of low-level grouping and metrical prominences. This effect reproduces the characteristic push and cut of a skate's blade, the interaction of effort, movement and then resistance produced by the skating motion.

In the second hemistich this syncopation continues, but in different patterns and with different effects. *Sweeps* reproduces almost exactly the phonetic and prosodic pattern of *skate's* (both words are weak clitic phrase peaks with a sCVCs phonetic pattern), but now the prosodic context allows *skate's* to be demoted, while the meter 'sweeps' on to the ictic onset of the second hemistich at *smooth*. The line then resolves by bringing together tactical beat and tonic syllable at *bow-bend*, now under waved and expanded clitic phrase contours and extensional prolongation.

This crossing of rhythmic energies at low levels is reproduced up the hierarchy at Levels 6 and 7. I group metrical line 7 with metrical line 8 ('the hurl and gliding rebuffed the big wind'). But this analysis is largely retrospective and misrepresents the complexity of the reading process. The *as*-clause in metrical line 7 is first grouped with metrical line 6 ('then off, off forth on swing'); then (at the colon after *bow-bend*) the line is regrouped with metrical line 8. Experientially, this also reproduces the crossing contours of force in the skating motion.

Like the other metrical lines, metrical line 7 is phonetically unified. Consonantally, sibilants abound (*as, skate's, sweeps, smooth*), appropriately rendering both the skate's 'smooth' movement and 'hissing' sound. Vocalically, tense vowels are prominent (*skate's, heel, sweeps, smooth, bow-(bend)*), presenting a sonic analogue of the skate's sharp 'cut'.

Like many other lines, metrical line 7 is also chiastic in many ways. At low levels, the three monosyllabic clitic phrases (*heel, sweeps, smooth*) are placed at the centre of the line, with the more expanded phrases (*as a skate's, on a bow-bend*) at the periphery. In the series of four consecutive lexical stresses in the line (*skate's heel sweeps smooth*), the two [i] vowels are placed at the centre, with constrasting vowels ([e] and [u]) at the periphery. Prolongational contours are also chiastic, the first phonological phrase being anticipational and the third extensional. And the central word in the line, *sweeps*, is multiply chiastic, beginning and ending with [s] and a preceding/following consonant and presenting visually doubled *es* medially.

5.2.7.8 Metrical line 8

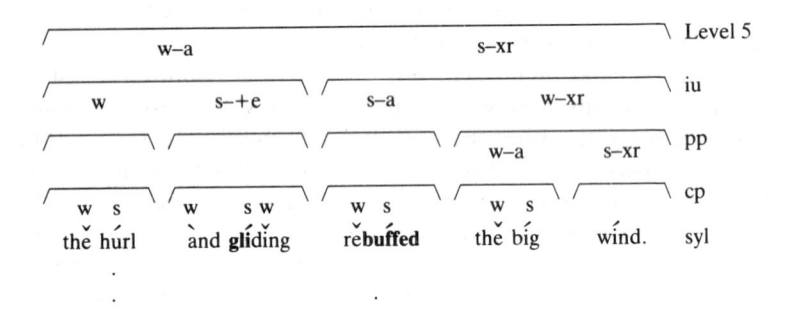

```
                                                              Level 5
            w–a                         s–xr
                                                              iu
    w             s–+e        s–a              w–xr
                                                              pp
                                      w–a            s–xr
                                                              cp
   w  s      w   s w      w  s      w    s
   the hurl  and gliding  rebuffed  the big    wind.          syl
```

At high levels, metrical line 8 is also congruent and symmetrical, dividing its ten syllables 5–5 into two tone units.

If metrical line 7 presents many types of crossing motion, metrical line 8 presents many sorts of *counter*-motion (as the skate 'rebuffs' the 'big wind'). In fact, in many ways metrical line 8 is a rhythmic 'negative' of metrical line 7. While the tone units in metrical line 7 are end-focused, the second tone unit in metrical line 8 is strong-initial ('**rebuffed** the big wind'). While the tone units in metrical line 7 arrive and then extend, the tone units in metrical line 8 extend and then arrive. While metrical line 7 places its 'scudding' syllables peripherally, metrical line 8 places its one pair of scudding syllables (*-ing*, *re-*) medially. And while metrical line 7 syncopates peaks and beats, metrical line 8 brings peaks and beats together, placing a tonic syllable (*-buffed*) on the strong beat of the second hemistich. Metrical line 8 is also the phonetic 'negative' of metrical line 7. While metrical line 7 presents kinaesthetically 'sharp' tense vowels and voiceless consonants (e.g. *skate's*), metrical line 8 is articulated with kinaesthetically 'blunt' mid central and lax vowels (e.g. *hurl*, *-buffed*) and voiced consonants (e.g. *rebuffed the big wind*).

This 'counter-motion' preserves much of the chiastic patterning of metrical line 7; therefore metrical line 8 also participates in the larger network of chiastic patterns in the text as a whole (GPR16 Unity, GPR17 Schemes). The most important chiastic pattern in metrical line 8, however, is new: the directionally chiastic (ws/sw) tone units.

5.2.7.9 Metrical line 9

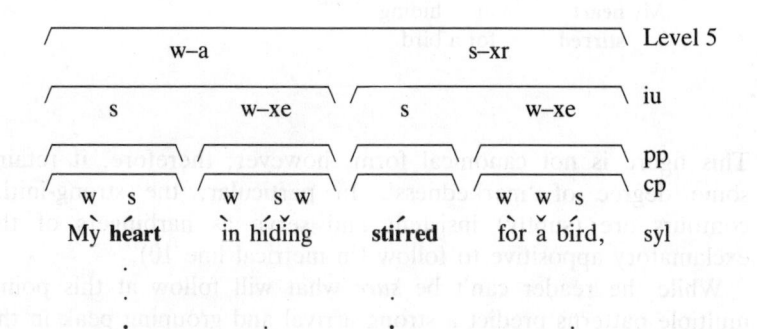

```
/─────────────────────────────\   Level 5
        w–a              s–xr
/──────────────\ /──────────────\  iu
    s    w–xe       s    w–xe
/─────\ /──────\ /─────\ /──────\  pp
/──\ /──\ /──\ /──\ /──\ /──\ /──\ cp
 w  s  w  s w    w   w  w  s
 My heart in hiding stirred for a bird,  syl
```

While metrical line 8 inverts many of the rhythmic and phonic patterns of metrical line 7, metrical line 9 *duplicates* many of the patterns of metrical line 8 (GPR14 Parallelism). The first hemistichs of the two lines are especially close, including a final rhyme (the juxtaposed 'b' rhymes in the abba pattern of the second visual quatrain).

  the hurl and gliding
  my heart in hiding

Like metrical line 8, the second tone unit of metrical line 9 is strong-initial ('**stirred** for a bird'). Like metrical line 8, the phonetic texture of metrical line 9 is muted with central vowels and voiced consonants. And like metrical line 8, metrical line 9 brings grouping peaks in line with strong metrical beats (the tonic syllables occur on the strong beats in the hemistichs).

Where metrical line 9 differs from metrical line 8 it *regularizes* rhythmic and phonetic patterning, producing a minimum of rhythmic tension, perhaps rendering the recessive, 'hidden' heart of the speaker. While metrical lines 7 and 8 contain dense sound patterning, for the first time metrical line 9 aligns this patterning with ictic syllables and metrical segmentation. The *heart–hiding* alliteration occupies the tactical beats in the first hemistich; the *stirred–bird* rhyme, the tactical beats in the second hemistich. Grouping and prolongational contours now run with meter as well. Both tone units fall and extend.

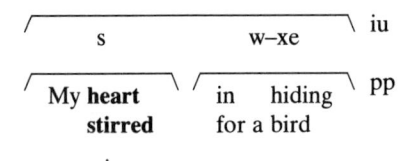

```
⌐─────────────────────────¬  iu
       s          w–xe
⌐──────────¬ ⌐──────────¬  pp
  My heart    in  hiding
  stirred     for a bird
      .
      .             .
```

This figure is not canonical form, however; therefore, it retains some degree of 'markedness'. In particular, the strong-initial contours are (subtly) insistent and serve as harbingers of the exclamatory appositive to follow (in metrical line 10).

While the reader can't be *sure* what will follow at this point, multiple patterns predict a strong arrival and grouping peak in the next metrical line; therefore, I notate metrical line 9 as anticipatory. In the visual form of text, metrical line 9 is in a penultimate position in the octave. The strong-initial tone units in metrical line 9 call out for resolution with end-focused units. The increasing rhythmic control in metrical lines 7–9 has reached a maximum, predicting some release of control. And the largely duple rising patterning within Level 7 leaves metrical line 9 without a complementing unit (and if this unit is to follow the rising pattern, this complementing unit should be a complementing *peak*).

5.2.7.10   *Metrical line 10*

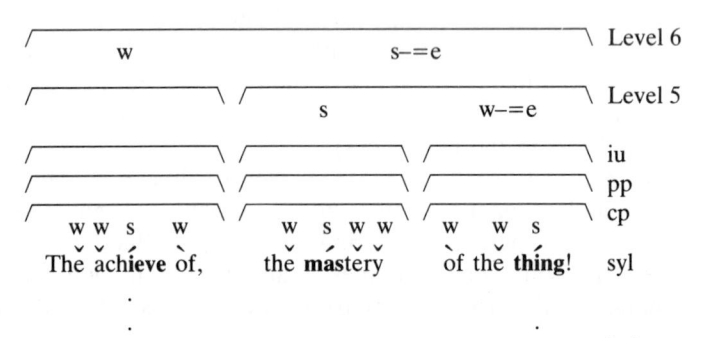

```
⌐──────────────────────────────────¬  Level 6
       w                  s–=e
⌐──────────────¬ ⌐─────────────────¬  Level 5
                      s        w–=e
⌐──────┬ ⌐──────┬ ⌐──────¬   iu
⌐──────┬ ⌐──────┬ ⌐──────¬   pp
⌐──────┬ ⌐──────┬ ⌐──────¬   cp
 w w s  w    w s w w    w  w  s
 The achieve of,  the mastery  of the thing!   syl
      .                                  .
      .           .             .       [ . ]
```

Metrical line 10 cadences the octave with an exclamatory appositive, completing the parallel with metrical lines 5–10 (and metrical lines 1–4 plus 'in his ecstasy'), thus establishing the duple rising movement of the octave as a whole at Level 10 (GPR14 Parallelism, GPR6 Change, GPR5 Return, GPR3 End-focus, GPR9 Binary Form).

In addition to its 'summarizing' and exclamatory content, this line presents various sorts of terminal modification and unification. At the middle levels it is composed of three tone units (without rejet or contre-rejet), the only line with this structure in the octave (GPR6 Change); and these three tone units are delivered without articulation at the phonological phrase and clitic phrase levels, also a unique gesture to this point (GPR4 Density).

On the other hand, many of the structures in metrical line 10 tie together the octave by recalling patterning that has preceded. At low levels, clitic phrases return to the quadruple movement of metrical lines 3 and 5 (e.g. *in his riding, of the rolling, underneath him, of a wimpling*). The tense vowel in *achieve* recalls the tense vowels in metrical line 7 (e.g. *heel sweeps*). The [m] in *mastery* recalls the opening alliterative motif in [m] (i.e. *morning–morning's–minion*). And *thing* delivers the culminating rhyme of the octave, linking back to the other a- rhymes (*king-, wing, swing*) in the abbaabba scheme for the octave – in addition to presenting an unstressed rhyme with the b- rhymes in the pattern well (*riding, striding, gliding, hiding*).

At higher levels of grouping, the figure presented by the three tone units in this line, a two-level triple, also recalls (GPR17 Unity) the triple appositives at the opening of the octave (*minion–dauphin–falcon*) and presages the two-level triples that will follow immediately at the opening of the sestet (*beauty–valour–act*, etc.), at the close of the first 'half' of the poem in visual line 11 (*lovelier–dangerous–chevalier*), and at the end of the poem as a whole (*fall–gall–gash*). It is significant that Hopkins rigorously varies the contours of these three-level triples.

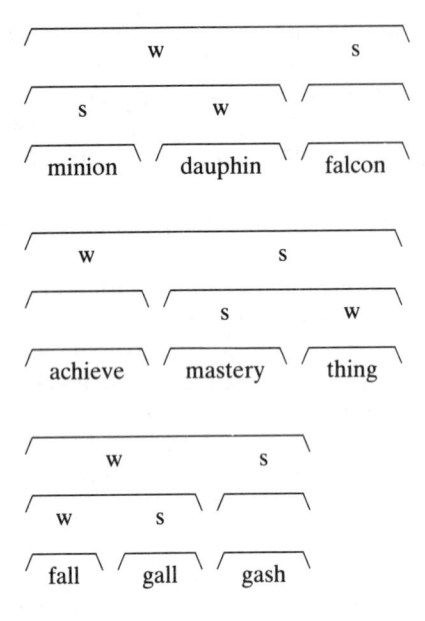

```
         ┌─────────────────────────────────┐
         │         w              s        │
       ┌─────────────┐  ┌──────────────────┐
       │  s     w    │  │                  │
     ┌────────┐ ┌────────┐ ┌────────┐
     │ minion │ │ dauphin│ │ falcon │
     └────────┘ └────────┘ └────────┘

       ┌─────────────────────────────────┐
       │     w              s            │
     ┌──────────┐  ┌──────────────────────┐
     │          │  │   s           w     │
     ┌────────┐ ┌────────┐ ┌────────┐
     │ achieve│ │ mastery│ │ thing  │
     └────────┘ └────────┘ └────────┘

       ┌─────────────────────────────────┐
       │       w              s          │
     ┌──────────────┐ ┌─────────┐
     │  w      s    │ │         │
     ┌──────┐ ┌──────┐ ┌──────┐
     │ fall │ │ gall │ │ gash │
     └──────┘ └──────┘ └──────┘
```

The multilevelled equative movement among the tone units in this line (and between this line and the rest of the octave) is especially effective as a cadential formula. The narrative, descriptive and logical progress of the text pauses while the speaker repetitively exclaims, naming and renaming his wonder and admiration for the bird and its flight.

As in many texts, metrical line 10 ends this large section of the poem with an implied beat (GPR12 Proximity). The three tonic syllables in the line (*-chieve*, *mas-* and *thing*) receive tactical beats, leaving the fourth tactical beat unrealized. This metrical pause reinforces the 'pause' in prolongation created by the multilevelled equative movement, further highlighting both the content of the exclamation and its cadential rhythmic function.

5.2.7.11 Metrical line 11

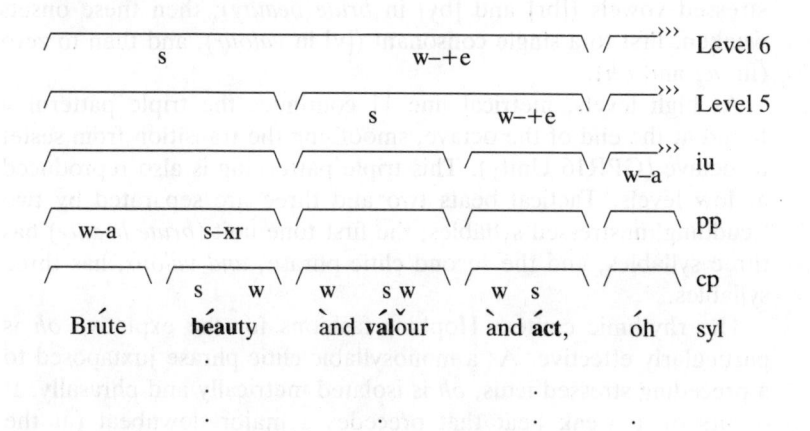

```
┌─────────────────────────────────────────┐ ┌────>>>   Level 6
        s                w–+e
┌──────────────┐ ┌────────────────────────┐ ┌────>>>   Level 5
                      s           w–+e
┌──────────────┐ ┌──────────┐ ┌───────────┐ ┌────>>>   iu
                                            w–a
┌──────┐ ┌─────┐ ┌──────────┐ ┌───────────┐ ┌──────┐   pp
  w–a    s–xr
         ┌─────┐ ┌──────────┐ ┌───────────┐ ┌──────┐   cp
           s  w   w    s w    w    s
  Brúte  beáuty  and válŏur  and áct,     ŏh    syl
```

Metrical line 11 begins the extended rise to the end of the first half of the text (the first unit at Level 12). This rise will traverse ten tone units in three visual lines, the most concentrated intonational articulation in the text.

At the beginning of this cadential rise, high levels of structure within metrical line 11 are strong-initial, extensional and additive – giving impulse and motion to this large phrasal onset (GPR16 Unity). To generate further impulsion, this line also returns to the enjambed structures we found at the beginning of the octave. The three tonic syllables in the line (*beau-*, *val-* and *act*) receive the first three tactical beats, leaving *oh* the fourth beat, but with grouping contours unresolved, *oh* being a weak anticipation of its tonic peak and arrival *air* in the next line. Higher levels add further impulsion. The duple rising pattern among units at Level 6 makes this line a weak rise to a following peak, and prolongationally the line as a whole, being a grammatical subject, anticipates its main verb *buckle* in the next metrical line.

Lower-level structures also generate strong-initial movement (GPR16 Unity). The only demotion in the line (*brute*) occurs at the beginning of the line; then the line runs more freely in its metrical-grouping relations. The most salient phoenetic pattern in the line, the partial reverse rhyme *brute beauty*, occurs at the beginning of the line, with the less salient assonance in *valour* and *act* occurring later on. Clitic phrase contours move from strong-initial (*beauty*), to waved (*and valour*), to strong-final (*and act*), an advancing grade

368 ANALYSIS

(GPR17 Schemes). And the line begins with strong syllabic onsets in stressed vowels ([br] and [by] in *brute beauty*); then these onsets weaken, first to a single consonant ([v] in *valour*), and then to zero (in *act* and *oh*).

At high levels, metrical line 11 continues the triple patterning found at the end of the octave, smoothing the transition from sestet to octave (GPR16 Unity). This triple patterning is also reproduced at low levels. Tactical beats two and three are separated by two 'scudding' unstressed syllables; the first tone unit (*brute beauty*) has three syllables; and the second clitic phrase, *and valour*, has three syllables.

The rhythmic context Hopkins fashions for the expletive *oh* is particularly effective. As a monosyllabic clitic phrase juxtaposed to a preceding stressed ictus, *oh* is isolated metrically and phrasally. It occurs on a weak beat that precedes a major downbeat (at the beginning of the next line), and its naturally anticipatory meaning is stranded at line end. This rhythmic articulation conspires to give the expletive an impulsion that reinforces its meaning (i.e. an exclamation of wonder, surprise, etc.).

5.2.7.12 Metrical line 12

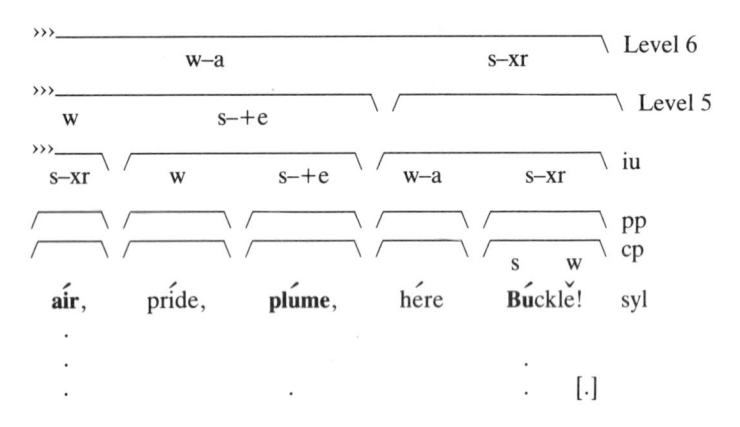

Metrical line 12 presents the peak and arrival of the structures in metrical line 11 and the culmination of the speaker's description of the Falcon's flight (anticipating the more interpretive comment to follow in metrical lines 13 and 14 and the more analogical and generalized comment to follow in the last tercet of the visual text).

'SPRUNG RHYTHM' 369

The last word in this line, *buckle*, is appropriately culminating, unifying with its polysemy the ironic implications of the poem's theme of beautiful sacrifice (GPR1 Information). As many have noted, *buckle* can mean both 'to join' and 'to give way', both 'to equip for battle' and 'to engage in battle'.

In many ways, metrical line 12 is rhythmically 'buckled' as well. Five of its six syllables are clitic phrase and phonological phrase peaks, and every other syllable is tonic. This is a near maximum of phrasal contraction. This phrasal reading is also somewhat strained, given the syntax of the line. I read *oh*, *pride* and *here* as intonationally subordinate to the syllables that they precede, but this prosodic reading overrides both syntax and punctuation and is enforced more by the meter and rhythmic preference than by the textual structure (GPR7 Beats).

Hopkins artfully distributes the prosodically knotted attributes of the Falcon so that they complete an elegant chiasmus with the structures in the preceding metrical line. With the main verb at the end of the line, the rhythmic contours of this line both peak and arrive at line end. By splitting the tone unit, *oh, air*, across metrical lines and strengthening the second tone unit, *pride, plume*, with the most prominent alliteration in the line (GPR4 Density), the first tone unit in the triple also rises to the second, producing a two-level rise, a contour that exactly inverts the two-level fall in metrical line 11 (GPR17 Schemes). Tone units in this line also incrementally expand (GPR16 Schemes): one syllable (*air*), then two syllables (*pride, plume*), then three syllables (*here buckle*), and the only complex clitic phrase, *buckle*, appears at line end – further influencing a 'rising' reading (GPR2 Weight).

This extended chiasmus is also punctuated with finer phonetic and rhythmic detail. *Brute beauty* in the first of the six tone units in the chiasmus is echoed (in both alliteration and stress contours) by *buckle* in the last of the six tone units in the pattern (GPR14 Parallelism), a parallel that is also reinforcd by the visual form of the text, which places *brute beauty* and *buckle* at the beginning of succeeding visual lines.

The two-level triple here also echoes the two-level triple in the exclamations at the end of the octave and the first half of the text, connecting this line with other large-scale grouping peaks in the text.

Like metrical line 10, this line ends with an implied beat. The three tonic syllables (*air*, *plume* and *bu-*) receive tactical beats,

370 ANALYSIS

leaving the fourth beat in the metrical space between the end of this line and the beginning of metrical line 13. This implied beat invites the reader to dwell on the thematic implication of *buckle*; further links the exclamation here with the exclamation at the end of the octave; and further punctuates the end of the extended chiasmus, the rhythmic contraction and, more generally, the extended description of the Falcon that has occupied the speaker to this point (GPR12 Proximity).

5.2.7.13 Metrical line 13

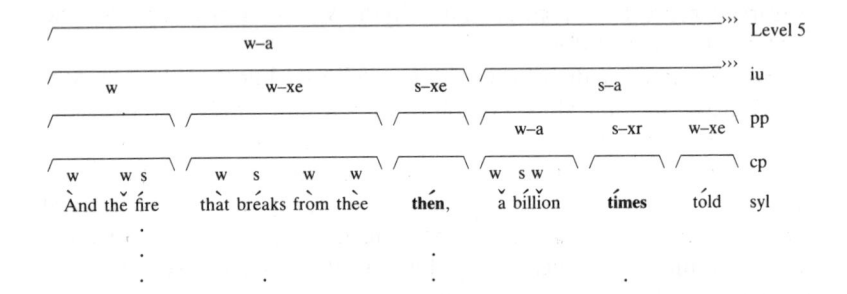

```
                                                              >>>  Level 5
         w–a                                                  >>>  iu
  w          w–xe         s–xe        s–a          w–xe       pp
                                w–a        s–xr               cp
  w    w s   w   s  w   w        w   s w
  And the fire  that breaks from thee  then,  a billion  times  told  syl
    .                           .                       .
    .              .            .              .
```

Metrical line 13 releases the rhythmic constriction and chiastic stasis of metrical lines 11 and 12 and begins the more expansive and volatile cadence to the first half of the text (delivered in the next metrical line).

At low levels, clitic phrases avoid duple movement and present rhythmic extremes, a jolting mixture of monosyllabic and polysyllabic (triple/quadruple) phrases that continues through the next line as well (GPR16 Unity, GPR17 Schemes).

Polysyllabic	Monosyllabic
AND the fire	
that breaks from thee	then
a billion	times
	told
lovelier	more
dangerous	O
my chevalier!	

Intonational units and phonological phrases also expand, showing some triple movement (e.g. a billion / times / told). Directional movement also shifts freely at all levels. Polysyllabic clitic phrases begin with an anapaestic rise (*and the fire*), then fall through a second paeonic pattern (*that breaks from thee*), then are waved (*a billion*). The only complex phonological phrase, *a billion times told*, is waved. And intonational units first rise in a triple pattern and then fall in a duple pattern (across the line break). Prolongational contours also avoid chiastic patterning, first extending and then being left unresolved and anticipatory at line end.

Significantly, the expanded triple movement in the first tone unit unbalances the line into an 8–5 syllabic distribution and places the tonic syllable, *then*, on the major beat of the second hemistich rather than at the end of the first hemistich, disturbing the duple metrical projection within the line. After this disturbance, the next tone unit rides out as a metrical upbeat to the next line, but in tune with the other volatile movement here, peaks early (at *times*), and then resolves its tail, *lovelier*, on the major beat in the next line, perpetuating both the metrical-grouping disturbance and the falling energy contours, which are not 'capped' with rising articulation until the end-focused clitic phrase *chevalier* in the next line. The metrical-grouping relations at *chevalier* perpetuate these metrical-grouping relations. *Chevalier* also delivers the peak of a tone unit that resolves on a strong (two-dot) beat. All of this expansive, varied yet tailing and resolving movement brings the first half of the text to a close.

While phrasal shapes in metrical line 13 are varied, phonetic patterns are still prominently chiastic, maintaining some formal connection between this line and the larger formal context. The [ay] assonance in *fire–times* surrounds the [b] alliteration in *breaks–billion*, which in turn surrounds the juxtaposed voiced interdentals at mid-line (*thee–then*).

And the fire that breaks from thee then, a billion times told

5.2.7.14 Metrical line 14

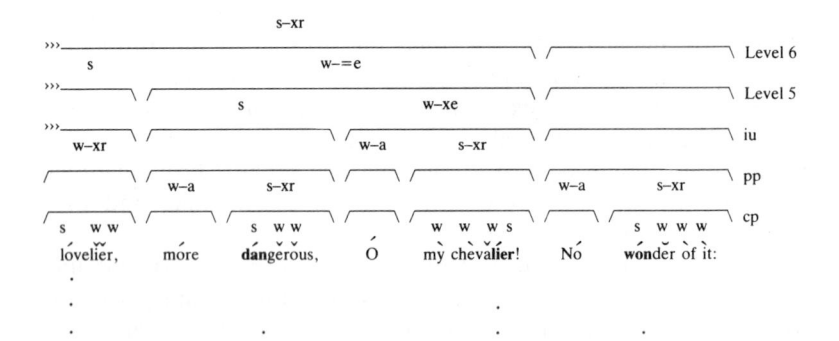

```
                          s–xr
»»——————————————————\  /————————————————\  Level 6
        s                 w–=e
»»———————————\  /———————————————————\  /—————————\  Level 5
              s                       w–xe
»»——————\  /——————————————\  /———————————\  /———————\  iu
  w–xr                w–a         s–xr
/————\  /————\  /————\  /——\  /————\  /————\  pp
        w–a       s–xr                w–a      s–xr
/s w w\ /s w w\ /w w w s\  /s w w w\  cp
 lovelier,  more   dangerous,  O    my chevalier!  No  wonder of it:
   .        .        .        .        .        .        .
   .        .        .        .        .        .        .
```

Metrical line 14 brings the first half of the text to a close and presents the dramatic upbeat, *No wonder of it:*, to the final three metrical lines.

In addition to patterning that we have already discussed, metrical line 14 intensifies the mixture of monosyllabic and polysyllabic clitic phrases begun in the last line by alternating their appearance, giving the peaks of the polysyllabic phrases metrical icti and scudding over the monosyllabic phrases between tactical beats (GPR16 Unity, GPR17 Schemes). This articulation is particularly effective. Each metrical valley is tensed with a demotion (*told, more, O, No*) while each ictus is delivered with an expansive release of tension, an accelerating movement, and a strong-initial contour (*lovelier, dangerous, wonder of it*).

```
/————\ /——————————\
         s   w w   w
 told    love li   er
 more    dan ger  ous
 no      won der of  it
         (.)
         (.)
          .
```

The significant exception to this pattern is *my chevalier*, which reproduces the metrical relations and phrasal spans of the other structures but differs in direction, closing the first half of the text with firm end-focus (GPR3).

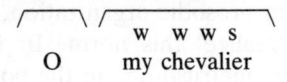

```
       w  w  w  s
O      my chevalier
                .
                .
```

This line is also unified phonetically. Nasal and liquid consonants are most prominent, but the [ʌ] assonance in *lovelier–wonder* and the [o] assonance in *more–O* are also salient.

We have discussed the rhythmic significance of *No wonder of it*, so I will not dwell on its significance further here.

The low-level expansion and contraction possible within Hopkins' meter is impressive. With its seventeen syllables, metrical line 14 is almost three times as long as metrical line 12, which has only six.

5.2.7.15 Metrical line 15

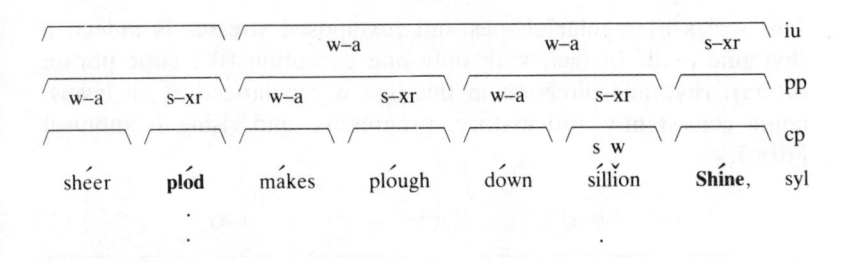

```
                            w–a              w–a          s–xr    iu
   w–a    s–xr    w–a    s–xr    w–a    s–xr              pp
                                              s  w                cp
  sheer   plod   makes   plough  down   sillion  Shine,   syl
```

No wonder of it serves as a transitional rise to the first analogical extension of the text's theme, the shining plough. The enormous compression of this extension and its late appearance give it a strong feeling of anticipation, however; therefore I read it as a cadential preparation for the closural image of the Christ-fire, which follows immediately in the next two metrical lines.

Thematically, the image of the plough is the antithesis of the Falcon: earth vs fire, bondage vs freedom, labor vs play, peasantry vs nobility, the common vs the unique; and Hopkins renders the image with a rhythmic antithesis as well. Prosodically, the dominant characteristics of the Falcon have been variety, virtuosity, a 'barbarous beauty'. In Hopkins' description, the ride and dive of the Falcon test the limits of prosodic coherence. Hopkins' description of the plough presents the prosodic opposite: a plodding normality.

Duple movement is a universal norm in prosodic organization, but metrical line 15 is the first line to 'realize' this norm. In fact, metrical line 15 is the *only* eight-syllable metrical line in the poem.

```
Line:       1  2  3  4  5  6  7  8  9 10 11 12 13 14 15 16 17
No. of syls: 9 11 18  6 12 11 10 10  9 11  9  6 13 17  8  9  9
```

Hopkins regularizes other aspects of this line's movement as well. The first three phonological phrases are regularly duple and rising, each with little articulation at the clitic phrase level (GPR3 End-focus, GPR9 Binary Form).

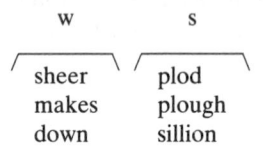

```
        w              s
     ┌──────\     ┌──────\
      sheer         plod
      makes         plough
      down          sillion
```

This series of regular shapes and juxtaposed stresses is indeed a rhythmic plod. In fact, with only one exception (the clitic phrase *sillion*), rhythmic direction in this line is regularized at all levels, being consistently anticipatory, progressive and rising (Canonical Form).

```
              w–a                              s–xr
     ┌─────────────────\          ┌────────────────────────\
       sheer                        plod
       makes                        plough
       down                         sillion
       makes plough [down sillion]  shine
       sheer plod                   makes plough down sillion shine
```

Even the major asymmetry in the phrasing, the intonational segmentation, could be seen as 'smoothing'. The ternary movement in the second tone unit levels the medial interaction between grouping and meter by 'bridging' the hemistich boundary. The metrical span of the line is projected at *plod* and completed at *shine*, without a medial peak on a weak metrical beat.

This line also preserves the static effect of the chiastic phonetic patterning that we have seen in other lines. The most prominent sonic echo, the [š] alliteration in *sheer–shine*, marks the limits of the line. Tactical beats within hemistichs are firmly marked with full or partial alliteration (*plod–plough* and *sillion–shine*). The middle of the line presents a prominent assonance (*plough–down*). And phonetic motives in [n] (*down–sillion–shine*) and [d] (*plod–down*) provide further unity. Vocalic pitch even makes a symmetrical dip and rise across the line, moving between the high front vowels at the periphery (*sheer–shine*) across the rounded back vowels in the centre (*plough–down*).

5.2.7.16 Metrical line 16

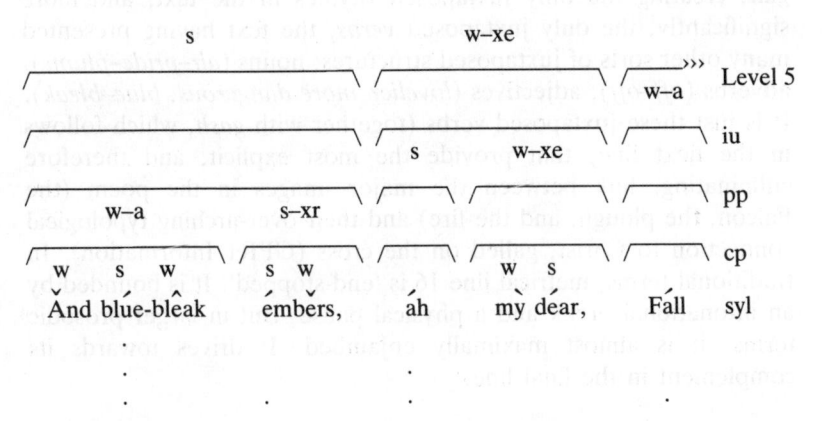

```
                    s                    w–xe
        ⌜‾‾‾‾‾‾‾‾‾‾‾‾‾‾‾⌝  ⌜‾‾‾‾‾‾‾‾‾‾‾‾‾‾‾⌝  ⌜‾‾‾‾≫≫
                                              w–a       Level 5
        ⌜‾‾‾‾‾‾‾‾‾‾‾‾‾‾‾⌝  ⌜‾‾‾‾‾‾‾⌝ ⌜‾‾‾‾‾‾‾⌝ ⌜‾‾‾⌝    iu
                               s        w–xe
        ⌜‾‾‾‾‾‾‾⌝ ⌜‾‾‾‾‾‾‾⌝ ⌜‾‾‾⌝ ⌜‾‾‾⌝ ⌜‾‾‾⌝ ⌜‾‾‾⌝    pp
          w–a        s–xr
        ⌜‾‾⌝  ⌜‾‾⌝ ⌜‾‾⌝ ⌜‾‾⌝ ⌜‾‾⌝ ⌜‾‾⌝ ⌜‾‾⌝ ⌜‾‾⌝       cp
         w s w   s  w        w   s
        And blue-bleak embers,  ah  my dear,  Fall syl
         ˘   ´   ^    ´    ˘   ´   ˋ  ´      ´
         .       .        .
```

Metrical line 16 begins the final image in the poem, the peak of the second 'half' of the text and therefore the peak of the text as a whole. At high levels, the dominant function of metrical line 16 is cadential preparation: a rising, anticipational drive towards closure.

As a penultimate preparation, metrical line 16 presents many sorts of counter-motion (GPR6 Change); then it hovers in anticipation of the textual close. The first tone unit delivers its tonic syllable on a weak beat in its hemistich, is weighted initially, is single, presents a rising, anticipational duple within its one phonological phrase, and presents weak-final structures within its two clitic phrases. The second tone unit delivers its tonic syllable on a strong beat in its hemistich, is duple, is weighted finally, presents a falling, extensional duple in its tone unit, and presents a strong-final structure in its one complex clitic phrase. This counter-motion is placed in relative congruence with metrical segmentation.

The post-tonic position of *my dear* makes it too weak to receive the fourth beat in the line, however, leaving the line with either an implied beat or a jolting one-syllable contre-rejet (of which I choose the latter). If we read *fall* as the fourth beat, this structure is radically unstable. While *fall* can be read as completing the syntactic prerequisites of the clause, this prosodic segmentation divides the line 8–1 in syllabic distribution, an enormously ungainly structure. Visual form also divides *fall* from the rest of metrical line 16. *Dear* completes the penultimate line in the visual text and delivers the last c- rhyme in the cdcdcd scheme for the sestet.

As we proceed, we also find *fall* linked significantly by rhyme to *gall*, creating the only juxtaposed rhymes in the text, and more significantly, the only juxtaposed *verbs*, the text having presented many other sorts of juxtaposed structures: nouns (*air–pride–plume*), adverbs (*off–off*), adjectives (*lovelier–more dangerous*, *blue–bleak*). It is just these juxtaposed verbs (together with *gash*, which follows in the next line) that provide the most explicit, and therefore culminating, link between the major images in the poem (the Falcon, the plough, and the fire) and their over-arching typological connection to Christ, galled on the cross (GPR1 Information). In traditional terms, metrical line 16 is 'end-stopped'. It is bounded by an intonational break and a physical pause. But in larger prosodic terms, it is almost maximally enjambed. It drives towards its complement in the final line.

5.2.7.17 Metrical line 17

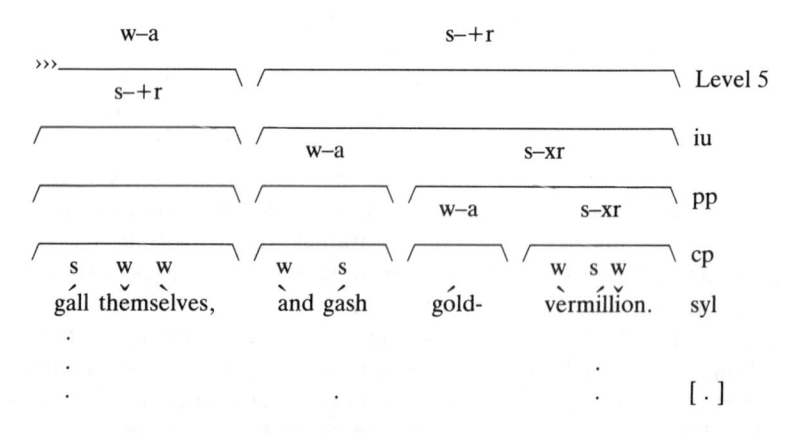

Metrical line 17 closes the poem. Given what has preceded, the formal pressures for closure are considerable.

This line completes the visual form of the text, delivering the last d-rhyme (billion–sillion–vermillion) of the cdcdcd scheme for the sestet, in addition to completing the 'sprung rhythm' meter and squaring out the presentation of the poem on the visual page.

At Levels 4 and 5, this line delivers the now expected two-level triple (fall–gall–gash) that has also cadenced the octave and the first 'half' of the text (GPR14 Parallelism, GPR16 Unity).

Level 6 presents a final chiastic figure, a figure that we also found at this level at the opening of the seset (GPR16 Unity).

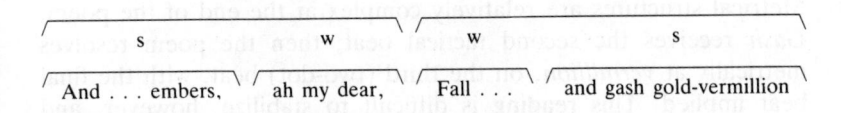

```
         s            w           w            s
⌐─────────────────⌐ ⌐─────────⌐ ⌐──────⌐ ⌐────────────────────⌐
 And . . . embers,   ah my dear,  Fall . . .  and gash gold-vermillion
```

At Level 9, this chiastic figure is also organized into a final rising duple, a figure that completes the series of rising duples at that level (GPR16 Unity, GPR17 Schemes).

| I caught . . . | My heart . . . |
| Brute beauty . . . | And the fire . . . |

(NO WONDER OF IT!)

| Sheer plod | makes plough . . . shine |
| and . . . embers | fall, gall . . . and gash . . . |

And this line competes the final end-weighted elaboration within the duple structure of the text as a whole (GPR2 Weight).

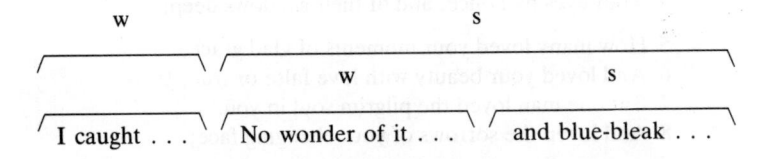

```
              w                           s
⌐──────────────⌐ ⌐─────────────────────────────────────────⌐
                            w                       s
                  ⌐─────────────────⌐ ⌐─────────────────────⌐
   I caught . . .   No wonder of it . . .   and blue-bleak . . .
```

This line also provides an arrival for the general prolongational anticipation that the text will tie up its imagery and argument, a task that Hopkins accomplishes with the verbs *gall* and *gash* and the dvandva compound *gold-vermillion* (GPR8 Arrivals).

Lower-level structures in this line are also interesting. Given that *Fall* receives the last beat in the preceding line, the heavy downbeat on *gall* is delivered after a metrical and prosodic pause and therefore arrives with considerable force, a force that is augmented by the extended and falling contours of the clitic phrase *gall themselves*. From this point, clitic phrases contract in span (3–2–1 syllables) and then end with a balanced wave on *vermillion*, a soft ending that is reinforced at high levels with the relatively mild additive elaboration (GPR16 Unity, GPR17 Schemes).

>   . . . and blue-bleak embers . . .
>   . . . and gash . . .

Metrical structures are relatively complex at the end of the poem. *Gash* receives the second tactical beat; then the poem resolves metrically at *vermillion*, on the third (two-dot) beat, with the final beat implied. This reading is difficult to stabilize, however, and many other readings are possible. The strong prosodic arrival at *gall* (together with the following tone-unit break and 'scud' of three unstressed syllables) invites an implied beat at mid-line, and the salience of *gold-* in the final dvandva compound invites a beat as well.

5.3 PENTAMETER

5.3.1 Text

> When You Are Old
>
> 1 When you are old and grey and full of sleep,
> 2 And nodding by the fire, take down this book,
> 3 And slowly read, and dream of the soft look
> 4 Your eyes had once, and of their shadows deep;
>
> 5 How many loved your moments of glad grace,
> 6 And loved your beauty with love false or true,
> 7 But one man loved the pilgrim soul in you,
> 8 And loved the sorrows of your changing face;
>
> 9 And bending down beside the glowing bars,
> 10 Murmur, a little sadly, how Love fled
> 11 And paced upon the mountains overhead
> 12 And hid his face amid a crowd of stars.

(W. B. Yeats)

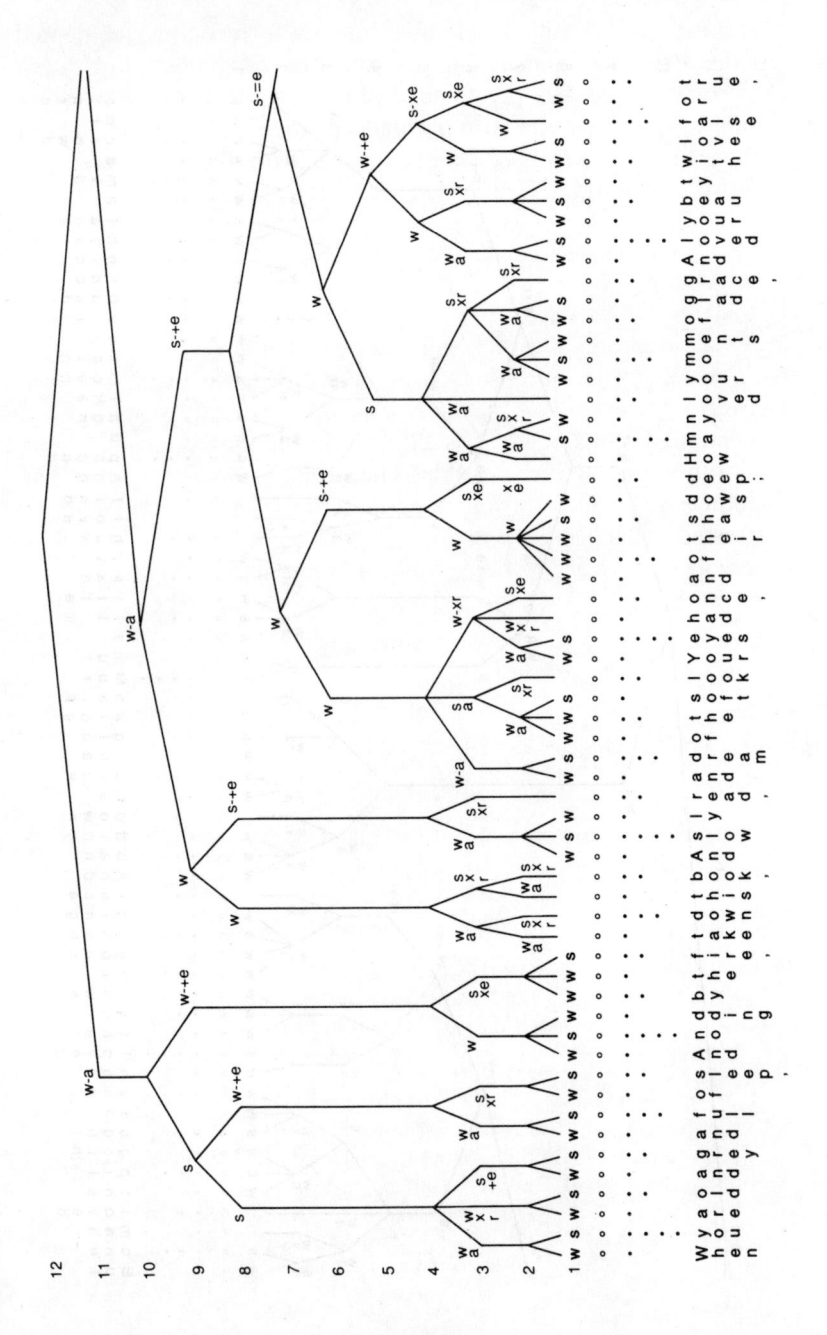

PENTAMETER 379

380 ANALYSIS

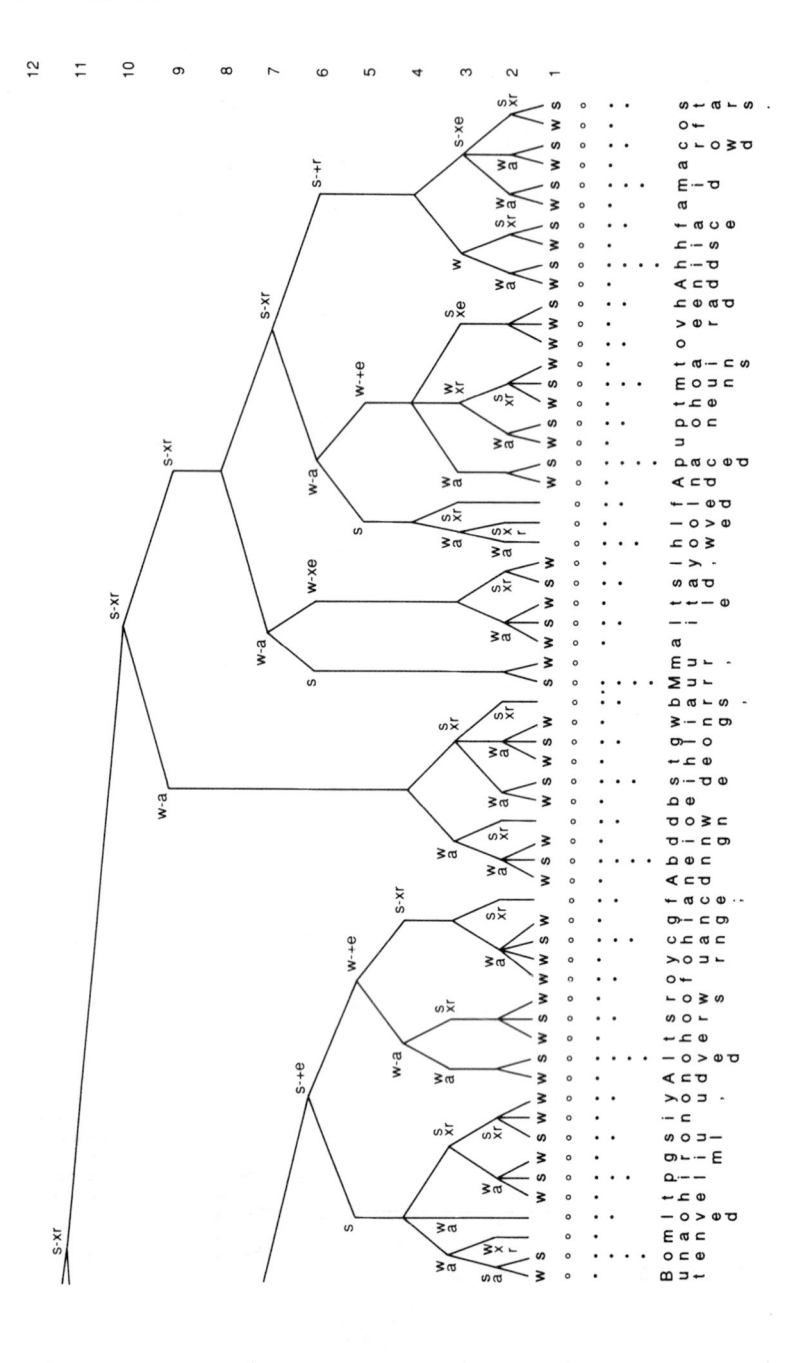

5.3.2 Higher-level phrasing: bracketing formalization

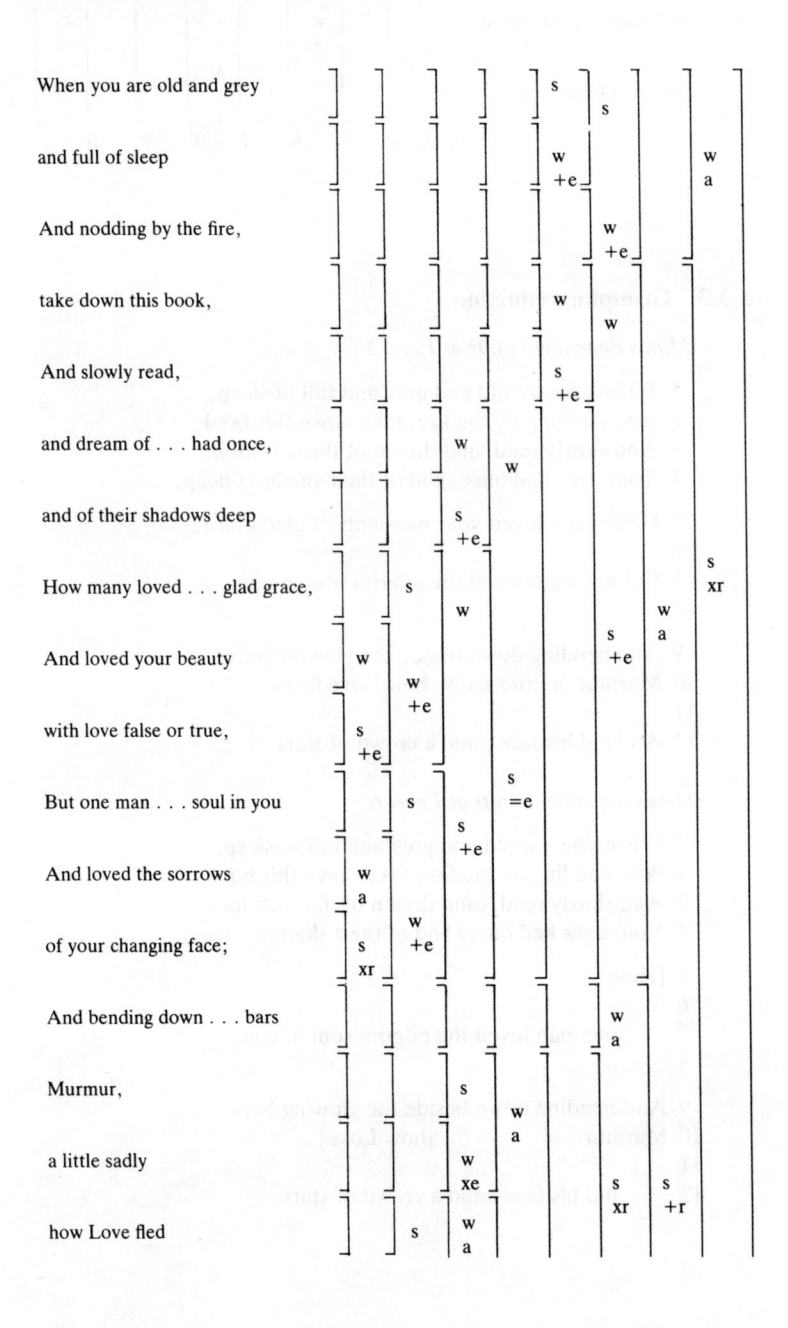

When you are old and grey	]	]	]	]	s]	s]		]
and full of sleep	]	]	]	]	w +e]		w a	
And nodding by the fire,	]	]	]	]	w +e]			
take down this book,	]	]	]	]	w w			
And slowly read,	]	]	]	]	s +e]			
and dream of . . . had once,	]	]	]	w w]				
and of their shadows deep	]	]	]	s +e]				s xr
How many loved . . . glad grace,	]	]	s w]			s +e	w a	
And loved your beauty	w]	w +e]						
with love false or true,	s +e]							
But one man . . . soul in you	]	s s +e]		=e				
And loved the sorrows	w a]	w +e]						
of your changing face;	s xr]							
And bending down . . . bars	]	]	]	]	w a]			
Murmur,	]	s w a]						
a little sadly	]	w xe]				s xr	s +r	
how Love fled	]]	s w a						

382 ANALYSIS

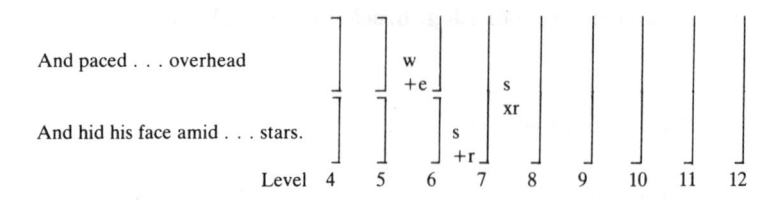

```
And paced . . . overhead      ⎤  ⎤   w   ⎤       ⎤   ⎤   ⎤   ⎤
                              ⎦  ⎦  +e   ⎦  s    ⎦   ⎦   ⎦   ⎦
                                             xr
And hid his face amid . . . stars. ⎤  ⎤  ⎤   ⎤   ⎤   ⎤   ⎤   ⎤
                                   ⎦  ⎦  ⎦ s ⎦   ⎦   ⎦   ⎦   ⎦
                                          +r
               Level  4   5   6   7   8   9   10  11  12
```

5.3.3 Grouping reduction

Minus dependent units at Level 5

1 When you are old and grey and full of sleep,
2 And nodding by the fire, take down this book,
3 And slowly read, and dream of the soft look
4 Your eyes had once, and of their shadows deep;

5 How many loved your moments of glad grace,
6
7 But one man loved the pilgrim soul in you,
8

9 And bending down beside the glowing bars,
10 Murmur, a little sadly, how Love fled
11
12 And hid his face amid a crowd of stars.

Minus dependent units at Level 6

1 When you are old and grey and full of sleep,
2 And nodding by the fire, take down this book,
3 And slowly read, [and dream of that soft look
4 Your eyes had once] and of their shadows deep;

5 [How]
6
7   one man loved the pilgrim soul in you,
8

9 And bending down beside the glowing bars,
10 Murmur   [how Love]
11
12   hid his face amid a crowd of stars.

Minus dependent units at Level 7

1 When you are old and grey and full of sleep,
2 And nodding by the fire, take down this book,
3 And slowly read,
4   [and dream of]

5 [How]
6
7   one man loved the pilgrim soul in you,
8

9 And bending down beside the glowing bars,
10 [Murmur]   [how Love]
11
12   hid his face amid a crowd of stars.

Minus dependent units at Level 8

1 When you are old and grey and full of sleep,
2
3   slowly read,
4   [and dream of]

5 [How]
6
7   one man loved the pilgrim soul in you,
8

9 And bending down beside the glowing bars,
10 [Murmur]   [how Love]
11
12   hid his face amid a crowd of stars.

Minus dependent units at Level 9

1 When you are old and grey
2
3
4   [dream of]

5 [How]
6
7   one man loved the pilgrim soul in you,
8

9 [And]
10 [Murmur]   [how Love]
11
12   hid his face amid a crowd of stars.

Minus dependent units at Level 10

```
 1  When you are old and grey
 2
 3
 4
 5
 6
 7
 8
 9
10  [Murmur]              [how Love]
11
12      hid his face amid a crowd of stars.
```

Minus dependent units at Level 11

```
 1
 2
 3
 4
 5
 6
 7
 8
 9
10  [Murmur]              [how Love]
11
12      hid his face amid a crowd of stars.
```

5.3.4 Prolongational reduction

Minus dependent units at Level 5

1 When you are old and grey and full of sleep,
2 And nodding by the fire, take down this book,
3 And slowly read, and dream of the soft look
4 Your eyes had once, and of their shadows deep;

5 How many loved your moments of glad grace,
6
7 But one man loved the pilgrim soul in you,
8

9 And bending down beside the glowing bars,

10 Murmur, a little sadly, how Love fled
11
12 And hid his face amid a crowd of stars.

Minus dependent units at Level 6

1 When you are old and grey and full of sleep,
2 And nodding by the fire, take down this book,
3 And slowly read, and dream of the soft look
4 Your eyes had once,

5 How many loved your moments of glad grace,
6
7
8

9 And bending down beside the glowing bars,
10 Murmur   [how Love]
11
12   hid his face amid a crowd of stars.

minus dependent units at Level 7

1 When you are old and grey and full of sleep,
2 And nodding by the fire, take down this book,
3 And slowly read, and dream of the soft look
4 Your eyes had once,

5
6
7
8

9 And bending down beside the glowing bars,
10 [Murmur]   [how Love]
11
12   hid his face amid a crowd of stars.

Minus dependent units at Level 8

1 When you are old and grey
2 And nodding by the fire, take down this book,
3   and dream of the soft look
4 Your eyes had once,

5
6
7
8

```
 9  And bending down beside the glowing bars,
10  [Murmur]              [how Love]
11
12       hid his face amid a crowd of stars.
```

Minus dependent units at Level 9

```
 1  When you are old and grey
 2                       , take down this book,
 3
 4
 5
 6
 7
 8
 9  [And]
10  [Murmur]              [how Love]
11
12       hid his face amid a crowd of stars.
```

Minus dependent units at Level 10

```
 1  When you are old and grey
 2
 3
 4
 5
 6
 7
 8
 9
10  [Murmur]              [how Love]
11
12       hid his face amid a crowd of stars.
```

Minus dependent units at Level 11

```
 1
 2
 3
 4
 5
 6
 7
```

```
 8
 9
10 [Murmur]              [how Love]
11
12      hid his face amid a crowd of stars.
```

5.3.5 General comments

'When You Are Old' is one of Yeats' most popular dramatic monologues written in the blurred focus of his early symbolist mode, which often explores the role of imaginative reverie as a mediator between temporal and transcendental experience. The poem was written shortly after the poet's first proposal of marriage to Maud Gonne in 1891; an early version of the poem appeared in a letter to Katharine Tynan (2 March 1892); the poem was first published in the *Countess Cathleen* volume of 1892; the final version of the poem appears in the *Collected Poems* between 'The Sorrow of Love' and 'The White Birds' in 'The Rose'.

The poem is written under Yeats' early mask of the courtly lover and has many counterparts elsewhere in his poetry, especially in 'The Wind Among the Reeds' (e.g. 'The Lover Tells of the Rose in his Heart', 'He Remembers Forgotten Beauty', 'He Gives his Beloved Certain Rhymes', 'He Tells of the Perfect Beauty', 'He Thinks of Those who have Spoken Evil of his Beloved', etc.). These poems generally have a vague setting and few concrete details. The lover appears in the guise of various synecdoches (hands, eyes, hair, etc.). The principal intent of these monologues is to embody a mood/passion purified of all external circumstances – in this case, failed love as a symbol of all hopeless passion, frustrated desire.

'When You Are Old' is often taken as a personal expression of Yeats' unhappy love for Maud Gonne, but many warn against an exclusively personal reading. In any case, the poem provides an interesting instance of Yeats' early style, especially his symbolic method and rhythmic craft.

5.3.6 Higher levels of phrasing: commentary

5.3.6.1 Level 11

The highest level is duple, rising and anticipatory. The initial time-adverbial (*When* . . .) is weak and anticipatory; the following main

clauses (*take down* ..., *read* ..., *dream* ..., *murmur* ...) form a strong, progressional arrival.
At this level, there are few uncertainties or alternatives in inclination. The main clauses are syntactically, semantically and physically stronger (GPR 1 Information, GPR 2 Weight, GPR 8 Arrivals). The major directives by the speaker are contained in the main clauses; the subordinate clause sets the directives in time and place.
The major uncertainty at this level is the segmentation. On the basis of semantic parallelism (GPR1 Information), I read the *when*-clause as superordinate rather than parallel to the other subordinate clauses in the text, in particular the clause in line 9 (*and bending down* ...). *And bending* ... is semantically parallel to *take down* ... *and read*. ... Both of these textual segments present physical actions that precede a 'world-creating' verb of saying/thinking (i.e. *dream* and *murmur*). The *when*- clause sets the larger spatial and temporal coordinates for both of these (more) mental actions.
The major effect of this segmentation is asymmetry. Given the extensional syntax in the text, the reader's perception of this asymmetry increases as the text progresses. Geometrically, this asymmetry gives the second half of the text a somewhat ungainly physical and semantic weight. Temporally, this asymmetry accentuates the digressional structure of the central sections of the monologue and therefore reinforces/dramatizes its emotive content. The prolongational anticipation at this level adds a forward movement, bringing all of the imagined actions and thoughts of the addressee under the same anticipatory adverbial.

5.3.6.2   Level 10

The first unit articulated at Level 11 is unarticulated at Level 10. The second is articulated into another rising, anticipatory duple, this time with an additive arrival.
Both grouping and prolongation are somewhat blurred at this level. I have already mentioned my motivations for segmenting the second unit at Level 11. *Take down* (etc.) is parallel to *bending down* (GPR 14 Parallelism).

take   down .... and dream ...   How many loved ... and loved ...
bending down ...   Murmur ... how Love fled ...   And paced ...

The repetition of *down* reinforces this parallel; these are the only two instances of *down* in the text (GPR 14 Parallelism). The subordinate clause in line 9 also interrupts the chain of conjunctional expansion in the main clauses in lines 2–8 and therefore suggests a rhythmic break (GPR 13 Similarity). The quatrain break also reinforces this segmentation (GPR 12 Proximity).

I read the second unit as strong because of its tropic intensity and symbolic depth: the personification of Love, the symbolic use of *face*, *mountains*, *crowd* and *stars*, etc. (GPR 1 Information). With the adverb *sadly*, the last quatrain also explicitly directs the mood of the addressee (GPR 1 Information). The implications of the past tense and perfective adverbials in lines 3–8 (*had*, *once*, *loved*) are also made explicit in the lexical content of the verbs in lines 9–12: *fled* and *hid* (GPR 1 Information). There is also a general tendency to view texts as climactic (GPR 3 End-focus).

The prolongational contours at this level are syntactically extensional, but I prefer to read them as thematically anticipatory. The first part of the doubled narrative arrives at a considerable thematic depth in the first two stanzas, but any repetitive reading of the poem (and acquaintance with Yeats) makes the reader anticipate the symbolic transmutation that follows (in the third stanza). Out of respect for the additive syntax and the narrative doubling, I label the third quatrain as an additive arrival, although the symbolic depth achieved at the end of the poem is strongly progressional in effect. A progressional labelling here would also be justified.

The major rhythmic effect of this level is to recover symmetry and deepen the climactic arrival in the third stanza. While the binary unit at Level 11 is unbalanced (over 1–5), the binary unit at this level is more balanced (just over 3–2). The binary unit at this level is also somewhat top-heavy, balancing the heavily end-weighted duple at Level 11.

This asymmetrical elaboration also allows a selective return (and thus modulation) of the semantic/narrative units presented in lines 3–8: the physical actions modulate from taking/reading to bending; the 'world-creating' actions, from dreaming to murmuring; the imagined worlds, from the remembered presence of love to the remembered absence of love; the agents of love, from concrete entities ('many' and 'one man') to a personified abstraction ('Love').

5.3.6.3 Level 9

Level 9 separates the verbs of physical action in the text (*take down, bend down,* etc.) from the 'world-creating' verbs (*dream, murmur,* etc.) with which they occur (GPR 1 Information). This parallel is fairly subtle and could be debated. The parallel is almost exclusively semantic/narrative, with little support from the syntax. The duple shape of these units is supported most clearly by the syntax in stanza 3. I justify the duple parsing of the corresponding parallels in stanzas 1 and 2 by implication from this clearer structure and from more minor considerations – for example the line break (. . . sleep, / And nodding . . .) between the units in the first duple (GPR 12 Proximity).

The strength assignments within these duples seem clear. *Dream* and *murmur* introduce the thematically central material in the text (GPR 1 Information), with the weak unit associated with *murmur* fully subordinate syntactically: *And bending down . . ., murmur . . .). When you are old and grey and full of sleep* presents the title of the poem and sets the basic temporal coordinates for the text: past-in-future, projected memory (GPR 1 Information). Predicates such as *old* and *full of sleep* also deal more centrally with states, especially states of mind; therefore, I read these forms in parallel with the verbs of mental action. *Nodding* is more physical (GPR 1 Information); therefore I read it in parallel with the verbs of physical action.

As a whole, this level defines three more duples (GPR 16 Unity), duples that are first top heavy (2–1) and then heavily end-weighted (1–6 and 1–3). The effect is an ebb and flow very important to the movement of the text. Because of their reduced size, the clauses that relate the physical actions (in the latter two units) move slowly. With their expanded shapes, the passages that convey the mental actions and their imagined worlds move quickly. Mimetically, this accentuates the 'flight' of memory in stanza 2 and the tropic flight of personified Love in stanza 3. Rhetorically, this accentuates the dramatic and emotive energy in these climactic sections of the poem. The differences in the relative proportions of the first duple and the second two duples also reinforce the higher-level segmentation at Level 11 between the superordinate *when*-clause and the rest of the text (GPR 13 Similarity).

The most heavily asymmetrical unit (1–6) occurs in the centre of the text and is counterbalanced (2–1) or partially controlled (1–3) by parallel structures that precede and follow.

The difference in inclination between the first duple and the second two is also productive. The falling and additively extensional contours in the first line and a half reinforce the somnolent mood of the opening of the poem as the speaker gently directs the addressee back into her projected reverie. The rising and, at the end of the poem, progressionally anticipatory contours in the last two duples render the heightened emotion and rhetoric within the body of the projected memory itself.

5.3.6.4 Level 8

This level represents the subordinate movement within the syntactic and semantic triples in the first stanza.

    old and grey . . . . full of sleep . . . nodding . . .
    take down . . .   read . . .   dream . . .

Strength assignment within these two duples is based on semantic and thematic considerations (GPR 1 Information). *When you are old and grey* presents both the title of the poem and its temporal coordinates and therefore is rhythmically strong. *Full of sleep* is a weaker, more subordinate elaboration, implied by what precedes (GPR 1 Information). On the other hand, *read* is closer to *dream* on a cline of mental to physical action. Therefore I read it as strong (GPR 1 Information). *Take down* is more exclusively physical. Therefore I read it as weak. Prolongation in these two duples is consistently additive and extensional.

These two-level triples organize the phrasal movement in the first stanza and give this stanza a distinct movement. The (two-level) triple movement is more asymmetrical, and with its two-level organization, proceeds from lower-level activity (a duple unit) to lack of activity (a single unit). This might further support the somnolent mood of the opening of the poem, a laxing movement that is furthered by the extensional prolongation as well. Given the high-level grouping break *between* these two duples, this uniform movement also helps connect the initial *when*-clause rhythmically to the following main clauses (GPR 14 Parallelism). On the other hand, the reversal in rhythmic direction between the two duples further accentuates the change in rhythmic energy in the middle of line 2 (GPR 16 Unity).

5.3.6.5 Level 7

Level 7 isolates the startling expansion in stanza 2 and its parallel in stanza 3. Again, this parallel is both strongly suggested and muted in various ways. The basic contours of the parallel are marked by the parallel 'world-creating' verbs *dream* and *murmur* and their following *how*-complements: *How many loved* . . . and *how Love fled* . . . (GPR 14 Parallelism). This parallel suggests a duple, rising structure. Both the internal rhythmic organization of the first stanza and its interpolated complement before the *how*-clause (*of the soft look your eyes had once* . . .) make the internal structures of these parallel units very different, however. Prolongationally, the first stanza stands complete and only then extends by apposition into the *how*-clause in stanza 2. The *how*-clause in stanza 3 is anticipated prolongationally and completes the structural prerequisites of *murmur*. This contrast accentuates both the psychologically digressive nature of stanza 2 and the culminating, closural symbolism in stanza 3. The proportions in the parts of these units are weighted 1–2. This reinforces the parallel and rhythmically dramatizes both the expansive reminiscence in stanza 2 and the concentrated troping in stanza 3.

5.3.6.6 Level 6

Level 6 isolates a pervasive distinction in the text between physical and spiritual aspects of the woman addressed, her *look*, *grace* and *beauty* vs her *soul* and *sorrows* (GPR 1 Information). This dichotomy is most evident in the second stanza, where the first distich refers to more physical qualities, the second distich to more spiritual qualities. The dichotomy also appears in the first stanza in the distinction between the 'soft look' of the woman's eyes vs their 'shadows deep'. This distinction is also implicit in the last stanza, between *murmur* and *a little sadly* and between the first two actions of Love (*fled*, *paced*) and the final action (*hid*). The spiritual qualities are associated with things deep, hidden and sorrowful; the physical qualities with things superficial, overt and 'glad'. Applied to the last stanza, this associates Love's 'hiding' with these more spiritual qualities; love's 'fleeing' and 'pacing' with the more physical qualities. This also associates the tone unit *a little sadly* with the spiritual qualities; the tone unit *murmur* with the more physical qualities.

The major effect of this level is to present the duple divisioning of the second stanza. The extensions of this pattern in stanzas 1 and 2 also seem important, however. With this duple pattern in stanza 1, the suprising appositional expansion in stanza 2 is somewhat controlled. Stanza 2 appears as a more symmetrical doubling of what appears in lines 3–4. The duple patterns at this level in stanza 3 support the *dream–murmur* parallel with 2x2 structures, echoing the 2x2 structure at this level in stanza 2 (GPR 16 Unity).

5.3.6.7 Level 5

Level 5 isolates the conjunctional elaboration within Level 6. These articulations are duple and falling. This falling movement is most salient in the second stanza. The quantifiers *how many* and *one* strengthen the odd lines, as do the diction and troping (*glad grace* and *pilgrim soul* vs *beauty* and *changing face*). The odd lines are also tonally unified, giving them a sweep and impulsion lacking in the even lines. The even lines break tonally at mid-line and then move to completion with another tone unit.

```
                          w                        s
iu    ╱ And loved your beauty  ╲ ╱ with love false or true  ╲
        And loved the sorrows       of your changing face.
```

The extensional prolongational contours between the odd and even lines also support this falling movement (GPR 8 Arrivals).

The falling movement is less salient in stanza 3, but is motivated there as well. Within the triple *fled*, *paced* and *hid*, *fled* and *hid* are more thematically central, *paced* more subordinate (GPR 1 Information). Both *fled* and *hid* indicate absence, loss – a central theme of the text.

The falling counter-motion at this level is an important part of the rhythmic structure of the text. With these contours, the distichs within the expansive second stanza present shapes that dramatize both their exclamatory insistence (strong-initial) and elegiac lament (weak-final). In stanza 3 this counter-motion stands as a penultimate variation before closure, a common aesthetic gesture (GPR 17 Schemes).

The extensional prolongation at this level in stanza 2 presents the last concentration of extensional departures that occupy the text at

Levels 5–10 in the first two quatrains. In stanza 3 these extensional contours will turn around and anticipate closure, completing the canonical chiastic patterning that characterizes prolongation at all levels (Canonical Form).

Looking down the hierarchy, Level 5 has only local articulation. Only two units at Level 5 are articulated at Level 4, the units that embrace lines 6 and 8. These units form rising duples. Prolongation is progressional, first extensionally then anticipationally.

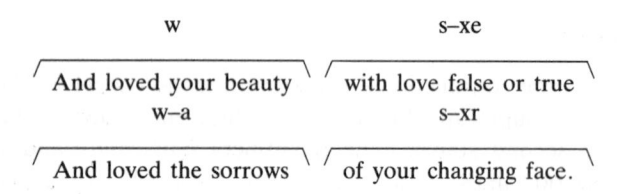

```
            w                         s–xe
  ┌─────────────────────┐  ┌─────────────────────────┐
    And loved your beauty      with love false or true
            w–a                         s–xr
  ┌─────────────────────┐  ┌─────────────────────────┐
    And loved the sorrows      of your changing face.
```

This local articulation further intensifies the alternating, binary shape of stanza 2 and deepens the articulation in the textual digression at this point.

5.3.6.8 *Level 4 (Intonational Units)*

Level 4 is composed of the nineteen tone units.

(1) When you are old and **grey**
(2) and full of **sleep**
(3) and nodding by the **fire,**
(4) take down this **book**
(5) and slowly **read,**
(6) and dream of the soft **look** your eyes had once
(7) and of their shadows **deep**;
(8) How many loved your moments of glad **grace,**
(9) And loved your **beau**ty
(10) with love false or **true,**
(11) But one man loved the pilgrim **soul** in you,
(12) And loved the **sor**rows
(13) of your changing **face**;
(14) And bending down beside the glowing **bars,**
(15) **mur**mur,
(16) a little **sad**ly,
(17) how love **fled**
(18) And paced upon the mountains over**head**
(19) And hid his face amid a crowd of **stars.**

While the intonational segmentation of a written text is often indeterminate, most of these segmentations are clear. Fourteen out of nineteen are marked with punctuation (GPR 12 Proximity). Two occur at unpunctuated line breaks, but in these cases the breaks are between clauses (or conjoined predicates), common points for intonational divisions (GPR 12 Proximity).

⌐ how Love fled ⌐/⌐ And paced . . . overhead ⌐/⌐ And hid his face . . . ⌐

Two of the remaining segmentations occur in the only lines to break 5–5 in syllable distribution, lines 6 and 8 (GPR 14 Parallelism). The informational prominences here are fairly well motivated at well. *Beauty* in line 6 is parallel to *grace* in line 5. *Sorrows* in line 8 alliterates with *soul* in line 7.

The most questionable segmentation is the first line. It could be read as one unit. If this were done, each stanza would have exactly six tone units. I like to read this break to maintain the two-level triple at Levels 8 and 9 (i.e. *old and grey, full of sleep, nodding*; *take down, read, dream*). A reading that left the first line as one tone unit would give up parts of the higher-level parallel.

Tone units adhere closely to the metrical frame. Six are coextensive with lines. Eleven others are coextensive with hemistichs, with lengths of four to six syllables, positioned squarely in the metrical frame. In its relation to meter, prominence within these tone units is also canonical. Eighteen of the nineteen tone units cadence lines or hemistichs. Eleven of the twelve rhymes are tone unit nuclei.

The only exceptions occur in lines 7 and 10. In line 7 the tone unit culminates on the eighth syllable in the line. In line 10, one tone unit culminates on the first syllable. These lines are marked in other ways. The tone unit nucleus in line 7 is the grouping peak of the second unit at Level 9. Line 10 is the only line with three tone units and the only line with tone units of less than four syllables.

The text has only one enjambment (lines 3–4), as enjambment is normally defined. This enjambment helps to break up the consistent lengths of the tone units in stanza 1 and provides a penultimate variation before the stanza's close. The early occurrence of the nucleus in this tone unit also foregrounds the contrast between the physical and spiritual qualities of the woman, an important thematic contrast maintained throughout the text.

396 ANALYSIS

All in all, the shapes of these tone units are canonical for the language (i.e. five to seven syllables, end-focus, etc.). The lengths of the tone units are artificially uniform, however. In most cases they are four, six, or ten syllables long, not three, seven, eight, nine or eleven – or any other quantity (fifteen, seventeen, one, etc.).

5.3.7 Lower levels of phrasing and meter: scansion and commentary

5.3.7.1 Line 1

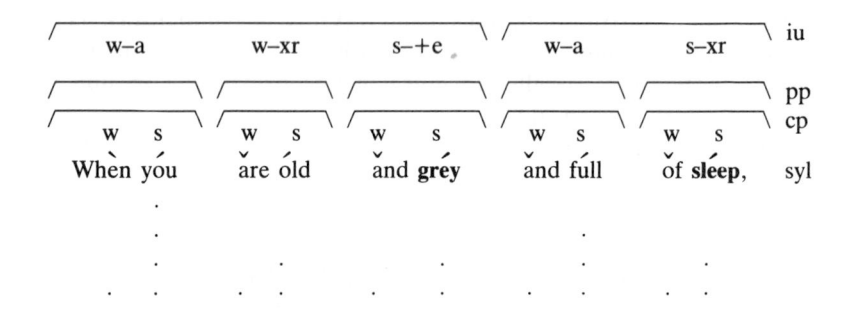

```
 /‾‾‾‾‾‾‾‾‾‾‾‾‾‾‾‾‾‾‾‾‾‾‾‾‾‾‾‾‾\ /‾‾‾‾‾‾‾‾‾‾‾‾‾‾‾‾‾‾‾\  iu
    w–a        w–xr       s–+e .     w–a         s–xr
 /‾‾‾‾‾\ /‾‾‾‾‾\ /‾‾‾‾‾\ /‾‾‾‾‾\ /‾‾‾‾‾\  pp
   w  s    w  s    w  s    w  s    w  s    cp
   ˋ  ´    ˇ  ´    ˇ  ´    ˇ  ´    ˇ  ´
  When you are old  and grey and full of sleep,  syl
   .        .        .        .        .
   .   .    .   .    .   .    .   .    .   .
```

The opening line has almost perfect canonical form. Prolongation is chiastic, first extensional and then anticipatory. Hemistichs are tone units. Clitic phrases are all iambic. This is an unusually regular shaping and an unusually close match between grouping spans and metrical spans. Intonational phrasing is also regularly iambic.

The duple clitic phrase movement is contracted compared with clitic phrase shapes in the language as a whole, and therefore slows the line. This slow, regular movement is also supported at higher levels. This line has a fairly superordinate position in the grouping structure as a whole (the tone unit hemistichs in this line are not grouped together until Level 9.) Consequently, lower-level groups are contracted relative to high levels, further slowing physical movement. The lack of phonological phrase articulation in the line produces further contraction and therefore further slowing.

The result of this patterning is a very relaxed movement, supportive of both sense and the rhetorical context. The rigidly repeating shapes at the individual levels are graded into alternating patterns at successively higher levels, producing smooth, multi-levelled alternation.

There are some indeterminacies with this reading. At the phonological phrase level, *and grey* and *of sleep* could be incorporated into preceding phrases, eliminating articulation within intonational units. The consequences of this alternative reading are not great. I read four phonological phrases to indicate the relative distinctness of the prominences in these units. Stress subordination is weak.

5.3.7.2 Line 2

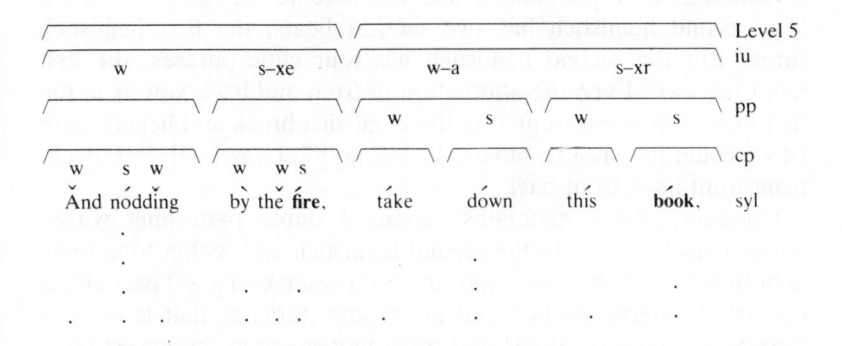

```
┌─────────────────────\┌─────────────────────\ Level 5
│  w           s-xe    ││  w-a         s-xr   │ iu
┌──────\┌──────\┌──────\┌──────\┌──────\┌──────\
│      ││      ││  w   │  s   ││  w   │  s    │ pp
┌──\┌──\┌──\┌──\┌──\┌──\┌──\┌──\┌──\┌──\       cp
│w  s w││w  w s││      ││      ││      ││      │
And nŏdding  by the fire,  take  down  this  book,  syl
```

Line 2 presents the highest grouping division in the text, the break between the opening adverbial (*When . . . fire*) and the rest of the text. Following the congruent patterning in the first line, this break is placed after the sixth syllable in the line, at the hemistich break. The first line is not enjambed, but the high-level contraction in the opening of the text gives this line the feel of a significant non-congruence. The two-level triple at Levels 8 and 9 (*old and grey*, *full of sleep*, *nodding*) is draped over the line break and resolves on the major beat of the second line. The nature of this movement and metrical resolution is also significant. Prolongation is regularly additive and extensional, and grouping is falling. This ebbing energy is further relaxed by the arrival of the four-dot beat in line 2 *before* the end of grouping triple and before the cadence of the first hemistich. The effect is indeed a rhythmic 'nod'.

These higher-level relations between grouping and meter are supported further at low levels. The consistently duple clitic phrase movement in the first line is expanded to triple movement in the first hemistich of the second line, and to a movement that is first lilting (*and nodding*) and then resolutionally peak-final (*by the fire*).

The overall effect is to reduce and relax activity at low levels, an effect that is heightened by the duple meter, which at *by* must find an ictus on a tertiary stress. The unarticulated phonological phrases in this first hemistich also support this relaxation.

On the other hand, the onset of the second half of the text is given a boldly contracted shaping at low levels. Clitic phrases are all monosyllabic, a striking departure after the expanded clitic phrases in the first hemistich. This contraction must also fight through the alternating meter, a struggle that is heightened by the energy of the three-dot beat at the onset of the second hemistich. The 6–4 divisioning of the pentameter line also accentuates this contraction. The second hemistich has two tactical beats; the first hemistich three. But the second hemistich has four clitic phrases, the first hemistich two. Even the alternation in front and back vowels in the first hemistich is interrupted at the hemistich break and begun again (if we count [ay] as a front vowel): [a], [ay]/ [e], [aw], [I], [U], back-front/front-back-front-back.

However, Yeats maintains canonical duple patterning within phonological phrases in the second hemistich and within tone units in both halves of the line, a gesture that preserves a good part of the pervasive congruence between meter and phrasing that is evident throughout the text. Single and triple movement at the lowest level and non-congruence at high levels are mediated by regularly duple and congruent patterning at mid levels.

The non-congruences between meter and phrasing in this line are typical of the non-congruences elsewhere in the text. Major grouping breaks and changes in rhetorical tenor are marked by low level non-congruences, while large-scale modulations in mood are marked by non-congruences between lineal and stanzaic patterning and syntactic levels in grouping.

This reading of line 2 is relatively clear. Clitic phrases centre on major category words, with the demonstrative *this* being the only exception (GPR 1 Information). Phonological phrases follow the four major syntactic phrases and take 'normal' prominence on syntactic heads or the particle in the phrasal verb (GPR 12 Proximity, GPR 1 Information, GPR 3 End-focus). Intonational phrasing is normally end-focused and is coextensive with clauses and punctuation (GPR 3 Proximity, GPR 3 End-focus).

5.3.7.3 Line 3

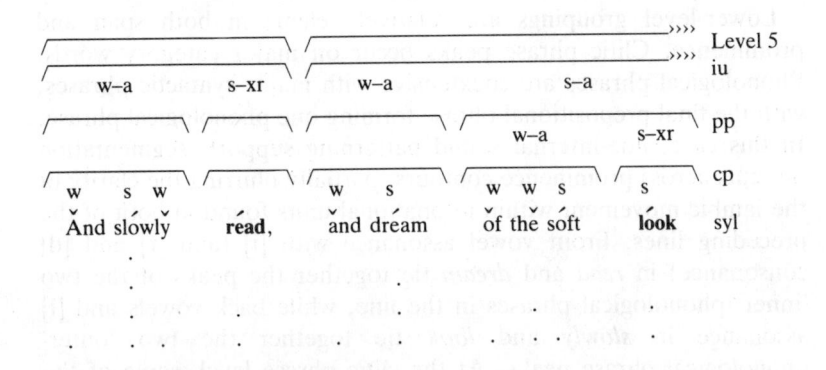

```
                                                          >>>>   Level 5
  ⌐─────────────────┐ ⌐──────────────────────────────┐  >>>>   iu
      w–a      s–xr        w–a              s–a
  ⌐────────┐ ⌐──────┐ ⌐──────────┐ ⌐─────────────────┐          pp
                            w–a              s–xr
  ⌐──────┐ ⌐────┐ ⌐───┐ ⌐───┐ ⌐──────┐ ⌐─────┐                  cp
   w  s  w         w   s     w  w  s    s
   ̆   ́  ̆     ́     ̆    ́     ̆   ̆   ́     ́
  And slowly    read,   and dream   of the soft   look    syl
```

At these lower levels, the most striking feature of this line is its enjambment. This is the only enjambment in the text. This enjambment gives some special salience to the second tone unit in the line and the 'look' that occurs at the nucleus of this tone unit. At this point, *look* is also linked with the end-rhyme *book* in the previous line, resolving the prolongation of the 'inner' rhyme pair of the envelope rhyme scheme and creating a further prolongation of the initial half of the 'outer' rhyme-pair *sleep–deep*. Metrically, the final stress-pairing at line end also syncopates *soft* against the metrical expectation of the line, a metrical tension that is immediately resolved at *look*. This highlights both *soft* and *look*.

The enjambed tone unit in this line begins an area of expansion and more detailed articulation in the grouping structure. This expansion accentuates the enjambment as the text moves more quickly at several lower levels. This expansion also gives end-weight to this second repetition of the two-level triple articulation (at Levels 8 and 9) of the first two units at Level 10, an end-weight that, in the next line, gives the stanza a satisfying close (before the syntax is surprisingly extended in stanza 2).

Globally, sound patterning links this line to line 1. *Slowly–read* recalls *old–grey*, both assonantally and consonantally. *Dream–look* inverts the vowels of *full–sleep* and presents echoing labials and liquids. As with the rhyme, this sound pattern cuts across (and therefore partially blurs) many of the segmentation and prominence contours in the two-level grouping parallel articulated at Levels 8 and 9 in this stanza and the next.

Hemistich articulation, however, links this line to line 4, against lines 1 and 2. Hemistich articulation in lines 1 and 2 is 6–4; hemistich articulation in lines 3 and 4 is 4–6.

Lower-level groupings are relatively clear, in both span and prominence. Clitic phrase peaks occur on major category words. Phonological phrases are coextensive with major syntactic phrases, with the final prepositional phrase forming one phonological phrase. In this case, line-internal sound patterning supports segmentation but cuts across prominence contours, partially blurring the clarity of the iambic movement within intonational units found in both of the preceding lines. Front vowel assonance with [i] (and [r] and [d] consonance) in *read* and *dream* tie together the peaks of the two 'inner' phonological phrases in the line, while back vowels and [l] assonance in *slowly* and *look* tie together the two 'outer' phonological phrase peaks. At the clitic phrase level, some of the triple movement begun in 2 is picked up again (*and slowly, of the soft*), but in a discontinuous and less metrically congruent and therefore less salient way. As in the preceding line, movement at the intonational and phonological phrase level (where articulated) is iambic.

5.3.7.4 Line 4

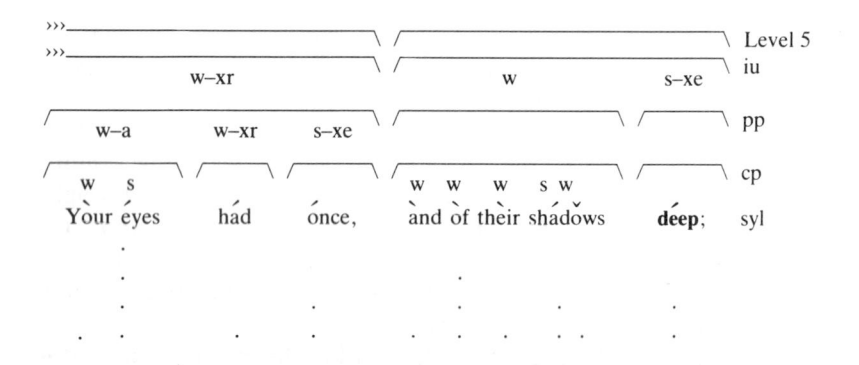

As we move from line 3 to line 4, the cataphoric *the* in *the soft look* and the unresolved 'outer' rhyme *sleep* maintain some forward energy, but in other respects the mid-level parallels in the grouping structure in this first stanza (e.g. the two-level triple) are completed at the end of line 3.

With line 4, however, Yeats plays out more fully the ongoing structural imperatives of the first three lines, bringing the stanza to a more satisfying close. The first hemistich in line 4 extends the tone unit at the end of line 3 and, in doing so, further accentuates the rhetorical emphasis on *soft look*, producing a ten-syllable phrase in cross-rhythm to the flow of the lines.

And dream of the soft look / your eyes had once

This tone unit is clearly the intonational 'sore thumb' of the stanza and acts as a semi-cadence that sets up a fuller cadence in the second hemistich in the line. Both the metrical demotion at *had* and the position of this post-tonic segment promote this feeling for (semi-)climax. The middle of the weak post-tonic phrase extending on from line 3 resolves on the strong beat of line 4; *had* presents a penultimate non-congruence; and then *once* delivers a (partially) canonical realignment of phrasing and meter. Sound also accentuates this cadential effect. The diphthong [ay] in *eyes* recalls the [ay] in both *by* and *fire*, which occur in the last unit of the first two-level triple in the stanza. Of course, the resolution of the expectations generated by the cataphoric *the* in *the soft look* also promotes a feeling for closure. This phonological phrase is also the only triple at this level in the stanza.

The final hemistich deepens this cadential close. This tone unit introduces another level in the grouping structure (Level 6), the thematically important level that distinguishes between physical and spiritual qualities of the addressee (e.g. beauty vs soul in stanza 2). This deepens the feeling of closure, provides another level of canonical iambic movement, and adds satisfying end-weight to the culmination of the two-level triple at Levels 8 and 9. This second hemistich also has many of the same features that make the first hemistich a satisfying close. The long clitic phrase *and of their shadows* produces an penultimate non-congruence that is largely decelerating (relative to a prose counterpart), being slowed by the three-dot beat in the meter at *of*. In another rhythmic context we might perceive this three-dot beat on *shadows* two syllables later, but the cadencing of the relatively high-level group in the first hemistich makes this second hemistich a significant grouping onset

402　ANALYSIS

for which we prefer a metrical projection; therefore we force a high-level beat upon a less preferred tertiary stress at *of*. At the end of this slow movement we get both the completion of this new projection and the satisfaction of the most highly prolonged and salient sonic pattern in the stanza, the 'outer' rhyme-pair *sleep–deep*. The satisfying nature of this close is heightened by many other formal patterns in the text as well: (1) the monosyllabic density of *deep* (GPR 4 Density); (2) the weak-final contour on the penultimate clitic phrase *and of their shadows*, a final weakness that *deep* turns to final strength, just as *by the fire* follows *And nodding* at the end of the first two-level triple (GPR 17 Schemes); and (3) the recurrence of [d] in the onset of *deep*: [d] occurs three other times in line 4 (in *had, and* and *shadows*) and eleven times elsewhere in the stanza (in *old, nodding, down, read, dream, crowd*, and in five other instances of *and*).

There are several uncertainies in this reading of line 4. The first hemistich is an unusually large post-tonic segment and therefore is somewhat anomalous in its grouping behaviour. None the less, I respond to this tone unit as a triple, with the relative clause in line 4 serving as the final weak segment in an amphibrachic contour. The grouping strength of *look* in line 3 is supported by its status as the first couplet rhyme (GPR 13 Parallelism), by its position at the end of the metrical projection of line 3 (Canonical Form), and by its resolution of the metrical–phrasal non-congruence at *soft* (GPR 5 Return). I also scan the poetically displaced post-modifier *deep* as its own phonological phrase. This preserves duple movement at the intonational unit level, an important global pattern in the first stanza (GPR 16 Unity).

5.3.7.5 Line 5

```
              w–a              w–a                      s–xr              iu
       w–a         s–xr                   w–a         w–a         s–xr   pp
                     s w                w   s w      w   s                cp
       How        many       loved      your moments  of glad   grace,   syl
```

Line 5 opens the second stanza. This second stanza is a major rhythmic event in the text, one of the most striking sources of horizontal asymmetry and vertical elaboration in the grouping structure. The onset of this stanza brings various sorts of rhythmic uncertainty as well. Initially, the *how*-clause that begins the stanza seems to stand as an independent exclamatory clause (e.g. *How many loved your moments of glad grace!*). This clause arrives at some distance from *dream*, and *dream* already receives the complement *of the soft look* . . .). Therefore, the reader does not expect another complement and is given no marking (in the form of a non-finite verb or an unequivocal subordinating conjunction) that indicates that this clause is dependent. As the poem proceeds (and more quickly on subsequent readings), this reading is rejected, however, and the clause is reinterpreted as a complement of *dream*, in apposition to the complement(s) in lines 3 and 4. This momentary ambiguity affects lower-level groupings in the line. The exclamatory reading gives more force to *how many*; the appositive complement reading lessens this force. I represent only this second reading. In this reading, *how many* is a weak phonological phrase within the intonational unit that embraces the line.

Like the beginning of the main clause in the text (in the second hemistich of line 2), this startling textual elaboration in stanza 2 is heavily marked in its lower-level articulation. The demotion in the first syllable (*How*) is the first line-initial demotion in the text. And the intonational triple is the first of its kind to span a line (the only other intonational triple so far is enjambed in lines 3–4). In fact, line 5 is the first line to be coextensive with an intonational unit, a major prosodic event. Some have argued that a triple structure is the most natural prosodic realization of the triadic structure of the English clause (subject–verb–object), and almost all claim that the most neutral phrasal realization of the line is the tone unit. The textual importance of line 5 is also signalled strongly by sonic patterns. This is the only line so far that contains full/partial consonantal alliteration and it occurs here twice: *many–moments* and *glad–grace*. Only one other line has consonantal alliteration, line 9.

In line 5 the phrasal patterns at the lowest level also become unusually smooth and continuous, although this smoothness is often dynamic and progressive. At the clitic phrase level, line 5 begins with peak-initial monosyllabic and trochaic phrases, moves through phrases that have medial peaks (*loved, your moments*), and ends with phrases that are peak-final (i.e. *of glad, grace*), forming a smoothly advancing grade. The placement of the only polysyllabic phrase with medial contours in the middle of the line accentuates this feeling of balance. Line 5 also has some pleasing interlevel harmony. The triple phrasing of the line (*How many // loved // your moments of glad grace*) is echoed at lower levels in the triple phrasing of the phonological phrase which stands at peak of the tone unit in the line (*your moments // of glad // grace*).

At the same time, relations between grouping and meter become chiastic. The non-congruent patterns in the line (the demotion of *How* and the stress-pairing on *glad grace*) are placed at the periphery of the line with more congruent patterns in between. As with the phrasal shapes, these patterns are also arranged to produce a natural movement from initiation to resolution. The demotion at *How* gives the line a strong impulsion; the stress-pairing at *glad grace* provides strong resolution. As far as possible, Yeats also arranges the triple structure of the line as whole so that it fits congruently with the duple structure of the pentameter line. Both the hemistich and the line are firmly and normatively cadenced, the first with a phonological phrase peak (*loved*), the second with a tonic syllable (*grace*).

There are some uncertainties with this reading. *Your moments of glad grace* could be read as two phonological phrases. The rhetorical weakness of *moments* compared with *sorrows* in line 4 (GPR 1 Information), the general impulsion and formal unity of the line (GPR 13 Similarity), and the architectural parallelism between this line and line 7 (GPR 14 Parallelism) make me prefer the intonationally continuous triple, however. The parallels between

5.3.7.6 Line 6

line 5 and line 7 are extensive, and these parallels play a significant role in the architectural organization of the second stanza as whole. Line 6 begins the alternation in stanza 2 between lines of one tone unit (lines 5 and 7) and lines of two (lines 6 and 8). Line 6 is also the first time that two consecutive lines are grouped together as units at some level in the grouping structure. These lines appear at Level 5 and are grouped together at Level 6. As we saw earlier, line 6 also introduces a double deepening of the grouping structure (at Levels 4 and 5), the 'deepest' articulation in the poem. Stanza 3 will become shallower and pick up high-level parallels from stanza 1. This rhythmic 'depth' gives stanza 2 a subtle intensity.

Line 6 is also the first line with a 'lyric/feminine' caesura. This lyric caesura will reappear in line 8. Against the background of the consistently masculine rhymes in the poem, these feminine endings are salient and support other sorts of formal alternation within the stanza. Lines 6 and 8 are also the only two lines in the poem that break 5–5 in syllabic composition. All of this patterning is evidence of exceptional order and constraint.

Many sorts of alternation, order and symmetry are evident at lower levels of phrasing in line 6 as well. Both the line itself and the intonational units are regularly iambic, with intonational nuclei (*beau-*, *true*) placed canonically at the end of metrical projections. The phonological phrases alternate in syllabic composition 2–3–2–3 (And loved // your beauty // with love // false or true). Clitic phrases alternate iambic phrases with phrases of other shapes (**And loved** // your beauty // **with love** // false // **or true**). The last intonational unit balances iambic phrases around a central single (**with love** // false // **or true**). Phonological phrase peaks alternate the morpheme *love* with other items (**loved**–your beauty–**with love**–or true). And the lack of lexical alternation in the even phonological phrase peaks is compensated for by internal rhyme (*beau-*, *true*), completing the alternating vocalic pattern in the line ([$\wedge$]-[u]-[$\wedge$]-[u] in *loved–beau-* *–love–true*). The peaks of clitic phrases which serve as phonological phrase peaks also alternate syllable shapes, both in onset and in coda. Onsets alternate simple–complex–simple–complex ([l]–[by]– [l]–[tr]); codas alternate filled–unfilled–filled–unfilled ([vd]–[ ]–[v]– [ ]).

5.3.7.7 Line 7

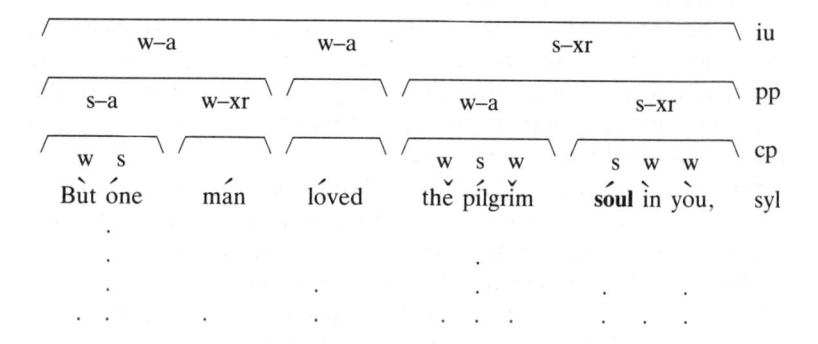

```
                                                                    iu
      ⌐ w–a          w–a              s–xr        ⌐
      ⌐ s–a    w–xr ⌐     ⌐ w–a              s–xr ⌐ pp
      ⌐ w  s  ⌐     ⌐     ⌐ w  s  w  ⌐ s  w  w    ⌐ cp
        But one   man    loved  the pilgrim  soul in you,  syl
         .        .       .       .           .    .
         .        .       .       .           .    .
            .        .       .          .     .    .
```

Line 7 is heavily parallel to line 5, furthering the symmetries in stanza 2. The initial adversative conjunction (*But*) splits the stanza in half, with this third line flanked by lines beginning with *But*'s additive counterpart *And*.

> How many loved . . .
> **And** loved . . . .
> **But** one man loved . . .
> **And** loved . . .

Many in line 5 becomes *one* in line 7. *Loved* is repeated, as is much of the syntactic shape of the noun phrase direct object of *loved*, with just a change in the position of an adjectival modifier from a premodification position to a position in the noun phrase object of the prepositional phrase post-modifier.

> your   moments of glad grace (line 5)
> the pilgrim soul   in   you (line 7)

Rhythmic parallels between lines 5 and 7 are also tight. Both lines are one anapaestic tone unit.

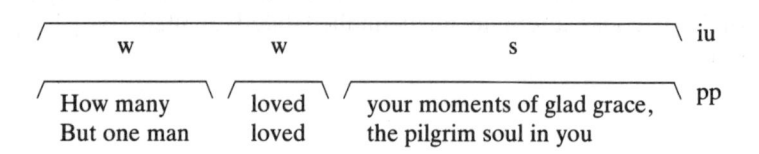

```
                                                              iu
        ⌐    w            w              s                ⌐
        ⌐ How many  ⌐ ⌐ loved  ⌐ your moments of glad grace, ⌐ pp
          But one man     loved     the pilgrim soul in you
```

The phonological phrases in the two lines have exactly the same syllabic composition and placement in the line (3–1–6). Both lines have a demotion in the first hemistich (*How* in line 5, *man* in line 7) and an amphibrachic clitic phrase opening the second hemistich (*your moments* in line 5, *the pilgrim* in line 7). And both lines have just one polysyllabic word, of trochaic shape, placed in the sixth and seventh syllables of the line (*moments* in line 5, *pilgrim* in line 7).

On the other hand, slight differences in form give line 7 a very different sound and feel to line 5. In line 7 the inclination of both the first phonological phrase (*But one man*) and the last clitic phrase (*soul in you*) are reversed, producing falling contours at line beginning and end; and line 7 loses a lexical stress at line end, reducing its number of clitic phrases from six to five. These changes create different intercomponential relations in the two lines at these levels. In line 5 the initial demotion is phrasally subordinate to a following phonological phrase peak; in line 7 the early demotion is phrasally subordinate to a preceding phonological phrase peak. The pattern in line 5 is more normal in metrical verse and somewhat less disturbing perceptually; a non-congruence is resolved in the next syllable by bringing together a higher-level peak and a higher-level beat in the *same* phrase. The pattern in line 7 is more unusual and more disturbing; a non-congruence is resolved in the next syllable by bringing together the metrical projection and the peak of a different phrase.

Similar differences in effect result from the slightly skewed parallels in the latter halves of these lines. In line 5 the consistently rising contours produce stress-final pairing, a fairly extreme but ultimately satisfying and end-weighted figure that reinforces a feeling of resolution. In line 7, however, the altered clitic phrase articulation produces a promotion at the final beat, a non-congruence that frustrates the metrical projection of the line at the point of highest expectation. With this promotion at line end, the prolongational arrival of the inner rhymes (*true–you*) of the envelope rhyme scheme is also backgrounded and, by implication, the more extreme prolongation of the outer rhymes (*grace–face*) is heightened.

These slight changes also have significant consequences for the overall symmetry of the two lines. While the reversed contours in line 7 now produce a satisfying chiastic pattern of both span and inclination at the phonological phrase level (sw // s // ws), a pattern that is lacking from line 5, both the interlevel harmony and the advancing grade (in the clitic phrases) of line 5 are now lost. Clitic phrases in line 5 present a more irregular pattern in inclination, and the duple and single patterning at the phonological phrase level is not echoed by the triple articulation of the intonational unit in the line. The result is again that line 7 is somewhat less ordered than line 5 in its prosodic contours, less satisfying and poetically canonical in the sweep of its global movement. Line 7 is the *only* line with reversed contours and disturbing intercomponential relations of this sort. It is the only line with a complex phonological phrase with strong-initial contours. It is the only line with a dactylic clitic phrase. It is the only line that does not match the end of its lineal projection with a tone-unit nucleus.

These differences give line 7 a spontaneous, prosaic effect. This tone is an important addition to the confessional content of line 7 in comparison with line 5 (i.e. the semantic movement from *many* to *one*, with the implication that the 'one man' is the poet or poetic speaker).

5.3.7.8 Line 8

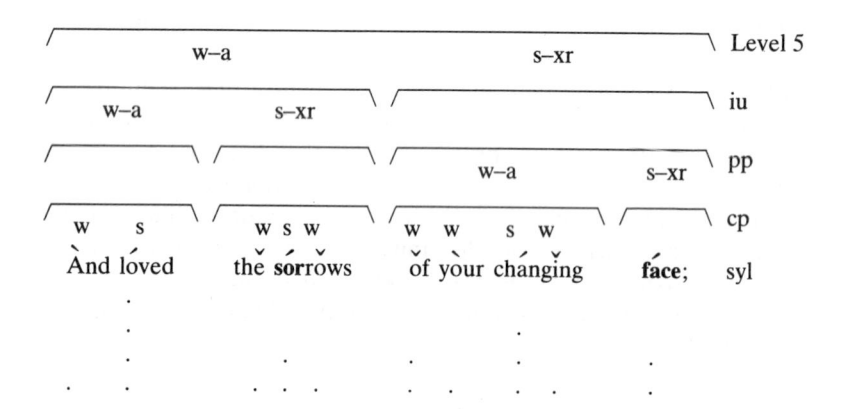

Line 8 completes the structural implications of the second stanza, with some terminal modification to secure closure and climax. Following the alternating structure of the stanza, line 8 returns to the duple patterning of line 6, providing complements for patterns begun there: the opening *And*, the duple rising pattern at level 5 and within intonational units, the 5–5 syllabic division of the line, the lyric caesura, the 2–3 iambic–amphibrachic articulation within clitic phrases in the first hemistich (*and loved // your beauty* in line 6; *and loved // the sorrows* in line 8), the repetition of *loved, your*, and a following trochaic word (*beauty* in line 6, *sorrows* in line 8), and so forth.

Where line 8 differs from line 6, it differs in the direction of grouping order and componential congruence, relaxing internal tension in the rhythm. The five clitic phrases in line 6 are reduced to four in line 8, with two clitic phrases to a hemistich: And loved / the sorrows // of your changing / face. The increased activity at the clitic phrase level in the second hemistich of line 6 is eliminated. And the 'rhythmical figures' in line 8 are made less jolting in their effect than those in line 6. The stress-pairing in line 6 becomes a promotion in line 8, a promotion that is centred in the line, flanked by balanced pairs of stressed beats.

Line 8 also supports its climactic effect with a multilevelled expansion in the grouping structure (i.e. an expanding grade). Clitic phrases present a capped expanding grade: 2–3–4–1.

```
         2              3              4            1
    ┌─────────┐   ┌─────────┐   ┌─────────────┐  ┌─────┐
    w    s        w   s   w    w    w   s   w       s
 And loved      the sorrows   of your changing    face;
```

After the first clitic phrase, this expanding grade also progressively advances the structural peak in these phrases (from medial, to penultimate, to final), another closural pattern.

    the **sor** rows
    of your **chan** ging
            face

Phonological phrases expand 2–3–5 in their syllabic composition and 1–1–2 in their clitic phrase composition.

410 ANALYSIS

```
        2–1              3–1                 5–2
      ⌐────⌐          ⌐────────⌐         ⌐──────────────────⌐
       And loved       the sorrows        of your changing / face;   pp
```

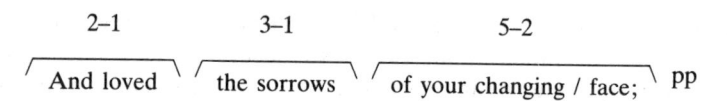

The final [e] assonance (in *changing face*) also reinforces closure. These are the only stressed assonantal vowels in the poem that occur in succession within the same phonological phrase.

Of course, with the final word in this line also comes the resolution of the outer rhymes (*grace–face*) in the envelope rhyme scheme and the completion of the 2x2x2x2x2 articulation in the grouping structure at Levels 5, 6, 7, 8 and 10, all of which rise except Level 6. This patterning satisfies the text's structural inertia and forward motion with psychologically and stylistically canonical structuring. If we refer to the tone units in the text by number, the second half of line 8 delivers the thirteenth tone unit at the end of a large step-wise crescendo.

```
 ⌐─────────⌐─────────────────────────────⌐  Level 10
               w                  s
         ⌐────⌐─────────────────────────────⌐  Level 9
              ⌐──────────────────────────⌐    Level 8
                   w              s
              ⌐────⌐──────────────────────⌐   Level 7
                      w              s
                    ⌐────⌐──────────────⌐     Level 6
                          s         w
                          ⌐────⌐────────⌐     Level 5
                                  w    s

 1   2   3   4   5   6   7   8   9  10  11   12  13
 W   a   A   T   a   a   a   H   A   W   B    A    o
 h   n   n   a   n   n   n   o   n   i   u    n    f
 e   d   d   k   d   d   d   w   d   t   t    d    
 n               e                       h         y
         f   n       d   o   m   l       o    l    o
 y   u   o   d   l   r   f   a   o   l   n    o    u
 o   l   d   o   o   e   .   n   v   o   e    v    r
 u   l   d   w   w   a       y   e   v        e    .
 .   .   i   n   l   m   h   .   d   e   m    d    .
 .   .   n   .   y   .   e   .   .   .   a    .    .
 .   .   g   .   .   .   i   .   .   .   n    .    .
 .   .   .   .   .   .   r   .   .   .   .    .    .
                                                        iu
```

5.3.7.9 Line 9

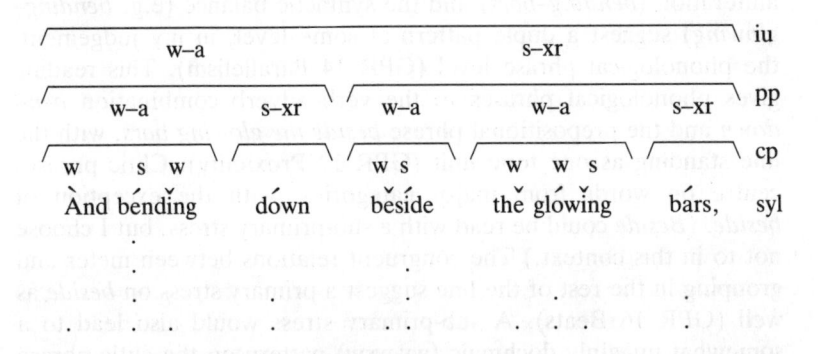

```
┌─────────────────────────────────────────────────────┐ iu
│        w–a                          s–xr            │
┌───────────────┐┌─────────────────────────────┐ pp
│   w–a    s–xr││   w–a         w–a      s–xr │
┌──────────┐┌───────┐┌─────────┐┌───────┐ cp
│  w  s  w ││  w  s ││  w   s  ││ w   s │
   And bénding    dówn    besíde   the glówing   bárs,   syl
```

Line 9 begins the third quatrain and the peak of the second half of the text. This line forms a large 'tower' in the grouping structure, remaining unarticulated for six consecutive levels (Levels 4–9). Given the depth of articulation in stanza 2, this creates an experiential *deceleration* at middle levels, a return to the pace of the first stanza rather than the second. This sudden shift from low levels to high has a kinaesthetic effect. We are literally 'lifted up' by the shift in vertical focus within the rhythmic articulation as the monologue pulls out of the reverie in stanza 2, moving back from memory to present action (dreaming becomes murmuring, nodding becomes bending, memory of past love becomes present sadness). The rhythmic 'elevation' here makes kinaesthetically palpable this shift in narrative focus.

At the same time, the sonic weight and rhythmic congruence of the line give it a quiescence that contrasts significantly with the lines in the second stanza, and in inclination the line changes from the mixture of falling and static contours in the second stanza to a mildly rising progression. The repeating pattern of falling movement between lines in the second stanza is suspended; the multilevelled symmetry at low levels is loosened up; and with its dependent syntax (i.e. *bending* . . .), its prolongational contours turn around in expectation of the main clause in line 10 and following (i.e. *murmur* . . .).

Segmentation and inclination in this line are fairly clear. Both the alliteration (*bending–bars*) and the syntactic balance (e.g. *bending–glowing*) suggest a duple pattern at some level, in my judgement, the phonological phrase level (GPR 14 Parallelism). This reading gives phonological phrases to the verb–adverb combination *bend down* and the prepositional phrase *beside the glowing bars*, with the line standing as one tone unit (GPR 12 Proximity). Clitic phrases centre on words from major categories, with the exception of *beside*. (*Beside* could be read with a sub-primary stress, but I choose not to in this context.) The congruent relations between meter and grouping in the rest of the line suggest a primary stress on *beside* as well (GPR 16 Beats). A sub-primary stress would also lead to a somewhat ungainly dochmaic (wwwsw) pattern on the clitic phrase *beside the glowing*, an oddity that doesn't seem motivated contextually (GPRs 9 and 10 Binary Form and Tri-max).

It is possible to read the line as two tone units (e.g. And bending down // beside the glowing bars), but several considerations weigh against this decision. One is the intense phonetic unity of the line. All but one of the consonants in the line are voiced, and these consonants are woven into intricate patterns, for example the patterning of [b], [d] and [n].

And b$_e$ nd$_{ing}$ d$_{ow}$ n b$_{esi}$ d$_e$ the glowing b$_{ars}$.

There is also a rhythmic regularity to the line that discourages its tonal division. If we opt to read the stress on *beside* as primary, the relations between grouping and meter are almost perfectly congruent at all levels of structure. The line divides 6–4 syllabically; it is iambic at the tone-unit level, with phonological phrase peaks normatively cadencing metrical projections; it is duple–triple and rising at the phonological phrase level; it has five clitic phrases with relatively controlled shapes; and it has no 'rhythmic figures'. This is the most congruent line so far in the poem. All of the other lines have rhythmic figures, except the first and last line. The stressed vowels in the line even form a continuously falling pattern in the second hemistich – [ay] in *beside*, [o] in *glowing*, [a] in *bars*. All of this patterning suggests a tonally unified reading of the line.

5.3.7.10 Line 10

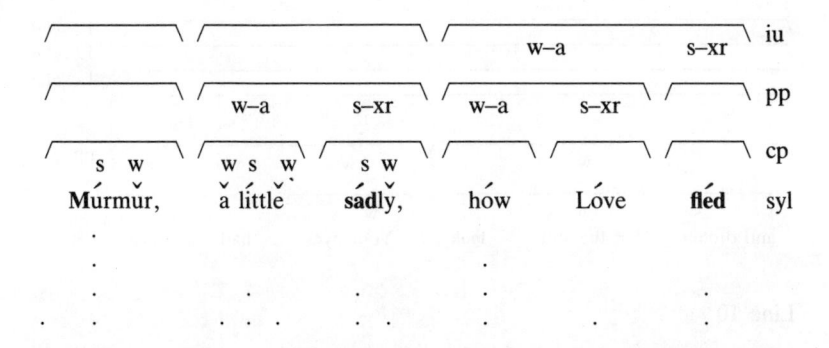

```
┌─────────┐┌─────────────┐┌─────────────────────────┐ iu
                            w–a           s–xr
┌─────┐┌──────────┐┌─────────────┐┌─────────────┐ pp
         w–a      s–xr    w–a      s–xr
┌─────┐┌──────────┐┌──────┐┌──────┐┌──────┐┌──────┐ cp
  s  w   w s  w    s  w
 Múrmur, a lĭttlĕ  sádlў,  how    Lóve    fled   syl
   .               .
   .  .    .   .   .    .    .    .
```

While line 9 presents the major narrative 'return' in the text, line 10 presents the most global *syntactic* return (i.e. the parallel between *dream* and *murmur* and their *how*-complements). The rhythmic structure of line 10 is more parallel to line 2 than to lines 3, 4 and following, however. As in line 2, line 10 polarizes at the hemistich break, most saliently in rhythmic direction. Grouping contours in the first hemistich are predominantly falling; grouping contours in the second hemistich are predominantly rising. All clitic phrases in the first hemistich are weak-final (*murmur, a little, sadly*); and the consistently rising iambic pattern within Level 6 is reversed here to a trochaic pattern.

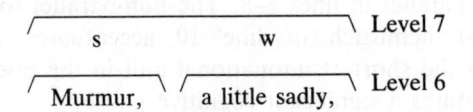

```
┌─────────────────────────────┐ Level 7
       s            w
┌─────────┐┌──────────────────┐ Level 6
 Murmur,    a little sadly,
```

Line 10 is also one of only three lines in the poem with a feminine caesura (the others being the even lines in the second stanza, lines 6 and 8). In the second hemistich, however, all prosodic units (the two clitic phrases and phonological phrases, and the one intonational unit) are strong-final and, as elsewhere in the poem, the line ends in a masculine rhyme. This reversal of rhythmic direction in the first hemistich intensifies the elegiac mood at this point relative to the narrative parallel in lines 3–4.

Lines 3–4

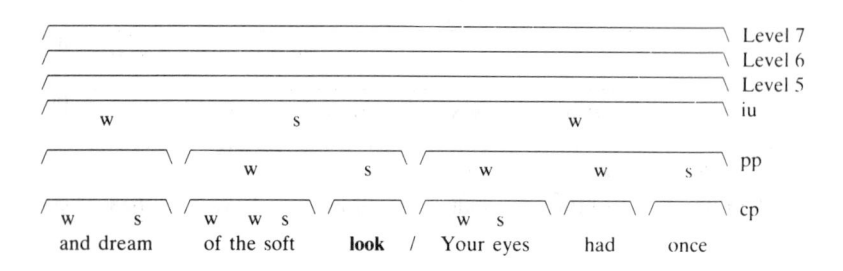

```
/─────────────────────────────────────────\ Level 7
 /────────────────────────────────────────\ Level 6
  /───────────────────────────────────────\ Level 5
   /──\                                   \ iu
    w          s                w
  /──────\ /──────────\ /──────────\        \ pp
        w        s     /   w    w     s
 /──\ /─────\ /──\ /─────\ /──\ /──\    \ cp
  w  s  w  w  s         w   s
 and dream of the soft  look / Your eyes had once
```

Line 10

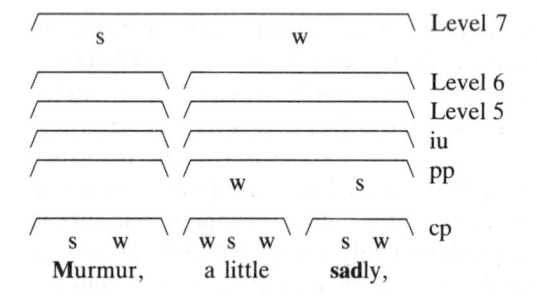

```
/──────────────\ Level 7
   s        w
/─────\ /──────\ Level 6
/─────\ /──────\ Level 5
/─────\ /──────\ iu
/─────\ /──────\ pp
          w    s
/────\ /─────\ /────\ cp
 s  w   w s w   s w
Murmur,  a little  sadly,
```

The (relative) contraction at low levels in line 10 further intensifies this elegiac mood. The narrative return in lines 10–12 is contracted 2–1 compared with its parallel in lines 3–8. The non-parallel tonal break within the first hemistich of line 10 accentuates this contraction. *Murmur* is the shortest intonational unit in the poem. Experientially, it constitutes a significant cognitive pause.

Other rhythmic features of line 10 also polarize at the hemistich break. The first hemistich contains a double offbeat; the second, a demotion. Clitic phrases in the first hemistich are all polysyllabic (*Murmur, a little, sadly*); clitic phrases in the second hemistich are all monosyllabic (*how, Love, fled*). Vocalic nuclei in the peaks of phonological phrases move from mid to low in the first hemistich (*mur-* to *sad-*) but from low to mid in the second hemistich (*Love* to *fled*). And so forth.

Line 10 resembles line 2 in other ways as well. Lines 2 and 10 are the only lines with six clitic phrases. Both contract syllabically (6–4 in line 2, 7–3 in line 10). The second hemistichs of both lines contain demotions and exclusively monosyllabic clitic phrases. The hemistichs in both lines exhibit various sorts of rhythmic balance at low levels: line 10 balances two trochaic clitic phrases around a central amphibrachic phrase (Murmur / a little / sadly); line 2 has many symmetries (e.g. its 2x2 structures and the balanced clitic phrase triples in the first hemistich, *and nodding, by the fire*).

The effect of this (narratively non-parallel) rhythmic parallel is to mark the major point of discontinuity in energy within this second half of the text with the somewhat milder rhythmic figures that marked a secondary discontinuity in energy in the first half of the text (the major discontinuity in the first half of the text being exactly the parallel presentation of the other *how*-clause in stanza 2). This modulates the text towards closure while economically re-using existing rhythmic materials elsewhere in the text.

While the discontinuity in rhythmic energy within line 10 is somewhat less than the startling syntactic interpolation in stanza 2, the rhythmic intensity of line 10 is still significant and presents a penultimate tensing before the double cadence in the last two lines. Line 10 is the only line with three intonational units, and these progressively expand at the clitic phrase level: 1–2–3.

   murmur
   a little / sadly
   how   / love / fled

Murmur is the only line-initial 'inversion' in the text. Line 10 is one of the most unbalanced lines in the text, dividing 7–3 in syllabic distribution. And the demotion in the second hemistich constitutes the most severe textual threat to the meter. As in line 7 (*and one man*), the demotion of *Love* occurs at the end of a phonological phrase, a jolting non-congruence, and this time the demotion is of the peak of the phrase (in line 7, *man* is prosodically subordinate to *one*; *fled* is not subordinate to *how*). The tension here is achieved by the most condensed means (meter-grouping relations at low levels); the tension in the parallel in the first half of the text is achieved by the most expansive means (meter-grouping relations at high levels).

The effect of this prosodic structure can be appreciated by considering an alternative version of the line that appeared in an earlier printing of the poem. I also include other changes that appeared in this version: the omission of the commas after *book*, *read* and *bars*; the strengthening of the semi-colons to full stops after *deep* and *face*; and the alterations in lines 11 and 12 in response to the alterations in line 10 – the capitalization of *He* to begin a new sentence after the period at the end of line 10, the substitution of *far above* for *overhead* to form a rhyme-mate for the new rhyme-word *Love* in line 10, and the closing of the quotes at the end of the poem.

> When you are old and grey and full of sleep,
> And nodding by the fire, take down this book
> And slowly read and dream of the soft look
> Your eyes had once, and of their shadows deep.
>
> How many loved your moments of glad grace,
> And loved your beauty with love false or true,
> But one man loved the pilgrim soul in you,
> And loved the sorrows of your changing face.
>
> And bending down beside the glowing bars
> Murmur, a little sad, 'From us fled Love.
> He paced upon the mountains far above,
> And hid his face amid a crowd of stars.'

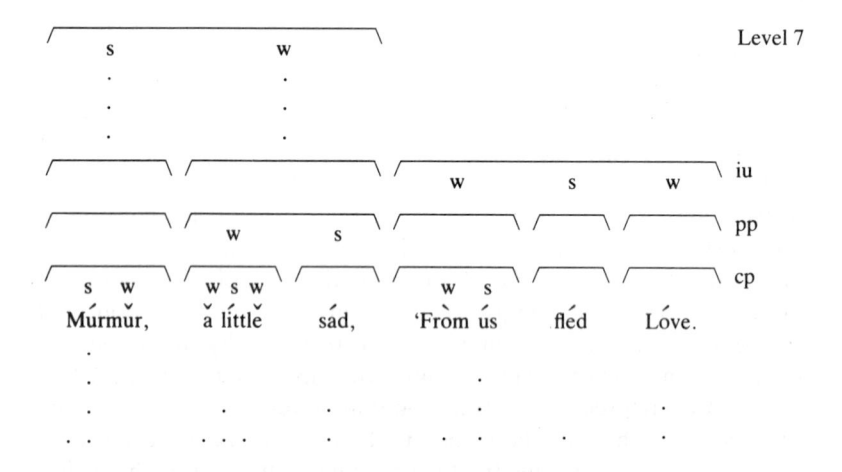

This other version of the line preserves many of the prosodic features of the final version: its rising contour between hemistichs, the three tone units and six clitic phrases (distributed 2–1 and 3–3 respectively within hemistichs), the falling contours between the tone units in the first hemistich, the progressive expansion of intonational units at the clitic phrase level, the initial inversion, the metrical figures at the peripheries and their polarization, the jolting demotion of the phonological phrase peak (*fled*) in the second hemistich, the low-level contraction from first to second hemistichs, the placement of the polysyllabic words *murmur* and *little* within the first hemistich, the trochaic shape of these polysyllables and the weak final clitic phrase *a little* in the first hemistich. Many of the effects of the final version, however, are lost.

The major weakness in this earlier line is its stilted syntactic inversion (*From us fled Love* for *Love fled from us*). This syntactic reordering achieves the intended rhetorical heightening but sacrifices the (more) conversationally natural syntax of the final version. This inverted syntax also moves the peak of the second hemistich on to a subtactical beat, a gesture that weakens the rhythmic energy of *fled* and produces a very tense cadence for the line, one that utilizes a somewhat subordinate grouping peak.

The loss of the parallel *how*-clause is also major. The repetitive *how*-clauses serve as important structural markers in the global architecture of the text. These lexical and syntactic parallels allow the reader to identify both the two units within the second half of the grouping structure (Level 11) and the two rising duples within Level 8, despite their asymmetrical shapes and (otherwise) non-parallel syntaxes. Without the parallel *how*-clauses, the second stanza tilts more towards a syntactically independent interpolation rather than a complement of *dream*. This reading destroys the controlled strain generated by the rhythmically asymmetric parallels in the final version.

This earlier version of the line also weakens the tight metrical parallel between line 10 and line 2. This undermines the textually unified (but subtle) modulation towards textual closure in the final version. With *sad* instead of *sadly*, the strongly falling contours of the first hemistich are diluted. The caesura becomes masculine, destroying the series of three consecutively weak-final clitic phrases. The truncation of *sad* also places a monosyllabic clitic phrase in the first hemistich, destroying the polarization of polysyllabic and monosyllabic clitic phrases in the two hemistichs. *Sad* also upsets the low-level rhythmic balance of the first hemistich (the 2–3–2 clitic phrase span becomes 2–3–1, a more varied, less balanced arrangement). The lower-level structure of the second hemistich also loses some of its intensity, formal unity and parallelism with line 2. *With us* breaks up the consistently monosyllabic structure of its clitic phrases. The extra syllable dilutes the second hemistich and squares out the line into a 6–4 syllabic arrangement. And the syntactic reordering and lexical substitutions alter the particular effectiveness of the phonetic patterning, both within the line as a whole and in the second hemistich in particular. The consistently rising vocalic pattern in the second hemistich in the original ([aw]–[ʌ]–[E]), which contrasts with the vocalic fall from *murmur* to *sadly* in the first hemistich, now becomes more balanced ([ʌ]–[E]–[ʌ]) and therefore less energetic and structurally polarizing.

Although this is not a prosodic matter, the explicit first person reference (*us*) in this alternative line also dilutes the dramatic tension between the intimately personal narrative pragmatics of the final version of the poem and its scrupulously generalized and 'distanced' references to the speaker. The final text strongly implies that the speaker is the author of 'this book' in line 2, the 'one man' in lines 7–8, and the earthly embodiment of 'Love' in lines 10–12; but these implications are left unspecified. The final text contains no first person reference. The *us* in this alternative line breaks this pattern and weakens this narrative effect.

5.3.7.11 Line 11

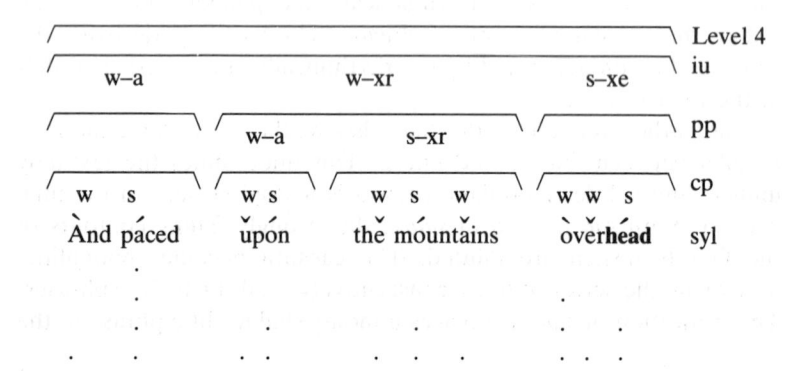

```
                                                                Level 4
 /─────────────────────────────────────────────────────────\    iu
 /              w–a              w–xr              s–xe    \
                                                                pp
 /───────────\ /─────────────────────\ /───────────────\
               w–a              s–xr                        cp
 /─────\ /─────\ /───────────────\ /───────────\
   w  s     w  s    w   s   w       w   w   s              syl
  And paced  upon  the mountains   overhead
    .           .        .              .
        .       .    .   .   .        .   .   .
```

PENTAMETER 419

The major function of line 11 is to provide a transition from the penultimate prosodic tension in line 10 to the final prosodic resolution in line 12. As in line 10, there is still some non-congruence between meter and grouping in line 11, but this non-congruence is comparatively mild (a promotion of the fourth tactical beat, the triple structures of the line and two of the clitic phrases, the general blurring of the grouping structure, etc.). Line 11 continues the steady (1–2–3) expansion of intonational units at the clitic phrase level that we found in line 10. The tone unit in line 11 has four clitic phrases; the tone unit in line 12 will have five. Line 11 establishes a second expansive pattern at the phonological phrase level. The last two tone units in line 10 have one and two phonological phrases; line 11 has three, as does line 12. (Therefore the last five intonational units in the poem expand 1–1–2–3–3.)

Compared with line 10, line 11 begins to regularize prominence contours at many levels, a regularization that will be completed in line 12. Line 10 has no iambic clitic phrases; line 11 has two (*And paced, upon*); line 12 will have five. Line 10 has three weak-final clitic phrases; line 11 has one (*the mountains*); line 12 will have none. Line 10 has three monosyllabic clitic phrases; line 11 has none, as does line 12. Line 10 has two unarticulated phonological phrases, as does line 11; line 12 will have none.

The global contours of the text at line 11 also strongly anticipate closure. Line 11 completes the last trochaic unit within Level 6, and remaining unresolved prolongationally, strongly anticipates the third verb (*hid*) that will both complete another two-level triple and provide a peak for the final iambic unit within Level 7. The nearly exact 2–1 ratio between the peaks of the last two units at Level 10 (lines 3–8 and 10–12) requires the last line to achieve this proportioning. And the rhyme *overhead* resolves the inner rhyme-pair and prolongs our anticipation of the final rhyme-mate *stars*.

Strength and segmentation in this line are somewhat blurred and leave considerable choice to the reader. As my scansion presents, I prefer to read the line as one tone unit, with three phonological phrases and four clitic phrases; but many of these choices are personal. As a post-modifier, *overhead* could be incorporated into the second phonological phrase, and with its close relation to the verb, *upon* might be grouped with *paced* at the phonological phrase level (the alliterating [p]s support this reading, as does the distribution of disyllabic and trisyllabic clitic phrases). As a function word, *upon* could also be read with a sub-primary stress, yielding a large dochmaic (wwwsw) clitic phrase in the centre of the line. Both the content of the line ('pacing', etc.) and the penultimate position of this line in the poem might support this physical expansion/ acceleration. Prominence within the one intonational unit in this line is also very balanced. I give the tone unit final prominence more on the basis of default than informational salience (GPR 3 End-focus). All of the phonological phrase peaks represent points of new information and textual interest. *Paced* is the second verb in the final triplet of actions in the text: *fled, paced, hid*. *Mountains* is important symbolically, adding conceptual breadth and distance to the final image. And *overhead* is important symbolically as well, pointing up to an 'overground' level of spiritual being 'above' the terrestrial and physical.

5.3.7.12 *Line 12*

	w			s–xe		iu
w–a	s–xr	w–a	w–a		s–xr	pp
w s	w s	w s	w s		w s	cp
And hid	his face	amid	a crowd		of stars.	syl

Line 12 is classically closural. Its most obvious closural feature is its metrical congruence. With the reading suggested above, relations between grouping and meter in line 12 are perfectly canonical. Clitic phrases are regularized into binary rising shapes. Phonological phrases follow the asymmetrical (2–3) structure of the pentameter and cadence the hemistichs. And the iambic tone unit both embraces and cadences the line as a whole.

Only two other lines in the text have no 'metrical figures', the first line and line 9. Only one other line in the text has one tone unit and two phonological phrases articulated into a 2–3 rising pattern, line 9. Prosodically, line 12 echoes line 9, placing a rhythmic frame around the third stanza (and peak of the second half of the text's grouping structure).

Many other features of line 12 are also closural. The final word *stars* provides the final rhyme and knits together the imagery of the text, linking back to *old, fire, soul, glowing,* and *loved/love/Love* within the structure of Yeats' extended 'elemental' mythology.

Elements	Water	Air	Fire	Earth
e	sorrow	hope	love	malevolence
x	blood	logic	soul	body/instinct
t	youth	maturity	old age	childhood
e	west	east	south	north
n	flood	wind	flames	woods
s	sunset	dawn	stars	night
i	.	.	.	.
o	.	.	.	.
n	.	.	.	.
s				

Hid provides the third unit in the two-level triple of verbs (*paced, fled* and *hid*) at Levels 6 and 7, a two-level triple that refers across levels and back in the text to the two two-level triples in the first stanza at Levels 8 and 9 (*old and grey, full of sleep, nodding by the fire; take down, read, dream*). *Hid* and *stars* provide the reference to spiritual being needed to link the last line to the peaks of the iambic patterning within Level 6 (shadows vs look, soul/sorrows vs grace/beauty, etc.). And this last line provides numerous phonic links both internally and across the text. *Face* echoes both *paced* in line 11 and the *grace–face* rhyme in the second stanza. The [m] and [aw] in *amid a crowd* echo *mountains* in line 11. And the many consonantal [d]s in the line reach back throughout the text: *old, nodding, down, read, dream, shadows, deep, loved, bending, beside, sadly, fled, overhead*.

This last line leaves various options for segmentation and prominence, but there is strong pressure for a very congruent reading (i.e. one tone unit, two phonological phrases, five clitic phrases). The line could be read in two tone units (i.e. And hid his face // amid a crowd of stars), but as with line 9, the pervasive phonetic unity of the line discourages this reading: the consonantal [d]s, *and, hid, amid, crowd*; the consonantal [z]s, *his, stars*; the reverse rhyme, *hid, his*; and the internal rhyme, *hid, amid* (GPR 13 Similarity). The serial expansion in the grouping structures begun in lines 10 and 11 also discourages this reading. A final intonational unit with five clitic phrases completes the expanding series begun with *murmur* two lines earlier (GPR 17 Schemes).

cps ›››	1	2	3	4	5
ius	murmur				
^	a little	sadly			
^	how	love	fled		
^	and paced	upon	the mountains	overhead	
^	and hid	his face	amid	a crowd	of stars

There is also general textual pressure for a unitary reading. If lines 9 and 11 are read as unitary, line 12 will tend this way as well (GPR 16 Unity).

Similarly, *amid* could be read with sub-primary stress, yielding an appropriately balanced line with four clitic phrases and a central promotion. Several considerations weigh against this reading as well, however: the internal rhyme *hid–amid* (GPR 14 Parallelism), the expanding clitic phrase pattern (GPR 17 Schemes), and the parallel assignment of strength to the other locative prepositions earlier in the stanza: *down, overhead, beside* and *upon* (GPR 14 Parallelism).

NOTE

1. 1981: 143.

Chapter 6
Implications

> Time does not make rhythm, but rhythm time.
>
> (Robert MacDougell)[1]

This book proposes solutions to several long-standing problems in prosodic study in the English tradition and therefore has various implications for further work.

6.1 ANALYSIS

The most important achievement of this book is the scansional system developed in Chapters 3 and 4 and illustrated in Chapter 5. This system makes possible for the first time a relatively complete and explicit representation of a rhythmic response to an individual text. The graphic conventions of this system are few and easy to use. The scansions themselves are relatively space-efficient (I get four or five lines of poetry to a page). The reductional technique developed in Chapter 4 is a useful heuristic for clarifying rhythmic intuitions and demonstrating the experiential contribution of individual levels of rhythmic structure. And the multilevelled organization of rhythm represented by the scansions yields readily to extraction and summary (through rhythmic 'sketches', etc.), a feature that enables the flexible presentation of analytical results within the larger context of a critical discourse as a whole.

6.2 RHYTHMIC COGNITION

Historically, the most important theoretical achievement of this book is the theory of rhythmic cognition presented in Chapter 3. While this theory is not original (as I explain, it is largely borrowed from cognitive psychology and music theory), it is new to prosodic theory and, with its extension to this domain, it gives prosodic study a much-needed theoretical centre from which other results, theoretical and practical, can follow.

While space does not permit me to pursue these matters here, this theory of rhythmic cognition also connects prosodic study with the exciting contemporary developments in cognitive science, the scientific study of mind, and therefore significantly broadens the theoretical implications of particular prosodic findings couched in this new theoretical context.[2] Poets craft their prosodic structures so that they perform certain poetic tasks. But in this crafting, they put to use in precise and complex ways one of our most fundamental powers of mind. For those interested in cognition, a body of precise, theoretically informed descriptions of these crafted constructions should provide important evidence for the nature of those mental abilities.

6.3 RHYTHM AND LANGUAGE

This book also helps to clarify the complex relations between rhythm and language. In a nutshell, this clarification is negative: rhythm is not linguistic and language, for the most part, is not especially rhythmic. While it seems evident that many linguistic structures are 'naturally' rhythmic in their effect and that many linguistic conventions have been significantly influenced by rhythmic considerations, linguistic competence and prosodic competence are largely independent in their function and design. Linguistic structures, while enabled by certain specific mental abilities, are largely social conventions. Rhythmic structures, while subject to the pervasive forces of conventionalization, are largely cognitive forms constructed naturally from stimuli presented on the spot. The term 'linguistic rhythm', if used at all, should be understood to refer to certain *responses* to linguistic structures, not to those linguistic structures themselves. In all cases (prosody, syntax, etc.), we find perfectly acceptable linguistic structures that are not significantly rhythmic, and rhythmic responses are in no way limited to linguistic stimuli.

On the other hand, this claim does not deny or underestimate the heuristic power of rhythmic analysis in descriptive and theoretical linguistics. In this respect I agree with Gil, the metrical phonologists and others who have been demonstrating that many long-standing problems in linguistic description and theory might best be handled in rhythmic terms. In fact, to the extent that the theory presented in this book clarifies the notion 'rhythmic response' and shows how such responses can be elicited from certain sorts of crafted language, it makes a significant contribution to this aspect of language study.

6.4 RHYTHM AND POETRY

The theory of rhythm developed in this book also helps to clarify the long-disputed relationship between rhythm and poetry. As with the relationship between rhythm and language, this clarification is largely negative: poetry need not be unusually rhythmic, nor rhythmic language unusually poetic.

Historically, prosodists have regularly distinguished between poetry and *verse*. But most critics still maintain that a text must be unusually rhythmic to be poetic. The major argument used to support this claim has been that most poetry, both metrical and 'free', is written in lines and that lines are necessarily rhythmic (because they present repeating forms and repeating forms, by definition, are rhythmic).

The argument I mount in this book questions such facile equations between repetitive form and rhythm. In the rhythmic theory I have developed here, rhythmic responses are distinguished sharply from rhythmic stimuli, and *rhythm* is defined in terms of canonical *shape* rather than in terms of formal repetition. In terms of the theory developed here, repeating forms are not rhythmic unless they elicit a levelled hierarchy of alternating beats, culminating phrases or goal-oriented regions. It is questionable whether a visual line alone elicits any of these responses. Therefore, lineation alone need not be rhythmic.

At the same time, this claim does not deny the many poetic functions of visual lines (and other sorts of repetitive forms), in both metered verse and 'free'. As we reviewed in Chapter 1, free verse prosodists have demonstrated at some length the many 'acts of attention' that visual forms in poetry can elicit and the centrality of these 'acts of attention' to the poetic intention of many contemporary poetic texts. In most cases these 'acts of attention' are generated across and against rhythmic response, however. Therefore they need not be rhythmic in themselves. The various non-rhythmic functions of other sorts of repetitive form in poetry have also long been documented and must be fully recognized by any adequate poetics.

6.5 SHAPE AND TIME

Internal to the theory, the most significant contribution of this book is its notion of rhythmic *shape*. Shape has long been a major concern of aestheticians and has been used in various ways in prosodic analysis. (Prosodists have developed various theories to refer to the shape of the metrical foot, the clitic phrase, the poetic line, the verse period, the stanza, the poetic form and other matters.) However, as we considered at some length in Chapter 2, many of these traditional references to rhythmic shape have been confused (e.g. the shape of the metrical foot) or inadequate (e.g. the tradition's 'flat' conception of meter), and many significant aspects of rhythmic shape have been overlooked entirely (e.g. prolongation and grouping at high levels). More important, perhaps, traditional considerations of prosodic shape have tended to isolate shapes at one level of structure from shapes at other levels of structure, and shape in one component of rhythmic organization from shapes in other components.

This book argues that rhythmic shape is essentially (1) multi-componential, and (2) vertically defined. In the theory of grouping developed in Chapter 4, grouping segmentation is essentially vertical, with structurally 'equivalent' units being grouped in terms of their association with a higher-level grouping peak. Once grouped, the shapes of units at any level are also defined in vertical terms (i.e. by the prominence relations among the immediate constituents in the group). The shape of a phonological phrase is determined by the prominence relations among its constituent clitic phrases (and so forth for the other levels of structure). Independent of hierarchical form, rhythmic groups in this theory have no specifiable shape at all. They can be characterized by size ('big', 'little', etc.) or by other diffuse formal qualities ('complex', 'irregular', etc.), but these characterizations are not specifications of rhythmic shape *per se*.

This clarification of the notion of rhythmic shape is the major critical pay-off of the theory presented here. The simultaneous arrays of projected beats, culminating groups and completing regions that constitute rhythmic structure define shapes of cognitive and physiological energy, shapes that, taken collectively and in concert, are some of the most precise analogues of our emotional energies. At this level of theorizing, descriptive precision necessarily fails, but this theory at least presents the possibility of gaining a clearer view of the deep human significance of our rhythmic experience of poetry and the other arts.

While these philosophical issues need much more consideration than I can give them here, one of the most significant effects of rhythmic shape is its creation of our experience of *time*. Most critical references to the temporal effects of poetic form are largely atheoretical references to the effects of rhythmic architecture. With its severe constraints on vertical scope, horizontal uniformity and duple–triple patterning, meter creates a relatively constant time that is the close textual analogue to the 'clock' time we use to regulate our everyday affairs. Within this constant 'measuring', horizontal expansions and contractions in grouping define various sorts of temporal acceleration and retardation, whose specific cognitive qualities are determined by their vertical positioning in the grouping hierarchy. And prolongation subjects these structural accelerations and retardations generated by grouping to the distorting temporal influence of our subjective desires for satisfying wholes and successful terminations. If this theory of rhythmic time is valid, the philosophical implications of the rhythmic theory presented here could be considerable. In this theory, rhythm creates time, not time rhythm – and the vexed issue of the oppositional relation between stasis and change, shape and process, in both art and human experience in general, dissolves (in part) into the larger unity of rhythmic cognition.

6.6 METER

While my focus in this book has been on phrasing, one of the significant results of this focus has been a clarification of its rhythmic complement, meter, and therefore a clarification of the central concern of the theoretical tradition. To my mind, meter still remains the most problematical aspect of rhythmic form in poetry. But the critique of the tradition presented in Chapter 2, the general theory of rhythm developed in Chapter 3, and the more detailed theory of phrasing developed in Chapter 4 help to dispel some of these problems.

First, this book proposes that what has been perceived in the tradition as metrical segmentation and direction be dissolved back into the more basic facts of hierarchical patterning, phasal relations and associative 'marking'. The most basic qualities of meter that distinguish it from the other components of rhythmic form are its horizontal uniformity, mandatory duple and triple patterning and limited vertical scope. Prosodic theories that see meter as composed of discrete segments (poetic feet, etc.), directional patterning ('rising', 'falling', etc.), quadruple and quintuple patterning (e.g. four-beat meters, pentameter, etc.), and such attribute to meter itself experiential effects that arise from meter's interaction with the other aspects of rhythm and other aspects of poetic form, and therefore mire themselves in overwhelming problems of definition, description and explanation. Traditional terms such as *accentual-syllabic meter*, *syllabic meter*, *iambic pentameter*, *dipodic meter*, *accentual meter* and so forth are misleading in the extreme, and if used at all should be taken to refer loosely to certain general systems of versification with certain general ranges of experiential effects, not to rhythmic experiences themselves.

This book also clarifies the function of meter in poetry. In essence, meter projects formal frames within which grouping and prolongation move to culmination and arrival. Normatively, meter is phasally afterbeating. Canonically, it marks the beginnings of phrases with strong beats that, in their hierarchical ordering, project measures composed of two subordinate levels of articulation. Opposed to the long tradition of comment on these issues, this theory emphatically denies that meter is some sort of regularized model of the pattern of linguistic prominences in the text. Rather, like grouping, meter is a rhythmic, not a linguistic, form, a rhythmic form with its own constraints on well-formedness, its own preferred relations to rhythmic stimuli, and its own particular function within rhythmic cognition as a whole. In fact, at higher levels at least, the major preference is for strong metrical prominences to be positioned on relatively weak linguistic prominences and for weak metrical prominences to be positioned on relatively strong linguistic prominences. With this patterning, the strong beats initiate groups and project their expected measures, while the strong linguistic prominences elicit the grouping peaks that cadence the rhythmic phrases and complete the projected measures.

6.7 METRICAL 'FIGURES'

The componential theory of rhythm developed in this book also helps to clarify the long-standing debates over the sources of certain experiential effects in poetic rhythm. The major innovation of this book is to claim a greater share of these effects for phrasing without denying the significant effects of meter. In particular, I have argued that many of what have been traditionally termed 'metrical figures' or 'metrical variations' are not essentially metrical at all and that many of the traditionally asserted connections between these 'metrical figures' and their experiential effects cannot withstand close examination.

6.8 PROSODIC HISTORY

The theory of poetic rhythm developed in this book also lays the foundation for an enriched rewriting of prosodic history. More than any other body of prosodic writing, our prosodic histories reflect the relative stagnation and confusion in prosodic theory. Despite significant theoretical advances on isolated problems, the failure of theoretical prosodists in this century to develop a generally accepted method of rhythmical analysis has made it impossible for literary historians and historically minded prosodists to take advantage of these advances in any coherent way. Since mid-century, most new work on prosodic 'style' has been undertaken within the context of specific 'schools' of prosodic theory (Slavic metrics, generative metrics, grammetrics, etc.), and as our historical survey in Chapter 1 has revealed, the analytical tools developed by these individual schools have all been directed at a relatively narrow range of prosodic structures and effects. As a result, the last half-century of prosodic study has produced no synthetic yet theoretically up-to-date prosodic histories. In the eyes of most literary historians, the standard prosodic histories are still the massive catalogues of verse forms produced by the German philological tradition (e.g. Schipper 1910) or the engagingly genteel, but largely pretheoretical, surveys produced by the English literary historians (e.g. Saintsbury 1906–10) – studies that are now almost a century old. Recent prosodic histories, even if limited in scope, have generally adopted one or another of these philological/pretheoretical formats (Allen 1935; Gross 1964; Piper 1969; Turco 1968; Wright 1988; Hartman 1980; Woods 1984; Hardison 1989, etc.).

While I have not attempted this historical task here, the theory presented in this book provides the analytical and theoretical tools for overcoming this historical stagnation and makes possible for the first time the production of a linguistically informed, theoretically sophisticated and critically relevant prosodic history. As Gil has

430 IMPLICATIONS

demonstrated in his analysis of non-canonical verse, an abstract, hierarchical representation of rhythmic response allows the prosodic stylistician to go 'beyond' syllable counts and stress profiles to a consideration of the typological shapes of poetic discourses as a whole, an analytical approach that can bring prosodic history in line with the central concerns of our stylistic histories of other 'elements' of poetic form (syntax, theme, image, voice, etc.). The multi-componential and multilevelled structure of the theory developed here would also allow for the productive coordination of individual studies by different hands focusing on the history of isolated aspects of prosodic structure (e.g. meter or grouping; phonological levels of grouping or syntactic levels, etc.) or of particular rhythmic shapes (e.g. rising vs falling grouping structures, duple vs triple forms, extensional vs anticipational prolongation, etc.) – a feature that would be essential for significant progress on these issues. It is reasonable to assume that no one prosodist will ever attempt to rewrite and update Saintsbury. But the theory presented here offers the possibility that prosodists as a collective scholarly community may one day be able to provide literary historians with just such a work.

6.9 RHYTHMIC PHRASING

More specifically, the central focus of this book has been to solve the long-standing problem of the role of caesurae, enjambment and other phrasal phenomena in verse rhythm, but in a way that generalizes these problems, expands their domain both upwards and downwards in the prosodic hierarchy, and, in the end, turns the tradition on its head.

As our survey in Chapter 1 documents, most of the 'schools' of prosodic analysis in the tradition have valorized meter at the expense of phrasing. Traditionally, meter has been seen as providing the dominant 'rhythms of English poetry', while phrasing has been seen as adding relatively 'free variation' to these metrical forms. This theoretical position is indefensible and reflects more the analytical limitations of the theoretical tradition than the nature of poetic rhythm *per se*. While meter is an important part of many verse rhythms, phrasal forms are the most universal, expressively powerful and theoretically central components of all verse rhythms, especially the rhythms of art verse, in which meter is often relatively flat and therefore perceptually weak. In almost all cases it is the phrasal rhythm of a poem that defines its unique rhythmic shape and therefore serves as the dominant vehicle of prosodic expression.

One of my major aims has been to show the complexity, coherence and relative independence of phrasal forms. In the tradition, many prosodists have argued that phrasal expressiveness is heavily dependent upon (if not derivative of) metrical form. This position is also indefensible. Meter in poetry has a very restricted scope. Some metrical forms do not project measures of over line length. Therefore, a theory of verse rhythm that takes meter as central and generative of other structures implicitly dismisses all of the global rhythmic organization in these texts as rhythmically peripheral, or, worse yet, arhythmical.

At the same time, the theory of rhythm in this book does not neglect meter or metrical–phrasal interaction. In fact, it enriches the theory of both meter and metrical–phrasal interaction in the tradition. In the theory presented here, most metrical poetry is considered as presenting three to eight levels of metrical beating and ten to fifteen levels of grouping and prolongation. In this theory, a phenomenon such as enjambment becomes not just a matter of the appearance or absence of an end-line pause, but our response to the transitional energies of the full grouping and prolongational hierarchies as these move across the termination and onset of the measure projected by the most salient level of beating. Here, the analysis of metrical–phrasal interaction is no longer a local affair. It demands that the prosodist consider the position of the metrical break in the shape of the grouping and prolongational hierarchies in the text as a whole.

The theory of phrase–meter interaction developed here is also more dynamically defined than in most traditional theories. Phrasal structures at high levels are represented as always moving towards or away from a point of informational culmination/arrival. This means that an enjambed structure in this theory does not just 'proceed beyond' a metrical break. In that 'proceeding', the enjambed phrase presents a detailed qualitative movement (e.g. rising progressional anticipation or falling additive extension) – a fact that greatly increases the critical acuity of the prosodic description. The analyses in Chapter 5 illustrate the critical power of such an enriched and dynamic theory of phrase–meter interaction.

In historical terms, the most important achievement of this theory of phrasing is that it solves the difficulty of the subjectivity and instability of phrasal interpretation, one of the major problems that has discouraged many prosodists from undertaking what I have undertaken here. Following the music theorists, I solve this problem by claiming that phrasal response is *preferential* in organization, that it is determined by a summative 'weighing' of a number of sometimes reinforcing, sometimes conflicting considerations. In Chapter 4 I show that these considerations are relatively simple and few and therefore can be coherently described, although I recognize that their selection and weighing in any given reading will always be somewhat individual, if not unique. This 'preferential' theory of phrasing overcomes the problem of phrasal variability by making this variability a design feature of the theoretical system. Therefore it makes possible for the first time a relatively substantial and stable theory of phrasal interpretation.

6.10 PROSE RHYTHM AND THE RHYTHM OF FREE VERSE

The theory of rhythm developed here also helps to dispel some of the traditional difficulties surrounding rhythm in prose, free verse and the prose poem. As we encountered in our historical survey in Chapter 1, many approaches to prosody have equated verse rhythm with either meter or versification, or at least have made non-metrical rhythm theoretically dependent in significant ways upon metrical rhythm or versification. In this theoretical context, ametrical verse ('free' verse), unversified poetry (the prose poem) and all non-poetic discourse (prose) by definition are arhythmical – a counter-intuitive, demonstrably unacceptable result.

I have argued that this 'metrification' of rhythm is unjustified and that any adequate theory of rhythm in metrical verse depends crucially on a theory of ametrical rhythm and therefore on a theory of rhythm in free verse, the prose poem and prose. In the theory I have developed here, the phrasal components (grouping and prolongation) serve as the complement to meter within rhythmic cognition as a whole and therefore consitute exactly a theory of rhythm in ametrical genres.

Given the history of comment on these issues, however, it is important to recognize the limitations in this result. As I have just stressed in 6.4 above, a rhythmic response, as I have defined it here, is only one, albeit a major, effect of the formal structure of a poetic discourse. Therefore, a theory of free verse rhythm must not be mistaken for a theory of free verse *in toto*. In both metrical verse and free, formal patterning can elicit many significant responses that are not rhythmic. These issues of definition are crucial to a coherent understanding of rhythmic form, both in verse and elsewhere.

6.11 POETIC PEDAGOGY

The theory of verse rhythm developed here also has important implications for poetic pedagogy. In their treatment of rhythm, almost all poetic pedagogies teach some version of traditional foot-substitution metrics. Given the partial and conflicting claims of the alternative approaches to verse rhythm we surveyed in Chapter 1, this is understandable. However, both these alternative approaches and the approach presented here offer strong arguments against the logical coherence and critical productivity of the foot-substitution system. Therefore, sooner or later this pedagogical practice should be changed.

Pedagogical issues in prosodic study should be strictly separated from theoretical issues. The problems in teaching beginning students about verse rhythm are considerable. None the less, it is also reasonable to expect that any significant change in theory should eventually be reflected in pedagogy. Therefore, as an advocate of a new theory of verse rhythm I might be expected to consider the pedagogical consequences of my proposals.

The major pedagogical implications of the theory developed here would be: (1) a revised definition of verse rhythm, (2) a clarification of the perceptual effects of meter, and (3) a greater concern for phrasing. Number (1) is relatively easy to accomplish. The generality of rhythmic response in human experience offers teachers of poetry many ways of introducing the basic intuitions represented by the rhythmic components and their interaction. For this task I find non-canonical verse (chants, cheers, etc.) and other media (e.g. music) especially useful. Number (2) is more difficult, but no more difficult than teaching foot-substitution prosody. Verse meters are difficult for many students to 'hear'. Therefore, this task is usually more an exercise in perceptual attention than in technical description. The major theoretical changes would involve (a) the introduction of meter without reference to foot boundaries, and (b) a demonstration of meter's canonically hierarchical, afterbeating structure. Given the complexity of rhythmic phrasing, task (3) is most difficult and I would assume that any detailed treatment of phrasing in a beginning class would be beyond the resources of class time and student ability/interest. None the less, the basic organization of rhythmic phrasing could be introduced and some salient levels of patterning could be examined in more detail.

The theory of rhythm developed here can contribute most significantly to higher levels in the curriculum. As it stands now, the logical confusions and critical weaknesses in traditional foot-substitution scansion necessarily exclude its effective incorporation into classes at higher levels in the curriculum. The system itself cannot withstand close examination by advanced students, and the classroom projects that the system enables are all relatively mechanical and uninteresting.

The theory of rhythm developed here offers a significant alternative to these curricular difficulties. The theoretical system I have developed yields wider and richer rewards as the student delves more deeply into its complexities. Therefore it lends itself naturally to a graded presentation at a continuous series of levels in the curriculum. Students introduced to verse rhythm at beginning levels could be given an opportunity to explore some of the technical difficulties in phrasal description in upper-level undergraduate classes. Then graduate-level courses could bring students to a professional competence in phrasal analysis. In sum, the system presented here holds the possibility of providing an engaging, graded curriculum that can both clarify the nature of verse rhythm for the casually interested non-professional and provide for the advanced training of professionals. The result could be a renewal of the study of verse rhythm in the English curriculum, a practice that is now effectively defunct.

6.12 POETRY AND MUSIC

The theory of rhythm developed here also has significant implications for the long discussion in Western philosophy and aesthetics of the relations between poetry and Western tonal music. The parallels that I draw in Chapters 3 and 4 between contemporary theories of rhythm in Western tonal music and rhythm in English poetry constitute one of the most detailed and explicit demonstrations of the experiential connections between music and poetry in the long history of comment on this issue. In my experience, most discussions of these connections have been either negative, emphatically rejecting the parallels I draw, or so general and/or partial as to be merely suggestive of the more detailed and explicit demonstration I present. The claim my argument suggests is that the most adequate and critically productive theory of rhythm in poetry is not just loosely parallel to the most respected and revealing theory of rhythm in Western tonal music. *These theories are one and the same.* While poetry and music are obviously different and therefore present reader–listeners with different rhythmic stimuli, both the cognitive representations that reader–listeners construct in response to these different stimuli and the relations between these cognitive representations and their phenomenal sources are based on *exactly the same* principles of rhythmic well-formedness and preference.

I also claim that this connection is not just fortuitous or even the product of the particular historical relations between the two art forms as they have developed in the West. Rather, following from my rejection of Myths 2 and 4 (Verse rhythm is linguistic and conventional) in Chapter 2 and my argument for a medium-independent rhythmic competence in Chapter 3, the theory I have developed here demands that this *must* be so. Therefore to the extent that it is, these cross-media correlations stand as independent evidence for the validity of my approach. I am linking my claims in the strongest way imaginable to another field of study. Therefore, those that would choose to reject the design of the theory of verse rhythm I have developed (by narrowing or broadening its scope, denying its componential or hierarchical organization, etc.) must claim either (1) that our rhythmic response to language is idiosyncratic and unconnected to our rhythmic response to other media, or (2) that the contemporary tradition of rhythmic analysis in music theory is misconceived and should be discarded. Either or both of these claims are possible, but convincing support for such claims would demand extensive and intricate argument.

At the same time, it is again important to understand the limitations of this interdisciplinary claim. To claim that we use the same basic rhythmic competence in our reactions to Western tonal music and English poetry is not to deny the strong forces of habituation and conventionalization that operate everywhere in cognitive response, especially our cognitive response to art. Biological and social determinants of experience are not mutually exclusive. Nor does this claim imply that the rhythms of Western tonal music 'sound' the same as the rhythms of English poetry. The well-formedness and preference rules that constrain the shape of our rhythmic intuitions are highly general principles that allow for a wide range of rhythmic organizations. For instance, if I could be allowed to speculate, it is my impression that, compared with English poetry, the rhythms of classical Western tonal music are more highly elaborated, more steeply vertical in their metrical organization, less congruent within their phrasal components, more dependent on equational elaboration in prolongation, more symmetrical and metrically congruent in their higher-level grouping, more symmetrical but less congruent in their lower-level grouping, and so forth. The fact that I can even articulate these differences, however, shows that these musical and poetic rhythms are profoundly similar in their basic organization. All rich contrast is based in equally rich similarity. Two radically distinct entities yield no productive differences.

These musical–poetic parallels also have significant implications for the separate study of rhythm in poetry. At this point, the most important implication for prosodic study is that all prosodists should make a significant attempt to become versed in contemporary music theory. This is not an easy task, but it is one that is motivated by several considerations and one that, if taken seriously, could transform prosodic study as we know it. Besides the evident similarity in phenomena being studied, the most important of these considerations is that music theorists at this historical moment have a more sophisticated understanding of the problems of rhythmic description than any prosodists in my experience. Many of the logical confusions in prosodic theory that I have tried to dispel in this book have long been recognized by music theorists and therefore music theory has long overcome the stagnating forces that have beset prosodic theory for so many centuries. The sheer complexity and theoretical centrality of formal elaboration in music has also driven music theorists to a level of descriptive intensity and rigour that has never been achieved (or even attempted) in prosodic theory. Therefore this work can serve as a model of what prosodic study, if pursued with equal energy and descriptive rigour, could become, both as field of scholarly endeavour and as an exciting and productive dimension of literary pedagogy. Contrary to what most of my literary readers might suppose, the theoretical and descriptive complexities that I have borrowed from music theory and applied to poetry form a relatively standard part of music education at advanced undergraduate levels. Therefore this curriculum stands as proof of the viability of the pedagogical proposals I have just suggested in 6.11 above.

For the same reason that linguistic theorists study many languages and literary theorists many literatures, the study of music theory can immeasurably enlarge a prosodist's perspective on rhythmic phenomena in language. The most insidious 'myth' of prosodic theory has been a textual (and therefore linguistic) preoccupation. Instead of listening to poems and trying to formalize the structure of their rhythmic intuitions, most prosodists, especially twentieth-century prosodists, have tried to formalize regularities in the linguistic surface of the text. As a result, the 'field' of prosodic study has developed more and more complex theories to predict the historical constraints on versification while making little progress in understanding the natural cognitive bases of rhythmic 'hearing'. The study of music can help to overcome this preoccupation. The complexities of the surface ornamentation in music make the seemingly chaotic notation of this musical surface palpably removed from the coherence of the cognitive experience this surface engenders. Unlike a comparable approach to poetic structure, the overwhelming problems in any attempt to elaborate a theory of 'musical versification' are immediately apparent and the theorist is naturally motivated to find a more abstract and indirect connection between the physical phenomena presented by the medium and their cognitive effect. It is just this perspective that can enrich prosodic theory and free it from its prolonged historical stagnation.

6.13 POETIC RHYTHM AND LITERARY CRITICISM

Finally, while my major focus has been more technical than philosophical, at this concluding point we might place these technical considerations within the larger realm of literary criticism and criticism of the arts in general.

Within traditional approaches to verse rhythm, in which meter is valorized over phrasing, our best prosodists have felt no lack in demonstrating convincingly and at length the diverse and significant aesthetic functions of meter: iconic, mimetic, associative, indexical, emotive, semantic, emblematic, allusive, emphatic, cohesive, reflexive, incantatory, etc. (e.g. Chatman 1965: 184–224; Hollander 1985: 135–211; Attridge 1982: 285–315). Throughout the centuries of comment on English verse, these demonstrations have been echoed in largely identical catalogues and with largely similar verse exemplars by prosodists within all of the various 'schools' of prosodic theory we reviewed in Chapter 1. Given that the prosodic theory I have developed in this book includes meter as a significant component of rhythmic form, I embrace these demonstrations, and given their ubiquity and quality, I feel no need to reproduce them here.

At the same time, I also recognize the larger critical (epistemological, metaphysical) aims of prosodists such as Tsur, Smith, Wesling and Meschonnic, who have found these demonstrations unsatisfying and, in their dissatisfaction, have sought broader theoretical contexts in which to place discussions of poetic rhythm. Even if we grant the many functions of meter, even if we continue to define poetry, as the tradition often has, as an inherently rhythmical (or 'musical') discourse, we must agree with critics such as Wesling and Meschonnic that an exclusively metrical defence of prosodic analysis inevitably peripheralizes the discussion of rhythm within a theory of poetic experience as a whole. As the most 'regular', flat, physically controlled and conventionally regulated component of rhythm, meter achieves its aesthetic ends by a somewhat polarized combination of highly general and highly local stylistic gestures. And even in these functions it is often heavily dependent on its interactions with phrasing to achieve its most salient effects.

Contrary to the tradition, I have argued that meter does not *create* phrasal expressiveness. Rather, with its pervasive presence, meter frames, intensifies, highlights and, by opposing, constrains the shapes and times inherent in the phrasing, shapes and times that would achieve a largely similar, albeit less effective and engaging, expressiveness without this metrical control. In fact, many metrical poems use meter as a relatively submerged expressive background, and as poetic practice for the last hundred years has demonstrated, poems can achieve astonishing rhythmic powers even though they dispense with meter altogether. In the normal case, rhythmic evaluation in critical response is rarely metrical in focus. Doggerel is not metrically regular or derivative verse; it is verse that is phrasally regular or derivative. Poets who write metrical verse rarely invent new meters. They invent new ways of moving phrasing through a historically recognizable meter. To reinvoke Frost's famous tennis analogy, meter in poetry is a type of rhythmical net that defines and constrains what rhythmical shots succeed and fail in the rhythmical game of poetry. But like spectators at a tennis match, we miss much, too much, if we focus more attention on the constraining net than on the nature of the rhythmic shots themselves, the global strategies of the rhythmical players, and the unfolding of those strategies in the quality of particular shot selections and executions.

On the other hand, in valuing this global rhythmic action and searching out its formal sources, I have chosen not to follow the theoretical path of prosodists such as Wesling, Tsur and Meschonnic. In developing the theory I present here, I have argued for a strict delimitation of prosodic study and have resisted the inclusion within prosodic analysis proper of the enormous cornucopia of experiential phenomena that constitutes poetic experience in its totality (i.e. 'style', 'voice', etc.). I have given *rhythm* a very broad definition, but I have argued that the experiential phenomena that are included within this definition are related in principled ways and that the theoretical coherence, if not the very possibility, of productive prosodic analysis depends on maintaining this strict delimitation. To return to Frost's metaphor, I have tried to reposition the metrical net within the larger dramatic action of the rhythmic game as a whole. The question we must now confront is: What is the function of this larger theory of rhythm within *its* larger context (i.e. poetic experience in general)?

Like the theory of verse rhythm I have developed, the stand I would like to take on this issue is largely borrowed from music theory and, to my knowledge, has been expressed most succinctly and eloquently (although certainly not originally) by Lawrence Kramer (1984) in the introduction to his study of the relations between music and poetry from the Romantics to the present. Although I wonder whether Kramer's analyses carry forward and illustrate his theorizing, I find his formulation of this theoretical issue excellent and therefore I defer to his wordings in this concluding comment.

Kramer notices and laments that neither twentieth-century literary theory nor twentieth-century music theory has done much to foster an interdisciplinary approach to music and poetry. In fact, speaking in 1984 he claims that 'none exists' (4). Part of the difficulty, he notes, is the general misunderstanding about the semiotic structures of the two art forms, their characteristic ways of making signs. Historically, many have argued that music is exclusively formal/combinatory/syntactic in its semiotic organization, developing forms that 'relate parts of the work to each other alone' (5), but that poetry is exclusively mimetic/connotative/ semantic, 'look[ing] outward toward the world or inward toward the self . . . invest[ing] significance in realities or fictions outside the work of art' (5). Both with argument and with specific examples,

Kramer rejects this dichotomy, claiming that each art form contains both semiotic 'dimensions', although he notes that poetry tends to be more explicitly connotative and only more tacitly combinative while music tends to be the opposite.

More positively, Kramer notes that poetry and music are the two arts 'uniquely dependent on the immediate tangible organization of the flow of time' (4), the two arts 'most dependent on giving a tangible contour and a distinctive texture to the lived present' (7). Unlike the movement of narrative fiction, Kramer claims, the movement of both music and poetry becomes 'compelling', not by 'fastening value on the outcome of imaginary events but by enveloping the reader or listener in a kind of polyphony of periodic forms', by 'transforming time into form' (7) – or, as I would prefer to put it, creating time with form. In poetry and music, Kramer claims, passing time is 'concretized and perceptually enriched between a definite beginning and a definite ending' so that it becomes 'invest[ed] with certain forms of expectancy and desire' (8).

Kramer stresses the multidimensionality of this enriched musical–poetic time sense. To organize time this way, he claims, 'several forms of periodicity have to exist at once, from the immediate levels of pulse or phrase-structure – which realize the shaped flow sensuously – to the consummatory level of a whole musical movement or poetic unit' (9). Kramer notes the special significance of forms at mid and high levels. 'Our concrete experience of reading or listening,' he claims, 'generally attaches to a variety of intermediate-range levels of action' which 'in turn, find their context, their horizon of significance, in the highest level – the pattern of tension and resolution which spans the whole' (9).

Kramer also stresses the structural integrity of this musical–poetic time sense. While he claims that its components are necessarily heterogeneous, he notes that this heterogeneity 'does not at all depend on a blurring or running together' of various shapes but on 'an interweaving and overlapping of *presences*', a 'coalescence of distinctness', which, in its unfolding, 'is like a slightly distanced form of the consciousness of internal time by which . . . we become aware of our own egos' (8).

What Kramer describes in a general way is very close to the theory of verse rhythm that I have developed here – and Kramer himself goes on to call this poetic–musical time sense *structural rhythm*. I would claim that the creation of this poetic–musical time sense is the major function of rhythm in poetry, and, following Kramer as well, I would oppose this poetic–musical time sense to the narrative time sense created in most prose fiction and therefore oppose it also to the usual array of experiential ends granted to literature by most contemporary literary theories.

The major accomplishment of the hierarchical, componential and preferentially based theory of verse rhythm I have developed in this book is to give this broader critical claim an explicit form, one that overcomes the traditional 'objections' in the tradition that any prosodic theory that attempts to represent such matters must, of necessity, be too complex or too subjective. In fact, comparable to the methods of interpretation that have been developed to explore the experiential effects of more connotative dimensions of literary experience, the theory of verse rhythm I have developed here for the first time offers a relatively explicit method by which such complex temporal effects of poetry can be explored and articulated in principled ways by different readers with different rhythmic sensitivities and preferences. Therefore, it brings these broader critical aims of prosodic analysis for the first time within the larger realm of productive humanistic discussion.

NOTES

1. 1902: 93.
2. For a general overview of the goals and methods of cognitive science, see Stillings *et al.* and the references cited there. For a particular argument, with language, music and vision as illustrations, see Jackendoff 1987.

References

Abercrombie, D. (1964a) 'Syllable quantity and enclitics in English' in Abercrombie, D. *et al.* (eds) *In Honour of Daniel Jones*, Longman, 216–22

Abercrombie, D. (1964b) 'A phonetician's view of verse structure' in *Studies in Phonetics and Linguistics*, Longman 1973, 17–25

Abrams, R.F. (1983) 'The skewed harmonics of English verse feet' *Language and Style* **16**: 478–503

Allen, D. and Tallman, W. (eds) (1973) *The Poetics of the New American Poetry*, Grove Press, New York

Allen, G.W. (1935) *American Prosody*, American Book Co., New York

Aronoff, M. (1977) 'The treatment of juncture in American linguistics' in Aronoff, M. and Kean, M.-L. (eds) *Juncture*, Anma Libri, Saratoga CA, 29–36

Armstrong, L.E. and Ward, I.C. (1926) *Handbook of English Intonation*, Teubner, Leipzig and Berlin

Attridge, D. (1982) *The Rhythms of English Poetry*, Longman

Attridge, D. (1987a) ' "Damn with faint praise": double offbeat demotion' *Eidos* **4**.1: 3–6

Attridge, D. (1987b) 'Poetry unbound? Observations on free verse' *Proceedings of the British Academy* **73**: 353–74

Attridge, D. (1988) 'Moving words', unpublished talk for Australian Broadcasting Company

Attridge, D. (1989) 'Linguistic theory and literary criticism: "The Rhythms of English Poetry" revisited' in Kiparsky, P. and Youmans, G. (eds), 183–99

Bailey, J. (1975) *Toward a Statistical Analysis of English Verse: The Iambic Tetrameter of Ten Poets*, Peter de Ridder Press, Lisse

Bardovi-Harlig, K. (1986) *Pragmatic Determinants of English Sentence Stress*, Indiana University Linguistics Club, Bloomington

Barnes, M. and Esau, H. (1979) 'Gilding the lapses in a theory of metrics' *Poetics* **6**: 489–90

Barry, Sister M.M. (1969) *An Analysis of the Prosodic Structure of Selected Poems of T.S. Eliot*, Catholic University of America Press, Washington DC

Barthes, R. (1974) *S/Z*, trans. R. Miller, Hill and Wang, New York

Baum, P.F. (1922) *The Principles of English Versification*, Harvard University Press, Cambridge MA

Baum, P.F. (1952) *. . . the other harmony of prose . . .* Duke University Press, Durham

Beardsley, M. (1972) 'Verse and music' in Wimsatt, W.K. (ed.) *Versification*, 238–52

de Beaugrande, R. and Dressler, W. (1981) *Introduction to Text Linguistics*, Longman

Beaver, J.C. (1968a) 'A grammar of prosody' *College English* **29**: 310–21

Beaver, J.C. (1968b) 'Progress and problems in generative metrics' in Darden, J.C. *et al.* (eds) *Papers from the Fourth Regional Meeting of the Chicago Linguistic Society*, University of Chicago Department of Linguistics, Chicago, 146–55

Beaver, J.C. (1969) 'Contrastive stress and metered verse' *Language and Style* **2**: 257–71

Beaver, J.C. (1970) 'A stress swapping rule in English verse' in *Papers from the Sixth Regional Meeting of the Chicago Linguistic Society*, University of Chicago Department of Linguistics, Chicago IL, 447–53

Beaver, J.C. (1971) 'The rules of stress in English verse' *Language* **47**: 586–614

Beaver, J.C. (1973) 'A stress problem in English prosody' *Linguistics* **95**: 5–12

Beaver, J.C. (1974) 'Generative metrics' in Preminger (ed.), 931–3

Benveniste, E. (1971) 'The notion of "rhythm" in its linguistic expression' in *Problems in General Linguistics*, trans. M.E. Meek, University of Miami Press, Coral Gables

Berg, Sister M.G. (1962) *The Prosodic Structure of Robert Bridges' 'Neo-Miltonic Syllabics'*, Catholic University of America Press, Washington DC

Bernhart, A.W. (1974) 'Complexity and metricality' *Poetics* **12**: 113–41

Bernstein, L. (1976) *The Unanswered Question*, Harvard University Press, Cambridge MA

Berry, E. (1981a) 'Syntactical and metrical structures in the poetry of William Carlos Williams', unpublished dissertation, University of Toronto

Berry, E. (1981b) 'Williams' development of a new prosodic form – not the "variable foot," but the sight-stanza' *William Carlos Williams Review* **8**, No. 2: 21–30

Berry, E. (1985) 'Arbitrary form in poetry and the poetic function of language' in Youmans, G. and Lance, D.M. (eds) *In Memory of Roman Jakobson: Papers from the 1984 MALC*, Linguistics Area Program, Columbia OH, 121–34

Berry, E. (forthcoming a) 'William Carlos Williams' triadic-line verse: an analysis of its prosody' *Journal of Modern Literature*

Berry, E. (forthcoming b) 'Visual form' in *Princeton Encyclopedia of Poetry and Poetics*, 3rd edn
Bing, J. (1979) 'Aspects of English prosody' unpublished dissertation, University of Massachusetts at Amherst
Birch, D. and O'Toole, M. (eds) (1988) *Functions of Style*, Pinter
Bjorklund, B. (1985) 'Review of Attridge (1982)' *Journal of English and Germanic Philology* **84**: 113–16
Bolinger, D. (1952) 'Linear modification' in Bolinger 1965: 279–307
Bolinger, D. (1957) 'Maneuvering for accent and position' in Bolinger 1965: 309–15
Bolinger, D. (1958) 'Stress and information' in Bolinger 1965: 67–83
Bolinger, D. (1965) *Forms of English*, Harvard University Press, Cambridge MA
Bolinger, D. (1972b) 'Accent is predictable (if you're a mind-reader)' *Language* **37**: 633–43
Bolinger, D. (1986) *Intonation and its Parts*, Stanford University Press, Stanford
Bollobas, E. (1986) *Tradition and Innovation in American Free Verse: Whitman to Duncan*, Akademiai Kiado, Budapest
Brazil, D. (1975) *Discourse Intonation*, University of Birmingham Department of English
Brazil, D. (1985) *The Communicative Value of Intonation in English*, English Language Research
Bridges, R. (1921) *Milton's Prosody*, Oxford University Press
Brogan, T.V.F. (1981) *English Versification, 1570–1980*, Johns Hopkins University Press, Baltimore MD
Brooks, C. and Warren, R.P. (1976) *Understanding Poetry*, 4th edn, Holt Rinehart and Winston, New York
Brown, E.K. (1950) *Rhythm in the Novel*, University of Toronto Press, Toronto
Byers, P. (1977) 'The contribution of intonation to the rhythm and melody of non-metrical English poetry', unpublished doctoral dissertation, University of Wisconsin–Milwaukee
Byers, P. (1979) 'A formula for poetic intonation' *Poetics* **8**: 367–80
Byers, P. (1980) 'Intonation prediction and the sound of poetry' *Language and Style* **13**: 3–14
Byers, P. (1983) 'The auditory reality of the verse line' *Style* **17**: 27–36
Cable, T. (1972) 'Timers, stressers, and linguists: contention and compromise' *Modern Language Quarterly* **33**: 227–39
Cable, T. (1976) 'Recent development in metrics' *Style* **10**: 313–28
Chafe, W.L. (1976) 'Givenness, contrastiveness, definiteness, subjects, topics, and point of view' in Li, C.N. (ed.) *Subject and Topic*, Academic Press, New York, 27–55
Chatman, S. (1965) *A Theory of Meter*, Mouton, The Hague

Chatman, S. and Levin, S.R. (1967) *Essays on the Language of Literature*, Houghton Mifflin, Boston

Chisholm, D. (1977) 'Generative prosody and English verse' *Poetics* **6**: 111–54

Chomsky, N. and Halle, M. (1968) *The Sound Pattern of English*, Harper & Row, New York

Christensen, F. and B. (1978) *Notes Toward a New Rhetoric: 9 Essays for Teachers*, 2nd edn, Harper & Row, New York

Ciardi, J. and Williams, M. (1975) *How Does a Poem Mean?*, 2nd edn, Houghton Mifflin, Boston MA

Clark, H.H. and E.V. (1977) *Psychology and Language*, Harcourt Brace Jovanovich, New York

Cobb, C.W. (1913) 'A scientific basis for metrics' *Modern Language Notes* **28**: 142–5

Cobb, C.W. (1917) 'A further study of the heroic tetrameter' *Modern Philology* **14**: 559–67

Cook, N. (1987) *A Guide to Musical Analysis*, George Braziller, New York

Cooper, G. and Meyer, L.B. (1960) *The Rhythmic Structure of Music*, University of Chicago Press, Chicago

Corbett, E.P.J. (1971) *Classical Rhetoric for the Modern Student*, 2nd edn, Oxford University Press, New York

Couper-Kuhlen, H.L. (1986) *An Introduction to English Prosody*, Edward Arnold

Creek, H.L. (1920) 'Rising and falling rhythm in English verse' *PMLA* **35**: 76–90

Croll, M. (1919) 'The cadence of English oratorical prose' in Patrick, J.M. and Evans, R.O. (eds) *Style, Rhetoric, and Rhythm: Essays by Morris W. Croll*, Princeton University Press, Princeton 1966, 303–55

Croll, M. (1929) 'The rhythm of English verse' in Patrick and Evans *op. cit.*, 365–429

Cruttenden, A. (1986) *Intonation*, Cambridge University Press

Crystal, D. (1969) *Prosodic Systems and Intonation in English*, Cambridge University Press

Crystal, D. (1975a) *The English Tone of Voice*, Edward Arnold

Crystal, D. (1975b) 'Intonation and metrical theory' in Crystal 1975a, 105–24

Crystal, D. and Davy, D. (1969) *Investigating English Style*, Longman

Crystal, D. and Davy, D. (1975) *Advanced Conversational English*, Longman

Crystal, D. and Quirk, R. (1964) *Systems of Prosodic and Paralinguistic Features in English*, Mouton, The Hague

Culler, J. (1975) *Structuralist Poetics: Structuralism, Linguistics, and the Study of Literature*, Cornell University Press, Ithaca

Cummings, D.W. (1965) 'Toward a theory of prosodic analysis for English metrical verse' unpublished dissertation, University of Washington
Cummings, D.W. and Herum, J. (1967) 'Metrical boundaries and rhythm-phrases', *Modern Language Quarterly* **28**: 405–12
Cummings, M. and Simmons, R. (1983) *The Language of Literature*, Pergamon
Cureton, R. (1985a) 'Rhythm: a multilevel analysis' *Style* **19**: 242–57
Cureton, R. (1985b) 'Review of Attridge (1982)' *American Speech* **60**: 157–61
Cureton, R. (1986a) 'Traditional scansion: myths and muddles' *Journal of Literary Semantics* **15**: 171–208
Cureton, R. (1986b) 'Visual form in e.e. Cummings' *No Thanks*' *Word & Image* **2**: 245–77
Cureton, R. (1986c) 'Review of Cushman (1985)' *William Carlos Williams Review* **12**: 34–52
Cushman, S. (1985) *William Carlos Williams and the Meanings of Measure*, Yale University Press, New Haven CT
Devine, A.M. and Stephens, L.D. (1975) 'The abstractness of metrical patterns: generative metrics and explicit traditional metrics' *Poetics* **4**: 411–30
Devine, A.M. and Stephens, L.D. (1978) 'The Greek appositives: toward a linguistically adequate definition of caesura and bridge' *Classical Philology* **73**: 314–28
Devine, A.M. and Stephens, L.D. (1981) 'A new aspect of the evolution of the trimeter in Euripedes' *Transactions of the American Philosophical Association* **111**: 43–64
Devine, A.M. and Stephens, L.D. (1983) 'Semantics, syntax, and phonological organization in Greek: aspects of the theory of metrical bridges' *Classical Philology* **78**: 1–25
Dewey, J. (1934) *Art as Experience*, Paragon, New York
Dillon, G. (1977) 'Kames and Kiparsky on syntactic boundaries' *Language and Style* **10**: 16–22
Dougherty, A. (1973) *A Study of the Rhythmic Structure of the Verse of William Butler Yeats*, Mouton, The Hague
Easthope, A. (1983) 'Review of Attridge (1982)' *Language and Style* **16**: 244–6
Eliot, T.S. (1965) 'Reflections on *vers libre*' in *To Criticize the Critic*, Faber and Faber, 183–9
Epstein, E.L. and Hawkes, T. (1959) *Linguistics and English Prosody*, Studies in Linguistics Occasional Papers, No. 7, University of Buffalo Department of Anthropology and Linguistics, Buffalo NY
Erlich, V. (1981) *Russian Formalism: History–Doctrine*, 3rd edn, Yale University Press, New Haven CT

Faure, G. (1970) *Les Eléments du rythme poétique en anglais moderne*, Mouton, The Hague

Firbas, J. (1959) 'Thoughts on the communicative function of the verb in English, German and Czech' *Brno Studies in English* **1**: 39–61

Firbas, J. (1961) 'On the communicative value of the modern English finite verb' *Brno Studies in English* **3**: 79–101

Firbas, J. (1964) 'On defining theme in functional sentence perspective' *Travaux linguistiques de Prague* **1**: 267–80

Firbas, J. (1965) 'A note on transition proper in functional sentence perspective' *Philogica Pragensia* **8**: 170–6

Firbas, J. (1966) 'Non-thematic subjects in contemporary English' *Travaux linguistiques de Prague* **2**: 239–54

Firbas, J. (1968) 'On the prosodic features of the modern English finite verb as means of functional sentence perspective' *Brno Studies in English* **7**: 11–48

Firbas, J. (1969) 'On the prosodic features of the modern English finite verb–object combination as means of functional sentence perspective' *Brno Studies in English* **8**: 49–59

Firbas, J. (1972) 'On the interplay of prosodic and non-prosodic means of functional sentence perspective' in Fried, V. (ed.) *The Prague School of Linguistics and Language Teaching*, Oxford University Press, 77–94

Firbas, J. (1974) 'Some aspects of the Czechoslovak approach to problems of functional sentence perspective' in Danes, F. (ed.), 11–41

Firbas, J. (1975a) 'On "existence/appearance on the scene" in functional sentence perspective' *Prague Studies in English* **16**: 47–69

Firbas, J. (1975b) 'On the thematic and non-thematic section of the sentence' in Ringbom, H. (ed.) *Style and Text*, Sprakfolaget Skriptor AB and Aba Akademi, Stockholm, 317–34

Firbas, J. (1976) 'A study in the functional perspective of the English and the Slavonic interrogative sentence' *Brno Studies in English* **12**: 9–63

Firbas, J. (1979) 'A functional view of "ordo naturalis" ' *Brno Studies in English* **13**: 29–59

Forster, E.M. (1927) *Aspects of the Novel*, Harcourt Brace Jovanovich, New York

Forte, A. and Gilbert, S. (1982) *Introduction to Schenkerian Analysis*, Norton

Fowler, R. (ed.) (1966a) *Essays on Style and Language*, Routledge & Kegan Paul

Fowler, R. (1966b) ' "Prose rhythm" and metre' in Fowler (ed.), 82–99

Fowler, R. (1966c) 'Structural metrics' in Fowler (ed.), 124–40

Fraisse, P. (1963) *The Psychology of Time*, trans. J. Leith, Harper & Row

Frank, R. and Sayre, H. (eds) (1988) *The Line in Postmodern Poetry*, University of Illinois Press, Urbana IL

Freeman, D.C. (1968) 'On the primes of metrical style' *Language and Style* **1**: 63–101

Freeman, D.C. (1969) 'Metrical position constituency and generative metrics' *Language and Style* **2**: 195–206

Freeman, D.C. (1972) 'Current trends in metrics' in Kachru, B.B. and Stahlke, H.F.W. (eds) *Current Trends in Stylistics*, Linguistic Research Inc., Edmonton, 67–80

Frost, R. (1949) 'The figure a poem makes' in Scully, J. (ed.), *Modern Poetics*, McGraw-Hill, New York 1965, 55–8

Fussell, P. (1979) *Poetic Meter and Poetic Form*, revised edn, Random House, New York

Gall, S.M. (1979) 'Pound and the modern melic tradition: towards a demystification of "absolute rhythm" ' *Paideuma* **8**: 35–47

Gasparov, M.L. (1987) 'A probability model of verse (English, Latin, French, Italian, Spanish, Portuguese)' *Style* **21**: 322–58

Giegerich, H.J. (1985) *Metrical Phonology and Phonological Structure: German and English*, Cambridge University Press

Gil, D. (1980) 'A note on quantifier scope, coreferentiality, and prosodic structure' *Journal of Literary Semantics* **9**: 30–3

Gil, D. (1985) 'What does grammar include?' *Theoretical Linguistics* **12**: 165–72

Gil, D. (1986) 'A prosodic typology of language' *Folia Linguistica* **20**: 165–231

Gil, D. (1987) 'On the scope of grammatical theory' in Modgil, S. and C. (eds) *Noam Chomsky, Nothing Wrong with Being Wrong, Consensus and Controversy*, Farmer, Barcombe, 119–41

Gil, D. (forthcoming) 'The Muwassah: artistic convention or cognitive universal?' in Somekh, S. (ed.) *Studies in Classical Arabic Poetics and Poetry*, Brill, Leiden

Gil, D. and Shoshani, R. (1984a) 'On the scope of prosodic theory' in Dressler, W.U., Pfeiffer, O.E. and Rennison, J.R. (eds) *Discussion Papers, Fifth International Phonology Meeting, June 25–28, 1984, Eisenstadt, Austria*, *Wiener Linguistische Gazette* Supplement/Beihelf **3**: 78–82

Gil, D. and Shoshani, R. (1984b) 'On the nature of prosodic competence', unpublished manuscript, Tel Aviv University

Gil, D. and Shoshani, R. (forthcoming) *Aspects of Prosodic Theory: Studies in Biblical Hebrew Poetry*, SUNY Press, Albany

Gleason, H.A. (1961) *An Introduction to Descriptive Linguistics*, revised edn, Holt Rinehart & Winston, New York

Golomb, H. (1979) *Enjambment in Poetry: Language and Verse in Interaction*, Porter Institute for Poetics and Semiotics, Tel Aviv University

Grammont, M. (1930) *Petit traité de versification française*, 7th edn, Armond Colin, Paris
Gray, G.B. (1972) *The Forms of Hebrew Poetry*, Ktav, New York
Gross, H. (1964) *Sound and Form in Modern Poetry*, University of Michigan Press, Ann Arbor
Gross, H. (ed.) (1979) *The Structure of Verse*, 2nd edn, The Ecco Press, New York
Guest, E. (1882) *A History of English Rhythms*, George Bell & Sons
Halle, M. (1970) 'On meter and prosody' in Bierwisch, M. and Heidolph, K.E. (eds) *Progress in Linguistics*, Mouton, The Hague, 64–80
Halle, M. and Keyser, S.J. (1966) 'Chaucer and the study of prosody' *College English* **28**: 187–219
Halle, M. and Keyser, S.J. (1971a) *English Stress: Its Form, its Growth, its Role in Verse*, Harper & Row, New York
Halle, M. and Keyser, S.J. (1971b) 'Illustration and defense of a theory of the iambic pentameter' *College English* **33**: 154–76
Halle, M. and Keyser, S.J. (1972) 'The iambic pentameter' in Wimsatt, W.K. (ed.) 217–37
Halle, M. and Vernaud, J.-R. (1987) *An Essay on Stress*, MIT Press, Cambridge
Halliday, M.A.K. (1963) 'The tones of English' *Archivum Linguisticum* **15**: 1–28
Halliday, M.A.K. (1966) 'Intonation systems in English' in MacIntosh, A. and Halliday, M.A.K. (eds) *Patterns of Language: Papers in General, Descriptive and Applied Linguistics*, Longman, 111–33
Halliday, M.A.K. (1967) *Intonation and Grammar in British English*, Mouton, The Hague
Halliday, M.A.K. (1970) *A Course in Spoken English: Intonation*, Oxford University Press
Halliday, M.A.K. (1985) *An Introduction to Functional Grammar*, Edward Arnold
Halliday, M.A.K. and Hasan, R. (1976) *Cohesion in English*, Longman
Hamer, E. (1930) *The Metres of English Poetry*, Macmillan, New York
Hanford, J.H. (1944) *A Milton Handbook*, 3rd edn, F.S. Crofts, New York
Hardison, O.B. Jr. (1989) *Prosody and Purpose in the English Renaissance*, Johns Hopkins University Press, Baltimore
Hartman, C.O. (1980) *Free Verse: An Essay on Prosody*, Princeton University Press
Hasan, R. (1985) *Linguistics, Language, and Verbal Art*, Deakin University Press, Victoria
Hascall, D.L. (1971) 'Trochaic meter', *College English* **33**: 217–26
Hascall, D.L. (1974) 'Triple meter in English verse', *Poetics* **12**: 49–71
Hayes, B. (1980/1985) *A Metrical Theory of Stress Rules*, Garland, New York

Hayes, B. (1984a) 'The phonology of rhythm in English' *Linguistic Inquiry* **15**: 33–74
Hayes, B. (1984b) 'Review of Attridge (1982)' *Language* **60**: 914–23
Hayes, B. (1988) 'Metrics and phonological theory' in Newmeyer, F. (ed.) *Cambridge Survey of Linguistics*, vol. 2, 221–49, Cambridge University Press
Hayes, B. (1989) 'The prosodic hierarchy in meter' in Kiparsky, P. and Youmans, G. (eds), 201–60
Heller, J.R. (1977) 'Enjambment as a metrical force in Romantic conversation poems' *Poetics* **6**: 15–26
Heller, J.R. (1978) 'Syntactic juncture and the Halle–Keyser theory of iambic pentameter' *Language and Style* **11**: 164–7
Hewitt, E.K. (1965) 'Structure and meaning in T.S. Eliot's *Ash Wednesday*' *Anglia* **83**: 426–50
Hill, A.A. (1958) *Introduction to Linguistic Structures: From Sound to Sentence in English*, Harcourt Brace & World, New York
Hockett, C.F. (1958) *A Course in Modern Linguistics*, Macmillan, New York
Hogg. R. and McCully, C.B. (1987) *Metrical Phonology: A Coursebook*, Cambridge University Press
Hollander, J. (1981) *Rhyme's Reason*, Yale University Press, New Haven CT
Hollander, J. (1985) *Vision and Resonance: Two Senses of Poetic Form*, 2nd edn, Yale University Press, New Haven CT
Hrushovski, B. (1960) 'On free rhythms in modern poetry' in Sebeok, T. (ed.), 173–90
Ihwe, J. (1975) 'On the foundations of "generative metrics" ' *Poetics* **4**: 367–400
Jackendoff, R. (1977) 'Review of Bernstein (1977)' *Language* **53**: 883–94
Jackendoff, R. (1987) *Consciousness and the Computational Mind*, MIT Press, Cambridge
Jackendoff, R. (1989) 'A comparison of rhythmic structures in music and language' in Kiparsky, P. and Youmans, G. (eds), 15–44
Jackendoff, R. and Lerdahl, F. (1980) *A Deep Parallel between Music and Language*, Indiana University Linguistics Club, Bloomington IN
Jackendoff, R. and Lerdahl, F. (1982) 'A grammatical parallel between music and language' in Clynes, M. (ed.) *Music, Mind, and Brain*, Plenum, New York, 83–177
Jakobson, R. (1960) 'Linguistics and poetics' in Jakobson 1987: 62–94
Jakobson, R. (1961) 'Poetry of grammar and grammar of poetry' in Jakobson 1987: 121–44
Jakobson, R. (1964) 'The grammatical texture of a sonnet from Sir Philip Sidney's *Arcadia*' in Jakobson 1981: 275–83

Jakobson, R. (1966a) 'Grammatical parallelism and the Russian facet' in Jakobson 1987: 145–79

Jakobson, R. (1966b) *Selected Writings IV: Slavic Epic Studies*, Mouton, The Hague

Jakobson, R. (1970a) 'Subliminal verbal patterning in poetry' in Jakobson 1987: 250–61

Jakobson, R. (1970b) 'On the verbal art of William Blake and other poet–painters' in Jakobson 1987: 479–503

Jakobson, R. (1970c) 'The modular design of Chinese regulated verse' in Jakobson 1979b: 433–85

Jakobson, R. (1979a) 'Retrospect' in Jakobson 1979b: 569–601

Jakobson, R. (1979b) *Selected Writings V: On verse, its Masters and Explorers*, Mouton, The Hague

Jakobson, R. (1981a) 'Retrospect' in Jakobson 1981b: 767–89

Jakobson, R. (1981b) *Selected Writings III: Poetry of Grammar and Grammar of Poetry*, Mouton, The Hague

Jakobson, R. (1987) *Language in Literature*, Harvard University Press, Cambridge MA

Jakobson, R. and Jones, L.G. (1970) 'Shakespeare's verbal art in "Th'Expence of Spirit" ' in Jakobson 1987: 198–215

Jakobson, R. and Lévi-Strauss, C. (1962) 'Charles Baudelaire's "Les Chats" ' in Jakobson 1987: 180–97

Jakobson, R. and Lotz, J. (1941) 'Axioms of a versification system exemplified by the Mordvinian folksong' in Jakobson 1979b: 160–6

Jakobson, R. and Rudy, S. (1977) 'Yeats' "Sorrow of Love" through the years' in Jakobson 1987: 216–49

Jannacone, P. (1973) *Walt Whitman's Poetry and the Evolution of Rhythmic Forms in Walt Whitman's Thought and Art*, trans. P. Mitilineos, National Cash Register Company, Washington DC

Jason, P.K. (1978) 'Stanzas and anti-stanzas' *College English* **39**: 738–44

Jesperson, O. (1900) 'Notes on metre' in Gross (ed.), 105–28

Jones, D. (1909) *Intonation Curves*, Teubner, Leipzig and Berlin

Jones, G.T. (1974) *Music Theory*, Harper & Row, New York

Jorgens, E.B. (1982) *The Well-tun'd Word*, University of Minnesota Press, Minneapolis

Kahn, D. (1976) *Syllable-based Generalizations in English Phonology*, Indiana University Linguistics Club, Bloomington IN

Kennedy, X.J. (1982) *An Introduction to Poetry*, 5th edn, Little Brown, Boston MA

Keyser, S.J. (1969) 'The linguistic basis of English prosody' in Reibel, D. and Shane, S. (eds) *Modern Studies in English*, Prentice-Hall, Englewood Cliffs NJ, 379–94

Kingdon, R. (1958) *Groundwork of English Intonation*, Longman

Kiparsky, P. (1975) 'Stress, syntax, and meter' *Language* **51**: 576–616

Kiparsky, P. (1977) 'The rhythmic structure of English verse' *Linguistic Inquiry* **8**: 189–247

Kiparsky, P. (1989) 'Sprung rhythm' in Kiparsky, P. and Youmans, G. (eds), 305–40

Kiparsky, P. and Youmans, G. (eds) (1989) *Phonetics and Phonology I: Rhythm and Meter*, MIT Press, Cambridge MA

Klein, W. (1974) 'Critical remarks on generative metrics' *Poetics* **12**: 29–48

Koelb, C. (1979) 'The iambic pentameter revisited' *Neophilologus* **63**: 321–9

Kopczynska, Z. and Pszczolowska, L. (1960) 'Le Rôle de l'intonation dans la versification' in Davie, D. *et al.* (eds), 215–24

Kramer, L. (1984) *Music and Poetry: The Nineteenth Century and After*, University of California Press, Berkeley CA

Krieger, M. (1988) *Words about Words about Words: Theory, Criticism, and the Literary Text*, Johns Hopkins University Press, Baltimore

Kugel, J.L. (1981) *The Idea of Biblical Poetry: Parallelism and its History*, Yale University Press, New Haven CT

Ladd, D.R. (1980) *The Structure of Intonational Meaning*, Indiana University Press, Bloomington IN

La Drière, J.C. (1943) 'Prose rhythm' in Shipley, J.T. (ed.) *Dictionary of World Literature*, Philosophical Library, New York

La Drière, J.C. (1974) 'Prosody' in Preminger, A. (ed.), 669–77

Langworthy, C.A. (1928) 'Verse-sentence patterns in English poetry' *Philological Quarterly* **7**: 283–98

Lanier, S. (1880) *The Science of English Verse*, Scribner's, New York

Leech, G.N. (1969) *A Linguistic Guide to English Poetry*, Longman

Leech, G.N. and Short, M.H. (1981) *Style in Fiction*, Longman

Lerdahl, F. and Jackendoff, R. (1983) *A Generative Theory of Tonal Music*, MIT Press, Cambridge MA

Levy, J. (1966) 'The meanings of form and the forms of meaning' in *Poetics 2*, Polish Scientific Publishers, Warsaw

Levy, K. (1983) *Music: A Listener's Introduction*, Harper & Row, New York

Liberman, M. (1975) 'The intonational system of English', doctoral dissertation, MIT

Liberman, M. and Prince, A. (1977) 'On stress and linguistic rhythm' *Linguistic Inquiry* **8**: 249–336

Liddell, M. (1902) *An Introduction to the Scientific Study of English Poetry*, Doubleday, New York

Lieberman, M. and P. (1972) 'The breath-group as a constructive element in Charles Olson's "projective verse" ' in *7th International Congress of the Phonetic Sciences*, University of Montreal, 1971, Mouton, The Hague, 949–56

Lindberg-Seyersted, B. (1968) *The Voice of the Poet: Aspects of Style in the Poetry of Emily Dickinson*, Harvard University Press, Cambridge MA

Linville, S.E. (1984) 'Enjambment and the dialectics of line form in Donne's *Holy Sonnets*' *Style* **18**: 64–82

Lowth. R. (1753) *Lectures on the Sacred Poetry of the Hebrews*, trans. G. Gregory, 4th edn, 1839, Thomas Tegg

Luecke, J. (1983) 'Toward a prosody of free verse' *Southwest Cultural Heritage* **3**: 65–73

MacDougall, R. (1902) 'Rhythm, time and number', *American Journal of Psychology* **13**: 88–97

Magnuson, K. (1974) 'Rules and observations in prosody: positional level and base' *Poetics* **12**: 143–54

Magnuson, K. and Ryder, F.G. (1970) 'The study of English prosody: an alternative proposal' *College English* **31**: 789–820

Magnuson, K. and Ryder, F.G. (1971) 'Second thoughts on English prosody' *College English* **33**: 198–216

Malof, J. (1970) *A Manual of English Meters*, Indiana University Press, Bloomington IN

Marr, D. (1982) *Vision*, W.H. Freeman, New York

Martin, H.R. and Pike, K. (1974) 'Analysis of the vocal performance of a poem: a classification of intonational features' *Language and Style* **7**: 209–18

McCreless, P. (1988) 'Roland Barthes's *S/Z* from a musical point of view', *In Theory Only* **10.7**: 1–29

Meijer, J.M. (1973) 'Verbal art as interference between a cognitive and an aesthetic structure' in Van Der Eng, J. and Grygar, M. (eds) *Structure of Texts and Semiotics of Culture*, Mouton, The Hague, 313–48

Meschonnic, H. (1982) *Critique du rythme: anthropologie historique du langage*, Verdier, Paris

Meyer, L.B. (1956) *Emotion and Meaning in Music*, University of Chicago Press, Chicago IL

Meyer, L.B. (1967) *Music, the Arts, and Ideas*, University of Chicago Press, Chicago IL

Meyer, L.B. (1973) *Explaining Music*, University of Chicago Press, Chicago IL

Mitchell, R. (1969) 'A prosody for Whitman?' *PMLA* **84**: 1606–12

Mitchell, R. (1970) 'Toward a system of grammatical scansion', *Language and Style* **3**: 3–28

Mukarovsky, J. (1933) 'Intonation as the basic factor of poetic rhythm' in Mukarovsky 1977, 116–33

Mukarovsky, J. (1977) *The Word and Verbal Art*, Burbank, J. and Steiner, P. (trans. and eds), Yale University Press, New Haven CT

Narmour, E. (1977) *Beyond Schenkerism*, University of Chicago Press, Chicago IL

Nash, W. (1980) *Designs in Prose*, Longman

Nespor, M. and Vogel, I. (1982) 'Prosodic domains of external sandhi rules' in van der Hulst, H. and Smith, N. (eds) *The Structure of Phonological Representations, Part I*, Foris, Dordrecht, 225–65

Nespor, M. and Vogel, I. (1983) 'Prosodic structure above the word' in Cutler, A. and Ladd, D.R. (eds) *Prosody: Models and Measurements*, Springer-Verlag, Berlin, 123–40

Nespor, M. and Vogel, I. (1986) *Prosodic Phonology*, Foris, Dordrecht

Nist, J. (1964) 'The word-group cadence: basis of English metrics' *Linguistics* 6: 73–82

O'Connor, J.D. and Arnold, G.F. (1961) *Intonation of Colloquial English*, Longman

Olson, C. (1950) 'Projective verse' in Allen and Tallman (eds), 147–58

Oras, A. (1960) *Pause Patterns in Elizabethan and Jacobean Drama*, University of Florida Monographs 3, University of Florida Press, Gainesville FL

Pace, G.B. (1961) 'The two domains: meter and rhythm' *PMLA* 76: 413–19

Palmer, H.E. (1922) *English Intonation, with Systematic Exercises*, Heffer

Patmore, C. (1856) 'Essay on English metrical law' in *Poems*, vol. 2, George Bell, 1894, 217–65

Pattison, B. (1948) *Music and Poetry of the English Renaissance*, Methuen

Perloff, M. (1973) 'Charles Olson and the "inferior predecessors": "projective verse" revisited' *ELH* 40: 285–306

Perloff, M. (1981) 'The linear fallacy' *Georgia Review* 35: 855–68

Perloff, M. (1985) *The Dance of the Intellect: Studies in the Poetry of the Pound Tradition*, Cambridge University Press

Perrine, L. (1982) *Sound and Sense*, 6th edn, Harcourt Brace Jovanovich, New York

Pierrehumbert, J.B. (1987) *The Phonology and Phonetics of English Intonation*, Indiana University Linguistics Club, Bloomington IN

Pike, K. (1947) *The Intonation of American English*, University of Michigan Press, Ann Arbor

Pike, K. (1959) 'Language as particle, wave, and field' *The Texas Quarterly* 2: 37–54

Pike, K. (1962) 'Practical phonetics of rhythm waves' *Phonetica* 8: 9–30

Pike, K. (1967) *Language in Relation to a Unified Theory of the Structure of Human Behavior*, 2nd edn, Mouton, The Hague

Pike, K. (1982a) *Linguistic Concepts: An Introduction to Tagmemics*, University of Nebraska Press, Lincoln NE

Pike, K. (1982b) 'Phonological hierarchy in a four-cell tagmemic representation from discourse to phoneme class' *Forum Linguisticum* 7: 65–91

Pike, K. and E. (1983) *Text and Tagmeme*, Ablex, Norwood NJ

Piper, W.B. (1969) *The Heroic Couplet*, Case Western Reserve University Press, Cleveland

Prall, D.W. (1936) *Aesthetic Analysis*, Thomas Crowell, New York
Preminger, A. (ed.) (1974) *Princeton Encyclopedia of Poetry and Poetics*, Princeton University Press
Prince, A. (1983) 'Relating to the grid' *Linguistic Inquiry* **14**: 19–100
Proffitt, E. (1981) *Poetry: An Introduction and Anthology*, Houghton Mifflin, Boston MA
Quirk, R. (1968) *Essays on the English Language Medieval and Modern*, Indiana University Press, Bloomington IN
Quirk, R. et al. (1985) *A Comprehensive Grammar of the English Language*, Longman
Ramsey, P. (1968) 'Free verse: some steps toward definition' *Studies in Philology* **65**: 98–108
Ranta, J. (1976) 'Palindromes, poems, and geometric form' *Visible Language* **10**: 157–72
Ranta, J. (1978) 'Geometry, vision, and poetic form' *College English* **39**: 707–24
Riffaterre, M. (1977) 'Semantic overdetermination in poetry' *Poetics and the Theory of Literature* **2**: 1–19
Riffaterre, M. (1978) *Semiotics of Poetry*, Indiana University Press, Bloomington IN
Saintsbury, G. (1906–10) *A History of English Prosody from the Twelfth Century to the Present Day* (3 vols), Macmillan
Saintsbury, G. (1910) *Historical Manual of English Prosody*, Macmillan
Saintsbury, G. (1912) *A History of English Prose Rhythm*, Macmillan
Salzer, F. (1952) *Structural Hearing*, Dover, New York.
Sayre, H.M. (1983) *The Visual Text of William Carlos Williams*, University of Illinois Press, Urbana IL
Schenker, H. (1932/1969) *Five Graphic Music Analyses*, Dover, New York
Schenker, H. (1935/1979) *Free Composition*, Ernst Oster (trans. and ed.), Longman, New York
Scherr, B.P. (1986) *Russian Poetry: Meter, Rhythm, and Rhyme*, University of California Press
Schipper, J. (1910) *A History of English Versification*, Clarendon
Schubiger, M. (1935) *The Role of Intonation in Spoken English*, W. Heffner & Sons
Schubiger, M. (1958) *English Intonation*, Max Niemeyer Verlag, Tübingen
Scott, J.H. (1925) *Rhythmic Verse*, University of Iowa, Iowa City
Scott, J.H. (1926) *Rhythmic Prose*, University of Iowa, Iowa City
Scripture, E.W. (1902) *The Elements of Experimental Phonetics*, Charles Scribner's Sons, New York
Sebeok, T.A. (ed.) (1960) *Style in Language*, MIT Press, Cambridge MA
Selkirk, E.O. (1972) 'The phrase phonology of English and French' doctoral dissertation, MIT

Selkirk, E.O. (1980a) 'Prosodic domains in phonology: Sanskrit revisited' in Aronoff, M. and Kean, M.-L. (eds) *Juncture*, Anma Libri, Saratoga CA, 107–29

Selkirk, E.O. (1980b) 'The role of prosodic categories in English word stress' *Linguistic Inquiry* **11**: 563–605

Selkirk, E.O. (1981) 'On the nature of phonological representation' in Meyers, T., Laver, J. and Anderson, J. (eds) *The Cognitive Representation of Speech*, North-Holland, Amsterdam, 379–88

Selkirk, E. (1984) *Phonology and Syntax: The Relation between Sound and Structure*, MIT Press, Cambridge MA

Shapiro, K. and Beum, R. (1965) *A Prosody Handbook*, Harper & Row, New York

Shoshani, R. (1986) 'Prosodic structures in Jeremiah's poetry' *Folia Linguistica Historica* **7**: 167–206

Skeat, W.W. (1894) 'Versification' in *The Complete Works of Chaucer*, Clarendon, vol. 6, lxxxii–lcvii

Skeat, W.W. (1898) 'On the scansion of English poetry' *Transactions of the Philological Society*, 484–503

Smith, B.H. (1968) *Poetic Closure: A Study of How Poems End*, University of Chicago Press, Chicago IL

Smith, E. (1923) *The Principles of English Metre*, Oxford University Press

Smith, H.L. Jr (1959) 'Toward redefining English prosody' *Studies in Linguistics* **14**: 68–76

Standop, E. (1975) 'Metric theory gone astray: a critique of the Halle–Keyser theory' *Language and Style* **8**: 60–77

Steele, J. (1779) *Prosodia Rationalis: Or, an Essay Toward Establishing the Melody and Measure of Speech, etc.*, T. Payne & Son

Steele, T. (1990) *Missing Measures: Modern Poetry and the Revolt against Meter*, University of Arkansas Press, Fayetteville AR

Stein, A. (1942) 'Donne and the couplet' *PMLA* **57**: 676–96

Stein, A. (1956) 'A note on meter' *Kenyon Review* **18**: 452–60

Stein, A. (1968) 'George Herbert's prosody' *Language and Style* **1**: 1–38

Stein, D. and Gil, D. (1980) 'Prosodic structures and prosodic markers' *Theoretical Linguistics* **7**: 173–239

Stevenson, C.L. (1970) 'The rhythm of English verse' in Gross (ed.), 194–224

Stewart, G. (1925) 'The iambic–trochaic theory in relation to musical notation in verse' *Journal of English and Germanic Philology* **24**: 61–71

Stewart, G. (1930) *The Technique of English Verse*, Henry Holt, New York

Stillings, N.A. et al. (1987) *Cognitive Science: An Introduction*, MIT Press, Cambridge MA

Sumera, M. (1970) 'The temporal tradition in the study of verse structure' *Linguistics* **62**: 44–65

Sutherland, R. (1958) 'Structural linguistics and English prosody' *College English* **20**: 12–17
Taglicht, J. (1971) 'The function of intonation in English verse' *Language and Style* **4**: 116–22
Taglicht, J. (1984) *Message and Emphasis*, Longman
Tarlinskaja, M. (1976) *English Verse: Theory and History*, Mouton, The Hague
Tarlinskaja. M. (1984) 'Rhythm–morphology–syntax–rhythm' *Style* **18**: 1–26
Tarlinskaja, M. (1987a) *Shakespeare's Verse*, Peter Lang, New York
Tarlinskaja, M. (1987b) 'Meter and mode: English iambic pentameter, hexameter, and septameter and their period variations' *Style* **21**: 400–26
Tarlinskaja, M. (1989) 'General and particular aspects of meter: literatures, epochs, poets' in Kiparsky and Youmans (eds), 121–54
Tempest, N.R. (1930) *The Rhythm of English Prose*, Cambridge University Press
Thomson, W. (1923) *The Rhythm of Speech*, Maclehose Jackson, Glasgow
Thompson, J. (1961) *The Founding of English Metre*, Columbia University Press, New York
Townsend, P. (1983) 'Essential groupings of meaningful force: rhythm in literary discourse' *Language and Style* **16**: 313–33
Trager, G.L. and Smith, H.L. Jr (1951) *An Outline of English Structure*, Studies in Linguistics Occasional Papers, No. 3, Norman OK
Tsur, R. (1972) 'Articulateness and requiredness in iambic verse' *Style* **6**: 123–48
Tsur, R. (1977) *A Perception-oriented Theory of Metre*, Papers on Poetics and Semiotics 7, Porter Institute for Poetics and Semiotics, Tel Aviv University
Tsur, R. (1983a) *What is Cognitive Poetics?*, Papers in Cognitive Poetics 1, Katz Research Instutute for Hebrew Literature, Tel Aviv University
Tsur, R. (1983b) *Poetic Structure, Information-processing, and Perceived Effects: Rhyme and Poetic Competence*, Papers in Cognitive Poetics 2, Katz Research Institute for Hebrew Literature, Tel Aviv University
Tsur, R. (1985) 'Contrast, ambiguity, double-edgedness' *Poetics Today* **6**: 417–45
Tsur, R. (1987a) *How Do the Sound Patterns Know They Are Expressive?: The Poetic Mode of Speech Perception*, Papers in Cognitive Poetics, Katz Research Institute for Hebrew Literature, Israel Science Publishers, Jerusalem
Tsur, R. (1987b) *The Road to Kubla Khan: A Cognitive Approach*, Papers in Cognitive Poetics, Katz Research Institute for Hebrew Literature, Israel Science Publishers, Jerusalem
Tsur, R. (1987c) *On Metaphoring*, Papers in Cognitive Poetics, Katz Research Institute for Hebrew Literature, Israel Science Publishers, Jerusalem

Tsur, R. (1989) 'Horror jokes, black humor, and cognitive poetics' *Humor* 2–3: 243–55

Turco, L. (1968) *The Book of Forms: A Handbook of Poetics*, E.P. Dutton, New York

Tynianov, Y. (1924/1981) *The Problem of Verse Language*, trans. M. Sousa, Brent Harvey. Ardis, Ann Arbor MI

van Draat, P.F. (1912) 'Rhythm in English prose' *Anglia* **36**: 1–58, 493–538

Weeks, R.M. (1921) 'Phrasal prosody' *English Journal* **10**: 11–19

Wellek, R. and Warren, A. (1949) 'Theory of literature', 3rd edn, Harcourt Brace, New York

Wertheimer, M. (1923) 'Laws of organization in perceptual forms' in Ellis, W.D. (ed.) *A Source Book of Gestalt Psychology*, Harcourt Brace, 1938, 71–88

Wesling, D. (1971) 'The prosodies of free verse' in Brower, R.A. (ed.) *Twentieth Century Literature in Retrospect*, Harvard University Press, Cambridge MA, 155–87

Wesling, D. (1975) 'Thoroughly modern measures' *Boundary 2* **3**.2: 455–71

Wesling, D. (1980a) *The Chances of Rhyme: Device and Modernity*, University of California Press, Berkeley CA

Wesling, D. (1980b) 'Augustan form: justification and breakup of a period style' *Texas Studies in Literature and Language* **22**: 394–428

Wesling, D. (1981) 'Difficulties of the bardic: literature and the human voice' *Critical Inquiry* **8**: 69–81

Wesling, D. (1982) 'Meter the scissors of grammar: grammar the scissors of meter', unpublished paper for the Conference on Lyric Poetry and the New New Criticism, University of Toronto

Wesling, D. (1985) *The New Poetries: Poetic Form since Coleridge and Wordsworth*, Bucknell University Press, Lewisburg PA

Wesling, D. (forthcoming) *The Scissors of Meter: Grammetrics and Interpretation*

Wexler, P. (1964) 'On the grammetrics of the classical alexandrine' *Cahiers de lexicologie* **4**: 61–72

Wexler, P. (1966) 'Distich and sentence in Corneille and Racine' in Fowler, R. (ed.) 1966: 100–17

Whaler, J. (1952) *Counterpoint and Symbol: An Inquiry into the Rhythm of Milton's Epic Style*, Haskell House, New York

Whitehall, H. (1951) 'From linguistics to criticism' *Kenyon Review* **13**: 710–14

Williams, J.M. (1981) *Style: Ten Lessons in Clarity and Grace*, Scott Foresman, Glenview IL

Williams, M. (1978) 'The line in poetry' *Antaeus* **30/31**: 309–13

Wimsatt, W.K. (1971) 'The rule and the norm: Halle and Keyser on Chaucer's meter' in Chatman, S. (ed.) *Literary Style: A Symposium*, Oxford University Press, 197–215

Wimsatt, W.K. and Beardsley, M. (1959) 'The concept of rhythm: an exercise in abstraction' in Chatman, S. and Levin, S.R. (eds), 91–114

Wimsatt, W.K. (ed.) (1972) *Versification: Major Language Types*, New York University Press

Winn, J.A. (1981) *Unsuspected Eloquence*, Yale University Press, New Haven CT

Winters, Y. (1943) 'The influence of meter on poetic convention' in *In defense of reason*, University of Denver Press, Denver CO, 103–50

Woods, S. (1984) *Natural Emphasis: English Versification from Chaucer to Dryden*, The Huntington Library, San Marino

Wright, G.T. (1983) 'The play of phrase and line in Shakespeare's iambic pentameter' *Shakespeare Quarterly* **34**: 147–58

Wright, G.T. (1988) *Shakespeare's Metrical Art*, University of California Press, Berkeley CA

Yoder, P. (1972) 'Biblical Hebrew' in Wimsatt, W.K. (ed.) *Versification: Major Language Types*, New York University Press

Youmans, G. (1974) 'Test case for a metrical theory: "La Belle Dame Sans Merci" ', *Language and Style* **7**: 283–305

Youmans, G. (1982) '*Hamlet*'s testimony on Kiparsky's theory of meter' *Neophilologus* **66**: 490–503

Youmans, G. (1983) 'Generative tests for generative meter' *Language* **59**: 67–92

Youmans, G. (1989) 'Milton's meter' in Kiparsky, P. and Youmans, G. (eds), 341–79

Youmans, G. (1989) 'Introduction: rhythm and meter' in Kiparsky, P. and Youmans, G. (eds), 1–14

Zirmunskij, V. (1925/1966) *Introduction to Metrics: Theory and History*, trans. C.F. Brown, Mouton, The Hague

Index

Abercrombie, David, 30
aesthetic function, 24, 64, 103, 120, 180
Allen, Gay Wilson, 14, 21, 82, 100, 429
Arnheim, Rudolph, 41
Aronoff, Mark, 29
Attridge, Derek, 42–6, 78–9, 88–90, 95–9, 109, 114–15, 128, 248, 250, 437

Bailey, James, 24
Bardovi-Harlig, K., 236
Barry, Sister M. Martin, 13–14
Barthes, Roland, 20
Baum, Paull F., 10, 15
Beardsley, Monroe, 10, 155
Beaver, Joseph C., 39
Benveniste, Emile, 68
Beowulf, 133
Berg, Sister Mary Gretchen, 13
Berry, Eleanor, 13, 22–3, 31, 78, 153, 181
Beum, Robert, 10
binary form, 58
binomials, 62
Blake, William
   'The Sick Rose', 1–8, 80–2, 101–2, 108
blank verse, 44, 83
Bolinger, Dwight, 49, 235–6
Bollobas, Eniko, 62
Book of Common Prayer, 15
Bridges, Robert, 13
Brogan, T. V. F., *xiv*, 15
Brooks, Cleanth, 88, 106
Brown, E. O., 20
Byers, Prudence, 181

cadence, 14, 28
caesura, 8–10, 79, 95, 97, 144, 430–2
Chafe, Wallace, 235–6

chants, 46–9, 120, 239
Chatman, Seymour, 88, 437
Chaucer, Geoffrey, 25
chiasmus, 23
Chomsky, Noam, 37, 39, 156, 242
Christensen, Francis and Bonniejean, 19
Ciardi, John, 93
clitic phrases, 51–2, 102, 239, 243, 256–7
closure, 6, 35–7, 125, 135, 153, 211–12
Cobb, Charles W., 85
cognitive
   competence, 179–80
   structure, 64
cohesion, 258
cola, 15–18, 115
commata, 15–18, 115
complexity, 38, 59
conditions, 43
constraints, 247
   horizontal uniformity, 56, 267
   monosyllabic word, 39
   stress maximum, 38–9, 41
   vertical continuity, 58, 121
   vertical uniformity, 59, 267
contre-rejet, 9, 266
conversation, 83
Cooper, Grosvenor and Leonard Meyer, 48, 85–6, 100, 154, 156, 170–6, 178, 184–6, 242, 245, 256
Corbett, Edward P. J., 19, 264
correspondence, 37–8, 273
Creek, Herbert L., 89
Croll, Morris, 12, 15–19, 84
Crystal, David, 31–2, 86–7, 181, 242, 265
Culler, Jonathan, 180
Cummings, Donald W., 13, 28, 89
Cummings, e.e.,
   'In Just–', 187–9

Cummings (*Cont.*):
  'be unto love a rain is unto colour; create', 223–4
  'so many selves (so many fiends and gods', 252–3
Cureton, Richard D., *xii*, 21, 181
cursus, 18–19, 83–4, 115
Cushman, Stephen, 8, 293

defamiliarization, 64
demotion, 45
Dewey, John, 106
Dickinson, Emily
  'After great pain, a formal feeling comes', 135
  'Conscious am I in my Chamber', 92
Dillon, George, 40
dipodic meter, 99
dol'nik, 25, 130
Donne, John
  'Love's Deity', 9
Dougherty, Adelyn, 13

Eliot, T. S., 14, 23
  'Ash Wednesday,' 29
elision, 45, 52
enjambment, 8–11, 23, 44, 79, 99, 144, 153, 265, 430–32
Epstein, Edmund L., 28, 32, 265
equivalence, 26, 31, 43, 67, 107, 122
Erlich, Victor, 24

Faure, G., 78
feet
  poetic, 7–12, 21, 28, 87–95, 97, 111
  rhythmic, 30
'A flea and a fly in a flue', 246
focus, 29–30
foot-substitution prosodists, 7–12, 77, 79, 101, 110, 112, 114
Forster, E. M., 20
Fowler, Roger, 8, 28
Fraisse, Paul, 124
Frank, Robert, 23
free verse and free verse prosodists, 6, 21–4, 77, 112, 120, 133, 277–323, 425, 432–3
Frost, Robert, 241, 438

'Birches', 86–7
'Design', 55
'Mending Wall', 8–9
'Nothing Gold Can Stay', 141–6, 150–2, 212, 236–8, 267
Fussell, Paul, 8, 81–2, 88, 91, 108

Gall, Sally M., 21
Gasparov, M. L., 24–5
generative metrists, 37–40, 56, 77, 79, 85, 88, 99, 102, 109–10, 113, 115, 429
gestalt psychology, 192–4
Gil, David, 56–62, 77, 79, 85, 87–8, 100, 103, 109, 115, 119, 135, 154, 239–41, 243, 429
Golomb, Harai, 9, 153
grades,
  in poetry, 269–71
  in prose, 15
'grammetric'
  coordinates, 66
  prosodists, 26, 62–7, 77, 97, 101, 265, 429
  relations, 14, 65–6
Grammont, Maurice, 9
Gray, Thomas,
  'Elegy Written in a Country Churchyard', 10, 91
Gross, Harvey, 22, 83, 439
grouping,
  ambiguity, 145–6
  bracketing formalization, 137–8, 282–3, 327–8, 381–2
  levels, 140, 186
    high discourse, 211–24
    low discourse, 224–32
    syntactic and prosodic, 232–8
  morphology, 139–41, 183
  overlap, 186–9
  peaks, *xiv*, 98, 115, 120, 136, 183–4
  preference, 140–1, 191–273
    GPR1 (Information), 195–238, 242, 244, 264, 301, 340–2, 344, 369, 376, 388–93, 398, 404
    GPR2 (Weight), 239–40, 244, 301, 342, 344, 357–8, 369, 377, 388
    GPR3 (End-focus), 241–3, 340–2, 344, 349, 352, 357, 360, 365, 370, 374, 389, 398, 420

GPR4 (Density), 243–4, 301, 340,
    342–3, 358, 365, 369, 402
GPR5 (Return), 244–6, 365, 402
GPR6 (Change), 246–7, 301, 342,
    344, 354, 358, 365, 375
GPR7 (Beats), 247–51, 265, 351,
    354–5, 369, 412
GPR8 (Arrivals), 251–3, 265, 344,
    351–2, 358, 377, 388, 393
GPR9 (Binary Form), 253–4, 260–1,
    267, 340–2, 344–5, 346–7, 352,
    360, 365, 374, 412
GPR10 (Singles), 254–6, 267
GPR11 (Tri-Max), 254–6, 267, 412
GPR12 (Proximity), 256–8, 302,
    366, 370, 389–90, 395, 398, 412
GPR13 (Similarity), 258–63, 267,
    300–4, 351, 389–90, 404, 422
GPR14 (Parallelism), 263–5, 267,
    300–2, 304, 308, 341, 343–4, 348,
    350, 355, 363, 365, 369, 377,
    388–9, 392, 395, 402, 404, 412,
    422
GPR15 (Measures), 264–7, 302,
    352, 354, 358, 360
GPR16 (Unity), 267–8, 303, 342,
    344, 346–50, 353–4, 356, 363, 365,
    367–8, 370, 372, 377–8, 390–3,
    422
GPR17 (Schemes), 268–71, 308,
    345, 346, 348–9, 363, 368–70, 372,
    378, 393, 402, 422
reduction, 137, 200–11, 283–8, 329–32,
    382–4
response, 124, 136–46
schemes, 140, 268–71
shape, 182–5, 268–71, 426–7
spans, 182–5, 268–71
tree formalization, 137–8, 279–81,
    324–6, 379–80
well-formedness, 139, 182–91
Guest, Edwin, 13

Halle, Morris, 37–40, 49, 181, 242
Halliday, M. A. K., 29–30, 122, 252
Hamer, Enid, *xiii*
Hanford, James Holly, 11
Hardison, O. B., Jr., 429

Hartman, Charles O., 22, 24, 429
Hasan, Ruqaiya, 258
Hawkes, Terrence, 28, 32, 265
Hayes, Bruce, 49, 51–6, 85–6, 90, 103–6,
    115, 154, 181
Herbert, George
    'Vertue', 246–7
Herum, John, 13, 89
Hewitt, Elizabeth, 28, 100
hierarchy
    caesural, 8
    constituent, 57, 122
    metrical, 48–50, 57–62, 104
    prosodic, 51–6, 85–6, 103, 115
    rhythmic, 114, 121–3
    syntactic, 8, 66, 122
    visual, 8, 23
Hill, Geoffrey,
    'The Kingdom of Offa', 96
Hogg, Richard and C. B. McCully, 181
Hollander, John, *xii*, 8, 153, 437
Hopkins, Gerard Manley,
    'The Windhover', 133, 150, 152–3,
    297, 323–78
Housman, A. E.
    'To an Athlete Dying Young', 248–53
Hrushovski, Benjamin, 1
Hughes, Langston
    'Harlen Sweeties', 131
    'Who but the Lord?', 32

iambicity, 62
information, 29–30
intonation and intonationalists, 4–5, 7,
    25, 27–33, 39, 41, 51, 79, 84, 95, 99,
    101, 103, 109–10, 115, 120, 242, 257,
    265
isochrony, 98, 106–7, 154

Jakobson, Roman, *xii*, 24, 26, 78, 102,
    115, 259
Jannaconne, P., 13–14, 21, 82, 100
Jesperson, Otto, 28
Jones, Lawrence G., 24, 26
Jorgens, Elise B., 154
juncture, 27–8

Kahn, D., 52
Keats, John,
    'Bright Star', 218–22, 234

Kennedy, X. J., 106
Keyser, Samuel Jay, 38–9
King James Version, *xi*
  Psalm 24, *xii*, 224–32
Kingdon, Roger, 30
Kiparsky, Paul, 38–40, 53–5, 90, 103, 265, 336, 339
Kramer, Lawrence, 155, 439–41
Krieger, Murray, 180

La Driere, J. Craig, 13, 15, 99, 115
Lawrence, D. H., *xi*
Lanier, Sidney, 12, 83, 115
Leech, Geoffrey, 12, 19, 264
Lerdahl, Fred, and Ray Jackendoff, *xiii*, 122, 125, 150, 156, 168–70, 174–8, 182, 185–6, 194, 273
Levi-Strauss, Claude, 26
Levy, Jiri, 67–8
Liberman, Mark, 46–9, 53, 85–7, 114–15, 154
Liddell, Mark H., 13–14, 100
Lindberg-Seyersted, Brita, 13
linguistic
  competence, 181–2, 424–5
  stylistics, 156
linkage, 10
literary competence 180–1
Linville, Susan, 9
Lotz, John, 26

Magnuson, Karl, 38
Malof, Josef, 8, 10, 22, 88
Marr, David, *xiv*
Martin, Howard R., 32
McCreless, P., 20
Meijer, Jan, 64
Meschonnic, Henri, 62, 67–70, 77–8, 94, 121, 154, 438–9
metrical
  alignment, 135
  beats, *xiv*, 12, 43–8, 83–4, 96, 98–100, 115, 120, 126–36, 247–51
  function, 428
  grids, 48, 85–6, 126–36
  measures, 12, 30, 124, 126–36, 264–6
  phonologists, 46–56, 77, 85–8, 99, 102–6, 109, 135
  preferences, 126–7

projection, 124–5, 127–9, 136
quantity, 12
response, 123–36
set, 128
style, 135–6
trees, 49, 53–4
variation, 135–6, 144, 428–9
Millay, Edna St. Vincent,
  'Spring', 212–18, 240, 267
Milton, John,
  Paradise Lost, 9–10, 12, 42, 55, 86, 89–90
  'Comus', 45
Mitchell, Roger, 13–14, 21, 82, 115
Mozart, Wolfgang Amedeus,
  'A-Major Sonata', 169–70, 172, 176–7
musical
  grouping, 170–4
  interpretation, 171
  melody, 162
  meter, 163–4
  overtones, 157
  phrasing, 162
  -poetic relations, 46, 120, 128, 154–7, 434–41
  progressions, 161
  prolongation, 164–70
  reduction, 176–7
  rhythm, 164
  scales, 158–60
  stability, 161–2
  triads, 157–8
myths of traditional prosody
  myth 1 (one-dimensionality), 79–98, 116
  myth 2 (concreteness), 98–106, 112, 116, 154, 156, 435
  myth 3 (regularity), 106–10, 113, 116, 154
  myth 4 (conventionality), 110–13, 116, 156, 435
  myth 5 (linearity), 113–16

Narmour, Eugene, 155–6
narrative structure, 3, 5, 36
Nash, Walter, 19–20
naturalness, 44
Nespor, Marina, 51–2, 181
Nist, John, 13

'No more pencils, no more books', 99, 130

objectivity, 23, 103
openness, 23
oppositional structure, 233, 236
organic form, 181, 267

pace, 88, 91–2
palatalization, 53
Palmer, Frank R., 29
parallelism, *xii*, 6, 23, 26–7, 35
parataxis, 35
Pattison, Bruce, 154
pauses, 8, 12–14
pentameter, 25, 38, 41–2, 53, 83, 113, 134, 254, 266, 378–422
periodicity, 43, 48
Perrine, Lawrence, 108
phonological
 clauses, 33
 domains, 51
 paragraphs, 33
 paragraph-complexes, 33
 phrases, 6, 33, 39–40, 51–2, 79–81, 90, 257
 sub-paragraphs, 33
 words, 25, 33, 39–40
phrasal prosodists, 13–15, 77, 82, 87–8
Pike, Eleanor, 32
Pike, Kenneth, 27, 32–3, 100, 115
Piper, William Bowman, 429
pitch, 27–8
poetic forms, 23, 34, 96
poetic function, the, 26
Pope, Alexander, 40
 'Epistle to a Lady', 96
 'Rape of the Lock', 245
positions, 37
pragnanz, 41
Prall, David, 85, 254
Prince, Alan, 49
principles,
 end-focus, 61, 84
 end-weight, 61
Proffitt, Edward, 88, 93
prolongational
 anticipation, 147
 arrival, *xiv*, 98, 115, 146

bracketing formalization, 147, 282–3, 327–8, 381–2
canonical form, 150, 343, 348, 394
extension, 147
-grouping relations, 251–3
levels, 149–53
morphology, 147
reduction, 152, 288–92, 332–6, 384–7
regions, 147
response, 124, 146–54
spans, 148–9
tree formalization, 282–3, 324–6, 379–80
types (equative, etc.), 147–8
prominence, 6, 13, 23–4, 59, 121–3, 196–200
promotion, 45
prose
 fiction, 20
 poem, 120, 133, 432
 rhythm, 8, 120, 432–3
 rhythmists, 6, 15–20, 100, 152
prosodic
 cometence, 61
 markers, 56–62
 theory, 6–7
proximity, 13
Pound, Ezra
 'The Seafarer', 133

Quirk, Randolph, 19, 241

Ramsey, Paul, 21–2
recursive form, 122
rejet, 9
regularity, 34, 67
relational form, 123
repetition, 6, 34, 43
resolution, 35
rhythmic
 cognition, 98, 423–4
 competence, 104, 116, 119–20, 182
 components, 123–54
 direction, 11, 15, 88–90, 92–5, 99, 127, 135
 function, 437
'Rock-a-bye, Baby', 2
Rudy, Stephen, 24, 26
rule
 bounding, 54–5

rhythmic (*Cont.*):
   disyllabic, 51, 105
   left-edge, 55
   nuclear stress, 39, 242
   phrasal, 51, 105
   quadrisyllabic, 51, 105
   rhythm, 49, 52, 105
   right-edge, 54–5
Ryder, Frank G., 38

Saint Augustine, 155
Saintsbury, George, 10, 11, 15, 165, 429–30
Sandburg, Carl, *xi*
Sayre, Henry, 23
Schenker, Heinrich, 156, 174
   Schenkerian analysis, 165–8, 174–8
Scherr, B. P., 24–5
Schipper, Jakob, *xiii*, 165, 429
Schubiger, M., 29
Scott, John H., 13, 15
Scripture, E. W., 99
secondary rhythmic features, 25
segmentation, 25
Selkirk, Elizabeth, 49, 51, 257
semantics, 59–61, 233–5
Shakespeare, William,
   Hamlet, 83
   King Lear, 10
   Romeo and Juliet, 56
   'Sonnet 1', 183–4
   'Sonnet 12', 56, 196–7, 259–61
   'Sonnet 15', 252
   'Sonnet 29', 90
   'Sonnet 33', 46
   'Sonnet 35', 134
   'Sonnet 42', 250–1
   'Sonnet 65', 10
   'Sonnet 73', 96
   'Sonnet 100', 55
   'Sonnet 121', 55
shape, 41, 108–9, 116, 123
Shapiro, Karl, 10
Shelley, Percy Bysshe
   'The Revolt of Islam', 55
Short, Michael, 19
Shoshani, Ronit, 56
Skeat, W. W., 13
Slavic metrists, 24–7, 78–9, 85, 88, 99, 101, 103, 109–10, 112–15, 130, 135, 156, 247, 265, 429
Smith, Barbara Herrnstein, 23, 35–7, 77–8, 141, 153, 211, 243, 245–8, 251. 259, 438
Smith, Egerton, 11
Smith, Henry Lee, Jr., 27–8, 115
song, 35
sound schemes, 6, 23, 25, 33, 44, 59, 80–1, 97, 102
spatiality, 23
sprung rhythm, 336–40
stanzas, 23, 96–7, 113–14
Stein, Arnold, 9, 28
Stein, David, 56
Stevens, Wallace
   'Sunday Morning', 93
Stevenson, Charles L., 89, 155
Stewart, George, 10, 89
stresses,
   degrees of, 27–9
   and grouping, 239
   ictic, 25, 38–9, 41–2, 45, 47–50, 80–1, 98, 247–54
   number of, 59–61
   phrasal, 39
   silent, 30
   statistical profiles of, 25
structural metrists, 27–9, 102
subject-predicate structure, 62
Swinburne, Algernon Charles, 25
syllables, 5, 23, 25, 33, 53, 59–60, 133, 257
syntax, 3, 4, 6, 8–10, 19–20, 26, 33, 52, 65–6, 80–1, 87, 91, 95, 97, 101–2, 115–16, 120–1, 152, 232–8, 241, 243

Taglicht, Josef, 31
Tarlinskaja, Marina, 24–6, 56, 102, 254, 265
Tempest, Norton R., 15
temporal prosodists, 14–15, 77, 79, 82–3, 87–8, 99, 101, 115, 120, 154, 259
tension, 23, 33, 65–6, 88, 90, 125, 135, 265
terminal modification, 34
tetrameter, 25, 44, 83, 266
text-tune alignment, 46–9
theme

discourse, 33–7, 199–200
  grammatical, 29, 233, 235, 241
Thomson, William, 12, 115
time, 427, 439–41
topic-comment structure, 62, 233, 235–6, 241
Townsend, Peter, 20
Trager, George L., 27–8, 115
transformational-generative grammar, 37–40
triadic line, 31, 85
Tsur, Reuven, 40–2, 77–9, 109, 114–15, 438–9
Turco, Lewis, 429
Tynianov, Jurii, 24, 198

universal grammar, 62

van Draat, P. Fijn, 49
Vernaud, Jean-Roger, 49, 181
verse
  alliterative, 133
  design, 24–5, 54
  instance, 24, 37, 54
  line, 25, 113, 114
  non-canonical, 56
  paragraph, 11–12, 15, 35
  period, 11
  syllabic, 133
versification, 112–15, 120
visual form, 8, 21–5, 31, 56, 79–80, 257–8, 295–8, 425
Vogel, Irene, 51–2, 181
voice, 64, 181, 439

Warren, Austin, 24, 88, 106

Weeks, Ruth M., 13, 21
Wellek, Rene, 24
well-formedness, 37, 42, 53–6, 98, 109, 122, 126–7
Wertheimer, Max, 192–4, 267
Wesling, Donald, 1, 62–7, 77–8, 86, 88, 100, 02, 115, 120, 153, 265, 438–9
Wexler, P. J., 65
Whaler, James, *xii*
Whitman, Walt, *xi*, 23, 82–3, 116,
  'Great are the Myths', 14
  'Song of Myself', 14, 261–3
  'When Lilacs Last in the Dooryard Bloom'd', 202–11, 240, 267
Williams, Joseph M., 191, 239
Williams, Miller, 93
Williams, William Carlos, 31, 85
  'Asphodel, That Greeny Flower', 31
  'Without invention nothing is well spaced', 277–323
Wimsatt, W. K., Jr., 109
Winn, James, 154
Winters, Yvor, 22
Woods, Susanne, 429
words, 23, 25–7, 34, 38, 97
Wordsworth, William, 307
Wright, George T., *xii*, 78, 248, 429

Yeats, William Butler,
  'After Long Silence', 93
  'The Pity of Love', 132–3
  'The Sorrow of Love', 259
  'When You Are Old', 378–422
Youmans, Gilbert, 254, 265

Zirmunskij, Viktor, 24, 26